The Indians of Central
and South America

The Indians of Central and South America

An Ethnohistorical Dictionary

James S. Olson

Greenwood Press
New York • Westport, Connecticut • London

Library of Congress Cataloging-in-Publication Data

Olson, James Stuart, 1946–
  The Indians of Central and South America : an ethnohistorical
dictionary / James S. Olson.
    p. cm.
  Includes bibliographical references and index.
  ISBN 0–313–26387–6 (alk. paper)
    1. Indians of Central America—History—Dictionaries. 2. Indians
of South America—History—Dictionaries. 3. Indians of Central
America—Social conditions—Dictionaries. 4. Indians of South
America—Social conditions—Dictionaries. 5. Ethnohistory—Latin
America—Dictionaries. I. Title.
F1434.045 1991
972.8′00497′003—dc20   90–47503

British Library Cataloging in Publication Data is available.

Library of Congress Catalog Card Number: 90–47503
ISBN: 0–313–26387–6

First published in 1991

Greenwood Press, 88 Post Road West, Westport, CT 06881
An imprint of Greenwood Publishing Group, Inc.

Printed in the United States of America

∞™

The paper used in this book complies with the
Permanent Paper Standard issued by the National
Information Standards Organization (Z39.48–1984).

10 9 8 7 6 5 4 3 2 1

CONTENTS

PREFACE

In recent years, the American public has become increasingly interested in Central and South American concerns. Political issues, such as the insurgency in Nicaragua and El Salvador or the question of Cuban involvement in hemispheric revolutionary activity, continue to affect public debate, but broader social and environmental issues are also becoming more urgent. Films like *The Emerald Forest* or *The Mission* have publicized the plight of surviving Amerindian groups, while many celebrities are expressing concern about the future of the Amazonian rain forest and the impact of its disappearance on the global climate. In the jungles of Colombia and Peru, drug traffickers and political revolutionaries like the Shining Path guerrillas produce the cocaine that is flooding American cities. Latin America looms large on the world's horizon, a place full of potential for political instability and ecological disaster.

I thought that a book providing information about the current status of the indigenous peoples of Central and South America would be a useful resource for scholars, students, and the general public. This ethnohistorical dictionary of Central and South American Indians is designed to serve as a reference guide providing basic information about the existing Amerindian tribes of Central and South America. Each entry provides a brief historical description of an existing tribe or group, with several bibliographical citations at the conclusion. It is important to note here that I have focused on those Indian groups and even isolated individuals who still maintain a sense of specific tribal identity. Throughout Central and South America, there are millions of people who no longer identify themselves as members of a particular indigenous tribe but who nevertheless understand that they are neither mestizos nor of European descent. They are Indians in a generic rather than a tribal sense. In El Salvador, for example, a common assumption has held that all but a few of their Indians have disappeared but in a 1989 edition of *Cultural Survival Quarterly*, Mac Chapin argued that there are more than 500,000 people in El Salvador who are essentially Indian, even though they speak Spanish, worship as Roman Catholics, work as peasants and day laborers, and dress like other working-class people. Similar groups exist throughout Central and South America, but these people are not the major subjects of this book. The use of the term "extinct" is meant to refer to a tribe that no longer functions as a sociological entity, even though there may be living members or descendents of the group who are aware of their tribal heritage.

I wish to express my gratitude to a host of librarians at Sam Houston State University, Texas A & M University, Brigham Young University, and the University of Texas who assisted me in locating hard-to-find materials, particularly articles from foreign journals. Ms. Shirley Parotti of the Newton Gresham Library at Sam Houston State University was particularly patient with my requests and very successful in securing the materials I needed.

James S. Olson
Huntsville, Texas

INTRODUCTION

Native American ethnicity is an extraordinarily complex subject. Thousands of tribes have become extinct since the Spanish and Portuguese arrived in the New World in the late fifteenth and early sixteenth centuries. A process of ethnogenesis is also at work as tribes merge with each other as well as with descendents of the European settlers to create new ethnic groups. The data about individual groups is often years old, and in a social landscape that changes so rapidly, the information is often outdated almost as soon as it is written. South American ethnicity is a bewildering kaleidoscope of diverse groups undergoing constant change, although the central theme of Amerindian history, today as well as five-hundred years ago, is still the story of tribal decay and social change. Those Indians who have survived and are experiencing population growth are also suffering from extreme poverty. In many regions of Central and South America, that poverty has spawned radical political movements among indigenous people. The processes of modernization, industrialization, and acculturation continue to inflict dramatic change on the native American communities.

Historians and anthropologists studying the indigenous people of the New World are usually amazed at the consistency of the historical dynamics at work, whether they are looking at the sixteenth or the twentieth century. Europeans and their descendents have routinely approached the indigenous people from one of two perspectives. On the one hand, the Europeans have lusted after Indian economic resources. They have created powerful negative stereotypes about the Indians, justifying the conflict necessary to drive them off the land. If the Indians really were bloodthirsty savages, they argued, society was better off without them. Over the centuries, the resources that Europeans wanted have changed. But whether it was the brazilwood of the sixteenth century in Brazil or the oil today in the Ecuadorian Amazon, Europeans have continually sought to push

Indians off the land. When the Indians would peaceably relocate to other less valuable areas, most Europeans were willing to leave them alone, but the key was removing them from the valuable land. If violence was necessary, so be it. All over the New World, these notions led to genocidal assaults on the Indian tribes. The irony, of course, was that time, technology, and population expansion eventually renders all land valuable. The penetration of Yanoama* land in northwestern Brazil by gold prospectors today is just the latest chapter in a long history of exploitation and invasion.

The second approach to indigenous people seemed more humane, at least superficially, and grew out of a combination of liberal guilt and missionary zeal. Dismayed by the violence inflicted upon indigenous people, some Europeans desired to protect them, to insulate them from the more aggressive, less morally restrained settlers. They also wanted to change the indigenous people. They accepted their humanity—as well as their cultural inferiority—but instead of annihilating them to clear the land, liberals and missionaries sought to assimilate Amerindians into European culture. That is, they sought to remake Indian society, transforming Indians into "law-abiding" farmers who believed in private property, nuclear families, individual aggrandizement, and Jesus Christ. The pattern has remained the same, whether it was the Jesuits of the sixteenth century or the New Tribes Mission or the Summer Institute of Linguistics in the 1980s. The irony is that although the methods of the assimilationists have been far more benign than the genocidal ravages of Indian haters, the results have been the same: the virtual elimination of indigenous cultures. History is repeating itself again and again.

Readers will note that there has been great variety in the spelling of tribal names. Over the centuries, thousands of Spanish, Portuguese, German, Dutch, French, British, and American explorers, missionaries, and anthropologists have observed the various Amerindian tribes, and they have often used different names and different spellings of the same names in describing individual tribes. In his 1989 book *To Weave and Sing*, David M. Guss reviews the history of the designations for the Yekuana* Indians of Venezuela. The Jesuit priest Manuel Román first called them the "Makiritaré" in 1744, and that name, with a variety of spellings, was used for two centuries. The word Makiritaré is of Arawak derivation and means "water people." But in 1847, the German ethnologist Robert Schomburgk reached the Yekuana with the help of Karib-speaking Pemón and Makushi guides. Those guides noticed the peculiar haircut worn by the Yekuana and called them "Maiongkong," which meant "Round Heads." The term Maiongkong, with a variety of spellings, also began to appear in the literature. The Pemón also referred to the Yekuana as the "Pawana" or the "Pabanotón." Theodor Koch-Grünberg first used the autochthonous term "Yekuana" in 1924. The Yekuana, of course, are hardly exceptional. Most of the tribes of indigenous people in Central and South America have been described with a variety of names by Europeans and by their own neighbors. I have included within the alphabetical listing of topics the names of tribes and subtribes that have most commonly appeared in the historical and anthropological literature. Readers encountering the same name to describe two very separate tribes should realize that this has not been an uncommon experience over the centuries. In most cases, I have noted the particular situation when a dual reference occurs.

This dictionary is a survey of those surviving Amerindians. Although brief citations at the end of each dictionary entry direct the reader to more in-depth coverage, there have been a number of works that I have used constantly throughout the book that deserve special citation. Foremost among them is the work of Julian H. Seward who edited the Smithsonian Institution's *Handbook of South American Indians*. The leading anthropologists in the world participated in the project, and most of the research was completed in the late 1930s and early 1940s. Seven volumes were published as Bulletin 143 of the Bureau of American Ethnology. Volume I, *The Marginal Tribes*, was completed in 1944; Volume II, *The Andean Civilizations*, was also completed that year. The next two volumes were ready in 1945. Volume III was entitled *The Tropical Forest Tribes* and Volume IV covered *The Circum-Caribbean Tribes*. World War II delayed the publication of the next two installments. Volume V, *The Comparative Ethnology of South American Indians*, appeared in 1947 and Volume VI, *Physical Anthropology, Linguistics and Cultural Geography of South American Indians*, came out in 1948. In 1957, the Smithsonian Institution published a comprehensive index to these six volumes; the *Index* appeared as Volume VII. Although subsequent research has resulted in a good deal of criticism and revision of the *Handbook of South American Indians*, it is nevertheless an extraordinary work, the place where all historians and ethnologists interested in the native cultures of South America must begin their work. To avoid redundancy, I have not cited the *Handbook of South American Indians* at the end of each entry in the dictionary, but the handbook was consulted for the vast majority of the essays in this book. I used several other works, which I have cited, of a broad, general nature, including the World Council of Churches' survey of the condition of the South American tribes, which was published in 1972 as *The Situation of the Indian in South America*, under the general editorship of Walter Dostal. I also referred to *The Indian in South America*, published in 1972 by the American West Center of the University of Utah under the editorship of S. Lyman Tyler, and to Scott S. Robinson, *La situación actual de los indígenas en el América del Sur*, 1971.

The whole question of South American languages and current population figures is a scholarly quagmire in which constant revision occurs as each new team of ethnologists and linguists returns from the field and enters data into the computer. The scholarly consensus is that there are hundreds of isolated Amerindian languages and dozens of language groups. In his influential recent book, *Language in the Americas* (1987), however, Joseph H. Greenberg argues that there are not hundreds of linguistic isolates, but that all Amerindian languages fall into just three groups: Na-Dene, which is concentrated in the western region of North America; Eskimo-Aleut; and what he calls Amerind, which includes 90 percent of all the aboriginal languages spoken in the Americas. Few topics in the social sciences are more complicated. The social structure in Central and South America is in a constant state of flux. Within a few years of publication, most information is already out-of-date. Defining just what constitutes an Indian is also a scholarly nightmare. Full-bloods, mixed-bloods, mestizos, and whites all look at the question from highly charged perspectives. For better or worse, I have relied on several basic works, including Desmond C. Derbyshire and Geoffrey K. Pullum, ed., *Handbook of Amazonian Languages*, 1986; Harriet E. Klein and Louisa R. Stark, *South American Indian Languages: Retrospect and Prospect*, 1985; Antonio Tovar, *Catálogo de las lenguas de América del Sur: Enumeración, con indicaciones tipológicas, bibliografía y mapas*, 1961; and Mario Montaño Aragón, *Guía etnográfica lingüística de Bolivia*, 1987. In 1987, the professional journal, *América Indígena*, published a series of articles on the Indian languages of individual Central and South American countries. I referred extensively to the following items: Arysteides Turpana, "Lenguas indígenas" [Panamá], 47:615–25; Robert Lee Spires, "As línguas faladas do Brasil," 47:455–79; Gloria Tujab, "Lenguas indígenas que se encuentran en vias de extinción," [Guatemala], 47:529–33; Gustavo Solís F., "Multilinguismo y extinción de lenguas de Perú," 47:631–45; Isabel Hernández, "Los pueblos y las lenguas aborígenes en la actualidad," [Argentina] 47:409–21; Graciela Zolezzi Ch. y Jürgen Riester, "Lenguas indígenas del oriente boliviano: Clasificación preliminar," 47:425–33; and Estéban Emilio Mosonyi, "La revitalización lingüística y la realidad venezolano," 47:553–61. I also relied on Mary Ritchie Key's *The Grouping of South American Indian Languages*, 1979; Cestmir Loukotka, *Classification of South American Indian Languages*, 1968, Melanie A. Counce and William V. Davidson, "Indians of Central America 1980s," *Cultural Survival Quarterly*, 13 (1989), 38–41; and Harriet E. Klein and Louisa Stark, "Indian Tribes of the Paraguayan Chaco," *Anthropological Linguistics*, 19 (1977), 378–402.

I used several other important works surveying the Amerindian tribes of particular countries extensively as well. On the Indians of Belize, I referred frequently to William V. Davidson, "The Amerindians of Belize, An Overview," *América Indígena*, 47 (1987), 9–22. For the Indians of Bolivia, I relied heavily on Mario Montaña Aragón, ed., *Guía etnográfia lingüística de Bolivia*, 1987; Pedro Plaza Martínez and Juan Carvajal Carvajal, *Étnias y lenguas de Bolivia*, 1985; Dick E. Ibarra Grasso, *Pueblos indígenas de Bolivia*, 1985; Jürgen Reister, *Indians of Eastern Bolivia: Aspects of Their Present Situation*, 1975; and Harold Key and Mary Key, *Bolivian Indian Tribes: Classification, Bibliography, and Map of Present Language Distribution*, 1967. John Hemming's books on the Brazilian Indians were invaluable: *Red Gold: The Conquest of the Brazilian Indians, 1500–1760*, 1978, and *Amazon Frontier: The Defeat of the Brazilian Indians*, 1987. For several generations, no historian will be able to analyze Brazilian ethnohistory without looking at Hemming's research. Other general surveys of the Brazilian tribes include Lucien Bodard, *Green Hell: Massacre of the Brazilian Indians*, 1971; Edwin Brooks, René Fuerst, John Hemming, and

Francis Huxley, *Tribes of the Amazon Basin, Brazil 1972*, 1973; Robin Hanbury-Tenison, *A Question of Survival for the Indians of Brazil*, 1973; Indígena and American Friends of Brazil, *Supysana, A Documentary Report on the Conditions of Indian Peoples in Brazil*, 1974; and Theodore L. Stoddard, ed., *The Indians of Brazil in the Twentieth Century*, 1967. On Colombia, I used Blaz Telban, *Grupos étnicos de Colombia*, 1987; Leah B. Ellis and Linda Criswell, eds., *Estudiemos las culturas indígenas de Colombia*, 1984; Myriam Jiméno and Adolfo Triana Antorveza, *Estado y minorías étnicas en Colombia*, 1985; Christine Hugh-Jones, *From the Milk River: Spatial and Temporal Processes in Northwest Amazonia*, 1979; Stephen Hugh-Jones, *The Palm and the Pleiades: Initiation and Cosmology in Northwest Amazonia*, 1979; Ministerio de Gobierno, *Aspetos de la cultura material de los grupos étnicos de Colombia*, 1979; and Gerardo Reichel-Dolmatoff, *Amazonian Cosmos: The Sexual and Religious Symbolism of the Tukano Indians*, 1971. I looked at the Cultural Survival organization's *El Salvador's Indians*, 1982, repeatedly for information on the Salvadoran tribes. W. George Lovell's "Surviving Conquest: The Maya of Guatemala in Historical Perspective," *Latin American Research Review*, 23 (Number 2, 1988), 25–58, was used often in writing about the Amerindians of Guatemala, as was C. Nelson and K. Taylor, *Witness to Genocide—The Present Situation of Indians in Guatemala*, 1983. For information on the Amerindians of Guyana, I repeatedly referred to W. Gibson and K. Gibson, "An Ethnohistory of Amerindians in Guyana," *Ethnohistory*, 26 (1979), 161–75, and Kenneth Sugrim, *Some Historical and Demographic Information on the Amerindians of Guyana*, 1977. When looking up information on the Amerindians of Honduras, I referred again and again to L. Fernando Cruz Sandoval, "Los indios de Honduras y la situación de sus recursos naturales," *América Indígena*, 44 (1984), 423–46. David Maybury-Lewis and James Howe, *The Indian Peoples of Paraguay: Their Plight and Their Prospects*, 1980, was used frequently, as was John Renshaw, "Property, Resources and Equality among the Indians of the Paraguayan Chaco," *Man*, 23 (1988), 334–52 and Miguel Chase-Sardi, *La situación actual de los indígenas del Paraguay*, 1972. For the Indians of Peru, I turned repeatedly to Stefano Varese, *The Forest Indians in the Present Political Situation of Peru*, 1972, and Darcy Ribeiro and Mary Ruth Wise, *Los grupos étnicos de la amazonia peruana*, 1978. On the Venezuelan tribes, I used Walter Coppens, *Los aborígines de Venezuela*, 1983, and Ministerio de Estado para la Cultura, *Arte Indígena de Venezuela*, 1983, frequently; on the population of the Venezuelan tribes, see Oficina Central de Estadistica Informatica, *Censo indígena de Venezuela*, 1985. I decided in the interest of space not to list any of the works cited above each time for individual entries.

The Indians of Central and South America

A

AAINGÁNG. See KAINGÁNG.

ABANI. See ACHAGUA.

ABIGIRA. See AWISHIRI.

ABIJIRA. See AWISHIRI.

ABIRA. See AWISHIRI.

ABIXIRA. See AWISHIRI.

ABUBAE. See BRUNKA.

ACAGUAYO. See AKAWÁIO.

ACAHUAYO. See AKAWÁIO.

ACATECO. The Acateco are a Mayan group of Amerindians whose native homeland is in the department of Huehuetenango, Guatemala. After throwing off Quiché* domination in the early 1500s, the Acateco suffered mass population decline at the hands of the Spanish conquerors who reached them in the 1530s. An agricultural people who raise maize and beans in communal plots, the Acateco population stabilized in the eighteenth century and began to increase in the nineteenth century. After World War II, the Acateco suffered from Guatemalan government policies designed to transform communal landholdings to private ownership. In the process, the Acateco acquired strong left-wing political leanings. Government repression in the 1980s inspired a mass emigration of more than half of the Acatecos who were living in Guatemala in 1980. Most of them ended up in Mexico, the United States, or refugee camps. Today there are approximately 15,000 Acateco speakers in Guatemala.

REFERENCES: Melanie C. Counce and William V. Davidson, "Indians of Central America 1980s," *Cultural Survival Quarterly*, 13 (1989), 38–41; Gloria Tujab, "Lenguas indígenas que se encuentran en vias de extinción," *América Indígena*, 47 (1987), 529–33.

ACAWÁI. See AKAWÁIO.

ACAWÓIO. See AKAWÁIO.

ACHAGUA. The Achagua are a tropical forest people scattered today from Venezuela to northeastern Colombia. At the time of the conquest, their tribal territory comprised what are today the states of Bolívar, Guárico, and Barinas in Venezuela. The main body of tribal members now resides near the confluence of the Meta and the Orinoco rivers. They are also located in the Intendancy of Arauca in Colombia. Historical synonyms and subtribes of the Achagua have included the Chiricoa,* Taparita, Otomaco, Yaruro,* Catarubén, Barria, Ucataquerri, Quirruba, Lizarva, Abani, Aycubaverrenay, Univerrenay, Amarizán, Amarizama, Sikuani* (Sicuani), and Issirriberrenai.

At the time of the conquest, the Achagua were primarily a farming tribe, raising bitter manioc, beans, and maize, although hunting provided an important dietary supplement. Near the end of the sixteenth century, Jesuit missionaries contacted the Achagua, and by the 1630s most of the Achagua had been gathered into Jesuit missions. There the Jesuits worked diligently at eliminating the Achagua practice of infanticide—killing each first-born daughter. There are 230 acculturated, mixed-blood Achaguas living on the Colombian Indian reservation of El Turpial y La Victoria. A small minority of the Achagua retreated into the Colombian mountains or the forests of southern Venezuela. Today the Achagua are almost completely acculturated, with Roman Catholicism the dominant religion and Spanish the language of formal and informal conversation among tribal members. The number of Achagua full-bloods is fewer than 100 people. Several Protestant evangelical groups have converted a number of Achagua in recent years.

REFERENCES: *Encyclopedia of Indians of the Americas*, 2(1974), 16–17; Francisco Ortiz Gómez, *Literatura oral Sikuani*, 1982; Nancy K. Morey, "Ethnohistory of the Colombian and Venezuelan Llanos," Ph.D. dissertation, University of Utah, 1975; Estéban Emilio Mosonyi, "La revitalización y la realidad venezolana," *América Indígena*, 47 (1987), 653–61; Francisco Pérez de Vega, *La Nación Achagua: Bosquejo histórico lingüístico*, 1963.

ACHÉ. The Aché are a stone-age tribe living in eastern Paraguay. Traditionally, they have been identified by the term "Guayakí" or "Guayaquí," but that is actually a racist term coined by the Guaraní tribe to describe the Aché, whom they consider subhumans. The term "Guayakí" literally means "rabid rats." For centuries, the Guaraní* have hunted and murdered the Aché, a foraging and fishing people who wander about in bands of approximately 20 people. They do not practice agriculture. In the mid-eighteenth century, some of the Aché were gathered into Spanish missions, but the attempt to "civilize" them was unsuccessful. In the 1970s, a near-genocidal war was carried out against the Aché by Paraguayans of Spanish and Guaraní descent. Government hydroelectric power projects and land policies encouraging immigration and settlement in eastern Paraguay brought more and more people to Aché territory. These policies reduced the land available for Aché hunting and foraging and increased the violence between the Indians and neo-Paraguayans. This extermination attempt captured world attention in the mid–1970s. Since then, several hundred Aché have been protected on a Protestant reservation, although others who live in the ancestral forests still face assault by neo-Paraguayans. The three major Aché settlements are the Colonia Nacional Guayakí, Cerro Moroti, and a Catholic reservation under the order of Verbo Divino near Curuguaty. The Aché economy has become increasingly mixed in recent years, with farming and part-time wage labor competing with hunting and gathering. At the present time the Aché number approximately 1,300 people.

REFERENCES: Richard Arens, *Genocide in Paraguay*, 1976; Pierre Clastres, "Guayakí Cannibalism," *Journal de la Société des Américanistes*, 57 (1968), 30–47; Kim Hill et al. "Men's Time Allocation to Subsistence Work among the Aché of Eastern Paraguay," *Human Ecology*, 13 (1985), 29–48; Kim Hill et al. "Seasonal Variance in the Diet of Aché Hunter-Gatherers in Eastern Paraguay," *Human Ecology*, 12 (1984), 101–35; David Maybury-Lewis and James Howe, *The Indian Peoples of Paraguay: Their Plight and Their Prospects*, 1980.

ACHÍ. The Achí are a group of Eastern Mayan* people living in the department of Baja Verapaz, Guatemala. They are subdivided into two groups, the Rabinal Achí and the Achí of Cubulco. In the fifteenth century, the Achí came under the domination of the Quiché* Maya, but that domination was largely over by the early 1500s. Pedro de Alvarado, the Spanish conqueror of Guatemala, tried to defeat the Achí several times in the 1520s and early 1530s, only to be driven back each time because of Achí fortifications and the rugged terrain. By the time Alvarado was ready to go after the Achí again, the Spanish priest Bartolomé de las Casas had risen to prominence in Guatemala. He brought the entire Achí region under church control, established mission settlements at Cubulco and Rabinal, and gathered the Indians to convert and protect them. The Achí suffered from the relocation and from disease, but they were saved from the military assaults of Spanish conquerors.

They did not fare so well against the nineteenth-century economic changes that brought more and more *ladino* settlers to Baja Verapaz, imposing great

pressures on Achí landholdings. Government policies in the late nineteenth century encouraged the transfer of land from communal to private holdings. In the
process, the Achí lost most of their aboriginal estate, becoming a peasant un-
derclass of tenant farmers and seasonal laborers. Today there are approximately
40,000 Rabinal Achí and 20,000 Achí of Cubulco.

REFERENCES: John E. Kelley, *Pedro de Alvarado, Conquistador*, 1932; W. George
Lovell, "Surviving Conquest: The Maya of Guatemala in Historical Perspective," *Latin
American Research Review*, 23 (1988), 25–58.

ACHIOTE. See WITOTO.

ACHOTE. See WITOTO.

ACHUAL. See ACHUARA.

ACHUARA. The Achuara (Achual, Achuare, Atchuara) are a tribe of Amerindians who are part of the isolated Jívaro* linguistic family of the Ecuadorian
and Peruvian montana. The Achuara live in the forests at the foothills of the
Andes Mountains, on both sides of the Pastaza River and on both sides of the
Peruvian-Ecuadorian border. At the time of the Spanish conquest of Peru,
the Incas were trying to subjugate the Jívaro tribes in general, an attempt that
failed after a series of bloody confrontations. The Achuara put up a similar
resistance to Spaniards, who came into their territory searching for placer gold.

Until the middle of the nineteenth century, the Achuara had only limited and
intermittent contact with the Spaniards. In the later years of the nineteenth
century, they increased their peaceful contact with neo-Ecuadorians and neo-
Peruvians in order to acquire trade goods, especially metal tools and manufactured cloth. During the first three decades of the twentieth century, there was
relatively little colonization of the Achuara area, except for successful Roman
Catholic missions by Salesians. A gold rush in the 1930s brought many outsiders,
precipitating violent confrontations. Under pressure from the Salesians, the Ecuadorian government established peaceful relations with the Achuara. During the
last four decades, contact between the Achuara and the larger society has been
characterized by relative peace and increasing acculturation, but the general
isolation of the Achuara tribal territory has helped them preserve a sense of tribal
identity.

The Achuara generally pursue a subsistence lifestyle, based on the production
of sweet manioc, maize, and a variety of other products in family gardens. The
need for cash to buy trade goods is steadily increasing, forcing them to spend
more and more of their time working as day laborers. At the present time, there
are approximately 15,000 members of the Achuara tribe.

REFERENCES: Michael J. Harner, *The Jívaro: People of the Sacred Waterfalls*, 1973;
Siro M. Pellizzaro, *Cantos de amor de la esposa Achuar*, 1978; Stefano Varese, *The
Forest Indians in the Present Political Situation of Peru*, 1972.

ACHUARE. See ACHUARA.

ACUTI-TAPUYA. See WAKUÉNAI.

ADZANENI. See CURRIPACO and WAKUÉNAI.

AENTS. See AGUARUNA.

AFOTIGÉ. See APINAYÉ.

AGAVOTOKÜENG. See AGAVOTOQÜENG.

AGAVOTOQÜENG. The Agavotoqüeng (Agavotoküeng) are a tropical forest tribe of Amerindians who today live in the southern reaches of the Xingú Indian Park in the state of Mato Grosso, Brazil. The tribal village is on the east side of the Xingú River, between the Kuluene and Kurizevo rivers. The tribe numbers fewer than 100 people. They speak a language very similar to that of the Iaualapití,* suggesting that the Agavotoqüeng were once part of the Iaualapití and broke away from them. The tribe maintains a strong isolation from surrounding groups in the Xingú Indian Park and pursues a lifestyle that retains many elements of its tropical forest, horticultural background.

REFERENCE: Orlando Villas Boas and Cláudio Villas Boas, *Xingú: The Indians, Their Myths*, 1973.

AGOUISIRI. See AWISHIRI.

AGUA. See OMÁGUA.

AGUA BLANCA. See TUNEBO.

AGUACATECO. See AGUATECA.

AGUAHÚN. See AGUARUNA.

AGUAJÚN. See AGUARUNA.

AGUANO. The Aguano (Aguanu, Awano, Uguano, Santacrucino) are today a highly integrated group of Amerindians who live on the lower Huallaga River and the upper Samiria River in the jungles of eastern Peru. They represent a case of ethnogenesis—the post-conquest fusion of the Aguano, Cutinana, and Maparina peoples. The Aguano subtribes include the Seculusepa, Chilacas, Meliquines, and Tivilos (Tibilos). They were living north of the Marañón River at the time of the arrival of the Spaniards in the sixteenth century. By the mid-eighteenth century, they had been decimated by European diseases, as well as by attacks from their traditional enemies, the Jívaro.* In order to protect them-selves from the Jívaro, they sought out the guardianship of the Spanish. The Aguano were concentrated near Santa Cruz on the lower Huallaga River in the nineteenth century, and as the processes of acculturation and detribalization took place, they began to call themselves Santacrucinos. Today they are an accul-turated, detribalized people who speak Spanish, worship as Roman Catholics, and work as subsistence farmers, but they still maintain a distinct ethnic identity.

REFERENCE: Darcy Riberio and Mary Ruth Wise, *Los grupos étnicos de la amazona peruana*, 1978.

AGUANU. See AGUANO.

AGUARUNA. The Aguaruna (Aguahún, Aguajún) are a branch of the Jívaro* people. They live in relatively dispersed communities along the Marañón, Nieva, Cenepa, Santiago, and Mayo rivers, as well as their major tributaries, in the tropical forests of northern Peru, especially in the departments of Amazonas, San Martín, and Loreto. They call themselves the Aents. Each community is a patrilineal group politically independent of the neighboring Aguaruna groups; they live in a single, large, thatched house that is approximately 80 feet long and 40 feet wide. Although the Aguaruna hunt and fish, they are primarily horticulturists who raise sweet manioc and plantains using swidden agricultural techniques. Today they also raise cotton, tobacco, and a variety of other crops. In addition, they collect rubber. Unlike most tribes of Central and South America, the Aguaruna still occupy land that they had held in the pre-conquest era. Only in recent years, however, have they been able to acquire complete legal title to their communal lands.

In the fifteenth and early sixteenth centuries, the Aguaruna successfully resisted attempts by the Inca Empire to subjugate them; in the process, they developed a fierce warrior culture that served them well after the arrival of Francisco Pizarro and the Spaniards in the 1530s. Spaniards first contacted the Aguaruna in 1549, but it was the expeditions led by Juan de Salinas in the 1550s that first threatened the tribe. Exposure to Spanish *encomenderos* led to dramatic population declines among the Aguaruna, but by 1600, the tribe had all but destroyed the Spanish settlements in their midst. Jesuit and later Franciscan attempts to missionize the Aguaruna failed in the eighteenth and nineteenth centuries. As late as the 1920s and early 1930s the Aguaruna were known for periodic attacks on white com-munities that they felt were encroaching on their land. By the 1980s, the Agu-arunas totaled approximately 27,000 people, virtually all of them still speaking the native language, although increasingly large numbers are also familiar with Quechua and Spanish. Despite continuing contact with Protestant missionaries and Peruvian schools, the Aguaruna maintain a powerful tribal identity.

REFERENCES: Michael F. Brown, "Power, Gender, and the Social Meaning of Aguaruna Suicide," *Man*, 21 (1986), 311–28; Michael F. Brown and Margaret L. Van Bolt, "Aguaruna Jívaro Gardening Magic in the Alto Río Mayo, Peru," *Ethnography*,

19 (1980), 169–90; Michael J. Harner, *The Jívaro: People of the Sacred Waterfalls*, 1972; Henning Siverts, *Tribal Survival in the Alto Marañón: The Aguaruna Case*, 1972; Martha Adrienne Works, "Aguaruna Agriculture in Eastern Peru," *The Geographical Review*, 77 (1987), 343–59.

AGUATECA. The Aguatecas (Aguacateco) are a small Mayan* enclave in the southeastern part of the department of Huehuetenango in the highlands of Guatemala. They are surrounded by the Ixil* on the east and the Mam* on the north and west. The Aguatecas were conquered by the Quiché* Maya early in the 1400s but cast off Quiché domination early in the 1500s, only to find a new master—the Spaniards—in the 1520s. Like the other highland Mayan groups, the Aguatecas experienced rapid population decline in the sixteenth century and stabilization in the seventeenth century. They were then an agricultural people whose economy revolved around the cultivation of maize and beans. The Aguatecos still live a settled agricultural lifestyle, raising maize, beans, and avocados for their own food and sugar cane for a cash crop. Although they maintain a number of communal agricultural plots, the transition to individual ownership, which government policies started at the end of the nineteenth century and accelerated after World War II, has been a continuing process. Guatemalan land policies have dramatically reduced Aguatecan land holdings, while the rise of large coffee plantations has turned many Aguatecas into agricultural laborers. In the 1980s, the Aguatecas, who call themselves "Balamiha," fled Guatemala in large numbers because of repressive government policies. Today there are approximately 16,000 Aguatecas living in Guatemala.

REFERENCES: Douglas E. Brintnell, *Revolt Against the Dead: The Modernization of a Mayan Community in the Guatemalan Highlands*, 1979; John Hawkins, *Inverse Images: The Meaning of Culture, Ethnicity, and Family in Postcolonial Guatemala*, 1984; John W. Fox, *Quiché Conquest: Centralism and Regionalism in Highland Guatemalan State Development*, 1978; W. George Lovell, "Surviving Conquest: The Maya of Guatemala in Historical Conquest," *Latin American Research Review*, 23 (Number 2, 1988), 25–58.

AGUTI. See SHARANÁHUA.

AHONEKENKE. See TEHUELCHE.

AHONICANKA. See TEHUELCHE.

AHONIKEN. See TEHUELCHE.

AHONNEKENKE. See TEHUELCHE.

AHOPOVO. See ARIKEN.

AHORIO. See AYOREO.

AHUISHIRI. See AWISHIRI.

AÍ. See PILAGÁ.

AIAPÍ. See OYANPÍK.

AIAYÉ. See GUAJÁ.

AIGNGUTDESU. See NAMBIQUÁRA.

AIKANÁ. The Aikaná people are a small group of Amerindians living today in the state of Rondônia in Brazil. They are the survivors of an isolated linguistic group of tribes that once included the Aikaná proper as well as the Huarí, Masaká, Tubarao, Kasupá, Mundé, and Corumbiara. The Aikaná culture was once typical of a tropical forest group, with the people living in small villages and subsisting by hunting, fishing, and raising manioc near rivers. They were first contacted in the 1730s when neo-Brazilian gold prospectors poured into their territory. The subsequent measles epidemics hurt them severely. Jesuit missionaries worked among them until 1750 when the Treaty of Madrid directed that territory north of the Guaporé River be given to the Portuguese. As gold mining declined in the later eighteenth century, a measure of peace returned to Aikaná territory. Until the early 1900s, the Aikaná were isolated from neo-Brazilian civilization, but the rubber boom brought hordes of collectors to their homeland. Epidemic disease, dislocation, and violence drastically reduced the tribal population to such an extent that mergers between the subtribes occurred. The rubber boom declined in the 1920s and 1930s, only to return during World War II, bringing with it another period of decline. In 1940, the Brazilian government settled a number of Aikaná, Kanoê,* and Mondé* Indians at a post on the Igarapé Cascata River, which is a tributary of the Pimenta Bueno River. Measles epidemics there, however, soon drove the Indians back into the forests. Demographers estimate that today there are only 80 Aikaná still alive who speak the aboriginal language. Most of them live on the headwaters of the Chupinguai River, east of the Pimenta Bueno River. They were moved there in the mid–1970s.

REFERENCES: David Price, "The Indians of Southern Rondônia," in David May-bury-Lewis et al., eds., *In the Path of the Polonoreste: Endangered Peoples of Western Rondônia*, 1981, 33–37; Robert Lee Spires, "As línguas faladas do Brasil," *América Indígena*, 47 (1987), 455–79.

AIMBORÉ. See BOTOCUDO.

AIMORÉ. See BOTOCUDO.

AINAWIMOMOWI. See GUAHIBO.

AIPATSÉ. The Aipatsé, also known as the Tsuva, were a tropical forest tribe who lived in the Xingú River drainage area of upper Mato Grosso, Brazil. They were a Karib* language people closely related to the Kuikúru.* The first European to reach them was the anthropologist Karl Von den Steinen in 1884, but by that time, they had already been badly devastated by disease and attacks from neighboring tribes. Early in the twentieth century, a new wave of epidemics all but obliterated the Aipatsé; by the early 1980s, the tribe had ceased to exist as a cultural unit. For years they lived with the Kuikúru Indians, and the few remaining Aipatsé intermarried with them. Most recently, two families, the only surviving Aipatsé, have been living with the Kalapalo* and Nafuquá* in the Xingú Indian Park.

REFERENCES: Orlando Villas Boas and Cláudio Villas Boas, *Xingú: The Indians, Their Myths,* 1973; Robert Lee Spires, "As línguas faladas do Brasil," *América Indígena,* 47 (1987), 455–79.

AIPÍ. See OYANPÍK.

AIWATERI. The Aiwateri are an unacculturated group of the Yanoama* linguistic family of southern Venezuela and northern Brazil. In particular, they are closely related to the Shiriana or Xiriana* branch of the Yanoama. They live along the Mapulau and Totobi rivers in several villages near the Venezuelan frontier in the territory of Amazonas, Venezuela, and the state of Amazonas, Brazil. See YANOAMA.

AJÁNA. See URUKUYÁNA.

AJURU. See WAYORO.

AKAWÁIO. The Akawáios are a Karib*-language tribe of Indians scattered widely throughout Guyana from the Venezuelan to the Brazilian borders and in eastern Venezuela. Well-known for their commercial skills and wide-ranging trading activities, as well as for their penchant for transplanting whole villages, the Akawáios live on the Cotinga River in northeastern Brazil and near the Guyana-Brazil-Venezuela boundary. They live on the Guyana frontier of the state of Bolívar in Venezuela. The bulk of them, however, are concentrated in the upper Mazaruni and on the Barama, upper Pomeroon, Demerara, Wenamu, and Upper Cuyuni rivers. Today they are a tropical forest people numbering more than 8,000 and living off a slash-and-burn agricultural economy. Historically, the Akawáios and their subtribes have been known as Acahuáyo, Aca-guáyo, Acawai, Acawóio, Akawóio, Guaica, Wacawai, Waica, Waika, Capohn, Kapohn, Capóng, Kapóng, and Patamuno.* Their self-designation is Kapón.

REFERENCES: Walter F. Edwards, *An Introduction to the Akawáio and Arekuna People of Guyana*, 1977; Andrew Sanders, *The Powerless People*, 1987; William Hen-ningsgaard, *The Akawáio, The Upper Mazaruni Hydroelectric Project and National Development in Guyana*, 1981; Estéban Emilio Mosonyi, "La revitalización lingüística y la realidad venezolano," *América Indígena*, 47 (1987), 553–61; Georg J. Seitz, "Epene, the Intoxicating Snuff Powder of the Waika Indians and the Tucano Medicine Man, Agostino," in D. H. Efron et al., eds., *Ethnopharmacologic Search for Psychoactive Drugs*, 1967, 315–38.

AKAWÓIO. See AKAWÁIO.

AKUAWA-ASURINÍ. See ASURINÍ.

AKUEN. See AKWĒ.

AKURIYÓ. The Akuriyó (Akuliyó) are a subtribe of the Tiriyó* people of the Brazilian-Surinamese border area. Their population today is approximately 100 people. Traditionally they were a hunting and gathering people, and they still prefer that economy, even though many have turned recently to a slash-and-burn agriculture typical of tropical forest people. They function socially in bands of 20 to 30 people. Europeans first contacted the Akuriyó in 1609, but it was not until 1937 that anything was really learned about them. Some Wayána* Indians contacted and described the Akuriyó in 1968, and in the 1970s several dozen Akuriyó were settled in a mission village among the Tiriyó. The Akuriyó remain extremely suspicious of outsiders, Indian as well as European.

REFERENCE: Walter Dostal, ed., *The Situation of the Indian in South America*, 1972.

AKWAWA. See ASURINÍ.

AKWĒ. The term "Akwē" (Akwén, A'we) refers to a group of Gê-speaking people that once included the Xavánte* (Chavánte, Shavánte), the Xerénte* (Cherénte, Sherénte), and the Xakriabá* (Chikriabá, Shakriabá). The Xakriabá are nearly extinct, except for a few isolated individuals in the state of Mato Grosso, Brazil, while the Xerénte and Xavánte still function as tribal entities.

REFERENCES: David Maybury-Lewis, *Akwē-Shavante Society*, 1974; David May-bury-Lewis, *Dialectical Societies: The Gê and Boróro of Central Brazil*, 1979.

AKWÉN. See AKWĒ.

AKWĒ-XAVÁNTE. See XAVÁNTE.

ALACALOUF. See ALACALUF.

ALACALUF. The Alacaluf (Halakwulup, Alakaluf, Alacalouf, Alaculuf, Alaculoof, Alucaluf, Alukoeluf, Alooculoof, Alookooloop, Alukulup, Alokolup,
Alikhoolip, Alikuluf, Alikaluf, and Alikoolif) were a hunting and foraging tribe
of Amerindians who lived on the island chain along the Chilean coast from the
Gulf of Peñas to the west of Tierra del Fuego. Totally without agriculture, the
Alacaluf were a nomadic people constantly on the move in small groups collecting
shellfish, hunting marine birds, sea lions, and porpoise, and fishing; they traveled
from island to island by canoe. Although there were isolated contacts between
Europeans and the Alacaluf in the sixteenth, seventeenth, and eighteenth centuries, there was nothing of a permanent nature. In the 1840s, however, when
steam navigation became common along the Straits of Magellan, the need for
permanent lighthouses developed. The Salesian missionaries established a mission for the Alacaluf in 1888. Both developments resulted in rapid population
decline among the Alacaluf because of imported diseases. By 1940, the Alacaluf
population had declined to fewer than 200 people, and today only a handful of
people can identify themselves as Alacaluf.
    REFERENCES: José Emperaire, *Los nomadas del mar*, 1963; Andrea T. Merrill,
Chile: A Country Study, 1982; Andrés Serbin, "Las organizaciones indígenas en la
Argentina," *América Indígena*, 41 (1981), 407–34.

ALACALUFAN. The term "Alacalufan" refers to a small group of Amerindian
languages that were once located in Chile. These included Aksanas, Alacaluf,*
and Caucau. Linguists surmise that the Alacalufan languages are closely related
to the Mataco* and Macá* languages of Argentina and Paraguay.
    REFERENCE: Harriet E. Klein and Louisa R. Stark, *South American Indian Lan-
guages: Retrospect and Prospect*, 1985.

ALACULOOF. See ALACALUF.

ALACULUF. See ALACALUF.

ALADNDESU. See NAMBIQUÁRA.

ALAKALUF. See ALACALUF.

ALAKATDESU. See NAMBIQUÁRA.

ALAMA. The Alamas are a Quechua*-speaking tribe of Amerindians who live
in the rugged territory extending from the Andean foothills near the town of

Puyo, Ecuador, east to the Peruvian border, primarily along the Curaray and Cononaco rivers. In Peru they live near the Tigre, Curaray, and Arabela rivers. The Alamas spent centuries, on and off, in Roman Catholic missions until the nineteenth century when those missions for the most part declined. Nevertheless, Roman Catholic missionaries have played a central role, through their schools, in acculturating the Alamas to neo-Ecuadorian institutions. In recent years, more and more Alama children have been attending public schools and learning Spanish, while their parents have become increasingly integrated into the regional economy. A modest technological acculturation is occurring, but the Alamas still function as a tribal people. Their subsistence economy is based on swidden slash-mulch techniques and only rarely by slash-and-burn cultivation of manioc, sweet potatoes, taro, plantain, maize, and palm. In the western areas of Canelo* territory, they are also beginning to raise cattle and horses. Increasing numbers of Alamas work for large landowners. By the late 1980s, the Alama population probably exceeded 2,500 people.

REFERENCES: Udo Oberem, "Trade and Trade Goods in the Ecuadorian Montana," *Folk*, 8–9 (1967), 243–58; Norman E. Whitten, Jr., "Ecological Imagery and Cultural Adaptability: The Canelos Quichua of Eastern Ecuador," *American Anthropologist*, 80 (1978), 836–59; Norman E. Whitten, Jr., *Ecuadorian Ethnocide and Indigenous Ethnogenesis: Amazonian Resurgence Amidst Andean Colombia*, 1976.

ALCOJOLADO. See PARAUJANO.

ALDEANO. The term "Aldeano" is used widely in Ecuador and northern Peru to describe village Indians who live near larger towns and often work as day laborers there. It is a term of social condescension among neo-Peruvians and neo-Ecuadorians.

REFERENCE: Albert William Bork and Georg Maier, *Historical Dictionary of Ecuador*, 1973.

ALIKALUF. See ALACALUF.

ALIKHOOLIP. See ALACALUF.

ALIKOOLIF. See ALACALUF.

ALIKULUF. See ALACALUF.

ALILE. See PARAUJANO.

ALMAGUERO. See QUECHUA.

ALOKOLUP. See ALACALUF.

ALOOCULOOF. See ALACALUF.

ALOOCULOOP. See ALACALUF.

ALUCALUF. See ALACALUF.

ALUCUYANA. See URUKUYÁNA.

ALUKOELUF. See ALACALUF.

ALUKULUP. See ALACALUF.

ALUKUYANA. See URUKUYÁNA.

AMACACORE. See IQUITO.

AMAGE. See AMUESHA.

AMAGUACO. See AMAHUACA.

AMAHUACA. The Amahuaca are a Panoan*-speaking people who dwell on the headwaters of the Ucayali, Juruá, Purús, Curanja, Inuya, and Sepahua rivers in the Amazon Basin of Peru and across the border in the western reaches of the states of Amazonas and Acre, Brazil. The Amahuaca have also been identified historically as the Amajuaca, Amawaka, Amahuaka, Amaguaco, Ameuhaque, Ipitnere, and Sayaco. Although they were historically a passive people, the Amahuaca did not convert to Hispanic culture, rejecting the teachings of missionaries and avoiding contact with Europeans. When first contacted by the Dominicans in 1686, the Amahuaca were widely scattered throughout the Amazon Basin in Eastern Peru. Slave raids and attacks by neighboring tribes in the nineteenth century forced them into the Amazon forests, where they lived in small groups of nomadic foragers. They adapted to a garden horticulture system and raised manioc, corn, and sugar cane. At the time of the conquest, there were approximately 8,000 Amahuacan Indians, but those numbers dropped to 3,000 in 1927, 1,500 in 1940, 500 in 1970, and 600 in the early 1980s. Most of them live in eastern Peru but there are a few in the state of Acre in Brazil. In recent years, they have made some adjustment to a rudimentary subsistence agriculture, producing a variety of crops, including caucho and chestnuts.

REFERENCES: Robert L. Carneiro, "Hunting and Magic Among the Amahuaca of the Peruvian Montana" *Ethnology*, 9 (1970), 331–41; Robert L. Carneiro, "The Amahuaca and the Spirit World," *Ethnology*, 3 (1964), 6–11; Gertrude E. Dole, "Endocannibalism Among the Amahuaca Indians," *Transactions of the New York Academy of Sciences*, 24 (1962), 567–73; Robert Lee Spires, "As línguas faladas do Brasil," *América Indígena*, 47 (1987), 455–79.

AMAHUAKA. See AMAHUACA.

AMAJÉ. See AMUESHA.

AMAJÓ. See AMUESHA.

AMAJUACA. See AMAHUACA.

AMAMATÍ. See YAMAMADÍ.

AMANAJÉ. See AMANAYÉ.

AMANAJÓ. See AMANAYÉ.

AMANAYÉ. The Amanayé are today a Tupi*-speaking people of Brazil, who live between the cities of Belém and Brasília on the Pindaré, Gurupí, Capim, Moju, and Tocantins rivers, in the state of Pará. Historically, they have also been known as the Manayé, Mananyé, Manazewá, Amanajó, Manajó, Manaxó, Ararandeuras, and Turiwa. Along with other Tupi tribes, the Amanayé practice a slash-and-burn agriculture and raise manioc, cotton, and tobacco. They originally came from the Pindaré River area of Maranhão, where they were probably closely related to the Tembé-Tenetehára* Indians. Systematic contact with the Portuguese developed in the mid-eighteenth century, and the Amanayé underwent a rapid population decline. By the mid-nineteenth century, the Amanayé were becoming increasingly acculturated. Although the Amanayé still survive as a conscious ethnic group, their contemporary culture provides little condemnation for intermarriage with mestizos or other Indians; as a result, their population is in a state of rapid decline, now numbering well below 100 people. Today the Amanayé are economically integrated with the non-Indian people of the headwaters of the Capim, Moju, and Cairari rivers.

REFERENCES: Paul L. Aspelin and Silvio Coelho dos Santos, *Indian Areas Threatened by Hydroelectric Projects in Brazil*, 1981; *Encyclopedia of Indians of the Americas*, 2 (1974), 124–25; Robert Lee Spires, "As línguas faladas do Brasil," *América Indígena*, 47 (1987), 455–79; Theodore L. Stoddard, ed., *Indians of Brazil in the Twentieth Century*, 1967.

AMARACAIRE. See AMARAKAERI.

AMARAKAERI. The Amarakaeri (Mashco, Amaracaire) are a small Amerindian group who comprise part of the Harakmbet* (Hate) linguistic family that once occupied large stretches of land in the province of Paucartambo, department of Cuzco, in eastern Peru, particularly in the Q'eros, Cosnipata, Pilcopata, Tonó, and Pini-pini river valleys. Today they live along the Colorado and Madre de Dios rivers. There are a number of identifiable subgroups among the Amarakaeri, including the Kochimberi, Küpondirideri, Wintaperi, Wakitaneri, and Kareneri. Over the years, their relative isolation at the headwaters of the Karené and Shilive rivers protected them from repeated, sustained contact. Although conquered by the Incas and then by the Spaniards, the Amarakaeri maintained a strong sense of tribal identity, even though epidemic disease repeatedly reduced the tribal population, but the great South American rubber boom between 1894 and 1920 devastated the Amarakaeri. In 1900, they totaled perhaps 500 people, but small-pox epidemics decimated them in the 1940s, reducing them to fewer than 100 people. When the rubber boom collapsed in the 1920s, Roman Catholic mis-sionaries moved in. The Amarakaeri were missionized by the Dominicans in the 1950s and settled in the Upper Madre de Dios mission of Shuntuya. Most of them fled those missions and established the present Amarakaeri communities of Puerto Luz, San José del Karené, Boca del Inambarí, and Barranco Chico. Subsequent intermarriage with such groups as the Machiguenga* and the Wach-ipaeri* have further reduced them, although there are perhaps 1,500 Indians and mixed-blood Indians who are aware of their Amarakaeri heritage. In the 1980s, Amarakaeri has been threatened by multinational oil companies exploring for new reserves. Some Amarakaeri have joined the Federation of Natives of Madre de Dios to protect their land claims.

REFERENCES: Andrew Gray, "Perspectives on Amarakaeri History," in Harald O. Sklar and Frank Salomon, eds., *Natives and Neighbors in South America: Anthropological Essays*, 1987, 299–328; Patricia Lyon, "Dislocación tribal y clasificaciones lingüísticas en la zona del Río Madre de Dios," *Actas y Memorias*, 5 (1975), 185–207; Thomas R. Moore, "La experiencia Amarakaeri," *América Indígena* 44 (1984) 25–48; Stefano Varese, *The Forest Indians in the Present Political Situation of Peru*, 1972.

AMARIBA. See WAPISHÁNA.

AMARIPA. See WAPISHÁNA.

AMARIZAMA. See ACHAGUA.

AMARIZÁN. See ACHAGUA.

AMATISENGE. See CAMPA.

AMAWAKA. See AMAHUACA.

AMBURÉ. See BOTOCUDO.

AMENA-DIAPA. See KATUKÍNA.

AMEUHAQUE. See AMAHUACA.

AMIEMHUACA. See CAMPA.

AMNIAPA. See AMNIAPE.

AMNIAPE. The Amniape (Amniapa, Koaratira, Guaratagaja) were once a Tupi*-speaking tribe of Amerindians who lived a riverine existence on the Mequenes River in the Guaporé River drainage area of southern Brazil, particularly in what is today the state of Rondônia. Their language was probably part of the Makurap* subfamily. They were an agricultural people who lived off maize and peanuts. The great Brazilian gold rush first brought neo-Brazilian prospectors and diseases to the Amniape in the 1730s and 1740s. Jesuit missionaries later worked briefly with the Amniape, until the expulsion of the Jesuits from the New World in 1767. When the gold rush played out, the Amniape were generally left alone until the late nineteenth and early twentieth centuries, when they were devastated by the rubber collectors who swarmed over their area. The tribe then entered a period of population decline from which they have never recovered. In the mid–1950s, anthropologists reported a small group of Amniape living along the Madeira-Mamoré Railroad. There are individual people in the Guaporé who are aware of their Amniape ancestry, but the tribe no longer functions as a differentiated social unit.

REFERENCES: David Price, ''The Indians of Southern Rondônia,'' in David Maybury-Lewis, ed., *In the Path of the Polonoreste: Endangered Peoples of Western Brazil*, 1981, 34–37; Theodore L. Stoddard, ed., *Indians of Brazil in the Twentieth Century*, 1967.

AMO. See CHIMANE.

AMOKEBIT. See MOCOVÍ.

AMORUA. The Amorua are a tropical forest, Amerindian people living along the Meta River, between Orocue and Puerto Carreno, in the territory of Vichada in Colombia and just across the border in Venezuela. More specifically, they can be found on the Ele, Lipa, and Bita rivers. Although the Amorua were victimized by Karib* slave traders in the seventeenth century and by Jesuit missionaries in the eighteenth, their relative isolation helped protect them from annihilation. Since the tribe values peace and tranquility, not aggressiveness, as the greatest of virtues, it was their geographic position, not their resistance, that preserved them from the ravages of European civilization. The Amorua also knew that deadly sicknesses always accompanied contact with whites, so they avoided whites whenever possible. The Amorua still live as they have for centuries. They hunt and fish but only to supplement their horticulture. The Amorua maintain individually owned gardens of two to four acres in which they raise their staple—bitter yucca—along with potatoes, squash, bananas, maize, pineapple, sugar cane, peppers, and cotton.

REFERENCES: Joanna Overing Kaplan, *The Piaroa: A People of the Orinoco Basin*, 1975; Estéban Emilio Mosonyi, "La revitalización lingüística y la realidad venezolano," *América Indígena*, 47 (1987), 553–61.

AMUEIXA. See AMUESHA.

AMUESHA. The Amuesha, an Arawakan*-speaking tribe of Amerindians, who closely related to the Campa* and live in the Peruvian montana along the Pozuzo, Churchuras, Huancabama, Palcazu, Pichi, Neguachi, Apuracayali, and Maís rivers in the departments of Pasco and Junín. They call themselves the Yanesha. Franciscan missionaries established contact with the Amuesha in 1635 when they constructed missions near Cerro de la Sal. Neo-Peruvian settlements appeared in the 1640s, but the Amuesha destroyed them by the 1650s. In the 1670s, the Franciscans had succeeded in bringing several thousand Amuesha into the missions, but the Indians rebelled in the early 1680s, killing several priests and driving the others out. Missionary work resumed in 1709 but ceased with the Atahuallpa Revolt of 1753. The Amuesha who lived along the Pozuzo River slowly adopted the Quechua* language and became widely known as the Lorenzo Indians. Late in the 1880s, the Franciscans resumed their missionary work among the Amuesha, establishing missions near Chanchamayo and Cerro de la Sal.

Today the Amuesha number approximately 8,000 people and pursue a subsistence agricultural lifestyle, except for a small amount of time spent earning wages for the purchase of trade goods such as shotguns, outboard motors and fuel, and metal tools. They also grow coffee and collect rubber to sell for cash. The Amuesha retain strong sense of tribal identity. Historically they have also been known as Amueshua, Amagé, Amueixa, Omagé, Amajó, Amajé, Lorenzo, and Amuetamo.

REFERENCES: Fernando Santos Granero, "The Moral and Social Aspects of Equality amongst the Amuesha of Central Peru," *Journal de la Société des Américanistes*, 72 (1986), 107–32; Fernando Santos Granero, "The Power of Love—the Moral Use of Knowledge amongst the Amuesha of Central Peru," Ph.D. dissertation, London School of Economics, 1986; Richard Chase Smith, *The Amuesha People of Central Peru: Their Struggle to Survive*, 1974; Richard Chase Smith, "Deliverance from Chaos for a Song: A Social and Religious Interpretation of the Ritual Performance of Amuesha Music, Ph.D. dissertation, Cornell University, 1972; Richard Chase Smith, *The Multinational Squeeze on the Amuesha People of Central Peru*, 1979.

AMUESHUA. See AMUESHA.

AMUETAMO. See AMUESHA.

ANAKÊ. See AUAKÊ.

ANAMARÍ. See YAMAMADÍ.

ANAMBÉ. The Anambé are a tiny group of Amerindians who originated in Tupi*-speaking people living in what is now the state of Maranhão, Brazil. Today they total fewer than 50 people and live on the headwaters of the Cairari River, which is a western tributary of the Moju River, in the state of Maranhão, Brazil. They live north-northeast of the Tucurui Dam site. The Anambé were first reported in the 1850s, when they were living on the left bank of the Tocantins River and on the headwaters of the Pacaja River, a little above Alcobaça. A series of severe epidemics in the 1880s devastated the Anambé. Although they are indistinguishable in terms of economics, dress, and housing from the surrounding mestizo population, they retain some elements of their Tupi language. Outside the home they are fluent in Portuguese. They also maintain a residential segregation from non-Indian people. Since the late 1940s, most of the Anambé people have been heavily in debt to a local merchant, for whom they hunt animal skins, meat, and forest vegetable products.

REFERENCE: Paul L. Aspelin and Silvio Coelho dos Santos, *Indian Areas Threatened by Hydroelectric Projects in Brazil*, 1981.

ANANA. See UANANA.

ANAPATI. See CAMPA.

ANAPIA. See OMÁGUA.

ANAUQUÁ. See NAFUQUÁ.

ANCASH. See QUECHUA.

ANCKUTERE. See SECOYA.

ANCUTENA. See SECOYA.

ANCUTERE. See SECOYA.

ANDAGUEDA. See CHOCÓ.

ANDE. See CAMPA.

ANDIRA. See MAWÉ.

ANDO. See SHIMIGAE.

ANDOA. See SHIMIGAE.

ANDOKE. The Andoke (Andaquí, Andoque) are a small tribe of about 150 Amerindians who live along the lower Aduche River, the Lower Araracuara

River, the Pedrera River, and stretches of the Caquetá River in the Colombian Amazon. There are also some Andoke, no more than a dozen people, living across the border in Peru. They are known to their Indian neighbors as the Paatsiaja, a name that they use to describe their ancestors. Approximately 106 of the Andoke Indians were living on the Colombian government's Indian reservation at Aduche in 1988. The Andoke are the last remnants of a once larger tribe that extended from the Caquetá River basin more than 300 miles west to the edge of the eastern Andes mountains. Although hunting and fishing consume much of their time and hold great symbolic importance in Andoke culture, most of the tribe's nutrients come from the manioc, maize, sweet potatoes, plantains, and bananas that they raise in tribal gardens. Until the end of the nineteenth century, the Andoke were a large tribe numbering more than 10,000 people, but the rubber boom of the 1890s and early 1900s devastated them. It brought thousands of neo-Colombians and their diseases into Andoke territory and drastically reduced their population. Although many linguists associate the Andoke language with that of the Witoto* people, there is considerable debate about its exact origins. The surviving Andoke Indians are today integrated with the Witoto people.

REFERENCE: Michael J. Eden and Angela Andrade, "Ecological Aspects of Swidden Cultivation among the Andoke and Witoto Indians of the Colombian Amazon," *Human Ecology*, 15 (1987), 339–59.

ANGAITÉ. The Angaité (Enslet, Kyoma) today are an Amerindian people who live in the Gran Chaco of Paraguay. In 1900 their homeland extended from San Salvador to Puerto Casado. When Paraguay and Bolivia fought the Chaco War between 1932 and 1935, large numbers of Angaité Indians died at the hands of Bolivian soldiers. In recent years, the construction of the Trans-Chaco Highway has opened up their land to settlement and development. There are Angaité Indians living between the Paraguay River and the Trans-Chaco Highway and from the Monte Lindo River to the San Carlos River in the department of Boquerón. The Angaité are part of the Mascoian* linguistic family, but during the twentieth century many of the Angaité have become completely acculturated to the surrounding society. Less than half of the Angaité speak the aboriginal language, while the rest use Guaraní as their primary tongue. They work as wage laborers in the regional economy and have adopted the material culture of neighboring non-Indians. At the same time, the Angaité have retained a sense of their tribal identity, still seeing themselves as Indians, quite distinct from other Indians, Europeans, and Mestizos. Those Angaité living on land held by the New Tribes Mission at San Carlos on the Paraguay River are better off than many of their other tribal members because of the stability of their land tenure. In the mid–1980s, there were approximately 2,400 Angaité Indians in Paraguay.

REFERENCES: Harriet Klein and Louisa Stark, "Indian Tribes of the Paraguayan Chaco," *Anthropological Linguistics*, 19 (1977), 378–402; David Maybury-Lewis and James Howe, *The Indian Peoples of Paraguay: Their Plight and Their Prospects*, 1980;

John Renshaw, "Property, Resources and Equality among the Indians of the Paraguayan Chaco," *Man*, 23 (1988), 334–52.

ANGOTERO. The Angotero (Angutera) are a highly assimilated group of Western Tukanoan* Amerindians who live along the left bank of the Napo River below the Aguarico River in Amazonian Peru and across the border in southern Colombia. In Colombia they are known as Macaguaje or Secoya.* Traditionally they raised manioc, yucca, and bananas in communal gardens, but they were decimated by the rubber booms of the late nineteenth and early twentieth centuries. Today there are approximately 200 Angoteros still aware of their tribal heritage, but their lifestyle is more consistent with that of surrounding neo-Peruvian mestizos.
REFERENCE: Stefano Varese, *The Forest Indians in the Present Political Situation of Peru*, 1972.

ANGUTERO. See ANGOTERO.

ANONOTHA. See NONUYA.

ANTANIRI. See CAMPA.

ANTE. See CAMPA.

ANUMANIA. The Anumania were of Tupi* linguistic extraction. At the time of the Portuguese conquest of Brazil, they probably lived close to the Atlantic coast, but the pressure of neo-Brazilian settlement drove them west into the Xingú River drainage area. There they lived a tropical forest existence on the shores of Lake Itavununo. The German explorer and anthropologist Karl Von den Steinen contacted the Anumania in 1884, but the tribe was not able to survive the diseases brought by rubber collectors in the early twentieth century and the murderous attacks by the Trumái* Indians. It was the Trumái attacks that eventually destroyed the Anumania people. Survivors of the Anumania went to live with the Auetí,* and there are probably a few individuals among the Auetí who are aware of their Anumania roots.
REFERENCE: Adrian Crowell, *The Tribe That Hides From Man*, 1979.

ANUU. See PARAUJANO.

ANUXA. See OCAINA.

AÓENI-KUNK. See TEHUELCHE.

AOGE. See APINAYÉ.

AÓNIK. See TEHUELCHE.

AÓNIKEN. See TEHUELCHE.

AÓNIKENKE. See TEHUELCHE.

AÓNIKO-TSHONK. See TEHUELCHE.

AÓNUKUN'K. See TEHUELCHE.

APACACHODEGODEGÍ. See KADUVEO.

APACACHODEGUO. See KADUVEO.

APACATCHUDEHO. See KADUVEO.

APACA-TSCHE-E-TUO. See KADUVEO.

APALAÍ. Also known historically as the Aparaí and Arakwayu, the Apalaí are a small Karib*-speaking people who live in a tropical forest environment northwest of the Amazon delta in Brazil, particularly along the Paru de Oeste, Jarí, Maicuru, and Curuá rivers in the territory of Amapá and the state of Pará. The tribe is loosely organized economically, numbers approximately 140 people, and survives in isolation by raising manioc and corn through slash-and-burn farming techniques, moving to a new agricultural area every five to ten years. They collect small animals and insects for food and hunt small game. The Apalaí are suspicious of outsiders, and many members of the tribe remain very isolated.

REFERENCES: *Encyclopedia of Indians of the Americas*, 2 (1974), 197–98; Robert Lee Spires, "As línguas faladas do Brasil," *América Indígena*, 47 (1987), 455–79; Theodore L. Stoddard, ed., *Indians of Brazil in the Twentieth Century*, 1967.

APALAKIRI. See KALAPALO.

APÂNIEKRA. The Apâniekra (Apânyekra) are an almost extinct group of Gê*-speaking Amerindians from Brazil who, after a serious population decline from contact with neo-Brazilians, ceased to exist as a tribal unit. Before their decline, they lived near Porquinhos on a small tributary of the Corda River in the state of Maranhão, Brazil. A few Apâniekra survivors merged with the Ramkóka-mekra, a closely related branch of the Canelas Indians. See CANELA.

APÂNYEKRA. See APÂNIEKRA.

APAPOKUVA. See AVÁ-CHIRIPÁ.

APARAÍ. See APALAÍ.

APEIRAN'DI. See KAWAHÍB.

APIACÁ. Before the Portuguese conquest, there were nearly 20,000 Apiacá (Apiaká) living in the northern Mato Grosso region of Brazil, at the junction of the Arinos and Juruena rivers. They were a Tupi*-speaking people who cultivated extensive manioc, maize, and potato gardens. The Apiacá were first contacted by Europeans in 1791, and after that contact, their numbers began to decline rapidly. By the middle of the nineteenth century, the Apiacá had declined in numbers to 2,700 people and had relocated to the São Manoel River to avoid increased Brazilian settlement in their aboriginal homeland. At this new location, they became known as the Pari-bi-tete, a Mundurukú* word for them. There the Apiacá assimilated gradually into the Mundurukú tribe or into the larger Brazilian population. By the mid-1980s, there were still perhaps 40 people alive who knew of their Apiacá heritage, even though they spoke either Portuguese or Mundurukú as their primary language. Only 2 people were alive who understood Apiacá. The surviving Apiacá lived along the middle and upper Tapajós River, the lower Juruena River, and between the Peixe River and the lower Teles Pires River in the states of Mato Grosso and Pará, Brazil.
  REFERENCES: *Encyclopedia of Indians of the Americas*, 2 (1974), 198–200; Robert Lee Spires, "As línguas faladas do Brasil," *América Indígena*, 47 (1987), 455–79; Theodore L. Stoddard, ed., *Indians of Brazil in the Twentieth Century*, 1967.

APIAKÁ. See APIACÁ.

APIEACA. See ARÁRA.

APINAGÉ. See APINAYÉ.

APINAJÉ. See APINAYÉ.

APINAYÉ. The Apinayé are a Gê* people who live in two villages—São José and Mariazinha—between the Tocantins and Araguaia rivers in the municipality of Tocantinopolis, which is located in the northern reaches of the state of Goiás in Brazil. Historically, the Apinayé have also been known as the Western Timbira, Pinaré, Pinagé, Apinagé, Apinajé, Oupinagee, Otogé, Afotigé, Aogé, Uhi-tische, and Utinsche. They build their villages on high ground between rivers as long as there are no trees to be cleared. The villages are circular, with houses surrounding a central plaza. The Apinayé were originally semi-nomadic hunters who regularly harvested the manioc and maize that they had planted before leaving on long hunting expeditions. First contacted by Europeans in the 1770s, the Apinayé quickly became dependent on iron tools and slowly made a transition to more systematic agriculture. Europeans came into the area to collect the babassu nut and to establish cattle ranches. Long hunting trips became less common. The Apinayé also began collecting the babassu nut as a cash crop. In 1824, the Apinayé population exceeded 4,000 people, but it declined to 2,000 in 1860, 400 in 1900, and 160 in 1940. By the 1980s, there were approximately 500 Apinayé still alive, although they were increasingly detribalized and being integrated into the larger economy.

REFERENCES: Roberto Da Matta, *A Divided World: Apinayé Social Structure*, 1982; Robert Lee Spires, "As línguas faladas do Brasil," *América Indígena*, 47 (1987), 455–79.

APINGUI. See ARÁRA.

APOPOKUVA. See AVÁ-CHIRIPÁ.

APURINÃ. The Apurinã (Ipurinã) are an Amerindian tribe of Arawak* extraction living along the middle Purús River in the state of Amazonas, Brazil. The Apurinã were a riverine people, living off fish and such river animals as large turtles, while also maintaining communal gardens. Late in the nineteenth century and early in the twentieth, neo-Brazilian rubber gatherers clashed repeatedly with the Apurinã, substantially reducing their population through disease, slavery, and outright slaughter. Today the Apurinã are highly acculturated with neo-Brazilian society. There are approximately 250 people with clear Apurinã roots and another 3,000 mestizo people closely associated with the Apurinã; these probably have Apurinã ancestors but no longer function culturally as Indians.

REFERENCES: Robert Lee Spires, "As línguas faladas do Brasil," *América Indígena*, 47 (1987), 455–79; Theodore L. Stoddard, ed., *Indians of Brazil in the Twentieth Century*, 1967.

APUTERE. See KAIWÁ.

ARABELA. The Arabela (Chiripuno) are an Amerindian group whose language is part of the Zaparo* linguistic family. They are concentrated on the Arabela River, a tributary of the Cururay River, and on the Rumiyacu River, in the province of Mayna, department of Loreto, in Peru. They call themselves the Tapueyocuaca. The first contact with the Arabela came in 1945 when a group of 27 of them came out of the jungle and met with Father Ismael Barrio, who baptized them as Roman Catholics. Since then their population has increased substantially. They practice a subsistence agriculture and hunt and fish to supplement their diets. The Arabela are increasingly integrated today with nearby Quechua*-speaking Indians. In the late 1950s, there were about 60 Arabela Indians who spoke the aboriginal language, but today that number has declined to only 10 people. The rest of the Arabela use Quechua as their primary language, although some of them also speak Spanish. Approximately 300 people consider themselves of Arabela descent, including the Vacacocha. Use of the native language is rapidly approaching extinction.

REFERENCES: Darcy Ribeiro and Mary Ruth Wise, *Los grupos étnicos de la amazona peruana*, 1978; Stefano Varese, *The Forest Indians in the Present Political Situation of Peru*, 1972.

ARACUNA. See AREKUNA.

ARAHUAC. The Arahuac are a generally highly acculturated group of Amerindian tribes in Venezuela. They descend from Arawak*-speaking tribes of the northern South American coast. A small group of highly acculturated, detribalized Arahuacs live as farmers as laborers on the Guyana frontier of the Delta Amacuro Territory of Venezuela. A larger group of Arahuac people—including the Baníwa,* Baré,* Guarequena,* Curripaco,* and Piapoco*—live in the Río Negro drainage area of Venezuela on the Colombian frontier of the territory of Amazonas. They too are highly integrated into the local economy, primarily as collectors of chiqui-chique fiber and the pandare gum. Their way of life today is characterized generally by extreme poverty.

REFERENCE: Walter Dostal, ed., *The Situation of the Indian in South America*, 1972.

ARAIBAYBA. See PAUSERNA.

ARAKWAYÚ. See APALAÍ.

ARAMACOUTOU. See ARAMAGOTÓ.

ARAMAGOTÓ. The Aramagotó (Aramgotó, Aramayana, Aramakotó, Aramogotó, Aramagotou, and Aramacoutou) are a subtribe of the Tiriyó* Indians of Brazil and Surinam. They number fewer than 100 people and can be found living in the region of the West Parú and Citare rivers. See TIRIYÓ.

ARAMAGOTOU. See ARAMAGOTÓ.

ARAMAKOTÓ. See ARAMAGOTÓ.

ARAMAYANA. See ARAMAGOTÓ.

ARAMGOTÓ. See ARAMAGOTÓ.

ARAMICHÓ. The Aramichó (Aramisó, Aramichaux, Aramihitcho, Aramisho) are a subtribe of the Tiriyó* Indians of the Brazilian-Surinam border. The traditional homeland of the Aramicho was near the Maroni River and its upper east bank tributaries. When the Bush Africans began arriving in this area, the Aramichó fled southward to live on the Amazonian side of the Tumuchumac Mountains, where they became part of the Tiriyó. See TIRIYÓ.

ARAMOGOTÓ. See ARAMAGOTÓ.

ARAONA. The Araona are a tiny Amerindian group from the Tacana* linguistic family who today live between the Madre de Dios River and the Madidi River in the department of La Paz in Bolivia. As late as the 1880s, there were a variety of Araona subtribes, including the Beyuma, Buda, Cahoco, Cama, Camaya, Camoavi, Canamary, Capa, Capanary, Capechene, Capaheni, Capu, Chumu, Cuesi, Curupi, Dejabi, Ecuary, Eno, Giry, Guajima, Habuwi, Hamapu, Huary, Huarymodo, Ino, Isebene, Jicho, Machui, Machuvi, Manipo, Mapumary, Marani, Maru, Masatibu, Mayupi, Moyana, Odoary, Sabatini, Sara, Tade, Taranu, Tuama, Tuno, Uaui, Uranico, and Yuma. Until the twentieth century, the Araonas numbered more than 20,000 people. During the conquest period, they provided much information to Spaniards about local geography and natural resources. Until fairly recently, the Araona remained hidden in their tropical forest, trying to stay away from neo-Bolivianos at all costs, except for peaceful contacts in the 1960s with the New Tribes Mission and the Summer Institute of Linguistics. In the 1970s and 1980s, their contacts with the outside world increased. The tribal population today is only about 60 people. They retain a highly pronounced sense of ethnic identity and still speak their own language exclusively. They still function in a subsistence economy based on hunting, fishing, foraging, and manioc gardens, live an essentially communal lifestyle, and are verging in extinction as a differentiated social unit.

REFERENCES: Brian M. Boom, *Ethnobotany of the Chácobo Indians, Beni, Bolivia*, 1987; Bani Hauli, *Historia Araona*, 1980; Harold Key and Mary Key, *Bolivian Indian Tribes: Classification, Bibliography, and Map of Present Language Distribution*, 1967; Pedro Plaza Martínez and Juan Carvajal Carvajal, *Etnías y lenguas de Bolivia*, 1985; Graciela Zolezzi and J. Riester, "Lenguas indígenas del Oriente boliviano clasificación preliminar," *América Indígena*, 47 (1987), 425–33.

ARAOTE. See WARRAÚ.

ARAPACO. See ARAPASO.

ARAPASO. The Arapaso Indians are a small subtribe of the Tukano* Indians, an Eastern Tukanoan language group. The Arapaso are located along the lower Vaupés River in Colombia, near the Brazilian border. Their population in the late 1980s was approximately 270 people. They live primarily as a fishing tribe. See TUKANO.

ARAPIUM. See MAWÉ.

ARÁRA. The Arára Indians are part of a Mondé*-linguistic family of Amerindian groups and are closely related to the Gavião* and Zoró* Indians of eastern Rondônia in Brazil. They are not to be confused with the Koaiá* Indians, who are sometimes called Arára, or the Kayapó*-Arára people of the Xingú River area. The Arára were at war with the Gaviãos in the 1950s, when the Brazilian government used the Gaviãos to contact and pacify the Arára. By 1966, there were only 50 Arára Indians still alive. Missionaries and physicians from the New Tribes Mission probably rescued the Arára from extinction by providing them with the medical care they needed to resist epidemic disease. The Arára then joined with the Gaviãos in living at several government posts in eastern Rondônia. Although the missionaries converted most of the Gaviãos to the Baptist church, the Arára have resisted and generally remained faithful to older, indigenous traditions. Government Indian agents have introduced a Brazil nut industry, which has allowed the Arára to remain in their area without venturing into local towns to search for jobs. In the 1980s, however, the Arára way of life has been threatened by the population explosion in Rondônia and the possibility of mineral reserves in the region. The Arára population today exceeds 200 people.
    REFERENCE: Denny Moore "The Gavião, Zoró, and Arára Indians," In David Maybury-Lewis, ed., *In the Path of the Polonoreste: Endangered Peoples of Western Brazil*, 1981, 46–54.

ARÁRA. The term Arára is a loose designation used for more than a century by Europeans to describe several closely related tropical forest Indian groups located on both sides of the upper Xingú River and between the Jiparaná and Tapajós rivers. Known also as the Yuma, Kre-akarôre, Apeiacá, Apiacá,* Apingui, Karo, Uruku, and Pariri,* the Arára called themselves the Opinadkom and are part of the larger Kayapó* Indian group. These are not to be confused with the Koaiá* Indians, sometimes referred to as Arára, who are living farther west in Rondônia, or the Mondé*-speaking Arára Indians who are living with the Gaviãos* near Ji-Paraná. At the time of the Portuguese conquest, they numbered more than 4,000 people and were known for their ferocity. Although the Arára planted some cotton and manioc, they were primarily a hunting and gathering people. In the eighteenth century, Jesuits missionized hundreds of Arára and set in motion a population decline that has not stopped even today. In the 1850s, some Arára appeared on the lower Xingú River, driven there by hostile Kayapó Indians. More than 130 Arára gathered at a new mission, São Francisco, on the Machado River in 1871 but they continued to die out. Their population is fewer than 100 people.

REFERENCES: *Encyclopedia of Indians of the Americas*, 2 (1974), 207–08; Robert Lee Spires, "As línguas faladas do Brasil," *América Indígena*, 47 (1987), 455–79; Theodore L. Stoddard, ed., *Indians of Brazil in the Twentieth Century*, 1967.

ARÁRA. See KOAIÁ.

ARARANDEURARAS. See AMANAYÉ.

ARARA-TAPUYA. See KARUTANA.

ARARAS. See ARÁRA.

ARASA. See ARASAERI.

ARASAERI. The Arasaeri (Arasaire, Arasa, Araza, Arasairi, Arazaire, and Careneri) are a small group of Amerindians from the Harakmbet* linguistic family. In the nineteenth century, they were located along the Marcapata or Arasa River, a tributary of the Inambari, in Peru. The rubber boom between 1894 and 1920 devastated them when neo-Peruvian rubber collectors either took them into slavery or killed them by distributing disease-infested blankets. They have also survived two gold rushes and the missionary activities of Protestants and Catholics. Today there are approximately 600 Arasaeri Indians, many of whom are mixed bloods, living in the region of the Madre de Dios River. There they pursue a largely subsistence, agricultural lifestyle, providing for their need for cash with day labor. Most of the Arasaeri live along the Maldonado-Cuzco Road. Also living with the Arasaeri are the Pukirieri, whom some scholars assume to be a former Arasaeri subgroup. The Pukirieri still have a sense of ethnic identity. Only a handful of the Arasaeri live today in a communal group; virtually all of them are bilingual. Their language will probably become extinct in the next two decades.

REFERENCES: Andrew Gray, "Perspectives on Amarakaeri History," in Harald O. Sklar and Frank Salomon, eds., *Natives and Neighbors in South America: Anthropological Essays*, 1987, 299–329; Stefano Varese, *The Forest Indians in the Present Political Situation of Peru*, 1972.

ARASAIRE. See ARASAERI.

ARASAIRI. See ARASAERI.

ARAUAK. See ARAWAK.

ARAUCANIAN. The Araucanians (Araucano) are one of the largest South American tribes of Amerindians. Alonso de Ercilla y Zúñiga, the sixteenth-century Spanish poet, first coined the term "Araucanian" to describe the fierce Amerindians of what is today Chile. During the period of Inca expansion and Spanish conquest in the fifteenth and sixteenth century, the Araucanians lived between the Choapa River in the north to northern Chiloé Island in the south of Chile. They included three major groups, who designated themselves by their geographical locations. The northern Araucanians were known as the Picunche*; the central and dominant Araucanians as the Mapuche*; and the southern Araucanians as the Huilliche.* In the seventeenth and eighteenth centuries, while they were resisting Spanish conquest, the Araucanians themselves expanded eastward and conquered the Pehuenche, Puelche, and Chiquillanes, all of which were absorbed into Araucanian culture. Other Araucanians, primarily Mapuche and Huilliche, expanded into Argentina, particularly southern Mendoza, Neuquén, and Buenos Aires provinces, where they became known as Aucas.*

Before the Spanish conquest, the Araucanians totaled more than one million people and practiced a slash-and-burn agriculture to raise maize, potatoes, beans, squash, chili peppers, and quinoa. They also domesticated the llama and a wild chicken. When Spaniards arrived, the Araucanians quickly adopted the cultivation of wheat, the use of the plow, and the domestication of cattle, horses, sheep, goats, mules, and pigs. Political cohesion was very loose among the Araucanians, with little emphasis on centralized values, but they fiercely resisted Spanish expansion. In 1541, Pedro de Valdivia, the Spanish explorer of the southern reaches of the continent, established the city of Santiago, but six months later the Araucanians destroyed the settlement. Valdivia then attacked the Araucanians with a vengeance, placing them on encomiendas and exacting tribute from them. By the end of the 1500s, the Araucanians had adopted the horse and had become expert guerrilla fighters. Still, the toll of war and disease on the Araucanians was great. By the early 1600s, the Araucanian population had been reduced to approximately 100,000 people and the Picunche were rapidly disappearing as an identifiable group. Araucanian culture by that time was confined primarily below the Bío-Bío River.

In the seventeenth century, Roman Catholic missionaries and neo-Chileno settlers began moving into Araucanian land, by now primarily Mapuche and Huilliche territory. During those years, they adopted many items from Spanish material culture, as well as a number of Roman Catholic values, first from the Jesuits until 1767, then the Franciscans until the mid–1850s, and finally the Capuchins. Throughout the 1700s and 1800s, there was violence between the

Spanish and the Araucanians and then between the Araucanians and the neo-Chilenos and the Chilean government. The Indians resented the increasing pressure of settlers on their lands and periodically rebelled. But in 1866, the government established the first reservations for the Araucanians, now primarily the Mapuche. In 1884, after the final subjugation, the reservations were implemented on a wide scale.

By the mid–1980s, the Mapuche numbered nearly 600,000 people living on several thousand reservations between the Laja River and the Gulf of Reloncavi in the region of La Araucania. Another 50,000 Mapuche lived in the cities of Santiago, Concepción, and Temuco, while more than 20,000 are Aucas living in Argentina. The Huilliche have for all intents and purposes ceased to exist as a separate social unit, having merged over the years with the expanding Mapuche people.

REFERENCES: Bernardo Berdichewsky, *The Araucanian Indian in Chile*, 1975; Maria P. Dillon, *The Fighting Araucanians*, 1964; Herbert Lee Ellis, *The Indian Policy of the Republic of Chile*, 1956; Louis Faron, *The Mapuche Indians of Chile*, 1986.

ARAUCANO. See ARAUCANIAN.

ARAUCO. See ARHUACO.

ARAVACO. See ARAWAK.

ARAWÁ. The term ''Arawá'' is used to describe a small linguistic family in South America. Today speakers of an Arawá language live primarily in the states of Acre and Amazonas in Brazil. They include the following groups: Banavá-Jafi,* Daní,* Jarauára,* Kanamantí, Kulína,* Paumarí,* and Yamamadí.* Arawá itself is part of the larger Arawakan group of languages.

REFERENCE: Robert Lee Spires, ''As línguas faladas do Brasil,'' *América Indígena*, 47 (1987), 455–79.

ARAWAK. The term ''Arawak'' is used to describe a wide variety of Amerindian groups native to the Greater Antilles and South America, as well as to a broad group of related languages. More particularly, Arawak (Aroaqui, Aruac, Aruaki, Aravaco, Arouage) refers to the Locono* (Lokono) groups, since the word ''Locono'' is a self-designation meaning ''Arawak proper.'' Those groups today are confined to the coastal and geographically related areas of Guyana, Surinam, and French Guiana. Most of the Locono Indians are bilingual in English, Dutch, or French, depending upon their residence. Many of them are in an advanced state of acculturation. The Locono population numbers approximately 13,000 people in about 40 villages, with the largest concentration in Guyana. Traditionally, the Locono were a horticultural people who lived off the production of manioc and other products, with hunting and fishing used as dietary supplements. But Western-style education as well as Western technologies have undermined that subsistence lifestyle, forcing increasing numbers of Locono to work as laborers in the regional cash economy. That economic integration has also politicized the Locono as they have worked to preserve their tribal land titles and fishing and hunting rights.

Before the arrival of Christopher Colombus and the Spaniards, the Arawakan Indians found themselves losing a struggle for survival with the more aggressive Karib* Indians, who were expanding out of South America into the Lesser Antilles. The Karibs had already conquered the Lesser Antilles and were poised to assault the Arawakan peoples on the Greater Antilles when Colombus arrived. In their conquest of the Arawak Indians, the Karibs often killed the men, married the women, and then witnessed the survival of the Arawakan language in their children. The arrival of the Spaniards stopped the Karib expansion.

The first people whom Colombus encountered in the New World were the Arawakan-speaking Taíno* people who occupied Cuba, the Bahamas, and Hispaniola. From the very beginning, the Spaniards classified the Arawaks as peaceful Indians and the Karibs as violent people, even cannibals. But despite their peaceful presence, the Arawakan peoples in the Greater Antilles did not survive Spanish contact. Scholars estimate that there were as many as two million Arawak Indians occupying the Greater Antilles at the time of the conquest; by 1519, only a few thousand were left, the others were victims of disease, violence, slavery, and environmental changes that occurred when the Europeans introduced new species of plants and animals to the islands. By 1600, Arawakan Indian society in the Greater Antilles had ceased to exist as a differentiated social unit.

Arawakan groups on the mainland of South America survived because they were more isolated and because European penetration occurred more slowly. Also, the Arawak groups of the continent were organized into small, secluded, and semi-nomadic societies, which allowed them to avoid European contact for a long time. The English in Guyana and the Dutch in Surinam approached the Arawak Indians from a commercial perspective rather than one of conquest, setting up trading posts along major rivers and encouraging the Indians to exchange forest products for metal goods and textiles. The Arawaks were drawn to the trading posts because they felt safer there, not so much from other Europeans as from their Karib enemies. Not surprisingly, they acculturated more quickly than Karibs to European ways. In the seventeenth and eighteenth centuries, when a plantation economy emerged in the Guianas and large numbers of African slaves were imported as workers, the planters paid money to the Indians to keep control of the slaves and track down those who escaped. The Indians lost that revenue when slavery was abolished in the 1830s and entered a long period of economic and population decline that did not stabilize until the twentieth century.

REFERENCES: *Encyclopedia of Indians of the Americas*, 2 (1974), 220–26; Fred Olsen, *On the Trail of the Arawaks*, 1971.

ARAWAKAN. The term ''Arawakan'' refers to an extensive linguistic family that existed widely throughout the West Indies and South America and that remains today one of the largest indigenous linguistic groups in the New World. Taíno* was once spoken on Hispaniola, Cuba, and the islands of the Greater Antilles, while the Arauan branch (Araua, Kulína,* Paumarí,* Yamamadí,* and Jaruára*) of the Arawakan family was spoken near the Purús and Juruá river drainages into the Amazon in central Brazil. Chamicuro,* Amuesha,* and Apolista were native to the mountains of Peru, while Uruan (Uru,* Shipaya,* and Puquina*) were found in the highlands of Bolivia. On the eastern foothills of the Andes and spreading from throughout western and central Brazil, eastern Ecuador, Colombia, Venezuela, Guyana, Surinam, and French Guiana are the enormous Maipurean group of Arawakan languages, which included the Moxo,* Baure,* Paiconeca, Paunaca,* Paraná, Teréno,* Chane, Inapari,* Ipurinã,* Kanamarí,* Píro,* Chontaquiro, Cuniba, Cujisenayeri, Cámpa,* Machiguenga,* Nomatsiguenga,* Waraicu, Guajiro,* Paraujano,* Baré,* Wirina, Guinau, Maipurean,* Yabarána,* Anauya, Cariaya, Araua, Manao, Yumana, Marawá, Piapoco,* Achagua,* Amarizina, Wainuma, Mariate, Pase, Cayuishana, Cauyari, Yukuna,* Guaru, Arekena, Resigaro,* Izaneni, Ipeca, Hohodene, Carutana, Catapolitani, Moriwene, Mapanai, Maulieni, Waliperi-Dakenai, Baníwa,* Suisi, Tariana, Mehinácu,* Iaualapití,* Custenau, Waurá,* Palikur,* Marawá, Yavitero, Parecí,* Saraveca,* Wapishána,* Shebayo, and Mandawáca.

REFERENCE: *Encyclopedia of Indians of the Americas*, 2 (1974), 226–27.

ARAWETÉ. See ARAWINE.

ARAWINE. The Arawine (Araweté) were a Tupi*-speaking group of Amerindians who in the late eighteenth and early nineteenth centuries moved into the upper Xingú River drainage region of Brazil from points east to escape the dislocations introduced by Portuguese settlers. They remained relatively isolated on a tributary of the Culuene River in what is today the state of Mato Grosso until the late nineteenth century when rubber collectors disrupted the region. The Arawine population decline that then set in was all but irreversible. Today there are perhaps 150 Arawine who live isolated in two villages near the Brazilian government Indian post on the Ipixuna River (an eastern tributary of the Xingú River). They live there primarily to be protected from the Parakána* Indians, who attacked them repeatedly in the late 1970s and early 1980s. Their recent contact with Brazilian society has caused problems of cultural dislocation for the Arawine, and the construction of the Carajas Dam will be even more disruptive. They live off the Brazil nut, wild cacao, inga, and the babassu palm. It has been only since 1976 that the Arawine have been in unarmed contact with the Brazilian government.

REFERENCES: William Balée, "Cultural Forests of the Amazon," *Garden*, 11 (1987), 12–14, 32; Robert Lee Spires, "As línguas faladas do Brasil," *América Indígena*, 47 (1987), 455–79; Theodore L. Stoddard, ed., *Indians of Brazil in the Twentieth Century*, 1967; Eduardo Viverios de Castro, "Arawete: Uma visão de cosmológia e da pessoa

Tupi-Guaraní,'' Ph.D. dissertation, Federal University of Rio de Janeiro-National Museum, 1984.

ARAZA. See ARASAERI.

ARAZAIRE. See ARASAERI.

ARÉ. The Aré (Curutón, Xetá) are descendents of a Tupi*-speaking group of Amerindians who were briefly contacted by neo-Brazilians early in the 1900s. A nomadic, foraging people who inhabited the open forests of the Ivai Valley in the state of Paraná in Brazil, the Aré came into intermittent contact with the Brazilian government's Indian service in 1952. Today there are fewer than 100 people who are even aware of their Aré heritage. The group is extinct as a social unit. Only 5 people still speak the aboriginal language. They live in the Barão de Antonina Indian Park in the state of Paraná, Brazil.

REFERENCES: Robert Lee Spires, ''As línguas faladas do Brasil,'' *América Indígena*, 47 (1987), 455–79; Theodore L. Stoddard, ed., *Indians of Brazil in the Twentieth Century*, 1967.

ARECUNA. See AREKUNA.

AREKUNA. The Arekuna, known also in the past as the Aracuna, Arecuna, Aricuni, Taulipáng, Taurepáng, Taurepa, Jaricuna, Jarecouna, and Pemóng, are a Karib*-language group of American Indians. They are also known as the Parukoto.* They once lived in the Vaupés River drainage region of Venezuela and Colombia. A tropical forest people whose life centers around slash-and-burn agriculture for the production of sweet manioc, the Arekuna did not migrate to Guyana until the 1920s when Seventh Day Adventist missionaries were expelled from Venezuela. The Arekuna followed the missionaries to a new mission in the Paruima area of Guyana. In recent years, the Arekuna have become increasingly acculturated to neo-Guyanese values and material artifacts. Today there are perhaps 1,500 Arekuna living in Guyana, Venezuela, and Brazil.

REFERENCES: Walter F. Edwards, *An Introduction to the Akawáio and Arekuna Peoples of Guyana*, 1977; Andrew Sanders, *The Powerless People*, 1987.

AREPINA. See MAWÉ.

AREQUENA. See WARIKYÁNA.

ARGENTINE TOBA. See TOBA.

ARHUAC. See ARHUACO.

ARHUACO. The Arhuaco (Aruac, Arauco, Arhuac, Auroguac) are descendents of a Chibchan*-speaking group of Amerindians who called themselves the Ika.*

There were several Arhuaco subtribes: the Bítuncua (Bíntuka), the Bucinka (Bucintaua), and the Ijka (Ijca, Iku). The term Arhuaco has also been used generically for several centuries to describe the Chibchan-speaking tribes of the Sierra Nevada mountains of Colombia, particularly such groups as the Cogui,* Búntigwa, Sanká (Sanhá), and Ika. At the time of the conquest in the sixteenth century, the Arhuaco were a large group scattered throughout what are today the departments of Magdalena and La Guajira in Colombia. In 1587, Luis de Tapia first encountered the Arhuaco, and Capuchin missionaries reached them in 1693. A sedentary, agricultural people, the Arhuaco were known for their peaceful ways and quickly adjusted to the Spanish empire, primarily by retreating upriver into the mountain ranges. Their population rapidly declined from disease and exploitation; the Arhuaco did not successfully resist acculturation. They live today on isolated farms on the southern slopes of the Sierra Nevada de Santa Marta mountains in northern Colombia. Most of them are included within the boundaries of the huge Arhuaco de la Sierra Nevada reservation in Colombia. Over the centuries, they tried to resist acculturation with European society by slowly migrating farther and farther upriver to avoid contact, but it was difficult. By the mid-nineteenth century, their aboriginal language had been replaced by Spanish. Today there are approximately 5,000 people in Colombia who are descendents of the Arhuaco and who still maintain an identity as Indians, although overt Arhuaco elements of that identity are increasingly less functional. Except for the adoption of such new plants as bananas, plantains, and sugar cane, the Arhuaco still practice a subsistence agriculture, with maize and manioc serving as dietary staples. They are more acculturated than their Cogui neighbors.

REFERENCES: Juan Friede, *Problemas sociales de los Arhuacos*, 1963; Vicencio Torres Marquéz, *Los indígenas Arhuacos y "la vida de la civilización,"* 1978; Alvaro Chaves Mendoza and Lucía de Francisco Zea, *Los Ijca*, 1977.

ARIANA. See OMÁGUA.

ARICAPÚ. See ARIKAPÚ.

ARICUNI. See AREKUNA.

ARIKAPÚ. The Arikapú (Aricapú), also known historically as the Maxubí or Maxukí, are a linguistically isolated group of Amerindians who live on the headwaters of the Río Branco River near the town of Vilhena in the State of Rondônia, Brazil. The language appears to be closely related to Jabutí.* The Arikapú were not exposed to Westerners until the 1730s when neo-Brazilian gold prospectors flooded into their territory, bringing violence and diseases, particularly measles, with them. The Arikapú population began a rapid decline. The gold boom ended by the early nineteenth century, and the Arikapú enjoyed a measure of peace. This calm was shattered early in the 1900s when the rubber boom brought new waves of settlers into their land. Today there are only about

40 of the Arikapú still living together as a people. Tribal ceremonial life has ceased to exist, and the Indians support themselves economically as small farmers and migrant laborers in the larger economy. Those still alive recognize their sense of tribal peoplehood even if the tribe barely functions as an overt social group. Still, the Arikapú are rapidly approaching extinction.

REFERENCES: David Price, "The Indians of Southern Rondônia," in David May-bury-Lewis, ed., *In the Path of the Polonoreste: Endangered Peoples of Western Brazil*, 1981, 33–37; Robert Lee Spires, "As línguas faladas do Brasil," *América Indígena*, 47 (1987), 455–79.

ARIKÊM. See ARIKÊN.

ARIKÊN. The Arikên (Ahopovo) were a Tupi*-Guaraní* tribe of Amerindians who once lived at the headwaters of the Jamari and Candeias rivers, both tributaries of the Madeira, in what is today the state of Rondônia, Brazil. At the time of the Portuguese conquest of Brazil, the Arikên probably exceeded 3,000 people. They pursued a horticultural lifestyle that revolved around the production of manioc, their staple; they also raised maize. Hunting and fishing supplemented their diet. But when Cândido Rondon discovered them in 1913, there were only 60 Arikên left alive. He transferred them to a government Indian post but their population decline continued and the tribe has ceased to exist as a differentiated social unit. Today the Arikên are nearly extinct, although a handful of older, detribalized people in Rondônia are aware of their Arikên heritage.

REFERENCE: Theodore L. Stoddard, ed., *Indians of Brazil in the Twentieth Century*, 1967.

ARIKIÉNA. See WARIKYÁNA.

ARIKPAKTSÁ. See ARIPAKTSÁ.

ARIMIGOTÓ. See ARIMIHOTÓ.

ARIMIHOTÓ. The Arimihotó (Arimikotó, Arimigotó, Arimiyana) are a sub-tribe of the Tiriyó* people of the Brazilian-Surinamese border area. Their population in the 1950s was approximately 100 people, but because of their friendly attitude toward outsiders, the Arimihotó have disappeared as an identifiable group. Those surviving members who still remember their Arimihotó heritage are pursuing a slash-and-burn agriculture typical of tropical forest people, but they are living amidst other Tiriyó people. See TIRIYÓ.

ARIMIKOTÓ. See ARIMIHOTÓ.

ARIMIYANÁ. See ARIMIHOTÓ.

ARIPAKTSÁ. Also known as the Erikpaktsá, Erigpactsá, Erigpatsá, Erig-baagtsá, Rikpakcá, and Rikpaktsá, the Aripaktsá are a tropical forest people who live near the junction of the Juruena, Sangue, and Arinos rivers in northwestern Mato Grosso state in Brazil. They were completely isolated from European culture until 1961 when Protestant missionaries first contacted them. At the time of the Portuguese arrival in Brazil in the 1500s, the Aripaktsá numbered approximately 3,000 people. Although they did not directly confront white people, they did encounter white diseases, which have plagued them then and now. The Aripaktsá total only 460 people today; they pursue a subsistence, agricultural lifestyle with major elements of their aboriginal culture still intact.

REFERENCES: Robert Hahn, "Missionaries and Frontiersmen as Agents of Social Change among the Rikpakcá," in Steve Hvalkof, ed., *Is God an American? An Anthropological Perspective on the Missionary Work of the Summer Institute of Linguistics*, 1981, 85–107; John Hemming, *Red Gold: The Conquest of the Brazilian Indians, 1500–1760*, 1978; Robert Lee Spires, "As línguas faladas do Brasil," *América Indígena*, 47 (1987), 455–79; Theodore L. Stoddard, ed., *Indians of Brazil in the Twentieth Century*, 1967.

ARITÍ. See PARECÍ.

AROAQUÍ. See TARUMA.

AROUÁ. See ARUÁ.

AROUAGE. See ARAWAK.

AROUEN. See ARUÁ.

ARTIEDA. See GUAYMÍ.

ARÚ. See JAQÍ.

ARUÁ. The Aruá (Arouén, Arouá) are a group of Amerindians who live in the state of Rondônia, Brazil. Some of them still live at the headwaters of the southern tributaries of the Ji-Paraná River. Their language is part of the Mondé* linguistic family. They were not contacted by Westerners until the 1730s when neo-Brazilian gold prospectors poured into southern Rondônia bringing measles and death with them. The Aruá population decline set in. A tropical forest people who lived off hunting and horticulture, the Aruá were later decimated by the rubber boom in Rondônia in the early 1900s and again during World War II.

The rubber collectors brought violence, disease, and forced labor to the Aruá people. Their population declined so drastically that they could no longer maintain traditional ceremonial life. In 1956, there were a number of Aruá living at Ribeirao on the Madeira-Mamoré Railroad in the territory of the Pakaanóva* Indians. There are reportedly some Aruá living at the headwaters of the Branco River as well. Today there are isolated groups of individuals living in Rondônia who are aware of their Aruá heritage, but the tribe is no longer an integrated social unit. A small group lives at the Ricardo Franco government post in southern Rondônia.

REFERENCES: David Price, "The Indians of Southern Rondônia," in David Maybury-Lewis, ed., *In the Path of the Polonoreste: Endangered Peoples of Western Brazil*, 1981, 33–37; Robert Lee Spires, "As línguas faladas do Brasil," *América Indígena*, 47 (1987), 455–79.

ARUAC. See ARHUACO.

ARUAKI. See ARAWAK.

ARUASHÍ. The Aruashí were once a tropical forest people living in the Guaporé River watershed of southeastern Rondônia. Their language was part of the Monde* linguistic family, and the Aruashí were closely related to the Gaviãos* and Zoró* Indians, their neighbors to the north. The Aruashí first encountered neo-Brazilian society in the 1730s when gold prospectors flooded Rondônia and brought diseases with them. The Aruashí population began a long decline that the rubber collectors of the early twentieth century only accelerated. By the 1960s, the Aruashí were not functioning as a tribal entity. Anthropologists have not seen any living Aruashí in several years, although it is certain that there are still individuals in southeastern Rondônia who, despite acculturation, are aware of their Aruashí roots.

REFERENCES: David Price, "The Indians of Southern Rondônia," in David Maybury-Lewis, ed., *In the Path of the Polonoreste: Endangered Peoples of Western Brazil*, 1981; Theodore L. Stoddard, ed., *Indians of Brazil in the Twentieth Century*, 1967.

ARUCUI. See URARINA.

ARUCUYI. See URARINA.

ARUPATI. The Arupati were a group of Tupi*-speaking Amerindians. At the time of the Portuguese conquest of Brazil in the sixteenth century, the Arupati lived much closer to the Atlantic coast. Waves of neo-Brazilian settlement gradually drove them farther west, while European diseases reduced their tribal population. They eventually made their way to the Ronura River in the Xingú River drainage area, where they pursued a typical tropical forest existence. Mortal enemies with the Kamaiurá,* the Arupati eventually fell victim to their genocidal attacks. All of the Arupati men died in the battles but many of the women were taken into captivity and absorbed by the Kamaiurá. There are probably still some members of the Kamaiurá tribe who are aware of their Arupati roots.

REFERENCE: Adrian Crowell, *The Tribe That Hides From Man*, 1979.

ARUTANI. See AUAKÊ.

ASHINANCA. The Ashinanca Indians are one of the main divisions of the Campa* people of Peru. They call themselves the Ashinanca and live today on the Bajo Apurimac, Ene, Tambo, Bajo Perené, and Satipo rivers in the jungles of the Peruvian Amazon, primarily at altitudes between 1,000 and 6,000 feet above sea level. They have traditionally lived in small groups governed by the heads of nuclear families. Although the Ashinanca, in relatively small numbers, intermarry with Quechua,* Amuesha,* Píro,* Machiguenga,* and other Campa subtribes, they are still primarily endogamous in their family and sexual relations. Historically, the Ashinanca were a seminomadic people, but in recent decades they have settled down into a subsistence agricultural lifestyle with their diets supplemented by hunting and fishing. To raise cash for trade goods, the Ashinanca produce and sell corn, rice, beans, coffee, cacao, and citrus fruits. In the Tambo region, a substantial number of Ashinanca work for padrone labor bosses. Today there are approximately 20,000 Ashinanca Indians in Peru.

REFERENCE: Darcy Ribeiro and Mary Ruth Wise, *Los grupos étnicos de la Amazona Peruana*, 1978.

ASHIRI. See AWISHIRI.

ASHLUSLAY. The Ashluslay are a Matacoan*-speaking people who today are concentrated north of the middle Pilcomayo River about 180 miles northwest of Asunción, Paraguay. They occupy both the Argentinian and Paraguayan sides of the river. They are divided into five major divisions: Tovok (Tte), Chishamne'e (Shicha'am), Yitaa (K'utja'am), Jotoy, and Tavashay. A small number, no more than 100, live in Bolivia, where they are severely persecuted by neo-Bolivians. Those in Argentina are concentrated on the Lamadrid River and around Fortin Nuevo, Pilcomayo, Laguna de los Pajaros, Tucumancito, and Misión de San Andrés. There they live in close proximity to the Matacos* and Chiriguanos.* Historically they have also been known at various times as Chunupí, Chulupí, Choropí, Sowa, Sowuash, Suhín, Sotiagai, Sotegaraik, Etehua, Nivaklé, and Tapieté.* They call themselves the Guisnai. When first contacted by Europeans in the 1830s, they were a nomadic hunting and foraging tribe who periodically practiced some horticulture. They were able to maintain their aboriginal lifestyle until the early 1900s, when increasing numbers of Ashluslay began finding work on ranches and sugar plantations in Paraguay and Argentina. After World War II, the Ashluslay abandoned their nomadic ways for permanent villages, and they added sheep raising as a major economic pursuit. Most of them also left the sugar plantations, where working conditions and wages were deplorable. Construction of the Trans-Chaco Highway in the 1970s and 1980s has brought more settlement and contact with neo-Paraguayans. Ashluslay territory now reaches from the Pilcomayo River on Paraguay's western border to the central Chaco around Filadelfia. Most Ashluslay live in settlements along the Paraguayan side of the Pilcomayo River at Roman Catholic missions of the Oblate Order and in agricultural colonies and worker villages in the region settled by Mennonites. Today there are approximately 10,000 Ashluslay who still identify themselves by their tribal membership. Although most of them are bilingual in Ashluslay and Guaraní* or trilingual in Ashluslay, Guaraní, and Spanish, they remain loyal to their aboriginal language and culture.

REFERENCES: Isabel Hernández, "Los pueblos y las lenguas aborígenes en la actualidad," *América Indígena*, 47 (1987), 409–23; David Maybury-Lewis and James Howe, *The Indian Peoples of Paraguay: Their Plight and Their Prospects*, 1980; Charles R. Wick and Migüel Chase-Sarcli, "Componential Analysis of Chulupí (Ashluslay) Kinship Terminology," *Ethnology*, 8 (1969), 484–93; Johannes Wilbert and Karin Simoneau, *Folk Literature of the Nivakle Indians*, 1987.

ASSURINÍ. See ASURINÍ.

ASURINÍ. The Asuriní (Assuriní, Assurinikin, Kuben-Kamrektí, Awaeté) are a tropical forest tribe who live along the Pacajá River, a tributary of the middle Xingú River in central Brazil. They managed to avoid sustained contact with Europeans until the 1890s when the rubber boom brought so many neo-Brazilians up the Xingú River. In 1894, they attacked a group of neo-Brazilian intruders near Praiá Grande, below Altamira and upstream from the Pacajá River. Other attacks took place in the 1890s, and the Asuriní became known as an extremely hostile tribe whose raids against incoming settlers continued well into the 1930s. The neo-Brazilian settlers even supplied weapons to the Arára* Indians to attack the Asuriní. Anthropologists from the Brazilian government did not establish formal contact with the Asuriní until 1972. They remained in violent contact with the rival neighbors, the Arawine,* into the 1970s. A farming people who raise a variety of manioc and maize plants, the Asuriní number fewer than 60 people today.

REFERENCES: Anton Lukesch, *Bearded Indians of the Tropical Forest: The Asuriní of the Ipiaçaba, Notes and Observations on the First Contact and Living Together*, 1976; Robert Lee Spires, "As línguas faladas do Brasil," *América Indígena*, 47 (1987), 455–79.

ASURINÍ. Not to be confused with the Asuriní of the middle Xingú River region, the Asuriní, also known as the Akwawa-Asuriní, are a Tupi*-speaking Amerindian group living on the left bank of the Tocantins River, below the Tucuri, Pacajá de Portel, and upper Pacajá rivers in the state of Pará, Brazil. Neo-Brazilians called them "Veados," an epithet synonymous with "homosexual." The Asuriní call themselves the Huriní, Suriní, or Uriní. The Brazilian

Indian Protection Service first pacified one group of these Asuriní in 1953, when they drifted into a government post for protection from other tribes. Although they left the post and returned repeatedly in the 1950s and early 1960s, their violent resistance had come to an end. Another group has had periodic contact since the 1920s, but has often broken off those contacts for years at a time. Like other tropical forest people, the Asuriní (Akwawa, Akuawa) raise maize, manioc, tobacco, and other crops using slash-and-burn horticultural techniques. The Asuriní came into contact with neo-Brazilians in the nineteenth century when collectors entered their territory to gather rubber and brazil nuts. The Asuriní fiercely attacked the intruders. Between 1927 and the early 1950s, there were repeated battles between the Asuriní and railroad workers who were constructing and maintaining a line through their territory. Since the 1960s, the pacified group of Asuriní has lived at the Trocara Indian Post, a small reservation maintained by the Brazilian National Indian Foundation. There are fewer than 150 members of the tribe still alive.

REFERENCES: *Encyclopedia of Indians of the Americas*, 3 (1974), 6–7; Carl H. Harrison, *Gramática Asuriní: Aspectos de uma gramatica transformacional e discursos monologados da língua Asuriní família Tupi Guaraní*, 1976; Robert Lee Spires, "As línguas faladas do Brasil," *América Indígena*, 47 (1987), 455–79.

ATCHUARA. See ACHUARA.

ATICUM. See ATIKUM.

ATIKUM. The Atikum (Aticum, Uamue) are a highly acculturated group of more than 1,500 Amerindians who have completely lost their aboriginal tribal heritage. They no longer speak an Indian language. Instead, they use Portuguese as their primary idiom, worship as Roman Catholics, work in the regional cash economy as laborers and small farmers, and function in the local mestizo culture. Today they live on a government Indian post just north of the municipality of Floresta in the state of Pernambuco, Brazil. From external appearances, the Atikum are not different from the surrounding mestizo society; internally, they retain an identity separate from that of neo-Brazilian society. Their current population probably exceeds 1,500 people. Like other Indian people in the region, the Atikum are threatened by the social, economic, and ecological changes that are inevitable as a result of the construction of the Itaparica Hydroelectric Project on the São Francisco River.

REFERENCES: Paul L. Aspelin and Silvio Coelho dos Santos, *Indian Areas Threatened by Hydroelectric Projects in Brazil*, 1981; Theodore L. Stoddard, ed., *Indians of Brazil in the Twentieth Century*, 1967.

ATIRI. See CAMPA.

ATONAXO. See MAXAKALÍ.

ATONTU'TUA. See TAUSHIRO.

ATORAD. See WAPISHÁNA.

ATORAI. See WAPISHÁNA.

ATORYA. See WAPISHÁNA.

ATROAHÍ. See ATRUAHÍ.

ATROAHY. See ATRUAHÍ.

ATROARÍ. See ATRUAHÍ.

ATRUAHÍ. The Atruahí (Atroahí, Atroahy, Atruahí, Atroarí) are a subtribe of the Yawaperi* Indians. An isolated group of Amerindians, the Atruahí live on the Alalau and Jauaperi rivers in northern Amazonas, Brazil. They number approximately 350 people. See YAWAPERI.

ATSIRÍ. See CAMPA.

ATTARAYA. See WAPISHÁNA.

ATTORRAIDI. See WAPISHÁNA.

AUAICU. The Auaicu (Awaikê, Awaika) are a little-known Amerindian tribe of tropical forest people who today live along the upper Paranajuva River in the Xingú Indian Park of upper Mato Grosso, Brazil. Extremely suspicious of all non-Auaicu, Brazilians as well as other Indians, the Auaicu have avoided all but the most accidental contact with other people. They remain in an aboriginal state, most likely without the use of iron and steel tools. Their tribal population probably numbers several hundred people.

REFERENCES: Robin Hanbury-Tenison, *A Question of Survival for the Indians of Brazil*, 1973; Orlando Villas Boas and Cláudio Villas Boas, *Xingú: The Indians, Their Myths*, 1973.

AUAKÊ. The Auakê (Anake, Awaikê, Aoaquis, Auaque, Oewaku, Arutaní, Urutaní, Uruak) are a tiny group of Amerindians who once extended from the upper Paragua River in Venezuela to the Uratani mountains and south to the Uraricoera River in Brazil. A tropical forest people, the Auakê practiced a slash-

and-burn agriculture to raise manioc, bananas, tobacco, yams, and some cotton. They also spent a good deal of their time hunting and fishing. Early in the 1800s, the Auakê were displaced by the expanding Kaliana* and Yanoama* Indians, and in the process their numbers were greatly reduced. Diseases from Europeans only accelerated their decline. By 1900, there were only about 70 Auakê still alive, and many of them began intermarrying with the Yanoama Indians. Today those surviving Auakê, perhaps 15 people, live at the headwaters of the Paragua and Uraricoera rivers at the Venezuelan-Brazilian border. Their self-designation is Uruak. Only a handful of people know the original tribal language, which is part of the larger Arawakan linguistic family.

REFERENCES: Walter Coppens, *Los aborígenes de Venezuela*, 1983; Walter Dostal, ed., *The Situation of the Indian in South America*, 1972; *Encyclopedia of Indians of the Americas*, 3 (1974), 22–24.

AUAQUE. See AUAKÊ.

AUCA. The term "Auca" (Auka, Aucano, Aucanian, Moluche, Maluche) is an Incan word referring to the unconquered Araucanian* Indians living between the Maipó and Bío-Bío rivers in Chile. In more recent years, this term and its synonyms have been used to describe the Araucanian Indians, primarily of Huilliche* and Mapuche* descent, who left Chile and migrated to Argentina, especially southern Mendoza, Neuquén, and Buenos Aires provinces, where they eventually took up trades as cattlemen, herders, horse traders, and migrant laborers. See ARAUCANIAN.

AUCANIAN. See AUCA.

AUCANO. See AUCA.

AUETÍ. The Auetí Indians, also known as the Awetí, Auetó, Autl, and Auití, are a Tupi*-speaking people who once lived on the left bank of the Culiseu River in the upper Xingú River area of Mato Grosso, Brazil. The German anthropologist Karl Von den Steinen first encountered them in the 1880s. They were, and remain today, a tropical forest people who survive off fishing, hunting, and raising maize, manioc, and tobacco. Although their population underwent a dramatic decline from disease in the first half of this century, they were saved as a cultural unit by the decision of the Brazilian government to establish the Xingú Indian Park in the 1960s. Another Tupi group, the Anumania, merged with the Awetí after being nearly destroyed by the Trumái.* Today there are fewer than 50 Auetí Indians living in the park. Although they still speak their own Tupi language, they closely cooperate in cultural and social matters with their immediate neighbors in and just outside the park—the Txikão,* Waurá,* Kamaiurá,* and Mehinácu.*

REFERENCES: Orlando Villas Boas and Cláudio Villas Boas, *Xingú: The Indians,*

Their Myths, 1973; Robert Lee Spires, "As línguas faladas do Brasil," *América Indígena*, 47 (1987), 455–79.

AUETÓ. See AUETÍ.

AUHISHIRI. See AWISHIRI.

AUISHIRI. See AWISHIRI.

AUITÍ. See AUETÍ.

AUKA. See AUCA.

AURA. See WAURÁ.

AUROGUAC. See ARHUACO.

AUSHIRI. See AWISHIRI.

AUTL. See AUETÍ.

AUVE. See IQUITO.

AUXIRA. See AWISHIRI.

AVÁ. The Avá, also known historically as the Canoiero (Canoeras), are a somewhat mysterious group of Tupi*-speaking Amerindians native to the state of Goiás in Brazil. Extremely suspicious of Europeans, the Avá put up a fierce resistance to neo-Brazilian expansion in the mid-nineteenth century. They lived a hunting and gardening existence on the Tocantins River and were widely known for their skills as guerrilla fighters. In the 1850s and 1860s, the Avá conducted a reign of terror throughout northern Goiás. Some anthropologists for a time assumed that the Avá were descendents of the Fulniô.* Today the Avá remain extremely isolated, living between the Araguaia and Tocantins rivers in the state of Goiás, east of the southern tip of Bananal Island. Current estimates place the tribal population at approximately 100 people.

REFERENCES: John Hemming, *Amazon Frontier: The Defeat of the Brazilian Indians*, 1987; Robert Lee Spires, "As línguas faladas do Brasil," *América Indígena*, 47 (1987), 455–79.

AVÁ-CHIRIGUANO. See CHIRIGUANO.

AVÁ-CHIRIPÁ. The Avá-Chiripá (Apapovoteng, Apopovoteng, Nhandeva, Nandeva, Apopokuva, Tanygua, Txiripa) call themselves the Avá-Katu-Ete.

They are part of the Guaraní* language family. Between 1630 and 1768, the Avá-Chiripá were residents of Jesuit missions, where they converted to Roman Catholicism, albeit a syncretic version. When the Jesuits were expelled from South America in 1767, the Avá-Chiripá returned to the forest and to a traditional lifestyle. In the twentieth century, government policies encouraged the economic development of Avá-Chiripá territory and settlement by neo-Paraguayans. In the process, the Avá-Chiripá, who did not have titles to their land, found themselves displaced. Today the Avá-Chiripá move around in the areas bordering the eastern Paraguayan localities of Laurel, Curuguaty, Yvyrarobana, Ytakyry, Hernandar-ías, Yerbal, and Santa Teresa. They can also be found in Brazil, particularly around Bananal, Arariba, Ytariri, Dourados, and Jacarei. The nomadic Apa-pokuva of southern Mato Grosso, Brazil, are a band of the Avá-Chiripá. The Avá-Chiripá are now among the most acculturated of the Guaraní tribes, espe-cially in terms of the pastoral economy of the area; they own horses and grazing animals and work as migrant laborers. Most of them are closely associated with Roman Catholic or German and Norwegian Lutheran missions in the area, or are subject to the economic control of local patrons and ranchers. Despite the economic integration, most of the nearly 5,000 Avá-Chiripá have a strong sense of tribal loyalty. The most important challenge facing the Avá-Chiripá today is the social and economic effect of the Itaipu Binational Paraná River Hydroelectric Project, which threatens to flood much land and bring tens of thousands of workers to their territory.

REFERENCES: Paul L. Aspelin and Silvio Coelho dos Santos, *Indian Areas Threat-ened by Hydroelectric Projects in Brazil*, 1981; Migüel Alberto Bartolomé, ''Shamanism Among the Avá-Chiripá,'' in David L. Browman and Ronald A. Schwartz, eds., *Spirits, Shamans, and Stars: Perspectives from South America*, 1979, 68–85; Robert Lee Spires, ''As línguas faladas do Brasil,'' *América Indígena*, 47 (1987), 455–79.

AVÁ-GUARANÍ. See CHIRIGUANO.

AVÁ-KATU-ETE. See AVÁ-CHIRIPÁ.

AVIJIRA. See AWISHIRI.

AVIRXIRI. See AWISHIRI.

AVIXIRA. See AWISHIRI.

AWAETÉ. See ASURINÍ.

AWAIKA. See AUAICU.

AWAIKÊ. See AUAKÊ.

AWANO. See AGUANO.

AWEIKOMA. The Aweikoma are an Amerindian tribe in Brazil. Closely related to the Kaingáng,* they belong to the southern branch of the Gê* family of

Amerindian languages. Over the years, they have also been known as Botocudo*
(not to be confused with the other Gê-speaking Botocudo tribe of eastern Brazil),
Xakléng, Xokléng, Shokléng, Xogléng, Xokréng, Xokré, and Bugré. At the
time of the Portuguese conquest in the sixteenth century, the Aweikoma lived
on a vast area of forest and savanna in what is today the state of Santa Catarina
in southern Brazil. By the nineteenth century, there were three Aweikoma communities in Brazil totaling more than 1,000 people. One group established peaceful contacts with the Indian Protection Service in 1914 and was relocated to a
reservation outside the town of Ibirama. That group of Aweikoma still survives
today with a population of approximately 650 people. The second Aweikoma
group came into peaceful contact with the Indian Protection Service in 1918,
although by that time they were in a state of disarray; a few of them survive
near the town of Porto União. The third Aweikoma group, which was still violent
toward neo-Brazilians in the 1930s, ceased to exist in the early 1940s.

The Aweikoma are a tribe of hunters, food gatherers, and agriculturalists who
place far more importance on hunting than on farming. Among their Kaingáng
neighbors, farming is a much more important part of economic life. The Brazilian
government has labored diligently to convert the Aweikoma on the Ibirama
reservation to settled agriculture, but it has been a difficult process at best for
Indians whose social life has traditionally revolved around semi-nomadism and
hunting. The Aweikoma today are either at the Ibirama reservation in the state
of Santa Catarina or at the Posto Laranjinhas in the municipality of Bandeirantes
in the state of Paraná. They are acculturated to neo-Brazilian clothing and technology, integrated into the local cash economy, and bilingual in Portuguese and
their own Gê language. Still, the surviving Aweikoma maintain a strong sense
of tribal identity, even if traditional ceremonies are disappearing. During the
1980s, one of the greatest threats to the Aweikoma Indians has been the construction of the Itajai River Flood Control Project, which threatens to flood more
than half of their land.

REFERENCES: Paul Aspelin and Silvio Coelho dos Santos, *Indian Areas Threatened
by Hydroelectric Projects in Brazil*, 1981; Jules Henry, *Jungle People: A Kaingáng Tribe
of the Highlands of Brazil*, 1941; David Hicks, "A Comparative Study of the Kaingáng
and Aweikoma of Southern Brazil," B.Litt. thesis, University of Oxford, 1965; Silvio
Coelho dos Santos, *Índios e Brancos do sul do Brasil: A dramatica experiencia dos
Xokléng*, 1973; Robert Lee Spires, "As línguas faladas do Brasil," *América Indígena*,
47 (1987), 455–79.

AWETÍ. See AUETÍ.

AWIRIMOMOWI. See GUAHIBO.

AWISHIRI. The Awishiri (Awishira, Avirxiri, Abixira, Avixira, Avijira, Abigira, Abijira, Auishiri, Agouisiri, Auhishiri, Aushiri, Auxira, Abira, Ahuishiri,
Ashiri, Huarani, Vacacocha, and Ixignor) are a group of Amerindians whose

original homeland was on the lower Curaray River and north to the Napo River in eastern Peru. Their linguistic origins are matters of scholarly debate, with some identifying them as a Panoan* people and others as Zaparoan.* Their self-designation is Tequiraca. Roman Catholic missionaries began extensive contacts with the Awishiri in 1620 and established a mission for them at San Miguel in 1665. The Awishiri maintained an intense hostility to neo-Peruvians as well as to other Indians, and their numbers declined rapidly because of disease, violence, and slavery. By the 1920s, there were only about 200 of the Awishiri still alive. They lived in two groups, one of them a detribalized community under the control of a Peruvian patron and another in the region of the Tiputini and Shiripuno rivers. The latter were living in an aboriginal state as semi-nomadic hunters and collectors. In 1956, the Awishiri attacked and killed six Protestant missionaries; as late as 1966, they attacked neighboring groups of Quechua* Indians. By that time, Quechua was increasingly becoming their primary language. The rubber boom of the World War II era struck a major blow at the Awishiri people, and a polio epidemic in 1969–1970 hurt them as well. Recently explorations by geologists for major petroleum companies have brought more disruptions to Awishiri land. The numbers of Awishiri are very few today, although there are probably other, more acculturated people in Ecuador and Peru who are aware of their Awishiri ancestry. There may also be a few older Awishiri who still understand the native language.

REFERENCES: Walter Dostal, ed., *The Situation of the Indian in South America*, 1972; Darcy Ribeiro and Mary Ruth Wise, *Los grupos étnicos de la Amazonia peruana*, 1978.

AYACUCHO. See QUECHUA.

AYAMARE. See AYMARA.

AYAPI. See OYANPÍK.

AYCUBAVERRENAY. See ACHAGUA.

AYMARA. The Aymara people constitute a vast Amerindian group second in size only to the Quechuan*-speaking group among the aboriginal people of South America. The Aymara language, part of the Jaqí* (Arú) language family, is spoken by more than 600,000 people in Argentina, Bolivia, Chile, and Peru. Perhaps 50,000 Aymara live in northern Chile. Before the Inca conquests of the fifteenth century and the Spanish conquest of the sixteenth century, there were several independent Aymara states, each of which had its individual Aymara dialect. The differences among the dialects, however, were quite minimal, and they were mutually intelligible. Those major Aymara groups were the following: the Canchi (in the Vilcanota Valley between Combapata and Tinta in what is today the department of Cuzco, Peru); the Cana (between Tinta and Ayaviri in the department of Puno, Peru); the Colla, Kolla, or Qolla* (on the plains of the Pucara and Ramis rivers north to the city of Puno, Peru); the Lupaca (on the southwestern shore of Lake Titicaca between the city of Puno and the Desaguadero River); the Collagua (north of the city of Arequipa, Peru, along the upper Colca River); the Ubina (east of the city of Arequipa, Peru, in the Tambo River drainage area of the department of Moquegua); the Pacasa or Pacaje (south of Lake Titicaca on both sides of the Desaguadero River in Bolivia; the Caranga or Caranca (south of the Desaguadero River to Lake Coipasa in Bolivia); the Charca (northeast of Lake Poopo near Chuquisaca in Bolivia); the Quillaca, Quilaco, or Quillagua (southeast of Lake Poopo in Bolivia); the Omasuyo (east of Lake Titicaca in Bolivia); and the Kollahuaya, Collahuaya, Kollasuyo, or Qollahuaya* (in the provinces of Muñecas and Caupolican in Bolivia. Other subtribes include the Sicasica and Paría. Although the forces of acculturation and assimilation are powerful in Peru and Bolivia, most of those subgroups still survive linguistically. Aymara has also spread to Mariscal Nieto province of Moquegua and to Tarata province of Tacna, Peru. Approximately 100,000 Aymara people, also known as Colla, live in Argentina, where they have migrated in recent years to find work. In many areas of Peru and Bolivia, Aymara has become the *lingua franca* of the general population, even among those people who no longer function socially as Indians. They live in the lowlands, central plateaus, and highlands of the Andes Mountains. A small number of Aymara dwell in the Yungas, a subtropical rain forest on the eastern slopes of the Andes. Most of the Aymara live in an area known as the Altiplano, a plateau at 12,000 to 14,000 feet elevation between the eastern and western ranges of Bolivia and Peru. They pursue an agricultural lifestyle in small villages of between 50 and 150 people. In the highlands, they raise potatoes, oca, quinoa, and barley; at lower altitudes, they produce wheat and maize. Along Lake Titicaca, they fish and raise beans and onions. At higher altitudes of 14,000 to 17,000 feet, Aymara herders graze alpacas, llamas, and sheep that provide the Aymara with cheese, fertilizer, milk, leather, wool, rope, and meat.

The Inca empire conquered the Aymara in the fifteenth century, scattering many of them to distant places; in the sixteenth century, the Spanish empire reduced the Aymara to near-slave status on the encomiendas. When the great mines opened up in Bolivia, the Aymara were forced to work and die in them. By 1600, there were only 35,000 Aymara still alive. Thus, more than 75 percent of the pre-conquest population was gone. In the 1600s, the Spanish tried to bring the Aymara on to *reducciones* where they could be converted to Roman Catholicism by Jesuit and Franciscan missionaries. On the reducciones, the Aymara were prohibited from speaking their own language, dressing like Indians, using body paint, or sleeping on the floor. Mass uprisings by the Aymara against Spanish rule occurred in 1781 and 1814. Since the period of Bolivian independence, the neo-Bolivian government has been trying to incorporate the Aymara into the larger political and social order through individual rather than communal land ownership and formal connections between Aymara political organizations and the local and national government. Increasingly large numbers of the Aymara people are today acculturating to neo-Peruvian and neo-Bolivian values—speaking Spanish or Quechua* as their primary language, accepting Roman Catholicism as their religion, attending state-run public schools, and becoming more and more integrated into the local regional economy. They are adapting to increasing land shortages by turning to cattle fattening, circular migration for temporary jobs, or permanent migration into the major cities to look for work. Approximately 600,000 of the nearly 1,800,000 Aymara people retain strong linguistic and religious ties to their aboriginal heritage, still speaking Aymara, avoiding contact with non-Indians, and practicing an ancient religion that involves worship of the earth and natural environment as the source of all life.

REFERENCES: Lucy Therina Briggs, "Dialectical Variation in the Aymara Language of Bolivia and Peru," Ph.D. dissertation, University of Florida, 1976; Hans C. Buechler, *The Bolivian Aymara*, 1971; Hans C. Buechler, *The Masked Media: Aymara Fiestas and Social Integration in the Bolivian Highlands*, 1980; T. C. Lewellen, *Peasants in Transition: The Changing Economy of the Peruvian Aymara, A General Systems Approach*, 1978; Harold Osborne, *Indians of the Andes: Aymaras and Quechuas*, 1952.

AYMORE. See AYMARA.

AYORE. See AYOREO.

AYOREO. The Ayoreo (Ahorio, Ayore, Zamuco, Moro, Muro, Muru, Morotoco, Ayoreode, Samococis, Potureros, Guaranoca, Ugaranos, Corazu, Kursu, Tynyro, Careluta, Caipotorades, Cucutades, Zatienos) are a Zamuco*-speaking Indian tribe of the Paraguayan Gran Chaco and the department of Santa Cruz in Bolivia. They were traditionally hunter-gatherers who fiercely resisted outside influences. When the Europeans first arrived on their land in the eighteenth century, the Ayoreo were a nomadic, foraging people with a simple material culture. Their mortal enemies, the Kaduveo,* regularly attacked and enslaved them, and the arrival of Europeans actually reduced that threat to the tribe. The Ayoreo were contacted widely by Spanish explorers in the eighteenth century, as well as by Jesuit missionaries, but they avoided friendly contacts until the 1940s. Today the Ayoreo have become somewhat more acculturated to European lifestyles, especially in their economic adjustment where they have made the transition to farm and ranch labor. They still retain, however, the use of their aboriginal language and a strong sense of tribal identity. Most of them work as wage laborers on the large Mennonite farms in the area or on small tribal plots of land and run a few head of cattle or sheep. In the 1970s, the Ayoreo were drawn to settle in two locations. Nearly 600 Ayoreo joined the New Tribes Mission at Faro Moro, north of Filadelfia; another 400 settled at a Salesian mission on the upper Paraguay River at María Auxiliadora. Several independent bands totaling about 150 people still pursue a nomadic, aboriginal lifestyle in the remote reaches of the Gran Chaco, where they avoid contact with whites and other settled Ayoreo. In the mid–1980s, there were approximately 1,200 Ayorean Indians in Paraguay and 2,500 in Bolivia.

REFERENCES: Brian M. Boom, *Ethnobotany of the Chácobo Indians, Beni, Bolivia*, 1987; Harold Key and Mary Key, *Bolivian Indian Tribes: Classification, Bibliography, and Map of Present Language Distribution*, 1967; Harriet Klein and Louisa Stark, "Indian Tribes of the Paraguayan Chaco," *Anthropological Linguistics*, 19 (1977), 378–402; David Maybury-Lewis and James Howe, *The Indian Peoples of Paraguay: Their Plight and Their Prospects*, 1980; John Renshaw, "Property, Resources and Equality among the Indians of the Paraguayan Chaco," *Man*, 23 (1988), 334–52; Graciela Zolezzi and J. Riester, "Lenguas indígenas del oriente boliviano clasificación preliminar," *América Indígena*, 47 (1987), 425–33.

AYOREODE. See AYOREO.

B

BACAIRÍ. See BAKIRÍ.

BACAJA. See XIKRÍN.

BAENAN. The Baenan (Baenna) were once part of an isolated linguistic group of Amerindians who lived on the left bank of the Pardo River in what is today the state of Bahia, Brazil. From the time of their first contact with neo-Brazilians, their population went into a rapid decline; by the 1940s, their small numbers prevented the maintenance of tribal ceremonial life. By the 1960s, anthropologists with the Brazilian government could identify only 20 Baenan who were still alive, and they were thoroughly detribalized. A few of those 20 are still alive today, living in the municipality of Itabuna in Bahia.

REFERENCE: Theodore L. Stoddard, ed., *Indians of Brazil in the Twentieth Century*, 1967.

BAENNA. See BAENAN.

BAGUAJA. See ESSEJJA.

BAGUAJAIRI. See ESSEJJA.

BAHUAJJA. See ESSEJJA.

BAKAIRÍ. See BAKIRÍ.

BAKIRÍ. The Bakirí (Bakairí, Bacairí, Kurá) are a Karib language tribe of Amerindians who today number approximately 400 people and live just outside the Xingú Indian Park in the state of Mato Grosso, Brazil. At the time of their discovery by anthropologist Karl Von den Steinen in 1884, they were divided into two groups, the Western Bakirí and the Eastern Bakirí. They lived then at the headwaters of the Paranatinga River. They were widely used, by neo-Brazilian traders as well as other Indian trading groups, as guides into the Xingú River area. Traditional warfare and influenza reduced their numbers in the twentieth century, but the population decline stabilized in the 1960s. Although the Bakirí today make extensive use of European metal technology and are thoroughly acculturated to local neo-Brazilian values, they have retained the use of the tribal language and maintain a powerful sense of separate ethnic identity.

REFERENCES: Orlando Villas Boas and Cláudio Villas Boas, *Xingú: The Indians, Their Myths*, 1973; Max Schmidt, "Comments on Cultivated Plants and Agricultural Methods of South American Indians," *Revista do Museu Paulista*, 5 (1951), 239–52; Robert Lee Spires, "As línguas faladas do Brasil," *América Indígena*, 47 (1987), 455–79.

BALÉ. See BARÉ.

BANAVÁ-JAFI. The Banavá-Jafi are a small group of Amerindians who speak a language that is part of the Arawa linguistic family. Relatively isolated until the twentieth century in what is today the state of Amazonas in western Brazil, the Banavá-Jafi experienced severe population decline in the early 1900s and again in the 1940s when neo-Brazilian rubber collectors entered their homelands, bringing disease and violence. A tropical forest people who survived off hunting, fishing, and the production of manioc in tribal gardens, the Banavá-Jafi acculturated themselves to metal technology and manufactured cloth, producing enough trade goods to purchase them. Today the group is very small, numbering fewer than 80 people. Extinction as a social unit is likely in the next few decades because tribal ceremonial life is becoming increasingly difficult to sustain.

REFERENCE: Robert Lee Spires, "As línguas faladas do Brasil," *América Indígena*, 47 (1987), 455–79.

BANÍBA. See BANÍWA.

BANÍUA DO IÇANA. See WAKUÉNAI.

BANÍVA. See BANÍWA.

BANÍWA. The Baníwa people are an Amerindian group living in southwestern Venezuela. They are often confused in terminology with another people called "Baníwa" by neo-Venezuelans, but this latter group is actually the Wakuénai.* The Baníwa proper speak an Arawakan* language that is not mutually intelligible with Wakuénai. Although the Baníwa live in proximity to the Wakuénai, there is little intermarriage. The Baníwa are fisher-horticulturalists. Jesuit missionaries reached the region in the early eighteenth century and began the acculturation process, but Portuguese slavers in the 1740s and 1750s reduced the Baníwa population, as did subsequent epidemics of measles, flu, and smallpox. In the mid-nineteenth century, Venancio Camico, a Baníwa leader, established a popular millenarian religious movement that gave the Baníwa a powerful sense of identity. To escape the military forces of dictator Tomás Fuñes, the Baníwa fled from Venezuela in the early 1900s to the Içana River in Brazil, where they remained for two generations. Not until the late 1940s did they begin to move back across the border. By that time, Colombian and Venezuelan authorities had moved the national boundary from the Guainía River eastward to Maroa. In order to escape the interference of Colombian authorities and to increase their trade with the Wakuénai, the Baníwa moved to the Venezuelan side of the Guainía River. They have become increasingly integrated into the urban and regional economy after 1960 as the acculturating pressures of representatives of the New Tribes Mission exerted more and more influence on them.

REFERENCE: Jonathan D. Hill and Robin M. Wright, "Time, Narrative and Ritual: Historical Interpretations from an Amazonian Society," in Jonathan D. Hill, ed., *Rethinking History and Myth: Indigenous South American Perspectives on the Past*, 1988, 78–105.

BANÍWA. The term Baníwa (Baníva, Baníba, Maníbas, Karutana, Carutana, and Korekaru) has traditionally been used by neo-Brazilians to describe the Arawakan*-language people called Wakuénai* Indians, who lived along the upper Guainía River in Venezuela and the Içana River in the territory of Amapá, Brazil. The more appropriate designation for these people is Wakuénai. See WAKUÉNAI.

BAPUA BARÁ. See BARASÁNA.

BARÁ. The Bará (Pokanga, Pokanga-Tapuya, Maku-Bará, Northern Barasána) are an Eastern Tukano* tribe of Amerindians who occupy land along the headwaters of the Tiquié River in the Vaupés River drainage area and along the Pirapiraná, Japú, Mitu, and Caruru rivers in Colombia. Some anthropologists consider the Bará to be a Barasána* group, more particularly the Northern Barasána, but they have a distinct identity. The Bará call themselves the Waimaha. There are also some Bará across the border in the state of Amazonas, Brazil. Historically, they were very closely related to the Tuyuka* and were most like a subtribe of the Tukano proper. They practice swidden agriculture to raise bitter manioc, their staple, and hunt and fish to supplement their diet. The Bará are especially adept as a riverine people. Like other tribes of the Vaupés, they had little contact with Europeans until the twentieth century. The Bará population stood at about 100 people in 1900; despite influenza epidemics since then, it has modestly increased, up to nearly 500 people in the 1980s. In those same years, the Bará have seen their traditional culture changed dramatically by contact with neo-Colombians and by integration into a cash-based regional economy.

REFERENCES: Christine Hugh-Jones, *From the Milk River: Spatial and Temporal Processes in Northwest Amazonia*, 1979; Jean E. Jackson, "Bará Zero Generation Terminology and Marriage," *Ethnology*, 16 (1977), 83–104; Jean A. Jackson, *The Fish People: Linguistic Exogamy and Tukanoan Identity in Northwest Amazonia*, 1983.

BARÁ. See BARASÁNA.

BARAFIRI. See YANOAMA.

BARAJIRI. See YANOAMA.

BARÁ MAKÚ. See MAKÚ.

BARASÁNA. The Barasána (Hanera, Palanoa, Southern Barasána, Barasáno, Bará) are an Eastern Tukano* language group of Amerindians who live along the Colorado, Yapú, Inambu, Macuco, and Tiquié rivers in the Vaupés River drainage area of Colombia. The major Barasána subtribes are the Waimaja, Wamutanara, Pamoa, Janena, Comía, Eduría, Bará,* Wanaco, and Bapua Bará. There were sporadic European contacts with the Barasána in the eighteenth and nineteenth centuries. Portuguese missions were temporarily established along the upper Vaupés in the 1780s, but systematic evangelization of the tribe did not begin until 1914 when Roman Catholic priests established missions in the area. Theodor Koch-Grünberg began ethnological studies of the Barasána at the same time. Protestant missionaries made their way into the region after World War II, eventually making nominal converts of a minority of Barasána. The tribal economy focuses on the production of bitter manioc and fishing; hunting is quite secondary, although in recent years the tribe has become increasingly dependent on such European technology as fishhooks, shotguns, and machetes, as well as increased manioc production for sale. Contact with whites has also led to the development of small-scale animal husbandry, primarily hogs and poultry. In the 1960s and 1970s, the Colombian government began to encourage colonization of the Vaupés River basin, but settlement there has been very slow. Since 1965, the Barasána have been in close contact with the Summer Institute of Linguistics. The Barasána interact with other Indian tribes in the area but less regularly with whites. Nevertheless, despite the geographic isolation of their region, the Barasána are facing increasing acculturation pressures. There are perhaps 500 Barasána today who acknowledge tribal membership, but fewer than 50 speak the native language. Except for ceremonial occasions, they wear neo-Colombian clothing.

REFERENCES: Alfonso Torres Laborde, *Mito y cultura entre los Barasána: Un grupo indígena Tukano del Vaupés*, 1969; Gerardo Reichel-Dolmatoff, *Amazonian Cosmos: The Sexual and Religious Symbolism of the Tukano Indians*, 1985; Stephen Hugh-Jones, "Male Initiation and Cosmology Among the Barasána Indians of the Vaupés Area of

Colombia,'' Ph.D. dissertation, Cambridge University, 1974; Ministerio de Gobierno, *Aspectos de la cultura material de grupos étnicos de Colómbia*, 1979.

BARASÁNO. See BARASÁNA.

BARAUÁNA. See BARAWÁNA.

BARAWÁNA. The Barawána (Baraúna, Barauána, Baranáwa) are an Arawak*-speaking tribe of Amerindians who lived on the upper Padauri River and its tributary, the Marari River, in the Río Negro drainage area of the state of Amazonas, Brazil. They have traditionally led a horticultural lifestyle based on the cultivation of manioc. Because of their location, they have managed to confine their contacts to trading items with neo-Brazilians as well as periodic contacts with anthropologists and missionaries. In recent years, the Barawána have established more permanent contacts because of their need for trade goods. Their population, once more than 3,000 people, is today smaller than 200.

REFERENCE: Theodore L. Stoddard, ed., *Indians of Brazil in the Twentieth Century*, 1967.

BARBADO. See UMOTINA.

BARBUDO. See MAYORÚNA.

BARÉ. The Baré (Barré) Indians once lived on the Guainía River in the Vaupés drainage region of Colombia and Venezuela. They were an Arawakan*-language people who lived in a horticultural economy revolving around the production of manioc and other crops. The first European contacts with the Baré, who call themselves the "Balé," took place at the end of the sixteenth century, when the Indians found themselves caught in the imperial struggles of the Spanish, Portuguese, and Dutch for control of northeastern South America. Between 1756 and 1761, large numbers of Baré were concentrated on Roman Catholic missions in Solano, Santa Rosa de Amanadona, and San Carlos de Río Negro. By the nineteenth century, the Baré language was in a state of rapid decline. In recent years, however, the Baré have become integrated into the regional economy and increasingly acculturated to European technology. Tribal membership today is approximately 2,000 people, but the Baré are largely detribalized. Only a handful of Baré still speak the native language. The rest have adopted either Tukano* or Nheengatú* as their primary language. They live in Colombia, Venezuela, and Brazil, particularly in Santa Rosa de Amanadona and San Carlos de Río Negro in the Federal Territory of Amazonas in Venezuela. Others are scattered along the Casiquiare River and near Manaus, Brazil.

REFERENCES: Lubio Cardozo, *Cuentas indígenas venezolanos*, 1968; Ministerio de Estado para la Cultura, *Arte indígena de venezuela*, 1983; Estéban Emilio Mosonyi, "La revitalización lingüística y la realidad venezolano," *América Indígena*, 47 (1987), 653–

61; Arthur P. Sorenson, Jr., "Multilingualism in the Northwest Amazon," *American Anthropologist*, 69 (1967), 670–84.

BARÍ. The Barí (Barira, Motilones, Mapé, and Dobozubi) are a group of tropical forest horticulturalists who live in the southwestern lobe of the Maracaibo basin in northeastern Colombia and northwestern Venezuela. Also known as the Southern Motilones, "Motilones Bravos," or the "Wild Motilones," the Barí are part of the Chibchan* language group. The tribal population exceeded 3,000 people by the early 1980s, equally divided between Venezuela and Colombia. There are 1,300 Barí living on the Colombian Indian reservation of Motilón Barí, and another 133 on the Gabarra Catalaura reservation. The first peaceful European contact with the Barí did not take place until 1772, but beginning in 1818 they retreated into the jungles to avoid contact with neo-Venezuelan society. Although the Barí came into continuous contact with neo-Colombian and neo-Venezuelan society early in the 1900s, they maintained a strong commitment to tribal traditions, with most individuals still living in longhouses in the 1980s. The years between 1910 and 1920 were especially violent because petroleum explorers invaded Barí land. Until 1960, contact between the Barí and neo-Colombian and neo-Venezuelan society was hostile and violent, but since then relations have been peaceful. The Barí are swidden agriculturalists, concentrating on the production of manioc and bananas but also cultivating plantains, sugar cane, tobacco, cotton, and a variety of other crops. In the 1970s and 1980s, increasing contact with neo-Colombians has brought social conflict, social immobility, and poverty to the Barí.

REFERENCES: Stephen Beckerman, "Barí Swidden Gardens: Crop Segregation Patterns," *Human Ecology*, 11 (1983), 85–191; Stephen Beckerman, "Carpe Diem: An Optimal Foraging Approach to Barí Fishing and Hunting," in Raymond B. Hames and William T. Vickers, eds., *Adaptive Responses of Native Amazonians*, 1983; Estéban Emilio Mosonyi, "La Revitalizacion linguistica y la realidad venezolano," *América Indígena*, 47 (1987), 653–61.

BARIRA. See BARÍ.

BARRÉ. See BARÉ.

BARRIA. See ACHAGUA.

BARRO NEGRA. See TUNEBO.

BATICOLA. See KAIWÁ.

BAURE. The Baure (Maure, Mojeno, Chiquimitica) are an Arawakan*-speaking group of Amerindians who today live in the departments of Beni and Santa Cruz between the Machupo, Alto Mamoré, and Baures rivers in Bolivia. The Baure are especially concentrated in the towns of Huacaraje, Trobi, San Ignacio,

Baures, Campo Santo, and La Cruz in the department of Itenez. There is still an uncontacted band of Baure Indians living between the Guaporé (Itenez) and Colorado rivers. The Baure were first reached by the Spanish in 1580. Spanish attempts to conquer them failed in 1617 and 1624, but Jesuit missionaries established peaceful contact with them in the late 1660s. Jesuit missions among the Baure were established at San Nicolás, San Joaquín, and Concepción in the seventeenth and early eighteenth centuries. When the Jesuits were expelled in 1767, the Baure fell victim to unscrupulous civil administrators and slavers, and, late in the nineteenth century, to rubber collectors. Their population fell from more than 40,000 people in the early 1700s to only 6,000 in the 1830s. Today there are approximately 7,000 Baure Indians. They are increasingly acculturated economically, working as farmers, herdsmen, or laborers, but the Baure nevertheless retain a strong sense of ethnic identity. Increasingly large numbers of them are using Spanish today.

REFERENCES: Brian M. Boom, *Ethnobotany of the Chácobo Indians, Beni, Bolivia*, 1987; Harold Key and Mary Key, *Bolivian Indian Tribes: Classification, Bibliography, and Map of Present Language Distribution*, 1967; Pedro Plaza Martínez and Juan Carvajal Carvajal, *Etnías y lenguas de Bolivia*, 1985; Graciela Zolezzi and J. Riester, "Lenguas indígenas del oriente boliviano clasificación preliminar," *América Indígena*, 47 (1987), 425–33.

BAWIHKA. See SUMU.

BAXUMOMOWI. See GUAHIBO.

BAYANO. See CUNA.

BEAUQUIECHO. See KADUVEO.

BEICO DO PAU. The Beico do Pau (Tapayúna, Tapanyúna, Tapanhúna, Western Suyá), a Gê*-speaking Amerindian tribe of Brazil, lived between the Arimos River and the Sangue River in Mato Grosso. Although there were sporadic contacts between the Beico do Pau and neo-Brazilians, it was not until 1968 that Brazilian anthropologists and journalists reached the Beico do Pau. They also brought a flu virus that reduced the tribal population from over 400 people to just 40. Like a number of other threatened Brazilian tribes, the Beico do Pau too then moved to the Xingú Indian Reserve in Brazil where they lived in close proximity to the Eastern Suyá.* By the mid–1980s, there were approximately 100 Eastern Suyá alive and about 50 Beico do Pau.

REFERENCES: Robin Hanbury-Tenison, *A Question of Survival for the Indians of Brazil*, 1973; Anthony Seeger, *Nature and Society in Central Brazil: The Suyá Indians of Mato Grosso*, 1981; Robert Lee Spires, "As línguas faladas do Brasil," *América Indígena*, 47 (1987), 455–79.

BELENISTA. See KADUVEO.

BELICHE. See HUILLICHE.

BEMONTIRE. See XIKRÍN.

BEN-DIAPA. See KATUKÍNA.

BETOI. Today "Betoi" is a generic term sometimes used to describe all of the Tukanoan* tribes of the Vaupés drainage area of southeastern Colombia. See TUKANO.

BETOI. The Betoi (Betoya, Betoye), also known as Betoi Jirarru, were a large and widely dispersed tribe of Amerindians who lived in the *llanos* of Colombia at the time of the Spanish conquest. Today they are a much smaller group that lives along the Cravo River near Tama in the intendency of Arauca in Colombia. Their language, which they no longer speak, is part of the Chibchan* linguistic family. Today they speak Spanish, but it is a peculiar dialect heavily mixed with Betoi words and grammatical structures. The Betoi are a subsistence agricultural group; they primarily raise maize, plantains, and manioc. For cash, they produce and sell rice, coffee, and cacao. The Betoi live in groups of two or more extended families and maintain a unique sense of identity.
    REFERENCE: Blaz Telban, *Grupos étnicos de Colombia*, 1987.

BETOI JIRARRU. See BETOI.

BETOYA. See BETOI.

BETOYE. See BETOI.

BEUTUEBO. See KADUVEO.

BEYUMA. See ARAONA.

BINTUCUA. See IKA.

BINTUKA. See IKA.

BINTUKWA. See IKA.

BISANIGUA. See GUAYABERO.

BITUNCUA. See IKA.

BLACK CARIB. See GARÍFUNA.

BLACK KARIB. See GARÍFUNA.

BOA. See SUMU.

BOCA NEGRA. The Boca Negra people are a small, isolated group of Amerindians who have descended from the Kawahíb* Indians. The Kawahíb once ranged over a large area of the Tapajós-Madeira River Basin in what is today the state of Amazonas, Brazil. In the eighteenth century, they dispersed into a series of many separate tribes because of the aggressive expansion of the Mundurukú* Indians. One of the small tribes emerging from the larger Kawahíb group was the Boca Negra. Rubber collectors and gold prospectors in the early twentieth century put more pressure on the tribe, drastically reducing their population to the point that ceremonial life was no longer possible. Today the Boca Negra are on the upper Machadinho, a tributary of the Roosevelt River, and total fewer than 100 people.

REFERENCE: Theodore L. Stoddard, ed., *Indians of Brazil in the Twentieth Century*, 1967.

BOCA PRETA. Until the eighteenth century expansion of the Mundurukú* Indians, the Boca Preta (Tenharém, Tenharím) were part of the larger Kawahíb* nation of Amerindians that roamed widely throughout the drainage area of the Tapajós and Madeira rivers in what are today the states of Pará and Amazonas, Brazil. The Mundurukú expansion dislocated and displaced the Kawahíb, breaking the tribe down into much smaller groups, one of which became known as the Boca Preta, a Kawahíb descendent of the Tupi*-language group. Rubber gatherers and gold prospectors settled their land in the early twentieth century and made life worse for the Boca Preta, and the tribal population declined rapidly. The Boca Preta have been in continuous contact with neo-Brazilian society now for more than 50 years. Although only 50 or so of the Boca Preta are still alive, most of them speak the native language as well as Portuguese.

REFERENCE: Theodore L. Stoddard, ed., *Indians of Brazil in the Twentieth Century*, 1967.

BOLAMOMOWI. See GUAHIBO.

BOLIVIAN TOBA. See TOBA.

BORA. The Bora (Boro, Miranha, Miranya, Miraña-Carapana-Tapuyo, Uirauasu-Tapuyo, Mirayo, Marayo, Miragua, Mariana, Miraña, Meamuyna) are a part of the Witoto* of the Colombian and Peruvian Amazon. They number approximately 2,500 people and live along the northeast border of Peru and southern Colombia, primarily along the Algodón, Ampiyacu, Cahuinari, Igará Paraná, Manay, and Yaguasyacu rivers. They call themselves the Miamunaa. A substantial number of detribalized Resigaro* Indians are also living with them. The Bora are divided into several subgroups based on different dialects: Miraña, Muruí,* Nonuya,* Imihita,* and Fa-ai.* The Bora-Muinane, or Muinane,* people are substantially different from the Bora Indians, and the two groups should not be confused. Although hunting and fishing consume a great deal of the Bora time and hold great symbolic importance in Bora culture, most of the tribe's nutrients come from the manioc, maize, sweet potatoes, plantains, and bananas that they raise in tribal gardens. Until the end of the nineteenth century, the Bora were a relatively large tribe, but the wild rubber boom of the 1890s and early 1900s devastated them, bringing thousands of neo-Peruvians and their diseases into Bora country and drastically reducing their population. The Bora population dropped from 15,000 people in 1910 to 12,000 in 1926 and to only 425 in 1940. Since that time the Bora population has increased to its present level of 2,500. Large numbers of those 2,500, however, represent a mixed population, since there has been considerable intermarriage in the last fifteen years with Ocaina,* Witoto, Cocama,* Orejón,* and Shipibo* Indians. Nevertheless, Bora culture, including older religious beliefs and customs, still survives. Public schools, however, are introducing Bora children to the larger national culture, as is the expanding cash economy.

REFERENCES: William M. Denevan et al., "Indigenous Agroforestry in the Peruvian Amazon: Bora Indian Management of Swidden Fallows," *Interciéncia*, 9 (1984), 346–57; Michael J. Eden and Angela Andrade, "Ecological Aspects of Swidden Cultivation among the Andoke and Witoto Indians of the Colombian Amazon," *Human Ecology*, 15 (1987), 339–59; Gustavus Solís F., "Multilinguismo y extinciones de lenguas," *América Indígena*, 47 (1987), 630–45.

BORAN. The term "Boran" refers to a small group of Amerindian languages that were once located in Colombia. Included in the Boran group were Bora* (Miraña), Emejeite, and Muinane.*

REFERENCE: Harriet E. Manelis Klein and Louisa R. Stark, *South American Indian Languages: Retrospect and Prospect*, 1985.

BORO. See BORA.

BORÓRO. The Boróro are a Gê*-speaking people who once occupied a vast territory in what is today north central Mato Grosso state in Brazil. At the time of the conquest, the Boróro were divided into two groups, the Eastern Boróro and the Western Boróro, together totaling about 15,000 people. The region was primarily a tropical savannah, which the Boróro preferred, although they also made use of tropical forests, fertile riverine areas, and swamps. Brazilian explorers reached Boróro territory in the 1720s, displacing the Indians and separating the Boróro into the Eastern and Western groups. The Western Boróro were concentrated near the Brazilian-Bolivian border around the Corixa, Cabacal, and Paraguai rivers, while the Eastern Boróro were at the confluence of the Piquiri and São Lourenço rivers and near present-day Rondônopolis, Poxoreu, Sangradouro, and Meruri.

In the late eighteenth and nineteenth centuries, gold and diamond prospectors entered Boróro territory in vast numbers, and violence was extensive. The Brazilian government launched military expeditions against the Boróro in the 1880s and invited Roman Catholic missionaries from the Salesian order to pacify the Indians. In the process, the Western Boróro were decimated; by the 1930s, the Western Boróro lived in a single village of perhaps 80 people and were almost completely acculturated, speaking Portuguese, working as laborers in the regional economy, and wearing Western clothing. Although a few Western Boróro Indians are still alive, there are isolated individuals functioning in neo-Brazilian society or living with the Eastern Boróro.

The Eastern Boróro live in three village clusters: at the mouth of the São Lourenço River, near the middle of the São Lourenço and Vermilho rivers, and in two Salesian missions at the headwaters of the Araguaia River. Those at the Salesian missions live in close contact with the Xavánte and are among the most acculturated of the Boróro. The Boróro at the Vermelho are the least acculturated of the tribe. The Boróro Indians totaled as many as 10,000 people in 1900, but by the 1980s their numbers stood at about 1,000 people. They consist of two subtribes, the Boróro Oriental and the Orari.

REFERENCES: J. Christopher Crocker, "Reciprocity Among the Eastern Bororo," *Man*, 4 (1969), 44–58; David Maybury-Lewis, *Dialectical Societies: The Gê and Bororo of Central Brazil*, 1979; Robert Lee Spires, "As línguas faladas do Brasil," *América Indígena*, 47 (1987), 455–79; Dennis Werner et al., "Subsistence Productivity and Hunting Effort in Native South America," *Human Ecology* 7 (1979), 303–15; Johannes Wilbert and Karin Simoneau, *Folk Literature of the Bororo Indians*, 1983.

BORÓRO ORIENTAL. See BORÓRO.

BORUCA. See BRUNKAS.

BORÚN. See BOTOCUDO.

BOTOCUDO. The term "Botocudo" has been used historically to refer to the Gê*-speaking Aweikoma* Indians and the Tupi*-speaking Xetá* Indians. They are not to be confused with the Botocudo proper, a tribe in the Macro-Gê linguistic family.

BOTOCUDO. The Botocudo (Engerakmung) people once occupied a wide stretch of forest between the Pardo River and the Doce River in what are today the states of Minas Gerais and Espirito Santo in Brazil. The Botocudo were a hunting and foraging people who ranged widely in search of food. They were widely known among the Portuguese for their fierce resistance to neo-Brazilian society. At the time of the conquest, the Botocudo were closely related to or part of the Aimore (Aimbore, Ambure) people. By the late nineteenth century, the Botocudo population exceeded 5,000 people and were divided into dozens of small bands. The last of the Botocudo bands was settled by the Brazilian Indian Protection Service in 1910, but they suffered rapid population decline. Today perhaps 50 Botocudo still survive, coming from one of two bands: the Krenák and the Nakrehé.

REFERENCES: *Encyclopedia of Indians of the Americas*, 3, 1974, 186–89; Wanda Hanke, *Os indios Botocudos de Santa Catarina, Brasil*, 1947; Robert Lee Spires, "As línguas faladas do Brasil," *América Indígena*, 47 (1987), 455–79.

BRIBRI. The Bribri are a Talamancan tribal group, part of the Chibchan* language family. At the time of the conquest, the Bribri inhabited the Lari, Uren, and Zhorquin River valleys on the east side of the Coen River in what is today Costa Rica. They managed to survive Spanish conquest, although their culture was substantially altered by the assimilation of a number of smaller, surrounding tribes. The Bribri once lived in large town settlements. By the 1980s, there were nearly 5,000 members of the Bribri tribe. Most of them lived on the Atlantic Coast from the Talamanca Valley to Panama and from the Lari River to the eastern bank of the Coen River. Approximately 500 Bribri were in Panama. The Pacific coast Bribri lived near the towns of Cabagra and Salitre. The Atlantic Bribri were more isolated than the Pacific Bribri and were consequently less assimilated to Hispanic culture. They still speak the tribal language, practice the tribal religion, and employ the pointed digging stick to raise tubers, cacao, bananas, and plantains. They own land communally through a clan system, with individual families using pieces of it and usually changing sites every year. The Pacific Bribri are more acculturated to Spanish, Roman Catholicism, and machete-hoe agriculture. Although the Pacific Bribri still think of land in communal terms, individual families occupy the same plots for years at a time and usually fence the property. The major dialects and subgroups of the Bribri were known as the Valiente, Talamanca, Viceita, Urinama, Tariaca (Teriaka or Teriaca), and Pocosí (Pokosí).

REFERENCES: Elías Zamora Acosta, *Etnografía Histórica de Costa Rica (1561–1615)*, 1980; Howard I. Blutstein, *Area Handbook for Costa Rica*, 1970; Melanie A. Counce and William V. Douglas, "Indians of Central America 1980s," *Cultural Survival Quarterly*, 13 (1989), 38–41.

BRUNCA. See BRUNKA.

BRUNKA. The Brunka are a mixture of a number of Indian tribes indigenous to the Terraba Plains of Costa Rica, as well as of other tribes that migrated into the area after the Spanish conquest. In the late sixteenth and seventeenth centuries, the Spaniards moved the Cotos, Turucacas, Texbis, Quepos, and Abubaes into concentrated communities in Brunka territory along the Pacific coast in southwestern Costa Rica. Over the years, these tribes assimilated with the Brunkas. The Brunka are thus actually a synthesis of tribes that once lived on the Pacific side from Quepos to the present border with Panama. Today there are more than 2,000 Brunka, most of whom are subsistence farmers working communal lands. Such Brunka subtribes as the Quepo (also known as Kepo), Coto (also known as Koktu), Texbi, Turucaca, Abubaes, and Osa are now extinct as languages. The vast majority of the Brunka speak Spanish as their primary language and are Roman Catholics, although folk elements of pre-Columbian beliefs still survive. The Brunka have also been known historically as Burica, Burucaca, Brunca, and Boruca.

REFERENCES: Elías Zamora Acosta, *Etnografía histórica de Costa Rica (1561–1615)*, 1980; Melanie A. Counce and William V. Douglas, "Indians of Central America

1980s,'' *Cultural Survival Quarterly*, 13 (1989), 38–41; Carlos Meléndez, *Legislación indigenista de Costa Rica*, 1957.

BUA. See PIRA-TAPUYO.

BÚCINKA. See IKA.

BÚCINTAUA. See IKA.

BUDA. See ARAONA.

BUE. See WITOTO.

BUEKETE. See GUAYMÍ.

BUGRÉ. See AWEIKOMA.

BUHAGANA. See BUHAYANA.

BUHAYANA. The Buhayana (Buhagana) are a small group of Amerindians who are very closely related to the Makuna.* Known as the "Blowgun People," they live on the Pira-Piraná and the Dyi-Igarape rivers in the Vaupés drainage area of southeastern Colombia. See MAKUNA.

BUIGANA. See BUHAYANA.

BUKINA. See URU.

BÚNTIGWA. See IKA.

BURICA. See BRUNKA.

BURUBORA. See PURUBORA.

BURUCACA. See BRUNKA.

BURURURAU. See TERRABA.

BUSADA. See PIRA-TAPUYA.

BÚSINKA. See IKA.

BÚSINTANA. See IKA.

BUSKIPANI. See KAPANÁWA.

BUSQUIPANI. See KAPANÁWA.

C

CABAHIBA. See KAWAHÍB.

CABAIVA. See KAWAHÍB.

CABANATITH. See TOBA-MASKOY.

CABÉCARE. The Cabécare are a Talamancan Indian tribe, part of the Chibchan* language family, living in Costa Rica. By the early 1980s, there were approximately 4,000 Cabecares in Costa Rica, most of whom lived on the eastern side of the Coen River to the Chirripo Valley. A small subtribe of the Cabécares are the Chirripo, who live isolated in the jungles of the Chirripo Valley and still have little contact with the outside world. These Cabécares on the Atlantic side still speak the ancient tribal language and maintain tribal religious practices. The Cabécares living in the General Valley of the Pacific Coast of Costa Rica are more acculturated to Hispanic values. Other subgroups and dialects of the Cabécare tribe include the Cavecara, Coen, Tucurriqui, Estrella, Garabito, Pacaca, and Corrhue. The Cabécares are subsistence farmers who raise manioc, corn, beans, bananas, and squash. Before the Spanish conquest, the Bribri conquered the Cabécare, assuming political and military control over them, but the Cabécare simultaneously became the spiritual leaders of both tribes. Today those political and spiritual distinctions no longer exist.

REFERENCES: Elías Zamora Acosta, *Etnografía histórica de Costa Rica (1561–1615)*, 1980; Howard I. Blutstein, *Area Handbook for Costa Rica*, 1970; Melanie A. Counce and William V. Davidson, "Indians of Central America 1980s," *Cultural Survival Quarterly*, 13 (1989), 38–41.

CABERRE. See PUINAVE.

CABISHÍ. See KABIXÍ.

CABISHI-PARECÍ. See KOZÁRENE.

CABISHINANÁ. See KABIXIANÁ.

CABIXÍ. See KABIXÍ.

CABIXIANÁ. See KABIXIANÁ.

CABIYARI. See KABIYERI.

CABIYERI. See KABIYERI.

CACAOPERA. The Cacaopera (Matagalpa) are a small group of Indians descended from a Matagalpan-speaking tribe of the pre-conquest era. When Pedro de Alvarado's expedition of conquest reached El Salvador in 1524, there were groups of Cacaopera all over northeastern El Salvador. By 1600, most of them had migrated to the towns of Cacaopera in Morazán department and Lislique in La Union department. Smaller groups of the Cacaopera have been located along the Nicaraguan-Honduras border. Another group lives in the highlands of the southwest corner of the department of El Paraiso, Honduras, where, although highly assimilated, the Cacaopera still practice communal ownership of farmland. Over the years, they have become strongly Hispanicized, with Spanish supplanting Cacaoperan as the primary language by the 1960s. Most of the Cacaopera Indians today live as small farmers and migrant workers on the large coffee plantations.

REFERENCES: Prospero Arauz, *El Pipil de la region de los Itzalcos*, 1960; Howard I. Blutstein, *Area Handbook for El Salvador*, 1971; Melanie A. Counce and William V. Douglas, "Indians of Central America 1980s," *Cultural Survival Quarterly*, 13, (1989), 38–41; J. Alden Mason, *The Maya and Their Neighbors*, 1940.

CACHIBO. See CASHIBO.

CACHOMASHIRI. See CAQUINTE.

CACIBO. See CASHIBO.

CACUA. See MAKÚ.

CADIOEO. See KADUVEO.

CADUVEO. See KADUVEO.

CAECENA. See CAYUISHÁNA.

CAGABA. See COGUI.

CAHIBO. See CASHIBO.

CAHOCO. See ARAONA.

CAHUAHIVA. See KAWAHÍB.

CAHUAPANA. See JEBEROAN.

CAHUARANO. The Cahuarano are a detribalized group of Amerindians numbering in the hundreds of people who today are dispersed throughout the area surrounding the Nanay River in the district of Alto Nanay in the province of Maynas, Loreto, in Peru. For years scholars associated the Cahuarano with the Iquitos*, a Zaparoan-speaking people, but the question remains controversial and undecided. Others surmise that the Cahuarano are descendents of the now extinct Maracano Indians. Spanish missionaries reached the Cahuarano in 1748; by a century later, the Indians were largely integrated into the local cash economy. Their population numbered more than 600 people in the 1920s, but they were increasingly acculturated. Since that time, because of disease but mostly because of integration into the national culture, the Cahuarano have all but disappeared. At the present time, there are only 1 or 2 Cahuarano who still understand words from the aboriginal language; the others speak Quechua* and/or Spanish. They are thoroughly detribalized but still maintain an identity as an Indian people. Only a handful of them, however, are actually aware of their Cahuarano heritage.

REFERENCES: Darcy Ribeiro and Mary Ruth Wise, *Los grupos étnicos de la amazona peruana*, 1978; Gustavus Solís F., "Multilinguismo y extinciones de lenguas," *América Indígena*, 47 (1987).

CAIABÍ. See KAIABÍ.

CAIAPO. See KAYAPÓ.

CAIMAN. See CUNA.

CAINGÁNG. See KAINGÁNG.

CAINGUA. See KADUVEO.

CAISHÁNA. See CAYUISHÁNA.

CAJAMARCA. See QUECHUA.

CAKCHIQUEL. The Cakchiquel (Kakchiquel) are a Quichean Mayan* tribe of Indians today living near Tecpan, Guatemala, and throughout the departments of Chimaltenango, Quiché, Guatemala, Solola, Escuintla, and Sacatepequez. In the fifteenth century, the Cakchiquel were conquered by the Quiché* Maya, but by the 1520s they had for the most part overthrown Quiché domination. When the Spaniards arrived in the 1520s, the Cakchiquel formed an alliance with the invaders and turned on their traditional enemies, the Quiché and the Tzutujil.* But the Cakchiquel soon found their Spanish allies to be their masters. They revolted against Spanish rule in 1526 but were defeated in a bloody war, after which the survivors retreated further into the highlands, where disease and cultural dislocation took its toll on their population.

By the 1600s, the Cakchiquel population had stabilized and they continued their settled, agricultural way of life, now under the tutelage of a variety of Spanish missionaries and government officials. In the nineteenth century, more and more Cakchiquel found themselves working as agricultural laborers on the large plantations of the Pacific Coast, even while Guatemalan government policies systematically converted their communal lands to private and eventually *ladino* ownership. By the twentieth century, the Cakchiquel had been reduced to a poverty-stricken, politically unstable lower class in Guatemala. With other poor Mayan groups, the Cakchiquel protested their lot in the 1970s and early 1980s, only to experience a reign of terror at the hands of the government. Large numbers of Cakchiquel fled Guatemala for Mexico and the United States. By the mid–1980s, there were approximately 420,000 Cakchiquel still living in Guatemala.

REFERENCES: W. George Lovell, "Surviving Conquest: The Maya of Guatemala in Historical Perspective," *Latin American Research Review*, 23 (1988), 25–58; Charles Nelson and Kevin Taylor, *Witness to Genocide—The Present Situation of Indians in Guatemala*, 1983.

CALAPALO. See KALAPALO.

CALCHAQUÍ. See DIAGUITA.

CALDONO. See PÁEZ.

CALIBÍ. See GALIBÍ.

CALINA. See KULÍNA.

CALLAHUAYA. See QOLLAHUAYA.

CALLISECA. See SHIPIBO.

CAMA. See ARAONA.

CAMACÁN. See KAMAKÁN.

CAMARACOTO. See PARUKOTÓ.

CAMAYA. See ARAONA.

CAMAYULA. See KAMAIURÁ.

CAMAYURÁ. See KAMAIURÁ.

CAMBA. The term "Camba" is a derogatory epithet used in Bolivia by mestizos and whites to refer to completely detribalized descendents of lowland Amerindians native to the jungles of the department of Santa Cruz. Cambas speak Spanish, wear Western clothing, worship as Roman Catholics, and work as subsistence farmers or day laborers. Although their lifestyles differ little from other mestizo campesinos, they are nevertheless an ethnically separate group.
REFERENCE: Thomas E. Weil, *Area Handbook for Bolivia*, 1973.

CAMBÉBA. See OMÁGUA.

CAMBÉLA. See OMÁGUA.

CAMEJEYA. See YUKUNA.

CAMOAVI. See ARAONA.

CAMPA. The Campa Indians (Kampa, Camba, Tampa, Thampa, Komparía, Kuruparía, Campiti, Ande, Anti, Chuncho, and Chascoso) are an Arawakan*-speaking tribe who today live in the eastern foothills of the Andes in Peru. Their territory includes the watersheds of the Apurimac, Ene, Perene, and Tambo rivers, plus the Gran Pajonal. Historically, scholars and missionaries have identified a number of Campa subgroups, including the Amiemhuaca, Anapati, Antaniri, Atiri, Amatsenge, Curano, Capiri, Cobaro, Chonta, Cuyentemari, Menearo, Manua, Nanerna, Nesahuaca, Pangoa, Pilcosumi, Pisiatari, Quintimiri, Satipo, Sepuanabo, Sangireni, Tasío, Unconino, and Zagoreni. Today, however, ethnologists and linguists recognize the following as the primary Campa subdivisions: the Ashaninca,* Caquinte,* Nomatsiguenga,* Pajonalino,* Campa del Alto Perené,* Campa del Pichis,* and the Ucayalino.* Although some scholars consider the Machiguenga* to be a Campa subgroup, the Machiguenga themselves have no such identity today. There are cultural differences between each of these groups, but there is also considerable interaction and intermarriage between the River Campa (also known as the Campa Ashinanca) of the Ené, Perené, and Tambo rivers.

Some of the Campa were gathered into Franciscan missions in the 1670s, but the Indians were restless there, periodically rebelling and escaping. Nevertheless, by 1735, the Franciscans had more than 8,000 Campa in 38 active missions. The tribe remained quite hostile to Europeans throughout the nineteenth century, accepting iron tools but preferring isolation. With the establishment of the Peruvian Corporation in 1889, which opened several million acres of land to neo-Peruvian settlement, the penetration of Campa land rapidly accelerated. The rubber boom of the early twentieth century devastated the Campa, but their population survived. They totaled approximately 20,000 people in 1896, only 10,000 in 1925, but today there are more than 40,000 Campa, most of whom speak Spanish and Quechua* in addition to their own language. They are the largest surviving tribe of the Amazon Basin. The various Campa subgroups pursue differing lifestyles, from the semi-nomadic to the agricultural.

REFERENCES: John W. Bodley, *Tribal Survival in the Amazon: The Campa Case*, 1972; William M. Denevan, "Campa Subsistence in the Gran Pajonal, Eastern Peru," *The Geographical Review*, 61 (1971), 496–518; Stefano Varese, *The Forest Indians in the Present Political Situation of Peru*, 1972; Gerald Weiss, "Campa Cosmology," *Ethnology*, 11 (1972), 157–72.

CAMPA ASHINANCA. See ASHINANCA.

CAMPA CAQUINTE. See CAQUINTE.

CAMPA DEL ALTO PERENÉ. The Campa del Alto Perené, who call themselves the Parenisati, are a major division of the Campa* Indians of the Peruvian Amazon. They live along the Alto Perené River and its major tributaries. The Campa del Alto Perené have been in permanent contact with neo-Peruvian civilization since the end of the nineteenth century, although their subjugation occurred earlier, in 1869, with the establishment of the community of La Merced. Today they are in an increasingly advanced state of acculturation, more so than the other Campa groups. Large numbers of the Campa del Alto Perené are bilingual. They support themselves through subsistence agriculture and also work as laborers, usually seasonally, for local neo-Peruvian landowners and businessmen. At present, the population of the Campa del Alto Perené exceeds 3,000 people.

REFERENCE: Darcy Ribeiro and Mary Ruth Wise, *Los grupos étnicos de la Amazona Peruana*, 1978.

CAMPA DEL PICHIS. The Campa del Pichis are a major division of the Campa Indians of the Peruvian Amazon. Their homeland is concentrated along the Pichis River and its tributaries—the Cocari, Nazaretequi, Azupizu, Quirishari, and Anacayali rivers. They are more isolated geographically than some of the other Campa groups and therefore less acculturated. The Campa del Pichis are subsistence horticulturalists whose staples are maize and manioc; they raise some rice to sell, even though cash markets are not readily available to them. In order to raise needed cash, large numbers of Campa del Pichis men leave their families seasonally to work on labor gangs. Their current population is approximately 3,000 people.

REFERENCE: Darcy Ribeiro and Mary Ruth Wise, *Los grupos étnicos de la Amazona Peruana*, 1978.

CAMPA NOMATSIGUENGA. See NOMATSIGUENGA.

CAMPA PAJONALINO. See PAJONALINO.

CAMPA UCAYALINO. See UCAYALINO.

CAMPÉ. The Campé Indians are a tiny remnant of a once much larger group of Amerindians. Their language is part of the Makuráp* family of languages, which are part of the larger Tupi* group. A tropical forest tribe who survived historically by fishing and garden horticulture, the Campé lived between the Arikapú* and the Amniape* Indians along the Mequenes River in southern Rondônia, Brazil. They were uncontacted by Europeans until the 1730s when hordes of neo-Brazilian gold prospectors flooded into their lands. A subsequent measles epidemic in the 1750s devastated the tribe. Jesuit missionaries worked among the Campé until 1750, when the Treaty of Madrid ceded all land north of the Guaporé River to the Portuguese. When the gold boom declined in the late eighteenth century, relative peace returned to the Campé, but that tranquility was shattered in the early 1900s when the world rubber boom brought a new invasion of neo-Brazilian collectors. The diseases they brought with them further decimated the Campé, as did the World War II rubber boom. Eventually, the Campé ceased to exist as a functioning social unit, even though isolated individuals still remain who are aware of their Campe background.

REFERENCE: David Price, "The Indians of Southern Rondônia," in David Maybury-Lewis et al., eds., *In the Path of the Polonoreste: Endangered Peoples of Western Brazil*, 1981, 33–37.

CAMPEBA. See OMÁGUA.

CAMPITI. See CAMPA.

CAMSÁ. See KAMSÁ.

CANA. See AYMARA.

CANAMARI. See KANAMARÍ.

CANAMARY. See ARAONA.

CANCHI. See AYMARA.

CANDOSHI. The Candoshi (Kandoshi) Indians are called the "Murato" by outsiders. That is an incorrect designation. The Murato Indians once lived near Lake Rimachi but have long been extinct as a tribe. The heart of Candoshi land is north and west of Lake Rimachi in the northwestern Peruvian Amazon. Along with the Shapra,* to whom they are closely related, the Candoshi are probably descendents of the now-extinct Maina tribe, which was devastated by Spanish *encomenderos*, who exploited Indian labor, and diseases in the late sixteenth and early seventeenth centuries. The Maina were living on the lower Maroni River in the late nineteenth century, but after that, the colonization of their lands along the Pastaza River was never effectively undertaken by neo-Peruvians. After the Jesuit expulsion in 1767, the entire area remained little traveled until well into the twentieth century. Early in the 1900s, when the wild rubber boom began, the Candoshi retreated to the headwaters of the Nucuray River, a tributary of the Marañon River. Today the Candoshi sell relatively little agricultural produce in the regional market; their agricultural practices are relatively unaffected by outside influences. The Candoshi raise plantains, maize, manioc, beans, peanuts, and sweet potatoes. Few of them speak Spanish, and their sense of tribal identity is strong. They are especially proud of their language and culture. Today the Candoshi population exceeds 3,000 people.

REFERENCES: Darcy Ribeiro and Mary Ruth Wise, *Los grupos étnicos de la Amazona Peruana*, 1978; Anthony Stocks, "Candoshi and Cocamilla Swidden in Eastern Peru," *Human Ecology*, 11 (1983), 69–84; Sheila C. Tuggy, "Candoshi Behavior Change," in William R. Merrifield, ed., *Five Amazonian Studies on World View and Cultural Change*, 1985, 5–40.

CANECHI. See CANICHANA.

CANELA. The Canela (Canelo, Canella, Kanela) are a Gê*-speaking, Eastern Timbira* tribe of Amerindians who live on the northern edge of the Central Brazilian plateau in the southwestern part of the state of Maranhão. There were several divisions of the Canela people, including the Ramkokamekra* (Rankó-kamekra, Ramcócamecra) or Kapiekran, who lived in the large village of Ponto near the headwaters of the Santo Estevao River; the Apânyekra* (Apânieka), who lived west of the Ramkókamekra on the upper Corda River; and the Ken-káteye, who lived in the village of Chinello. Before contact with neo-Brazilians, the Canela raised manioc, maize, beans, and sweet potatoes, but they were also a hunting people. From Europeans, they adopted the cultivation of rice, bananas, watermelon, sugar cane, and a number of other products. By the early 1800s, the Canela were raiding plantations and killing cattle. For a hunting tribe, the lure of cattle was irresistible. A smallpox epidemic devastated the tribe in the 1810s and 1820s. Periodically in the nineteenth century, the neo-Brazilians used the Canela to attack other tribes. The Kenkateye have largely merged with the other Canela groups. Today the Ramkókamekra number more than 700 people and the Apânyekra about 300, and they live in circular villages about 30 miles from each other.

REFERENCES: William H. Crocker, "Canela Marriage: Factors in Change," in Kenneth M. Kensinger, ed., *Marriage Practices in Lowland South America*, 1984, 169–84; William H. Crocker, "Extramarital Sexual Practices of the Ramkokamekra-Canela Indians: An Analysis of Socio-Cultural Factors," in Patricia J. Lyon, ed., *Native South Americans: Ethnology of the Least Known Continent*, 1974, 184–94; Curt Nimuendajú, *The Eastern Timbira*, 1946; Dennis Werner et al., "Subsistence Productivity and Hunting Effort in Native South America," *Human Ecology*, 7 (1979), 303–15.

CANELLA. See CANELA.

CANELO. The Canelo, not to be confused with the Gê*-speaking Canela of Brazil, are a Quechua*-speaking tribe of Amerindians who live in the rugged territory extending from the Andean foothills near the town of Puyo, Ecuador, east to the Peruvian border. Their contemporary population exceeds 12,000 people, and they maintain a powerful sense of ethnic identity. The Canelo are actually a product of the colonial period when remnants of the Quijo,* Zaparo,* and Jívaro* tribes of the northern Bobonaza region merged. They are a classic case of ethnogenesis. The Canelos spent centuries, on and off, in Roman Catholic missions until the nineteenth century when those missions for the most part disappeared. In recent years, more and more Canelo children are attending public schools and learning Spanish, while their parents have become increasingly integrated into the regional economy. A modest technological acculturation is occurring, but the Canelos still function as a tribal people. Their subsistence economy is based on swidden slash-mulch and only rarely by slash-and-burn cultivation of manioc, sweet potatoes, taro, plaintain, maize, and palm. The Canelos gather nuts, fish, and hunt. In the western areas of Canelo territory, they are also beginning to raise cattle and horses. In increasing numbers, the Canelos are intermarrying with the Achuara, a Jívaro group.

REFERENCES: Udo Oberem, "Trade and Trade Goods in the Ecuadorian Montana," *Folk*, 8–9 (1967), 243–58; Norman E. Whitten, Jr., "Ecological Imagery and Cultural

Adaptability: The Canelos Quichua of Eastern Ecuador,'' *American Anthropologist* 80 (1978), 836–59; Norman E. Whitten, Jr. *Ecuadorian Ethnocide and Indigenous Ethnogenesis: Amazonian Resurgence Amidst Andean Colombia*, 1976; Norman E. Whitten, Jr., and Dorothea S. Whitten, ''The Structure of Kinship and Marriage among the Canelos Quichua of East-Central Ecuador,'' in Kenneth M. Kensinger, ed., *Marriage Practices in Lowland South America*, 1984.

CANESI. See CANICHANA.

CANGA-PEBA. See OMÁGUA.

CANICHANA. The Canichana (Canesi, Canisi, Canechi, Kanisiana) Indians are a small group of Bolivian people who represent an isolated linguistic group. They live today dispersed along the right bank of the Mamoré River in the department of El Beni in Bolivia. Agustín Zapata visited the Canichana in 1693 and estimated their population at approximately 5,000 people. In 1695, the Jesuits settled about 1,200 Canichana Indians on a mission. They are in an advanced state of detribalization and have all but lost use of the aboriginal language. The Canichana economy revolves around subsistence agriculture, hunting, fishing, and seasonal labor to generate cash. In the past, the Canichana preferred hunting and fishing to agriculture, but in recent years they have turned more and more to subsistence agriculture. Because of rapidly declining numbers, the Canichana will soon cease to exist as a functional social group and will probably disappear into the larger mestizo population. Today there are fewer than 40 people who identify themselves as Canichana; only a dozen of them speak the aboriginal language, but several hundred other detribalized people are aware of their Canichana roots.

REFERENCES: Harold Key and Mary Key, *Bolivian Indian Tribes: Classification, Bibliography, and Map of Present Language Distribution*, 1967; Pedro Plaza Martínez and Juan Carvajal Carvajal, *Etnías y lenguas de Bolivia*, 1985; Graciela Zolezzi and J. Riester, ''Lenguas indígenas del oriente boliviano clasificación preliminar,'' *América Indígena*, 47 (1987), 425–33.

CANISI. See CANICHANA.

CANNIBAL. See POTIGUARA.

CANNIBALIER. See POTIGUARA.

CANOEIRO. See AVÁ.

CANOERA. See AVÁ.

CAPA. See ARAONA.

CAPAHENI. See ARAONA.

CAPANAGUA. See KAPANAWÁ.

CAPANAHUA. See KAPANAWÁ.

CAPANARY. See ARAONA.

CAPANAWÁ. See KAPANAWÁ.

CAPAPACHO. See CASHIBO.

CAPECHENE. See ARAONA.

CAPIRI. See CAMPA.

CAPOHN. See AKAWAIO.

CAPONG. See AKAWAIO.

CAPOSHO. See MAXACALÍ.

CAPU. See ARAONA.

CAPUIBO. See PACANUARA.

CAQUINTE. The Caquinte are a major division of the Campa* Indians of Peru. They call themselves the Caquinte or Poyenisati, although non-Caquinte call them the Cachomashiri, a term the Caquinte consider an epithet. Today they live on the banks of the Alto Poyeni, Shireni, Tireni, Ayeni, Yori, Alto Sepa, Urubamba, Mayapo, and Picha rivers in the department of Junín of the Peruvian Amazon. Although they are in permanent contact with the Machiguenga* Indians, most of the Caquinte Indians still function on the periphery of the regional cash economy. They are primarily a subsistence agricultural community, raising manioc as their protein staple and supplementing their diet by hunting and fishing. At present, there are approximately 1,000 of the Caquinte Indians, and their contact with the larger Peruvian society remains somewhat sporadic.

REFERENCE: Darcy Ribeiro and Mary Ruth Wise, *Los grupos étnicos de la amazona peruana*, 1978.

CARABAYO. See KARABAYO.

CARABERE. See PAUSERNA.

CARACATÍ. See KRIKATÍ.

CARAJÁ. See KARAJÁ.

CARAMANTA. The Caramanta (Karamanta) were a group of Amerindians located in the Cauca Valley of Colombia, primarily in Cristiana in the municipality of Jardín Antioquia. There are thousands of their descendents still living there, working as subsistence farmers and wage laborers, but the aboriginal culture did not survive the conquest. The term "Caramanta" is still occasionally used to refer to the Indian people of the region, but the people themselves are thoroughly detribalized and pursue lifestyles indistinguishable from those of lower-class mestizos and neo-Colombianos.
    REFERENCE: Myrian Jiméno and Adolfo Triana Antorveza, *Estado y minorias étnicas en Colombia*, 1985.

CARANA-CUNA. See MAKIRITARÉ.

CARANGA. See AYMARA.

CARAPANA. See KARAPANÃ.

CARA PRETA. See MUNDURUKÚ.

CARAVARE. See KURUÁYA.

CARELUTA. See AYOREO.

CARENERI. See ARASAIRE.

CARIB. See KARIB.

CARIBE. See KARIÑA.

CARIHONA. See KARIJONA.

CARIJONA. See KARIJONA.

CARINA. See KARIÑA.

CARINYA. See KARIÑA.

CARIPUNA. See KARIPÚNA.

CARIRÍ. See KARIRÍ.

CARITIÁNA. See KARITIÁNA.

CARNIJÓ. See FULNIÔ.

CARUTANA. See BANÍWA.

CASHARARI. See KAXARARÍ.

CASHIBO. The Cashibo (Cacibo, Caxibo, Casibo, Cachibo, Cahivo, Managua, Hagueti, and Capapacho) are a Panoan*-speaking group of Amerindians who live near the Aguaytia, San Alejandro, Cushucayo, and Manoa rivers on the left bank of the Ucayali River on the east side of the Andes in the jungles of central Peru. Spanish missionaries did not reach the Cashibo until 1757, but the Cashibo maintained a determined hostility to Europeans and other Indians. When increased settlement reached their homeland, the Cashibo retreated further into the interior. Demographers estimate that their population totaled approximately 4,000 people in the 1930s but that epidemic diseases have hurt them since then. Today there are approximately 2,500 Cashibo Indians. Some of them are increasingly acculturated to the neo-Peruvian economy, while others prefer the communal, subsistence horticultural existence traditional to their aboriginal way of life. Today there are a few highly isolated Cashibo communities, but most of them are in permanent contact with neo-Peruvian society. Most Cashibo men speak Spanish, and there has been a good deal of intermarriage with neo-Peruvians and with Shipibo* Indians. The Cashibo are primarily subsistence farmers who supplement their incomes by wage labor.

REFERENCES: Darcy Ribeiro and Mary Ruth Wise, *Los grupos étnicos de la amazona peruana*, 1978; Stefano Varese, *The Forest Indians in the Present Political Situation of Peru*, 1972; Lila May Wistrand, *Folkloric and Linguistic Analysis of Cashibo Narrative Prose*, 1969.

CASHINAHUA. See KAXANÁWA.

CASHINAWA. See KAXANÁWA.

CASHINITI. See PARECÍ.

CASIBO. See CASHIBO.

CATAMARCA-LA RIOJE. See QUECHUA.

CATARUBEN. See ACHAGUA.

CATATHOY. See KAMAKÁN.

CATAWIAN. See KATAWIAN.

CATAWISHI. See KATUKÍNA.

CATÍO. See KATÍO.

CATOMAE. See GUAHIBO.

CATUKÍNA. See KATUKÍNA.

CATUKINARU. See KATUKÍNA.

CATUKÍNO. See KATUKÍNA.

CATUQUINA. See KATUKÍNA.

CAUHUAHIPE. See KAWAHÍB.

CAUISHÁNA. See CAYUISHÁNA.

CAUIXÁNA. See CAYUISHÁNA.

CAUJÁNA. See CAYUISHÁNA.

CAUXÁNA. See CAYUISHÁNA.

CAUYARY. See KABIYERI.

CAVÉCARA. See CABÉCARE.

CAVIÑA. See CAVINEÑA.

CAVINEÑA. The Cavineña (Caviña) Indians today live in the department of El Beni in Bolivia, between the Beni, Medio, Biata, and Genesoguaya rivers. In particular, they live on a mission complex of the upper Beni River where they engage in cattle raising and subsistence farming. Spaniards first contacted the Cavineña in the 1530s when the expedition of Pedro Anzules de Campo-Redondo reached the Beni River. Franciscan missionaries established missions among them at the end of the seventeenth century, converting them to Roman Catholicism. Many Cavineña also adopted the Quechua* language at the time because of its use by the missionaries. Today there are approximately 1,800 Cavineña living in Bolivia. Most of them live in a single community. In traditional Cavineña culture, fishing was particularly important, but in recent years most of them have become laborers, subsistence farmers, and cattle raisers. Their language, which today is spoken by fewer than 200 of the Cavineñan people, is part of the Tacana* family, although linguists suspect that the Cavineña adopted their Tacana dialect fairly recently, abandoning a more isolated language.

REFERENCES: Brian M. Boom, *Ethnobotany of the Chácobo Indians, Beni, Bolivia*, 1987; Harold Key and Mary Key, *Bolivian Indian Tribes: Classification, Bibliography, and Map of Present Language Distribution*, 1967; Pedro Plaza Martínez and Juan Carvajal Carvajal, *Etnías y lenguas de Bolivia*, 1985; Graciela Zolezzi and J. Riester, "Lenguas indígenas del oriente boliviano clasificación preliminar," *América Indígena*, 47 (1987), 425–33.

CAVUA. See KADUVEO.

CAWAHÍB. See KAWAHÍB.

CAWAHIWA. See KAWAHÍB.

CAXIBO. See CASHIBO.

CAYABÍ. See KAIABÍ.

CAYAMÓ. See KAYAPÓ.

CAYAPA. The Cayapa (Chachi) are a Chibchan*-speaking people who live scattered along the banks of the Cayapas River and its tributaries—the Onzole, Estero de Camaroner, Zapallo Grande, and San Miguel rivers—in Esmeraldas Province in northwest Ecuador. Others live along the Santiago River. Along with the Colorado* Indians, they are the last surviving group of indigenous people in coastal Ecuador. They were traditionally a riverine people scattered throughout the jungles of Esmeraldas Province and managed to resist the worst depredations of the Spanish settlers who devastated the highland tribes. Within the last half-century, however, the Cayapa have been pushed back into the Andes foothills by mestizo and black settlers. The Cayapa are subsistence farmers who raise plantains, bananas, sugar cane, coca, manioc, maize, and yams, but their riverine origins also make the Cayapa a fishing and hunting people as well. They have been integrated into the slash-and-burn cultivation system used by mestizo and black settlers surrounding them. Over the years, more and more black and mestizo settlers have immigrated to Cayapa land; in the process, they have launched the Cayapa on the road to acculturation. The Summer Institute of Linguistics maintains a bilingual school for Cayapa children, and various other Protestant and Catholic missionaries work among them as well. Most Cayapa are Roman Catholics in religion, although many aboriginal folk beliefs still survive. There are approximately 3,000 Cayapo Indians today.

REFERENCES: Milton Altschuler, "The Cayapa: A Study in Legal Behavior," Ph.D. dissertation, University of Minnesota, 1964; Thomas E. Weil, *Area Handbook for Ecuador*, 1972; Neil Wiebe, "The Structure of Events and Participants in Cayapa Narrative Discourse," in Robert E. Longacre, ed., *Discourse Grammar: Studies in Indigenous Languages of Colombia, Panama, and Ecuador*, 2 (1977), 191–228.

CAYAPÓ. See KAYAPÓ.

CAYUA. See KADUVEO.

CAYUBABA. See CAYUVAVA.

CAYUBICENA. See CAYUISHÁNA.

CAYUISHÁNA. The Cayuishána (Caiushána, Cauixána, Caishána, Caujána, Cauxána, Caecena, Cujubicena, Cayubicena) were an Arawakan* group of Amerindians who lived west of Acunauy Lake on the Mauapari River in Brazil. They were a tropical forest people who did not survive the nineteenth and early twentieth century neo-Brazilian influx into their traditional tribal homeland. The Cayuishána numbered approximately 600 people in 1820, but that dropped to 400 people in 1860. By 1920, there were only 50 or so Cayuishána left alive, and they were on the Mauapari River. There may be detribalized Indians living in the area who are aware of their Cayuishána heritage.

REFERENCES: John Hemming, *Red Gold: The Conquest of the Indians of Brazil, 1500–1760*, 1978; John Hemming, *Amazon Frontier: The Defeat of the Brazilian Indians*, 1987.

CAYUVAVA. The Cayuvava (Cayubaba) Indians are a small group of Bolivian people who represent an isolated linguistic group. The Jesuit priest Agustín Zapata estimated in 1693 that the Cayuvava totaled approximately 12,000 people, but those numbers declined to 3,000 people in 1749, 2,000 in 1831, and only 100 in 1910. They live today in widely dispersed, tiny village groups between the Mamoré and Alto Yata rivers in the province of Yacuma in the department of El Beni in Bolivia. They are in an advanced state of detribalization and have all but lost the use of the aboriginal language. The Cayuvava economy revolves around subsistence agriculture, hunting, fishing, and seasonal labor. Most of their disposable income is generated through cattle raising on the open plains west of the Mamoré River. Because of rapidly declining numbers, the Cayuvava have ceased to exist as a functional social group and will probably disappear into the larger mestizo population. Demographers estimate that there are only 55 Cayuvava Indians still alive who possess a clear sense of their ethnic identity, along with several hundred other Bolivians who are vaguely aware of their Cayuvava heritage.

REFERENCES: Brian M. Boom, *Ethnobotany of the Chácobo Indians, Beni, Bolivia*, 1987; Harold Key and Mary Key, *Bolivian Indian Tribes: Classification, Bibliography, and Map of Present Language Distribution*, 1967; Pedro Plaza Martínez and Juan Carvajal Carvajal, *Etnías y lenguas de Bolivia*, 1985; Graciela Zolezzi and J. Riester, "Lenguas indígenas del oriente boliviano clasificación preliminar," *América Indígena*, 47 (1987), 425–33.

CENO. See SIONA.

CEONA. See SIONA.

CHACHI. See CAYAPA.

CHÁCOBO. The Chácobo (Chakobo) Indians of Bolivia are a Panoan*-language group who live in the department of El Beni in the area of the Ivon y Medio River and the Benicito River. A small, isolated band of the Chácobo lives today on the left bank of the Yata River. The Chácobo dwell in fairly concentrated village groups and now number approximately 300 people, with most of them at a Summer Institute of Linguistics mission at Río Ivón. Despite being surrounded by neo-Bolivian and other tribal cultures, the Chácobo have maintained a profound sense of identity and still function exclusively, with few exceptions, in their aboriginal language. The vast majority of them are not familiar with Spanish. Traditionally, they were a nomadic people, surviving from hunting, fishing, and foraging, with agriculture playing only a small role in their economy. In recent years, as the neo-Bolivian economy has expanded, however, more and more Chácobo have begun to support themselves through subsistence agriculture and migrant labor. Because of declining numbers, there are doubts among ethnologists if Chácobo tribal identity will survive the next generation.

REFERENCES: Brian M. Boom, *Ethnobotany of the Chácobo Indians, Beni, Bolivia*, 1987; Harold Key and Mary Key, *Bolivian Indian Tribes: Classification, Bibliography, and Map of Present Language Distribution*, 1967; Marian D. Prost, *Costumbres, habilidades, y cuadro de la vida humana entre los Chácobos*, 1970; Jürgen Riester, *Indians of Eastern Bolivia: Aspects of Their Situation*, 1975; Graciela Zolezzi and J. Riester, "Lenguas indígenas del oriente boliviano clasificación preliminar," *América Indígena*, 47 (1987), 425–33.

CHAGOTEO. See KADUVEO.

CHAGUAN. See CHIRIGUANO.

CHAGUANACO. See CHIRIGUANO.

CHAGUANE. See CHIRIGUANO.

CHAKE. See YUKPA.

CHAKOBO. See CHÁCOBO.

CHALIVA. See GUAYMÍ.

CHAMA. See ESSEJJA.

CHAMA. See SHIPIBO.

CHAMACOCO. The Chamacoco (Chamakoko), known to themselves and neighboring tribes as the Ishir (Ishira), live along the east bank of the Paraguay River from the Bolivian border to Puerto Casado in Paraguay and between Bahia Negra and Puerto Olimpo in the Paraguayan Chaco. There are three Chamacoco subtribes: the Orio (Xorshio, Horio, Ochiro, Isira, and Ishir proper) in the northern Chamacocoan region; the Ebidoso (Ebitoso) in the central region; and the Tomraxo (Tomarxa, Tumrah, Timinaba, Timiniha) in the southern region. When the Europeans first arrived on their land in the eighteenth century, the Chamacoco were a nomadic, foraging people with a simple material culture. Their mortal enemies, the Kaduveo,* regularly attacked and enslaved them, and the arrival of Europeans actually reduced that threat to the tribe. Today the Chamacoco have become somewhat more acculturated to European lifestyles, especially in their economic adjustment, where they have adapted to farming and ranching labor. Like other Indian groups along the Paraguay River, the Chamacoco have been dramatically affected by contact with Paraguayan sailors and soldiers and Salesian missionaries; they work as commercial hunters, lumberjacks, ranch laborers, and tannin-processors. Still, the Chamacoco have maintained a strong sense of tribal identity and have studiously avoided migrating away from the river toward Mennonite farms and ranches, where jobs but also acculturation wait for them. The vast majority of the Chamacoco still speak the aboriginal language. In the mid–1980s, there were approximately 1,000 Chamacoco in Paraguay.

REFERENCES: Johannes Wilbert and Karin Simoneau, *Folk Literature of the Chamacoco Indians*, 1987; Edgardo Jorge Cordeu, ''Aishtuwente: Las ideas de diedad en la reliosidad Chamacoco,'' Ph.D. dissertation, University of Buenos Aires, 1980; Branislava Susnik, *Chamacocos*, 1969.

CHAMAKOKO. See CHAMACOCO.

CHAMBIRA. See URARINA.

CHAMBIRINO. See URARINA.

CHAMÍ. The Chamí are an Amerindian people who are widely considered part of the larger Chocó* or Embera* group of Indians in western Colombia. By the late 1980s, there were more than 3,000 Chamí Indians, most of whom lived in the northwest corner of the departments of Chocó and Risaralda, especially along the middle and upper San Jorge River. They are in an increasingly advanced state of acculturation and live as subsistence farmers, raising maize, plantains, and sugar cane. The Chamí have for the most part abandoned indigenous clothing in favor of Western dress, and their extended families are breaking down into patriarchal, nuclear families. Most of the Chamí have become nominal Roman Catholics, although a variety of Protestant evangelical groups are working among them. The Chamí are very closely related to the Embera and Katío; in fact, they are part of those groups, except for their designation as Chamí by outsiders.

REFERENCE: Blaz Telban, *Grupos étnicos de Colómbia: Etnografía y bibliografía*, 1987.

CHAMICOLO. See CHAMICURO.

CHAMICURA. See CHAMICURO.

CHAMICURO. The Chamicuro (Chamicura, Chamicolo) are an Arawakan* linguistic group living on the Huallaga River near Lagunas in the province of Alto Amazonas, Loreto, in Peru. Until the 1760s, they resided on the Samiria River, but a devastating smallpox epidemic forced many of them to move. They relocated to Santiago de la Laguna on the Huallaga River. The rubber boom in the early twentieth century dispersed them throughout the regional cash economy, and the forces of acculturation have been working steadily on the Chamicuro. Today there are approximately 150 Chamicuro Indians, but only a handful speak the aboriginal language. All of the rest are monolingual in Spanish. They are completely integrated into the local mestizo society.

REFERENCES: Darcy Ribeiro and Mary Ruth Wise, *Los grupos étnicos de la amazona peruana*, 1978; Gustavus Solís F., "Multilinguismo y extinciones de lenguas," *América Indígena*, 47 (1987), 630–45.

CHAMILA. See CHIMILA.

CHANA. See LAYANA.

CHANA. See TERÉNO.

CHANA-BOHANE. See TERÉNO.

CHANA-MBEGUA. See TERÉNO.

CHANA-TIMBU. See TERÉNO.

CHANCA. See AYMARA.

CHANCO. See AYMARA.

CHANDINÁHUA. See SHAHINDÁWA.

CHANE. See TERÉNO.

CHANGO. The term "Chango" is used in northern Chile today, primarily in the coastal zones of the provinces of Atacama and Coquimbo, to describe the descendents of an early Amerindian group that migrated there during the period of Inca expansion in the fifteenth century. Although they understand the nature of their Amerindian roots, the Changos today retain none of the aboriginal culture. They speak Spanish, worship as Roman Catholics, and live as small farmers and laborers in the regional economy.

REFERENCE: Francisco L. Cornely, *Cultura Diaguita Chilena y cultura del Molle*, 1966.

CHANGUENA. The Changuena, or Changuina, were a Chibchan*-language people of the Talamancan group living in the central highlands of Costa Rica, southwest of Almirante Bay, along the Robalo River, and around the headwaters of the Changuena, Bun, and Puan rivers. Under the impact of the Spanish conquest, English pirate raids, and attacks by Miskito* Indians, the Changuena mixed with the surrounding Bribri,* Terraba,* and Guaymí* Indians. In 1900, there were a few dozen descendents of the Changuenos, known as the Chelibas. Although there are a few descendents of the Chelibas still alive near the head-waters of the Changuinola River, the tribe has ceased to function.

REFERENCE: Elias Zamora Acosta, *Etnografía histórica de Costa Rica (1561–1615)*, 1980.

CHANGUINA. See Changuena.

CHANINÁWA. See YAMINÁWA.

CHAPACÚRA. See TXAPAKÚRA.

CHAPAKÚRA. See TXAPAKÚRA.

CHAPARRO. See YUKPA.

CHAQUE. See YUKPA.

CHARARANA. See TERÉNO.

CHARCA. See AYMARA.

CHARRUAN. The term "Charruan" refers to a small group of Amerindian languages closely related to the Guaycuru* languages. The Charruan languages once included Chana and Charrua, both of which are today extinct as languages and ethnic entities. At the time of the European conquest in the sixteenth century, the Charruan languages were located in what are today Uruguay, Argentina, and Brazil.

REFERENCE: Helen E. Manelis Klein and Louisa R. Stark, *South American Indian Languages: Retrospect and Prospect*, 1985.

CHASCOSO. See CAMPA.

CHASUTINO. See QUECHUA.

CHAVANTE. See AKWĒ.

CHAYABITA. See CHAYAVITA.

CHAYAHUITE. See CHAYAVITA.

CHAYAVITA. The Chayavita (Chayawita, Chayabita, Chayahuita, Chayhuita, Tshaahui, Shayabit, and Chawí) are a group of Amerindians who are closely related linguistically to the Jebero* Indians and are part of the Cahuapana or Jeberoan language family. Originally they lived at the headwaters of the Sillay River in Peru, but seventeenth-century slavers greatly reduced them in number. The Chayavita scattered widely throughout the region of the headwaters of the Paranapura River. The slaving expeditions severely damaged Chayavita life and population size. For a few years after 1654, many Chayavita joined Jeberos and Muniche* on a Jesuit mission, but the Chayavita gradually returned to the jungles. Today the Chayavita are in permanent contact with neo-Peruvian social and economic life, although a subsistence horticultural economy remains their preferred lifestyle. Increasing numbers of Chayavita are turning to commercial agriculture to sell rice, beans, and chickens. They are overwhelmingly monolingual in their aboriginal language. Approximately 6,500 Chayavita Indians are scattered throughout the region drained by the Huallaga, Shanusi, and Cahuapana rivers.

REFERENCES: Darcy Ribeiro and Mary Ruth Wise, *Los grupos étnicos de la amazona peruana*, 1978; S. Lyman Tyler, *Indians of South America*, 1976; Stefano Varese, *The Forest Indians in the Present Political Situation in Peru*, 1972.

CHAYAWITA. See CHAYAVITA.

CHAYHUITA. See CHAYAVITA.

CHEBERO. See JEBERO.

CHEBERO-MUNICHI. See PARANAPURA.

CHEHUELCHU. See TEHUELCHE.

CHELIBAS. See CHANGUENA.

CHEPEO. See SHIPIBO.

CHEPO. See CUNA.

CHEQUELCHO. See TEHUELCHE.

CHERENTE. See XERÉNTE.

CHEUELCHU. See TEHUELCHE.

CHIBCHA. The Chibcha, or Muisca (Musica, Muysca, Mosca), were native to the high plateau of Colombia at the time of the Spanish conquest. Living an Andean lifestyle, they were farmers who cultivated maize, potatoes, and a variety of other crops and lived in large towns. At the beginning of the sixteenth century, there were approximately 500,000 Chibcha Indians in central Colombia, including a settlement near present-day Bogotá that had more than 20,000 houses. They produced cotton textiles as well as gold and emerald jewelry. The Chibcha were organized politically into city-states that often had elaborate and violent rivalries with one another. Although not as technically sophisticated as the Inca empire to the south, the Chibcha were one of the great Amerindian civilizations.

Rodrigo de Bastidas, one of the first Spanish explorers to reach present-day Colombia, arrived with a conquering expedition at Santa Marta, in what later became the department of Magdalena, in 1525. Cartagena, the present-day capital of the department of Bolívar, was founded by Pedro de Heredia in 1533. Between 1531 and 1539, the Spaniards completed their conquest of the northern Andes interior of Colombia. Gonzalo Jiménez de Quesada entered Chibchan territory in 1536; within the next five years, the Spaniards conquered the Chibcha Indians. The Indians staged a completely ineffective resistance. Population decline set in immediately after the arrival of the Spaniards, and Chibchan tribal culture went into a long period of decline. By the early 1700s, the Chibchan* dialect had become extinct and the surviving Indians were rapidly acculturating. Today there are thousands of detribalized descendents of the Chibcha Indians living in and around Bogotá, Colombia, where they pursue lifestyles indistinguishable from those of the local mestizo population.

REFERENCES: Howard I. Blutstein, ed., *Area Handbook for Colombia*, 1977; José Clements Markham, *The Conquest of New Granada*, 1912; Pérez de Barradas, *Los Musicas antes de la conquista*, 1951.

CHIBCHAN. The term "Chibchan" refers to a large linguistic family of Amerindian languages native to northern South America and Central America. At the time of the Spanish conquest, the Chibchan family included Boruca, Bribri,* Cabecare,* Chiripo, Corobisi, Guatuso,* Guetar, Camachi, and Terraba* in Costa Rica; Cuna,* Guaymí,* Changuena,* Chumula, and Mové in Panama; Rama* in Nicaragua; Mapé in Venezuela; Panazelo, Cara, Cayapa,* and Colorado* in Ecuador; and Andoke,* Cagaba, Guamaca, Tairona, Motilón,* Bairira, Betoi,* Pasto,* Coaiquer,* Muellama, Telembi, Katío,* Nutabe, Chibcha* (Muisca), Tunebo,* Chimila,* Malibu, Coconuco, Guambiana, Moguex, Totoro, Kamsá,* and Quillacinga* in Colombia. In addition to the Chibchan proper family of Amerindian languages, there is a larger group of Macro-Chibchan languages scattered throughout the region more distantly related to the others. At the time of the Spanish conquest, the Macro-Chibchan group included the Esmeralda and Matagalpa in Ecuador; the Yaruro,* Sanumá,* Waika and Warao* in Venezuela; the Itonama* in Bolivia; the Jinotega, Sumu,* Miskito,* and Ulua in Nicaragua; the Paya* in Honduras; and the Shamatari, Shiriana, and Yanoama* in Brazil.

REFERENCES: Pérez de Barradas, *Los Musicas antes de la conquista*, 1951; Joseph H. Greenberg, *Language in the Americas*, 1987.

CHICANA. See HOTI.

CHICOA. See CHIRICOA.

CHIKRIABA. See XAKRIABÁ.

CHILACA. See AGUANO.

CHIMAKU. See URARINA.

CHIMANE. The Chimane (Amo, Chimanisa, Chumano, Mosetene, Nawezi-Montji, Tsimane) are a small group of Amerindians from the isolated Mosetene linguistic family who today live in the department of El Beni between the Maniqui and Cheverecure rivers in central Bolivia. Francisco de Angulo first mentioned them in 1588 when they described their appreciation for Francisco Pizarro's conquest of the Incas who had been trying to subjugate the Chimane. Roman Catholic missionaries first reached the Chimane in 1621, but it was not until the mid-1650s that Franciscan missionaries succeeded in large-scale conversions of the Chimane. By that time, smallpox epidemics had decimated the tribe. Beginning in 1804, the Roman Catholic mission of San Miguel de Muchanes began the acculturation process to convert the Chimane to neo-Bolivian institutions, but the Chimane managed to maintain a strong sense of ethnic identity, although the pace of cultural transformation is accelerating. Today the Chimane number approximately 4,500 people. They tend to live in small villages of five to six families. Their traditional economy was based on fishing, but many of them today are engaged in cattle ranching. Some of the Chimane are also subsistence farmers, raising manioc and bananas. Others continue as subsistence farmers, with hunting and fishing on the side to supplement their diet. The Chimane maintain a strong ethnic identity and still speak the indigenous language.

REFERENCES: Harold Key and Mary Key, *Bolivian Indian Tribes: Classification, Bibliography, and Map of Present Language Distribution*, 1967; Jürgen Riester, *Canción y producción en la vida de un pueblo indígena: los Chimane, tribu de la selva oriental*, 1978; Graciela Zolezzi and J. Riester, "Lenguas indígenas del oriente boliviano clasificación preliminar," *América Indígena*, 47 (1987), 425–33.

CHIMANISA. See CHIMANE.

CHIMIGAE. See SHIMIGAE.

CHIMILA. The Chimila (Chamila, Chimile, Simiza, Simza, and Shimizya) are a group of Amerindians from a Chibchan dialect who once lived all along the western foothills of the Sierra Nevada mountains and the lowlands south and west of Santa Marta, Colombia. They live today in four departments of Colombia: Antioquia, Caldas, Risaralda, and Valle. When Santa Marta was founded in 1525, the Chimila came into contact with Spanish explorers and settlers; because of that contact, they did not survive as a distinct political group with a functional tribal organization. Since 1969, the Summer Institute of Linguistics has maintained a presence among the 400 or so Chimila Indians who are not integrated into Colombian society. Another 8,000 or so more acculturated people are conscious of their Chimila heritage, but they function much like surrounding mestizo farmers. Most of the Chimila Indians who maintain the indigenous culture live on or near the government Indian reservation of Chami Margen Izquierda R. S. Juan, near San Angel in the department of Magdalena. Another group of Chimila lives near El Dificil: they are primarily subsistence farmers raising maize and sweet manioc.

REFERENCES: Walter Dostal, ed., *The Situation of the Indian in South America*, 1972; Blaz Telban, *Grupos étnicos de Colómbia: Etnografía y Bibliografía*, 1988.

CHIMILE. See CHIMILA.

CHIPAYA. See SHIPAYA.

CHIPEO. See SHIPIBO.

CHIPIO. See SHIPIBO.

CHIQUILLAM. See PUELCHE.

CHIQUIMITACA. See BAURE.

CHIQUITANO. The Chiquitano (Paumuca) are a group of Amerindians whose language is part of the larger Chiquito family. Today they live in the province of Velasco in the department of Santa Cruz, Bolivia. There are also some Chiquitano Indians on the Brazilian side of the Guaporé River, primarily along the Colorado and Mequenes rivers. They are concentrated largely in the provinces of Velasco, Nuflo de Chavez, Chiquitos, and Sandoval. Their traditional territory is bordered on the south by the Santa Cruz-Corumba Railway, on the east by Brazil, on the north by the Río Itenes, and on the west by the Río Grande. They were first contacted by Europeans in 1542 when Domingo Martínez de Irala ascended the Paraguay River. They were conquered between 1557 and 1560 by Ñuflo de Chávez. Late in the 1500s, many of the Chiquitano fled Spanish missions and returned to a foraging lifestyle, raiding Spanish settlements frequently. Beginning in the late seventeenth century, Portuguese slavers from Brazil decimated the people. Only the defensive resistance of Jesuit priests stopped the slavers from completely destroying the Chiquitano. Most of the Chiquitano stayed in Jesuit missions until 1767 when the Jesuits were expelled from South America. The Jesuits often used Chiquitano as a *lingua franca* for teaching other Indians. After that, many Chiquitano retreated to an aboriginal lifestyle of hunting and foraging, as well as the cultivation of sweet manioc. Portuguese slavers continued to attack the Chiquitano in the 1800s and the tribal population declined. Between 1880 and 1945, thousands of Chiquitanos died as the virtual slaves of the rubber collectors; the tribe did not begin to recover until the twentieth century. Today there are approximately 45,000 Chiquitano Indians in Bolivia. They are widely scattered and increasingly detribalized, with Spanish and Quechua* replacing their native tongue. They work as subsistence farmers, fishing and hunting to augment their diet, and they work as laborers in the regional economy to generate cash. Debt peonage and virtual enslavement to rubber collectors still affect hundreds of Chiquitanos today. Thousands of Chiquitanos are servants in neo-Bolivian homes and work as impoverished laborers on large ranches owned by the Catholic Church and private capitalists. In fact, much of the local economy depends on the exploitative labor system that maintains the Chiquitanos in poverty.

REFERENCES: Brian M. Boom, *Ethnobotany of the Chácobo Indians, Beni, Bolivia*, 1987; Harold Key and Mary Key, *Bolivian Indian Tribes: Classification, Bibliography, and Map of Present Language Distribution*, 1967; Pedro Plaza Martínez and Juan Carvajal Carvajal, *Etnías y lenguas de Bolivia*, 1985; Jürgen Riester, *Indians of Eastern Bolivia: Aspects of Their Present Situation*, 1975; Graciela Zolezzi and J. Riester, "Lenguas indígenas del oriente boliviano clasificación preliminar," *América Indígena*, 47 (1987), 425–33.

CHIQUITO. See MONCOCA.

CHIRICAU. See CHIRICOA.

CHIRICOA. The Chiricoa (Chiricua, Chicoa, Chiricau, Chiricoy) Indians are a subtribe of the Guahibo* people of Venezuela and Colombia. Like the other Guahibo tribes, they call themselves "Hiwi." Actually, the term "Chiricoa" is ambiguous, inconsistent, and not a tribal division recognized by the Guahibo people. It is instead a designation imposed on one large group of Guahibo Indians. The term Chiricoa is actually the word used by the Yaruro* Indians to refer to Guahibo Indians. In Venezuela and Colombia, the Chiricoa total several thousand people. A foraging people who generally disdain agriculture, they range widely across the Capanaparo, Ariporo, Agua Clara, and Meta River drainage systems in the savannahs of western Venezuela and eastern Colombia. They were contacted by Europeans in the seventeenth century, but the Chiricoa survived the contact. Unlike the riverine Indians who occupied the major routes of penetration of the South American interior and were devastated by frequent contact by Europeans, the Chiricoa were a nomadic hunting and gathering people, an interfluvial group, who were able to maintain their isolation at least until recent years, when economic development and settlement of eastern Colombia has increased the contact with neo-Colombians and neo-Venezuelans.
REFERENCE: Walter Coppens, *Los aborígenes de Venezuela*, 1983.

CHIRICOY. See CHIRICOA.

CHIRICUA. See CHIRICOA.

CHIRIGUA. See ACHAGUA.

CHIRIGUANO. The Chiriguanos (Guarayo,* Izoceño,* Avá-Chiriguano, Avá-Guaraní,* Chaguanaco, Giriguanos) were at the time of the Spanish conquest a slash-and-burn agricultural group of Amerindians who lived in southeastern Bolivia and raised maize, beans, potatoes, and a variety of other crops. Originally a Tupi-Guaraní people who descended from the Paraguayan Guaraní, the Chiriguanos migrated from the area of the Gran Chaco to settle along the Andes foothills between the upper Pilcomayo River to the upper Río Grande in southeastern Bolivia. The migration occurred in successive waves during the sixteenth century. Before the migration, they were primarily a hunting and foraging people, but after arriving in what is today Bolivia, they adopted agriculture, raising maize, pumpkins, beans, sweet potatoes, sweet manioc, peanuts, cotton, and tobacco.

The Chiriguano resisted Spanish conquest, fighting a guerrilla war against Spanish expeditions throughout the sixteenth century. Franciscans, Dominicans, and Jesuits all established missions among the Chiriguanos, but the Indians rose up and destroyed them in 1727. Later in the eighteenth century, new Franciscan and Dominican missions began to succeed in converting the Chiriguano; by the nineteenth century, those missions were acculturating the Indians to the neo-Bolivian economy and material culture. There was still violence, however. In 1866, 1874, and 1892, the Chiriguanos revolted because of heavy in-migration by neo-Bolivian settlers. The Roman Catholic mission system exposed the Chiriguanos to a regimented labor system. Late in the nineteenth century, the Chiriguano migration to the cattle ranches and sugar plantations of Argentina began. There they became increasingly integrated into the regional cash economy. In 1891–1892, a massacre of the Chiriguanos took place in Bolivia, after which large numbers of them were enslaved on agricultural and cattle-raising haciendas.

The Chiriguano population today exceeds 70,000 people, of whom 40,000 live in Bolivia. In Bolivia, there are two centers of Chiriguano Indians: the eastern Andean foothills from Abapo through Monteagudo and from Cuevo to Camantinoi, bordered on the east by a line extending from Santa Cruz to Bacuiba, Buenos Aires; and the Río Parapeti region. The Chiriguanos in the Andean foothills are known as Avá-Chiriguano, while those in the Rio Parapeti area are the Izoceño-Chiriguano. Most of them resent the term Chiriguano and prefer the reference of Avá or Izonceño. Approximately 1,600 Chiriguanos have migrated to the Paraguayan Gran Chaco in the past several decades, and several thousand are still on the secularized missions in Bolivia where they work as craftsmen, truck drivers, teachers, and blue-collar workers. There are more than 28,000 Chiriguano in Argentina. They live primarily in the departments of El Carmen, Ledesma, San Pedro, and Santa Barbara in Jujuy and in the departments of Orán and San Martín in Salta. Most of them work in sugar mills, live with Franciscan missionaries, or function in the local economy as laborers. The Chiriguano have a powerful sense of ethnic identity; most still speak the native language, although increasing numbers are bilingual. A closely related subtribe, also known as Avá-Guaraní, are the Simba, who total approximately 500 people and live in the province of Luis Calvo in the department of Chuquisaca in Bolivia.

REFERENCES: Isabel Hernández, "Los pueblos y las lenguas aborígenes en la actualidad," *América Indígena*, 47 (1987), 409–23; Erick D. Langer, "Franciscan Missions and Chiriguano Workers: Colonization, Acculturation, and Indian Labor in Southeastern Bolivia," *The Americas*, 43 (1987), 305–27; John Renshaw, "Property, Resources and Equality among the Indians of the Paraguayan Gran Chaco," *Man*, 23 (1988), 334–52; Pedro Plaza Martínez and Juan Carvajal Carvajal, *Etnías y lenguas de Bolivia*, 1985; Graciela Zolezzi and J. Riester, "Lenguas indígenas del oriente boliviano clasificación preliminar," *América Indígena*, 47 (1987), 425–33.

CHIRIPÁ. See AVÁ-CHIRIPÁ

CHIRIPUNO. See ARABELA.

CHIRRIPO. The Chirripo are a subtribe of the Cabecares* of Costa Rica. Today the Chirripo live isolated on the mountain slopes of the Chirripo Valley where they number only a few hundred people. The Chirripo are extremely suspicious of outsiders. Because the jungles where they live are almost impenetrable, the tribe still lives an indigenous lifestyle. See CABECARES.

CHISHAMNE'E. See ASHLUSLAY.

CHIVARI. See JÍVARO.

CHIWARO. See JÍVARO.

CHOANIK. See TEHUELCHE.

CHOARANA. See TERÉNO.

CHOCÓ. The Chocó Indians are a tropical forest people occupying the southeastern area of Darién Province in Panama and the northern Pacific coast of Colombia. Actually, Chocó is a generic term referring to a number of Amerindian groups in western Colombia and Panama. Their current population of approximately 45,000 people is evenly divided between Panama and Colombia. Vasco Núñez de Balboa first contacted the Chocó in 1511 and encountered fierce resistance; after those first encounters, there was little contact until 1654 when Spanish missions worked to concentrate and convert the Chocó. Large numbers of Chocó resisted the concentration efforts by moving farther upriver from the Panamanian and Colombian coasts. The tribe practices a slash-and-burn agriculture and lives primarily on plantains, bananas, sweet manioc, sugar cane, and maize. They usually live in round houses without walls. Most of the Chocó speak Spanish, and since World War II, they have increasingly intermarried with black Colombians migrating to the Pacific Coast of Colombia. Some Chocó have moved farther upriver to avoid contact with blacks, while others have headed for Chocó territory in Panama.

Anthropologists divide the Chocó into three groups: the Southern Chocó, the Northern Chocó, and the Katío* (Catío). The Southern Chocó consist primarily of the Waunana* (Nonama, Noanama), who live along the San Juan and Taparal Rivers in Chocó Province near the Pacific Coast of Colombia. The Noanama total approximately 1,500 people; the Summer Institute of Linguistics works among them. The Northern Chocó include the Embera,* also known as the Empera or Emberak, who live in the northern, Pacific coastal region of Chocó Province in Colombia—especially at the headwaters of the Atrato River, around San Juan, and on the coast to the south of San Buenaventura—as well as such subtribes of the Chocó proper in Panama as the Cholo, Citara, Paparo, and Andagueda. The Embera total more than 20,000 people, of whom 5,000 now live in Panama. A number of government Indian reservations serve the Embera Indians. The Katío (Catío) live in the eastern regions of the Atrato River Valley in Colombia, in the departments of Córdoba, Chocó, and Antioquia, with increasing numbers of them in the outskirts of Bogotá. There are nearly 40,000

CHOLÓN   91

Katío Indians, most of whom live in small groups along small river systems where they work as subsistence farmers. Most Katío are bilingual, speaking Katío and Spanish. The Caramantas* are also included in the Choco group.

REFERENCES: Constancio Pinto García, *Los Indios Katíos: Su cultura-su lengua*, 1978; Jean Jackson, "Recent Ethnography of Indigenous Northern Lowland South America," *Annual Review of Anthropology*, 4 (1975), 307–37; David P. Pavy, "The Negro in Western Colombia: An Investigation of Social Change and Personality," Ph.D. dissertation, Tulane University, 1966; J. W. L. Robinson, "Chocos of the Taparal: Indians of Colombia Face Social Changes," *Natural History*, 74 (1975), 47–51; J. W. L. Robinson and A. R. Bridgeman, "Los Indios Noanama del Río Taparal," *Revista Colombiana de Antropología*, 14 (1966–69), 177–200; Ministerio de Gobierno, *Aspetos de la cultura material de los grupos étnicos de Colómbia*, 1979; Arysteides Turpana, "Lenguas indígena," *América Indígena*, 47 (1987), 614–25; Luis Guillermo Vasco, *Jaibanes: Los verdaderos hombres*, 1985.

CHOLO. Throughout western Colombia, the term "Cholo" is used generically by mestizo people to refer to local Indians, most of whom are members of the Chocó linguistic family.

REFERENCE: Leah B. Ellis and Linda Criswell, *Estudiemos las culturas indígenas de Colómbia*, 1984.

CHOLO. Throughout Peru, Bolivia, and Ecuador, the term "Cholo" is used to describe a Quechuan*-speaking Indian who exhibits characteristics of Indian as well as mestizo society. Although the Cholo speaks a Quechua dialect as a mother tongue and as a private language in home, he or she also speaks at least some Spanish, which is necessary for any measure of success in the workplace. Cholos have abandoned traditional Indian dress for Western clothing. Most Cholos have attended at least a few years of public school. Although most Cholos work as farmers, they supplement their incomes by hiring out as manual laborers in order to earn cash. In short, the Cholo is an individual in the process of making the transition between Indian and neo-Peruvian society.

REFERENCE: Sarah K. Myers, *Language Shift Among Migrants to Lima, Peru*, 1973.

CHOLÓN. The Cholón Indians are a small Amerindian group of people whose tribal homeland existed on the upper Huallaga River between Tingo María and Río del Valle in central Peru. Franciscan missionaries first reached the Cholón in 1661 and placed many of them on missions. Father Francisco Gutiérrez de Porres lived among them and wrote a Cholón dictionary and grammar. By the early 1800s, the Cholón totaled approximately 1,000 people living on six Roman Catholic missions in the Huallaga River valley. A tropical forest people, they lived a subsistence existence of hunting monkeys and peccaries and planting bananas, manioc, peanuts, cotton, and coca. Gradually during the nineteenth and twentieth centuries, the Cholón became steadily detribalized, adopting Quechua* as their language and acculturating to the larger Quechua Indian community in central Peru. By the early 1980s, there were only two Indians alive who still spoke Cholón and only two more who understood it.

REFERENCE: Gustavus Solís F., "Multilinguismo y extinciones de lenguas," *América Indígena*, 47 (1987), 455–79.

CHOLOS PENONOMENOS. The term "Cholos Penonemenos" is used in Panama to describe a completely detribalized group of people who are descendents of the Penonomeno Indians, a Guaymí* subtribe. They speak Spanish, worship as Roman Catholics, and work as subsistence farmers or wage laborers. None of the aboriginal culture has survived, except for certain folkloric health practices, but they are aware of their Indian background.
REFERENCE: S. Lyman Tyler, *Indians of South America*, 1976.

CHOLUTECA. See CHOROTEGA.

CHON. The term "Chon" refers to a small group of Amerindian languages that were part of the larger Panoan*-Tacanan* group. Included in the Chon affiliation were the Huash, Selk'nam,* and Tehuelche* tribes of Argentina.
REFERENCE: Harriet E. Manelis Klein and Louisa R. Stark, *South American Indian Languages: Retrospect and Prospect*, 1985.

CHONECA. See TEHUELCHE.

CHONIK. See TEHUELCHE.

CHONTA. See CAMPA.

CHONTADER. See PÍRO.

CHONTAL. The term "Chontal" is derived from the Nahuatl word "chontalli," which translates as "rustic or backward person." The Spanish invaders of Central America used the word Chontal as a generic description for all Indian tribes who did not exhibit a high level of civilization. The term specifically referred to a subgroup of the Matagalpan language who lived in eastern El Salvador at the time of the Spanish conquest. It came into general use to describe rural, unacculturated Indians in Nicaragua and Costa Rica. It does not refer to a specific tribe.
REFERENCES: Philip F. Flemion, *Historical Dictionary of El Salvador*, 1972; Linda Newsom, *Indian Survival in Colonial Nicaragua*, 1987.

CHONTAQUIRRO. See PÍRO.

CHOONKE. See TEHUELCHE.

CHORÍ. See SIRIONÓ.

CHOROPÍ. See ASHLUSLAY.

CHOROTÉ. The Choroté, also known historically and by their subtribes as the Chorotí, Eklejuy, Manjuy, Manuk, Maniuk, Solotí, Tsolotí, Yofuaha, and Zolota, are a Matacoan*-language Indian tribe of the Gran Chaco in South America. At the time of the Spanish conquest of the New World, the Choroté occupied the upper Bermejo River, but in the seventeenth and eighteenth centuries, they migrated north to the Pilcomayo River under the pressure of Toba* and Mocoví* expansion. They were extremely hostile to outsiders, whether Indian or Europeans. As late as 1900, the Choroté were attacking groups of European settlers, missionaries, and anthropologists. Not until the 1920s did Choroté men begin working as seasonal laborers on ranches and sugar plantations, precipitating the acculturation process. The Choroté call themselves the Yoxwaha and today constitute approximately 2,500 people, divided into several groups. The Southern Choroté (or Yoxwaha proper) live along the right bank of the upper Pilcomayo River near the town of Tartagel, Argentina. A splinter Yoxwaha group lives along the left bank of the Pilcomayo northeast of Colonia Pedro P. Peña. The Northern Choroté, which includes the Yowuxua and the Xuikina-wo, live along the upper Pilcomayo near the western border of Paraguay. In the 1970s, the Paraguayan government outlawed the sale of animal skins, which hurt many Choroté commercial hunters. Although there are probably still a few nomadic Choroté avoiding contact with white and mestizo society, most of them have become more settled and accessible in the 1970s and 1980s. They work on ranches and military outposts in the western Chaco or on Mennonite ranches and farms, while perhaps 200 farm and raise livestock at a New Tribes mission at Santa Rosa, Paraguay. Several hundred others are at the Chaco Salteño Mission in Argentina. Those Choroté living in the department of Rivadavia in the province of Salta are closely associated with Chulupí, Toba, and Mataco Indians, while those in the department of San Martín live with the Mataco and Ashluslay. They have a strong sense of tribal identity, and most speak the aboriginal language.

REFERENCES: Isabel Hernández, "Los pueblos y las lenguas aborígenes en la actualidad," *América Indígena*, 47 (1987), 409–23; David Maybury-Lewis and James Howe, *The Indian Peoples of Paraguay: Their Plight and Their Prospects*, 1980; Johannes Wilbert and Karin Simoneau, *Folk Literature of the Chorote*, 1985.

CHOROTEGA. The Chorotega Indians today live in northern Costa Rica and on the Gulf of Fonseca in El Salvador; they are also known as the Chorotega-Mangue. Anthropologists suspect that the Chorotegas were early migrants to Costa Rica from Mexico and that they were composed of several tribes. The

Choluteca lived along the northern shore of the Gulf of Fonseca. Mangue was a dialect spoken between Lake Managua and the Pacific Coast, with subdialects known as Nagrandan and Dirian. The Orotina lived in the Nicoya area east to Lake Nicaragua, as well as on the north shore of the Gulf of Nicoya west of Puntarenas. At the time of the Spanish conquest, there were more than 13,000 Chorotegas in Costa Rica and surrounding areas. They were an agricultural people who lived in large towns and had their own hieroglyphic writing. In 1522, half the Chorotegas were converted to Roman Catholicism by missionaries accompanying the conquest expeditions. The Spaniards then left the Chorotegas largely alone, and the tribe gradually intermarried with European settlers, creating a mestizo people. By the 1980s, the tribe had ceased to exist as a self-conscious unit and only a few hundred people even identified themselves as Chorotega or Chorotega-Mangue. All of them spoke Spanish as their primary language. Most of the Chorotega are subsistence farmers who prefer growing maize over manioc. They raise some cotton and also work frequently as day laborers for cash.

REFERENCES: Howard I. Blutstein, *Area Handbook for Costa Rica*, 1970; Philip L. Wagner, *Nicoya, A Cultural Geography*, 1958.

CHOROTEGA-MANGUE. See CHOROTEGA.

CHOROTÍ. See CHOROTÉ.

CHORTÍ. The Chortí are a highland Maya* tribe. Approximately 4,000 of them live in the hills of western Copán Department, Honduras, while a much larger group of 52,000 are in the department of Chiquimula in Guatemala; there are also some Chortí in northeastern El Salvador. The Chortí were first conquered by Spaniards in the 1520s, after having already spent a century under the domination of the Quiché.* The Chortí are more closely related to the lowland Maya of the Yucatán and Belize than to the highland Maya of Guatemala. During the sixteenth and early seventeenth centuries, the Chortí population dropped precipitously because of disease, warfare, and relocation into Spanish missions, but by the eighteenth century it had stabilized. The Chortí practiced a maize and bean agriculture, even though they lost much of their land in the nineteenth century when the Guatemalan government began turning communal lands over to private ownership. More recently, in the 1980s, approximately one in four Chortí have fled Guatemala because of political instability there and headed to the United States.

REFERENCES: Charles Wisdom, *The Chortí Indians of Guatemala*, 1940; W. George Lovell, "Surviving the Conquest: The Maya of Guatemala in Historical Perspective," *Latin American Research Review*, 23 (1988), 25–58; L. Fernando Cruz Sandoval, "Los Indios de Honduras y la situación de sus recursos naturales," *América Indígena*, 44 (1984), 423–46.

CHOUQUÍ. See TEHUELCHE.

CHUALA. See TERÉNO.

CHUCUNA. See CUNA.

CHUCUNAQUE. See CUNA.

CHUH. See CHUJ.

CHUJ. The Chuj, or Chuh, are a small Mamean Maya* group of Indians who live in the highlands of the department of Huehuetenango in Guatemala. Their language is closely related to the Mamean linguistic group. In the fifteenth century, they fell under the domination of the Quiché* Maya. Although they overthrew Quiché oppression early in the 1500s, they fell under Spanish control in the 1530s. Disease, relocation, and warfare dramatically reduced the Chuj population in the sixteenth century, but it stabilized in the 1600s. Like other Mayans, the Chuj were a settled, agricultural people who lived off the cultivation of maize and beans. In the late 1800s, the government of Guatemala, pressured by powerful agricultural interests, began forcibly transferring tribal land to private ownership, reducing most Chuj people to peasant or migrant laborer status. Their poverty produced political unrest after World War II and bloody reprisals against Mayan activists. In the 1980s, perhaps 25 percent of the Chuj tribe emigrated to the United States, leaving approximately 30,000 members behind in Guatemala.

REFERENCES: Jim Handy, *Gift of the Devil: A History of Guatemala*, 1984; W. George Lovell, *Conquest and Survival in Colonial Guatemala: A Historical Geography of the Cuchumatan Highlands, 1500–1821*, 1984; W. George Lovell, "Surviving Conquest: The Maya of Guatemala in Historical Perspective," *Latin American Research Review*, 23 (1988), 25–58.

CHULUPÍ. See ASHLUSLAY.

CHUMANO. See CHIMANE.

CHUMU. See ARAONA.

CHUNCHO. See CAMPA.

CHUNCHO. See GUAYARU.

CHUNCHO. See YURACARÉ.

CHUNUPÍ. See ASHLUSLAY

CHUNUPÍ. See MATACO.

CHURITANA. See MUNICHE.

CHURUPA. The Churupa are a group of Amerindians whose language is part of the larger Chiquito family. Today they live in the provinces of Sara and C. Buena Vista in the department of Santa Cruz, Bolivia. They were first contacted by Europeans in 1542 when Domingo Martínez de Irala ascended the Paraguay River. They were conquered between 1557 and 1560 by Nuflo de Chavez. Late in the 1500s, many of the Churupa fled Spanish missions and returned to a foraging lifestyle, raiding Spanish settlements frequently. Beginning in the late seventeenth century, Portuguese slavers from Brazil decimated the people. Only the defensive resistance of Jesuit priests stopped the slavers from completely destroying the Churupa. Most of the Churupa stayed in Jesuit missions until 1767 when the Jesuits were expelled from South America. After that, many Churupa retreated to an aboriginal lifestyle of hunting and foraging, as well as cultivating sweet manioc. Portuguese slavers continued to attack the Churupa in the 1800s, and the tribal population declined. Today there are approximately 500 Churupa Indians in Bolivia. They are rapidly being detribalized by acculturation and assimilation into the neo-Boliviano mestizo society. They support themselves through subsistence agriculture and migrant labor.

REFERENCE: Graciela Zolezzi and J. Riester, "Lenguas indígenas del oriente boliviano clasificación preliminar," *América Indígena*, 47 (1987), 425–33.

CHUUNAKE. See CUNA.

CIAWANI. See CHAGUAN.

CICAQUE. See JICAQUE.

CIEGUAJE. See SECOYA.

CINTA LARGA. The Cinta Larga are a tribe of Amerindians who are members of the Tupi*-Kawahíb* language group and who live with the Suruí* Indians in the Aripuana Indian Park of the state of Rondônia in Brazil. Their homeland lies between the left bank of the Roosevelt River and the right bank of the Aripuaña River. They are more specifically part of the Mondé* linguistic family. The name Cinta Larga was given to them by the neo-Brazilians, and it means "Broad Belt Indians." Actually, the Cinta Larga consist of three subgroups, each with a very distinct sense of identity. Those groups are the Ma, the Kaki, and the Kaba. Until the 1960s, the Cinta Largas managed to fight off the advances of rubber collectors and diamond prospectors on their land, but in 1963 the Arruda and Junquiera Company, a large Brazilian rubber concern, launched a military strike against the Cinta Largas, using mercenaries to conduct air strikes against tribal villages. The company was after the mineral cassiterite, an essential ingredient in the production of tin. By the late 1960s, a number of multinational corporations were investing in Rondônia, assisted by the completion of several government highways through the area. To protect the Cinta Largas, the government established formal contact with them in 1967 and created the Aripuaña Indian Park. The Cinta Largas and the Suruí, together numbering approximately 1,600 people, hoped to live within the protection of the park. No sooner had the government established the park than another government agency allowed mining companies to begin prospecting and colonizing inside it. Clashes with the Cinta Largas and the Suruí were inevitable, as were the diseases that the settlers brought with them. By the mid–1970s, both the Suruí and the Cintas Largas were suffering population declines because of influenza and tuberculosis. Nearly 75 percent of the members of the Cinta Largas and the Suruí suffered from one or both of the diseases. By the early 1980s, instead of prosperity and protection in the Aripuanã Indian Park, the Cinta Largas and Suruí were suffering from widespread poverty and disease. The population decline, however, has been stabilized and demographers have estimated the Cinta Larga population at around 900 people. Most of them are increasingly dependent upon the local cash economy.

REFERENCES: Shelton H. Davis, *Victims of the Miracle: Development and the Indians of Brazil*, 1977; Robin Hanbury-Tenison, *A Question of Survival for the Indians of Brazil*, 1973; David Maybury-Lewis, *In the Path of the Polonoreste: Endangered Peoples of Western Brazil*, 1981, 55–58.

CIONA. See SIONA.

CIRABO. See MAYORÚNA.

CIRIANA. See SANUMÁ.

CITARA. See CHOCÓ.

COAIQUER. The Coaiquer (Cuaiker, Cuaiquer, Cuayker, Kwaiker) are a group of Amerindians living in the department of Nariño, primarily along the Guabo, Cuaiquer, San Juan, Guiza, and Mira rivers in southwestern Colombia. They are descendents of Chibchan*-language peoples and probably an example of ethnogenesis—the creation of a new tribe from the intermingling of such now-extinct groups as the Telembies, Barbacoas, Iscuandes, Nulpes, Puntales, Pialpies, Mayasqueres, and Sinduaguas. Another group of Coaiquer lives on both sides of the Colombian-Ecuadorian border. Originally a nomadic foraging people, the Coaiquer maintained that type of existence until well into the twentieth century, avoiding contact with neo-Colombian civilization as well as with the African-Colombians who migrated in large numbers to the western departments of Colombia. The cultural life of the Coaiquer has survived the processes of conquest and assimilation because of their powerful sense of ethnic identity even though in recent years they have increasingly settled down into patterns of subsistence agriculture and migrant labor. At present, there are more than 4,000 Coaiquer Indians, of whom approximately 500 live in northwestern Ecuador. Another 15,000 detribalized people are aware of their Coaquier background. There are 155 Coaiquer Indians at the Colombian government reservation at Cuambi-Yasiambi and 123 at the Cuaiquer o Awua del Alto Albi reservation.

REFERENCES: Walter Dostal, ed., *The Situation of the Indian in South America*, 1972; Robert E. Longacre, ed., *Discourse Grammar: Studies in Indigenous Languages of Colombia, Panama, and Ecuador*, 2 (1977), 43–68; Myrian Jiméno and Adolfo Triana Antorveza, *Estado y minorias étnicas en Colombia*, 1985.

COAJIRO. See GUAJIRO.

COBARI. See YANOAMA.

COBARO. See CAMPA.

COBBEO. See CUBEO.

COBEWA. See CUBEO.

COCAMA. The Cocama (Kokama, Ucayali) are a Tupi*-Guaraní* speaking tribe that occupied the Ucayali River in northeastern Peru at the time of the Spanish conquest. They have also been known as the Ucayali. Archaeological records indicate that the Cocama had moved to the area around A.D. 1250 and lived by practicing tropical forest swidden farming and fishing. When Spaniards first arrived on the scene in the 1500s, the Cocama numbered perhaps 7,000 people scattered throughout a dozen villages. In 1557, the Spanish explorer Juan Salinas Loyola led an expedition along the Ucayali River and made first contact with the Cocama. In the mid–1600s, the Jesuits established a mission among the Cocama at Santa María de Ucayales, and a rapid population decline set in, reducing the Cocama to fewer than 800 people by 1700. They served as canoemen and guides for the Spanish, and a number of the Cocama became agricultural laborers and peons. After the expulsion of the Jesuits from the New World in 1767, the Cocama came under military jurisdiction.

The Cocama were moved from Santa María de Ucayales to the region of Lagunas in the 1680s after a disastrous smallpox epidemic, where they formed their own barrios, along with the Cocamilla* and the Chipeo. From 1767 to the independence of Peru, the Cocama served as forced laborers in Lagunas, working on haciendas and in the extractive mineral and timber industries. After independence in 1827, some of the Cocama relocated back to the Ucayali River area, while others, in search of new farmland, made their way to the floodplains of the Marañon, Pastaza, Nucuray, and Urituyacu Rivers. Their population growth in the twentieth century has been sustained at about 1.5 percent annually; in the early 1980s there were more than 20,000 people of Cocama descent in Peru. Several hundred Cocama also live across the border in Brazil, and another 500 are in southern Colombia. Very few of the Cocama still speak or even understand the aboriginal language. They are in an advanced state of assimilation.

REFERENCES: Robert Lee Spires, "As línguas faladas do Brasil," *América Indígena*, 47 (1987), 455–79; Gustavus Solís F., "Multilinguismo y extinciones de lenguas,"

América Indígena, 47 (1987), 630–45; Anthony Stocks, "The Invisible Indians: A History and Analysis of the Relations of the Cocamilla Indians and the State," Ph.D. dissertation, University of Florida, 1978.

COCAMILLA. The Cocamilla live in the floodplain of the lower Huallaga River in northeastern Peru. Their language, Cocama*, is a member of the Tupi*-Guaraní* family. They are very closely related to the Cocama Indians. Over the years, they have also been known as the Huallaga, Pambadeque, and Pandabequeo. The Cocamilla have traditionally been fishermen and tropical forest swidden farmers; they raise plantains, manioc, maize, bananas, chick-peas, taro, beans, sweet potatoes, rice, peppers, and squashes. Around the fourteenth century, the Cocamilla split from the Cocama tribe on the Ucayali River and moved to the lower Huallaga River. At the time of the Spanish conquest in the sixteenth century, the Cocamilla had assimilated to the clothing and economic life of the neighboring Jebero* Indians.

In 1557, Juan Salinas Loyola led an expedition to the lower Ucayali River and the lower Huallaga River and made contact with the Cocamilla. At the time, the Cocamilla numbered approximately 1,600 people in several villages. By 1600, Spanish contacts with the Cocamilla were more frequent. By the 1640s, the Cocamilla were employed as guides and canoemen on Spanish expeditions into the interior. The Jesuits established a mission among the Cocamilla at Santa María de Huallaga in 1649. The Cocamilla population entered a steep decline because of missionization, smallpox and other diseases, and repeated rebellion against the Spanish. By 1682, their numbers were fewer than 100 people, and they were relocated to Lagunas.

The Jesuits were expelled from South America in 1767. The Cocamilla then came under military rule, although the labor exploitation continued. By the early nineteenth century, as haciendas moved up the Huallaga River, the Cocamilla fell under new labor institutions, producing salt, fish, turtles, and white wax for the white-mestizo economy. But the population began to increase, and the Cocamilla began to disperse. In the late nineteenth century, a rubber boom brought more white-mestizo settlers into Cocamilla areas, as did the demand for barbasco, an ingredient in insecticides, in the 1940s and 1950s. Surrounded by large numbers of white-mestizos, the Cocamilla adopted white-mestizo dress and house styles and spoke Spanish publicly, although many Cocama retained their private idiom. By the late 1980s, the Cocamilla population totaled nearly 7,000 people, making them one of the largest tribes in the area, but they are in an advanced state of acculturation and assimilation.

REFERENCES: Anthony Stocks, *Los nativos invisibles: Notas sobre la historia y realidad actual de los Cocamilla del Río Huallaga, Peru*, 1981; Anthony Stocks, "Native Enclaves in the Upper Amazon: A Case of Regional Non-Integration," *Ethnohistory*, 30(1986), 77–92.

COCHABOTH. See MACÁ.

COCHÉ. See KAMSÁ.

COCONUCO. See GAMBIANO.

COFÁN. See KOFÁN.

COFANE. See KOFÁN.

COGAPACORI. See MACHIGUENGA.

COGUI. Also known as the Kogui, Kogi, Kigi, Gagaba, Kagaba, and Cagaba, the Cogui are a Chibchan*-language tribe of Amerindians who today live on isolated farms on the northern and western slopes of the Sierra Nevada de Santa María mountains in northern Colombia, primarily in the department of Magdalena. They are called Pebos by neighboring mestizos. Their tribal territory rests between 5,000 and 7,000 feet in altitude, and they live in small villages of homes occupied by nuclear families. Over the centuries they have resisted acculturation with European society, slowly migrating farther and farther upriver to avoid contact, even though there has been persistent contact with priests, explorers, anthropologists, and government officials for four hundred years. Except for the adoption of such new plants as bananas, plantains, and sugar cane, the Cogui still practice a subsistence agriculture, with maize and manioc serving as dietary staples. They also raise chickens and hogs. Although demographers are uncertain about Cogui population, most estimate that today there are several thousand Cogui Indians in Colombia. The vast majority live at the Kogui Malayo reservation.

REFERENCES: Linda Gawthorne, "Cogui Kinship," in William R. Merrifield, ed., *South American Kinship: Eight Kinship Systems From Brazil and Colombia*, 1985, 54–70; Gerardo Reichel-Dolmatoff, *Los Kogi: Una tribu de la Sierra Nevada de Santa Mariá*, 1950; Gerardo Reichel-Dolmatoff, "Training for the Priesthood among the Kogi of Colombia," in Johannes Wilbert, ed., *Enculturation in Latin America: An Anthology*, 1976, 265–88.

COIBA. See CUNA-CUEVA.

COLINA. See KULÍNA.

COLLA. See QOLLA.

COLLAGUA. See AYMARA.

COLLAHUAYA. See QOLLAHUAYA.

COLORADO. The Colorado (Tsatchela, Tsatchila, Zatchila) Indians are a Chibchan*-speaking group who, along with the Cayapa,* are the only surviving indigenous people in the western lowlands of Ecuador. Their tribal homeland centered on the western slope of the Andes Mountains in Pichincha Province, particularly in the area near Santo Domingo. They call themselves the Tsatchela or Tatchila. Their name came from the tribal practice of plastering their hair with red dye from the achiote. They are a tropical forest people who raise plantain as their staple as well as yams, yucca, peppers, maize, rice, manioc, sugar cane, and pineapples. At the beginning of the nineteenth century, the Colorados numbered more than 3,000 people, but their numbers have declined rapidly. Their homeland in western Pichincha Province has been subject to heavy settlement in recent years, and large numbers of Colorados have ended up as laborers on large plantations. In recent years, increasing numbers of Colorados have abandoned subsistence agriculture in favor of raising cattle, while others have taken jobs as laborers in towns and cities, particularly Santo Domingo de los Colorados. The government has recently established reservation-like communes of 600 to 2,000 hectares of land for the Colorados. The land is protected from mestizo settlers. In the 1970s and 1980s, there has also been an increasing number of marriages between Colorado Indians and either Quechua* Indians or neo-Ecuadoreans. There are approximately 700 people today who claim a Colorado heritage. Most of them live in seven communities on the Chihuipe, Baba, Tahuazo, and Poste Rivers.

REFERENCES: Elisabeth Elliot, *These Strange Ashes*, 1975; Victor W. Von Hagen, *The Tsatchela Indians of Western Ecuador*, 1939; Thomas E. Weil, *Area Handbook for Ecuador*, 1972.

COMIA. See BARASÁNA.

CONIBO. The Conibo (Conivo, Cuniba, Cunivo, Curibeo) are a Panoan*-speaking tribe of Amerindians living near the Ucayali River in the selva of eastern Peru. Before Spanish soldiers and missionaries reached them in the 1680s, the Conibo were known widely for the raiding and slaving expeditions, the goods from which they traded to the Cocama* for iron tools. The Spanish had little trouble bringing the Conibo into Jesuit missions because of the Indians' desire for metal technology. They remained under Jesuit influence between 1686 and 1698 before rebelling and killing the missionaries. Jesuit and Franciscan missionaries succeeded in bringing large numbers of Conibo back to the missions by the 1760s. By that time the tribal population had stabilized. Today there are more than 20,000 Conibo Indians living in a floodplain environment that provides fertile soil for their staple product—the banana—as well as for maize, beans, and manioc; they also hunt and fish. Until the 1960s, the Conibo maintained a largely indigenous lifestyle. By the 1970s, they were being drawn inexorably into the regional cash economy because of their use of outboard motors and fuel, shotguns and ammunition, and manufactured clothing. Today it is almost impossible for the outside observer to distinguish between the Shipibo* and Conibo communities. Both peoples live along the Ucayali River and many of its tributaries, with the town of Pucallpa a rough dividing line between them. The

Shipibo live to the north and the Conibo to the south. The two languages are very similar, except for some pronunciation and lexical differences. Extensive intermarriage in recent years has further blurred the dividing lines between the Shipibo and Conibo.

REFERENCES: Clifford A. Behrens, "The Cultural Ecology of Dietary Change Accompanying Changing Activity Patterns among the Shipibo," *Human Ecology*, 14 (1986), 367–96; Lucille Eakin, Erwin Lauriault, and Harry Boonstra, *People of the Ucayali: The Shipibo and Conibo of Peru*, 1986; Angelika Gebhart-Sayer, *The Cosmos Encoiled: Indian Art of the Peruvian Amazon*, 1984; Guillermo Arevalo Valera, "El Ayahuasca y el curandero Shipibo-Conibo del Ucayali (Peru)," *América Indígena*, 46 (1986), 147–61; Stefano Varese, *The Forest Indians in the Present Political Situation of Peru*, 1972.

CONIS. See YURACARÉ.

COPANE. See KOFÁN.

CORAZO. See AYOREO.

COREGUAJE. The Coreguaje are a Western Tukano*-speaking people who consist of a mixture of Coreguaje, Tama,* and Karijona* Indians who intermarried. They call themselves the Korebahu. Today the tribe lives along the tributaries of the Orteguaza River below Caquetá in the department of Caquetá, Colombia, and along the tributaries of the Caquetá River below Puerto Solano. The tribal population today is approximately 1,500 people, the vast majority of whom speak Coreguajean as their primary language. They live in scattered villages of between 60 and 80 people each. There are 162 Coreguaje Indians living at the Puerto Naranjo, Peñas Rojas, Cuerazo, and El Diamente reservations, as well as 96 at the Gorgonía reservation, 21 at the La Esperanza reservation, and 220 at the Aguanegra reservation. Although they are becoming increasingly integrated into the regional cash economy as wage laborers and are surrounded by neo-Colombiano settlers, the Coreguaje still maintain a strong identity as an Indian people. Most of them are subsistence farmers who raise maize and rice.

REFERENCES: William R. Merrifield, ed., *South American Kinship: Eight Kinship Systems From Brazil and Colombia*, 1985; Ministerio de Gobierno, *Aspetos de la cultura material de los grupos étnicos de Colómbia*, 1979.

CORINTO. See PÁEZ.

COROA. See KAYAPÓ.

COROADO. See KAINGÁNG.

COROASO. See KAINGÁNG.

CORRHUE. See CABECARE.

CORUMBIARA. See AIKANÁ.

COSINA. See GUAJIRO.

COTÓ. See OREJÓN.

COTOGEHO. See KADUVEO.

COTOGUDEO. See KADUVEO.

COYA. See QOLLA.

COYAIMA. The Coyaimas and Natagaimas today constitute one of the largest Indian groups in Colombia. They number more than 80,000 people. From the beginning of the colonial period, they have been lumped together as one people. The Coyaima live between the Saldana, Chenche, and Hilarco rivers in the department of Tolima. They are called Natagaima in the municipios of Natagaima, Prado, and Dolores. In the municipios of Coyaima, Ortega, and Natagaima, they constitute more than 80 percent of the population. They are for the most part farmers who grow maize, sweet manioc, beans, plantains, sorghum, and coffee. Coffee is a cash crop for them. Coyaima men also work part-time as laborers in the regional economy. The Coyaima and Natagaima have lost their language and most of their aboriginal culture in the last several decades, but they retain a strong sense of being Indians. In the 1980s, they have also established a political interest group—the Consejo Regional Indígena—to promote their point of view.
    REFERENCE: Kenneth Renner Verlag, *El Sistema médico entre los Coyaimas y los Natagaimas*, 1986.

COZARINI. See KOZARENE.

CRISHANA. See YAWAPERI.

CUACUA. See MAPOYO.

CUAIQUER. See COAIQUER.

CUAYKER. See COAIQUER.

CUBEO. The Cubeo are a tropical forest Indian people who today live primarily along the left bank of the Vaupés River, between its headwaters and the Querari River, in Colombia. There are also several small groups of the tribe living near the headwaters of the Ayari River, a tributary of the Içana River in Brazil. They call themselves the Pamiwa, but they have also been described by various Europeans as the Kubeo, Kubeu, Kubewana, Cobbeos, Cobewa, Kobewa, and the Kobeua. The Cubeo are members of the Eastern Tukano* language family. There were sporadic European contacts with the Cubeo in the eighteenth and nineteenth centuries. Portuguese missions were established temporarily along the upper Vaupés in the 1780s, but systematic evangelization of the tribe did not begin until 1914 when Roman Catholic priests established missions in the area. Theodor Koch-Grünberg began ethnological studies of the Cubeo at the same time. Protestant missionaries made their way into the region after World War II, eventually making nominal converts of a minority of Cubeo. The tribal economy focuses on the production of bitter manioc and fishing; hunting is quite secondary, although in recent years the tribe has become increasingly dependent on such European technologies as fishhooks, shotguns, and machetes, as well as increased manioc production for sale. Contact with whites has also led to the development of small-scale animal husbandry, primarily hogs and poultry. In the 1960s and 1970s, the Colombian government began to encourage colonization of the Vaupés River basin, but settlement there has been very slow. The Cubeo interact with other Indian tribes in the area but less often with whites. They wear Western clothing and have adopted Roman Catholicism. There are approximately 12,000 Cubeo today who live at the Parte Oriental del Vaupés reservation in Colombia. Approximately 100 of them live in Brazil. Missionaries and anthropologists from the World Evangelization Crusade and the Summer Institute of Linguistics have worked with the Cubeo since the 1950s and 1960s respectively.

REFERENCES: Irving Goldman, *The Cubeo: Indians of the Northwest Amazon*, 1963; Gerardo Reichel-Dolmatoff, *Amazonian Cosmos: The Sexual and Religious Symbolism of the Tukano Indians*, 1985; Robert Lee Spires, ''As línguas faladas do Brasil,'' *América Indígena*, 47 (1987), 455–79.

CUBEO MAKÚ. See MAKÚ.

CUBEUS. See CUBEO.

COCHIS. See YURACARÉ.

CUESI. See ARAONA.

CUEVA. See CUNA-CUEVA.

CUFAN. See KOFÁN.

CUIBA. See CUIVA.

CUIBO. See CUIVA.

CUICURO. See KUIKÚRU.

CUICUTL. See KUIKÚRU.

CUIPOCO. See PIAPOCO.

CUIVA. The Cuiva (Wamonae, Cuiba, Kuiba, Kuiva, Cuybas, Cuibos, and Quiva) Indians are a subtribe of the Guahibo* people of Venezuela and Colombia. Like the other Guahibo tribes, they call themselves "Hiwi." Actually, the term "Cuiva" is ambiguous, inconsistent, and not a tribal division recognized by the Guahibo people. It is, instead, a designation imposed on one large group of Guahibo Indians. In Venezuela and Colombia, the Cuiva total several thousand people. A foraging people who generally disdain agriculture, the Cuiva range widely across the Capanaparo, Ariporo, Agua Clara, and Meta River drainage systems in the savannahs of western Venezuela and eastern Colombia. They live right in the middle of the Orinoco plains, an area of immense, grassy savannas dotted with palms and small shrubs. Because Cuiva territory is at the crossroads of the main water routes into the South American interior, they have had contact with Europeans since the beginning of the conquest of the New World. The Spanish explorer Alonso de Herrera first reached the Cuiva in 1533 when he ascended the Meta River. In 1650, Jesuit missionaries established missions on the upper Meta and Casanare Rivers where they converted large numbers of Guahibo, Sáliva*, and some Cuiva. After the expulsion of the Jesuits in 1767, the savannas were opened up to neo-Venezuelan and neo-Colombian cattle ranchers. Violence between the nomadic Cuiva and the ranchers has been consistent for two centuries. Even in the 1970s and 1980s, the settlers launched extermination campaigns against the Cuiva.

The Cuiva economy revolves around the collection of roots, fish, and small game. The Cuiva do not have permanent houses of any kind and do not practice agriculture. A nomadic people, they change locations every few days. The Cuiva initiated hostile contact with neo-Colombian and neo-Venezuelan society in the early 1950s, attacking cattle ranches that were limiting their foraging territory. By the late 1960s, the Cuiva were living in two main locations: near Caribali on the right bank of the Capanaparo River and near San Estéban. The Summer Institute of Linguistics has been working among both Cuiva groups since 1965. Although some Cuiva work on the ranches as laborers, hostility still prevails between cattle ranchers and the Cuiva Indians. In 1988, there were 39 Cuiva Indians living on the government reservation of Los Iguanitos, as well as 2,500 at the Cano Mochuelo-Hato Corozál reservation.

REFERENCES: Bernard Arcand, *The Urgent Situation of the Cuiva Indians of Colombia*, 1972; Walter Coppens, *Los Cuiva de San Estéban de Capanaparo: Ensayo de Antropologia Aplicada*, 1975; A. Magdalena Hurtado and Kim R. Hill, "Early Dry Season Subsistence Ecology of Cuiva (Hiwi) Foragers of Venezuela," *Human Ecology*, 15 (1986), 163–88.

CUJAREÑO. The Cujareño are a tiny, Panoan*-speaking group of Amerindians who live in the Peruvian Amazon. In particular, their tribal homeland is concentrated along the Cujar and Mishagua rivers. They are a highly isolated, nomadic group of foragers and hunters, whose tribal population today is fewer than 100 people. Some anthropologists believe that the Cujareno separated from the Masronahua, a subgroup of the Yamanawa, in the 1940s and evolved a separate identity. Little is known about the Cujareño. Today they remain very isolated.

REFERENCE: Darcy Ribeiro and Mary Ruth Wise, *Los grupos étnicos de la amazona peruana*, 1978.

CUJUBICENA. See CAYUISHÁNA.

CULANTRO. See GUAYMÍ.

CULINA. See KULÍNA.

CULINO. See KULÍNA.

CUMANÁ. See PIRITU-TAPUYA.

CUMANASHO. See MAXAKALÍ.

CUNA. The Cuna Indians today occupy the northeast Atlantic Coast of Panama, as well as a small area across the border in the departments of Antioquia and Chocó in Colombia. They have also been known as Kuna. Totaling approximately 38,000 people, they occupy 39 villages on the San Blas Islands, a series of coral atolls near the coast, and 9 mainland villages on the Caribbean shore. The Cuna on the islands are known as San Blas Cuna, while those on the mainland are referred to as Mainland Cuna. The Mainland Cuna are also known as the Cunacuna, while subtribes and pseudonyms for the San Blas Cuna have included the Chucuna, Tule, Mandinga, Bayano, Chepo, Chucunaque, Chuunake, Caiman, and Yulé. The Mandinga term comes from a people who are descended from a mixture of Cuna Indians and migrating blacks from Colombia. Each Cuna settlement lies within a few hundred yards of a mainland river, and each village has its own sense of ethnic identity. There is relatively little intermarriage between the San Blas and Mainland Cuna. The Cuna land is all included within the Comarca de San Blas, a government-owned reservation, approximately 125 miles long and 15 miles wide. They practice a slash-and-burn agriculture that produces plantains, sugar cane, maize, rice, yams, and sweet manioc, and they earn cash by selling bananas and coconut palm (copra) to Colombia. They call themselves the "Olotule," a term that was occasionally used by Spaniards and other Indians to describe the Cuna.

At the time of the Spanish conquest, which first reached the Cuna early in the 1500s, the tribe totaled as many as 700,000 people living in large villages with circular thatched huts. The reign of Pedro Arias de Ávila, who was known as "Pedrarias the Cruel," proved devastating to the Cuna Indians and the other tribes of Panama and northern Colombia. Wanton slaughter, disease, and relocation decimated the tribal population, but enough escaped to the San Blas Islands for the tribe to survive. Their isolation there protected them, and no attempts were made to place them in Roman Catholic missions. From the 1600s to the early 1900s, Cuna men worked as crew members on English ships, so an understanding of English was widespread among them.

The Cuna were and remain a fiercely independent people. As late as 1925, some of them participated in a revolt against the Panamanian government over forced attempts to place them in schools. Nevertheless, by the 1980s, more than 40 percent of the Cuna were literate and 20 percent of them spoke Spanish in their homes. Increasingly large numbers of Cuna are migrating to the larger Panamanian cities in search of jobs. A number of Baptist missions funded in the United States work among the Cuna. In Colombia, 350 Cuna live at the government Indian reservation of Caiman Nuevo, as well as 49 at the Cuti reservation and 210 at the Arquia reservation.

REFERENCES: Regina Holloman, "Developmental Changes in San Blas," Ph.D. dissertation, Northwestern University, 1969; James Howe, "The Effects of Writing on the Cuna Political System," *Ethnology*, 18 (1979), 1–16; Fritz W. Kramer, *Literature Among the Cuna*, 1970; David B. Stout, *San Blas Cuna Acculturation: An Introduction*, 1947; Alexander Moore, "Lore and Life: Cuna Indian Pageants, Exorcism, and Diplomacy in the Twentieth Century," *Ethnohistory*, 30 (1983), 93–106.

CUNA-CUEVA. The term "Cuna-Cueva" generally refers today to the Cuna Indians. Early Spaniards identified two languages spoken in the Darién region of Panama: Cueva and Coiba. Anthropologists suspect that the Cueva were ancient ancestors of the modern Cuna and that some of the Cueva language still survives among Mainland Cuna in Colombia. The Cueva have also been known as the "Coiba." See CUNA.

CUNACUNA. See CUNA.

CUNUANA. See YEKUANA.

CURABARE. See KURUÁYA.

CURANO. See CAMPA.

CURIBARY. See KURUÁYA.

CURIERAI. See KURUAYA.

CURIUÁIA. See KURUÁYA.

CURIUÁYE. See KURUÁYA.

CURIVARE. See KURUÁYA.

CUROTÓN. See ARÉ.

CURRICARO. See WAKUÉNAI.

CURRIPACO. The Curripaco (Curripako, Kurripako, Kuripako, Koripako), including the Yavarete-Tapuya, are a subtribe of the Wakuénai,* a group of Amerindians living today in the Vaupés drainage area of northwestern Amazonia in Colombia and Venezuela. In Brazil and Venezuela they are called Baníwa.* Their self-designation is "Kurrim." Although Curripaco is the term widely used in Colombia and Venezuela to refer to this Wakuénai group, it is not really accurate. It actually refers to the Adzaneni subgroup of the Wakuenai people who live along the Guainía River. In particular, they inhabit the area around Victorio in the department of Casiquiare in the federal territory of Amazonas in Venezuela, as well as the areas drained by the Atabapo, Ventauri, and Orinoco rivers. The Curripaco in Colombia live in the territory of Guanía along the Isana, Guainía, Inirida, and Guaviare rivers. A riverine people with great skills at navigating canoes along rivers and streams, the Curripaco live by fishing, hunting river animals, and practicing a slash-and-burn agriculture to raise bitter manioc. In recent years, they have switched to boats with outboard motors instead of canoes for their primary transportation. Because of the extreme geographic isolation of the Vaupés River area, the Curripaco were relatively unmolested by neo-Colombians until rubber gatherers and missionaries penetrated the region late in the nineteenth century, introducing European technology as well as diseases. At the present time, the Curripaco are being increasingly integrated into the regional cash economy. Most of them are bilingual in Curripaco, an Arawakan* language, and Spanish. There are approximately 124 Curripaco Indians living on a government reservation at Laguna Negra y Cacao and 124 at the El Venado reservation. Today the Curripaco number approximately 2,500 people. The World Evangelization Crusade has had missionaries among the Curripaco since the early 1960s.

REFERENCES: Jonathan D. Hill and Robin M. Wright, "Time, Narrative, and Ritual: Historical Interpretation from an Amazonian Society," in Jonathan D. Hill, ed., *Rethinking History and Myth: Indigenous South American Perspectives on the Past*, 1988, 78–105; Robert Holmes, "Diet, Nutritional Status and Acculturation Among the Curripaco Indians of the Amazon Territory," M. A. thesis, Instituto Venezolano de Investigaciones Científicas, 1981; Ministerio de Estado para la Cultura, *Arte indígena de Venezuela*, 1983; Estéban Emilio Mosonyi, "La revitalización lingüística y la realidad venezolano," *América Indígena*, 47 (1987), 653–61.

CURRIPAKO. See CURRIPACO.

CURUÁHE. See KURUÁYA.

CURUÁRA. See KURUÁYA.

CURUARI. See KURUÁYA.

CURUAYA. See KURUÁYA.

CURUÁYE. See KURUÁYA.

CURUBARE. See KURUÁYA.

CURUEYE. See KURUÁYA.

CURUPÍ. See ARAONA.

CUSHMA. The Cushma are a nearly extinct group of jungle-dwelling Amerindians native to the provinces of Napo and Pastaza in Ecuador. They were isolated until the rubber boom of the early twentieth century, when disease and exploitation dramatically reduced their population. When the Capuchin order created the mission of Apostolic Prefecture of Aguarico in 1954, several hundred Cushma settled there and lived among Siona,* Kofán,* Tetete,* Yumbo,* and Auca* Indians. They are a tropical forest people whose traditional lifestyle valued hunting and fishing over agriculture, although in recent years they have become more adept at raising manioc and bananas. Capuchin schools are helping to acculturate the Cushma, while the presence of so many other Indians is bringing about their detribalization.
    REFERENCE: S. Lyman Tyler, *Indians of South America*, 1976.

CUSTENAU. See KUTENABU.

CUTASHO. See KAMAKÁN.

CUTINANA. See AGUANO.

CUTU. The term "Cutu" is widely used among Quechuan-speaking Indians in Ecuador and northern Peru to describe those individuals who are acculturating more rapidly to neo-Ecuadorian and neo-Peruvian values. The equivalent term among Spanish-speaking people is "Cholo."
    REFERENCE: Albert William Bork and Georg Maier, *Historical Dictionary of Ecuador*, 1973.

CUTUGUEO. See KADUVEO.

CUYBA. See CUIVA.

CUYENTEMARI. See CAMPA.

CUZCO. See QUECHUA.

D

DACHSEA. See TUKANO.

DAHSEYE. See TUKANO.

DALLUS. See MAYORÚNA.

DANÍ. The Daní (Dení) are a small tribe of Amerindians who speak an Arawá* language. They live in a vast territory extending from the headwaters of the Purús River to the headwaters of the Xirua River in the state of Amazonas, Brazil. They are a tribe, however, only in the sense that they have a common language. Their primary political and social focus is on a local region rather than on all who share the Daní language. The major Daní subgroups are the Upanavadení on the Mamoría River; the Dimadení, located where the Mamoría River flows into the Purús River; the Kamadení and Tamikuridení, at the headwaters of the Mamoría River; the Shivakuadení, on the Inauini River; the Kunivadení on the Xiruã River; and the Varashedení on the Aruã River. Their home consists of four clustered villages. Relatively isolated in what is today the state of Amazonas in western Brazil until the twentieth century, the Daní experienced severe population decline in the early 1900s and again in the 1940s when neo-Brazilian rubber collectors entered their homeland and brought disease and violence. A tropical forest people who have survived by hunting, fishing, and the production of manioc in tribal gardens, the Daní remain somewhat isolated today, preferring association with the members of their own tribe to contact with other Indians and neo-Brazilians. They have adopted some of the metal and textile artifacts of neo-Brazilian society but maintain a strong sense of tribal identity.

The Daní are known to reside for only five or six years at a single location before relocating. There are approximately 560 members of the Daní tribe.

REFERENCES: Gordon Koop and Sherwood G. Lingenfelter, *The Dení of Western Brazil: A Study of Sociopolitical Organization and Community Development*, 1980.

DATSEA. See TUKANO.

DATUANA. The Datuana (Detuana) are a surviving subtribe of the Yahuna,* a Tukanoan* group of Amerindians who lived on the lower Apaporis River in the Vaupés River drainage region of Colombia. A tropical forest people, the Datuana have maintained their cultural isolation from Europeans primarily because of the limited settlement on their tribal land. At present, there are approximately 150 Datuana Indians.

REFERENCE: Arthur P. Sorenson, Jr., "Multilingualism in the Northwest Amazon," *American Anthropologist*, 69 (1967), 670–84.

DECANO. See DESANA.

DECUANA. See DEKUANA.

DE'CUANA. See DEKUANA.

DEJA. See PIAPOCO.

DEJABAI. See ARAONA.

DEKUANA. The term "Dekuana" (Decuana, De'cuana, Dekuhana) refers to a group of Yekuana* Indians of Venezuela living on the middle and lower Ventauri River. See YEKUANA.

DEKUHANA. See DEKUANA.

DENÍ. See DANÍ.

DEPSO. See TÉRRABA.

DESA. See DESANA.

DESANA. The term "Desana" or a related word is frequently used in western Colombia to refer to several Arawakan*-speaking groups of Amerindians, as well as to the Eastern Tukanoan* group described below. The Tariana* are sometimes referred to as "Detsana" or "Detsenei," while the Ipeka are often called the "Desa."

REFERENCE: Blaz Telban, *Grupos étnicos de Colombia: Etnografía y bibliografía*, 1987.

DESANA. The Desana (Decano, Desano, Wina), who call themselves the "Wira," are an Eastern Tukanoan* language group of Amerindians who today live on the Papuri and Tiquie rivers in the upper Vaupés region of Colombia and across the border in the western reaches of the state of Amazonas, Brazil. They resent the word "Desana," which they consider an epithet, but it is widely used throughout the region. In particular, they occupy places on the right bank of the Vaupés from the rapids of Yurupuri downriver and below Mitu on the Cucura, Abiyu, Timbo, and Murutinga tributaries of the Vaupés. Most of the Desana live in the basin of the Papuri River, especially along the Macu-paraná, Virari, and Cuyucu tributaries. They can also be found in the settlements of Wainambi and La Estrella in Teresita.

There were sporadic European contacts with the Desana in the eighteenth and nineteenth centuries. Portuguese missions were established temporarily along the upper Vaupés in the 1780s, but systematic evangelization of the tribe did not begin until 1914 when Roman Catholic priests established missions on the Papuri River. Theodor Koch-Grünberg began ethnological studies of the Desana at the same time. Protestant missionaries made their way into the region after World War II, eventually making nominal converts of a minority of Desana. The tribal economy focuses on the production of bitter manioc and fishing; hunting is quite secondary, although in recent years the tribe has become increasingly dependent on such European technology as fishhooks, shotguns, and machetes, as well as on increased manioc production for sale. Contact with whites has also led to the development of small-scale animal husbandry, primarily hogs and poultry.

In the 1960s and 1970s, the Colombian government began to encourage colonization of the Vaupés River basin, but settlement there has been very slow. The Desana interact with other Indian tribes in the area but rarely with whites, except for missionaries and rubber collectors. There are approximately 1,700 Desana today who acknowledge tribal membership and speak the native language.

REFERENCES: Jean A. Jackson, *The Fish People: Linguistic Exogamy and Tukanoan Identity in Northwest Amazonia*, 1983; Umbusin P. Kumu, *Antes o mundo nao existia, a mitológia heróica dos indios Desana*, (1980); Gerardo Reichel-Dolmatoff, "Desana Curing Spells: An Analysis of Some Shamanistic Metaphors," *Journal of Latin American Lore*, 2 (1976), 157–210; Gerardo Reichel-Dolmatoff, "Desana Animal Categories, Food Restrictions, and the Concept of Energies," *Journal of Latin American Lore*, 4 (1978), 243–91; Robert Lee Spires, "As línguas faladas do Brasil," *América Indígena*, 47 (1987), 455–79.

DESANA MAKÚ. See MAKÚ.

DESANO. See DESANA.

DETSANA. See DESANA.

DETSENEI. See DESANA.

DETUANA. See DATUANA.

DE-USHENE. See TEHUELCHE.

DIAGUITA. The Diaguita and their major subtribe, the Calchaquí, are today a highly assimilated Amerindian group in northwestern Argentina. At the time of the Spanish conquest, they were one of the largest tribes in Argentina, but their tribal origins are definitely Andean. When the Spanish arrived, the Diaguita were a sedentary people who raised corn, squash, potatoes, beans, and quinoa. They constructed elaborate irrigation systems to water their mountainside farms and raised llamas for wool, meat, and as beasts of burden. The Diaguita population declined as a result of contact with Spaniards, but the processes of assimilation were far more powerful in eliminating tribal identity. Today there are approximately 100,000 people of Diaguita-Calchaquí descent living in Argentina but they are thoroughly assimilated into the regional cash economy and into the Spanish-speaking, Roman Catholic culture.

REFERENCES: Francisco L. Cornely, *Cultura Diaguita Chilena y cultura del Molle*, 1966; *Encyclopedia of Indians of the Americas*, 2, (1974), 257–63; Isabel Hernández, "Los pueblos y las lenguas aborígenes en la actualidad," *América Indígena*, 47 (1987), 409–23; Andrés Serbin, "Las organizaciones indígenas en la Argentina," *América Indígena*, 47 (1987), 407–34.

DIAHÓI. See DIARRÓI.

DIARRÓI. The Diarrói (Diahói) are a small and isolated group of Amerindians, closely related to the Parintintín,* living on the Preto River near the border of the states of Amazonas and Rondônia in Brazil; the Preto River is an upper tributary of the Marmelos. The Diarrói people have declined in population because of imported diseases, although their geographical isolation has kept them from a great deal of contact with neo-Brazilians. The Diarrói population has slipped below 20 people. They manage to maintain a sense of tribal integrity and aboriginal values, but their traditional ceremonial life can no longer sustain itself.

REFERENCES: Robert Lee Spires, "As línguas faladas do Brasil," *América Indígena*, 47 (1987), 455–79; Theodore L. Stoddard, ed., *Indians of Brazil in the Twentieth Century*, 1967.

DIGUT. See GAVIÃO.

DIMADENÍ. See DANÍ.

DIOKAYA. See OCAINA.

DIORE. See XIKRÍN.

DIRIAN. See MANGUE.

DITIAPODE. See PIRA-TAPUYA.

DIURHET. See PUELCHE.

DJORE. See XIKRÍN.

DOBOZUBI. See BARÍ.

DOCHKAFUARA. See TUYUKA.

DOHKAPOARA. See TUYUKA.

DOWNSTREAM HALOTESU. See NAMBIQUÁRA.

DUHAIMOMOWI. See GUAHIBO.

DUKAIYA. See OCAINA.

DUKAIYA. See WITOTO.

DUUXUGA. See TUKUNA.

DZASE. See PIAPOCO.

DZAWINAI. See WAKUÉNAI.

DZUBUKUA. See KARIRI.

E

EASTERN BAKIRÍ. See BAKIRÍ.

EASTERN BORÓRO. See BORÓRO.

EASTERN SUYÁ. See SUYÁ.

EASTERN TIMBIRA. The Eastern Timbira is a Gê*-speaking group of people in central Brazil that today includes the Canela,* Krikatí,* Krahô,* and Gavião* tribes. They live in the high steppes and dry forests of the Maranhão region and support themselves by raising maize, manioc, and beans and by hunting and fishing.
   REFERENCE: Curt Nimuendaju, *The Eastern Timbira*, 1946.

EASTERN TOBA. See TOBA.

EBIDOSO. See CHAMACOCO.

EBITOSO. See CHAMACOCO.

ECHENOANA. See TERÉNO.

ECHIGUEGUO. See KADUVEO.

ECHOALADI. See TERÉNO.

ECHOJA. See ESSEJJA.

ECUARY. See ARAONA.

EDIU-ADIG. See KADUVEO.

EDJEHO. See KADUVEO.

EDURÍA. The Eduría are an Eastern Tukanoan* language tribe of Amerindians who live in the Vaupés River drainage region of Colombia. The upper Vaupés River has been a very isolated place until recently, even though various anthropologists, Roman Catholic priests, and Protestant missionaries have moved into the area since 1900. The Colombia government today is trying to encourage settlement of the region, but development has been very slow. The Eduría have contacts with many other Indian tribes but not much contact with Europeans. The tribe now includes several hundred people. They are part of the Barasána* people.

REFERENCE: Arthur P. Sorenson, Jr., "Multilingualism in the Northwest Amazon," *American Anthropologist*, 69 (1967), 670–84.

EH-HEN. See WAKUÉNAI.

EINONTU'TUA. See TAUSHIRO.

EJUEO. See KADUVEO.

EKLEJUY. See CHOROTÉ.

EMBERA. The Embera Indians, also known as Northern Chocó,* Empera, or Emberak, live in a broad region along the Pacific Coast of Colombia and Panama. They are a large group who are also known as the Chocó, Katío,* and Chamí,* depending on where they reside. In Panama, the Embera live along the Chorcí River and its tributaries—the Jurubida, Bojaya, Uva, Pogue, Cuia, and Baudo rivers. In the area of the middle Baudo River, they live along the Catru, Dubasa, Ancoso, Nuquí, Panguí, Joví, Arusí, Evarí, Pavasita, Pavasa, Siviru, and Purricha rivers. Those Embera known as the Chocó live along the Capa, Quito, and Pato rivers in the region of the upper Atrato River, around San Juan, and on the coast to the south of San Buenaventura. Some of these subtribes are known as the Citara, Paparo, and Andagueda. They are frequently referred to as "Cholos" by local mestizos. In Colombia, the people known as the Katío live in the area of Dabeiba, Frontino, Ituango, Murindo, Chigorodo, and Urrao, along the Esmeraldas and Verde rivers, and along the upper San Jorge river. In the departments of Cauca and Nariño, the Embera live along the Micay, Saija, Satinga, and Saquianga rivers. The Embera known as the Chamí live along the middle and upper San Juan River in the departments of Chocó and Risaralda.

They are primarily a farming people, raising maize, rice, plantains, and sugar cane, as well as a variety of domesticated livestock. Their principal means of transportation is the canoe. The Embera, including the Katío and Chamí, total more than 50,000 people, of whom approximately 10,000 now live in Panama. A number of government Indian reservations serve the Embera Indians. There are 414 Embera at the Guangui reservation; 219 at the Infi reservation; 336 at the Río Verde reservation; 1,054 at the Tahami del Andagueda reservation; 533 at the Ríos Uva y Pogue reservation; 144 at the Ríos Lañas o Capa reservation; 218 at the Ríos Valle y Boroboro reservation; 174 at the Jagual-Río Chintado reservation; 127 at the Río Nuquí reservation; 617 at the Ríos Catru y Dubasa reservation; 800 at the Ríos Jurubida, Cholrí y Alto Baudo reservation; 151 at the Río Panguí reservation; 175 at the El Veinte, Playalta y El Noventa reservation; 2,101 at the Chamí Río San Juan Margen Derecha reservation; 1,500 at the Chamí Río Carraparas reservation; 184 at the Iguanas reservation; 303 at the Salaquí-Pavarando reservation; 109 at the Bete, Auro Bete y Auro del Buey reservation; 161 at the Calle Santa Rosa reservation; 109 at the Río Domingodo reservation; 102 at the Río Quiparado reservation; 200 at the Río Torreido Chimani reservation; 111 at the Río Mumbu reservation; 68 at the Río Jarapero reservation; 61 at the Quebrada Canaveral Río San Jorge reservation; 83 at the Río Icho y Quebrada Baratudo reservation; 88 at the Río Negua reservation; 104 at the Alto Río Tagachi reservation; 81 at the Alto Río Buey reservation; 382 at the Alto Río Bojaya reservation; 152 at the Alto Río Cuia reservation; 111 at the Napipi reservation; 215 at the Opogado reservation; 355 at the Río Murindo reservation; 67 at the Caimanero de Jampapa reservation; 96 at the Guayabal de Partado reservation; 231 at the Polines reservation; and 55 at the Motordo reservation. There are also several hundred Embera in Panama. Episcopalian missionaries currently work among them.

The Embera are in a process of rapid acculturation and detribalization. Their region of western Colombia and Panama is a multiracial area with rapid settlement by mestizos, blacks, and other detribalized Indians. To deal with the problems of land tenure and title, education, and poverty that settlement has brought to the region, the Embera have joined with the Waunana Indians in forming OREWA (Organización Regional de Embera y Waunana Aborígenes) to exert some political pressure on Colombian authorities.

REFERENCES: Leah H. Ellis and Linda Criswell, eds., *Estudiemos las culturas indígenas de Colómbia*, 1984; Blaz Telban, *Grupos étnicos de Colómbia: Etnografía and bibliografía*, 1987.

EMBERAK. See EMBERA.

EMERILLON. See EMERION.

EMERILON. See EMERION.

EMERION. The Emerion, also known as the Emerillon or Emerilon, lived on the east Brazilian coast from the mouth of the Amazon River north to the border of present-day French Guiana. Under the impact of Portuguese occupation, they migrated north into French Guiana but their population declined rapidly. By 1870, there were only about 150 Emerion still alive, and they were living in close proximity to the Oyanpík.* By the late 1950s, there were still approximately that number of Emerion alive, but they were suffering from the impact of alcoholism and prostitution. A number of the Emerion were also virtual slaves of West Indian gold-washers. In the 1960s, Surinamese government officials expelled the West Indians and provided medical assistance to the Emerion. In the process, the group began to recover. By the 1980s, the Emerion population was just over 100 people, with settlements on the Camopi River and on the Tampok River upstream from Maripasoula.

REFERENCES: Walter Dostal, ed. *The Situation of the Indian in South America*, 1972; John Hemming, *Amazon Frontier: The Defeat of the Brazilian Indians*, 1987; Jean Hurault, "Les Indiens Emerillon de la Guyane Française," *Journal de la Société des Américanistes*, 2 (1963), 133–56.

EMOA. See MAKUNA.

EMOAMASA. See MAKUNA.

EMOK. See TOBA.

EMPERA. See EMBERA.

ENAGUA. See PIAPOCO.

E'NAPA. See PANARE.

ENAWENE-NAWE. See SALUMA.

ENCABELLADO. See SECOYA.

ENCAGA. See KADUVEO.

ENCOGIDO. The term "Encogido" is used in Ecuador and northern Peru to describe an Indian who has no interest in acculturating or assimilating into neo-Ecuadorean or neo-Peruvian society. Encogidos are willing to accept their identity as Indians.

REFERENCE: Albert William Bork and Georg Maier, *Historical Dictionary of Ecuador*, 1973.

ENETES. See YURACARÉ.

ENGARICO. See INGARIKÓ.

ENGERAKMUNG. See BOTOCUDO.

E'NIEPA. See MAPOYO.

ENI-MACA. See MACÁ.

ENIMAGA. See MACÁ.

ENO. See ARAONA.

ENSLET. See ANGAITÉ.

ENTHLIT. See LENGUA.

ENTRÓN. In Ecuador and northern Peru, the term "Entrón" is used disparagingly to describe upwardly mobile Indians who want access to higher levels of society. More properly, Entrón means social climber.

REFERENCE: Albert William Bork and Georg Maier, *Historical Dictionary of Ecuador*, 1973.

EPEÑA. The Epeña are a group of Amerindians who today live in the departments of Nariño, Cauca, and Valle in western Colombia. They tend to be concentrated at the mouths of the Saija, Guangui, and Ifni del Cauca rivers on the Pacific Coast. Their language forms part of the Chocó* subfamily of the larger Chibchan* linguistic group. They are an agricultural people who primarily raise sugar cane and plantains, along with maize and rice as secondary products. Although they raise some domestic livestock, most of their meat protein comes from hunting. In recent years, the increasing settlement of the Pacific Coast by mestizos and blacks has increased the pressures of acculturation on the Epeña. At present, there are approximately 2,000 members of the Epeña group.

REFERENCE: Leah B. Ellis and Linda Criswell, eds., *Estudiemos las culturas indígenas de Colombia*, 1984.

EQUIJATI. See ESSEJJA.

EQUILIQUINAO. See KINIKINÃO.

EQUINIQUINAO. See KINIKINÃO.

ERAHIDAUNSU. See NAMBIQUÁRA.

ERIGBAAGTSÁ. See ARIPAKTSÁ.

ERIGBACTSÁ. See ARIPAKTSÁ.

ERIGPATSÁ. See ARIPAKTSÁ.

ERIKBAKTSÁ. See ARIPAKTSÁ.

ESA-EXA. See ESSEJJA.

ESEEXA. See ESSEJJA.

ESSEJJA. The Essejja (Ese-eja, Echoja, Esa-exa, Eseexa, Chama) are a Tacana*-speaking group of Amerindians who today live in the department of Pando, between the Madre de Dios and Beni rivers in Bolivia, where they are concentrated near Riberalta and Rurrenabaque. Those who live in Peru refer to themselves as Bahuajjas (Baguaja, Baguajairi), while those living near the Heath River are known as Soneñes. Historically they have also been known as the Guarayo* or Huarayo (not to be confused with the Guaranian-speaking Guarayo of central Bolivia), Quinaqui, Tambopata, Tambopata-Guarayo, Tiatinagua, Mohino, and Guacanahua. The Essejja on the Beni River are the Equijati. They live across the border in southeastern Peru as well. They are still a technologically primitive people who prefer a nomadic to a settled existence. At the time of the Spanish conquest, they were a slash-and-burn agricultural group living in south-eastern Bolivia and raising maize, beans, potatoes, and a variety of other crops. Originally a Tupi*-Guaraní* people who descended from the Paraguayan Guar-aní, the Essejja migrated from the area of the Gran Chaco to settle along the Andes foothills between the upper Pilcomayo River to the upper Río Grande in southeastern Bolivia. The migration occurred in successive waves during the sixteenth century. In the 1700s, the Jesuits tried but failed to gather them into their mission system. After arriving in what are today Bolivia and eastern Peru, they adopted agriculture, raising maize, pumpkins, beans, sweet potatoes, sweet manioc, peanuts, cotton and tobacco. By the late nineteenth and early twentieth centuries, however, the Essejja were becoming increasingly acculturated, with large numbers of them abandoning the aboriginal life in favor of migrant and unskilled labor on cattle ranches, missions, and farms; there their lifestyle came to resemble those of forced laborers and landless peasants. Today there are approximately 1,400 Essejja living in Peru and approximately 7,000 in Bolivia, most of them in the province of Nuflo de Chavez in the department of Santa Cruz, between the San Pablo and Blanco rivers. They maintain a strong sense of identity and still function in their aboriginal language, although the forces of acculturation are accelerating among them. The Essejja economy revolves around subsistence agriculture, hunting, fishing, and seasonal labor, with agriculture the most important activity.

REFERENCES: Brian M. Boom, *Ethnobotany of the Chácobo Indians, Beni, Bolivia*, 1987; Mary Ritchie Key, *Comparative Tacanan Phonology: With Cavinena Phonology and Notes on Pano-Tacanan Relationship*, 1968; Pedro Plaza Martínez and Juan Carvajal Carvajal, *Etnías y lenguas de Bolivia*, 1985; Darcy Ribeiro and Mary Ruth Wise, *Los grupos étnicos de la amazona peruana*, 1978.

ETABOSLE. See MACÁ.

ETEHUA. See ASHLUSLAY.

ETELENA. See TERÉNA.

ETHELENA. See TERÉNA.

EWARHOYÁNA. The Ewarhoyána (Ewarhoyána-Kahyawa) are a small tribe of Karib*-speaking Amerindians who today live in the northwestern region of the state of Pará, Brazil. They live in the Tumucumaque Indian Park south of the Brazil-Surinam border. The Ewarhoyána are a riverine people who live on the Paru do Este River, where they fish, hunt river animals, and plant small gardens. They have accepted the metal tools of neo-Brazilian society and engage in work and exchanges with the local cash economy in order to purchase trade goods, but their sense of tribal identity is still intact. But because their population has dropped to only about a dozen people, it has become impossible for them to maintain their tribal ceremonial life. The Ewarhoyána tribe is verging on extinction.

REFERENCES: Edwin Brooks, *Tribes of the Amazon Basin, Brazil 1972*, 1973; Robin Hanbury-Tenison, *A Question of Survival for the Indians of Brazil*, 1973; Robert Lee Spires, "As línguas faladas do Brasil," *América Indígena*, 47 (1987), 455–79; Theodore L. Stoddard, ed., *Indians of Brazil in the Twentieth Century*, 1967.

EWARHOYÁNA-KAHYAWA. See EWARHOYÁNA.

EYIBOGODEGI. See KADUVEO.

F

FA-AI. The Fa-ai are a subtribe of the Bora* Indians. They were first contacted by Europeans in the early seventeenth century, but sustained contact did not come until the late nineteenth century. Although hunting and fishing consume a great deal of their time and hold great symbolic importance in Fa-ai culture, most of the tribe's nutrients come from the manioc, maize, sweet potatoes, plantains, and bananas that they raise in tribal gardens. Until the end of the nineteenth century, the Fa-ai were a large group numbering several thousand people. The wild rubber boom of the 1890s and early 1900s devastated them, bringing thousands of neo-Colombians and their diseases into their territory and drastically reducing their population. The Fa-ai were dislocated and moved, the vast majority of them dying from disease or being assimilated into neo-Colombian society. See BORA.

FARUTE. See WARRAU.

FIAROA. See PIAROA.

FIAROANKOMO. See PIAROA.

FITITA. See WITOTO.

FRENTONE. See MOCOVÍ.

FRENTONE. See TOBA.

FUEGINO. The term "Fuegino" was used for years in Chile to describe the nomadic, fishing, and foraging tribes of Tierra del Fuego. Those tribes consisted for the most part of the Alacaluf,* Yahgan,* and Selk'nam.* Because those groups have all drifted into tribal extinction or near extinction in recent years, use of the term "Fuegino" has also declined.

REFERENCE: S. Lyman Tyler, *Indians of South America*, 1976.

FULNIÔ. The Fulniô, also known historically as the Carnijó (Karnijó) or Yatê, are members of an isolated linguistic family. Today they number approximately 4,000 people and live in the Dantas Barreto Indian Park and near the city of Aguas Belas in the state of Pernambuco, Brazil. In all of northeastern Brazil, they are the most ethnically conservative of the Indian groups. They still prefer to speak the tribal language, although large numbers of them also understand Portuguese. Central concepts in the ancient tribal religion still survive in thought as well as in ceremonialism. Most of the Fulniô people live on a government Indian post. Although they are increasingly integrated into the local cash economy, the Fulniô are a separate, tribal people in terms of their primary social loyalties.

REFERENCES: Robert Lee Spires, "As línguas faladas do Brasil," *América Indígena*, 47 (1987), 455–79; Theodore L. Stoddard, ed., *Indians of Brazil in the Twentieth Century*, 1967.

G

GAE. See SHIMIGAE.

GAGABA. See COGUI.

GAIQUERÍ. See GUAYQUERÍ.

GALERA. The Galera are a subtribe of the Nambiquára* Indians. Today there are fewer than 100 Galera Indians living in several villages on the Galera River in the southern region of the state of Mato Grosso, Brazil. See NAMBIQUÁRA.

GALIBÍ. The Galibí Indians of Brazil and French Guiana are part of the Karib* linguistic family. A slash-and-burn horticultural people, they function today in two separate groups, although at the time of the Portuguese and French conquest of the area, they totaled more than 5,000 people in a series of scattered villages. Approximately 500 Galibí live in a single village on the Uaca River in the territory of Amapá, Brazil. They are highly acculturated and pursue a subsistence, agricultural lifestyle supplemented by seasonal migrant labor to provide money for the cash economy. These Galibí no longer use their aboriginal language, speaking only Portuguese and a local Creole. The second group is the Galibí-Marworno (Galibí-Marworne), of whom approximately 200 live on the Brazilian side of the Oiapoque River and another 2,000 in many villages on the French Guiana side. Many of these Indians still speak Galibí, although they are highly integrated into local society and speak French, Portuguese, and Creole as well. French schools, military experience in the French Army, and tourists crowding their traditional homeland have all accelerated their acculturation. In the last decade, most of the Galibí children have moved out of tribal and into mestizo life.

REFERENCES: Expedito Arnaud, *Os indios Galibí do Río Oiapoque*, 1966; Jean Baptiste Delawarde, *Promenade en Guyane avec les Indiens Galibi*, 1980; Robert Lee Spires, "As línguas faladas do Brasil," *América Indígena*, 47 (1987), 455–79; Theodore L. Stoddard, ed., *Indians of Brazil in the Twentieth Century*, 1967.

GALIBÍ-MAWORNE. See GALIBÍ.

GALIBÍ-MAWORNO. See GALIBÍ.

GAMAKÁN. See KAMAKÁN.

GAMBIANO. The Gambiano (Silvenos, Coconuco, Moguex, Guambiano, Guanbiano) Indians are agriculturalists who live on the eastern slopes of the central Cordillera mountain range in the Andean valleys of southwestern Colombia. Smaller Gambiano settlements can be found on the western slopes of the mountains as well as on the Pacific Coast and in the eastern lowlands. Francisco Benalcazar first conquered them in 1562. The Gambiano raise maize, beans, potatoes, sugar cane, coca, manioc, plantains, and bananas, along with some coffee that they use as a cash crop. In recent years, they have also turned to raising dairy livestock as well. Politically they are organized into reservation communities presided over by councils called *cabildos*. All property is owned communally, not individually.

The Gambiano resisted Spanish conquest and drifted to the Andean valleys from points further east to avoid contact. Many of them, however, came under control of the *encomiendas*. In the eighteenth century, the colonial encomiendo gave way to wage labor systems, especially when neo-Colombians became interested in producing chinchona bark. During the twentieth century, the Gambiano Indians have become more politically active in protecting their way of life from government intrusion. Since 1929, the Christian and Missionary Alliance has had missionaries among the Gambiano, and the Summer Institute of Linguistics has been working with them since the mid–1960s. Along with the neighboring Páez Indians, they established the *Commando Quintín Lame*, a guerrilla organization, in 1985. Government attempts to question Gambiano title to their land have inspired the guerrilla activity. There are approximately 15,000 members of the Gambiano Indian group. The majority live on a reservation near the town of Popayán. Although most of them are Roman Catholics and recognize the political authority of the state, they nevertheless maintain their language and ethnic identity.

REFERENCES: Harold López Mendez, *Guambia*, 1980; Jorge P. Osterling, *Democracy in Colombia: Clientelist Politics and Guerrilla Warfare*, 1989; Joanna Rappaport, "Territory and Tradition: The Ethnohistory of the Páez of Colombia," Ph.D. dissertation, University of Illinois, 1982; Juan Bautista Sanchez, *The Drama of Life: A Study of Life Cycle Customs Among the Guambiano, Colombia, South America*, 1978.

GARÍFUNA. The Garífuna, also known historically as "Black Karibs," now live along the Atlantic Coast of Central America from Belize to Nicaragua. Their numbers exceed 110,000 people, with the majority (over 63,000) in Honduras and smaller numbers in Nicaragua, Belize, and Guatemala. They originated as an ethnic group on St. Vincent island in the Caribbean in the seventeenth century when escaped African slaves mixed with the Karib* Indians. By the early eighteenth century, they had become a new ethnic group, neither African nor Indian. In 1783, England took control of St. Vincent and in the 1790s fought an extended guerrilla war against the Garífuna. The Garífuna were finally defeated in 1796, and the English promptly relocated 5,000 of them to the Bay Islands of the Gulf of Honduras. From there they have migrated north and south along the coast, becoming a large working-class population of farmers, laborers, and artisans.

REFERENCES: Nancie L. González, *Sojourners of the Caribbean: Ethnogenesis and Ethnohistory of the Garifuna*, 1988; C. J. Gullick, *Exiled from St. Vincent: The Development of Black Carib Culture in Central America to 1945*, 1976; L. Fernando Cruz Sandoval, "Los Indios de Honduras y la situación de sus recursos naturales," *América Indígena*, 44 (1984), 423–46.

GATUYA PAIN. See SIONA.

GAVIÃO. The Gaviãos (Gavioes) are a Gê*-speaking, Timbira* tribe of Amerindians who live in Brazil. They are divided into two separate groups. The Gavião of the state of Pará, concentrated near the city of Jacunda on the right bank of the Tocantins River, are known as the Parakáteye and number approximately 175 people. The other group of Gavião live to the north of Imperatriz in the state of Maranhão and are known as Pukobyé (Pukopyé); they number over 300 people. They should not be confused with the Mondé*-speaking Gaviãos* of Rondônia. The Gaviãos resisted neo-Brazilian expansion into their territory until the 1850s, destroying a number of bandeirantes sent against them. But in 1857, an army of extermination nearly obliterated the Gaviãos and set them on the road to pacification and economic and social decline. Today tribal ceremonial life is all but impossible to maintain and the tribe has been reduced to nearly complete dependency on government or philanthropic handouts. In the mid–1950s, neo-Brazilian nut gatherers decimated the Gaviãos. After the Gaviãos were "pacified" in the mid–1950s, epidemic diseases almost wiped them out. When the state of Pará constructed Highway PA–70 straight through their territory, they were also hurt by the economic development and settlement that came in its wake. They live in desperate economic conditions, ameliorated only recently by the University of São Paolo's project to assist them to develop their own nut-gathering business. A future threat to them will be the impact of the construction of an electrified railway from the iron mines of the Serra dos Carajas São Luis in the state of Maranhão.

REFERENCES: Paul L. Aspelin and Silvio Coelho dos Santos, *Indian Areas Threatened by Hydroelectric Projects in Brazil*, 1981; Robin Hanbury-Tenison, *A Question of Survival for the Indians of Brazil*, 1973; Robert Lee Spires, "As línguas faladas do

Brasil,'' *América Indígena*, 47 (1987), 455–79; Theodore L. Stoddard, ed., *Indians of Brazil in the Twentieth Century*, 1967.

GAVIÃO. The Gaviãos (Ikoro, Digút), not to be confused with the Gê*-speaking Gaviãos, are a tribe of approximately 220 Amerindians who live in the state of Rondônia, Brazil. Their language is part of the Mondé* linguistic family. They call themselves the Ikoleec. A tropical forest people who lived off hunting and horticulture, the Gaviãos were decimated by the rubber boom in Rondônia in the early 1900s and again during World War II. The rubber collectors brought violence, disease, and forced labor to the Gavião people, and their population declined so drastically that they had difficulty maintaining their traditional ceremonial life. In the 1940s, the Gavião suffered severely from colds and pneumonia acquired from neo-Brazilians. They survived primarily because their homeland, in what is today the Lourdes government Indian post, was nearly 45 miles from the town of Ji-Paraná and the rapids along the Jiparaná River prevented easy access. In 1966, missionaries and physicians from the New Tribes Mission arrived to work with the Gaviãos, and their health conditions improved dramatically. At the time there were fewer than 100 Gaviãos still alive. The Gavião population increased to 143 people by 1977 and more than 200 by the late 1980s. The Brazilian government clearly demarcated their land in 1977 and gave them clear title to it. By the early 1980s, almost all of the Gaviãos had been converted to the Baptist religion. The major threat to the Gaviãos today, however, is the continuing population boom and economic growth in Rondônia which threaten to put pressure on their land.

REFERENCES: Denny Moore, "The Gavião, Zoró, and Arara Indians," in David Maybury-Lewis, ed., *In the Path of the Polonoreste: Endangered Peoples of Western Brazil*, 1981, 46–54; Robert L. Spires, "As línguas faladas do Brasil," *América Indígena*, 47 (1987), 455–79.

GAVIOE. See GAVIÃO.

GÊ. The term "Gê," also known as "Jê," refers to one of the four main language groups of the Brazilian Indians. The Gê-speaking tribes once occupied the Brazilian coastline. A few centuries before the arrival of the Portuguese, they were driven into the interior by the northeastern expansion of the Tupi,* who were moving out from their homelands in Bolivia and Paraguay. The Gê ended up on the plateaus and scrublands of central and eastern Brazil, generally avoiding the tropical forests. Historically the major tribes of the Gê linguistic family included the Akroa, Xakriabá,* Xavánte,* Xerénte,* Apinayé,* Kayapó,* Eastern Timbira,* Suyá,* Kaingáng,* and Xokléng.*

REFERENCES: John Hemming, *Red Gold: The Conquest of the Brazilian Indians, 1500–1760*, 1978; Johannes Wilbert, *Folk Literature of the Ge Indians*, 1984.

GERAL. Geral is a Tupi*-Guaraní*-based language that was brought to the northwest Amazon by Jesuit missionaries and has evolved into a *lingua franca* for many different tribes in the area. It is also known as Nheengatú.* See NHEENGATÚ.

GHUYLLICHE. See HUILLICHE.

GÍBARI. See JÍVARO.

GINABO. See PACANUARA.

GIRIGUANA. See CHIRIGUANO.

GIRY. See ARAONA.

GITIBO. See SETEBO.

GÍVARO. See JÍVARO.

GOAHIBO. See GUAHIBO.

GOAHIVO. See GUAHIBO.

GOAJIR. See GUAJIRO.

GOAJIRO. See GUAJIRO.

GOIANAZ. See KAINGÁNG.

GOROTÍRE. The Gorotíre are a Gê*-speaking, Northern Kayapó* tribe of Amerindians who today live on the Fresco River, a tributary of the middle Xingú River, in the municipality of Altamira in the state of Pará, Brazil. The Gorotíre first encountered neo-Brazilian settlers early in the 1800s, but they resisted contact, sometimes violently, fleeing into uninhabited regions where they could pursue their hunting and foraging lifestyle. Early in the 1900s, rubber gatherers battled with the Gorotíre and severely reduced their population, but in 1936 the Brazilian government Indian service pacified them. They had just recently, only a year before, split from the Kuben-Kran-Kêgn,* another Northern Kayapó group. The Gorotíre are the parent group to such other Northern Kayapó people as the Mekranotí* and Mentuktíre.* Today the Gorotíre number approximately 1,050 people and live in permanent contact with neo-Brazilian society. They have adapted to European technology and dress; they work in the regional cash economy in addition to their agricultural pursuits, but they still receive assistance from the government, identify themselves as a separate people, and speak Portuguese and their Gê language.

REFERENCES: Robin Hanbury-Tenison, *A Question of Survival for the Indians of Brazil*, 1973; Robert Lee Spires, "As Línguas Faladas do Brasil," *América Indígena*, 47 (1987), 455–79; Theodore L. Stoddard, ed., *Indians of Brazil in the Twentieth Century*, 1967.

GOTOCOGEGODEGI. See KADUVEO.

GOYANA. See KAINGÁNG.

GRITONE. See PACANAURA.

GUACANAHUA. See ESSEJJA.

GUACURURE. See PILAGÁ.

GUAGIBO. See GUAHIBO.

GUAGIVA. See GUAHIBO.

GUAHARIBO. See YANOAMA.

GUAHARIVO. See YANOAMA.

GUAHIBA. See GUAHIBO.

GUAHIBO. The Guahibo (Guajibo, Goahibo, Guayba, Guagiva, Guaiba, Guaibo, Guayva, Guaiva, Goahivo, Guagibo, Guajivo) are an Amerindian people living in small groups in the savannas of eastern Colombia and western Venezuela. They call themselves the Hivi (Hiwi). Over the years, anthropologists have identified four subtribes of the Guahibo: the Guahibo, Chiricoa,* Cuiva,* and Sikuani.* These subdivisions are ambiguous, inconsistent, and not recognized by the Guahibo themselves. At one time, there were 26 Guahibo subtribes, but today only ten survive with a social identity. They are known as the Awirimomowi or Bolamomowi, the Baxumomowi or Duhaimomowi, the Hamaruamomowi or Ainawimomowi, the Huramomowi, the Kabalemomowi, the Kawirimomowi, the Mahamomowi, the Metsahamomowi, the Newithimomowi, and the Okoromomowi. Known for their wide-ranging migration patterns, the Guahibo live between the Meta and Vichada rivers in Colombia; along the Sipapo, Mundauapo, Vicharo, and Morrocoy Rivers in western Venezuela; and in the Federal Amazonas Territory and the states of Apure and Bolívar in Venezuela. They moved into the area after the disappearance of many agricultural tribes in the sixteenth century and then absorbed many of the smaller remaining tribes. At different times of the year and in different eras, the Guahibo, a culturally flexible people, use nomadic foraging or subsistence agriculture as their economic base. Different Guahibo groups many also emphasize a nomadic, semi-sedentary, or sedentary life. Nomadism was so constant among the Guahibo that early Spanish explorers referred to them as the Gypsies of the Indies. Late in the 1940s, large-scale migrations of neo-Colombian and neo-Venezuelan settlers into the llanos and selva areas forced the Guahibo to abandon the land or face extermination. They moved southward in Colombia and eastward in Venezuela and also took to cyclical migrations to nearby towns and cities to look for work. That pattern continues to describe the Guahibo today. They spend much of the year working their land as settled, subsistence farmers, but also spend time laboring in the regional cash economy. Large numbers have moved in recent years into the cities of Puerto Ayacucho, San Juan de Manapiare, and El Amparo, where they are rapidly acculturated. The Guahibo in the state of Apure are terribly persecuted and live in desperate poverty. Although most Guahibo speak some Spanish, they still prefer their native tongue. Today more than 25,000 Guahibo Indians in Colombia and Venezuela retain a strong sense of their tribal identity. The hostility between Guahibo and the ranchers and settlers remains intense, even though some Guahibo now work as day laborers. The World Evangelization Crusade and the Summer Institute of Linguistics have been among the Guahibo since the early 1960s.

In Colombia, large numbers of Guahibo live on government reservations, including 78 at the Cano Negro reservation; 239 at the Corocito-Yopalito-Gualabo reservation; 2,500 at the San Rafael, Abariba, and Ibibi reservation; 241 at the Vencedor, Piriri, Guamito y Matanegra reservation; 375 at the El Tigre reservation; 82 at the Cano Jabón reservation; 77 at the Cano Ovejas o Betania-Corocito reservation; 205 at the Río Siare o Barranco Lindo reservation; 3,500 at the El Unuma reservation; 729 at the Saracure y Río Cada reservation; 702 at the Cano Cavasi reservation; 877 at the Ríos Muca y Guarrojo reservation; 580 at the Canos Cuna Tsepajibo Warracha reservation; 803 at the Santa Teresita del Tuparro reservation; 608 at the Ríos Tomo Weberi reservation; 259 at the San Luis del Tomo reservation; 216 at the La Pascua reservation; 149 at the La Llanura reservation; 3,347 at the Bajo Río Vichada o Santa Rita reservation; 60 at the Gano Claro reservation; 118 at the Egua Guariacana reservation; 446 at the Atana Pirariami reservation; 68 at the Cenareros reservation; 59 at the Macarieros reservation; 709 at the Roqueros reservation; 26 at the Puyeros reservation; 65 at the Parreros reservation; 53 at the Julieros 7 Velasqueros reservation; 105 at the Cano Guaripa reservation; 27 at the Cano La Hormiga reservation; 43 at the Cano Bachaco reservation; 116 at the Merey La Veraita reservation; 294 at the Guacamayas-Mamiyare reservation; 158 at the Laguna Anguilla-La Maracena reservation; 102 at the Arrecifal reservation; 242 at the Barranquito Laguna Colorado reservation; 86 at the Carrizal reservation; 350 at the Carpintero Palomas reservation; 172 at the El Vigía reservation; 91 at the Campoalegre y Ripialito reservation; 74 at the Laguna Curvina-Sapuara reservation; 112 at the Sejalito-San Bernio reservation; and 70 at the La Esmeralda reservation.

REFERENCES: Bernard Arcand, *The Urgent Situation of the Cuiva Indians of Colombia*, 1972; Mary Ellen Conaway, *Still Guahibo, Still Moving: A Study of Circular Migration and Marginality in Venezuela*, 1984; Robert Morey, *The Guahibo: People of the Savannah*, 1974.

GUAHIBOAN. The term "Guahiboan" refers to a small group of Amerindian languages closely related to the longer Arawakan* grouping. Historically, the Guahiboan tribes lived in Colombia and Venezuela and included the Chiricoa,* Guahibo,* Churuya, and Guayabero* languages.

REFERENCES: Joseph H. Greenberg, *Language in the Americas*, 1987; Harriet E. Manelis Klein and Louisa R. Stark, *South American Indian Languages: Retrospect and Prospect*, 1985.

GUAIANA. See KAINGÁNG.

GUAIAPY. See OYANPÍK.

GUAIBA. See GUAHIBO.

GUAIBO. See GUAHIBO.

GUAICA. See AKAWÁIO.

GUAICA. See YANOAMA.

GUAICURU. See GUAYCURU.

GUAIKA. See YANOAMA.

GUAIKIARE. See WOKIARE.

GUAIKURU. See GUAYCURU.

GUAIPUINAVE. See PUINAVE.

GUAIQUAIRO. See YABARANA.

GUAIVA. See GUAHIBO.

GUAJÁ. The Guajá (Wazaizara, Aiaye) are a Tupi*-speaking tribe of Amerindians who migrated among locations in the jungles between the Capim and upper Gurupí rivers and between the Gurupí and Pindaré rivers in the state of Maranhão, Brazil. A foraging and hunting people who were not agricultural, the Guajá were traditional enemies of the Urubús.* Well into the twentieth century, the Guajá were still employing stone tools and avoiding contact with neo-Brazilians. Agents of the Brazilian Indian Service did not make peaceful contact with the Guajá until 1975. Since then, most of the violence between the Guajá and the Urubú has disappeared. At most there may be 250 Guajá still functioning as a tribal people, with permanent contact established with them only in the last decade. They reside between the upper Gurupí and the Pindaré rivers. Many of the Guajá still avoid contact with neo-Brazilian society. They live primarily on the fleshy pulp of the babassu palm. The Guajá are one of the few remaining nomadic, foraging tribes in Brazil. Today the Guaja are threatened by the Carajas Project, which is involved in heavy mining practices and reforestation programs that are damaging the Guajá habitat.

REFERENCES: William Balée, "Cultural Forests of the Amazon," *Garden*, 11 (1987), 12–14, 32; "Doctrine of National Security Threatens Brazil's Indians," *Cultural Survival Quarterly*, 11 (1987), 63–65.

GUAJAJÁRA. The Guajajára are a Tupi*-speaking tribe of Amerindians who were first contacted by the Portuguese early in the 1600s. They fought pitched battles with the incoming settlers. They call themselves the Tenetahara; a subtribe is the Tembé. In the 1650s, some of the Guajajára settled on a Jesuit mission near Itaqui in what is today the state of Maranhão, but when the priests tried to get them to work the tobacco plantations, the Indians fled back into the forests where they were able to maintain their existence as a large warrior tribe. They lived on the Pindaré, Mearim, and Grajau rivers. As late as 1830, they numbered more than 12,000 people, scattered over a broad area, with more than 5,000 on rivers south of Belém in the state of Pará and the others on the upper Pindaré and Gurupí rivers in what is today the state of Maranhão. In the 1850s, the Brazilian government and the church made another concerted attempt to convert the Guajajára to Christianity and "useful work." In 1860, the Guajajára rose up in rebellion, killed several neo-Brazilians, and fled back into the wilderness from the new aldeias. New attempts to pacify the Guajajára developed in the 1890s, but Italian Capuchin missionaries were brutal in forcing religion on them so they rebelled again in 1900 after a severe measles epidemic. This rebellion led to a near genocidal reaction against the Guajajára. After that rebellion, the Guajajára were essentially pacified, and because the missionaries encouraged them to have large families, their population stabilized and increased. Today there are more than 6,700 people in the state of Maranhão, between the Pindaré and upper Mearim rivers, who know of their Guajajára heritage. They are in a state of advanced acculturation and completely integrated into the local cash economy.

REFERENCES: William Balée, "Ka'apór Ritual Hunting," *Human Ecology*, 13 (1985), 485–510; Robert Lee Spires, "As línguas faladas do Brasil," *América Indígena*, 47 (1987), 455–79; Theodore L. Stoddard, ed., *Indians of Brazil in the Twentieth Century*, 1967.

GUAJARIBO. See YANOAMA.

GUAJIBO. See GUAHIBO.

GUAJIMA. See ARAONA.

GUAJIRO. The Guajiro, also known as the Coajiro, Goajiro, Guayu, Cosina, Goajir, and Wayuu, are a pastoral, Arawak*-speaking people occupying the Guajiro Peninsula of Venezuela and Colombia. Their self-designation is Wayuu. When the Spanish first encountered the Guajiro in 1499, they were a hunting people, but the introduction of cattle by Spaniards early in the 1500s transformed Guajiro life. They adapted quickly to a pastoral lifestyle, raising cattle over an area of more than 5,000 square miles. The Guajiro acquired the livestock by raiding white settlements and then grazed them all over the "shrubland" of the Guajiro Peninsula. Today there are more than 100,000 members of the Guajiro tribe. Perhaps 25,000 of them in Venezuela and 65,000 in Colombia live as stock raisers and breeders. Approximately 10,000 Guajiro live on the outskirts of Maracaibo and work in urban jobs. Others live in such cities as Santa Barbara, Sinamaica, and Paraguaipoa. Hunting and fishing have become quite secondary to the Guajiro economy. They are increasingly affected by the expansion of European civilization. The Summer Institute of Linguistics and the South American Indian Mission have worked among the Guajiro since the early 1960s. In Colombia, 45,000 Guajiro Indians live on the government reservation at Alta y Media Guajira, 575 at the El Zaino, Guayabito, Muriaytuy reservation, 357 at the Wayuu de Lomamato reservation, and 1,000 at the Carraipa reservation.

REFERENCES: Michel Perrin, *The Way of the Dead Indians: Guajiro Myths and Symbols*, 1976; Johannes Wilbert and Karin Simoneau, *Folk Literature of the Guajiro Indians*, 1986; Lawrence C. Watson, "Sexual Stratification in Guajiro Society," *Ethnology*, 11 (April 1972), 150–56.

GUAJIVO. See GUAHIBO.

GUAMBIA-COCONUCO. See GUAHIBO.

GUAMBIANO. See GAMBIANO.

GUAMO. See GUAYQUERÍ.

GUANA. See KASKIHA.

GUANA. See TERÉNO.

GUANANO. See UANANA.

GUANBIANO. See GAMBIANO.

GUAPORÉ NAMBIQUÁRA. See NAMBIQUÁRA.

GUARANÍ. Guaraní is an Indian language spoken today by more than 2,500,000 people in Bolivia, Paraguay, northern Argentina, and southern Brazil. Because of its physical isolation from primary trade routes in South America and its lack of attractive resources, Paraguay did not attract massive settlement. There the Spanish language, instead of replacing Guaraní, co-existed with it. The entire population of Paraguay is bilingual, in Spanish and Guaraní, although Spanish tends to be the language of business and government while Guaraní is the private language of friends and family. Another 1,000 people of Indian descent who speak Guaraní live in Argentina, and 14,000 Brazilian Indians—Kaiwá,* Mbüa (Mbiá), and Nhandéva (Nandéva)—speak Guaraní as well. They are widely dispersed throughout a variety of government Indian parks in southern Brazil.

When the Spaniards first encountered the Guaraní in eastern Argentina in the early 1500s, the Indians lived in town systems of communal houses and practiced slash-and-burn argriculture. Before the arrival of the Spanish, many Guaraní had migrated into Bolivia where they reached the outskirts of the Inca Empire. Attracted by Incan wealth, the Guaraní welcomed the Spaniards as potential allies in securing some of the riches of Incan civilization. After the establishment of Asunción in 1537, the Guaraní worked as warriors and porters for Spanish expeditions. In Paraguay and northern Argentina, Guaraní and Spanish civilization produced a mestizo culture. The society was bilingual in Spanish and Guaraní. Those Guaraní who did not adapt to mestizo culture in the towns were gathered by Jesuits into the mission system, where they converted to Roman Catholicism and European agricultural patterns.

REFERENCES: Moíses Santiago Bertoni, *La civilisación Guaraní*, 1956; Philip Caraman, *The Lost Paradise: The Jesuit Republic in South America*, 1976; Isabel Hernández, "Los pueblos y las lenguas aborígenes en la actualidad," *América Indígena*, 47 (1987), 409–23; Arthur P. Sorenson, Jr., "South American Indian Linguistics at the Turn of the Seventies," in Daniel R. Gross, ed., *Peoples and Cultures of Native South America*, 1973; Robert Lee Spires, "As línguas faladas do Brasil," *América Indígena*, 47 (1987), 455–79.

GUARANNE. See WARRAU.

GUARANU. See WARRAU.

GUARAÓ. See WARAÓ.

GUARAON. See WARRAU.

GUARAOUN. See WARRAU.

GUARAOUNO. See WARRAU.

GUARAOUNOE. See WARRAU.

GUARARINI. See WARRAU.

GUARASUG'WE. See PAUSERNA.

GUARATAGAJA. See GUARATEGÁJA.

GUARATEGÁJA. The Guarategája (Guaratagája) were a tribe of Tupi*-speaking Amerindians who once numbered in the thousands in the Guaporé drainage area of Brazil. They lived off black beans, maize, and peanuts, as well as by fishing and hunting. The rubber boom of the late nineteenth and early twentieth centuries throughout the state of Rondônia started the Guarategája on the road to extinction because of disease and relocation at the hands of the rubber collectors. By the 1940s, the Guarategája had ceased to exist as a differentiated social unit. Today there are just a handful of people still alive in the Guaporé region of Rondônia who are aware of their Guarategája origins.

REFERENCE: Theodore L. Stoddard, ed., *Indians of Brazil in the Twentieth Century*, 1967.

GUARAU. See WARRAU.

GUARAUNA. See WARRAU.

GUARAUNAN. See WARRAU.

GUARAUNE. See WARRAU.

GUARAUNO. See WARAÓ.

GUARAYO. See CHIRIGUANO.

GUARAYO. See ESSEJJA.

GUARAYO. The Guarayo are a group of Amerindians whose homeland today is in Paraguay. They speak a Guaraní* language and refer to themselves as the Guaraní or Mbya Guaraní. Some scholars believe that they are the Chiriguano* Indians. During the eighteenth century the Guarayo migrated to their present location from Bolivia. Today the Guarayo population is approaching 2,000 people. They are located across a broad area of the Paraguayan Gran Chaco. In the extreme western region of Paraguay, there are Guarayo living in Nueva Asunción and in the Immaculate Heart of Mary Mission near Colonia Pedro P. Peña. In the central part of the Gran Chaco, Guarayo live in Mariscal Estigarriba and in the Mennonite colonies near Filadelfia. In the eastern Chaco, they live scattered along the Puerto Casado Railroad. Large numbers of the Guarayo work as laborers in the Gran Chaco. As a people, they tend to be less acculturated to the larger society than most other indigenous people of the Chaco.

REFERENCE: Miguel Chase-Sardi, *La situación actual de los indígenas del Paraguay*, 1972.

GUARAYU. See ESSEJJA.

GUAREQUENA. The Guarequena are a subgroup of the Wakuenai* people. Their current habitat is near Gavilán and Guzmán Blanco in southwestern Venezuela. See WAKUENAI.

GUAREQUENA. See WARIKYÁNA.

GUARIBA. See MAKÚ.

GUARIBO. See YANOAMA.

GUARIQUENA. See WARIKYÁNA.

GUARPE. See HUARPE.

GUASURANGO. See TAPIETÉ.

GUATÓ. The Guató were once members of a linguistically isolated group living a riverine existence on the banks of the Paraguay River in the state of Mato Grosso, Brazil. By the early 1900s, their population was in a state of rapid decline because of contact with neo-Brazilians. They have recently ceased to function as a differentiated social group. There are approximately 225 people today who have a recollection of their Guató origins, but they have intermarried with neo-Brazilians and today live in the lake district north of Corumba in the state of Mato Grosso.

REFERENCES: Robert Lee Spires, "As línguas faladas do Brasil," *América Indígena*, 47 (1987), 455–79; Theodore L. Stoddard, ed., *Indians of Brazil in the Twentieth Century*, 1967.

GUATUSOS. The Guatusos are a contemporary Indian tribe living in three small villages—Margarita, El Sol, and Tonjibe—in the district of San Rafael de Guatuso, Costa Rica. They are probably descendents of the Corobici and Voto tribes, which are now extinct. There are only 100 Gautusos still alive and functioning in an indigenous lifestyle, raising tubers, bananas, and white cacao on communal land. They live in multifamily houses without walls. The tribe is in a state of rapid decline and destined to extinction. The Guatusos are subsistence farmers who work communal plots of land.

REFERENCES: Elías Zamora Acosta, *Etnografía historia de Costa Rica (1561–1615)*, 1980; Howard I. Blutstein, *Area Handbook for Costa Rica*, 1970.

GUAVIARE. The Guaviare are a small group of Amerindians who live between the Guaviare and Inirida rivers in the territory of Vaupés in southeastern Colombia. They are a nomadic hunting and gathering people who are probably closely associated with the Makú* Indians. The Guaviare studiously avoid much contact with neo-Colombians unless such contact is unavoidable, and they tend to associate themselves, often as servants, with other tribes. At present, there are several hundred Guaviare Indians.

REFERENCE: Leah B. Ellis and Linda Criswell, eds., *Estudiemos las culturas indigenas de Colombia*, 1984.

GUAYABERO. The Guayabero (Kunimia, Bisanigua) are a tropical forest group of Amerindians who at the time of the conquest lived on the Orinoco River north of the Atuares Rapids to the mouth of the Arauca River, as well as along the Cinaruco River. They call themselves the Mitua. Their language is part of the Guahibo* family. Like other tropical forest people, the Guayabero were primarily farmers who raised sweet manioc, maize, and chili peppers. After the arrival of the Spaniards, they adopted banana cultivation as a major horticultural endeavor as well. The Guayabero came under attack from Karib* Indians in the early eighteenth century and fled south toward the Vichada River. Many of them joined Jesuit missions there until the expulsion of the Jesuits in 1767. Today the Guayabero live along the Gauviare River near the junction of the departments of Vaupés, Meta, Guainía, and Vichada in Colombia. Their principal communities are Barrancón, La Sal, La Fuga, Barrano Salado, Barrano Colorado, Barrano Ceiva, and Macuare. They maintain a strong sense of Indian identity even though they are acculturating to the neo-Colombian economy. Their population totals approximately 700 people living in ten settlements along the Guaviare River. Most of them work as farmers raising manioc, plantains, bananas, corn, and rice. Although older adults still wear aboriginal clothing, younger people have adopted Western dress. The New Tribes Mission and the Summer Institute of Linguistics have been in contact with the Guayabero since the early 1960s. In 1988, there were approximately 120 Guayabero living on the Colombian Indian reservation of Venezuela, as well as 125 at the Barrancón reservation, 90 at the La Fuga reservation, 103 at the Barranco Ceiba y Laguna Araguato reservation, 105 at the La Sal reservation, and 107 at the Macuare reservation.

REFERENCES: Nancy Morey, "Ethnohistory of the Colombian and Venezuelan Llanos," Ph.D. dissertation, University of Utah, 1975; Myriam Jiméno and Adolfo Triana Antorveza, *Estado y minorias étnicas in Colombia*, 1985; Ministerio de Gobierno, *Aspetos de la cultura material de los grupos étnicos de Colombia*, 1979.

GUAYAKÍ. See ACHÉ.

GUAYÁNA. See WAYÁNA.

GUAYÁNA. See KAINGÁNG.

GUAYÁNO. See KAINGÁNG.

GUAYAPÍ. See OYANPÍK.

GUAYAQUÍ. See ACHÉ.

GUAYBA. See GUAHIBO.

GUAYCARÍ. See GUAYQUERÍ.

GUAYCURU. The term Guaycuru (Guaykuru, Guaikuru) refers to a large linguistic group of Amerindians living at the time of the Spanish conquest in what today is Argentina. They included such tribes as the Abipón, Mocoví,* Pilagá,*

Mbayá, and Payaguá.* Before the sixteenth century, when they migrated to the Gran Chaco, the Guaycuruans had lived as nomadic hunters and gatherers in Patagonia. In the seventeenth century, they adopted the use of the horse and became even more nomadic, raiding Spanish settlements and other Indians. Not until the nineteenth century were they pacified. In the twentieth century, the Guaycuruans generally assimilated into neo-Argentinian life.

REFERENCE: Felix A. Chaparro, *Los Guaycurus*, 1947.

GUAYKURU. See GUAYCURU.

GUAYMÍ. The Guaymí today are a tribe of approximately 60,000 Indians living in the provinces of Bocas del Toro, Chiriqui, and Veraguas in Panama. Approximately 2,000 Guaymí also live in Costa Rica. Pedro de Gómez launched the conquest of the Guaymí in 1516, but Spaniards had little success, especially in the highland areas. During the sixteenth century, small groups of the Guaymí separated from the main tribe and migrated west to a number of locations near the mountains of the Caribbean coast. Dominican and Jesuit missionaries tried to convert the Guaymí in the seventeenth century, as did Franciscans in the eighteenth, but the Indians resisted. Some of them were moved to new locations in southwestern Panama in the seventeenth century, although substantial numbers of the Guaymí retreated further east into the coastal lowlands of Chiriquí. Those Guaymí who remained on the plains of Chiriquí and Veraguas provinces gradually blended into the campesino population. They speak a Chibchan* language, which most Guaymí still use in their homes and in private conversation, although Spanish is becoming an increasingly common public language, spoken by a large minority.

The Guaymí are generally divided into two groups. The Northern Guaymí, a tropical forest tribe, live in round and square homes with conical roofs. Several tribes make up the Northern Guaymí. The Mové live in the Miranda Valley and on the Caribbean slopes of the mountains between Laguna de Chiriquí and the Belén River. The Murire live in the eastern regions of the Serrania de Tabasara and along the Caribbean coast as far east as the Northern Cocle River. The Muoi were a Northern Guaymí subtribe who once lived along the Fonseca River in Chiriquí Province. The Chaliva, Artieda, Nuite, Norteño, Buekete, and Culantro are other small tribelets or pseudonyms for the Northern Guaymí. The Southern Guaymí occupy the uplands of the Pacific Coast. Like the Northern Guaymí, they still live in small, dispersed hamlets and raise maize, beans, lima beans, sweet manioc, papaya, avocado, yams, plantains, and bananas using slash-and-burn farming techniques. After 1900, substantial numbers of Guaymí also began raising cattle. Guaymí Indians can also be found working for the large fruit companies as day laborers, clearing land, planting banana plants, spraying insecticides, harvesting crops, and doing general maintenance.

REFERENCES: University of Panama, *Los Indios Guaymies*, 1969; Philip D. Young, "Notes on the Ethnohistorical Evidence for Structural Continuity in Guaymí Society,"

Ethnohistory, 17 (1970), 11–30; Arysteides Turpana, "Lenguas indígenas," *América Indígena*, 47 (1987), 614–25.

GUAYNUNGOMO. See MAYONGÓNG.

GUAYQUERÍ. The Guayquerí (Guayquirí, Gaiquerí, Guaycarí, Guamó) were once a large Amerindian tribe scattered throughout the Venezuelan llanos from an area north and west of the Orinoco River to the Andes foothills in the east and to the Vichada River basin in the south. Fish and shellfish were the most important parts of their diet, although the Guayquerí also hunted river animals. They knew little of agriculture. In the twentieth century, the Guayquerí have become a highly acculturated group of Indians, speaking Spanish as their primary language and adopting Roman Catholicism as their religion, although the religion still has some older folk elements to it. Economically, the Guayquerí have become integrated into the regional economy as wage laborers, small-scale livestock raisers, and small farmers. Today approximately 6,000 people in Venezuela are aware of their Guayquerí ancestry, although the tribe as a functional social unit has all but ceased to exist. A large concentration of Guayquerí people live in El Poblado on Margarita Island in the state of Nueva Esparta.

REFERENCES: Walter Dostal, ed. *The Situation of the Indian in South America*, 1972; Nancy Morey, "Ethnohistory of the Colombian and Venezuelan Llanos," Ph.D. dissertation, University of Utah, 1975.

GUAYQUIRÍ. See GUAYQUERÍ.

GUAYÚ. See GUAJIRO.

GUAYVA. See GUAHIBO.

GUENTUSE. See MACÁ.

GUEREN. Several thousand people, now living a completely mestizo lifestyle, are spread throughout the region of Olivenca in the state of Bahia, Brazil. They are most likely descendents of the original Gueren and Botocudo* Indians who lived in the area, but the disruptions of Portuguese conquest reduced them from as many as 20,000 people in the seventeenth century to an assimilated group by the nineteenth. Today the Gueren retain none of their aboriginal culture and function within neo-Brazilian society. Nevertheless, despite their cultural integration and high rates of intermarriage with neo-Brazilians, the Gueren retain a certain ethnic identity that distinguishes them from the larger society. They speak Portuguese, and most live in the region of Olivenca in the state of Bahia.

REFERENCE: Theodore L. Stoddard, ed., *Indians of Brazil in the Twentieth Century*, 1967.

GUETAR. See RAMA.

GUETEADEGUO. See KADUVEO.

GUETIADEGODI. See KADUVEO.

GUETIADEO. See KADUVEO.

GUICÚRU. See KUIKÚRU.

GUILICHE. See HUILLICHE.

GUILLICHE. See HUILLICHE.

GUINAU. See WINAO.

GUIRIGUANA. See CHIRIGUANA.

GUISNAI. See ASHLUSLAY.

GUISNAI. See MATACO.

GUISNAY. See MATACO.

GUITOTO. See WITOTO.

GUNUNA-KENE. See TEHUELCHE.

GUOCOTEGODI. See KADUVEO.

GUUYLLICHE. See HUILLICHE.

GUYANA. See URUKUYÁNA.

GUYAPI. See OYANPÍK.

H

HABUWI. See ARAONA.

HAGUETI. See CASHIBO.

HALITI. See PARECÍ.

HALOTESU. See NAMBIQUÁRA.

HAMACORE. See IQUITO.

HAMAPU. See ARAONA.

HAMARUAMOMOWI. See GUAHIBO.

HANERA. See BARASÁNA.

HARAKMBET. The term "Harakmbet," also known as Hate, refers to an isolated linguistic family that once occupied much of the Alto Madre de Dios drainage area in southeastern Peru. The group included such tribes as the Wachipaeri* (Huachipairi), Toyeri,* Sirineiri,* Amarakaeri* (Amarakairi), Arasaeri,* Kisambaeri,* Pukirieri, Shiliveri, and Suweri. Since the conquest, the area covered by the Harakmbet has been drastically reduced by population decline. Remnants of the Harakmbet, primarily the Amarakaeri and Wachipeiri groups, still reside at the Roman Catholic mission in Shintuya, Peru.

REFERENCES: Andrew Gray, "Perspectives on Amarakaeri History," in Harald O. Sklar and Frank Salomon, eds., *Natives and Neighbors in South America: Anthropological Essays*, 1987, 299–328; Patricia J. Lyon, "Dislocación tribal y clasificaciones lingüísticas en la zona del Río Madre de Dios,'' *Actas y Memorias*, 5 (1975), 185–207; Stefano Varese, *The Forest Indians in the Present Political Situation of Peru*, 1972.

HARWANEKI. See TEHUELCHE.

HATE. See HARAKMBET.

HAUANIKER-TSONIK. See TEHUELCHE.

HAVENIKEN. See TEHUELCHE.

HAWANEKI. See TEHUELCHE.

HECHOALADI. See TERÉNO.

HETÁ. The Hetá Indians are a tiny group of Amerindian people in Brazil. Linguists have identified their language as being of Tupi* extraction. The Hetá were virtually unknown in recorded history until December 8, 1954, when they voluntarily approached some neo-Brazilian farmers in the northeastern region of the state of Paraná. They were a forest people of the Serra dos Dourados in Paraná. Although anthropologists suspect that the Hetá might once have been a horticultural people, they had become, by the mid-twentieth century, a nomadic hunting and foraging people with only the most rudimentary technology. Although they probably numbered several hundred people in the 1940s, the spread of coffee plantations in Paraná has deforested their habitat. The Hetá declined in numbers because of acculturation and disease. By the mid–1980s, there were only a handful of acculturated Hetá still alive.
   REFERENCE: Vladimir Kozak, *The Hetá Indians: Fish in a Dry Pond*, 1979.

HIANACOTO. See KARIJONA.

HIANACOTO-UMAUA. See KARIJONA.

HÍBARO. See JÍVARO.

HICAQUE. See JICAQUE.

HINGUTDESU. See NAMBIQUÁRA.

HISKARYÁNA. See HIXKARUYÁNA.

HITOTE. See WITOTO.

HIVI. See GUAHIBO.

HIWI. See GUAHIBO.

HIXKARYÁNA. The Hixkaryána (Hiskaruyána) are a subtribe of the Parukoto* Indians, a Karib*-speaking people, who live in the states of Pará and Amazonas, Brazil. Most of the Hixkaryána live near the junction of the Mapuera and Trombetas rivers. At present, they total approximately 300 people. See PARUKOTO.

HOHODENE. See WAKUENAI.

HORIO. See CHAMACOCO.

HOTÍ. The Hotí are an Amerindian people who live near the Panare* Indians in the southwestern part of the state of Bolívar and the northeastern portion of the federal territory of Amazonas in Venezuela. In particular, they live in the forested region between the Kaima, Asita, Parucito, and Cuchivero rivers. They have also been known in the past as "Chicanas" (Shikana). Local mestizos refer to the Hotí as the Waruwaru or Ongwa, while missionaries from the New Tribes Mission call them the Yowana or Yuana. Their language appears to be independent. They live in small villages of two or three families totaling 15 to 20 people. While Hotí women practice agriculture, the men hunt, fish, and forage. Although the Hotí have historically had to deal with a succession of Jesuit and Capuchin missionaries, settlers, anthropologists, and government officials, they have maintained a remarkable cultural identity, resisting all but the most rudimentary examples of European technology, such as metal tools. Part of the reason for their success in maintaining a cultural identity is the geographic isolation and relative inaccessibility of their territory. They usually live at the junction of the savanna and the forests, and they plant gardens along fertile river bottoms. Although the bulk of their nourishment comes from agriculture, the Hotí still view hunting and fishing as more important activities. By the early 1980s, the Hotí numbered approximately 500 people living in a dozen villages.

REFERENCES: Walter Coppens, *Los aborígenes de Venezuela*, 1983; Ministerio de Estado para la Cultura, *Arte indígena de Venezuela*, 1983; Estéban Emilio Mosonyi, "La revitalización lingüística y la realidad Venezolano," *América Indígena*, 47 (1987), 553–61.

HOUAROUX. See WARRAU.

HUACHIPAIRE. See WACHIPAERI.

HUACHIPAIRI. See WACHIPAERI.

HUACHIPAIRY. See WACHIPAERI.

HUALLAGA. See COCAMILLA.

HUAMBISA. The Huambisa (Huambiza, Wambisa) are a branch of the Jívaro* language group. They live in Peru's north central montana, beginning at the village of Galilea on the lower Santiago River and extending northward along the upper Santiago River to the Ecuadorean border. Each community is a patrilineal group politically independent of the neighboring Huambisa groups; each group lives in a single large, thatched house that is approximately 80 feet long and 40 feet wide. Although the Huambisa hunt and fish, they are primarily horticulturists who raise sweet manioc and plantains using swidden agricultural techniques. Today they also raise cotton, tobacco, and a variety of other crops. Unlike most tribes of Central and South America, the Huambisa still occupy land that they held in the pre-conquest era. Only in recent years, however, have they been able to acquire complete legal title to their communal lands.

In the fifteenth and early sixteenth centuries, the Huambisa successfully resisted attempts by the Inca Empire to subjugate them, and in the process they developed a fierce warrior culture that served them well after the arrival of Francisco Pizarro and the Spaniards in the 1530s. Spaniards first contacted them in 1549, but it was the expeditions led by Juan de Salinas in the 1550s that first threatened the tribe. Exposure to Spanish *encomenderos* led to dramatic population declines among the Huambisa, but by 1600 the tribe had nearly destroyed Spanish settlements in their midst. Jesuit and later Franciscan attempts to missionize the Huambisa failed in the eighteenth and nineteenth centuries; as late as the 1920s and early 1930s, the Huambisa were known for periodic attacks on white communities that they felt were encroaching on their land. By the 1980s, the Huambisa totaled approximately 5,000 people, virtually all still speaking the native language, although increasingly large numbers are familiar with Quechua and Spanish. Despite continuing contact with Protestant missionaries and Peruvian schools, the Huambisa maintain a powerful tribal identity.

REFERENCES: Brent Berlin and Elois Ann Berlin, ''Adaptation and Ethnozoological Classification: Theoretical Implications of Animal Resources and Diet of the Aguaruna and Huambisa,'' in Raymond B. Hames and William T. Vickers, eds., *Adaptive Responses of Native Amazonians*, 1983; M. J. Harner, *The Jívaro: People of the Sacred Waterfalls*, 1973; Darcy Ribeiro and Mary Ruth Wise, *Los grupos étnicos de la amazona peruana*, 1978.

HUAMBIZA. See HUAMBISA.

HUANUCO. See QUECHUA.

HUANYAM. See PAKAANÓVA.

HUANYAM. See WANAM.

HUARANI. See AWISHIRI.

HUARAYO. See ESSEJJA.

HUAYARU. See ESSEJJA.

HUARI. The Huarí (Massaca) today are a nearly extinct tribe of Amerindians who once numbered in the thousands at the headwaters of the Corumbiara River, a tributary of the Guaporé River, in the state of Rondônia, Brazil. They lived off black beans, maize, and peanuts, as well as by fishing and hunting. The rubber boom of the late nineteenth and early twentieth centuries throughout Rondônia started the Huarí on the road to extinction because of death, disease, and relocation at the hands of the rubber collectors. By the 1940s, the Huarí had ceased to exist as a differentiated social unit. Today there are just a handful of people still alive in the Corumbiara River region of Rondônia who are aware of their Huarí origins.

REFERENCE: Theodore L. Stoddard, ed., *Indians of Brazil in the Twentieth Century*, 1967.

HUARIAPANO. See PANOBO.

HUARY. See ARAONA.

HUARYMODO. See ARAONA.

HUASIPUNGUERO. The term "Huasipunguero" is used in Ecuador to describe Amerindians who are detached from a tribal setting and permanently attached to a hacienda or latifundia estate as permanent peasants. They have no land of their own and are usually caught in extraordinarily difficult economic situations.

REFERENCE: S. Lyman Tyler, *Indians of South America*, 1976.

HUESHUO. See MATACO.

HUIKNU. See MAKAGUANE.

HUILICHE. See HUILLICHE.

HUILLI. See HUILLICHE.

HUILLICHE. The Huilliche (Huiliche, Huilli, Guiliche, Guilliche, Ghuylliche, Veliche, and Beliche) were the southernmost of the Araucanian* Indian people of Chile. Their traditional homeland was south of the present-day city of Valdivia. Although the Mapuche* Indians, the largest group of the Araucanian people, have survived, the Huilliche underwent rapid deculturation beginning in the mid-nineteenth century when the Chilean government succeeded in relocating them. Most of the Huilliche were absorbed into mestizo society in the late 1800s and throughout the 1900s, although there remain a few thousand of them living south of Valdivia on reservations. These are far more acculturated than their Mapuche neighbors. See ARAUCANIANS.

HUITATO. See WITOTO.

HUITNU. See MAKAGUANE.

HUITO. See WITOTO.

HUITOTO. See WITOTO.

HUMURANA. See OMURANO.

HUNO. See URU.

HÚPDA. See MAKÚ.

HÚPDU. See MAKÚ.

HURAMOMOWI. See GUAHIBO.

HURINÍ. See ASURINÍ.

HUUMBO. See YUMBO.

HUYUPURINĀ. See IPURINĀ.

HYPURINĀ. See IPURINĀ.

I

IAMAMADÍ. See YAMAMADÍ.

IAMINÁWA. See YAMINÁWA.

IAUALAPITÍ. The Iaualapití, also known as the Iwalapití, Yawalapití, Yauapití, and Yaulapití, are a small tropical forest tribe living near the headwaters of the Xingú River in central Brazil. The tribe speaks an Arawakan* language, although today it is laden with Karib* words as well. They were not contacted by Europeans until surveying and anthropological expeditions made it up the Xingú River in the late nineteenth century. The Iaualapití lived at the time on the left bank of the Culiseu River, north of the Mehinácu.* By the 1940s, the Iaualapití population had fallen to only a few families who were scattered out among the Kuikúru* and Kamaiurá* Indians. Orlando Villas Boas and Cláudio Villas Boas persuaded them to build a village of their own, relocate all of the scattered families, and try to preserve their sense of ethnicity. All of the Iaualapití today live in a single village and total approximately 135 people, dwelling in several households. They fish and practice a slash-and-burn agriculture to produce their staple—manioc. Today the Iaulapití are protected by their residence in the Xingú Indian Park.

REFERENCES: Orlando Villas Boas and Cláudio Villas Boas, *Xingu: The Indians, Their Myths*, 1973; Robert Lee Spires, "As línguas faladas do Brasil," *América Indígena*, 47 (1987), 455–79.

IAWALAPITÍ. See IAUALAPITÍ.

IAWANO. The Iawano (Iawavo) are a Panoan*-speaking tribe of Amerindians who live on the Amenia River, a tributary of the Juruá River, in the state of Acre in Brazil as well as across the border in eastern Peru; more than 1,500 Iawano are on the Brazilian side and an equal number in Peru. Although the Iawano are in permanent contact with neo-Brazilian and neo-Peruvian society, most of them still speak the native language, maintaining their tribal ceremonial life and a powerful sense of ethnic identity. They pursue a subsistence, agricultural lifestyle but also work as laborers part-time in the regional cash economy in order to purchase trade goods.

REFERENCE: Theodore L. Stoddard, ed., *Indians of Brazil in the Twentieth Century*, 1967.

IAWAVO. See IAWANO.

IBO'TSA. See OCAINA.

ICAGUATE. See SECOYA.

ICHAGOTEGUO. See KADUVEO.

IDEMASA. See MAKUNA.

IEKUANA. See YEKUANA.

IGNACIANO. See MOXO.

IGNACIO. See MOXO.

IHURUHANA. Also known as the "Headwater" people, the Ihuruhana are one of the four subtribes of the Yekuana* Indians of Venezuela. They live in the vast region of mountains, savannas, and rain forests stretching from the right bank of the upper Orinoco to the lower Caura and Ventauri rivers. See YEKUANA.

IJCA. See IKA.

IJKA. See IKA.

IKA. The Ijka (Ijca, Ijka, Iku) are an Amerindian group of people who live in the southeastern region of the Sierra Nevada de Santa Marta mountains of Colombia. They are concentrated along the banks of the Ariguani, Guatapuri, and San Sebastián rivers and in the cooler valleys of the mountains. Their language is part of the Chibchan* linguistic family. Over the years, they have also been identified as Busintana, Bíntucua, Businka, Bíntukwa, Vintukua, and Arhuaco.*

The Ika Indians today are primarily subsistence farmers who raise maize, manioc, and plantains. They are also known to relocate their gardens frequently, making them a semi-nomadic people. The Ika population today exceeds 8,000 people.

REFERENCE: Blaz Telban, *Grupos étnicos de Colombia: Etnografía y bibliografía*, 1987.

IKAKE. See JICAQUE.

IKITO. See IQUITO.

IKORO. See GAVIÃO.

IKU. See IKA.

IMAPARI. See IÑAPARI.

IMIHATA. The Imihata are a subtribe of the Bora* Indians. They were first contacted by Europeans in the early seventeenth century, but sustained contact did not come until the late nineteenth century. Although hunting and fishing consume much of their time and have great symbolic importance in Imihata culture, most of the tribe's nutrients come from the manioc, maize, sweet potatoes, plantains, and bananas they raise in tribal gardens. Until the end of the nineteenth century, the Imihata numbered several thousand people, but the wild rubber boom of the 1890s and early 1900s devastated them, bringing thousands of neo-Colombians and their diseases into Imihata territory and drastically reducing their population. The Imihata were dislocated and moved, the vast majority dying from disease or being assimilated into neo-Colombian society. See BORA.

IMIKIE. See YUKUNA.

IÑAKEN. See TEHUELCHE.

IÑAPARI. The Iñapari (Imapari) are a tribe of Arawakan*-speaking Amerindians who once lived in small scattered groups in the forests between the upper Iaço and Acre Rivers in the state of Acre, Brazil, and across the border in Peru. Their particular homeland was near the junction of the Brazilian-Bolivian-Peruvian borders. They were often considered a subtribe of the Masco* Indians. An interfluvial people, the Iñapari generally avoided river life, preferring to gather food and hunt in the open forests between the rivers. A succession of epidemics reduced their population in the twentieth century, and the Iñapari lost their sense of tribal identity as families dispersed. Although there are individuals in Peru and Bolivia today who are aware of their Iñapari heritage, they no longer function as a sociological entity.

REFERENCES: Darcy Ribeiro and Mary Ruth Wise, *Los grupos étnicos de la amazona peruana*, 1978; Robert Lee Spires, "As línguas faladas do Brasil," *América Indígena*, 47 (1987), 455–79; Theodore L. Stoddard, ed., *Indians of Brazil in the Twentieth Century*, 1967; Stefano Varese, *The Forest Indians in the Present Political Situation of Peru*, 1972.

INCA. See QUECHUA.

INEKATÚ. See NHEENGATÚ.

INGA. The Inga (Ingano) are a group of Amerindians who inhabited the upper Putumayo River in southwestern Colombia, from the region of Santiago and Sibundoy to the equator. Their homeland has historically been the eastern side of the Sibundoy Valley. Today the Inga can be found scattered throughout the mountains at higher altitudes as well as in the towns of Santiago, Colón, and San Andrés. They also live in Yunguillo in the lower Putumayo River and in Puerto Umbria in the department of Cauca. In the department of Caquetá, there are Inga living on the Orteguaza, Caguan, and Pescado rivers. Some Inga have also moved to Bogotá in search of work. Others can be found around Lake Anatico and the Pastaza, Huasaga, and Urituyaca rivers in Peru. Jesuit missionaries reached them in 1600, as did Franciscans in 1635, but the Indians rebelled against the missions and the priests abandoned them. The Jesuits and Franciscans returned in the early 1700s, but the Inga rebelled again in the 1740s, forcing the abandonment of the missions. By the nineteenth century, however, the Inga had adopted metal technology to improve their hunts and their manioc gardens. Slowly they became more and more integrated into the regional cash economy. Today there are approximately 7,000 Inga Indians, most of whom live in the eastern sector of the Sibundoy Valley, at the headwaters of the Caquetá River, in the department of Putumayo, and along the eastern cordillera of the department of Nariño in Colombia. Approximately 60 Inga live on the Colombian government reservation of San Antonio del Fragua; some are also across the border in adjacent areas of Ecuador. The others are scattered downriver where they have mixed with the white and black population. Most Inga have adopted Western dress and food, plant cash crops, and speak Quechua as a first language. In fact, Inga Quechua is the northernmost Quechua language known in South America.

REFERENCES: Myriam Jiméno and Adolfo Triana Antorveza, *Estado y minorias étnicas de Colómbia*, 1985; Steven H. Levinsohn, *The Inga Language*, 1976.

INGAÍN. See KAINGÁNG.

INGANO. See INGA.

INGARICO. See INGARIKÓ.

INGARIKÓ. The Ingarikó (Ingaricó, Engaricó) are a small group of several hundred Karib*-speaking Amerindians who live on the Mau River and in its surrounding area on the border between Brazil and Guyana. They are intimately related historically to the Kapóng and Akawáio.* Because of their location, the Ingarikó had relatively little contact with neo-Brazilians until the twentieth century, and as a result they survived as a people. The Ingarikó are a horticultural people who raise manioc as their staple crop. They also hunt and fish to supplement their diet. Although they are in permanent contact with neo-Brazilian society, most of them speak their tribal language and maintain an active tribal ceremonial life. In order to raise cash to purchase such trade goods as cloth and metal tools, some Ingarikó work part-time in the regional cash economy. At present, the tribal population is approximately 450 people.

REFERENCES: Robert Lee Spires, "As línguas faladas do Brasil," *América Indígena*, 47 (1987), 455–79; Theodore L. Stoddard, ed., *Indians of Brazil in the Twentieth Century*, 1967.

INI-MACA. See MACÁ.

INKA. See QUECHUA.

INO. See ARAONA.

INTOGAPÍD. See ITOGAPÚK.

IPEWÍ. See KREEN-AKARÔRE.

IPITINERE. See AMAHUACA.

IPOTEWÁT. The Ipotewát today are a tiny tribe of Tupi*-speaking Amerindians who once numbered in the thousands in the Jiparaná River drainage area of Brazil. They lived off black beans, maize, and peanuts, as well as fishing and hunting. The rubber boom of the late nineteenth and early twentieth centuries throughout the state of Rondônia started the Ipotewát on the road to extinction because of death, disease, and relocation at the hands of the rubber collectors. By the 1940s, the Ipotewát had ceased to exist as a differentiated social unit. Today just a handful of people still live in the Jiparaná region of Rondônia who are aware of their Ipotewát origins.

REFERENCE: Theodore L. Stoddard, ed., *Indians of Brazil in the Twentieth Century*, 1967.

IPURICOTO. See PARUKOTO.

IPURINĀ. The Ipurinā (Hypurinā, Hyupurinā, Jupurinā, Kangutú, Kangite, Kangití, Kankití, and Kankete) are an Amerindian tribe of Arawak* extraction living on the right bank of the Acre and Seruini rivers and the left bank of the Ituxi River in the state of Amazonas, Brazil. The Ipurinā were a riverine people, living off fish and such river animals as large turtles, while also maintaining communal gardens. Late in the nineteenth century and early in the twentieth century, neo-Brazilian rubber gatherers clashed repeatedly with the Ipurinã, substantially reducing their population through disease and slaughter. Today the Ipurinã are in permanent contact with neo-Brazilian society and increasingly acculturated. They number approximately 500 people, most of whom speak Portuguese as well as their tribal tongue.

REFERENCE: Theodore L. Stoddard, ed. *Indians of Brazil in the Twentieth Century*, 1967.

IQUITA. See IQUITO.

IQUITO. The Iquito (Iquita, Ikito, Amacacore, Hamacore, Quiturran, and Puca-uma) are an Amerindian group whose language is part of the Zaparo* linguistic family. Originally there were three Iquito subtribes: the Iquito proper, the Maracano, and the Auve. They are concentrated in Alto Nanay in the province of Maynas, Loreto, in Peru, along the Pintoyacu, Chambira, and Nanay rivers, all three of which are tributaries of the Amazon. Spanish missionaries first reached them in 1737 and settled them in two missions, but the Indians soon scattered. Today there are approximately 125 Iquito Indians who still speak the aboriginal language, but almost all of them are trilingual in Spanish and Quechua as well; another 500 Iquito Indians do not use the aboriginal language at all. Use of the native language is declining rapidly. The Iquito practice subsistence agriculture in communal areas and engage in part-time labor to generate the cash they need. Today they are integrated into neo-Peruvian society.

REFERENCE: Darcy Ribeiro and Mary Ruth Wise, *Los grupos étnicos de la amazona peruana*, 1978.

IRÁNSHE. See IRÁNTXE.

IRÁNTXE. Very closely related to the Parecí* and perhaps one of their subtribes, the Irántxe (Irántze, Iránxe, Muynku, Mynky, Münkü) are an Arawaken*-speaking group of Amerindians today living on the Cravari River near Utiariti in the state of Mato Grosso, Brazil. The rubber collectors of the late nineteenth and early twentieth centuries nearly destroyed the Irántxe. Today there are approximately 195 Irántxe, but only a few dozen are consciously aware of their language and culture. Although they are for the most part deculturated from tribal ways, those surviving are still conscious of their Irántxe heritage.

REFERENCES: Adalberto Holanda Pereira, *Historia dos Muynku (Iránxe)*, 1975; Robert Lee Spires, "As línguas faladas do Brasil," *América Indígena*, 47 (1987), 455–79; Theodore L. Stoddard, ed., *Indians of Brazil in the Twentieth Century*, 1967.

IRÁNTZE. See IRÁNTXE.

IRÁNXE. See IRÁNTXE.

IRAPA. The Irapa (Tukuku) are a subtribe of the Yukpa* Indians of northwestern Venezuela. They pursue a horticultural lifestyle in the tropical forests near the Tukuku River and today number more than 700 people. See YUKPA.

IRA-TAPUYA. See WAKUÉNAI.

IROKA. The Iroka are a subtribe of the Yuko* Indians of northeastern Colombia. A tropical forest people, they pursue a subsistence lifestyle based on manioc horticulture and live along the Iroka River. Today the Iroka total approximately 400 people. See YUKO.

ISCOBAQUEBU. See ISCONAHUA.

ISCONAHUA. The Isconahua are a Panoan*-speaking group of Amerindians who today live along the Calleria River in the province of Coronel Portillo, Ucayali, in Peru. They call themselves the Iscobaquebu. By the 1980s, the tribal population had fallen below 50 people. Although most of them still understood their aboriginal language, they were also bilingual, speaking Shipibo* and/or Spanish, depending upon the major direction of their non-Isconahua social and economic contacts. The Isconahua lost much of their aboriginal ceremonial life because population declines had destroyed the critical mass necessary to sustain the tribe as a sociocultural unit. Nevertheless, the Isconahua still viewed their ethnic identity in tribal terms. Today the Isconahua number only 50 people who are increasingly integrated with the neighboring Shipibo Indians.
    REFERENCES: Darcy Ribeiro and Mary Ruth Wise, *Los grupos étnicos de la amazona peruana*, 1978; Gustavus Solís F., ''Multilinguismo y extinciones de lenguas,'' *América Indígena*, 47 (1987), 630–45.

ISCUANDE. See COAIQUER.

ISEBENE. See ARAONA.

ISHIR. See CHAMACOCO.

ISHIRA. See CHAMACOCO.

ISIRA. See CHAMACOCO.

ISOSEÑO. See IZOCEÑO.

ISSIRRIBERRENAI. See ACHAGUA.

ITACAYUNA. See XIKRÍN.

ITATÍN. See PAUSERNA.

ITÉN. See MORÉ.

ITÉNEZ. See MORÉ.

ITOEBEHE. See KAWAHÍB.

ITOGAPÚK. The Itogapúk (Ntogapíg, Ntogapíd, Intogapíd) people are a tiny group of Kawahíb* Indians. The Kawahíb once ranged over a large area of the Tapajós-Madeira river basin in what is today the state of Amazonas, Brazil, but in the eighteenth century they dispersed into a series of many separate tribes because of the aggressive expansion of the Mundurukú* Indians. One of the small tribes emerging from the larger Kawahíb group was the Itogapúk. Rubber collectors and gold prospectors in the early twentieth century put more pressure on the tribe, drastically reducing their population to the point that ceremonial life was no longer possible. There are still approximately 90 Itogapúk living between the Jiparaná and Roosevelt rivers near the border between the states of Mato Grosso and Rondônia.

REFERENCES: Robert Lee Spires, "As línguas faladas do Brasil," *América Indígena*, 47 (1987), 455–79; Theodore L. Stoddard, ed., *Indians of Brazil in the Twentieth Century*, 1967.

ITONAMA. The Itonama (Saeamo) are a small group of Amerindians who are part of an independent linguistic family. They live in dispersed, multifamily settlements near the Baure, San Simón, and Itenez rivers in the department of El Beni in Bolivia. They are especially concentrated in the towns of Magdalena, San Ramón, and Huacaraje. In the early 1700s, their population totaled about 6,000 people. Today their tribal numbers are declining rapidly because of the processes of assimilation and acculturation; aboriginal ceremonies have disappeared. The Itonama no longer speak their aboriginal language and make their living as subsistence farmers and cattle raisers. Their major crops are maize, manioc, rice, and tobacco. From outside appearances, their lifestyle is no different from that of non-Indian mestizos living near them. Still, the Itonama know of their Indian heritage. Their present population totals approximately 2,000 people, of whom perhaps only 100 speak the tribal language.

REFERENCES: Brian M. Boom, *Ethnobotany of the Chácobo Indians, Beni, Bolivia*, 1987; Harold Key and Mary Key, *Bolivian Indian Tribes: Classification, Bibliography, and Map of Present Language Distribution*, 1967; Pedro Plaza Martínez and Juan Carvajal Carvajal, *Etnías y lenguas de Bolivia*, 1985; Graciela Zolezzi and J. Riester, "Lenguas indigenas del oriente boliviano clasificación preliminar," *América Indígena*, 47 (1987), 425–33.

ITUCALE. See URARINA.

ITUKALE. See URARINA.

ITZÁ. The Itzá are a small tribe of Amerindians who are scattered throughout the department of Petén in Guatemala. In recent years, because of their population dispersal, most of the Itzá have become bilingual, speaking Spanish in most of their public and commercial transactions and retaining Itzá as a private language. There are approximately 3,000 Itza Indians living in Guatemala, but they have become regionally integrated into the cash economy and live similarly to the surrounding mestizo people. Only about 500 of them have a strong sense of their tribal roots. The Itzá are in a state of rapid acculturation.

REFERENCES: Melanie A. Counce and William V. Davidson, "Indians of Central America 1980s," *Cultural Survival Quarterly*, 13 (1989), 38–41; Gloria Tujab, "Lenguas indígenas que se encuentran en vias de extinción," *América Indígena*, 47 (1987), 529–33.

IXIGNOR. See AWISHIRA.

IXIL. The Ixil are a Mayan* tribe, part of the Mamean people, who occupy the eastern Cuchumatane mountains of the Guatemalan highlands, particularly in the departments of Quiché and Huehuetenango. Early in the fifteenth century, they fell under the domination of the Quiché* Mayans, but by the beginning of the sixteenth century the Ixil had once again asserted their independence. It was to be shortlived. The Spanish conquest of Mexico took place in the early 1520s, and shortly thereafter the Spaniards turned their attention to Central America. In 1524, Pedro de Alvarado launched the conquest of the lowland tribes of present-day Guatemala and El Salvador, but the Spanish conquistadores did not reach the Guatemalan highlands until 1529, when they encountered fierce resistance from the Ixil. Nevertheless the Spaniards persisted and had pacified the Ixil by 1540.

The Spaniards then relocated the Ixil into *congregaciones*, where missionary priests taught them Christianity and labor contractors worked them to death. During the sixteenth and early seventeenth centuries, the Ixil population dropped by a precipitous 90 percent because of disease, relocation, and attacks by other Indians, particularly the Lacandones. Some Ixil, however, remained outside the jurisdiction of the *congregaciones*, and lived scattered and isolated in the highlands. The Ixil population stabilized by the later seventeenth century.

During the late eighteenth and nineteenth centuries, labor contractors took large numbers of Ixil down to the Pacific Coast plantations. Thousands of Ixil workers never returned and the closed corporate nature of Ixil community life broke down. In 1871, the Guatemalan government began a land reform program that gradually abolished communal tribal property in favor of individual ownership. The rise of the coffee plantations late in the nineteenth century accelerated the loss of Ixil communal land, which had diminished by half between 1871 and 1910. By the 1970s, the average Ixil family owned about four acres of land. Men had to spend part of the year laboring on coffee, cotton, and sugar plantations along the Pacific Coast in order to support their families. Some Ixil leaders turned to counterinsurgency tactics, demanding land reform, but the government brutally repressed their protests in the 1970s. The Ixil population reached 80,000 people by the early 1980s. By that time, however, more than 20,000 Ixil had fled the highlands for Guatemalan cities or the United States, trying to escape political persecution.

REFERENCES: W. George Lovell, *Conquest and Survival in Colonial Guatemala: A Historical Geography of the Cuchumatan Highlands, 1500–1821*, 1985; W. George Lovell, "Surviving Conquest: The Maya of Guatemala in Historical Perspective," *Latin American Research Review*, 23 (1988), 25–58; B. Colby and P. Van Den Berghe, *Ixil Country: A Plural Society in Highland Guatemala*, 1969.

IYEMI. See KARUTANA.

IZOCENIO. See IZOCEÑO.

IZOCEÑO. At the time of the Spanish conquest, the Izoceño (Isoseño) were a slash-and-burn agricultural group of Amerindians who lived in southeastern Bolivia and raised maize, beans, potatoes, and a variety of other crops. Originally a Tupi*-Guaraní* people who were descended from the Paraguayan Guaraní, the Izoceños migrated from the area of the Gran Chaco to settle along the Andes foothills between the upper Pilcomayo River to the upper Río Grande in southeastern Bolivia. The migration occurred in successive waves during the sixteenth century. Before the migration, they were primarily a hunting and foraging people, but after arriving in what is today Bolivia they adopted agriculture, raising maize, pumpkins, beans, sweet potatoes, sweet manioc, peanuts, cotton, and tobacco. Today there are approximately 5,500 Izoceño living in Bolivia, most of them in the department of Santa Cruz in the province of Cordillera, near the Parapeti River. They retain a powerful sense of ethnic identity, and most still speak the aboriginal language. The Izoceño make a living as small ranchers, subsistence farmers, and seasonal laborers, but most of them suffer from a desperate poverty. They are also known as Izoceño-Chiriguano.

REFERENCES: Jürgen Riester, *Indians of Eastern Bolivia: Aspects of Their Present Situation*, 1975; Graciela Zolezzi and J. Riester, "Lenguas indigenas de oriente boliviano clasificación preliminar," *América Indígena*, 47 (1987), 425–33.

J

JABOTÍ. See JABUTÍ.

JABUTÍ. The Jabutí (Jabotí, Yabutí) are a tribe of Amerindians who once numbered in the thousands at the headwaters of the Branco River, a tributary of the Guaporé River, in the state of Rondônia, Brazil. They lived on black beans, maize, and peanuts, as well as by fishing and hunting. During the gold boom of the 1730s, neo-Brazilian prospectors flooded their territory, bringing disease and death with them. Although relative peace returned to the Jabutí in the 1800s, the rubber boom of the late nineteenth and early twentieth centuries throughout the Rondônia started the Jabutí on the road to extinction because of death, disease, and relocation at the hands of the rubber collectors. By the 1940s, the Jabutí had ceased to exist as a differentiated social unit. Today there are just a handful of people still alive in the Branco River region of Rondônia who speak Jabutí and another 50 or so who are aware of their Jabutí origins. Most live on the Río Guaporé government Indian post and make a living by selling latex, ipecac, Brazil nuts, and fish.

REFERENCES: David Maybury-Lewis, *In the Path of the Polonoreste: Endangered Peoples of Western Brazil*, 1981; Robert Lee Spires, "As línguas faladas do Brasil," *América Indígena*, 47 (1987), 455–79; Theodore L. Stoddard, ed., *Indians of Brazil in the Twentieth Century*, 1967.

JACALTECO. The Jacalteco are a Western Mayan* language group living in the department of Huehuetenango in the highlands of Guatemala. Today they total more than 32,000 people. They still make a living from the production of corn and beans on communal lands, although in recent years their increasing poverty, as well as government policies that convert large amounts of their land to individual ownership, have forced thousands of Jacalteco men to seek employment as migrant laborers. Until the 1970s, the Jacalteco settlements could be reached only by footpath. This situation had protected them from the worst depredations of European and mestizo civilization, but completion of a dry-weather road in 1970 ended that isolation. In the 1980s, political repression of the Jacalteco by a right-wing government in Guatemala precipitated a large-scale emigration of Jacaltecans to the United States.

REFERENCES: Colette Grinevald Craig, *Jacaltec: The Structure of Jacaltec*, 1977; Christopher Day, *The Jacaltec Language*, 1973; Helen L. Neuenswander, *Cognitive Studies of Southern Mesoamerica*, 1981; W. George Lovell, "Surviving Conquest: The Maya of Guatemala in Historical Perspective," *Latin American Research Review*, 23 (1988), 25–58.

JAHUI. See KAWAHÍB.

JAMAJIRI. See YAMAMADÍ.

JAMAMADÍ. See YAMAMADÍ.

JAMAMANDÍ. See YAMAMADÍ.

JAMBALO. See PÁEZ.

JAMINAUA. See YAMINÁWA.

JAMINÁWA. See YAMINÁWA.

JANENA. See BARASÁNA.

JAPRERÍA. The Japrería (Sabril, Sapriría) are a subtribe of the Yukpa* Indians of northwestern Venezuela, especially in the state of Zulia. Today they number approximately 70 people and live a horticultural lifestyle along the Palmar River. Their self-designation is Yokpa. See YUKPA.

JAQARÚ. The Jaqarú are a relatively large group of Amerindians descended from a Jaqí*-speaking linguistic family. Closely related to the Aymara* of southern Peru and Bolivia, the Jaqarú are an Andean subculture whose traditional economy revolved around the production of maize, potatoes, and llama. In recent years, however, the Jaqarú have been dramatically influenced by rapid economic change. Today there are more than 2,000 Jaqarú Indians living primarily in the province of Yauyos of the department of Lima in Peru, approximately 240 kilometers southeast of Lima. They constitute a linguistic island in a sea of Quechuan*-speaking people. Large numbers of the Jaqarú have also migrated toward the city in recent years in search of employment. Linguists and ethnologists estimate that virtually the entire Jaqarú population, except for the oldest members, are bilingual in Spanish or Quechua. Although the Jaqarú are Roman Catholic, there are still powerful remnants of earth worship in their religion, an aboriginal survival from earlier days.

REFERENCES: Martha J. Hardman, *Jaqarú: Compendio de estructura fonológia y morfológica*, 1983; Gustavus Solís F., ''Multilinguismo y extinciones de lenguas,'' *América Indígena*, 47 (1987), 630–45.

JAQÍ. The term ''Jaqí'' refers to a small group of Amerindian languages native to Peru and Bolivia. The most significant of them, at least in terms of population, is the Aymara* language, now spoken by more than 600,000 people in Peru, Bolivia, Chile, and Argentina. The other Jaqí languages are Jaqarú* and Kawkí*, spoken in Tupe and Cachuy respectively, in the province of Yauyos, approximately 150 miles south of Lima, Peru. Although Jaqarú still has some vitality, Kawkí is almost extinct. Aymara retains great linguistic vitality.

REFERENCES: Lucy Therina Briggs, *Dialectical Variation in the Aymara Language of Bolivia and Peru*,'' Ph.D. dissertation, University of Florida, 1976; Pedro Plaza Martínez and Juan Carvajal Carvajal, *Etnías y lenguas de Bolivia*, 1985.

JARAWÁRA. See JARUÁRA.

JARECOUNA. See AREKUNA.

JARICUNA. See AREKUNA.

JARÚ. See JORA.

JARÚ. See PAKAANÓVA.

JARUÁRA. The Jaruára (Jarawára) are a subtribe of the Yamamadí,* an Arawa*-speaking people of the Juruá-Purús region in the state of Amazonas, Brazil. There are approximately 120 members of the Jaruára people living in two villages. They are in permanent contact with neo-Brazilian society, and virtually all of the Jaruára work as laborers for local businesses, plantations, and ranches. Because of their increasing integration into the regional cash economy, most of the Jaruára are bilingual, speaking the aboriginal language as well as Portuguese. See YAMAMADÍ.

JARUYA. See WITOTO.

JAVAÉ. The Javaé (Javahé, Javajé) are a subgroup of the Karajá* tribe in Brazil. Today there are approximately 1,200 Javaé living on the southern portion of the island of Bananal in the Araguaia River. See KARAJA.

JAVAHÉ. See JAVAÉ.

JAVAJÉ. See JAVAÉ.

JÊ. See GÊ.

JEBERO. The Jebero (Chebero, Xevero, Xebero, Shiwila) originally lived between the Marañon and Huallaga rivers in the Amazonian jungles of north central Peru. Jesuit missionaries established the Concepción de Xeveros Mission in 1640, but the Jebero abandoned it in 1643, afraid that the church was giving their names to encomenderos. Late in the seventeenth century, they joined another mission—Concepción de María—which included such other tribes as the Cocamilla,* Jívaro,* Cutinana (Aguano), and Mayorúna. The Jebero population steadily declined over the next two hundred years, and the rubber boom of the early 1900s devastated them. By the 1920s, their numbers had declined to fewer than 1,000 people, most of whom spoke Quechua* instead of Jebero. Since then the Jebero population has recovered to approximately 3,000 people, but the vast majority of them speak Quechua and only the elderly among them understand Jebero. The aboriginal language is in danger of rapid extinction. Today the Jebero live along the Platanayacu River and the Papayucu Lagoon, on the right bank of the Marañon River. Although they are effectively integrated into the surrounding mestizo society, they still live in their own cluster of communities and retain a sense of identity.

REFERENCES: Darcy Ribeiro and Mary Ruth Wise, *Los grupos étnicos de la amazona peruana*, 1978; Gustavus Solís F., "Multilinguismo y extinciones de lenguas," *América Indígena*, 47 (1987), 630–45; Stefano Varese, *The Forest People in the Present Political Situation of Peru*, 1972.

JEBEROAN. The term "Jeberoan" refers to a small group of Amerindian languages that were once concentrated in Peru; they are sometimes collectively called the Cahuapanan languages. The Jeberoan languages once included Cahuapana, Chayavita,* Jebero,* Miquira, and Yamorai.

REFERENCE: Harriet E. Manelis Klein and Louisa R. Stark, *South American Indian Languages: Retrospect and Prospect*, 1985.

JERUIWA. See YUKUNA.

JÍBARO. See JÍVARO.

JICAQUE. The Jicaque are an Indian tribe living primarily in Honduras. Although scholars disagree about the classification of their language, most suspect that it is similar to the Hokan-Siouan language group of the United States, which might explain the tribe's origins. The Jicaque have also been known by the following names: Tol, Tolpan, Torrupan, Xicaque, Cicaque, Hicaque, Ikake, Taguaca, and Taupane. The Jicaque originally lived along the northern coast from the Aguan River west to the Sierra de Omoa and bordering Lenca land in the interior. In the nineteenth century, two events altered Jicaque settlement patterns. Black Karibs, or Garífuna,* began settling the coastal region, driving some of the Jicaque into the southern section of the department of Yoro. Then Father Manuel Jesús de Subiriana, a Roman Catholic priest, gathered most of the Jicaque into central villages and taught them how to raise corn. Over the years, those Jicaque assimilated into ladino society. Some Jicaque, however, stayed on the coast or gathered into centralized farming villages. They retreated to the region of the Montaña de la Flor where they lived in isolation, retaining their language and practicing subsistence horticulture. The government established a 1,900 acre reservation for them there; by the early 1980s, their numbers exceeded 600 people. There are another 8,000 people who are relatively acculturated but who are identified as Jicaque Indians.

REFERENCES: Wolfgang Von Hagen, *The Jicaque (Torrupan) Indians of Honduras*, 1969; Howard I. Blutstein, *Area Handbook for Honduras*, 1971; L. Fernando Cruz Sandoval, "Los Indios de Honduras y la situación de sus recursos naturales," *América Indígena*, 44 (1984), 423–46.

JICHO. See ARAONA.

JITIPO. See SETEBO.

JÍVARA. See JÍVARO.

JÍVARO. The Jívaro are a linguistically isolated group of five tribes living in the montana of Eduador as well as in the contiguous areas of northern Peru. The five tribes consist of the Jívaro (Jíbaro) proper, or Shuar* (Shuara), and the Aguaruna,* Huambisa,* Achuara* (Atchuara, Achual), and Mayna.* Together the Jívaro tribes number approximately 50,000 people.

REFERENCES: Michael J. Harner, *The Jivaro: People of the Sacred Waterfall*, 1973; Michael J. Harner, "The Sound of Rushing Water," *Natural History Magazine*, (1968), 28–33, 60–61; Martha Adrienne Works, "Aguaruna Agriculture in Eastern Peru," *The Geographical Review*, 77 (1987), 343–58.

JÍVARO. The Jívaro (Jíbaro, Chíwaro, Síwaro, Gíbari, Xívari, Chívari, Gívaro, Zíbaro, Jívara, Híbaro, and Jívira, Shuar,* Shuara) are a tribe of Amerindians who are part of the isolated Jívaro linguistic family of the Ecuadorian and Peruvian montana. They call themselves the Aents, Jíbaro, or Mainu (Macusari). The Jívaro live in the forests at the foothills of the Andes Mountains, on both sides of the Zamora, Upano, and Paute rivers. At the time of the Spanish conquest of Peru, the Incas were trying to subjugate the Jívaro, an attempt that failed after a series of bloody confrontations. The Jívaro put up a similar resistance to Spaniards, who came into their territory searching for placer gold. Until the middle of the nineteenth century, the Jívaro had only limited and intermittent contact with the Spaniards. In the later years of the nineteenth century, the Jívaro increased their peaceful contact with neo-Ecuadorians and neo-Peruvians in order to acquire trade goods, especially metal tools and manufactured cloth. During the first three decades of the twentieth century, except for successful Roman Catholic missions by Salesians, there was relatively little colonization of the Jívaro area; but a gold rush in the 1930s eventually brought outsiders, precipitating a violent reaction by the Jívaro. Under pressure from the Salesians, the Ecuadorian government established a church-administered reservation for the Jívaro, and the violence stopped. During the last four decades, contact between the Jívaro and the larger society has been characterized by relative peace and increasing acculturation. Those Jívaro west of the Cordillera de Cútucu are far more acculturated than the interior Jívaro east of the mountains. The Jívaro generally pursue a subsistence lifestyle revolving around the production of sweet manioc, maize, and a variety of other products in family gardens, but the need for cash to buy trade goods is steadily increasing, forcing more and more of them to spend their time working as day laborers. At present, there are approximately 5,000 members of the Jívaro tribe.

REFERENCES: Michael J. Harner, *The Jívaro: People of the Sacred Waterfalls*, 1973; Darcy Ribeiro and Mary Ruth Wise, *Los grupos étnicos de la Amazona Peruana*, 1978.

JÍVIRA. See JÍVARO.

JORA. The Jora (Jaru) were a group of Amerindians of Guaraní* descent who occupied the middle Guaporé River in northeastern Bolivia near the Brazilian border. Like other Guaranian Indians, they probably migrated into the region from points east in Paraguay and Brazil beginning in the late fifteenth century. The Jora did not survive the twentieth century. By the 1940s, they had ceased to function as a differentiated social unit because of population decline. There were only 10 members of the tribe who still spoke the aboriginal language in the early 1960s, and only 8 were still alive in the 1970s. They lived between the San Simón and Itenez rivers in the department of El Beni.

REFERENCES: Harold Key and Mary Key, *Bolivian Indian Tribes: Classification, Bibliography, and Map of Present Language Distribution*, 1967; Jürgen Riester, *Indians of Eastern Bolivia: Aspects of Their Present Situation*, 1975.

JOTOY. See ASHLUSLAY.

JUINA KITAUNLHU. See NAMBIQUÁRA.

JUKUMANI. The Jukumani are a group of 9,000 Amerindians living today in the northern tip of the department of Potosí in Bolivia. All but a few hundred reside in the highlands. Since the sixteenth century, most of them have been involved in the regional cash economy, primarily delivering native fuels like quinua, thola, and dry llama dung to the silver and later the tin mines of Potosí. The Jukumanis also raised wheat and barley to make their tribute payments to the Spanish and to raise money for trade goods. Today the majority of the

Jukumanis are landless peasants who work as migrant laborers, ranch hands, and tenant farmers. The Jukumani population has risen from 1,000 people in 1817 to 1,600 in 1877 to more than 9,000 today.

REFERENCE: Ricardo Godoy, "Ecological Degradation and Agricultural Intensification in the Andean Highlands," *Human Ecology*, 12 (1984), 359–84.

JÚMA. The Júma are an isolated tribe of Tupi*-speaking Amerindians who live on the tributaries of the Macuim River in the state of Amazonas, Brazil. Although the Júma at one time numbered more than 1,000 people, they were decimated by genocidal attacks by rubber gatherers beginning in the early 1900s. Those attacks continued into the 1950s, reducing the Júma tribe to fewer than 30 people. Extremely suspicious of contact with outsiders, the Júma maintain a largely aboriginal lifestyle, except for the introduction of metal tools and some trade goods, which requires increasing contact with neo-Brazilians. Only a handful of Júma still understand the aboriginal dialect, and tribal ceremonial life can no longer sustain itself because of the severe population decline.

REFERENCES: Robert Lee Spires, "As línguas faladas do Brasil," *América Indígena*, 47 (1987), 455–79; Theodore L. Stoddard, ed., *Indians of Brazil in the Twentieth Century*, 1967.

JUNIKUIN. See KAXINÁWA.

JUNIN. See QUECHUA.

JUPDE. See MAKÚ.

JUPICHIYA. See MATAPI.

JUPURINA. See IPURINÃ.

JURUHUNA. See JURUNA.

JURUMI. See YUKUNA.

JURUNA. In the seventeenth and eighteenth centuries, the Juruna (Juruhuna, Yuruna) lived at the mouth of the Xingú River where it meets the Amazon. At the time, they numbered more than 3,000 people. Until 1767 they were under Jesuit control, but they slowly despaired of European values and began moving upriver on the Xingú. They eventually covered more than 1,000 miles, at which point they came into conflict with the Suyá* and Txukahamãi.* Prince Adalbert of Prussia visited them in 1843, by which time they had migrated above the great bend in the lower Xingú River. Adalbert discovered approximately 2,000 Juruna living in nine villages. Between 1860 and 1880, 250 Juruna Indians lived in a Roman Catholic mission sponsored by the provincial government of Pará.

Disease and alcoholism, however, were taking their toll on the Juruna. When Karl Von den Steinen reached the Juruna in 1884, he could locate only 205 members of the tribe living in five villages. The rubber boom of the 1890s decimated the Juruna, reducing the tribal population to 150 people in 1900. Most of them were virtual slaves on large rubber plantations. The tribe saved itself from extinction in 1916 by fleeing up the Xingú River, above the Von Martius Rapids. In 1949, Orlando Villas Boas and Cláudio Villas Boas contacted them, but they numbered only about 20 people then. They subsequently moved to the Xingú Indian Park. Today the tribe numbers about 100 people and lives in the Xingú Indian Park of Mato Grosso, Brazil.

REFERENCES: Orlando Villas Boas and Cláudio Villas Boas, *Xingu: The Indians, Their Myths*, 1973; Robin Hanbury-Tenison, *A Question of Survival for the Indians of Brazil*, 1973; John Hemming, *Amazon Frontier: The Defeat of the Brazilian Indians*, 1987; Robert Lee Spires, ''As línguas faladas do Brasil,'' *América Indígena*, 47 (1987), 455–79.

JURUTI. See YURUTI-TAPUYA.

K

KA'APÓR. See URUBÚ.

KABA. See CINTA LARGA.

KABALEMOMOWI. See GUAHIBO.

KABIRIARI. See KABIYERI.

KABIXÍ. The Kabixí (Cabishí, Cabixí, Kabishí) were once a very docile group of Arawakan*-speaking Amerindians who lived west of the Boróro* in what are today the states of Mato Grosso and southern Rondônia, Brazil. Although primarily a hunting and foraging tribe, the Kabixí raise manioc and maize during the rainy season. During the eighteenth century, their population dropped dramatically when Portuguese slavers took hundreds of them into captivity and diseases killed hundreds more. Gold prospectors during those same years brought measles and epidemic death. By the 1870s, the Kabixí were violently resisting neo-Brazilian expansion, attacking settlers and driving off as many as possible. Their attacks closed down mining camps throughout that region of Mato Grosso. The rubber boom of the early twentieth century, however, brought more disease and death to the Kabixí. Those Kabixí Indians living on the San Miguel River were pacified by the Wanám* Indians and even adopted their language. In recent years, the Kabixí have been known for their extreme sense of isolation on the upper Guaporé River near Vila Bela, where violence with the neo-Brazilians is still known to happen. The Kabixí remain culturally isolated and number only a few hundred people.

REFERENCES: David Price, "The Indians of Southern Rondônia," in David Price, et al., eds., *In the Path of the Polonoreste: Endangered Peoples of Western Brazil*, 1981, pp. 33–37; Theodore L. Stoddard, ed., *Indians of Brazil in the Twentieth Century*, 1967.

KABIXÍ. See SARARÉ.

KABIXIÁNA. The Kabixiána (Cabishiána, Cabixiána, Kabishiána) are a tribe of Tupi*-speaking Amerindians who once numbered in the thousands at the headwaters of the Corumbiara River, a tributary of the Guaporé River, in the state of Rondônia, Brazil. They lived on black beans, maize, and peanuts, as well as by fishing and hunting. The rubber boom of the late nineteenth and early twentieth centuries throughout Rondônia started the Kabixiána on the road to extinction because of death, disease, and relocation at the hands of the rubber collectors. By the 1940s, the Kabixiána had ceased to exist as a differentiated social unit. Today there are just a handful of people still alive in the Corumbiara River region of Rondônia who are aware of their Kabixiána origins.
REFERENCE: Theodore L. Stoddard, ed., *Indians of Brazil in the Twentieth Century*, 1967.

KABIYARI. See KABIYERI.

KABIYERI. The Kabiyeri (Cabiyari, Cabiyeri, Cauyary, Kabiriari, Kabiyari, Kawillary) are a small Amerindian tribe today living at the confluence of the Cananari and Apapori rivers in the Vaupés River drainage area of the territory of Vaupés in southeastern Colombia. They speak an Arawakan* language. The nuclear family is the primary economic and social unit of Kabiyeri society. A riverine people, the Kabiyeri are skilled canoemen and fishermen who live off the fish and river animals of the area. They also practice a slash-and-burn agriculture to raise manioc. Although they are gradually being integrated into the regional cash economy, the approximately 450 members of the Kabiyeri tribe retain a sense of tribal identity. Only 50 of them still speak Kabiyeri, while others have adopted Barasána.
REFERENCES: Jean A. Jackson, *The Fish People: Linguistic Exogamy and Tukanoan Identity in Northwest Amazonia*, 1983; Myriam Jimeno and Adolfo Triana Antorveza, *Estado y minorias étnicas en Colómbia*, 1985.

KACHARADI. See KAXARARÍ.

KACHARARÍ. See KAXARARÍ.

KADIU-DIAPA. See KATUKÍNA.

KADIWÉU. See KADUVEO.

KADUAPURITANA. See WAKUÉNAI.

KADUVEO. The Kaduveo (Cadioeo, Caduveo, Cavua, Cayua, Kaiwa, Kadiwéu, Kaingua, Caingua, Guaraní) today are a fairly large Guaraní*-speaking tribe of Amerindians who live in the Bodoquena hills and Pantanal swamps of the Paraguay River in southern Mato Grosso, Brazil, and in the forests of eastern Paraguay near Guaira. They call themselves the Ediu-Adig. The Kaduveo are descendents of the once mighty Mbya (Mbaya, Mbaia, Mbaye, Mbia, Mbüa) tribe that fiercely resisted Portuguese expansion in the eighteenth century and were one of the subtribes of the Guaycuru.* At that time, the Guaycuru (Guaik-uru, Guaicuru) numbered approximately 4,000 people, although they rigidly controlled tribal population by the widespread practice of abortion. They considered themselves superior to all other people, Indian or European, and earned a reputation for military prowess and resistance to acculturation. In the later eighteenth century, their population began a precipitous drop, however, because of smallpox and influenza, and the tribe declined in significance. Most of the subtribes (Guetiadegodi, Gueteadeguo, Guatiadeo, Uatadeo, Ouaitiadeho, Ua-teo-te-uo, Oleo, Apacachodegodegi, Apacachodeguo, Apacatchudeho, Pacaju-deus, Apaca-tsche-e-tuo, Belenistas, Lichagotegodi, Ichagoteguo, Xagueteo, Chagoteo, Eyibogodegi, Echigueguo, Tchiguebo, Edjeho, Ejueo, Enacaga, Go-tocogegodegi, Guocotegodi, Ocotegueguo, Cotogudeo, Cotogeho, Cutugueo, Venteguebo, Beutuebo, and Beauquiechos) became extinct.

In 1865, when Paraguay invaded the Mato Grosso, the Kaduveo allied themselves with the Brazilians and repelled the attack. As a reward, Brazil granted the Kaduveo a huge stretch of land in the Pantanal and Serra da Bodoquena. Most of that land has since been leased out or sold to cattle ranchers, and many Kaduveo live at a remote outpost of the Brazilian Indian Service. Today the Kaduveo number more than 7,000 people but they are scattered widely and intermixed in small communities and family groups with the larger neo-Brazilian and neo-Paraguayan society. Kaduveo and their descendents can be found in the states of Paraná, Santa Catarina, and Río Grande do Sul and between the Apa, Paraguay, and Paraná rivers in Paraguay. Nearly 1,000 Kaduveo also live across the Paraná River in northern Argentina where they migrated after 1870.

REFERENCES: Robin Hanbury-Tenison, *A Question of Survival for the Indians of Brazil*, 1973; John Hemming, *Red Gold: The Conquest of the Brazilian Indians, 1500–1760*, 1978; Darcy Ribeiro, "Kadiwéu Kinship," *Revista do Museu Paulista*, 2 (1948), 175–92; Egon Schaden, "Aspectos específicos de la cultura Mbüa-Guaraní, *Revista de Antropológia de São Paulo*, 2 (1963), 83–94; Robert Lee Spires, "As línguas faladas do Brasil," *América Indígena*, 47 (1987), 455–79.

KAGABA. See COGUI.

KAGWAHIV. See KAWAHÍB.

KAHEPAIA. See KOFÁN.

KAIABÍ. See KAYABÍ.

KAIABY. See KAYABÍ.

KAIAPÓ. See KAYAPÓ.

KAIMBÉ. Today there are approximately 500 people who know of their descent from the Kaimbé (Caimbé) Indians of northeastern Brazil. They live in Massacara in the state of Bahia and function like the rest of the lower-class mestizo society—as small farmers, ranch hands, and laborers. The Kaimbé have become completely acculturated to neo-Brazilian society: They speak Portuguese and remember none of their tribal language, they are Roman Catholics in terms of religion, and they are integrated into the regional cash economy. What sets the Kaimbé apart, however, is their surviving recollection of an Indian heritage and their sense of ethnic separation today. They live today at the Caimbé Indian Park near Mirandela.

REFERENCE: Theodore L. Stoddard, ed., *Indians of Brazil in the Twentieth Century*, 1967.

KAIMÉ. See WITOTO.

KAINGÁNG. The Kaingáng (Kaingangue, Ingain, Caingáng, Aaingáng, Coroasos, Coroado) are a Gê*-speaking group of Amerindians who pursue a semi-nomadic, foraging lifestyle in the savannas and forests of southern Brazil. They once lived by hunting monkeys, tapir, and peccaries and by collecting the Araucaria pine nut, which they converted to flour and bread. The Kaingáng also practiced a small-scale agriculture, although nothing on the scale of the neighboring Tupi* tribes. The Kaingáng are descendents of the Guayána (Guaiana, Goianaz, Goyána, Wayanazes) Indians, a warlike people of the sixteenth and seventeenth centuries. They originally lived in the open savannas but moved into the forests to escape other attacking tribes as well as Portuguese slavers. Unlike most other Brazilian tribes, the Kaingáng were indifferent to European trade goods, which made it all but impossible for Jesuit missionaries, as well as government agents, to attract them into peaceful contact and concentrated settlements. They were extremely suspicious of Europeans. Early in the 1800s, the Brazilian government launched a terrible war against the Kaingáng, allowing neo-Brazilian settlers who captured members of the tribe to enslave them, even though Indian slavery in Brazil had been outlawed for more than 50 years; at the time, the Kaingáng totaled approximately 6,000 people living in twelve separate villages. By the mid-nineteenth century, a number of Kaingáng groups were cooperating with neo-Brazilians in conquering other tribes, and increasing numbers of Kaingáng were being brought to centralized aldeia settlements. Because hunting grounds were inadequate in the area, intertribal warfare erupted among the different Kaingáng groups competing for use of the land. Not until the 1860s did peace return to the Kaingáng region. The last Kaingáng group to be peacefully settled were those along the Tiete River in the state of São Paolo in 1911. Today the Kaingáng number approximately 10,400 people living on eighteen government Indian reservations in the state of Paraná. Some Kaingáng groups have acculturated heavily while others remain loyal to tribal ceremonies and language and function more in their aboriginal subsistence economy than in the regional cash economy. Recent hydroelectric development projects in their traditional homelands are threatening the Kaingáng Indians with imminent relocation and all its social consequences.

REFERENCES: Paul L. Aspelin and Silvio Coelho dos Santos, *Indian Areas Threatened by Hydroelectric Projects in Brazil*, 1981; *Encyclopedia of Indians of the Americas*, 3 (1974), 293–96; Jules Henry, *Jungle People: A Kaingáng Tribe of the Highlands of Brazil*, 1941; Robert Lee Spires, "As línguas faladas do Brasil," *América Indígena*, 47 (1987), 455–79.

KAINGANGUE. See KAINGÁNG.

KAINGUA. See KADUVEO.

KAIOVÁ. The Kaiová (Kayová, Teui, Tembekua) are a Guaraní*-speaking group of Amerindians who number more than 1,000 people and are scattered in villages and government Indian posts throughout the states of Mato Grosso, Santa Catarina, Rio Grande do Sul, São Paolo, and Paraná in Brazil. By the 1970s, the Kaiová were thoroughly integrated into neo-Brazilian society. They spoke Portuguese rather than Guaraní, worked as small farmers or laborers in the regional cash economy, and were Roman Catholic in religion. From all external appearances they were no different from the surrounding mestizo society. On another level, the Kaiová remember that their origins were different and that they had Guaraní ancestry that set them apart from the Portuguese base of the rest of Brazilian society. The Kaiová still know that they are Indians, even though the external manifestations of Indian culture no longer exist.

REFERENCES: Robert Lee Spires, "As línguas faladas do Brasil," *América Indígena*, 47 (1987), 455–79; Theodore L. Stoddard, ed., *Indians of Brazil in the Twentieth Century*, 1967.

KAIWÁ. The Kaiwá (Mbia, Tambeope, Aputere, Baticolas) are a large tribe of Guaraní*-speaking Amerindians who today live in the southern reaches of the state of Mato Grosso, Brazil, near the Paraguay border. Jesuit missionaries pacified and converted the Kaiwá in the seventeenth century. In 1830 Silva Machado, the Baron of Antonina, established a mission for them that was administered by Capuchin priests. He organized a number of expeditions in the 1830s and 1840s to reach remote Kaiwá Indians and convince them to cease their nomadic ways and settle at the mission. They were a peaceful people who, although suspicious of neo-Brazilians and neo-Paraguayans, eventually accommodated themselves. The Paraguay frontier region remained quite isolated until 1864 when the Brazil-Paraguay War erupted. The fighting led to the deaths of many Kaiwá Indians; many others migrated into Brazil during the conflict. Today there are more than 7,000 Kaiwá Indians living in southern Mato Grosso, with a few others on the other side of the Paraná River in Paraguay.

REFERENCES: Robert Lee Spires, "As línguas faladas do Brasil," *América Indígena*, 47 (1987), 455–79; Theodore L. Stoddard, ed., *Indians of Brazil in the Twentieth Century*, 1967.

KAJABÍ. See KAIABÍ.

KAKCHIQUEL. See CAKCHIQUEL.

KAKI. See CINTA LARGA.

KAKWA. The Kakwa (Cucua, Kama, Cubeo Maku) are a subtribe of the Maku* (Macu), an Amerindian group of independent linguistic stock who today dwell in central northwest Amazonia, particularly at the headwaters of the Curicuriari River, the Makuparaná River, and the Tuyuka River in southeastern Colombia and northwestern Brazil. The Kakwa live on tributaries of the Vaupés and Papuri rivers. Scholars speculate that anciently the Kakwa had Tupi* origins, but that assumption is problematic at best. Unlike the surrounding Tukanoan* tribes, who are sedentary, agricultural, and riverine, the Kakwa are an interfluvial foraging people who practice some agriculture but primarily stay on the move hunting and gathering food. Periodically over the years, the Kakwa have practiced a temporary assimilation with one of the horticultural tribes in the region, occupying a subservient position in the social structure and functioning as servants in return for food and protection. Today the Kakwa population numbers approximately 300 people.

REFERENCE: Marilyn E. Cathcart and Stephen H. Levinsohn, "The Encoding of Chronological Progression in Cacua Narratives," in Robert E. Longacre, ed., *Discourse Grammar: Studies in Indigenous Languages of Colombia, Panama, and Ecuador*, 2 (1977), 69–94.

KALAPALO. The Kalapalo (Apalakiri) Indians are a Karib*-speaking people who live in the northeastern Mato Grosso region called the Upper Xingú Basin. Because the Xingú River was never a prominent route for expansion into the Brazilian interior by missionaries, settlers, or slavers, the Kalapalo people were completely isolated until the late nineteenth century when European anthropologists first reached the area. The many waterfalls and rapids on the Xingú River made exploration of the region difficult, and the ferocity of the neighboring Xavánte* and Kayapó* Indians discouraged settlement as late as the 1950s. In 1961, the Brazilian government established the Xingú National Park and placed the Kalapalo, along with several other small tribes, on 8,530 square miles of land and prohibited all non-Indian settlement, economic development, and tourism there. Safe and protected, the Kalapalo have followed an indigenous lifestyle that includes fishing and horticulture—the production of manioc, piqui, and corn. The Kalapalo discourage hunting and the eating of animal flesh, which they feel create too much aggressiveness in their society. By the early 1980s, there were nearly 200 Kalapalo living in the single village of Aifa in Xingú National Park.

REFERENCES: Ellen B. Basso, "A Husband for His Daughter, a Wife for Her Son: Strategies for Selecting a Set of In-Laws among the Kalapalo," in Kenneth M. Kensinger, ed., *Marriage Practices in Lowland South America*, 1984; Ellen B. Basso, *The Kalapalo Indians of Central Brazil*, 1973; Robert Lee Spires, "As línguas faladas do Brasil," *América Indígena*, 47 (1987), 455–79.

KALIANA. The Kaliana, also known as the Sapé, by which name they call themselves, are a linguistically isolated group of Amerindians living at the headwaters of the Paragua River in the state of Bolívar, Venezuela. The Kaliana claim to be descendents of the extinct Marakana people. Actually, there are only about 15 Kaliana still alive, and they live in three separate groups. One group is along the Lower Paragua River on the Isla El Casabe. A second group lives along the Middle Kerun River, a tributary of the Middle Paragua River. The third lives near Cosoiba on the Upper Paragua River. They are widely known and respected among other Indians for their elaborate healing and religious rituals. A riverine people who live by hunting and fishing as well as the production of manioc in communal gardens, the Kaliana Indians are few in number today. In fact, their population is so low that the Kaliana will soon be functionally extinct as a viable social group.

REFERENCES: Marc de Civrieux, *Watunna: An Orinoco Creation Cycle*, 1980; Waltger Coppens, *Los aborígenes de Venezuela*, 1981.

KALINO. The term Kalino (Kalina) is based on the Karib word for the Karib Indians proper, distinct from all of the diverse tribes speaking a Karib language. See KARIB.

KALLAWAYA. See QOLLAHUAYA.

KAMÃ. See MAKÚ.

KAMACÁN. See KAMAKÁN.

KAMADENÍ. See DANÍ.

KAMAIURÁ. The Kamaiurá, also known historically as the Kamayurá, Camayurá, and Camayulá, are a Tupi*-speaking people who once lived on Lake Ipavu near the left Culiseu River in the upper Xingú River area of Mato Grosso, Brazil. The German anthropologist Karl Von den Steinen first encountered them in the 1880s. They were and remain today a tropical forest people who survive off fishing, hunting, and raising maize, manioc, and tobacco. Although their population underwent dramatic decline from disease in the first half of the twentieth century, they were saved as a cultural unit by the decision of the Brazilian government to establish the Xingú Indian Park in the 1960s. Today there are approximately 200 Kamaiurá Indians living in the park in a single village on Lake Ipavu. Although they still speak their own Tupi language, they cooperate closely in cultural and social matters with their immediate neighbors in the park, the Txikão and Waurá.*

REFERENCES: Pedro Agostinho, *Mitos e outras narrativas, Kamayhurá*, 1974; Robin Hanbury-Tenison, *A Question of Survival for the Indians of Brazil*, 1973; Orlando Villas Boas and Cláudio Villas Boas, *Xingú: The Indians, Their Myths*, 1973; Robert Lee Spires, "As línguas faladas do Brasil," *América Indígena*, 47 (1987), 455–79.

KAMAKÁN. The Kamakán (Gamacán, Camacán, Kamacán, Catathoy, Cutasho, Masacara, Massacara, and Menian) were part of an isolated linguistic group of Amerindians. Portuguese settlers, led by people like João Gonçalves da Costa, began attacking the Kamakán in the early 1800s in their homeland near the Gongori, Cachoeira, and Pardo rivers in what is today the state of Bahia, Brazil. The Kamakán put up a fierce resistance. Eventually, however, they joined with the Portuguese in attacking their mortal enemies, the Botocudo. Capuchin missionaries tried to settle the Kamakán on missions in the early 1800s but the Indians resisted. They had a healthy disgust for neo-Brazilian society, except for metal tools, but were not able to survive even their minimal contacts with neo-Brazilians. Their population steadily declined until the tribe nearly became extinct in the 1940s. A few surviving Kamakán live on a government Indian post in the municipality of Itabuna in the state of Bahia.

REFERENCE: Theodore L. Stoddard, ed., *Indians of Brazil in the Twentieth Century*, 1967.

KAMARACOTO. See PARUKOTO.

KAMARÚ. See KARIRÍ.

KAMAYURÁ. See KAMAIURÁ.

KAMBEBA. See OMÁGUA.

KAMBIWA. There are several hundred Kambiwa families scattered widely throughout the state of Pernambuco in Brazil. Until forty years ago, the Kambiwa lived in relative isolation, but since the 1940s incoming neo-Brazilian settlers living and farming in the Serra Negra have displaced them from their land. The Kambiwa are being rapidly integrated into the neo-Brazilian economy and society. Now employing Portuguese, they no longer speak Kambiwa as their primary language, and the tribe no longer functions as a social unit. In terms of economic life, the Kambiwa cannot really be distinguished from the local mestizo society in which they work as poor laborers. They are concentrated especially in the Talhada highlands in the center of the state of Pernambuco.

REFERENCE: Theodore L. Stoddard, ed., *Indians of Brazil in the Twentieth Century*, 1967.

KAMENTXA. See KAMSÁ.

KAMILLARY. See KABIYERI.

KÁMPA. The Kámpa are an Arawakan*-speaking group of Amerindians today living at the headwaters of the Juruá River in the state of Acre, Brazil, very near the Peruvian border. There are approximately 235 people there who claim a Kámpa heritage. They are related closely to the Arawakan-speaking Campa* of Peru, from whom they probably separated early in the 1900s during the worst times of the rubber boom when so many western Amazonian tribes were disrupted. They are increasingly integrated into the local cash economy in order to secure trade goods, but the Kámpa maintain a strong sense of Indian identity.

REFERENCES: Robert Lee Spires, "As línguas faladas do Brasil," *América Indígena*, 47 (1987), 455–79; Walter Dostal, ed., *The Situation of the Indian in South America*, 1972.

KAMSÁ. The Kamsá (Camsá, Coché, Kamentxa, Koché, Kotze, Kochi, Sibundoy, Sebondoy) people are a detribalized group of Amerindians who are descendents of Coché-speaking Sebondoy and Quillacinga* Indians in southwestern Colombia, especially the eastern sector of the Sibundoy Valley in the department of Putumayo. They call themselves the Sibundoy and today number nearly 3,000 people. They function economically in the regional cash economy as subsistence farmers who sell surplus products, raise some livestock, and work as migrant laborers. There are approximately 320 Kamsá Indians living on a government Indian reservation known as Sibundoy Parte Alta. Although they cannot be distinguished from the surrounding mestizo population in terms of their dress and economic lifestyle, the Kamsá nevertheless maintain an understanding of their Indian heritage, even if much of the aboriginal culture has disappeared. They also tend to travel widely to visit other Indians as they have done for hundreds of years, which makes it difficult for Kamsá children to attend school regularly.

REFERENCE: Myriam Jimeno and Adolfo Triana Antorveza, *Estado y minorias étnicas en Colómbia*, 1985.

KANAMANTÍ. See KANAMARÍ.

KANAMARÍ. Not to be confused with the Panoan*-speaking Kanamarí* (Tamanáwa) outside of Feijo on the border between the states of Amazonas and Acre, nor with the Katukinan Kanamarí* of the upper Inauini, Juruá, Massipira, Jurupari, and Pauini rivers, the Kanamarí (Kanamantí, Canamarí) are descendents of an Arawá*-speaking people who lived in the interfluvial areas between the Acre and Iaco rivers in what is today the state of Acre. They remained quite isolated until the rubber boom of the late nineteenth and early twentieth centuries, when permanent contact with neo-Brazilian society was established. Today the Kanamarí are completely integrated into neo-Brazilian political and economic life, speaking Portuguese and working in the cash economy like other mestizo people. Although tribal society does not function anymore, there are still several hundred Kanamarí who are aware of their tribal heritage and still feel an ethnic separation from the larger society.

REFERENCES: Robert Lee Spires, "As línguas faladas do Brasil," *América Indígena*, 47 (1987), 455–79; Theodore L. Stoddard, ed., *Indians of Brazil in the Twentieth Century*, 1967.

KANAMARÍ. The Kanamarí (Kanawarí, Canamarí) were once a tropical forest people who spoke a Katukína* language and lived at several scattered locations in what are today the states of Amazonas and Acre in Brazil. In particular, they lived on the upper Ianuini River, the left bank of the Juruá River, on the Massipira River, between the Jurupari and Pauini rivers, and between the Tapaua and upper Tefé rivers. They are not to be confused with the Panoan*-speaking Tamanáwa tribe who called themselves Kanamarí or the Arawakan*-speaking Kanamarí* on the Acre River. The Katukína Kanamarí established permanent contact with neo-Brazilian society in the early 1900s during the rubber boom, and the tribe suffered rapid population decline from disease, dislocation, and conflict. Those Kanamarí who survived went to work for rubber collectors or on rubber plantations. There are still approximately 650 individuals who claim a Kanamarí heritage, but the tribe no longer functions as a viable social entity.

REFERENCES: Robert Lee Spires, "As línguas faladas do Brasil," *América Indígena*, 47 (1987), 455–79; Theodore L. Stoddard, ed., *Indians of Brazil in the Twentieth Century*, 1967.

KANDOSHI. See CANDOSHI.

KANELA. See CANELA.

KANGITE. See IPURINÃ.

KANGITI. See IPURINÃ.

KANGUTU. See IPURINÃ.

KANHOBAL. See KANJOBAL.

KANISIANA. See CANICHANA.

KANJOBAL. The Kanjobal (Kanhobal) are an Eastern Mayan* group of Indians living primarily in the department of Huehuetenango, Guatemala. The conquest of the Kanjobal came in three distinct stages in Guatemalan history. In the 1520s, Pedro de Alvarado led an expedition of conquest against the Indians of the Guatemalan highlands; the Kanjobal soon found themselves succumbing in large numbers to disease, military attack, and the rigors of relocation into missions.

Kanjobal numbers declined precipitously in the sixteenth century before stabi-
lizing in the mid–1600s. The second wave of conquest occurred in the mid- to
late nineteenth century when coffee cultivation boomed in Guatemala, creating
enormous pressure for new land. Between 1880 and 1920, the Kanjobal lost
more than 70 percent of their lands to *ladinos*, and they were gradually reduced
to the economic status of peasant farmers and seasonal migrant laborers. The
third stage has developed recently. Because of their miserable economic circumstances, the Kanjobal have been susceptible to left-wing propaganda and rhetoric,
especially to promises of land reform. In response, the Guatemalan government
launched a campaign of violent repression against the Kanjobal and a number
of other highland Mayan groups in the 1970s and 1980s, forcing thousands of
Kanjobal to flee the country. By the mid–1980s, there were approximately
110,000 Kanjobal Maya living in Guatemala.

REFERENCES: Shelton H. Davis, "Land of Our Ancestors: A Study of Land Tenure
and Inheritance in the Highlands of Guatemala," Ph.D. dissertation, Harvard University,
1970; W. George Lovell, "Surviving Conquest: The Maya of Guatemala in Historical
Perspective," *Latin American Research Review*, 23 (1988), 25–58.

KANKETE. See IPURINÃ.

KANKITI. See IPURINÃ.

KANOÊ. The Kanoê, also known as the Kapixána, are a group of Amerindians
from an isolated linguistic family, although some scholars think they are distantly
related to the Nambiquára* Indians. A tropical forest people, the Kanoê live on
the Guajajus River in southern Rondônia. They first encountered neo-Brazilian
settlers in the 1730s when gold prospectors flooded their territory; the Kanoê
suffered in subsequent malaria epidemics. Although relative peace returned in
the 1800s, the Kanoê became victims of the great rubber booms of the early
1900s and the 1940s, when neo-Brazilian rubber collectors poured into Rondônia
and brought with them disease, violence, and slave labor systems. The Kanoê
population declined so rapidly that tribal ceremonial life was badly damaged by
the early 1950s. Today demographers estimate that there are approximately 20
people in Rondônia who are still familiar with the Kanoê language. They live
at the Rio Guaporé Indian Post and in Guajara Mirim.

REFERENCES: David Price, "The Indians of Southern Rondônia," in David May-
berry-Lewis, ed., *In the Path of the Polonoreste: Endangered Peoples of Western Brazil*,
1981, 34–37; Robert Lee Spires, "As línguas faladas do Brasil," *América Indígena*, 47
(1987), 455–79.

KAPANA. See YAMAMADÍ.

KAPANAWÁ. The Kapanawá (Capanawá, Capanahuá, Kapanahu, Capangua,
Buskipani, Busquipani) were once a large tribe of Panoan*-speaking Amerindians
living in the tropical forests of western Brazil and eastern Peru. The Kapanawá

call themselves the Nuquencaibo. Their particular habitat was east of the Ucayali River near the Javari River, on the upper Maquea River, on tributaries of the upper Juruá River, and at the headwaters of the Javari, Tapiche, Blanco, and Guanache rivers. A Franciscan attempt to missionize the Kapanawá failed in the early 1800s when epidemic disease forced the Indians back into the forests. In the late nineteenth and early twentieth centuries, the rubber boom further devastated them, forcing the survivors onto local haciendas and plantations as laborers. By the 1920s, there were only 100 Kapanawá still alive. Tuberculosis has been an especially severe problem for them. Attacks by the Mayorúna* Indians as well as the dissolution of their tribal culture have also inspired migration of many Kapanawá to such areas as Requeña, Iquitos, and Pucallpa, where they have looked for work. The Kapanawá practice a subsistence agriculture, although in recent years many of them have switched to commercial rice production. They number approximately 500 people today, but among them are large numbers of Kapanawá who speak Spanish as their primary language and are fully integrated into local mestizo society. There are also some thoroughly detribalized people in Brazil and Peru who are aware of their Kapanawá ancestry.

REFERENCES: Darcy Ribeiro and Mary Ruth Wise, *Los grupos étnicos de la amazona peruana*, 1978; Theodore L. Stoddard, ed., *Indians of Peru in the Twentieth Century*, 1967; S. Lyman Tyler, *Indians of South America*, 1976.

KAPIEKRAN. See CANELA.

KAPINAMARÍ. See YAMAMADÍ.

KAPIXANA. See KANOÊ.

KAPOHN. See AKAWÁIO.

KAPÓN. See AKAWÁIO.

KAPÓNG. See AKAWÁIO.

KARABAYO. The Karabayo are a tiny group of Amerindians, numbering no more than 200 people, who live in the territory of Amazonas in southeastern Colombia. Their homeland is along the Caquetá River and its tributaries. A tropical forest people who raise manioc as a protein source and supplement their diet through fishing and hunting, the Karabayo have suffered a severe population decline in the twentieth century, primarily because of the diseases they have caught from their contact with neo-Colombian settlers, missionaries, explorers, and rubber collectors. Although the Karabayo have recently become better integrated into the regional cash economy, they still practice an essentially subsistence lifestyle.

REFERENCE: Leah B. Ellis and Linda Criswell, eds., *Estudiemos las culturas indígenas de Colómbia*, 1984.

KARAJÁ. The Karajá (Carajá) are an Amerindian tribe who for at least the past five centuries have occupied the island of Bananal near the great fork of the Araguaia River in the state of Goiás, Brazil. The island is nearly 200 miles long, but the Karajá have also ranged far upstream and downstream along the Araguaia. They are divided into three subgroups: the Karajá proper, the Javaé* (Javahé) on the southern part of Bananal Island, and the Xambioá* (Shambioá) who live north near the Araguaia Rapids. Their language is an isolate, unrelated to any other Native American dialect. The Karajá are accomplished potters, musicians, and boatsmen. The Karajá encountered Jesuit missionaries in the seventeenth century, but their first encounter with hostile whites came in the 1750s when Portuguese slavers slaughtered thousands of them. Attempts to missionize the Karajá failed in the late eighteenth century. Over the years, however, the Karajá gradually developed peaceful relations with neo-Brazilians, adopting their metal technology, textiles, shotguns, and sugar in return for skins and fish. The Brazilian government estimates that in the early 1980s there were more than 1,800 Karajá along the Araguaia. The Karajá proper numbered approximately 1,300 people, while the Javaé totaled 400 people and the Xambioá only 100 people.

REFERENCES: Nathalie Petesch, "Divinités Statiques, Homme en Mouvement: Structure et dynamique cosmique et sociale chez les Indiens Karaja du Brésil Central," *Journal de la Société des Américanistes*, 73 (1987), 75–92; Robert Lee Spires, "As línguas faladas do Brasil," *América Indígena*, 47 (1987), 455–79; Christopher J. Tavener, "The Karajá and the Brazilian Frontier," in Daniel R. Gross, ed., *Peoples and Cultures of Native South America*, 1973, 433–62.

KARAMANTA. See CARAMANTA.

KARAPANÃ. The Karapanã (Karapanã-Tapuya, Carapanã), who call themselves the Mochda (Mutea, Mehta), are an Eastern Tukanoan* language group of Amerindians who today live along the Ti River, a tributary of the Vaupés River, and at the headwaters of the Para-paraná River in both Colombia and across the border in the state of Amazonas, Brazil. The Karapanã are a highly skilled, semi-nomadic riverine people whose lifestyle revolves around the river. There were sporadic European contacts with the Karapanã in the eighteenth and nineteenth centuries. Portuguese missions were established temporarily along the upper Vaupés in the 1780s, but systematic evangelization of the tribe did not begin until 1914 when Roman Catholic priests established missions in the area. Theodor Koch-Grünberg began ethnological studies of the Karapanã at the same time. Protestant missionaries made their way into the region after World War II, eventually making nominal converts of a minority of Karapanã. The tribal economy focuses on the production of bitter manioc and fishing; hunting is quite secondary, although in recent years the tribe has become increasingly dependent on such European technology as fishhooks, shotguns, and machetes, as well as increased manioc production for sale. Contact with whites has also led to the development of small-scale animal husbandry, primarily hogs and poultry. In the 1960s and 1970s, the Colombian government began to encourage colonization of the Vaupés River Basin, but settlement there has been very slow. The Karapanã interact with other Indian tribes in the area but less so with whites, except for missionaries and rubber collectors, because of the extreme geographical isolation of the area. There are more than 1,500 Karapanã today who acknowledge tribal membership and speak the native language. Approximately 50 of them are in Brazil.

REFERENCES: Jean A. Jackson, *The Fish People: Linguistic Exogamy and Tukanoan Identity in Northwest Amazonia*, 1983; Gerardo Reichel-Dolmatoff, *Amazonian Cosmos: The Sexual and Religious Symbolism of the Tukano Indians*, 1985; Robert Lee Spires, "As línguas faladas do Brasil," *América Indígena*, 47 (1987), 455–79.

KARAPANÃ-TAPUYA. See KARAPANÃ.

KARARAIHO. See KARARAÔ.

KARARAÔ. The Kararaô (Kararaiho) are a tiny remnant of a Gê*-speaking group of Amerindians who are part of the Northern Kayapó* group. At the time of the Portuguese conquest, the Kararaô were part of the original Kayapó village of Pykatoti in what is today the state of Pará in Brazil. In 1933, they split off from Pykatoti, as Kayapó people do so frequently; they then numbered approximately 200 people. They soon divided into three villages. One of those was contacted by neo-Brazilians in 1940. They had crossed the Iriri River and headed north near Porto de Moz at the mouth of the Xingú River. Most of them immediately became ill and died. The survivors were induced to come into Altamira where they were shotgunned one evening; only one individual survived. The second village was contacted in 1957, and its population was moved to a government Indian post on the Curua River. Flu epidemics killed half of them within two years. The third Kararaô group, living along the Iriri River, was contacted in 1972. The Kararô Indian Reservation was established for them, but in 1979 they were summarily moved to the Xikrín Kayapó Bacaja Reservation. Several died on the way. Terrible measles epidemics further decimated the tribe in the 1960s. They never recovered their population. Today the Kararaô number only a handful of people and are under the care of the Brazilian Indian Service. Although tribal identity is still powerful among surviving Kararaô, ceremonial life no longer functions because the critical population mass does not exist.

REFERENCES: Paul L. Aspelín and Silvio Coelho dos Santos, *Indian Areas Threatened by Hydroelectric Projects in Brazil*, 1981; Edwin Brooks et al., *Tribes of the Amazon Basin in Brazil 1972*, 1973; Robin Hanbury-Tenison, *A Question of Survival for the Indians of Brazil*, 1973; Robert Lee Spires, "As línguas faladas do Brasil," *América Indígena*, 47 (1987), 455–79.

KAREKATEYÉ. See KRENKATEYÉ.

KARENERI. See AMARAKAERI.

KARIB. The word "Karib" (Carib) has been used by ethnologists to describe an Amerindian group as well as a large group of Amerindian languages. Those languages today are scattered widely throughout Venezuela, Colombia, Brazil, Guyana, Surinam, French Guiana, Belize, Peru, Honduras, and the Antilles. Included in this group were the Chocó* languages of Colombia, as well as Karijona,* Carare, Pijiao, Muzo, Motilón, and Opone; Acawái, Pemón, Yek-uana,* Yauarana, and Panare* in Venezuela; Rucuyen in French Guiana; Colan and Patagón in Peru; Oyana and Tiriyó* in Surinam; Garífuna* in Belize and Honduras; and the Apalaí,* Aracaju, Upurui, Apiacá,* Atroahí, Waimiri, Na-hukua, Parukoto,* Waiwai,* Waiboi, Caxuiana, Saluma,* Shikiana, Makushí,* Zapara, Yekuana, Pawishána, and Pianokoto in Brazil. The Kariban languages remain one of the most extensive language groups among indigenous poeple in the New World.

Most ethnologists today argue that the Karib tribes were once a warlike group of Amerindians who lived in the Amazon River Valley. Beginning in the 1200s, some of them started migrating to the northeast where they spread throughout the Guianas. Around 1300, their migrations pushed them out from northeastern South America to the islands of the Caribbean Sea, where they conquered the more peaceful Arawakan* tribes. The Karib Indians were farmers who raised cassava and lived in small, independent villages. Those Karib groups that con-quered the Arawak usually killed the men and married the women; the women and their children continued to speak the Arawakan languages while the Karib men spoke the Karib language. By the second generation on the islands, the Karib languages had died out. By the middle of the fifteenth century, the Karibs had taken over the Lesser Antilles, but their expansion to the Greater Antilles was blocked by the arrival of the Spanish explorers early in the sixteenth century.

The Karib Indians did not survive the presence of the Spaniards. War and disease decimated their numbers, virtually depopulating the islands of Amer-indians. On St. Vincent, the surviving Karibs intermarried freely with escaped African slaves, creating a new ethnic group known as Black Karibs or Garífuna. They revolted against British rule on St. Vincent in 1795, but the British crushed the rebellion and deported 5,000 Garífuna to the island of Roatan off the coast of Honduras. There they multiplied and eventually migrated to the coast, where they now constitute a large ethnic group of 100,000 people in Belize, and Nicaragua, Honduras.

The Karib Indians proper, who use the word Kalino* (Kalino, Calina, Caribe, Galibí*) to describe themselves, still exist today, though in reduced numbers. On the island of Dominica, there are approximately 400 of them living on a government reservation; thousands more live in scattered tribal groups in Guyana, Surinam, and French Guiana.

REFERENCES: Kathleen Adams, *Barama River Carib Narratives*, 1979; Ellen B. Basso, *Carib-Speaking Indians: Culture, Society, and Language*, 1977; Marc de Civrieux, *Los Caribes y la conquista de la Guayana Española*, 1976; William Curtis Farabee, *The Central Caribs*, 1924; Peter Kloos, *The Maroni River Caribs of Surinam*, 1971.

KARIJONA. The Karijona (Carijona, Carihona, Hianacoto-Umaua) are a Karib*-speaking group of Amerindians who live near the headwaters of the Vaupés River and on the upper Apaporis River in the northwestern Amazonian drainage region of Colombia. They live in the territory of Guaviare. Another group of Karijona lives in the department of Caquetá along the Yari and lower Caquetá rivers. Today the Karijona include the Hianacoto subtribe. A riverine people who navigate the rivers in the area with great skills, the Karijona live on fish and river animals; they also practice a slash-and-burn agriculture to raise bitter manioc. Beginning in the nineteenth century, sustained contact with rubber gatherers, missionaries, and settlers introduced devastating diseases into Karijona life. Today the tribe numbers around 1,000 people who are becoming increasingly detribalized. Survival of the Karijona people as a differentiated social unit is problematic at best.

REFERENCES: Jean A. Jackson, *The Fish People: Linguistic Exogamy and Tukanoan Identity in Northwest Amazonia*, 1983; Blaz Telban, *Grupos étnicos de Colómbia: Etnografía y bibliografía*, 1987.

KARIÑA. Today there are approximately 7,000 Kariña (Cariña, Carinya, Caribe, Karinya) Indians scattered in tribal groups throughout the mesas and llanos of northeastern Venezuela and northwestern Brazil. Their self-designation is Matiuhana. They came from a Karib* linguistic background. Their population center is near Guanipa in the state of Anzoategui. In the seventeenth and eighteenth centuries, they allied themselves with the Dutch against the Spanish and the Portuguese. Recent industrial development in the area, particularly steel fabrication and production factories and oil drilling and refining, have had a profound impact on the Kariña. They are becoming increasingly acculturated and bilingual; more and more Kariña now live in small towns and cities. They have adopted the Roman Catholic faith, although it is laced with aboriginal elements, particularly the Kariña faith in tribal healers. Nevertheless, the Kariña maintain a strong sense of Indian identity.

REFERENCES: Estéban Emilio Mosonyi, "La revitalización lingüística y la realidad venezolano," *América Indígena*, 47 (1987), 553–61; Karl H. Schwerin, "Processes of Karinya Culture Change in Response to Industrial Development," Ph.D. dissertation, University of California at Los Angeles, 1965.

KARINYA. See KARIÑA.

KARIPÚNA. The Karipúna (Caripúna), not to be confused with the Tupi*-speaking Karipúna of the territory of Amapá in Brazil, are a tribe of Panoan*-speaking Amerindians who once lived on the Capivari River in the state of

Rondônia, Brazil. In the nineteenth century, they were known as a peaceful tribe who lived near the rapids of the Mamoré and Madeira rivers. They traded with travelers and worked by helping them portage their canoes. In 1848, the Karipúna population exceeded 1,000 people. Rubber collectors completely disrupted Karipúna life in the late nineteenth and early twentieth centuries, triggering a population decline from which the tribe has never recovered. The Karipúna no longer function as a well-differentiated social unit, although their sense of tribal identity is still intact. A small group of Karipúna on the Jaçi-Paraná River managed to evade neo-Brazilians until the 1980s. The Conselho Indigenista Missaionario group of Protestant missionaries estimated that there were approximately 150 Karipúna still alive in the area.

REFERENCES: David Maybury-Lewis, *In the Path of the Polonoreste: Endangered Peoples of Western Brazil*, 1981; Robert Lee Spires, "As línguas faladas do Brasil," *América Indígena*, 47 (1987), 455–79; Theodore L. Stoddard, ed., *Indians of Brazil in the Twentieth Century*, 1967.

KARIPÚNA. The Karipúna (Caripúna) are a tribe of Amerindians who trace their language and ethnic origins back to ancient Tupi* Indians in Brazil. Until neo-Brazilian rubber gatherers destabilized their tribal homeland in the mid–1800s, the Karipúna were known for their docility and willingness to share the fruits of their peaceful, horticultural life with outsiders. When railroad construction workers entered the area and treated the Karipúna with a measure of civility, the Indians responded quickly, supplying them with turtles, fish, and manioc. At the time of the Portuguese conquest, the Karipúna numbered approximately 3,000 people, but today there are only approximately 500. They are highly acculturated and no longer speak the aboriginal language. It has been replaced by Portuguese and a Portuguese-Karipúna Creole. The Karipúna live in a single village on the Caripi River in the Luiz Horta Indian Park in the territory of Amapá, Brazil, where they receive assistance from a post of the Brazilian government's Indian Service.

REFERENCE: Theodore L. Stoddard, *Indians of Brazil in the Twentieth Century*, 1967.

KARIRÍ. The term Karirí refers to a group of Brazilian Amerindian languages that once included Kamaru, Dzubukua, Kipea, and Sapuya. Today there are descendents of those groups living in the municipality of Itabuna in the southern reaches of the state of Bahia. They are a highly assimilated group of people who retain none of the Karirí language or tribal ceremonies and who have no real tribal identity. They work in the regional cash economy as small farmers and laborers and are indistinguishable from the surrounding mestizo society. The only thing that sets them apart is a personal knowledge of their Amerindian ancestry.

REFERENCES: María de Lourdes Bandeira, *Os Karirís de Mirandela: Um grupo indígena integrado*, 1972; Theodore L. Stoddard, ed., *Indians of Brazil in the Twentieth Century*, 1967.

KARITIÁNA. The present Karitiána (Caritiána) are descendents of the once-large Karitiána tribe, a group of Tupi*-speaking Amerindians who occupied a wide range of Madeira River watershed in what are today the states of Amazonas and Rondônia in Brazil. Their Tupi dialect was part of the Arikên* language family. Before the arrival of neo-Brazilian settlers, the Karitiána population exceeded 1,000 people, but a succession of gold prospectors, slavers, and rubber collectors brought disease and devastation to the Indians. Only about 150 Karitiána are alive today, and most of them work as laborers in the local neo-Brazilian economy approximately 60 miles from the city of Porto Velho in Rondônia, Brazil. Another group is located at the Post Karitiána, on the Rio das Gorgas, a tributary of the Candeias River. The Summer Institute of Linguistics is working among them. A number of Karitiána now speak Portuguese and have adopted the use of rifles.

REFERENCES: Rachel M. Landin, "Nature and Culture in Four Karitiana Legends," in William R. Merrifield, ed., *Five Amazonian Studies on World View and Cultural Change*, 1985, 53–69; David Maybury-Lewis, *In the Path of the Polonoreste: Endangered Peoples of Western Brazil*, 1981; Robert Lee Spires, "As línguas faladas do Brasil," *América Indígena*, 47 (1987), 455–79; Theodore L. Stoddard, ed., *Indians of Brazil in the Twentieth Century*, 1967.

KARNIJÓ. See FULNIÔ.

KARO. See ARÁRA.

KARU. See WAKUÉNAI.

KARUPAKA. See WAKUÉNAI.

KARUTÁNA. The Karutána are a subtribe of the Baníwa* people and are located on the lower Içana River in the northeastern part of the state of Amazonas, Brazil. They consist of a number of individual clans, including the Yawarete-Tapuya, Yurapari-Tapuya (Yurupari-Tapuya, Iyemi), Urubú-Tapuya, and Arára-Tapuya. See BANÍWA and WAKUÉNAI.

KASHARARÍ. See KAXARARÍ.

KASHINITÍ. The Kashinití (Cashinití, Kaxinití) are a subgroup of Amerindians whose larger tribal affiliation is with the Parecí* Indians of Brazil. They speak an Arawak* language and live on the Sumidouro, Agua Verde, and Sepotuba rivers. Although the Kashinití intermarry freely with other Parecí subgroups, they nevertheless maintain a strong sense of Kashinití identity. See PARECÍ.

KASKIHA. The Kaskiha today are an Amerindian people who live in the Gran Chaco of Paraguay. In 1900 their homeland was in the interior of the Chaco, approximately 100 miles northwest of Puerto Casado. They numbered several thousand people, but since then there has been a dramatic population decline, caused by disease as well as acculturation. The Kaskiha, once known as the Guaná, were part of the Mascoian* linguistic family, but during the twentieth century, they have become completely acculturated to the surrounding society. They no longer speak the tribal language, work exclusively as wage laborers in the regional economy, and have adopted the material culture of neighboring non-Indians. At the same time, the Kaskiha have retained a sense of their tribal identity, still seeing themselves as Indians, quite distinct from other Indians, Europeans, and mestizos. In the mid–1980s, there were approximately 750 Kaskiha Indians in Paraguay. Salesian missionaries maintain a presence among Kaskiha Indians near Maria Casilda in the department of Boqueron.

REFERENCES: Harriet Klein and Louisa Stark, "Indian Tribes of the Paraguayan Chaco," *Anthropological Linguistics*, 19 (1977), 378–402; David Maybury-Lewis and James Howe, *The Indian Peoples of Paraguay: Their Plight and Their Prospects*, 1980; John Renshaw, "Property, Resources and Equality among the Indians of the Paraguayan Chaco," *Man*, 23 (1988), 334–52.

KASUPA. See AIKANÁ.

KATAWIAN. The Katawian (Catawian) tribe is a group of Karib*-speaking Amerindians who today live a relatively isolated existence in the tropical forests of Brazil and Surinam, primarily along the Anamu River, which is a tributary of the Trombetas, in the northwestern region of the state of Pará, Brazil. There they pursue a subsistence horticultural life revolving around the production of manioc. They also hunt and fish. Anthropologists describe them as a people having intermittent contact with neo-Brazilian and neo-Surinamese society, which means that they need trade goods in the form of cloth and metal tools and work or trade to get them. Their tribal identity, along with the language and ceremonial life, is still intact. Increasingly, the Katawian people, however, are becoming familiar with Portuguese and the frequency of their contacts is on the rise.

REFERENCE: Theodore L. Stoddard, ed., *Indians of Brazil in the Twentieth Century*, 1967.

KATAWISHI. See KATUKÍNA.

KATAWIXÍ. The Katawixí are a tiny subtribe of a Katukína* linguistic group. There are only 10 surviving members of the tribe, and they live on the Mucuim River in the state of Amazonas, Brazil. See KATUKÍNA.

KATDITAUNLHU. See NAMBIQUÁRA.

KATÍO. The Katío (Catío) are one of the Chocó* or Embera* groups of western Colombia. Today they number approximately 15,000 people, although the large majority of them are highly acculturated, Spanish-speaking people who live lives indistinguishable from those of surrounding mestizo farmers. The Katío people are especially concentrated in the northwest area of the department of Antioquio in Colombia, particularly near the Esmeraldas, Verde, and San Jorge rivers, as well as in the communities of Dabeiba, Frontino, Ituango, Murindo, Chogorodo, and Urrao. Most Katío are subsistence farmers who raise maize, sugar cane, manioc, and a variety of other products. They also hunt and fish to provide themselves with protein supplements. Increasing numbers of Katío are abandoning agriculture altogether and heading for the cities looking for work.

REFERENCE: Blaz Telban, *Grupos étnicos de Colombia: Etnografía y bibliografía*, 1987.

KATUKÍNA. Katukína (Catukína, Catukíno, Katukíno, Catuquíno, Catukinaru) is a South American linguistic group concentrated in Brazil, especially in the states of Amazonas and Acre. Today there are as many as 1,000 people who still speak one of the Katukínan dialects, which includes the Katukína proper, also known as the Kutia-Diapá (Katukína do Bía/Jutaí) and Pida-Diapá of the middle Jutaí River and the Mutum and Bía rivers; the Kanamarí*; the Tukun-Diapá (Txunhuã-Djabá, Tucundiapá) groups of the Pedras River; the Ben-Diapá group of the São Vicente River; the Puku-Diapá (Tawai) of the Restauração River; the Wadiuparanin and Urubú-Diapá of the Restauração River; the Amena-Diapá and the Kadíu-Diapá near São Felipe; and the Katawixí (Catawishí, Katawishí) on the Mucuim River. Until the late nineteenth century, the Katukína groups were quite isolated from neo-Brazilian settlers except for rare contacts, but the rubber boom of the 1890s and early 1900s brought them into permanent contact and greatly reduced tribal populations. Today most Katukína are indistinguishable in appearance from surrounding mestizo neo-Brazilians, in terms of their dress and economic lifestyle, for they are farmers and migrant laborers. But they are still aware of their Katukínan heritage and maintain a separate sense of identity.

REFERENCES: Joseph H. Greenberg, *Language in the Americas*, 1987; Robert Lee Spires, "As línguas faladas do Brasil," *América Indígena*, 47 (1987), 455–79; Theodore L. Stoddard, ed., *Indians of Brazil in the Twentieth Century*, 1967.

KATUKÍNA. Not to be confused with the Katukína* language groups, there is a small group of Panoan*-speaking Amerindians who call themselves Katukína (Wanináwa). They total approximately 350 people and live in scattered villages on the Bía and Jandiatuba rivers, with another settlement outside of Feijo, on the border between the states of Amazonas and Acre in western Brazil. They are in permanent contact with neo-Brazilian society, and most of them speak Portuguese as well as the native dialect. They are integrated into the regional cash economy and are having an increasingly difficult time maintaining any unique ceremonial life, although their tribal identity is still strong.

REFERENCES: Robert Lee Spires, "As línguas faladas do Brasil," *América Indígena*, 47 (1987), 455–79; Theodore L. Stoddard, ed., *Indians of Brazil in the Twentieth Century*, 1967.

KAVIXÍ. See KABIXÍ.

KAWAHÍB. At the time of the Portuguese conquest of Brazil, the Kawahíb (Kagwahíb) were a powerful Amerindian tribe of between 10,000 and 20,000 people living near the Mundurukú* in the heavy forests west of the upper Tapajós and Juruena rivers. Bitter wars with the Mundurukú eventually shattered the Kawahíb into a number of subgroups, including the Paii, Diahoi (Jahui), Tenharím (Tenharém), Apeiran'di, Paranawat,* Parintintín,* Boca-Negra,* Tapayuna, Wirafed,* Takuatep,* Itogapúk,* Ipotewat,* Tukumanfed, Mialat, Jabutifed, and Ramaráma.* They migrated west to the Madeira River, a tributary of the Amazon in Brazil. Historically the Kawahíb have been known as the Parintintín, which was actually a Mundurukú word meaning "enemy." They have also been known by a variety of other European and Indian terms, including Kagwahiv, Kawahyb, Kawahiv, Cawahíb, Cawahiwa, Cabahiba, Cabaiva, Cauhuahipe, Cahuahiva, Tupi-Cawahíb, Paritín, Wahai, Toepehe, Topehe, Toypehe, Toebehe, Nakazeti, Itoebehe, Tapakara, and Yawareta-Tapiiya. They are a Tupi*-speaking people who long ago lived along the Atlantic Coast near the outlet of the Amazon River.

During the second half of the nineteenth century, the Kawahíb put up an intense resistance to European settlement on the rubber frontier. Not until late in the 1800s did the rubber extractors subdue the Kawahíb by employing other Indians in their destruction. Peaceful contact with the Kawahíb was not established until 1923 when the German anthropologist Curt Nimuendajú reached them and pacified them with a wealth of steel tools. At the time, the Kawahíb were at war with neo-Brazilians, the Mura-Piraha, and their own Kawahíb-speaking relatives, the Paii, Diahói, Tenharím, and Apeiran'di. Today there are two principal subdivisions of the Kawahíb—the Parintintín-Kawahíb and the Tupi-Kawahíb, or Tenharím. The Parintintín number approximately 120 people and the Tenharím around 250 people. The tiny Diarrói* and Júma* are also Kawahíb subgroups. They live in small settlements of three or four nuclear families along the banks of tributaries and subtributaries of the Madiera and Machado rivers. They practice a slash-and-burn agriculture to raise sweet manioc and corn, and they hunt and fish to supplement their diet. The Kawahíb still speak the tribal language, although increasing numbers of young people are also fluent in Portuguese. Although the Kawahíb are nominally Roman Catholic, the religion is laced with tribal beliefs and ceremonies. In the mid–1980s, there were approximately 400 members of the Kawahíb tribe.

REFERENCES: Waud H. Kracke, *Force and Persuasion: Leadership in an Amazonian Society*, 1980; Robert Lee Spires, "As línguas faladas do Brasil," *América Indígena*, 47 (1987), 455–79.

KAWAHÍV. See KAWAHÍB.

KAWAHYB. See KAWAHÍB.

KAWA-TAPUYA. See WAKUÉNAI.

KAWILLARY. See KABIYERI.

KAWIRIMOMOWI. See GUAHIBO.

KAWIYERI. See KABIYERI.

KAWKI. The Kawki are a tiny group of Amerindians who live in a small village west of Tupe, in the province of Yauyos in the department of Lima, Peru. Closely related linguistically to the Jaqarú,* they are subsistence farmers surrounded by Jaqarú and Quechua*-speaking Indians. Today only a few elderly people still speak aboriginal Kawki, while most members of the group speak Jaqarú. Intermarriage with the Jaqarú has all but completely blurred the ethnic divisions between the two peoples.
    REFERENCE: Martha J. Hardman, *Jaqaru: Compendio de estructura fonología y morfológica*, 1983.

KAXANÁWA. See KAXINÁWA.

KAXARARÍ. The Kaxararí (Casharari, Kacharari, Kacharadí) are descendents of a larger, tropical forest tribe of Amerindians who spoke a Panoan* language and lived at the headwaters of the Curequete River, a right tributary of the upper Ituxi River, in what is today the state of Amazonas, Brazil. The tribe was decimated by the rubber boom of the late 1800s and early 1900s, when large numbers of the Kaxararí were either slaughtered or enslaved by rubber collectors. Today the tribe no longer functions as a strong social unit. All of the Kaxararí speak Portuguese, with only a few still employing their aboriginal tongue. Approximately 110 Kaxararí are still aware of their tribal heritage, but they work as laborers for local rubber collectors and other businessmen and do not function as an economic unit.
    REFERENCES: Robert Lee Spires, "As línguas faladas do Brasil," *América Indígena*, 47 (1987), 455–79; Theodore L. Stoddard, ed., *Indians of Brazil in the Twentieth Century*, 1967.

KAXINAUA. See KAXINÁWA.

KAXINÁWA. The Kaxináwa (Cashináwa, Cashinahua, Kaxanáwa, Kashináwa, Kaxinaua) are a small, Panoan*-speaking tribe of Amerindians, numbering about 2,000 people. They live along the Acre and Muru Rivers in eastern Brazil in the states of Amazonas and Acre, near the Peruvian border, and along the Curanja and Alto Purús rivers in Peru. They call themselves the Junikuin. An agricultural tribe, they raise sweet manioc on large, cultivated fields, as well as maize, cotton, and peanuts. The tribe supplements its diet through hunting, fishing, and foraging. Because of the extreme geographical isolation of their territory, the Kaxináwa did not have significant contact with neo-Brazilians until the later nineteenth century, but that contact set in motion a rapid population decline. Although the Kaxináwa waged war against rubber collectors in the early 1900s, by 1910 the Kaxináwa population was down to only 200 people. In 1946, several Kaxináwa came down from the headwaters of the Taraya River, a tributary of the Curanja River, in search of metal axes and machetes. Before then they had ambushed travelers to secure those goods. At that time, their population exceeded 400 people, but the new contact with neo-Brazilians brought the inevitable epidemics, killing about 80 percent of the adult population. Today the tribe is in permanent contact with neo-Brazilian society, still pursuing a subsistence, horticultural existence but supplementing that with migrant labor to provide cash for trade goods. The Kaxináwa are in the process of acculturation but still maintain a sense of their ethnic identity, even though their population is so scattered that maintaining ceremonial life is increasingly difficult. The geographic isolation of the area has prevented heavy settlement and limited opportunities for participation in the cash economy. By the late 1980s, there were approximately 1,000 Kaxináwa living in Peru and another 2,000 living in Brazil. Although the tribe has adopted metal tools from Europeans and practices a very limited wage labor, the tribal identity remains very strong. Most of them live on the Chandless, Muru, and upper Juruá rivers and near Feijo.

REFERENCES: Jane Powell Dwyer, ed., *The Cashinahua of Eastern Peru*, 1975; Kenneth M. Kensinger, "An Emic Model of Cashinahua Marriage," in Kenneth M. Kensinger, ed., *Marriage Practices in Lowland South America*, 1984; Kenneth M. Kensinger, "Cashinahua Medicine and Medicine Men," in Patricia J. Lyon, ed., *Native South Americans: Ethnology of the Least Known Continent*, 1974; Robert Lee Spires, "As línguas faladas do Brasil," *América Indígena*, 47 (1987), 455–79; Theodore L. Stoddard, ed., *Indians of Brazil in the Twentieth Century*, 1967; S. Lyman Tyler, *Indians of South America*, 1976.

KAXINITI. See PARECÍ.

KAXUIÁNA. The Kaxuiána (Kaxuyáma, Kaxuyána) are a small tribe of Karib*-speaking Amerindians who today live in the northwestern region of the state of Pará, Brazil. They are a riverine people who live on the Cachorro River, fish, hunt river animals, and plant small gardens. They have accepted the metal tools of neo-Brazilian society and engage in work and exchanges with the local cash economy in order to generate the revenue to purchase trade goods, but their sense of tribal identity is still intact. Today their total population is just under 200 people.

REFERENCES: Robert Lee Spires, "As línguas faladas do Brasil," *América Indígena*, 47 (1987), 455–79; Theodore L. Stoddard, ed., *Indians of Brazil in the Twentieth Century*, 1967.

KAXUYÁMA. See KAXIUÁNA.

KAXUYÁNA. See KAXIUÁNA.

KAYABÍ. The Kayabí (Cayabí, Kaiaby, Kayabí, Parua, Caiabí, and Kajabí) are a tropical forest tribe of Tupi*-speaking Indians who live in the Tapajós River Basin and in the Xingú Indian Park along the Xingú River in upper Mato Grosso, Brazil. The expansion of the Maundurukú* Indians eventually pushed the Kayabí toward their present locations in Mato Grosso, Brazil. Although Karl Von den Steinen first encountered some Kayabí in 1886, extensive and hostile contacts between Europeans and the tribe did not begin until the 1880s when rubber gatherers entered Kayabí land. The Kayabí numbered in the thousands at the time of the Portuguese conquest. The Kayabí were devastated by rubber collectors and the violence and diseases they brought with them. The Brazilian government Indian service pacified the Kayabí in 1924 when they were living in a half dozen villages between the Verde and São Manoel rivers. By the 1930s, peaceful Kayabí settled near the São Manoel-Paranatinga River. Orlando and Cláudio Villas Boas contacted them in 1950, and in 1952 the first small group of Kayabí relocated inside the Xingú Indian Park. During the 1960s and 1970s, most of the other Kayabí moved into the park as well. A few Kayabí still live outside the park in the Teles Peres area. Because of their extensive contacts with rubber collectors throughout the twentieth century, the Kayabí are the most acculturated Indians living in the Xingú Indian Park today. There are approximately 650 members of the tribe.

REFERENCES: F. L. Black et al., "Prevalence of Antibody Against Viruses in the Tiriyó, An Isolated Amazon Tribe," *American Journal of Epidemiology*, 91 (1970), 430–38; Robin Hanbury-Tenison, *A Question of Survival for the Indians of Brazil*, 1973; Robert Lee Spires, "As línguas faladas do Brasil," *América Indígena*, 47 (1987), 455–79; Orlando Villas Boas and Cláudio Villas Boas, *Xingú: The Indians, Their Myths*, 1973.

KAYAPÓ. The Kayapó—also known historically as the Cayamó, Coroa, Cayapó, Caiapó, Kaiapó, and Northern Kayapó—are a Gê*-speaking tribe of Amerindians who once lived in a huge expanse of territory in southern Pará and northern Mato Grosso, Brazil. The term Northern Kayapó was used to distinguish them from the Southern Kayapó, an unrelated tribe in southern Mato Grosso that is now extinct. Known for their aggressiveness and military skills, the Kayapó raided widely against other Indian tribes and against the Portuguese settlers, from the portage of Camapua in the south to the mines of Goiás in the north. In the 1740s, the Portuguese allied themselves with the Boróro,* the traditional enemies of the Kayapó, and launched military expeditions against them. In response, the Kayapó killed slaves, attacked and burned farm houses, and slaughtered cattle. They even attacked Goiás itself in 1751. Peace did not come until the 1770s when the end of the gold rush reduced the influx of settlers. Those neo-Brazilians remaining turned to farming and ranching, pursuits somewhat less threatening to the Kayapó. Most Kayapó relocated to a government aldeia near Goiás in 1781, and the fighting stopped.

These model villages of Kayapó survived intact until the 1870s when new increases in neo-Brazilian settlement threatened Kayapó land. The Kayapó began attacking farms and ranches again, and by 1889 they were threatening Goiás. In 1897, Roman Catholic missionaries from the Dominican order established a mission among some Kayapó on the Araguaia River about 60 miles downstream from the town of Santa María. Although those Kayapó became increasingly peaceful, others continued their violence against neo-Brazilians into the 1950s. In the 1960s and 1970s, the construction of the Trans-Amazon Highway through their land, along with the waves of new settlement it has inspired, has hemmed in the Kayapó and drastically reduced their mobility. The Kayapó traditionally dispersed in small groups for foraging activities during the dry season from April to October, but their inability to range widely in recent years has caused them to increase their horticultural activities. Their need for manufactured goods and medical services has also tied them increasingly to the larger society. Today there are approximately 1,700 members of the Kayapó tribe.

Historically, the Kayapó people have been known for their factionalism and the frequency of group splits, expulsion of dissidents, and formation of new groups. In Brazil today, there are more than a dozen tribes of Amerindians whose tribal ancestry is Northern Kayapó in origin, including the Kuben-Kran-Kêgn,* the Kuben Kragnotíre,* Kokraimôro,* Gorotíre,* Mentuktíre,* Mekranotí,* Xikrín,* Suyá,* Beico do Pau,* and Kararaô.*

REFERENCE: David Maybury-Lewis, *Dialectical Societies: The Ge and Bororo of Central Brazil*, 1979.

KAYAPWE. See ZAPARO.

KAYOVÁ. See KAIOVÁ.

KEDADA. See PIRA-TAPUYA.

KEKCHÍ. Along with the Pokomchí* and Pocomán,* the Kekchí are a Kekchian Maya* group of Indians living north of the city of Cobán in the department of Alta Verapaz, Guatemala. They are also scattered throughout the departments of Petén, Izabal, and Baja Verapaz, as well as in Belize. Small numbers of Kekchí also live in Mexico. In the fifteenth century, they fell under the domination of the Quiché* Maya; although they overthrew Quiché oppression early in the 1500s, they fell under Spanish control in the 1530s. Disease, relocation, and warfare dramatically reduced the Kekchí population in the sixteenth century, but it stabilized in the 1600s. Like other Mayans, the Kekchí were a settled agricultural people who lived by the cultivation of maize and beans. In the late 1800s, the government of Guatemala, pressured by powerful agricultural interests, began forcibly transferring tribal land to private ownership, reducing most Kekchí to peasant or migrant laborer status. Their poverty produced political unrest after World War II and bloody reprisals against Mayan activists, most notably the 1978 slaughter of more than 100 Kekchí men, women, and children by government troops. In the 1980s, perhaps 25 percent of the Kekchí emigrated to the United States, leaving approximately 360,000 members of the tribe behind in Guatemala and Belize. Of that total, only about 4,000 live in Belize.

REFERENCES: William E. Carter, *New Lands and Old Traditions: Kekchi Cultivators in the Guatemalan Lowlands*, 1969; Jim Handy, *Gift of the Devil: A History of Guatemala*, 1984; W. George Lovell, *Conquest and Survival in Colonial Guatemala: A Historical Geography of the Cuchumatan Highlands, 1500–1821*, 1984; W. George Lovell, "Surviving Conquest: The Maya of Guatemala in Historical Perspective," *Latin American Research Review*, 23 (1988), 25–58; Ruth Carlson and Francis Eachus, "The Kekchí Spirit World," in Helen L. Neuenswander, *Cognitive Studies of Southern Mesoamerica*, 1981.

KEKCHIAN. The term "Kekchian" refers to a language group within the larger group of Mayan* languages. The Kekchian group includes Kekchí,* Pokomchí,* and Pocomán.*

REFERENCE: Richard E. Moore, *Historical Dictionary of Guatemala*, 1973.

KENK. See TEHUELCHE.

KENKATEYE. See CANELA.

KEPIKERIWAT. See KEPIKIRIWAT.

KEPIKIRIWAT. The Kepikiriwat (Kepikeriwat) were Tupi*-speaking Amerindians whose homeland was on the Pimenta Bueno River, a tributary of the Jiparaná River in the state of Rondônia, Brazil. Their population underwent a dramatic decline in the late nineteenth and early twentieth centuries when neo-Brazilian rubber collectors brought violence and disease to their tribal homeland. The Rondônia Commission first pacified the Kepikiriwat in 1912 but they could not stop the inexorable process of demographic decline. By the 1940s, the tribe was no longer able to sustain any ceremonial life; soon after that it lost its social cohesion, breaking up into family groups that either intermarried with other Indians or died out. Today there are a handful of elderly people in Rondônia who are aware of their Kepkiriwat heritage.

REFERENCES: David Price, "The Indians of Southern Rondônia," in David Maybury-Lewis, ed., *In the Path of the Polonoreste: Endangered Peoples of Western Brazil*, 1981, 33–37; Theodore L. Stoddard, ed., *Indians of Brazil in the Twentieth Century*, 1967.

KICHO. See QUIJO.

KIGI. See COGUI.

KILEMOKA. The Kilemoka are a tiny group of Amerindians who once lived in the province of Velasco in the department of Santa Cruz in Bolivia. Spanish explorers ascending the Paraguay in the mid- and late sixteenth century probably encountered the Kilemoka, who were then a tropical forest people who hunted and fished for their livelihood. Always a small group, the Kilemoka avoided contact with neo-Bolivians until the rubber boom of the late nineteenth and early twentieth centuries devastated them. The Kilemoka population declined rapidly because of disease and exploitation. The tribe had ceased to function as a differentiated social unit by the late 1950s. Today there are only 20 members of the tribe still alive.

REFERENCE: Pedro Plaza Martínez and Juan Carvajal Carvajal, *Etnías y lenguas de Bolivia*, 1985.

KILLACINGA. See QUILLACINGA.

KINIKINÃO. The Kinikinão (Equiniquinao, Quainaconas) were an Arawakan*-speaking group of Amerindians located in the Gran Chaco area of what is today far southern Mato Grosso in Brazil. They were a foraging and hunting people. The Kinikinão had a population of approximately 1,000 people in the mid-nineteenth century, but experienced a rapid population decline in the last half of the 1800s. Italian Capuchin missionaries established a mission among them in 1852. By that time, they, along with the Teréno* tribe, were the only surviving subtribes of the Guaná people. The Paraguayan-Brazilian War of the 1860s, with its violent fighting in southern Mato Grosso, was especially devastating to the Kinikinão. Their population decline has continued in the twentieth century, and the last surviving group of Kinikinão lived in the Paraiso village in the municipality of Aquidauana in southern Mato Grosso. Within the last several decades, they joined with one of their surviving related tribes, the Teréno, and ceased to exist as a functioning tribe. There are probably still a few descendents of the Kinikinão who are aware of their ethnic origins.

REFERENCE: Theodore L. Stoddard, ed., *Indians of Brazil in the Twentieth Century*, 1967.

KIRIKIRIGOTÓ. The Kirikirigotó are a small subtribe of the Tiriyó* Indians of the equatorial forests on the Brazilian-Surinam border. Like other people of the tropical forests, they practice a subsistence, slash-and-burn horticulture, but contact with Protestant and Catholic missionaries in the last three decades has launched them on the acculturation process. See TIRIYÓ.

KIRIRÍ. Today there are approximately 1,000 people living near Mirandela in the state of Bahia, Brazil, who are aware of their Kirirí Indian ancestral heritage. A mestizo people who work as subsistence farmers or laborers, the Kirirí retain none of their tribal language, religion, or culture. Still, they sense an ethnic separation from neo-Brazilian society and maintain a unique identity.

REFERENCE: Theodore L. Stoddard, ed., *Indians of Brazil in the Twentieth Century*, 1967.

KIRISHÁNA. See YANOAMA.

KISAMBAERI. The Kisambaeri are the tiny remnant of a once larger Harakmbet* (Hate) language group of Amerindians who once lived on the Wasorokwe River, a tributary of the Karene River, in southeastern Peru. They are closely related linguistically to the Amarakaeri.* The rubber boom of the early 1900s started the Kisambaeri on a long, sustained population decline, a process that was accelerated by smallpox and influenza epidemics in the 1950s and 1960s. Today there are only a handful of Kisambaeri and they live on the Pukiri River with the Sapiteri Indians.

REFERENCE: Andrew Gray, "Perspectives on Amarakaeri History," in Harald O. Sklar and Frank Saloman, eds., *Natives and Neighbors in South America: Anthropological Essays*, 1987, 299–329.

KITAUNLHU. See NAMBIQUÁRA.

KJOTSUNI. See URU.

KOAIÁ. The Koaiá, also known as the Arára, are a group of Amerindians from an isolated linguistic family. They are not to be confused with the Kayapó*-based Arára* of the Xingú River area. They Koaiá were first contacted in the 1730s when gold prospectors reached the upper Guaporé River in what became the state of Mato Grosso. Malaria epidemics appeared by the 1750s. Many of the Koaiá fled into what became Rondônia. At the same time, they lived near the Pimenta Bueno River. The Koaiá population declined so rapidly that tribal ceremonial life was badly damaged by the early 1950s; the tribe ceased to exist as a functional social unit soon after. Demographers then estimated that there were only 7 people who still used the Koaiá language, but in the 1960s there was evidence that some extremely isolated Koaiá still survived. In 1970, neo-Brazilian engineers, surveying for the proposed Transamazon Highway west of Altamira, Brazil, found a Koaiá village abandoned only hours before. The Brazilian government then established the Arára Attraction Area in hopes of bringing the Koaiá Indians out of isolation. In the early 1970s, the Transamazon Highway cut right through their traditional territory, dividing the Koaiá into two groups, the Southern Koaiá and the Northern Koaiá.

From examination of their abandoned artifacts, anthropologists suspect that the Koaiá are probably a group of Karib*-speaking Indians. In the late 1970s and early 1980s, there were apparently some Koaiá living on the Jiparaná River at the mouth of the Agua Azul River and a few people who claimed to be Koaiá working as laborers in the city of Rondônia. Many Koaiá, however, are still highly isolated. They are facing extreme pressure from the development brought by the Transamazon Highway, the expansion of agribusiness concerns intent on converting subsistence farming areas to commercial production, and the persistent efforts of the government Indian service to establish permanent contact with them. In 1979 and again in the early 1980s, Koaiá attacked government agents trying to establish contact with them.

REFERENCES: Paul L. Aspelin and Silvio Coelho dos Santos, *Indian Areas Threatened by Hydroelectric Projects in Brazil*, 1981; David Price, "The Indians of Southern Rondonia," in David Maybury-Lewis, *In the Path of Polonoreste: Endangered Peoples of Western Brazil*, 1981, 33–37; Robert Lee Spires, "As línguas faladas do Brasil," *América Indígena*, 47 (1987), 455–79.

KOARATIRA. See AMNIAPE.

KOBEUA. See CUBEO.

KOBEWA. See CUBEO.

KOCHÉ. See KAMSÁ.

KOCHÍ. See KAMSÁ.

KOCHIMBERI. See AMARAKAERI.

KOFÁN. The Kofán (Cofán, Cofane, Kofane, Cufán, Kahepain, and Copane) are a thoroughly detribalized group of Amerindians who once lived in the upper Aguarico River area, especially near its junction with the Azuela River in the Ecuadorian and Colombian montana. Their primary residence today is still in the northwestern-most region of Ecuador's Oriente. In 1599, Jesuit missionaries reached the Kofán and established several missions among them, but the Jesuits and later the Franciscans could not protect the Kofán from the raids of Spanish slavers. The Kofán steadily declined in population during the seventeenth, eighteenth, and nineteenth centuries, becoming either Quechua* or Spanish-speaking Roman Catholics and losing virtually all of their aboriginal culture. The Kofán who did survive lived under the protection and exploitation of large neo-Ecuadorian landowners. In the 1940s, there were more than 200 descendents of Kofán Indians living and working as laborers in the montana; today those numbers have declined further. In recent years, Kofán territory has been invaded by three groups. First, exploration and drilling activities by the Texaco Oil Company and Gulf Oil have been extensive in the Kofán region and have brought large numbers of foreigners into the area. Second, large numbers of neo-Ecuadorian and neo-Colombian settlers have moved up the Aguarico River in search of land. Finally, large numbers of Quechua-speaking Quijos* Indians have migrated there from the Napo River area. The Kofán are either fleeing crowded conditions on their traditional lands or looking for work with oil contractors. The Kofán have lost much of their aboriginal culture and tribal political organization, although most of them still understand the tribal language. The Kofán traditionally avoided agriculture, but in recent decades many of them have made that transition. They usually refuse to work continually in the cash economy, except for a few months a year to earn some cash. There are approximately 1,800 Kofán Indians in Ecuador and Colombia, although border patrols, especially a military garrison at Santa Cecilia, prevent movement back and forth across the frontier by the Indians. Their principal villages are along the Aguarico, San Miguel, Guamues, and Putumayo rivers. In 1988, approximately 207 Kofán were living on a government Indian reservation at Yarina, as well as 80 on the Luzón reservation, 71 on the Santa Rosa de Sucumbios reservation, 150 on the Santa Rosa de Guamuez reservation, and 36 on the Afilador reservation.

REFERENCES: Myriam Jiméno and Adolfo Triana Antorveza, *Estado y minorias étnicas en Colombia*, 1985; Manuel Lucena Salmoral, *Las ultimas creencias de los indios Kofán: magia, selva y petroleo en el alto Putumayo*, 1977.

KOFANE. See KOFÁN.

KOGI. See COGUI.

KOGUI. See COGUI.

KOKAMA. See COCAMA.

KOKRAIMÔRO. The Kokraimôro (Kokraymôro) are a Northern Kayapó* group of Amerindians who today live on the upper Xingú River in the southern reaches of the state of Pará, Brazil, as well as in the Econtrada highlands of Pará. A tribal forest people, the Kokraimôro have survived by hunting and fishing, with manioc from tribal gardens supplementing their diet. Like Northern Kayapó people in general, the Kokraimôro are a fractious people. They separated from the Kuben-Kran-Kêgn*, moved west across the Xingú River, and settled between it and the middle Iriri River. There they split into northern and southern groups and engaged in violent resistance to rubber collectors in the area. Suspicious of outsiders, the Kokraimôro avoided contact with neo-Brazilians until 1957, but when that contact began it was devastating to the tribe. Population declined dramatically, falling below 50 people in the 1960s. In recent years, the Kokraimôro population has recovered somewhat and has reached nearly 100 people today, especially after the two groups reunited and moved to the banks of the Xingú River. Although the Kokraimôro want and trade for metal tools and other European technologies, they maintain a strong sense of ethnic identity. The greatest threat to them in recent years has been the prospect of the Kaiapó Dam on the Xingú River.

REFERENCES: Paul L. Aspelin and Silvio Coelho dos Santos, *Indian Areas Threatened by Hydroelectric Projects in Brazil*, 1981; Edwin Brooks et al., *Tribes of the Amazon Basin in Brazil 1972*, 1973; Robert Lee Spires, "As línguas faladas do Brasil," *América Indígena*, 47 (1987), 455–79.

KOKRAYMÔRO. See KOKRAIMÔRO.

KOLÍNA. See KULÍNA.

KOLLA. See QOLLA.

KOLLASUYO. See AYMARA.

KOLLÍNA. See KULÍNA.

KOLOMISI. See SABANE.

KONEA. See TUKANO.

KOREBAHU. See COREGUAJE.

KORIPAKO. See CURRIPACO.

KOTEDIA. See WANANA.

KOTEMOKA. See PAKAANÓVA.

KOTIRIA. See UANANA.

KOTITIA. See UANANA.

KOTÓ. See OREJÓN.

KOTZE. See KAMSÁ.

KOZÁRENE. The Kozárene are a subgroup of Amerindians whose larger tribal affiliation is with the Parecí* Indians of Brazil. They speak an Arawak* language and live along the headwaters of the Verde, Sacre, Papagaio, Juba, Cabacal, Jaurú, Guaporé, and Juruena. Historically, they were also known as the Cabishí-Parecí. Although the Kozárene intermarry freely with other Parecí subgroups, they nevertheless maintain a strong sense of group identity. See PARECÍ.

KOZÁRINI. See KOZÁRENE.

KRAHÔ. The Krahô are a Gê*-speaking people who today live on a 1,000-square-mile government Indian reservation near the town of Itacaja, on the right bank of the Tocantins River, south of Carolina, in the state of Goiás, Brazil. Although the Krahô had violent confrontations with some Europeans in the seventeenth century, they have been in peaceful contact with neo-Brazilians since 1809. They frequently assisted neo-Brazilians in conquering other tribes in the region, and the government tended to look with favor upon them. At the time of the conquest, the Krahô numbered approximately 5,000 people, but those numbers declined rapidly, as did those of all other South American Indian tribes. In the mid-nineteenth century, Roman Catholic missionaries from the Capuchin order established a mission among the Krahô, and many members of the tribe made at least a nominal conversion to Christianity. By that time, the tribal population was rapidly declining from disease and alcoholism. The mission survived until the 1880s, when the Krahô left and returned to an aboriginal lifestyle. They became embattled with local ranchers, who accused the Krahô of hunting and killing their cattle. In 1940, after a group of ranchers killed 23 Krahô in retaliation for the loss of cattle, the Brazilian government designated a reservation for the tribe and placed an Indian Protection Service post on it. The Krahô population stood at about 500 people in the early 1960s and had expanded to approximately 900 people by the late 1980s. Most of the Krahô have not taken up cattle raising as an economic pursuit, and there are still problems with local ranchers because some Krahô continue to treat cattle as game animals.

REFERENCES: Robin Hanbury-Tenison, *A Question of Survival for the Indians of Brazil*, 1973; David Maybury-Lewis, *Dialectical Societies: The Ge and Bororo of Central Brazil*, 1979; Julio Cezar Melatti, "Myth and Shaman," *Revista do Museu Paulista*, 14 (1963), 60–70; Julio Cezar Melatti, *Indios e criadores: A situação dos Krahô na area pastoril do Tocantins*, 1967; Robert Lee Spires, "As línguas faladas do Brasil," *América Indígena*, 47 (1987), 455–79.

KRANHACARÔRE. See KREEN-AKARÔRE.

KRE-ANKÔRE. See ARÁRA.

KREEN-AKARÔRE. The Kreen-Akarôre (Kranhacarôre, Kreen-Akrôre, Ipewi, Miahao), also known as the "shaven heads" by surrounding tribes, are a Gê*-speaking people who live at the headwaters of the Iriri River in central Brazil. In 1950, Orlando and Cláudio Villas Boas saw Kreen-Akarôre villages from the air, but the tribe was not contacted by Europeans until 1961 when an expedition of anthropologists and geographers from the Royal Geographical Society of London came across them. When a small band of Kreen-Akarôre showed up outside the Cachimbo Air Force Base in 1968, the Villas Boas brothers set out to establish permanent relations with the tribe, but the Kreen-Akarôre only retreated deeper into the Cachimbo forest. But in the early 1970s, construction of the Santarem-Cuiaba Highway forced the Kreen-Akarôre out of hiding. By 1974, the Kreen-Akarôre had been reduced from 300 people to only 135, and they were living near the Peixoto de Azevedo and Teles Pires rivers, as well as in the Cachimbo highlands, in the states of Mato Grosso and Pará. They had abandoned their gardens and were living along the highways begging for food from passersby. Later in the year, the Villas Boas brothers convinced the Kreen-Akarôre to relocate to the Xingú National Park, where their population stabilized and they were able to return to a tropical forest existence of swidden agriculture, raising manioc, fishing, and hunting. Demographers estimate the tribal population at fewer than 100 people.

REFERENCES: Adrian Cowell, *The Tribe that Hides from Man*, 1973; Shelton H. Davis, *Victims of the Miracle: Development and the Indians of Brazil*, 1977; Robin Hanbury-Tenison, *A Question of Survival for the Indians of Brazil*, 1973; John Hemming, *The Tribes of the Amazon Basin in Brazil*, 1972; Robert Lee Spires, ''As línguas faladas do Brasil,'' *América Indígena*, 47 (1987), 455–79.

KREEN-AKRÔRE. See KREEN-AKARÔRE.

KREM-YÉ. The Krem-yé (Kren-yé, Krēyé, Krenjé) were once a Gê*-speaking Timbira* people who lived in what is today the northern region of the state of Maranhão, Brazil. During the early 1800s, the Krem-yé put up a fierce resistance to neo-Brazilian settlement, and the Indians experienced rapid population decline because of disease and violence. Not until the 1850s did the Krem-yé establish peaceful contact with neo-Brazilians and begin to present themselves in increasing numbers near Bacabal on the lower Mearim River. The Krem-yé were attracted by trade goods and food. Soon after their arrival there, the Krem-yé suffered a terrible epidemic and declined rapidly in population. The survivors then fled northeast to settle on the upper Gurupi River, but the tribe did not survive as a differentiated social unit. They also suffered from attacks by their neighbors, the Urubú, as well as from incoming neo-Brazilian gold prospectors, rubber collectors, farmers, and resin gatherers. Today there are still a few people in Brazil, perhaps 30, who claim a Krem-yé heritage, but they are thoroughly detribalized and living near the government Indian post at Gonçalves Dias.

REFERENCES: Robert Lee Spires, ''As línguas faladas do Brasil,'' *América Indígena*, 47 (1987), 455–79; Theodore L. Stoddard, ed., *Indians of Brazil in the Twentieth Century*, 1967.

KRENAK. See BOTOCUDO.

KRENJÉ. See KREM-YÉ.

KRENKATĒYÉ. The Krenkatēyé (Kenkatēyé, Karekatēyé) were a tribe of Gê*-speaking Amerindians who once lived along the Itapicuru River in the Tocantins-Araguaia drainage area of Brazil. Neo-Brazilians waged a war of extermination

against them in 1814, killing or selling most of the Krenkatēyé into slavery in
the state of Pará. In 1913, neo-Brazilian settlers attacked the one surviving
Krenkatēyé village in the state of Maranhão. The surviving members of the tribe
scattered widely, joining other tribes and ceasing to exist as a sociological unit.
By the 1970s, Brazilian anthropologists reported some surviving Krenkatēyé,
primarily isolated elderly people, living with the Krahó. See KRAHÓ.

KRÊYÉ. See KREM-YÉ.

KRIKATÍ. The Krikatí (Krinkatí, Caracatí, Gaviāno) are a Gê*-speaking people
who live today in the southwest part of the state of Maranhão, Brazil. Their six
villages are in two clusters near the towns of Amarante and Montes Altos. They
claim today to be mixed descendents of now-extinct Eastern Timbira* tribes,
particularly the Ronhugatí, Pihugatí, and Pukobké. By the 1920s, the Krikatí
were nearly extinct as a tribe, reduced by disease to fewer than 100 people, but
their numbers stabilized, increasing to 350 people in 1960 and more than 500
in 1980. Their tribal territory is surrounded by tens of thousands of poor neo-
Brazilian backwoodsmen, and although the Krikatí still practice subsistence
farming and foraging, they are becoming increasingly integrated as laborers into
the surrounding commercial economy. The government's Indian Protection Service maintains a post for the Krikatí.

REFERENCES: David Maybury-Lewis, *Dialectical Societies: The Gê and Boróro of
Central Brazil*, 1979; Robert Lee Spires, "As línguas faladas do Brasil," *América Indígena*, 47 (1987), 455–79.

KRINKATÍ. See KRIKATÍ.

KRISHANA. See YAWAPERI.

KRIXANA. See YAWAPERI.

KU. See SUMU.

KUBEN-KAMREKTÍ. See ASURINÍ.

KUBEN-KRAGNOTÍRE. The Kuben-Kragnotíre (Kuben-Krangnotí) are a
Gê*-speaking Amerindian people who are part of the Northern Kayapó* group
of tribes. Because of their geographical isolation and extreme suspicion of outsiders, the Kuben-Kragnotíre lived in a largely aboriginal state as hunters and
foragers until the 1960s, even though they did suffer a population decline because
of indirect contact with Europeans and their diseases. Today there are approximately 150 members of the Kuben-Kragnotíre tribe. They live along the tributaries of the Xingú River, near the headwaters of the Iriri River, in the state
of Pará, Brazil. Although their contact with neo-Brazilians in recent years has
increased, they remain quite isolated.

REFERENCES: Robert Lee Spires, "As línguas faladas do Brasil," *América Indígena*, 47 (1987), 455–79; Theodore L. Stoddard, ed., *Indians of Brazil in the Twentieth Century*, 1967.

KUBEN-KRANGNOTÍ. See KUBEN-KRAGNOTÍRE.

KUBEN-KRAN-KÊGN. The Kuben-Kran-Kêgn (Kubenkranken, Kubenkrankêgn) are a Gê*-speaking Northern Kayapó* group of Amerindians who today live in a relatively isolated condition between the Xingú and Iriri rivers just north of the Mato Grosso border in the state of Pará, Brazil. Extremely suspicious of outsiders, the Kuben-Kran-Kêgn maintained their separation from neo-Brazilians until the 1950s when they were finally pacified. A hunting and foraging people with only marginal interest in agriculture, the Kuben-Kran-Kêgn still speak the native language and maintain native customs, except for an increasing use of European technology. They are in permanent contact with a post of the government Indian service and frequent contact with a variety of missionaries in the area, but they still maintain a strong sense of cultural isolation. The Kuben-Kran-Kêgn today number approximately 400 people. The greatest threat to the Kuben-Kran-Kêgn Indians in recent years has been the construction of the Kaiapó and Gorotíre Dams on the Xingú River.

REFERENCES: Paul L. Aspelin and Silvio Coelho dos Santos, *Indian Areas Threatened by Hydroelectric Projects in Brazil*, 1981; Robin Hanbury-Tenison, *A Question of Survival for the Indians of Brazil*, 1973; Robert Lee Spires, "As línguas faladas do Brasil," *América Indígena*, 47 (1987), 455–79; Theodore L. Stoddard, ed., *Indians of Brazil in the Twentieth Century*, 1967.

KUBENKRANKEN. See KUBEN-KRAN-KÊGN.

KUBEO. See CUBEO.

KUBEU. See CUBEO.

KUBEWA. See CUBEO.

KUBEWANA. See CUBEO.

KUGAPAKORI. See MACHIGUENGA.

KUIBA. See CUIVA.

KUIKÚRO. See KUIKÚRU.

KUIKÚRU. The Kuikúru (Cuicuro, Kuikúro) Indians are an Amerindian tribe whose language is part of the larger Karib* group. When they were first discovered by anthropological expeditions in the 1880s and 1890s, the Kuikúru

(Guicúru or Cuicutl) were a tropical forest tribe living between the Culiseu and Culuene rivers in the upper Xingú River drainage area of Mato Grosso, Brazil. The tribe suffered from the attacks of other tribes as well as from influenza epidemics in the twentieth century, but since the 1960s they have found relative peace in the Xingú Indian Park, where today they pursue a largely traditional lifestyle. There are approximately 220 members of the tribe living there in a village on the edge of open savannas full of game for hunting. Although they still speak their own Karib dialect, they share a great deal socially and culturally with other Xingú tribes, particularly with the Iaualapití,* Matipú,* and Nafuquá* who have decided to live near them.

REFERENCES: Gertrude E. Dole, "The Structure of Kuikúru Marriage," in Kenneth M. Kensinger, ed., *Marriage Practices in Lowland South America*, 1984; "Slash-and-Burn Cultivation Among the Kuikúru and its Implications for Cultural Development in the Amazon Basin," *Antropológica*, Suppl. 2 (1961), 47–65; Orlando Villas Boas and Cláudio Villas Boas, *Xingú: The Indians, Their Myths*, 1973; Robert Lee Spires, "As línguas faladas do Brasil," *América Indígena*, 47 (1987), 455–79.

KUIVA. See CUIVA.

KUKRA. See SUMU.

KUKUYÁNA. The Kukuyána are a subtribe of the Pianokotó, who are today completely merged with other Tiriyó* Indians along the border between Brazil and Surinam. See TIRIYÓ.

KULÍNA. The Kulína Indians, also known historically as the Kulíno, Kolína, Kollína, Kurína, Culíno, and Culína, are an Arawá*-speaking tribe of Amerindians who today live in far western Brazil. They call themselves the Madija. They are concentrated in several villages on the Chandless River, at Manoel Urbano on the Purús River, and to the west on the Acarau River. They are also near the Santa Rosa River. In 1877, the Kulína were devastated by a measles epidemic, and in the early twentieth century they had to flee the depredations of rubber collectors. A smallpox epidemic hurt them in 1950. In recent years, some Kulína have migrated west across the international border to Peru. Demographers estimate that there are approximately 2,500 Kulína Indians. All of them are in permanent contact with neo-Brazilian society and are being assisted by a branch of the government Indian service. Those Kulína who have migrated into Peru tend to be somewhat more acculturated; they number approximately 500 people.

REFERENCES: Donald K. Pollock, "Health Care Among the Culina, Western Amazonia," *Cultural Survival Quarterly*, 12 (1988), 28–32; Darcy Ribeiro and Mary Ruth Wise, *Los grupos étnicos de la amazonia peruana*, 1978; Theodore L. Stoddard, ed., *Indians of Brazil in the Twentieth Century*, 1967; Stefano Varese, *The Forest Indians in the Present Political Situation of Peru*, 1972.

KULÍNO. See KULÍNA.

KUMADAMNAINAI. See WAKUÉNAI.

KUNA. See CUNA.

KUNIMIA. See GUAYABERO.

KUNIVADENÍ. See DANÍ.

KUNUANA. See KUNUHANA.

KUNUHÁNA. The Kunuhána (Kunuána) are a subtribe of the Yekuana* Indians. They live along the Kunukunuma and Padamo rivers in Brazil. See YEKUANA.

KUPONDIRIDERI. See AMARAKAERI.

KURA. See BAKIRÍ.

KURASKIANA. See YABARÁNA.

KURIŃA. See KULÍNA.

KURIPAKO. See CURRIPACO.

KURRIM. See CURRIPACO.

KURRIPAKO. See CURRIPACO.

KURSU. See AYOREO.

KURUÁYA. The Kuruáya (Curuáya, Caravare, Curibary, Curivere, Curubare, Curabare, Curuahe, Curierai, Curuara, Curuaye, Curiuaye, Curueye, and Curiuaia) are a nearly extinct group of Tupi*-speaking Amerindians who lived along the Jamanxim and Curua rivers in what is today the state of Pará, Brazil. In the seventeenth century, the Kuruáya lived between the Xingú and Tapajós rivers. Although they had periodic contacts with neo-Brazilian society, nothing permanent developed until after anthropologists visited them in the early 1900s. In 1934, expanding bands of Kayapó* Indians attacked and dispersed the Kuruáya, putting them on the road to extinction. By the late 1940s, there were fewer than 50 Kuruáya still alive. Today there are only a few isolated individuals still aware of their Kuruáya heritage.

REFERENCE: Theodore L. Stoddard, ed., *Indians of Brazil in the Twentieth Century*, 1967.

KURUKURU. See PAUMARÍ.

KURUPARIA. See CAMPA.

KUSIKIA. The Kusikia were a group of Amerindians who lived in the province of Velasco in the department of Santa Cruz in Bolivia. Spanish explorers ascending the Paraguay in the mid- and late sixteenth century probably encountered the Kusikia, who were then a tropical forest people who hunted and fished for their livelihood. Always a small group, the Kusikia avoided contact with neo-Bolivians until the rubber boom of the late nineteenth and early twentieth centuries devastated them. The Kusikia population declined rapidly because of disease and exploitation. The tribe had ceased to function as a differentiated social unit by the late 1950s. Today there are only 10 members of the tribe still alive.

REFERENCE: Pedro Plaza Martínez and Juan Carvajal Carvajal, *Étnias y lenguas de Bolivia*, 1985.

KUSTENAU. See KUTENABU.

KUTENABU. The Kutenabu, also known historically as the Custenau or Kustenau, were once an Arawak*-language people living on the Batovi River in the Xingú River drainage area of upper Mato Grosso, Brazil. The first European to reach them was the anthropologist Karl Von den Steinen in 1884, but by that time they had already been badly devastated by disease and the attacks from neighboring tribes. They had probably migrated to the area from the Guianas and Caribbean region. Early in the twentieth century, a new wave of epidemics all but obliterated the Kutenabu. By the early 1980s, the tribe had ceased to exist, and only two people were alive who claimed Katenabu membership, an older woman and her son. Both of them lived with the Waura* tribe in the Xingú Indian Park.

REFERENCE: Orlando Villas Boas and Cláudio Villas Boas, *Xingú: The Indians, Their Myths*, 1973.

KUTIA-DIAPÁ. See KATUKÍNA.

KUTJA'AM. See ASHLUSLAY.

KWAIKER. See COAIQUER.

KWALINSADNDESU. See NAMBIQUÁRA.

KYISAPANG. See SANAPANA.

KYOMA. See ANGAITÉ.

L

LACANDON. The Lacandon are a group of Mayan* Indians whose traditional homeland has been in the Chiapas region of Mexico; a much smaller number lived across the border in northwestern Guatemala. Like the other Mayan groups, the Lacandones suffered mass population decline at the hands of the Spanish conquerors who reached them in the late 1520s and 1530s. An agricultural people who raise maize and beans in communal plots, the Lacandon population stabilized in the eighteenth century and began to increase in the nineteenth. After World War II, the Lacandones in Guatemala suffered from government policies designed to transform communal landholdings to private ownership; as a result, some Lacandones acquired strong left-wing political leanings. Government repression in the 1980s has inspired a mass emigration of Guatemalan Lacandones, most of whom have ended up in Mexico, the United States, or refugee camps. Today there are only a few dozen Lacandones left in Guatemala.

REFERENCE: Melanie A. Counce and William V. Davidson, "Indians of Central America 1980s," *Cultural Survival Quarterly*, 13 (1989), 38–41.

LAKONDÉ. See NAMBIQUÁRA.

LAMA. The Lamas (Lamista, Lamisto, Lamano) are a Quechua*-speaking group of Amerindians who live along the Lamas River and the lower Huallaga River in Peru. They call themselves the Llakwash. Scholars do not know anything about their aboriginal language since they had adopted Quechua (Río Napo variety) by the time of the Spanish conquest. Pedro de Ursúa first reached the Lamas in 1554. The Jesuits converted most of the tribe in 1654 and resettled them in a mission, Santa Cruz de los Motilones y Lamas. Others settled in the Mission of San Francisco Regis on the Paranapura River. In 1767, when the

Jesuits were expelled from the New World, the Lamas came under the jurisdiction of the Franciscans. Most of the Lamas were agricultural serfs by that time. Over the course of the next two centuries, the Lamas gradually acculturated to neo-Peruvian society, retaining use of Quechua but adopting an economic lifestyle consistent with that of the surrounding mestizo population. Although they retain a distinct sense of ethnic identity, the Lamas are in an advanced state of acculturation. They number approximately 19,000 people today.

REFERENCES: Darcy Ribeiro and Mary Ruth Wise, *Los grupos étnicos de la amazonia peruana*, 1978; Stefano Varese, *The Forest Indians in the Present Political Situation of Peru*, 1972.

LAMANO. See LAMA.

LAMISTA. See LAMA.

LARI. See TÉRRABA.

LAS CANDELAS. The Las Candelas Indians are a subtribe of the Yuko* Indians of northeastern Colombia. Traditionally they pursued a subsistence, horticultural lifestyle along the Cascara River. Today their numbers are fewer than 20 people, and the sense of group identity is disappearing. See YUKO.

LATUNDE. See NAMBIQUÁRA.

LAYANA. The Layana (Chana) are a nearly extinct group of Brazilian Indians. Originally a subtribe of the Guaná, they spoke an Arawakan* language and occupied the eastern reaches of the Paraguay Basin. They were a peaceful farming people who were often subjugated by more warlike tribes. The Niguecactemic (Neguecatemiji) were a subtribe of the Layana. In 1766, Roman Catholic missionaries established a mission for the Layana on the western side of the Paraguay River near the mouth of the Apa River. In 1800, there were approximately 2,000 members of the Layana, but they were unable to withstand attacks from other tribes and European diseases. The Layana population had dropped to only 300 people by 1850. By the early twentieth century, the Layana population reached the point where ceremonial life was seriously affected by lack of numbers. As late as the 1960s, there were still a few Layana on the banks of the Miranda River in southern Mato Grosso, Brazil. A few others were living with the Teréno* tribe.

REFERENCE: Theodore L. Stoddard, ed., *Indians of Brazil in the Twentieth Century*, 1967.

LAYMÍ. The Laymí are an Aymara*-speaking group of Amerindian people who live in the region of northern Potosí, Bolivia. There are approximately 9,000 Laymí Indians today; about two-thirds of them live in the highlands above 10,000 feet while the other third are in the temperate area between 6,000 and 10,000 feet. They pursue a broad subsistence economy. In the highlands they raise llamas and sheep as well as tubers, wheat, barley, and beans. The Laymí in the temperate area raise sheep, goats, maize, beans, wheat, barley, and squash. Their only export commodity is woven cloth products that provide them with a minimal amount of cash. Most of the Laymí live in small villages scattered throughout the region. The center of Laymí culture is located at Qalaqala. Ever since the nineteenth century, the Laymí have resisted attempts by the Bolivian government to implement "land reform" policies designed to individualize land-ownership and impose uniform taxes on all smallholders. They much prefer their communal systems.

REFERENCE: Olivia Harris, "Labour and Produce in an Ethnic Economy, Northern Potosí, Bolivia," in David Lehman, ed., *Ecology and Exchange in the Andes*, 1982, 79–96.

LECO. The Leco, also known as the Chuncho, are members of an isolated language group today confined to a small area in the department of La Paz in Bolivia, primarily near the upper Madadi River and the Huanay River and its tributaries, the Tipuani, Mapiri, Turiapo, and Yuyo rivers. They call themselves the Yuguru. The Spanish explorer Miguel Cabello de Balboa first contacted them in the 1580s, and in the early 1620s they were located on the Cacamayo River. By the beginning of the nineteenth century, the Leco were concentrated in the Mission of Huanay at the confluence of the Mapiri and Tipuani rivers; their numbers were declining. Today the few surviving Leco work as subsistence farmers, ranchers, and seasonal laborers. They are rapidly being assimilated into the surrounding mestizo society. Leco subsistence farmers raise maize and plantains. Little of their aboriginal culture remains. They have a population of approximately 200 people.

REFERENCES: Brian M. Boom, *Ethnobotany of the Chácobo Indians, Beni, Bolivia*, 1987; Pedro Plaza Martínez and Juan Carvajal Carvajal, *Etnías y lenguas de Bolivia*, 1985; Graciela Zolezzi and J. Riester, "Lenguas indígenas del oriente boliviano clasificación preliminar," *América Indígena*, 47 (1987), 425–33.

LENCA. The Lenca (Opatoro) Indians today number approximately 95,000 people and live in Honduras, especially in the departments of La Paz, Intibuca, and Lempira in the southwestern mountains. Some have also migrated to El Salvador. Most scholars believe that the Lenca were originally migrants to Honduras from South America who were strongly influenced by Mayan* culture. At the time of the Spanish conquest, the Lenca were also concentrated farther north in what is today the department of Francisco Morazán and on the east side of the Lempa River. Large numbers of Lenca have also migrated to coffee and banana plantations, mining communities, and major cities looking for work in recent years. When the Spaniards first arrived in Honduras in the 1520s, the Lenca were a peaceful, settled agricultural people, numbering as many as 300,000 people. The Spanish presence triggered a massive population drop because of disease, forced labor, and mistreatment. By 1550, the Lenca population had declined to only 25,000 people, at which point it stabilized. The Lenca gradually became acculturated to many European institutions. Roman Catholicism became the prominent religion among the Lenca, although the Indians have retained many earlier practices in a form of folk Catholicism. In Lenca areas, farmland is still owned communally and worked with simple tools, but this practice is becoming less and less economical. The Spanish language is now the predominant form of communication among the Lenca.

REFERENCES: Robert S. Chamberlain, *The Conquest and Colonization of Honduras 1520–1550*, 1967; Howard I. Blutstein et al., *Area Handbook for Honduras*, 1971; L. Fernando Cruz Sandoval, "Los Indios de Honduras y la situación de sus recursos naturales," *América Indígena*, 44 (1984), 423–46.

LENGUA. With a population of just under 10,000 people, the Lengua are today the largest Indian tribe of the Paraguayan Gran Chaco. They are part of the Lengua-Maskoy linguistic family. They call themselves the Eenthlit. A large, powerful nation before the Spanish conquest, the Lengua were reduced to near extinction by 1800, after which their population stabilized and began a steady increase. During the Chaco War between 1932 and 1935, large numbers of Lengua Indians died at the hands of Bolivian soldiers. Anglican missionaries and Mennonite farmers and ranchers, as well as the construction of the Trans-Chaco Highway, have integrated the Lengua into the local economy and Christian religion. Although the Lengua still retain a strong Indian identity, they are increasingly being integrated into the regional cash economy as ranch and farm hands, migrant workers, and wage laborers. They are a poor, lower-class people, subject to discrimination at the hands of mestizos and people of European descent in Paraguay. A host of Christian missionary groups, including Salesians, the Mennonite Central Committee, and the South American Missionary Society, work among the Lengua Indians.

REFERENCES: Pastor Arenas, *Etnobotánica Lengua-Maskoy*, 1981; Harriet Klein and Louisa Stark, "Indian Tribes of the Paraguayan Chaco," *Anthropological Linguistics*, 19 (1977), 378–402; John Renshaw, "Property, Resources and Equality among the Indians of the Paraguayan Chaco," *Man*, 23 (1988), 334–52.

LETUAMA. See LETUANA.

LETUANA. The Letuana (Letuama, Letuara) are a small Amerindian tribe today living at the confluence of the Pira-paraná and Apaporis rivers in the Vaupés drainage area of southeastern Colombia. They are part of the Arawak* linguistic family. A riverine people, the Letuana are skilled canoemen and fishermen who live off the fish and river animals of the area. They also practice a slash-and-burn agriculture to raise manioc. Although they are gradually being integrated into the regional cash economy, the approximately 100 members of the Letuana tribe retain a sense of tribal identity. The Portuguese first reached Letuana territory in 1750; Roman Catholic missionaries entered the area by 1786. Around 1900, Colombian and Brazilian rubber-gatherers entered the area in large num-

bers, and the Letuana fled upstream on the rivers to avoid them. The rubber
boom declined in the 1930s but resumed again during World War II. Measles
and influenza decimated the Letuana, while the war economy integrated many
of them into the regional cash economy. Most Letuana began working seasonally
as migrant laborers to generate cash. Still, traditional religious and cultural values
still thrive among the Letuana.

REFERENCES: Christine Hugh-Jones, *From the Milk River: Spatial and Temporal
Processes in Northwest Amazonia*, 1979; Jean A. Jackson, *The Fish People: Linguistic
Exogamy and Tukanoan Identity in Northwest Amazonia*, 1983.

LETUARA. See LETUANA.

LICHAGOTEGODI. See KADUVEO.

LIMA. See QUECHUA.

LÍNGUA GERAL AMAZÔNICA. See NHEENGATÚ.

LIZARVA. See ACHAGUA.

LLAGUA. See YAGUA.

LLAWASH. See LAMA.

LOCOMO. See LOCONO.

LOCONO. The Locono (Lokono) are an Arawak*-speaking people who today
inhabit the coastal areas of eastern Venezuela, Guyana, Surinam, and French
Guiana. They are descended from the first Arawak people who migrated from
the Orinoco/Río Negro area before the arrival of Europeans. Today they number
approximately 10,000 people, although there are thousands of other people there
who have Arawak ancestry but are highly acculturated. The Locono occupy the
northern coast of South America from the Moruca River in Guyana to the
Brazilian-French Guiana boundary. Their population is growing, unlike those
of many other South American Indian tribes. The Locono, also known historically
as the Lokomo, are characterized by a matrilineal social structure. For several
generations, they have supplemented their traditional slash-and-burn economy
by selling fish and timber for cash or taking jobs as migrant laborers in the
regional economy. In the process, the Locono have become increasingly integrated into national political and economic life.

REFERENCES: Walter F. Edwards and Kenneth Gibson, "An Ethnohistory of Amerindians in Guyana," *Ethnohistory*, 26 (1979), 161–75; Kenneth Sugrim, *Some Historical
and Demographic Information on the Amerindians of Guyana*, 1977; Estéban Emilio
Mosonyi, "La revitalización lingüística y la realidad venezolano," *América Indígena*,
47 (1987), 553–61.

LOKONO. See LOCONO.

LONGO. The term "Longo" is used in Ecuador as a derogatory reference to Indian and even mestizo people who reside in highland areas.
    REFERENCE: Albert William Bork and Georg Maier, *Historical Dictionary of Ecuador*, 1973.

LORENZANO. See MOXO.

LORENZO. See AMUESHA.

LUGARE. See MATACO.

LUNA. See TUNEBO.

LUPACA. See AYMARA.

M

MA. See CINTA LARGA.

MACA. The Maca (Maka, Mak'a, Enimaga, Eni-maca, Ini-maca, Toothle, Towothli, Estabosle, Guentuse, Quentuse, and Cochaboth) are a Matacoan*-speaking people who once occupied a large area of the Gran Chaco in Argentina and Paraguay. Toba* and Pilagá* warriors drove them north into the upper Verde River area where further warfare with other Indian tribes and epidemic disease reduced their numbers. For an extended period in the late eighteenth and early nineteenth centuries, the Maca lived with the Lengua*; they separated from them in the mid–1800s. Until the Chaco War of the 1930s, the Maca maintained an aboriginal lifestyle, but that came to an end when large numbers of troops occupied their territory and brought with them diseases and acculturation pressures. Bolivian soldiers also killed large numbers of the Maca.

In recent years, hundreds of Maca have moved to a site across the river from the botanical gardens north of Asunción. Although they continue to hunt and fish, they also support themselves by selling paintings to tourists and sponsoring guided tours through their village. By the mid–1980s, Paraguayan officials estimated that there were perhaps 800 Maca in the Gran Chaco, most of whom were working as wage laborers on ranches in Laguna Guasu, Nanawa, and Cuatro Vientos in the department of Presidente Hayes and near Fray Bartolomé de las Casas near Asunción.

REFERENCES: José Antonio Gómez-Perasso, *Estudios Mak'a, cultura material*, 1977; Harriet Klein and Louisa Stark, "Indians of the Paraguayan Chaco," *Anthropological Linguistics*, 19 (1977), 378–402; David Maybury-Lewis and James Howe, *The Indian Peoples of Paraguay: Their Plight and Their Prospects*, 1980; John Renshaw, "Property, Resources and Equality among the Indians of the Paraguayan Chaco," *Man*, 23 (1988), 334–52.

MACAGUAJE. See SECOYA.

MACAGUANE. See MAKAGUANE.

MACANIPA. See OMÁGUA.

MACHICUY. See TOBĄ-MASKOY.

MACHIGANGA. See MACHIGUENGA.

MACHIGUENGA. The Machiguenga (Machiganga, Matsiganga, Matsigenka) Indians speak an Arawakan* language and live in the Upper Amazon basin of southeastern Peru, especially on the Misahua, Alto Urubamba, Camisea, Manu, and Alto Madre de Dios rivers. The Cogapacori (Kugapakori, Pucapacuri) are a subtribe of the Machiguenga. At the time of the Spanish conquest, they were known as the Manaries. They are closely related to the Amuesha,* Campa,* and Píro* Indians who also inhabit the montana of southeastern Peru.

The Machiguenga were first contacted by the Spanish in 1572; Jesuits began working with them in the seventeenth century. The Jesuits were expelled from South America in 1767, and in 1798 the Franciscans started mission work among the Machiguenga. They live as single families or in small hamlets along a stream providing clean water for household needs, near a river for fishing, and in close proximity to forests for hunting and planting gardens. Although the Machiguenga spend a great deal of time hunting and fishing, the bulk of their nutrition comes from their cultivated gardens, in which they raise sweet manioc as their staple, as well as maize, pineapples, yams, cotton, papaya, coffee, and cacao. Until recently, the Machiguenga preferred to do without trade goods in order to avoid contact with neo-Peruvian society, but in the 1970s and 1980s they adopted the shotgun and other technologies. The Peruvian public school has steadily enrolled more and more Machiguenga children in recent years. Still, only 2 percent of Machiguenga work time is spent earning money for trade goods; the rest is spent in the traditional activities of slash-and-burn agriculture, hunting, and fishing. The Machiguenga population by the mid–1980s was approximately 13,000 people.

REFERENCES: Allen Johnson, "Time Allocation in a Machiguenga Community," *Ethnology*, 14 (July 1975), 301–10; Allen Johnson, "Machiguenga Gardens," in Raymond B. Hames and William T. Vickers, eds., *Adaptive Responses of Native Amazonians*, 1983; William Keegan, "The Optimal Foraging Analysis of Horticultural Production," *American Anthropologist*, 88 (1986), 92–107.

MACHUI. See ARAONA.

MACHUVI. See ARAONA.

MACO. See MACOITA.

MACO. See PIAPOCO.

MACOAS. See MACOITA.

MACOITA. The Macoita (Macoas, Maco) are a subtribe of the Yukpa* Indians of northwestern Venezuela. They traditionally pursued a subsistence, horticultural lifestyle along the Apón River. Today the Macoita number approximately 300 people. See YUKPA.

MACONAGUA. See MAYORÚNA.

MACONI. See MAXAKALÍ.

MACÚ. See MAKÚ.

MACUNA. See MAKUNA.

MACUNÍ. See MAXAKALÍ.

MACURAP. See MAKURÁP.

MACUSARI. See JÍVARO.

MACUSHÍ. See MAKUSHÍ.

MACUSÍ. See MAKUSHÍ.

MACUSY. See MAKUSHÍ.

MADIJA. See KULÍNA.

MAHAMOMOWI. See GUAHIBO.

MAHIBAREZ. See NAMBIQUÁRA.

MAHINACU. See MEHINÁCU.

MAINA. See CANDOSHI.

MAINA. See MAYNA.

MAINGCÓNG. See YEKUANA.

MAINLAND CUNA. See CUNA.

MAINU. See JÍVARO.

MAIONGCÓNG. See YEKUANA.

MAIONGKING. See YEKUANA.

MAIONGKÓNG. See YEKUANA.

MAIONGÓNG. See YEKUANA.

MAIPUREAN. The term "Maipurean" refers to a large, complicated group of Amerindian languages that were part of the larger Arawakan* language group. On the eastern foothills of the Andes and spreading throughout western and central Brazil, eastern Ecuador, Colombia, Venezuela, Guyana, Surinam, and French Guiana, the enormous Maipurean group of Arawakan languages included the Moxo,* Baure,* Paiconeca, Paunaca,* Parana, Tereno,* Chane, Iñapari,* Ipurinã,* Kanamari,* Piro,* Chontaquiro, Cuniba, Cujisenayeri, Campa,* Machiguenga,* Nomatsiguenga,* Waraicu, Guajiro,* Paraujano,* Baré,* Wirina, Guinau, Maipure, Yabarána,* Anauya, Cariaya, Aráua, Manao, Yumana, Marawa, Piapoco,* Achagua,* Amarizina, Wainuma, Mariate, Pasé, Cayuishana, Cauyari, Yukuna,* Guarú, Arekena, Resigaro,* Izaneni, Ipeca, Hohodene, Carutana, Catapolitani, Moriwene, Mapanai, Maulieni, Waliperi-Dakenai, Baníwa,* Suisi, Tariana, Mehinácu,* Iaualapití,* Custenau, Waura,* Palikur,* Marawa, Yavitero, Parecí,* Saraveca,* Wapishána,* Shebayo, and Mandawaka.*
    REFERENCE: *Encyclopedia of Indians of the Americas*, 2 (1974), 226–27.

MAIPURIDJANA. See OKOMOYÁNA.

MAITSI. See YEKUANA.

MAJUBIM. See PARANAWAT.

MAJURUNA. See MAYORÚNA.

MAKA. See MACA.

MAK'A. See MACA.

MAKAGUANE. The Makaguane are a small tribe of Amerindians who live in the llanos of the intendency of Arauca in Colombia. They call themselves the Huitnu. Most of them are scattered in small settlements along the Colorado

River, a tributary of the Ele River. They are closely related historically to the Guahibo,* and some people consider them a subtribe of the Guahibo. Their language is part of the Guahibo group of languages. They were traditionally a semi-nomadic people who fished, hunted, and collected fruits, insects, and nuts. The first European interruption of Makaguane life began in the seventeenth century when Jesuit missionaries arrived to work among them. After the expulsion of the Jesuits in 1767, missionaries from the Capuchin order replaced them among the Makaguane. Large-scale mestizo settlement of Makaguane territory began in the 1930s, but the Makaguane were not terribly affected by it because of their homelands in the jungles. Indians living in the llanos, however, were devastated by the settlement.

Today the Makaguane practice a subsistence agriculture, raising plantains, maize, manioc, and sugar cane, as well as chickens and pigs. They supplement their protein needs by hunting. They generally wear Western clothing. Rates of intermarriage with mestizos and other Indians are rising rapidly. In the mid–1980s, the Makaguane population stood at nearly 500 people. Most of them live on government reservations where the Catholic Church maintains the elementary schools.

REFERENCES: Leah B. Ellis and Linda Criswell, eds., *Estudiemos las culturas indígenas de Colombia*, 1984; Blaz Telban, *Grupos Étnicos de Colombia: Etnografía y bibliografía*, 1987.

MAKIRITÁRE. See YEKUANA.

MAKÚ. The term "Maku" is a generic word widely used in southern Colombia when referring to "wild" Indians—the most isolated, least acculturated, nomadic Amerindians of the region. Even members of the various Eastern Tukanoan* tribes use the term in this fashion.

REFERENCE: Jean A. Jackson, *The Fish People: Linguistic Exogamy and Tukanoan Identity in Northwest Amazonia*, 1983.

MAKÚ. They Makú (Macú) are an Amerindian group of independent linguistic stock who today dwell in central northwest Amazonia, particularly at the headwaters of the Curicuriari River, the Makuparaná River, and the Tuyuka River in southeastern Colombia and in northwestern Brazil. They are also referred to as the Makunabodo. Scholars speculate that in ancient times the Makú had Tupi* origins, but that assumption is problematic at best. Unlike the surrounding Tukanoan* tribes who are sedentary, agricultural, and riverine, the Makú are an interfluvial foraging people who practice some agriculture but primarily stay on the move hunting and gathering food. There are several linguistic groups among the Makú: the Cacua (Kakwa, Kama, Cubeo Makú) who number approximately 300 people; the Júpda (Úbde, Tukano Maku, Húpda, or Húpdu) who number nearly 1,500 people; the Yohop (Yahup, Desana Makú) who total approximately 300 people; the Makú-Bará who are highly isolated and total perhaps 150 people; the Nadeb who total nearly 300 people; and the Guariba (Wariwa-Tapuya) who are fewer than 200 people. Over the years, the Makú have practiced a temporary assimilation with one of the horticultural tribes in the region, occupying a sub-servient position in the social structure and functioning as servants in return for food and protection. Today the Makú remain a relatively unacculturated group and number more than 2,700 people. The most isolated of the Makú live on the left bank of the Japura River between Pure and Cumpai and are known as Makú-Bravos (hostile Makú).

REFERENCES: Kaj Arhem, "The Makú, the Makuna, and the Guaina System: Trans-formation of Social Structure in Northern Lowland South America," *Ethnos*, 54 (1989), 5–22; Christine Hugh-Jones, *From the Milk River: Spatial and Temporal Processes in Northwest Amazonia*, 1979; Jean A. Jackson, *The Fish People: Linguistic Exogamy and Tukanoan Identity in Northwest Amazonia*, 1983; Robert Lee Spires, "As línguas faladas do Brasil, *América Indígena*, 47 (1987), 455–79.

MAKÚ-BARÁ. See MAKÚ.

MAKUNA. The Makuna (Buhagana, Buigana, Emoa, Masa, Macuna, Mak-unabodo, Poza, Wuhana, and Yauna) are a small group of Eastern Tukano*-speaking Amerindians who live in the Vaupés River drainage region of Colombia. They are particularly concentrated on the Comena River, a tributary of the Piraparana River, and along the Piraparaná and Apaporis rivers. There are seven subtribes of the Makuna: the Idemasa, Roeamasa, Emoamasa, Yebamasa, Umu-amasa, Suroamasa, and the Tabotirojejeamasa. There were sporadic European contacts with the Makuna in the eighteenth and nineteenth centuries. Portuguese missions were established temporarily along the upper Vaupés in the 1780s, but systematic evangelization of the tribe did not begin until 1914 when Roman Catholic priests established missions in the area. Anthropologists reached the Makuna early in the 1900s, and Protestant missionaries made their way into the region after World War II. The tribal economy focuses on the production of bitter manioc and fishing; hunting is quite secondary, although in recent years the tribe has become increasingly dependent on such European technologies as fishhooks, shotguns, and machetes, as well as on increased manioc production for sale. Contact with whites has also led to the development of small-scale animal husbandry, primarily hogs and poultry. In the 1960s and 1970s, the Colombian government began to encourage colonization of the Vaupés River basin, but settlement there has been very slow. The process of acculturation is accelerating among the Makuna, who today wear Western clothing and rely increasingly on Western technologies. There are approximately 500 Makuna today who acknowledge tribal membership and speak the native language.

REFERENCES: Kaj Arhem, *Makuna Social Organization: A Study in Descent, Al-liance and the Formation of Corporate Groups in the North-Western Amazon*, 1981; Gerardo Reichel-Dolmatoff, *Amazonian Cosmos: The Sexual and Religious Symbolism of the Tukano Indians*, 1985; Arthur P. Sorenson, Jr., "Multilingualism in the Northwest Amazon," *American Anthropologist*, 69 (1967), 670–84.

MAKUNABODO. See MAKÚ.

MAKURÁP. The Makuráp were a tribe of Tupi*-speaking Amerindians who once lived in the Guaporé drainage area of what is today the state of Rondônia, Brazil. They probably migrated into Rondônia from the east under the pressure of the Portuguese conquest. Neo-Brazilians caught up with them in the late nineteenth century when rubber collectors poured into the area and ravaged the various Indian tribes. The Makuráp adapted to the rubber collectors better than most tribes, setting themselves up as intermediaries between the neo-Brazilians and other tribes. For a while, Makuráp was the *lingua franca* of the area. They too, however, eventually succumbed to epidemic diseases. By the early twentieth century, their population had dropped below 100 because of violent death and disease; their numbers continued to decline. In the late 1950s, there were a few Makuráp living at Ribeirão on the Madeira-Mamoré railroad. Others can be found living at the Roman Catholic mission at Sagarana. Today there are a few elderly Makuráp full-bloods and mixed-bloods living on the Branco River in Rondônia who are acutely aware of their Makuráp heritage and another 200 more acculturated individuals with Makuráp roots.

REFERENCES: David Maybury-Lewis, *In the Path of the Polonoreste: Endangered Peoples of Western Brazil*, 1981; Robert Lee Spires, "As línguas faladas do Brasil," *América Indígena*, 47 (1987), 455–79; Theodore L. Stoddard, ed., *Indians of Brazil in the Twentieth Century*, 1967.

MAKUSHÍ. The Makushí (Makuxí, Macusy, Macusí, Makusí) are a tropical forest tribe of Amerindians living in the central Rupununi savannah north of the Kanuku Mountains and on the southern Pakaraimas in Guyana and southeastern Venezuela. A Karib*-language tribe, the Makushí originally lived along the Orinoco River. They are closely related to the Pemón Indians and were once a subtribe of theirs. They were first contacted by Europeans when Sir Walter Raleigh encountered them in 1595 during his search for the fabled El Dorado. Over the subsequent centuries, they migrated to Guyana, probably because they were fleeing the expansion of the Wapishána.* Today the Makushí are highly acculturated to neo-Guyanese values and material technology. They include approximately 15,000 people between the Ireng, Takutu, and Rupununi rivers on the Brazilian-Guyana border. Several thousand Makushí live in the savannas of the upper Branco River in Brazil. The source of their acculturation recently has been the adoption and spread of cattle raising among them, which has involved them in local marketing arrangements in the regional cash economy.

REFERENCES: W. Edwards and K. Gibson, "An Ethnohistory of Amerindians in Guyana," *Ethnohistory*, 26 (1979), 161–75; M. M. Holden, "Daily Routine of a Makushí Family," *Bulletin of the Amerindian Languages Project*, 2 (1978), 1–5; Andrew Sanders, *The Powerless People*, 1987; Robert Lee Spires, "As línguas faladas do Brasil," *América Indígena*, 47 (1987), 455–79; Kenneth Sugrim, *Some Historical and Demographic Information on the Amerindians of Guyana*, 1977.

MAKUXÍ. See MAKUSHÍ.

MALAYO. The Malayo (Sanja, Sanka) are descendents of a Chibchan*-speaking group of Amerindians who today live on isolated farms on the southeastern slopes of the Sierra Nevada de Santa Marta in northern Colombia. They call themselves the Wiwi. Over the centuries, they have resisted acculturation with European society, slowly migrating farther upriver to avoid contact. At the time of the conquest in the sixteenth century, the Malayo were a large group scattered throughout what are today the departments of Magdalena, northern Cesar, and La Guajira in Colombia. In 1587, Luis de Tapía first encountered the Malayo; Capuchin missionaries reached them in 1693. A sedentary, agricultural people, the Malayo were known for their peaceful ways and quickly adjusted to the Spanish empire, primarily by retreating upriver into the mountain ranges. Their population rapidly declined from disease and exploitation. The Malayo did not successfully resist acculturation; by the mid-nineteenth century their aboriginal language had been replaced by Spanish. Except for the adoption of such new plants as bananas, plantains, and sugar cane, the Malayo still practice a sub-sistence agriculture, with maize and manioc serving as dietary staples. Today there are approximately 7,000 people in Colombia who are descendents of the Malayo and still maintain their identity as Indians although they are detribalized. Approximately 800 Malayo Indians still understand the native dialect. They live primarily in the valleys of El Cerro, Cherua, Pozo de Humo, Guamaca, and the Barcino River in the Sierra Nevada de Santa Marta in northern Colombia.

REFERENCES: Leah B. Ellis and Linda Criswell, eds., *Estudiemos las culturas indígenas de Colombia*, 1984; Myriam Jiméno and Adolfo Triana Antorveza, *Estado y minorias étnicas en Colombia*, 1985; Gerardo Reichel-Dolmatoff, *Los Kogi: Una tribu de la Sierra Nevada de Santa Maria*, 1950; "Funerary Customs and Religious Symbolism Among the Kogi," in Patricia J. Lyon, ed., *Native South Americans: Ethnology of the Least Known Continent*, 1974.

MALBALA. See MATACO.

MALEKU. The Maleku are a thoroughly detribalized group of Amerindians living today in the north central reaches of Costa Rica, just south of the Nicaraguan border. At the time of the Spanish conquest, they covered a much larger area in northern Costa Rica, but disease and dislocation drastically reduced their numbers. Today they number under 200 people, and most are highly acculturated mixed bloods who speak Spanish as their primary language and are Roman Catholics.

REFERENCES: Melanie A. Counce and William V. Douglas, "Indians of Central America 1980s," *Cultural Survival Quarterly*, 13 (1989), 38–41.

MALUCHE. See AUCA.

MAM. The Mam are a large Mayan* tribe in Guatemala whose language is part of the larger Eastern Maya group. Today the Mam are located in the departments of Huehuetenango, Quezaltenango, and San Marcos, Guatemala, as well as in southern Mexico. Gonzalo de Alvarado conquered the Mam in 1525 after the tribe put up a fierce resistance. They experienced a rapid population decline in the sixteenth century, primarily because of disease. The Spaniards forcibly put as many Mam as possible into their mission *congregaciones*, while other Mam escaped into more remote areas of the highlands. The Mam population stabilized in the seventeenth century, and they continued to pursue a settled agricultural lifestyle based on the cultivation of maize and beans.

During the nineteenth century, the Mam found themselves assaulted from a different direction. Large-scale plantation agriculture, particularly the cultivation of coffee, appeared in Guatemala in the mid-nineteenth century, creating a new demand for agricultural labor. At the same time, government land policies were designed to convert Mayan communal lands into individual holdings. The combination of those two trends, which continued into the twentieth century, gradually transformed the Mam people into a poverty-stricken lower class of migrant workers and peasants with fewer than three acres of land each. After World War II, left-wing political movements promising a redistribution of land found a sympathetic audience among the Mam, triggering a series of bloody reprisals by conservative Guatemalan politicians interested in maintaining the status quo. Repression and murder became official policies to crush Mam insurgency during the 1970s and 1980s. In the process, large numbers of Mam fled Guatemala for the United States. In the mid–1980s, there were still approximately 650,000 Mam living in Guatemala, second in numbers only to the Quiché* Maya.

REFERENCES: J. L. Fried, *Guatemala in Rebellion: Unfinished History*, 1983; W. George Lovell, "Surviving Conquest: The Maya of Guatemala in Historical Perspective," *Latin American Research Review*, 23 (1988), 25–58.

MAMAINDÉ. The term "Mamaindé" is sometimes used in Brazil as a generic name to describe the Northern Nambiquára* Amerindians. See NAMBIQUÁRA.

MAMAINDÉ. The Mamaindé (Mamainé) are a small subtribe of the Northern Nambiquára* Indians of Brazil. They live today in an area bounded by the Cabixí River on the west and the north, the Pardo River on the south, and the Cuiaba-Porto Velho Highway on the east. They prefer to live in the open spaces of the savannah, with their villages located close to forested areas where they can hunt and fish. The Mamaindé have been contacted sporadically by neo-Brazilians, first by telegraph line construction workers in 1909 and then by rubber gatherers during World Wars I and II. The opening of the Cuiaba-Porto Velho Highway between 1960 and 1962 brought many neo-Brazilian settlers to the Mamaindé villages, triggering a rapid population decline. The Mamaindé have adopted neo-

Brazilian technology—guns, metal tools, mirrors, and clothing—but still maintain a sense of separation. The Mamaindé population had dropped below 50 people by the 1980s.

REFERENCES: Paul Leslie Aspelin, *External Articulation and Domestic Production: The Artifact Trade of the Mamainde of Northwestern Mato Grosso*, 1975; Paul Leslie Aspelin, "Food Distribution and Social Bonding among the Mamainde of Mato Grosso, Brazil," *Journal of Anthropological Research*, 35 (1979), 309–27.

MAMAINE. See MAMAINDÉ.

MAMBARÉ. See PARECÍ.

MAMBYUÁRA. See NAMBIQUÁRA.

MAMEAN. The term "Mamean" refers to a large linguistic group within the Mayan* system of languages. The Mamean languages are concentrated in southern Mexico and in the departments of Huehuetenango, Quezaltenango, Quiché, and San Marcos in Guatemala. The Mamean dialects include Mam,* Aguateca,* Ixil,* Jacalteco,* Kanjobal,* and Solomec.

REFERENCE: Richard E. Moore, *Historical Dictionary of Guatemala*, 1973.

MANAGUA. See CASHIBO.

MANAIRISU. The Manairisu are most likely a subtribe of the Nambiquára* Indians. They number fewer than 100 people and live west of Highway BR29, about 25 miles from the Bolivian-Brazilian border in the state of Rondônia in Brazil. See NAMBIQUÁRA.

MANAJÓ. see AMANAYÉ.

MANAMABOBO. See SHIPIBO.

MANANYÉ. See AMANAYÉ.

MANARIES. See MACHIGUENGA.

MANAURE. The Manaure are a subtribe of the Yuko* Indians of northeastern Colombia. They traditionally pursued a subsistence, horticultural lifestyle in the tropical forests. Today the Manaure total fewer than 50 people and are having difficulty in maintaining tribal cultural traditions. See YUKO.

MANAVA. See SHIPIBO.

MANAXÓ. See AMANAYÉ.

MANAYÉ. See AMANAYÉ.

MANAZEWA. See AMANAYÉ.

MANCHINERE. See MAXINÉRI.

MANDAHUACA. See MANDAWAKA.

MANDAWAKA. The Mandawaka (Mandahuaca) live on the upper Orinoco River in Venezuela and on the upper Cauabori River in the state of Amazonas in Brazil. Their language derives from the Arawakan* language group. Compared to most other Brazilian and Venezuelan tribes of Amerindians, the Mandawaka remain highly isolated, pursuing a semi-nomadic, subsistence lifestyle in which horticulture plays a secondary role to hunting and fishing. Except for their need for certain trade goods, such as metal tools and some clothing, the Mandawaka maintain a strong sense of tribal identity and an aboriginal lifestyle. There are fewer than 200 members of the tribe.

REFERENCES: Robert Lee Spires, "As línguas faladas do Brasil," *América Indígena*, 47 (1987), 455–79; Theodore L. Stoddard, ed., *Indians of Brazil in the Twentieth Century*, 1967.

MANDINGA. See CUNA.

MANETENÉRI. See MANITENÉRI.

MANETINÉRI. See MANITENÉRI.

MANGUE. The Mangue were an Indian tribe living between Lake Managua and the Pacific Coast of Central America at the time of the Spanish conquest. Small subtribes of the Mangue were the Nagrandans and the Dirians. Large numbers of the Mangue converted to Roman Catholicism in the 1520s and were left alone to continue farming their tribal land. Over the years, they melted into the larger Chorotega* community, becoming known as the Chorotega-Mangue. See CHOROTEGA.

MANÍBA. See BANÍWA.

MANICHENÉRI. See MANITENÉRI.

MANIENÉRI. See MANITENÉRI.

MANIPO. See ARAONA.

MANITENEIRI. See MANITENÉRI.

MANITENÉRI. The Manitenéri (Manetenéri, Manetinéri, Manienéri, Maniteneiri, Manitinéri, and Manicheneri) are a tribe of Arawakan*-speaking Amerindians who live in small scattered groups in the forests between the upper Iaco and Acre rivers in the state of Acre, Brazil. Their particular homeland is near the junction of the Brazilian-Bolivian-Peruvian borders. An interfluvial people, the Manitenéri generally avoid river life, preferring to gather food and hunt in the open forests between the rivers. In Peru, the Manitenéri are known as the Píro* Indians. In Peru and Brazil, the Manitenéri number approximately 530 people.

REFERENCES: Robert Lee Spires, "As línguas faladas do Brasil," *América Indígena*, 47 (1987), 455–79; Theodore L. Stoddard, ed., *Indians of Brazil in the Twentieth Century*, 1967.

MANITINÉRI. See MANITENÉRI.

MANIUK. See CHOROTÉ.

MANJUY. See CHOROTÉ.

MANOA. See PANOBO.

MANOITA. See SETEBO.

MANUA. See CAMPA.

MANUK. See CHOROTÉ.

MANUQUIARI. See TOYERI.

MANWORNE. See GALIBÍ.

MANWORNO. See GALIBÍ.

MAOPIDIAN. See MAPIDIAN.

MAOPITYAN. See MAPIDIAN.

MAPARINA. See AGUANO.

MAPÉ. See BARÍ.

MAPESHÁNA. See WAPISHÁNA.

MAPIDIAN. The Mapidian (Maopityan, Pidian, Moonpidenne) are a subtribe of the Wapishána*, an Arawakan*-speaking group of Amerindians. They remain today an isolated group of several hundred people. In the 1880s, they lived on the Brazilian slopes of the Acarai Mountains near the headwaters of the Curucuri River, but in the twentieth century they wandered to the Surinam border. Today they live between the headwaters of the Cafuini and Mapuera rivers in the northwest section of the state of Pará, Brazil. See WAPISHÁNA.

MAPOYO. The Mapoyo (Nepoyo, Cuacua, Yuhuana, Mpoyo, Mapollo), who call themselves the "Wanai," are a tiny Karib*-speaking tribe of Amerindians who live between the Paruaza, Suapure, Caripo, and Villacoa rivers, tributaries of the Orinoco River, in the north part of the state of Bolívar, Venezuela. An interfluvial people who were scattered in large numbers throughout the Venezuelan savannas, they have declined in population to the point of near-extinction today. Ethnohistorians suspect that the Mapoyo are descended from a now extinct group, the Quaqua. Approximately 50 years ago, the Mapoyo began intermarrying with local mestizos or with members of other Indian tribes; in the process, their own numbers declined rapidly. Some Mapoyo have also migrated to various Venezuelan towns and cities in search of work, and have also been lost to the tribe. There are only 115 members of the Mapoyo tribe who are aware of their aboriginal identity, and only 10 people, all of them aged, speak the tribal language. There is also a small group of people called the E'niepa who are a subtribe of the Mapoyo and still have a sense of subtribal identity, although their numbers no longer permit traditional ceremonial life. Most of the Mapoyo are today small, subsistence farmers who raise corn, beans, manioc, plantains, and rice; they also raise chickens and burros.
    REFERENCES: Walter Coppen, *Los aborígenes de Venezuela*, 1983; Ministerio de Estado para la Cultura, *Arte indígena de Venezuela*, 1983; Estéban Emilio Mosonyi, "La revitalización lingüística y la realidad Venezolana," *América Indígena*, 47 (1987), 653–61.

MAPUCHE. The Mapuche (Mapunche, Mupudungun), with more than 500,000 tribal members, is the largest Amerindian tribe in Chile and one of the largest tribes in all of North and South America. They are part of the Araucanian* Indians of Chile. The Mapuche have for centuries exhibited a powerful sense of tribal identity and a resiliency to external pressure. In the fifteenth century, the Incas tried and failed to subjugate the Mapuche. Pedro de Valdivia, the

Spanish *conquistadore*, established Santiago as a military outpost in 1540 and set out to conquer the Araucanians in general and the Mapuche in particular. At the time, the Mapuche were a settled, agricultural people. Valdivia succeeded quickly in conquering the Picunche, an Araucanian people north of the Mapuche, but when they proved too few in numbers to work the Spanish mines and ranches, Valdivia headed south of the Bío-Bío River and went after the Mapuche. The Mapuche proved to be more than a match for the Spaniards. For the next 250 years, they resisted Spanish penetration with the violence and hostility of true guerrilla fighters. Spain never did conquer the Mapuche, even though the crown invested millions in the effort. The Mapuche population, however, suffered from the wars and from European diseases, for which the Indians had no immunity.

After Chile achieved independence in 1818, the government worked to protect the Mapuche from further depredations while at the same time encouraging settlement in the frontier. It was an impossible dream. The government established a reservation policy in 1866, but in 1869–1870 the Mapuche launched a widespread rebellion against incoming mestizo settlers. They revolted again, on a much larger scale, in 1880. A new reservation system went into effect in 1884, and from that time until the 1920s the Mapuche relocated to them. Today the more than 500,000 Mapuche Indians live on 2,200 reservations between Concepción and Valdivia, Chile. Another 22,000 Mapuche live in the southwestern portion of Neuquén Province in Argentina where they fled to avoid the violence of neo-Chilenos; they are far more acculturated than the Mapuche of Chile. Finally, approximately 50,000 Mapuche work as laborers in such cities as Santiago, Valdivia, Concepción, and Temuco. The Mapuche still have a profound sense of tribal identity, even though the Spanish language, via the public school system, is gaining ground among the youngest generation.

REFERENCES: Louis C. Faron, *The Mapuche Indians of Chile*, 1986; Isabel Hernández, "Los pueblos y las lenguas aborígenes en la actualidad," *América Indígena*, 47 (1987), 409–23.

MAPUMARY. See ARAONA.

MAPUNCHE. See MAPUCHE.

MAQUIRITÁRE. See YEKUANA.

MARACA. The Maraca are a subtribe of the Yuko* Indians of northeastern Colombia. Traditionally they were a subsistence, horticultural people living along the Socorpas River. Today they number approximately 140 people. See YUKO.

MARACANO. See CAHUARANA.

MARACANO. See IQUITO.

MARACHÓ. See PIANOKOTÓ.

MARAHTXO. See PIANOKOTÓ.

MARAHUA. See MAYORÚNA.

MARAKANA. See KALIANA.

MARANI. See ARAONA.

MARASO. See PIANAKOTÓ.

MARAYO. See BORA.

MARIANA. See BORA.

MARINÁHUA. See SHARANÁHUA.

MARINÁWA. The Marináwa (Aguti, Marináhua) are a highly acculturated group of formerly Pano*-speaking Amerindians who today are scattered along the upper Envira River, a tributary of the Tarauaca River, in the state of Acre, Brazil, with some others on the Curanja and Purús rivers in eastern Peru. They are a primary division of the Sharanáhua. Because of the excellent water routes for transportation in the state of Acre, most of the tribe there, including the Marináwa, were devastated by the rubber boom of the late nineteenth and early twentieth centuries. See SHARANÁHUA.

MARIUSA. The Mariusa are a subtribe of the Warrau* who live between the Imataca River, the Macareo River, and the Manamo River of Guyana. See WARRAU.

MARKIRITÁRE. See YEKUANA.

MAROBA. See MARUBO.

MAROPA. See MARUBO.

MAROVA. See MARUBO.

MARU. See ARAONA.

MARUBA. See MARUBO.

MARUBO. The Marubo (Maroba, Maropa, Marova, and Maruba) are a relatively isolated tribe of Amerindians who are related to the Mayorúna* and speak a language that is part of the Panoan* family. They live in several closely related villages at the headwaters of the Itui and Curaca rivers in the state of Amazonas, Brazil. The Marubo land is approximately 100 miles east of the Peruvian border. Because of their extreme isolation, the Marubo had no permanent contact of any sustained kind with neo-Brazilians until the early twentieth century. They violently resisted rubber collectors and settlers well into the 1950s. The Marubo still pursue a subsistence, horticultural lifestyle revolving around the production of manioc and other crops, with hunting and fishing supplementing their diet. In recent years, they have developed a need for trade goods, requiring participation in the cash economy as laborers during seasonal periods. There are approximately 500 members of the Marubo tribe who, despite permanent contact now with neo-Brazilian society, maintain a powerful sense of tribal identity.

REFERENCES: Norman Elder, *This Thing of Darkness: Elder's Amazon Notebooks*, 1979; Robert Lee Spires, "As línguas faladas do Brasil," *América Indígena*, 47 (1987), 455–79; Theodore L. Stoddard, ed., *Indians of Brazil in the Twentieth Century*, 1967.

MASA. See MAKUNA.

MASACARA. See KAMAKÁN.

MASAKA. See AIKANÁ.

MASATIBU. See ARAONA.

MASCHONGKÓNG. See YEKUANA.

MASCO. The Masco (Mashco, Moeno) are a collective group of several Amerindian tribes who today live along the Los Amigos, Madre de Dios, and Inambari rivers in southeastern Peru, primarily in the departments of Cuzco and Madre de Dios. Their historic subtribes included the Amarakaeri,* Wachipaeiri,* Zapiteri, Careneri, Puquiri, Toyeri,* and Iñapari* (Iñamari). Although there were no doubt earlier contacts by Europeans, it was not until the nineteenth century that the Masco came into frequent contact with missionaries, explorers, and anthropologists. Like other tropical forest people, the Masco suffered dramatically from the early twentieth century rubber boom, and their population began a steady decline. Today the Masco are integrated into the regional economy, although most of them are subsistence farmers and wage laborers. They are becoming increasingly acculturated and detribalized.

REFERENCES: Mario Califano and Alicia Fernando Distel, "The Use of Hallucinogenous Plants among the Mashco" (Southeastern Amazonia, Peru), *Zeitschrift für Ethnologie*, 107 (1982), 129–52; S. Lyman Tyler, *Indians of South America*, 1976.

MASCOI. See TOBA-MASKOY.

MASCOIAN. The term "Mascoian" is used to refer to a small group of Amerindian languages that were concentrated in Paraguay at the time of the European conquest in the sixteenth century. The Mascoian languages included Angaite,* Kashika,* and Lengua.*

REFERENCE: Joseph H. Greenberg, *Language in the Americas*, 1987.

MASCOY. See TOBA-MASKOY.

MASHACALÍ. See MAXAKALÍ.

MASHCO. See MASCO.

MASHONGCÓNG. See YEKUANA.

MASHONGKÓNG. See YEKUANA.

MASKOY. See TOBA-MASKOY.

MASRODAWA. See YAMINÁWA.

MASRONHUA. See YAMINÁWA.

MASSACA. See HUARI.

MASSACARA. See KAMAKÁN.

MASTANAHUA. The Mastanahua (Mastanawa) are a group of Amerindians descended from Panoan*-speaking people and living in the region of eastern Peru drained by the Curanja River. They are a subgroup of the Sharanáhua*. Once a horticultural people who lived off the production of manioc, the Mastanahua remain a subsistence agricultural people, but they are now in permanent contact with the neo-Peruvian economy and work part-time and seasonally as laborers to raise cash for trade goods. See SHARANAHUA.

MASTANAWA. See MASTANAHUA.

MATACO. The Mataco Indians, also identified historically by the terms Chunupi, Guisnai, Guisnay, Lugare, Malbala, Matako, Mataguayo, Noctene, Ocoles, Vejos (Vejoz), Wejwos, and Hueshuos, are a tribe of the Gran Chaco living between the Bermejo and Pilcomayo rivers in northwestern Argentina, with several thousand living across the border in Bolivia and Paraguay. The Mataco were historically a hunting and foraging people who lived on fish and small game, although they adopted a light maize horticulture from the Andes tribes and infrequent manioc production from the Amazonian tribes. They were first contacted by Europeans in 1628, when they numbered more than 20,000 people, but they resisted acculturation. By the 1700s, however, thousands of Mataco were living either in Jesuit missions in the Gran Chaco or working as farm laborers, lumberjacks, ranch hands, or near slaves on sugar plantations. In the centuries since then, their numbers have declined and they have become increasingly acculturated, although there are still approximately 24,000 Mataco people living in the Gran Chaco who are aware of their tribal identity; there are also approximately 2,500 Mataco Indians living in the department of Tarija in Bolivia. Most Matacos earn their living by fishing and the sale of tribal articles, especially plaited straw items made out of an agave fiber they call "caraguata," to mestizo middlemen. Between May and October, most Matacos leave their villages and settle in temporary huts of straw along river banks where they can fish. They join in groups of up to 30 families for communal net fishing, and merchants come in refrigerated trucks to purchase the whole catch. There are also Mataco bands living an aboriginal, nomadic existence; several thousand other Mataco live at missions such as the Anglican Mission, La Paloma Evangelical Mission, the Chaco Mission, the Hickman Anglican Mission, and the Embarcación. To boost the prices they receive for the fish, the Matacos have recently considered establishing unions or cooperatives, but their efforts have not yielded success yet.

REFERENCES: Miguel Alberto Bartolomé, "Lamitología del contacto entre los Mataco: una respuesta simbólica al conflicto interétnico," *América Indígena*, 36 (1976), 517–57; Niels Fock, "Mataco Law," *Actas y Memorias, XXXII Congreso Internacional de Americanistas, España, 1964*, 3 (1966), 349–53; Isabel Hernández, "Los pueblos y las lenguas aborígenes en la actualidad," *América Indígena*, 47 (1987), 409–23; Pedro Plaza Martínez and Juan Carvajal Carvajal, *Etnías y lenguas de Bolivia*, 1985; Johannes Wilbert and Karin Simoneau, *Folk Literature of the Mataco Indians*, 1982.

MATACOAN. The term "Matacoan" is used to refer to a group of Amerindian languages. At the time of the Spanish conquest of the New World in the sixteenth century, the major Matacoan languages included Ashluslay,* Choroté,* Enimaga, and Maca in Paraguay, and Chorotí, Choropí, and Mataco* in Argentina.

REFERENCE: Joseph H. Greenberg, *Language in the Americas*, 1987.

MATAGALPA. See CACAOPERA.

MATAGUAYO. See MATACO.

MATAMBÚ. The Matambú are a thoroughly detribalized group of Amerindians living today in the north central reaches of Costa Rica, just south of the Nicaraguan border. At the time of the Spanish conquest, they covered a much larger area in northern Costa Rica, but disease and dislocation drastically reduced their numbers. Today they number under 400 people, and most of them are highly acculturated mixed bloods who speak Spanish as their primary language and are Roman Catholics.

REFERENCE: Melanie A. Counce and William V. Douglas, "Indians of Central America 1980s," *Cultural Survival Quarterly*, 13 (1989), 38–41.

MATAPI. The Matapi are a small group of Amerindians who live along the Río Miriti-Paraná in the Vaupés River drainage area of the territory of Amazonas, Colombia. Their language, which they no longer speak, was part of the larger Arawakan* linguistic family. The Matapi call themselves the Jupichiya. The Matapi are a riverine people known for their excellence as canoemen and river navigators. They make a living fishing and hunting river animals, as well as cultivating bitter manioc and a variety of other crops in tribal gardens. They remained almost completely isolated until neo-Colombian rubber gatherers penetrated their territory in the late nineteenth century, as did missionaries who brought Christianity and European diseases. During the Peruvian-Colombian War of 1933–1934, the Matapi sided with the Colombians and were devastated. Most Matapi men died of war and measles. The Yukuna* adopted their children, and the Matapi adopted the Yukuna language. Only a handful of the Matapi who remember their tribal heritage are still alive.

REFERENCES: Christine Hugh-Jones, *From the Milk River: Spatial and Temporal Processes in Northwest Amazonia*, 1979; Myriam Jiméno and Adolfo Triana Antorveza, *Estado y minorias étnicas en Colombia*, 1985; Pierre Yves-Jacopin, "On the Syntactic Structure of Myth, or the Yukuna Invention of Speech," *Cultural Anthropology*, 3 (1988), 131–59.

MATIPÚ. The Matipú (Matipuhy) Indians are an Amerindian tribe whose language is part of the larger Karib* group. When they were first discovered by anthropological expeditions in the 1880s and 1890s, the Matipú were a tropical forest tribe living between the Culiseu and Culuene Rivers in the upper Xingú river drainage area of the state of Mato Grosso, Brazil. The area was a main trade route, and the Matipú fell victim to European diseases even before the Europeans had arrived. The tribe suffered from the attacks of other tribes as well as influenza epidemics in the twentieth century. By the 1930s, their population had dropped below the point at which ceremonial life can be maintained, and the Matipú,* along with the Nafuquá,* moved in to live with larger Kuikúru* and Kalapalo* groups. Since the 1960s, they have found relative peace in the

Xingú Indian Park, where today they pursue a largely traditional lifestyle. There are fewer than 50 members of the tribe living there, and although they still speak their own Karib dialect, they share a great deal socially and culturally with other Xingú tribes, especially with their immediate neighbors, the Kalapalo and the Nafuquá (Nahukwá) with whom they now share their village.

REFERENCES: Orlando Villas Boas and Cláudio Villas Boas, *Xingú: The Indians, Their Myths*, 1973; Myriam Jiméno and Adolfo Triana Antorveza, *Estado y minorias étnicas de Colombia*, 1985; Robert Lee Spires, "As línguas faladas do Brasil," *América Indígena*, 47 (1987), 455–79.

MATIPUHY. See MATIPÚ.

MATIS. See MATSES.

MATIUHANA. See KARIÑA.

MATSES. The Matses (Matis) are a Panoan*-speaking tribe of Amerindians who today live on tributaries of the Yavari River along the border between Peru and Brazil. There are several hundred members of the tribe, most of whom live on the Peruvian side of the river. Extremely suspicious of neo-Peruvians and neo-Brazilians, the Matses did not accept peaceful contact with outsiders until the late 1970s. Although they have accepted trade goods and metal tools, they still pursue an aboriginal lifestyle and try to avoid unnecessary contacts. They practice a swidden horticulture revolving around the production of maize, manioc, and a variety of other crops. Although agriculture provides the bulk of their dietary needs, they invest great physical and cultural energy in hunting. Today the Matses number approximately 150 people.

REFERENCES: Steven Rolmanoff, "El uso de la tierra por los Matses," *Amazonia Peruana*, 1 (1976), 97–130; Steven Rolmanoff, "Women as Hunters Among the Matses of the Peruvian Amazon," *Human Ecology*, 11 (1983), 339–43; Robert Lee Spires, "As línguas faladas do Brasil," *América Indígena*, 47 (1987), 455–79.

MATSIGANGA. See MACHIGUENGA.

MATSIGENKA. See MACHIGUENGA.

MAUÉ. See MAWÉ.

MAUITZI. See YEKUANA.

MAURE. See BAURE.

MAUZUNA. See MAYORUNA.

MAWÉ. The Mawé (Maue, Andira, Arapium, Sateré, Sataré) are descendents of a Tupi*-speaking people who once occupied a broad stretch of territory bounded by the lower Tapajós, the Amazon, and the Uraria rivers in what are today the states of Pará and Amazonas, Brazil. Jesuit missionaries first contacted the Mawé in the 1690s, and, except for random acts of violence, there was peace between the Indians and neo-Brazilians in the seventeenth and eighteenth centuries. Early in the nineteenth century, the Carmelites established successful missions among the Mawé, and the Indians rapidly acculturated. Early in the 1900s, however, rubber collectors destroyed many of the Mawé settlements. Roman Catholic missionaries and then Seventh Day Adventist missionaries returned to the region in subsequent years, and the Mawé became even more integrated into neo-Brazilian society. Today there are approximately 3,000 Mawé Indians in an advanced state of acculturation living in villages along the Andira, Marau, Miriti, Maues-Acu, Mariaqua, Gurumatuba, Mamuru, Uaicurapa, and Arya rivers.

REFERENCES: Francisco M. Salzano et al., "Demography and Genetics of the Satere-Mawé and Their Bearing on the Differentiation of the Tupi Tribes of South America," *Journal of Human Evolution*, 14 (1985), 647–55; Robert Lee Spires, "As línguas faladas do Brasil," *América Indígena*, 47 (1987), 455–79.

MAXAKALÍ. The Maxakalí people are part of the larger Gê linguistic group that once included such Amerindian tribes as the Caposhó, Cumanashó, Monoshó (Atonaxó, Monaxó), Macuní, and Maxakalí (Mashacalí) proper. They originally lived near the borders of the states of Minas Gerais, Porto Seguro, and Bahia in Brazil, until the Botocudo* Indians drove them toward the coast. In the eighteenth century, the Maxacalí put up a violent resistance to neo-Brazilians moving onto their land, but their fears of the Botocudo were even greater. By the 1790s, some of the Maxacalí had come into permanent contact with Roman Catholic priests and were serving as allies of the Portuguese in fighting the Botocudo. The Maxakalí have been suspicious of contact with neo-Brazilians and have maintained a strong affinity for their tribal language; increasingly large numbers of them are bilingual, however. Today there are fewer than 500 members of the Maxakalí tribe. Although they are in permanent contact with the larger society, they live at government Indian posts—Mariano de Oliveira and Pradinho Indian Parks—outside the city of Machacalis in the state of Minas Gerais.

REFERENCES: Robert Lee Spires, "As línguas faladas do Brasil," *América Indígena*, 47 (1987), 455–79; Theodore L. Stoddard, ed., *Indians of Brazil in the Twentieth Century*, 1967.

MAXARÚNA. See MAYORÚNA.

MAXINÉRI. The Maxinéri (Manchinere) are a tribe of Arawakan*-speaking Amerindians who live in small scattered groups in the forests between the upper Iaço and Acre rivers in the state of Acre, Brazil. Their particular homeland is near the junction of the Brazilian-Bolivian-Peruvian borders. An interfluvial people, the Maxinéri generally avoid river life, preferring to gather food and hunt in the open forests between the rivers. In Peru, the Maxinéri, along with

nitenéri,* are known as the Píro* Indians. In Peru and Brazil, the Maxinéri
er approximately 345 people.
FERENCES: Robert Lee Spires, "As línguas faladas do Brasil," *América Indígena*,
4, (987), 455–79; Theodore L. Stoddard, ed., *Indians of Brazil in the Twentieth Century*,
1967.

MAXIRÓNA. See MAYORÚNA.

MAXUBÍ. See ARIKAPÚ.

MAXUKÍ. See ARIKAPÚ.

MAYA. The Mayan Indians had one of the great civilizations of Mesoamerica.
Highly influential throughout southern Mexico, Guatemala, Belize, El Salvador,
and Honduras, Mayan civilization declined inexplicably long before the arrival
of the Spanish conquistadors. Archeologists estimate that the peak of classic
Mayan civilization developed between A.D. 600 and 800—a period in which the
Maya developed sophisticated ideas concerning astronomy, sculpture, architec-
ture, and hieroglyphic writing. Mayan civilization was then centered in lowland
Yucatán and Guatemala. The collapse of this civilization occurred between A.D.
800 and 925, and the Indians relocated to the upper Yucatán peninsula. Today
a series of Mayan languages and tribes survive in southern Mexico, Guatemala,
Belize, and El Salvador. Linguists divide the Maya into four general groups:
Huastec, Yucatec, Western Maya, and Eastern Maya. Huastec includes the
Huastec and Chicomuceltec dialects. The Yucatec dialects are Yucatec, Lacan-
dón,* Itza, and Mopán.* The Western Maya group consists of Tzeltal, Chontal,*
Chol, Chortí,* Tzutujil, Tojolabal, Chuj,* Kanjobal,* Acateco,* Jacaltec,* and
Motozintlec. Finally, the Eastern Mayan dialects include Quiché,* Cakchiquel,*
Mam,* Teco, Aguateca,* Ixil,* Uspantec,* Sacapultec,* Sipacapense,* Po-
comám,* Pokomchí,* and Kekchí.*
REFERENCE: J.E.S. Thompson, *The Rise and Fall of Maya Civilization*, 1966.

MAYÁ. Not to be confused with the large groups of Mayan* Indians in Mexico
and Central America, the Mayá (Mayó, Mayú) are a Panoan*-speaking tribe of
Amerindians who are closely related to the Mayorúna.* The Mayá today total
approximately 100 people living on the Curuca River and on the Javarí River
in the state of Amazonas in far western Brazil. There are isolated Mayá across
the border in Peru, since the village on the Javarí River is right on the Peruvian-
Brazilian border. They were first contacted by the Spanish in 1790, but because
of the extreme geographical isolation of the region, the Maya did not have
sustained contact with neo-Brazilians and neo-Peruvians until the 1950s. They
remained a violent people toward settlers well into the 1970s, even forcing settlers
out of the area. In the 1980s, the Mayá remain one of the few Brazilian tribes
whose behavior toward settlers is quite unpredictable. They continue to pursue

a largely aboriginal lifestyle of subsistence manioc horticulture, hunting, and fishing.

REFERENCES: Robert Lee Spires, "As línguas faladas do Brasil," *América Indígena*, 47 (1987), 455–79; Theodore L. Stoddard, ed., *Indians of Brazil in the Twentieth Century*, 1967.

MAYA-MOPAN. See MOPAN.

MAYASQUERE. See COAIQUER.

MAYIRÚNA. See MAYORÚNA.

MAYNA. The Mayna (Maina, Rimachu) are the smallest, most isolated tribe of Amerindians who comprise the isolated Jívaro* linguistic family of the Ecuadorean and Peruvian montana. The Mayna are also the easternmost of the Jívaroan people, living east of the Pastaza River and just south of the Peruvian-Ecuadorean border in the forests at the foothills of the Andes Mountains. At the time of the Spanish conquest of Peru, the Incas were trying to subjugate the Jívaro tribes in general, an attempt that failed after a series of bloody confrontations. The Mayna put up a similar resistance to Spaniards, who came into their territory searching for placer gold. Until the middle of the nineteenth century, the Mayna had only limited and intermittent contact with the Spaniards, but they later increased their peaceful contact with neo-Ecuadoreans and neo-Peruvians in order to acquire trade goods, especially metal tools and manufactured cloth. During the first three decades of the twentieth century, except for missionary contacts by Roman Catholic Salesians, there was relatively little colonization of the area. A gold rush in the 1930s eventually brought more and more outsiders, precipitating violent confrontations. Under pressure from the Salesians, the Ecuadorean government established peaceful relations with the Mayna. During the last four decades, contact between the Mayna and the larger society has been characterized by relative peace and increasing acculturation. Still, the general isolation of the Mayna tribal territory has helped them to preserve their sense of tribal identity. The Mayna generally pursue a subsistence lifestyle revolving around the production of sweet manioc, maize, and a variety of other products in family gardens. The need for cash to buy trade goods is steadily increasing, forcing more Mayna to spend more time working as day laborers. At present, there are several hundred members of the Mayna tribe.

REFERENCE: Michael J. Harner, *The Jívaro: People of the Sacred Waterfalls*, 1973.

MAYÓ. See MAYÁ.

MAYONGGÓNG. See MAYONGÓNG.

MAYONGÓNG. The Mayongóng (Maingcóng, Maiongkíng, Maiongcóng, Maiongkóng, Maiongóng, Mayonggóng, Maschongcóng, Maschongkóng, Munangomo, Waiomgomo, and Yekuana*) are the Brazilian branch of the Karib*-

speaking Makiritáre people of southern Venezuela. Extremely isolated and still speaking their Karib dialect, the Mayongóng total approximately 200 people and live in a single village located on the upper Auaris River. See YEKUANA.

MAYORÚNA. The Mayorúna (Mayú, Maxurúna, Magirona, Majurúna, Mayirúna, Maxiróna, Mayuzúna, Barbudo, Dallus) are an indigenous people who live in the swamps and jungles in the state of Amazonas, Brazil, south of the Amazon River between the lower Ucayali and Jutahy rivers, on the upper Javari and upper Curuca rivers, and across the border in northeastern Peru, along the Yaquerana River and its tributaries. They speak a Panoan* language. The Mayorúna are an interfluvial people who generally avoided life on the major tributaries. Although they raise manioc today, they were originally a semi-nomadic tribe who subsisted by gathering palm fruits in the marshes and catching turtles. Jesuit missionaries reached the Mayorúna in the mid-seventeenth century and settled several hundred of them on missions. When the Jesuits were expelled from the New World in 1767, the Mayorúna returned to their semi-nomadic existence. In the nineteenth century, the Mayorúna suffered from enslavement at the hands of the Conibo* Indians. During the early 1970s, petroleum exploration companies entered Mayorúna land looking for oil, but their presence provoked few hostilities. The Peruvian government established a reservation for the Mayorúna between the Yaquerana and Galvez rivers in 1973. Today there are approximately 1,300 members of the Mayorúna tribe. More than 1,000 of them live on the Brazilian side of the border.

REFERENCES: Harriet Fields, *Parentesco Mayorúna (Pano)*, 1976; Darcy Ribeiro and Mary Ruth Wise, *Los grupos étnicos de la amazona peruana*, 1978; Gustavo Solís F., "Multilinguismo y extinciones de lenguas," *América Indígena*, 47 (1987), 630–45; Robert Lee Spires, "As línguas faladas do Brasil," *América Indígena*, 47 (1987), 455–79.

MAYÚ. See MAYÁ.

MAYÚ. See MAYORÚNA.

MAYUPI. See ARAONA.

MBAIA. See KADUVEO.

MBAYA. See KADUVEO.

MBAYE. See KADUVEO.

MBIA. See GUARANÍ.

MBIA. See KAIWÁ.

MBIA. See SIRIONÓ.

MBOYÓ. See MAPOYÓ.

MBUA. See KADUVEO.

MBYA. See KADUVEO.

MEAMUYNA. See BORA.

MEHINÁCU. The Mehinácu, sometimes called the Mahinácu, Mehináku, Meináco, or Mináco, are a small tropical forest tribe living on the left bank of the Culiseu River, a tributary near the headwaters of the Xingú River in central Brazil. The tribe speaks an Arawakan* language. The Mehinácu were not contacted by Europeans until surveying and anthropological expeditions made it up the Xingú River in the late nineteenth century. At that point, they suffered from the incoming European diseases, which drastically reduced the Mehinácu population. All of the Mehinácu live in a single village and total approximately 125 people dwelling in several households. In terms of residence, the Mehinácu live in extended family households. The society places a great value on those relationships. They fish and practice a slash-and-burn agriculture to produce their staple, manioc. Today the Mechinácu are protected by their residence in the Xingú Indian Park.

REFERENCES: Thomas A. Gregor, *Anxious Pleasures: The Sexual Lives of an Amazonian People*, 1985; "Exposure and Seclusion: A Study of Institutionalized Isolation Among the Mehináku Indians of Brazil," *Ethnology*, 9 (1970), 234–50; *Mehináku: The Drama of Daily Life in a Brazilian Indian Village*, 1977; "Publicity, Privacy, and Mehinácu Marriage," *Ethnology*, 13 (1974), 333–50.

MEHINÁKU. See MEHINÁCU.

MEHTA. See KARAPANÃ.

MEINÁCO. See MEHINÁCU.

MEKÉM. The Mekém traditionally lived in what is now the state of Rondônia, Brazil. Their language is part of the Mondé* linguistic family. A tropical forest people who lived off hunting and horticulture, the Mekém were decimated by the rubber boom of Rondônia in the early 1900s and again during World War II. The rubber collectors brought violence, disease, and forced labor to the Mekém people. Their population declined so drastically that they could no longer maintain traditional ceremonial life. Today there are approximately 40 people living in Rondônia who are aware of their Mekém heritage and understand the language, but the tribe is no longer a viable social unit.

REFERENCE: Robert Lee Spires, "As línguas faladas do Brasil," *América Indígena*, 47 (1987), 455–79.

MEKKA. See WITOTO.

MEKRANGNONTÍ. See MEKRANOTÍ.

MEKRANOTÍ. The Mekranotí (Menkrononty, Mekrangnontí, Menkranotíre, Mekronotíre) are a small tribe of Amerindians who speak a Gê* language and are part of the Northern Kayapó* culture group in Brazil. They split off from the original Kayapó village of Pykatoti in 1905 and moved west across the Xingú River to a region between the Jarina River and the middle Iriri River. Since then, there have been a number of divisions and recombinations of the Mekranotí. In 1953, the Mekranotí split with the Mentuktíre,* who moved into the Xingú Indian Reserve in the upper regions of the state of Mato Grosso, Brazil. The Mekranotí today number several hundred people and live in four locations: the Mekrangnotí Post on the Iriri River; the Bau Post on the Curua River, a western tributary of the Iriri River; the Kretíre Post in the northern part of the Xingú Indian Park; and the Jarina Post on the western bank of the Xingú River. These last two groups of Mekranotí have often been called the Txukaharamãe or Txukahama. Today they pursue a traditional lifestyle based on some agriculture and on hunting, fishing, and gathering. They are widely known for their extensive "treks" in which large portions of the village population travel extensively gathering food. Through the Brazilian Indian Foundation, the Mekranotí trade Brazil nuts and handicrafts for medicine, shotguns, metal tools, and ammunition. Only one or two members of the tribe speak Portuguese. They remain relatively unacculturated.

REFERENCES: Dennis Werner, "Fertility and Pacification Among the Mekranotí of Central Brazil," *Human Ecology*, 11 (1983), 227–45; Dennis Werner, "Paid Sex Specialists among the Mekranotí," *Journal of Anthropological Research*, 40 (1984), 394–405; Dennis Werner, "Are Some People More Equal than Others? Status Inequality among Mekranotí Indians of Central Brazil," *Journal of Anthropological Research*, 37 (1981), 360–73.

MEKRONONTY. See MEKRANOTI.

MEKRONOTÍRE. See MEKRANOTÍ.

MENEARO. See CAMPA.

MENECA. See WITOTO.

MENEKKA. See WITOTO.

MENGALA. In Guatemala, the term "Mengala" is used in derogatory fashion to refer to mestizos and ladinos who have learned a local Indian—usually Mayan*—dialect and who have chosen to live in heavily populated Indian regions, adopting Indian cultural habits in many instances.

REFERENCE: Richard E. Moore, *Historical Dictionary of Guatemala*, 1973.

MENIEN. See KAMAKÁN.

MENKRANOTÍRE. See MEKRANOTÍ.

MENTUKTÍRE. The Mentuktíre (Metuktíre, Metotíre, Metoctíre), also known as the Txukahamai (Txukahamãe, Txukahami, Txukarramãe, Shakahamai) are a Gê*-speaking, Northern Kayapó* tribe of Amerindians living along the Xingú River just below the Martius Falls on the border between the states of Pará and Mato Grosso, Brazil. They migrated into the upper Xingú River area late in the 1880s after Karl Von den Steinen's expedition to the area and immediately established themselves as the most aggressive and dominant group in the region. A hunting and foraging people who were only tangentially interested in agriculture, the Mentuktíre had heavy contact from neo-Brazilian settlers in the nineteenth century and then resisted rubber collectors in the early 1900s. They fiercely resisted contact until well into the 1950s; by that time they had earned a reputation for violence because of their attacks on cattle ranches on the Araguaia Plains and on other Indian tribes in the Xingú River drainage area. In 1953, the Mentuktíre, like so many other Northern Kayapó peoples, split off from the Mekranotí and assumed an independent identity. The government Indian service pacified the Mentuktíre in 1954 but they have remained isolated. Members of the Brazilian Indian Protection Service contacted the Mentuktíre in 1954. Today there are approximately 1,500 Mentuktíre Indians living in the Xingú Indian Park. They are divided into two groups who live very close to one another near the headwaters of a tributary of the Jarina River, approximately 25 miles from the left bank of the Xingú, just above the Von Martius Falls. They are still known to raid down the middle Xingú River, and Mentuktíre settlements include other Brazilians and Indians captured as children in tribal raids.

REFERENCES: Orlando Villas Boas and Cláudio Villas Boas, *Xingu: The Indians, Their Myths*, 1973; Robert Lee Spires, "As línguas faladas do Brasil," *América Indígena*, 47 (1987), 455–79; Theodore L. Stoddard, ed., *Indians of Brazil in the Twentieth Century*, 1967.

METOCTÍRE. See MENTUKTÍRE.

METOTÍRE. See MENTUKTÍRE.

METSAHAMOMOWI. See GUAHIBO.

METUKTÍRE. See MENTUKTÍRE.

MIAHAO. See KREEN-AKARÔRE.

MIAMUNAA. See BORA.

MIARRA. The Miarra are a little-known Amerindian tribe of tropical forest people who today live at the headwaters of the Arraias River, a tributary of the Maritsaua River in the Xingú Indian Park of upper Mato Grosso, Brazil. Extremely suspicious of all non-Miarra, Brazilians as well as other Indians, the Miarra have avoided all but the most accidental contact with other people. They remain in an aboriginal state. Their tribal population, no doubt, is quite small, probably fewer than 100 people.

REFERENCE: Orlando Villas Boas and Cláudio Villas Boas, *Xingú: The Indians, Their Myths*, 1973.

MINÁCU. See MEHINÁCU.

MIRAGUA. See MIRAÑA.

MIRAÑA. The Miraña (Mirania, Miraño, Miragua, Miranha, Miranya, Mirayo, Miraña-Carapana-Tapuyo) are a small group of Amerindians who today live along the lower Caquetá River in the territory of Amazonas in southeastern Colombia. They speak a Bora* dialect. The Miraña are a tropical forest group who raise manioc as their staple product and hunt and fish to supplement their diets. In recent decades, they have adopted European hunting and fishing technologies, but they have resisted assimilation. Their tribal history is closely associated with that of the Bora Indians. The Miraña population today is between 100 and 200 people.

REFERENCE: Leah H. Ellis and Linda Criswell, eds., *Estudiemos las culturas indígenas de Colombia*, 1984.

MIRAÑA-CARAPANA-TAPUYO. See MIRAÑA.

MIRANHA. See MIRAÑA.

MIRANIA. See MIRAÑA.

MIRANO. See MIRAÑA.

MIRANYA. See MIRAÑA.

MIRAYO. See MIRAÑA.

MIRITI. See MIRITI-TAPUYA.

MIRITI-TAPUYA. The Miriti-Tapuya are an Eastern Tukano* language group of Amerindians living along the Papuri and Tikié rivers in the Vaupés River drainage area of Colombia. There were sporadic European contacts with the Miriti* in the eighteenth and nineteenth centuries. Portuguese missions were established temporarily along the upper Vaupés in the 1780s, but systematic evangelization of the tribe did not begin until 1914 when Roman Catholic priests established missions on the Papuri River. Theodor Koch-Grünberg began ethnological studies of the Miriti-Tapuya at the same time. Protestant missionaries made their way into the region after World War II, eventually making nominal converts of a minority of Miriti-Tapuya. The tribal economy focuses on the production of bitter manioc and fishing; hunting is quite secondary, although in recent years the tribe has become increasingly dependent on such European technology as fishhooks, shotguns, and machetes, as well as increased manioc production for sale. Contact with whites has also led to the development of small-scale animal husbandry, primarily hogs and poultry.

In the 1960s and 1970s, the Colombian government began to encourage colonization of the Vaupés River basin, but settlement there has been very slow. The Miriti-Tapuya interact with other Indian tribes in the area but less often with whites, except for missionaries and rubber collectors, because of the extreme geographical isolation of the area. There are several hundred Miriti-Tapuya today who acknowledge tribal membership and speak the native language.

REFERENCE: Gerardo Reichel-Dolmatoff, *Amazonian Cosmos: The Sexual and Religious Symbolism of the Tukano Indians*, 1985.

MISHARA. See YAGUA.

MISKITO. The Miskito Indians, also known historically as the Moscos, Mosquitos, Moustiquais, and Moustiques, live in the coastal Caribbean lowlands of Central America, from Belize to northern Nicaragua. Today they total more than 100,000 people and still make their living from subsistence agriculture, hunting, and fishing; increasing numbers of them are migrant laborers in order to earn a small cash income. In terms of religion, large numbers of the Miskitos are Protestants because of the efforts of German Moravian missionaries in the seventeenth and eighteenth centuries and the influence of the British. Great Britain controlled British Honduras (Belize) as a colony and in 1687 established a Protectorate of Mosquitia over the Indians in Nicaragua. It was not until 1896 that sovereignty over that area was given to Nicaragua. In the 1980s, the Miskito experienced considerable discrimination from the Sandinista government in Nicaragua, and approximately 15,000 of them fled to Honduras; today approximately 25,000 Miskito Indians live in Honduras. The largest group is still in Nicaragua. The Miskito are subsistence farmers who raise bananas, yams, rice, corn, beans, cotton, and sugar cane. To earn cash for purchases of gunpowder, salt, and tobacco, the Miskito extract the sap of wild rubber trees and trap fur animals. They also work as laborers for fruit companies, mahogany timber operations, and gold mines. Since the 1979 Sandinista Revolution in Nicaragua, the government has worked to incorporate the Miskito region, politically and economically, into the larger society. The Miskito have perceived a loss of independence in the process and have resisted the government programs. Thousands of Miskito refugees have crossed the border out of Nicaragua to escape government persecution.

REFERENCES: David Dodds, "Miskito and Sumo Refugees: Caught in Conflict in Honduras," *Cultural Survival Quarterly*, 13 (1989), 3–5; Mary W. Helms, *Asang: Ad-*

aptations to Culture Contact in a Miskito Community, 1971; Barbara Nietschmann, *Between Land and Water: The Subsistence Ecology of the Miskito Indians*, 1973; L. Fernando Cruz Sandoval, "Los indios de Honduras y la situación de sus recursos naturales," *América Indígena*, 44 (1984), 423–46.

MITUA. See GUAYABERO.

MOCHDA. See KARAPANÃ.

MOCOBÍ. See MOCOVÍ.

MOCOVÍ. The Mocoví, also known historically as the Mocobí, Mosobiae, Mogosnae, Amokebit, and Frentones, and to themselves as the Mokoit, are a society of Guaicuruan-speaking people who occupy a large section of the southern Gran Chaco in Argentina. They live in the departments of O'Higgins, Chacabuco, Fontana, and San Lorenzo in the province of Chaco and in the departments of Garay, Obligado, San Javier, San Justo, and Vera in the province of Santa Fe. At the time of the Spanish conquest, the Mocoví occupied the area of the middle Bermejo River, but they gradually migrated to the southeast. In the early eighteenth century, most of the Mocoví tribe was gathered into Franciscan and Jesuit missions where the missionaries tried to transform the equestrian, hunting people into settled farmers. The acculturation process began then and has continued today. Mocoví settlements today interact constantly with the surrounding mestizo society. Most of the Indians work as farmers, lumberjacks, sawmill laborers, ranch hands, migrant pickers, domestics, and day laborers. Only about 1,500 of the 10,000 Mocoví alive today still speak the Indian language. Most of them use Spanish as their primary language and are in a state of rapid acculturation.

REFERENCES: Isabel Hernández, "Los pueblos y las lenguas aborígenes en la actualidad," *América Indígena*, 47 (1987), 409–23; Johannes Wilbert and Karin Simoneau, *Folk Literature of the Mocovi Indians*, 1988.

MOENO. See MASCO.

MOGOSNAE. See MOCOVÍ.

MOGUEX. See GAMBIANO.

MOHINO. See ESSEJJA.

MOJENO. See BAURE.

MOJO. See MOXO.

MOKOIT. See MOCOVÍ.

MOLUCHE. See AUCA.

MONAXÓ. See MAXAKALÍ.

MONCOCA. The Moncoca (Monkoka, Chiquito) are a group of Amerindians whose language is part of the larger Chiquito family. They live today in southeastern Bolivia, primarily in the department of Santa Cruz in the province of

Ñuflo de Chávez. They were first contacted by Europeans in 1542 when Domingo Martínez de Irala ascended the Paraguay River. They were conquered between 1557 and 1560 by Ñuflo de Chávez. Late in the 1500s, many of the Moncoca fled Spanish missions and returned to a foraging lifestyle, raiding Spanish settlements frequently. Beginning in the late seventeenth century, Portuguese slavers from Brazil decimated the Moncoca people. Only the defensive resistance of Jesuit priests stopped the slavers from completely destroying the Moncoca. Most of the Moncoca stayed in Jesuit missions until 1767 when the Jesuits were expelled from South America. After that, many Moncoca retreated to an aboriginal lifestyle of hunting and foraging, as well as the cultivation of sweet manioc. Portuguese slavers continued to attack the Moncoca in the 1800s, and the tribal population declined. It did not begin to recover until the twentieth century. Today there are approximately 18,000 Moncoca Indians in Bolivia. They maintain a strong sense of tribal identity, and many still speak the aboriginal language, although most are fluent in Spanish. They make a living through subsistence agricultural, livestock, and seasonal labor.

REFERENCES: Pedro Plaza Martínez and Juan Carvajal Carvajal, *Etnías y lenguas de Bolivia*, 1985; Graciela Zolezzi and J. Riester, "Lenguas indígenas del oriente boliviano clasificación preliminar," *América Indígena*, 47 (1987), 425–33.

MONDÉ. The term "Mondé" refers to a linguistic family within the larger Tupi* group. Included in the Mondé family are the Aruá,* Cinta Larga,* Gavião* (Ikõrõ, Digút), Mekém,* Mondé proper (Sanamaikã, Salamãi), Suruí* (Paitér), and Zoró.* These are located in Western Brazil, primarily in the states of Rondônia and Mato Grosso.

REFERENCE: Robert Lee Spires, "As línguas faladas do Brasil," *América Indígena*, 47 (1987), 455–79.

MONDÉ. The Mondé (Sanamaikã, Salamãi) are today a nearly extinct tribe of Tupi*-speaking Amerindians who once lived in the state of Rondônia, Brazil, primarily along the right bank of the Pimenta Bueno River. A riverine people who also planted manioc gardens, the Mondé were first reached by neo-Brazilians in the 1730s when gold prospectors by the thousands flooded their territory. A malaria epidemic devastated the Mondé in the 1750s. The gold prospectors were gone by the 1800s and relative peace returned to the area, but the tribe was decimated by neo-Brazilian rubber collectors in the early twentieth century. The Mondé population decline was never arrested. Surviving Mondé were gathered together by the Indian Protection Service in 1940 and placed on a post on the Igarape Cascata River. Measles and flu epidemics in the 1940s and 1950s drove the survivors back into the forests. During the late 1950s and early 1960s, a group of Mondé were found living at Ribeirão near the Madeira-Mamoré railroad. Today there are a few Mondé Indians living with the Pakaanóva* tribe at the Post Lage and another group along Highway 364 near Porto Velho. Today there are still a few isolated individuals who are aware of their Mondé ancestry, but the tribe no longer functions as a social unit.

REFERENCES: David Maybury-Lewis, *In the Path of the Polonoreste: Endangered Peoples of Western Brazil*, 1981; Robert Lee Spires, "As línguas faladas do Brasil," *América Indígena*, 47 (1987), 455–79; Theodore L. Stoddard, ed., *Indians of Brazil in the Twentieth Century*, 1967.

MONICHI. See MUNICHE.

MONKOKA. See MONCOCA.

MONOSHÓ. See MAXAKALÍ.

MOPAN. The Mopan, or Mopanero, are a Yucatec Mayan* people. At the time of the Spanish conquest, the Mopan were living in Mexico. The conquest dramatically reduced the Mopan population, and they became a small community. During the heavy taxes, forced labor, and military unrest of the Caste War in Mexico between 1847 and 1853, the Mopan fled Mexico in favor of west central Guatemala and the western Cayo district of Belize. Military repression in Guatemala after World War II caused more Mopan to flee Guatemala for Belize. By the 1980s, there were approximately 10,000 Mopan people equally divided between Guatemala and Belize. Because of their proximity to the much larger Mayan Kekchí* tribe, however, many of the Mopan are becoming bilingual, speaking Kekchí as well as their own aboriginal language.

REFERENCES: William V. Davidson, "The Amerindians of Belize, An Overview," *América Indígena*, 47 (1987), 9–22; W. George Lovell, "Surviving Conquest: The Maya of Guatemala in Historical Perspective," *Latin American Research Review*, 23 (1988), 25–58; J. Eric Thompson, *The Maya of Belize*, 1977; Gloria Tujab, "Lenguas indígenas que se encuentran en vias de extinción," *América Indígena*, 47 (1987), 529–33; D.A.G. Waddell, *British Honduras: A Historical and Contemporary Survey*, 1981.

MOPANERO. See MOPAN.

MORÉ. The Moré (Itén, Iténez) are a small group of Txapakuran*-speaking people. Originally they lived in the large triangle between the Mamoré and Guaporé rivers and the Machupo and Itonama rivers. In the early 1700s, the Moré population exceeded 3,000 people, but epidemic disease came to them from eighteenth-century gold prospectors and slavers and early twentieth-century rubber collectors. By the nineteenth century, some of the Moré had moved across the Guaporé River from Bolivia to Brazil. They are a tropical forest people who practice manioc horticulture. The Moré farmers also raise maize, cotton, and plantains. Today the Moré verge on extinction. Many of them live under the protective care of ranchers between the Mamoré and Iténez rivers in the department of El Beni in Bolivia. They probably number no more than 150 people.

REFERENCES: Brian M. Boom, *Ethnobotany of the Chácobo Indians, Beni, Bolivia*, 1987; Harold Key and Mary Key, *Bolivian Indian Tribes: Classification, Bibliography, and Map of Present Language Distribution*, 1967; Pedro Plaza Martínez and Juan Carvajal

Carvajal, *Etnías y lenguas de Bolivia*, 1985; Graciela Zolezzi and J. Riester, "Lenguas indígenas del oriente boliviano clasificación preliminar," *América Indígena*, 47 (1987), 425–33.

MORENO. In Guatemala, the term "Moreno" is used to refer to "Black Karibs" or Garífuna* people who inhabit the coastal regions. See GARIFUNA.

MOREREBI. The Morerebi are a small and isolated group of Amerindians living on the Preto River near the border of the states of Amazonas and Rondônia in Brazil. The Preto River is an upper tributary of the Marmelos River. Although the Morerebi people have declined in population because of imported diseases, their geographical isolation has kept them from a great deal of contact with neo-Brazilians. The Morerebi population has slipped below 100 people but they manage to maintain a sense of tribal integrity and aboriginal values.

REFERENCE: Theodore L. Stoddard, ed., *Indians of Brazil in the Twentieth Century*, 1967.

MORO. See AYOREO.

MOROTOCO. See AYOREO.

MORUBA. See MAYORÚNA.

MORUNAHUA. The Morunahua are a Panoan*-speaking group of Amerindians whose homeland is along the Embira River in the Peruvian Amazon. The Kaxináwa* Indians, as well as several other groups, often referred to them as the Nishinahua. They have also been referred to as the Paconahua. Several neighboring Panoan people like the Yamináwa* understand the Morunahua language. The Morunahua are a semi-nomadic, extremely isolated people whose economy revolves around hunting, fishing, foraging, and some horticulture. Little is known about them in the anthropological literature, but neighboring tribes indicate that they have adopted European metal technologies. The Morunahua population is estimated at approximately 150 people.

REFERENCE: Darcy Ribeiro and Mary Ruth Wise, *Los grupos étnicos de la amazona peruana*, 1978.

MOSCA. See CHIBCHA.

MOSCO. See MISKITO.

MOSETEN. See CHIMANE.

MOSOBIAE. See MOCOVÍ.

MOSQUITO. See MISKITO.

MOTEREQUOA. See PAUSERNA.

MOTILONES. The term "Motilones" (Dzubukua, Djobokubi, Mapes) was first used in the seventeenth century by European explorers to describe the Amerindians living in the area west of Lake Maracaibo in Colombia and Venezuela. Generally the term was used indiscriminately to refer to all Indians who wore a cropped hairstyle. Although the term is still used somewhat indiscriminately, it is usually employed when referring to the Barí.

REFERENCE: Myriam Jiméno and Adolfo Triana Antorveza, *Estado y minorias étnicas en Colombia*, 1985.

MOUSTIQUAIS. See MISKITO.

MOUSTIQUES. See MISKITO.

MOVÉ. See GUAYMÍ.

MOVIMA. The Movima (Movina) are a small group of Amerindians who are part of an isolated language family. They live in dispersed, multifamily settlements on the left bank of the Yacuma River in the department of El Beni in Bolivia and along the lower Rapula River, the Matos River, and the Apere River. Today their tribal numbers are declining rapidly because of the process of assimilation and acculturation. Aboriginal ceremonies have disappeared. Although some scholars have estimated the Movima population to be around 10,000 people, most ethnologists would put the number closer to 2,000. The Movima no longer speak their aboriginal language; they make their living as subsistence farmers and as peons and cowboys on cattle ranches. Many of them still work as oarsmen and tappers in the rubber forests. The local economy has all but reduced them to a state of servitude. From outside appearances, their lifestyle is no different from that of non-Indian mestizos living near them. Still, the Movima know of their Indian heritage.

REFERENCES: Brian M. Book, *Ethnobotany of the Chácobo Indians, Beni, Bolivia*, 1987; Harold Key and Mary Key, *Bolivian Indian Tribes: Classification, Bibliography, and Map of Present Language Distribution*, 1967; Pedro Plaza Martínez and Juan Carvajal Carvajal, *Etnías y lenguas de Bolivia*, 1985; Jürgen Riester, *Indians of Eastern Bolivia: Aspects of Their Present Situation*, 1975; Graciela Zolezzi and J. Riester, "Lenguas indígenas del oriente boliviano clasificación preliminar," *América Indígena*, 47 (1987), 425–33.

MOVINA. See MOVIMA.

MOXO. The Moxo (Mojo) are an Arawakan*-speaking group of Amerindians who today live in the department of El Beni in Bolivia. The most important Moxo villages are Trinidad, San Ignacio, San Lorenzo, and San Loreto, but the Moxo can be found scattered throughout the lowlands of Beni because of the forced labor systems imposed during the rubber boom between 1880 and 1945. The Moxo were first reached by the Spanish in 1580. Spanish attempts to conquer them failed in 1617 and 1624, but Jesuit missionaries established peaceful contact with them in the late 1660s. Jesuit missions among the Moxo were established at Loreto in 1684, Trinidad in 1687, and San Ignacio in 1689. By 1715, there were 15 Moxo missions. When the Jesuits were expelled in 1767, the Moxo fell victim to unscrupulous civil administrators and slavers, and, in the late nineteenth century, to rubber collectors. During the rubber boom, the Moxos were forced to work in the forests of the department of Pando, gathering rubber as peons and servants or working as oarsmen transporting the rubber to Riberalta, Mato Grosso, and Guajaraminim. Their population declined rapidly. Many of the Moxo Indians joined the Lomo Santa religion, a messianic faith that developed a strong resentment toward neo-Bolivian society and frequently bordered on military resistance to exploitation. The Moxos' wanderings did not really end until the early 1950s, when they settled into permanent residences. Today there are approximately 17,000 Moxo, half of them known as Ignacios (Ignacianos, Zamucos) or Lorenzanos and the other half as Trinitarios because of their departmental residences. They are an acculturated people who work as farmers, herdsmen, or laborers. Most are bilingual and retain a strong sense of ethnic identity. About 90 percent of Moxo farm products—manioc, bananas, and maize—are produced for subsistence.

REFERENCES: Brian M. Boom, *Ethnobotany of the Chácobo Indians, Beni, Bolivia*, 1987; Harold Key and Mary Key, *Bolivian Indian Tribes: Classification, Bibliography, and Map of Present Language Distribution*, 1967; Pedro Plaza Martínez and Juan Carvajal Carvajal, *Etnías y lenguas de Bolivia*, 1985; Jürgen Riester, *Indians of Eastern Bolivia: Aspects of Their Present Situation*, 1975; Graciela Zolezzi and J. Riester, "Lenguas indígenas del oriente boliviano clasificación preliminar," *América Indígena*, 47 (1987), 425–33.

MOYANA. See ARAONA.

MUCHIMO. See MUNICHE.

MUDJETÍRE. See SURUÍ.

MUENANE. See MUINANE.

MUINANE. See WITOTO.

MUINANE. The Muinane, or Bora-Muinane, are a small tribe of Amerindians whose language is of the Bora* linguistic family. They should not be confused with another group of people called the Bora who are actually a subgroup of the Witoto* tribe. Their homeland today is near the headwaters of the Cahuinari River near Araracuara in the territory of Amazonas in southern Colombia. They were first contacted by Europeans in the early seventeenth century, but sustained contact did not come until the late nineteenth century. Although hunting and fishing consume a great deal of their time and hold great symbolic importance in Muinane culture, most of the tribe's nutrients come from the manioc, maize, sweet potatoes, plantains, and bananas they raise in tribal gardens. Until the end of the nineteenth century, the Muinane were a large tribe numbering several thousand people, but the wild rubber boom of the 1890s and early 1900s devastated them, bringing thousands of neo-Colombians and their diseases into Muinane territory and drastically reducing their population. The Muinane were dislocated and moved, the vast majority dying from disease or being assimilated into neo-Colombian society. Their numbers today are approximately 160 people, of whom 125 live on a government Indian reservation at Nunuya de Villazul in the Colombian Amazon. Another 40 or so live across the border in Peru.

REFERENCES: Darcy Ribeiro and Mary Ruth Wise, *Los grupos etnicos de la Amazona Peruana*, 1978; Blaz Telban, *Grupos étnicos de Colombia: Etnografía y bibliografía*, 1988.

MUISCA. See CHIBCHA.

MUJETÍRE. See SURUÍ.

MUNANGÓNE. See MAYONGÓNG.

MUNDÉ. See AIKANÁ.

MUNDRUCÚ. See MUNDURUKÚ.

MUNDURUCÚ. See MUNDURUKÚ.

MUNDURUKÚ. The Mundurukú are a Tupi*-speaking language group of Amerindians who today live in the region east of the upper Tapajós River. Their population totals approximately 1,500 people, scattered in small villages along the Tapajós and Cururu rivers, at the Roman Catholic mission on the Cururu River, at the Mundurukú Post of the Brazilian Indian Protection Service, and in traditional villages between the headwaters of the Cururu and Tropas rivers. The Mundurukú have been known historically as Mundurucú, Mundruca, Moturicú, Weidyenye (their name for themselves), and Wiaunyen. Brazilians have also called them the Cara Pretas and Paikise (Paiquize, Paikyce). They first came to the attention of Europeans in 1770 when they began a series of widespread attacks on Brazilian settlements along the Amazon River. The Portuguese pacified the Mundurukú in the 1790s and then used the tribe extensively in their attacks on other Indian groups. By the mid-nineteenth century, the Mundurukú of the lower Tapajós River were busy collecting rubber and selling it for Brazilian goods, becoming completely integrated into the regional cash economy. Assimilation soon followed. By 1900, they had largely disappeared into the local mestizo society, wholeheartedly embracing the Roman Catholic religion. The Mundurukú on the Madeira River still maintained a separate identity but had largely lost the use of the tribal language. A closely related tribe to the Mundurukú are the Kuruáya,* who today number only about 50 people. Only the Mundurukú of the upper Tapajós River valley have maintained the tribal identity as well as the tribal language, although today they are surrounded by the larger Brazilian society as well as by Catholic and Protestant missionaries. Since the 1950s, the Mundurukú economy has changed from a trade economy in wild rubber using a barter-credit system to a cash economy with individual status increasingly being determined by personal wealth.

REFERENCES: S. Brian Burkhalter and Robert F. Murphy, "Tappers and Sappers: Rubber, Gold, and Money Among the Mundurukú," *American Ethnologist*, 16 (1989), 100–17; Robert F. Murphy, *Headhunters Heritage: Social and Economic Change Among the Mundurucú Indians*, 1960; Yolanda Murphy and Robert F. Murphy, *Women of the Forest*, 1974; Robert Lee Spires, "As línguas faladas do Brasil," *América Indígena*, 47 (1987), 455–79.

MUNICHE. The Muniche (Munichi, Otanave, Otanabe, Munitsche, Munichino) originally lived between the Marahon and Huallagua rivers in the Amazonian jungles of north central Peru. Although scholars still disagree, they suspect that Muniche is a Tukano* language. The Muniche call themselves the Monichi. Jesuit missionaries reached them in the 1640s but the Muniche fled, afraid that the church was giving their names to *encomenderos*. The two major subgroups of the Muniche are the Churitana and the Muchimo. Late in the seventeenth century, they relocated to what is today Munichis on the Paranapura River. The Muniche population steadily declined over the next several decades, falling to only 150 people in 1737. It had recovered to nearly 1,000 people by the late nineteenth century when the rubber boom brought more diseases, death, and dislocation. By the 1920s, their numbers had declined to only 200 people. Today there are only 10 people who still understand the aboriginal language. The others speak Quechua instead of Muniche and are completely integrated into the larger society. The aboriginal language is in danger of rapid extinction. Despite the linguistic decline, the Muniche retain a strong sense of being Indians.

REFERENCES: Darcy Ribeiro and Mary Ruth Wise, *Los grupos étnicos de la amazona peruana*, 1978; Gustavus Solís F., "Multilinguismo y extinciones de lenguas," *América Indígena*, 47 (1987), 630–45.

MUNICHI. See MUNICHE.

MUNICHINO. See MUNICHE.

MUNITSCHE. See MUNICHE.

MÜNKÜ. See IRÁNTXE.

MUOI. See GUAYMÍ.

MURÁ. The Murá Indians are a tribe of Brazilian Indians who today live in small groups scattered along the Marmelos, Maici, Manicore, and Capana rivers in the state of Amazonas. Along with the Pirahã,* they are the only representatives of the isolated Murá linguistic family. Throughout the eighteenth century, the Murá were extremely hostile to neo-Brazilians, and their subtribe, the Pirahã, was absolutely paranoid about outsiders and completely uninterested in European technologies. By 1800, the combination of European diseases, neo-Brazilian wars of extermination, and attacks by the expanding Mundurukú Indians had badly weakened the Murá. Although there were sporadic acts of violence during the nineteenth century, the Murá were actually pacified. A riverine people, they preferred to live near rivers and live off fish, river animals, and the small gardens they planted. Permanent contact with neo-Brazilian society changed the Murá, gradually integrating them until they had fully acculturated. From external appearances, it is impossible to distinguish the Murá from the larger society, but the 1,500 people who are aware of their tribal heritage still maintain a separate ethnic identity.

REFERENCES: Robert Lee Spires, "As línguas faladas do Brasil," *América Indígena*, 47 (1987), 455–79; Theodore L. Stoddard, ed., *Indians of Brazil in the Twentieth Century*, 1967.

MURATO. The term "Murato" is used today in Surinam to describe a group of subsistence farmers and wage laborers who are descendents of Karib* Indians and African settlers. They are concentrated primarily in communities along the rivers of western Surinam.

REFERENCE: Walter Dostal, ed., *The Situation of the Indian in South America*, 1972.

MURATO. The term "Murato" (Murata) is used by mestizo people of the Pastaza River area of the northwestern Peruvian Amazon to refer to the Candoshi* and Shapra* Indians. Actually, the word is a misnomer, since the original Murato Indians, who once lived in the vicinity of Lake Rimachi, have long been extinct.

REFERENCE: Sheila C. Tuggy, "Candoshi Behavior Change," in William R. Merrifield, ed., *Five Amazonian Studies on World View and Cultural Change*, 1985, 5–40.

MURIRE. See GUAYMÍ.

MURO. See AYOREO.

MURU. See AYOREO.

MURUI. The Murui are a subtribe of the Witoto* Indians of Colombia. Their language is Tupian in its origins but of the Bora* linguistic family. Their homeland today is on the frontier between Colombia and Peru, in the territory of Amazonas of Colombia, along the Igara Paraná, Chorrera, San Francisco, and Carapana rivers, all of which are tributaries of the Putumayo River. The Murui were first contacted by Europeans in the early seventeenth century, but sustained contact did not come until the late nineteenth century. Although hunting and fishing consume a great deal of their time and have great symbolic importance in Murui culture, most of the tribe's nutrients come from the manioc, maize, sweet potatoes, plantains, and bananas they raise in tribal gardens. Until the end of the nineteenth century, the Murui were a large tribe numbering several thousand people, but the wild rubber boom of the 1890s and early 1900s devastated them, bringing thousands of neo-Colombians and their diseases into Murui territory and drastically reducing their population. The Murui were dislocated and moved, the vast majority dying from disease or being assimilated into neo-Colombian society. Their numbers today are approximately 2,000 people, with more than 1,000 in Colombia, 800 in Peru, and perhaps 100 in Brazil.

REFERENCE: Blaz Telban, *Grupos étnicos de Colombia: Etnografía y bibliografía*, 1988.

MUSICA. See CHIBCHA.

MUTEA. See KARAPANÃ.

MUYNKA. See IRÁNTXE.

MUYSCA. See CHIBCHA.

MYNKY. See IRÁNTXE.

N

NACTOCORIT. See TOBA.

NADEB. See MAKÚ.

NAFUGUÁ. See NAFUQUÁ.

NAFUQUÁ. The Nafuquá (Nafukwá, Nafuguá, Nahukwá, Nahuquá, and An-auquá) were once a Karib*-speaking language group who lived independently on the right bank of the Culiseu River in the Xingú River drainage river of northern Mato Grosso, Brazil. That location, however, was along one of the main Brazilian trading routes, so the Nafuquá were early recipients of European diseases. Europeans first came across the Nafuquá in the 1880s, but by that time their tribal population had already dropped because of disease and attacks from other Xingú tribes. Influenza epidemics in the twentieth century finished the tribe off as a cultural unit because the population dropped too low. By the 1930s, the Nafuquá no longer existed as a separate tribal unit, and they had taken up residence with the Kalapalo* and Kuikúru* peoples. In the 1960s, Orlando and Cláudio Villas Boas persuaded the Nafuquá to revive their separate tribal existence by living separately from, if near, the Kuikúru and Kalapalo. By the early 1980s, there were approximately 80 Nafuquá still alive, but they were living with the Kalapalo in the Xingú Indian Park.

REFERENCES: Orlando Villas Boas and Cláudio Villas Boas, *Xingú: The Indians, Their Myths*, 1973; Robert Lee Spires, "As línguas faladas do Brasil," *América Indígena*, 47 (1987), 455–79.

NAGRANDAN. See MANGUE.

NAHUA. See NICARAO.

NAHUKUÁ. See NAFUQUÁ.

NAHUKWA. See NAFUQUÁ.

NAKAZETI. See KAWAHÍB.

NAKREHE. See BOTOCUDO.

NAMBICUÁRA. See NAMBIQUÁRA.

NAMBIKUÁRA. See NAMBIQUÁRA.

NAMBIKWÁRA. See NAMBIQUÁRA.

NAMBIQUÁRA. The Nambiquára, also known historically as the Nambikuára, Nambikwára, Nambicuára, Mambyuára, and Mahibarez, today live in western Mato Grosso and southern Rondônia, Brazil. They live on the Parecís Plateau between the tributaries of the Juruena and Guaporé rivers, up to the headwaters of the Ji-Paraná and Roosevelt rivers. To the southwest, the plateau falls away into the Guaporé Valley. The plateau is a savanna and scrub region, while the Guaporé Valley is heavily forested. The Nambiquára live right on the line between the forest and the savanna; more precisely, they live in the savanna but plant their gardens in the forest. The tribe and its related groups are part of the isolated Nambiquára language group. They are comprised of three groups that share a culture but whose languages are mutually unintelligible. The Southern Nambiquára (Campo Nambiquára) live on the Chapada dos Parecís and include such subgroups as the Munduka, Siwaihsú, Hìngutdésú, Niyalhósú, Kitaunlhú, Juina Kitaunlhú, Sawedndésú, Halótésú, Downstream Halótésú, Wakalitdésú, Âigngùtdésú, Nandésú, Kwalinsàdndésú, Yódunsú, Erahidaunsú, Âladndésú, Alakatdésú, Wâikatdésú, Wasùhsú, and Katditalhú. The second group—the Sabané or Kolimisi—live northwest of Vilhena. The Northern Nambiquára, also called the Mamaindè, include the Tawandê (Tagnani, Taundê, Tauarde), Tawende, Tocokiru, Taiaté, Yaludnde, Lakondê, Latundê, Mamaindè,* and Nagarotú (Negaroté).

The Nambiquára were first contacted by Europeans in 1770 when João Leme do Prado reached them and called them the "Tamare." By the nineteenth century, they were thrown together with the Kabixí.* Gold brought neo-Brazilian prospectors to Nambiquára land in the 1700s, and in the 1830s the gathering of ipecac, a medicinal herb, brought others. In 1907, Rondon mistakenly called them the "Nambiquára," a name that stuck. The real Nambiquára were actually the group currently called the Beiço de Pau.* Some Nambiquára came into permanent contact with Brazilian society around 1920, when telegraph lines were

completed through their lands. Others remained isolated until 1960 when Highway BR–364 reached them. In the early 1900s, the Nambiquára totaled more
than 6,000 people. Disease soon took its toll, reducing the tribal population to
only 600 people by 1960. Today they live near the Parecí* tribe in villages of
30 to 40 people each. The Nambiquára build their villages on the savannas in
order to avoid the insects and humidity of the forest, but they plant their gardens
among the trees. Their population today is approximately 750 people. They are
known for a fierce independence among the various tribal groups. The Nambiquára Indians living in the Guaporé Valley have suffered the most from contact
with whites. Disease and penetration of their land by huge agribusinesses have
all but destroyed their way of life. The Mamaindé Indians live in the Kabixí
River watershed a few miles west of Highway BR–29. Closely related to the
Nambiquara are the Manairisu* Indians, a small group located about 30 miles
south of the Mamaindè. The Galera* subgroup includes several small villages
along the Galera River and the Kabixí (Sararé) subgroup totals perhaps 75 people
and lives on the Sararé River. Protestant missionaries first reached the Nambiquára in 1924. Since then, missionaries from the following groups have worked
among them: the South America Mission, the New Tribes Mission, the Missao
Crista Brasileira, and the Summer Institute of Linguistics.

REFERENCES: David Price, "Nambiquára Geopolitical Organization," *Man* 22
(1987), 1–24; David Price, "Nambiquara Society," Ph.D. dissertation, University of
Chicago, 1972; Robert Lee Spires, "As Línguas Faladas do Brasil," *América Indígena*,
47 (1987), 455–79.

NAME. See WAKUÉNAI.

NANAIGUA. See TAPIETÉ.

NANDESU. See NAMBIQUÁRA.

NANDÉVA. See AVÁ-CHIRIPÁ.

NANDÉVA. See GUARANÍ.

NANERNA. See CAMPA.

NANUYA. See NONUYA.

NAPO. See QUIJO.

NARUVOT. The Naruvot (Naravute) were once a Karib*-speaking tribe of the
Xingú River drainage area of upper Mato Grosso, Brazil. The first European to
reach them was the anthropologist Karl Von den Steinen in 1884, but by that
time they had already been badly devastated by disease and the attacks from

neighboring tribes. Early in the twentieth century, a new wave of epidemics all but obliterated the Naruvot. By the early 1980s, the tribe had ceased to exist, and only three or four people were alive who claimed Naruvot membership. They lived with the Kalapalo* tribe in the Xingú Indian Park.

REFERENCE: Orlando Villas Boas and Cláudio Villas Boas, *Xingú: The Indians, Their Myths*, 1973.

NASA. See PÁEZ.

NATAGAIMA. See COYAIMA.

NATA-KEBIT. See TOBA.

NATEKEBIT. See TOBA.

NATÚ. The Natú are a nearly extinct group of Amerindians from an isolated linguistic family. Little is known about their history except for their presence near Pacatuba in the state of Sergipe, Brazil. A few people with Natú roots still live in the area but they are completely detribalized and virtually indistinguishable from surrounding neo-Brazilians. The Natú tribe, culture, and language have ceased to exist.

REFERENCE: Theodore L. Stoddard, ed., *Indians of Brazil in the Twentieth Century*, 1967.

NAWAZI-MONTJI. See CHIMANE.

NEENOA. See MIRITI-TAPUYA.

NEGARÓTE. See NAMBIQUÁRA.

NEGUECAGA TEMIGII. See LAYANA.

NEGUECAGA TEMIGII. See TERENO.

NEGUECATEMIGI. See LAYANA.

NEGUECATEMIGI. See TERÉNO.

NEGUECOGATEMIGI. See LAYANA.

NEGUECOGATEMIGI. See TERÉNO.

NEGUICACTEMI. See LAYANA.

NEGUICACTEMI. See TERÉNO.

NEPOYO. See MAPOYO.

NESAHUACA. See CAMPA.

NEWITHIMOMOWI. See GUAHIBO.

NHANDÉVA. See AVÁ-CHIRIPÁ.

NHANDÉVA. See GUARANÍ.

NHEENGATÚ. Nheengatú, also known as Nyengatú, Inekatú, Lingua Geral Amazônica, and Tupi Moderno, is a *lingua franca* in the region of Colombia and Brazil drained by the Vaupés River and its tributaries. It is a Tupi-Guaraní language that was brought into the area during the rubber boom between 1875 and 1920. Jesuits originally brought the language up the Amazon in the eighteenth century as a language of mission instruction. Among multilingual neo-Brazilians and various Indian tribes, Nheengatú became a way of communicating. In the last several decades, its use has declined, although the language can still be heard along the lower Vaupés River. Today approximately 10,000 people speak Nheengatú.

REFERENCES: Edwin Brooks et al., *Tribes of the Amazon Basin, Brazil, 1972*, 1973; Arthur P. Sorenson, Jr., "Multilingualism in the Northwest Amazon," *American Anthropologist*, 69 (1967), 670–84; Robert Lee Spires, "As línguas faladas do Brasil," *América Indígena*, 47 (1987), 455–79.

NICARAO. The Nicarao (Nahua) were a Nahuat-speaking tribe who lived in central and southern Mexico until around A.D. 700. Because of the collapse of Teotihuacan and the expansion of the Toltec empire in central Mexico, the Nicarao, who at the time were united with the Pipil,* began a southern movement that eventually carried them to Central America. By A.D. 1200 the Nicarao had split with the Pipil, who settled in southeastern Guatemala and western and central El Salvador. The Nicarao continued south until they settled in Nicaragua, first as far as Panama before they returned north and settled near Lake Managua. They then moved near Chorotega* land near Ometepe Island, but moved again after a war with the Chorotega and the Sumu.* By the time of the Spanish conquest, the Nicarao lived on the Isthmus of Rivas and south along the Tempisque River in Nicaragua, and they occupied part of the Guanacaste region of Costa Rica. The tribe did not survive the conquest. Slave traders and Spanish missionaries removed the Nicarao from their land, while war and epidemic disease devastated their numbers. A few Nicarao people were living in southern Nicaragua and El Salvador in the mid-twentieth century, but they did not survive much longer as a self-conscious ethnic group. Instead they became thoroughly detribalized Indians vaguely aware of their tribal ancestry.

REFERENCES: William R. Fowler, "Ethnohistoric Sources on the Pipil-Nicarao of Central America: A Critical Analysis," *Ethnohistory*, 32 (Number 1, 1985), 37–62; Linda

Newson, "The Depopulation of Nicaragua in the Sixteenth Century," *Journal of Latin American Studies*, 14 (1982), 253–86; S. Lyman Tyler, *Indians of South America*, 1976.

NIGUECACTEMIC. See LAYANA.

NIGUECACTEMIC. See TERÉNO.

NIGUICACTEMIA. See LAYANA.

NIGUICACTEMIA. See TERÉNO.

NIHAMWO. See YAGUA.

NINAM. See YANOAMA.

NISHIDAWA. See YAMINÁWA.

NISHINAHUA. See MORUNAHUA.

NISHINAHUA. See YAMINÁWA.

NIVAKLE. See ASHLUSLAY.

NIXAMVO. See YAGUA.

NIYALHOSU. See NAMBIQUÁRA.

NOANAMA. See WAUNANA.

NOANAME. See WAUNANA.

NOCTENE. See MATACO.

NOMATSIGUENGA. The Nomatsiguenga, who call themselves the Matsiguenga or Atiri, are a major division of the Campa* Indians of the Peruvian Amazon. They live on the Alto Pangoa, Sanibeni, Añapati, Ene, Mazamari, and Kiatari rivers, and they usually make their homelands in the upper jungles between 2,500 and 5,000 feet above sea level. The rivers are not navigable, which has protected the Nomatsiguenga and limited neo-Peruvian settlement in their region. The completion of a highway into their region in 1954, however, brought thousands of settlers and ended their relative isolation. Diseases accompanying the settlers also hurt the Indians. In some areas, like San Ramón de Pangoa, the Nomatsiguenga are rapidly acculturating, while in other regions they are more isolated. Still, most Nomatsiguenga men speak Spanish as well as their own dialect. There is an extremely close relationship between the Nomatisguenga and the Ashinanca.* They are primarily a subsistence agricultural people, but increasingly large numbers of them are working seasonally for colonists to earn cash. They also make money selling coffee. At present, there are approximately 4,000 Nomatsiguenga Indians.

REFERENCE: Darcy Ribeiro and Mary Ruth Wise, *Los grupos étnicos de la amazona peruana*, 1978.

NONAMA. See WAUNANA.

NONUYA. The Nonuya (Nanuya, Nyonuxa) are a relatively small group of Amerindians living in Colombia. Linguists still debate whether their language is Bora* or Witoto* in its origin. Their self-designation is Anonotha. They were first contacted by Europeans in the early seventeenth century, but sustained contact did not come until the late nineteenth century. Although hunting and fishing consume a great deal of their time and have great symbolic importance in Nonuya culture, most of the tribe's nutrients come from the manioc, maize, sweet potatoes, plantains, and bananas they raise in tribal gardens. Until the end of the nineteenth century, the Nonuya were a large group numbering several thousand people, but the wild rubber boom of the 1890s and early 1900s devastated them, bringing thousands of neo-Colombians and their diseases into Nonuya territory and drastically reducing their population. The Nonuya were dislocated and moved, the vast majority dying from disease or being assimilated into neo-Colombian society. Today the Nonuya live in small groups along the banks of the Cahuinari and upper Igara-Paraná rivers. Some are also living in Tarapaca and on the lower Caquetá River. Their population today is approximately 1,000 people.

REFERENCE: Blaz Telban, *Grupos étnicos de Colombia: Etnografía y bibliografía*, 1987.

NORTEÑO. See GUAYMÍ.

NORTHERN BARASÁNA. See BARÁ.

NORTHERN CAYAPÓ. See KAYAPÓ.

NORTHERN CHOCÓ. See EMBERA.

NORTHERN CHOROTÉ. See CHOROTÉ.

NORTHERN KAIAPÓ. See KAYAPÓ.

NORTHERN KAYAPÓ. See KAYAPÓ.

NORTHERN NAMBIQUÁRA. See NAMBIQUÁRA.

NORTHERN TEHUELCHE. See TEHUELCHE.

NOVA. See PAKAANÓVA.

NTOCOUIT. See TOBA.

NTOGAPÍD. See ITOGAPÚK.

NTOGAPÍG. See ITOGAPÚK.

NTOKOWIT. See TOBA.

NUITE. See GUAYMÍ.

NUKAK. The Nukak are a small group of Amerindians very closely related to the Makú* Indians. Gerardo Reichel Dolmatoff identified them in 1967. At the time, there were two groups of the Nukak, one living deep in the rain forest in the Papunaua and Inirida Basin of Colombia, about 50 to 100 miles from Calamar, and the other in the marshy jungle between the Inirida River's northern shore and the Guaviare River. Both regions are all but inaccessible, and for that reason, the Nukak were able to maintain their isolation. But in April 1988, the Nukak began a migration out of those deep rain forests to more heavily populated areas near the town of Calamar; another group of Nukak headed for the town of Jabón on the Guaviare River. Together they totaled about 80 people, and they claimed that they were fleeing "bad spirits," probably a cold virus, in their traditional homeland. Because the Nukak are completely unacculturated, Colombian authorities are trying to relocate them today near other Makú groups so that they can survive.

REFERENCE: Leslie Wirpsa and Hector Mondragón, "Resettlement of Nukak Indians, Colombia," *Cultural Survival Quarterly*, 12 (1988), 36–40.

NUKUÍNI. The Nukuíni are a Panoan*-speaking group of Amerindians who are today scattered from the Moa River to the Rio Sungaru in the northwestern section of the state of Acre, Brazil. Although their population once numbered in the thousands, it has been drastically reduced by disease and dislocation. Today there are just under 250 members of the Nukuíni tribe, and they live in permanent contact with neo-Brazilian society in Acre. Although most of them speak Portuguese and dress and work as other mestizos do, they maintain a cultural identity as Indians and Nukuini that has not been destroyed yet by the acculturation process.

REFERENCE: Robert Lee Spires, "As línguas faladas do Brasil," *América Indígena*, 47 (1987), 455–79.

NULPE. See COAIQUER.

NUMBIAI. The Numbiai, also known as the Orelha de Pau, are a tiny tribe of Amerindians who lived between the Preto River, a tributary of the Marmelos River, and the Aripuanã River in what is today the state of Amazonas, Brazil. They were much larger in numbers during the nineteenth century, but rubber collectors and other neo-Brazilian settlers brought conflict and disease, so the Numbiai population declined. Today there are a few isolated individuals and families still living near the Preto River who are aware of their immediate Numbiai heritage, but the tribe no longer functions as a differentiated social unit. Their population today is only around 25 people.

   REFERENCE: Theodore L. Stoddard, ed., *Indians of Brazil in the Twentieth Century*, 1967.

NUMURANA. See OMURANO.

NUQUENCAIBO. See KAPANÁWA.

NYENGATÚ. See NHEENGATÚ.

NYONUXA. See NONUYA.

O

OAIAPÍ. See OYANPÍK.

OCAINA. The Ocaina (Anuxa, Okaina, Orebe) are a tribe of Amerindians who live along the Ampiyacu, Putumayo, and Yaguasyacu rivers in the district of Pebas y Putumayo in the province of Maynas, Loreto, in the Peruvian Amazon, as well near San Andrés on the territory of Amazonas in Colombia. They call themselves the Diokaya. The two Ocaina subgroups are the Dukaiya and the Ibo'tsa. Of the 380 Ocaina Indians, perhaps half are bilingual. A substantial number of detribalized Resigaro* Indians are also living with them. Scholars are undecided whether the Ocaina language is Witoto* or Bora* in its origins. Although hunting and fishing consume much of their time and have great symbolic importance in Ocaina culture, most of the tribe's nutrients come from the manioc, maize, sweet potatoes, plantains, and bananas raised in tribal gardens. Until the end of the nineteenth century, the Ocaina were a large tribe numbering thousands of people, but the wild rubber boom of the 1890s and early 1900s devastated them, bringing thousands of neo-Peruvians and their diseases into Ocaina country and drastically reducing their population. A group from the Summer Institute of Linguistics has been with them since 1964.

REFERENCES: Michael J. Eden and Angela Andrade, "Ecological Aspects of Swidden Cultivation among the Andoke and Witoto Indians of the Colombian Amazon," *Human Ecology*, 15 (1987), 339–59; Gustavus Solís F., "Multilinguismo y extinciones de lenguas," *América Indígena*, 47 (1987), 630–45; Stefano Varese, *The Forest Indians in the Present Political Situation of Peru*, 1972.

OCHIRO. See CHAMACOCO.

OCHOMAZO. See URU.

OCHOZUMA. See URU.

OCOLE. See MATACO.

OCTENAI. See MATACO.

ODOARY. See ARAONA.

OEPOEROEI. See WAYÁNA.

OFAYÉ. The Ofayé (Ofayé-Xavánte*) are a tiny, nearly extinct group of Amerindians who probably come from an isolated linguistic family. Today there are only 20 members of the tribe still surviving. Because of those small numbers, traditional ceremonial life has become impossible to sustain. They live in the southern reaches of the state of Mato Grosso, Brazil, with assistance from the Brazilian Indian Service. Most demographers believe that the Ofayé will cease to exist as a self-conscious social unit in the next generation.

REFERENCE: Robert Lee Spires, ''As Línguas Faladas do Brasil,'' *América Indígena*, 47 (1987), 455–79.

OFAYÉ-XAVÁNTE. See OFAYÉ.

OH-HON. See WAKUENAI.

OHLWA. See SUMU.

OIAMPÍK. See OYANPÍK.

OICO. See YANOAMA.

OJANA. See URUKUYÁNA.

OKAINA. See OCAINA.

OKOMOYÁNA. The Okomoyána, also known as Maipuridjana or Waripi, are a subtribe of the Tiriyó* of the Brazilian-Surinam border. They traditionally pursued a slash-and-burn form of subsistence agriculture, but in recent years, because of their friendly reaction to contact with Protestant and Catholic missionaries, they have accepted some neo-Brazilian technologies and begun the acculturation process. They number fewer than 100 people. See TIRIYÓ.

OKOROMOMOWI. See GUAHIBO.

OLEO. See KADUVEO.

OLOTULE. The term "Olotule" was a term the Cuna* Indians of Panama used when referring to themselves. To some extent, neighboring tribes and Spaniards in Panama used the term as well. See CUNA.

OLUA. See SUMU.

OMAGE. See AMUESHA.

OMÁGUA. At the time of the conquest, the Omágua (Kambéba) were a huge tribe of 20,000 Tupi*-speaking Amerindians living along the Amazon River in what is today the state of Amazonas, Brazil. Spanish explorers first encountered them in 1542 and were immediately impressed with the level of their social organization and technology, particularly Omágua glazed pottery, which they considered equal to European work. In 1560, the Omágua fought a pitched battle with a group of Spanish explorers attempting to descend the Amazon from Peru in search of the fabled riches of El Dorado. Throughout the sixteenth and seventeenth centuries, the Spanish and then the Portuguese marvelled at the sophistication of the Omágua way of life, such as their ability to plant huge gardens of manioc along the river and raise turtles for meat. By 1681, because of widespread slave expeditions against the Omágua, their population had declined to only 7,000 people. Jesuit missionaries worked among the Omágua until their expulsion from the New World in 1767. By that time, periodic outbreaks of dysentery and smallpox had reduced the Omágua to fewer than 1,000 people. In the struggle between the Portuguese and Spanish for control of South America, the Omágua were caught in the middle in the eighteenth century and eventually abandoned their lands to avoid the conflict, retreating into Peru. Their population dropped to only 150 people in the 1920s and then began a modest recovery. Today there are approximately 350 individuals in Brazil and several hundred in Peru who are detribalized people aware of their Omágua heritage. Most of them are integrated into Cocama* or mestizo society. Otherwise, the tribe does not function as a social unit.

REFERENCES: John Hemming, *Red Gold: The Conquest of the Brazilian Indians, 1500–1760*, 1977; John Hemming, *Amazon Frontier: The Defeat of the Brazilian Indians*, 1987; Darcy Ribeiro and Mary Ruth Wise, *Los grupos étnicos de la amazona peruana*, 1978; Gustavus Solís F., "Multilinguismo y extinciones de lenguas," *América Indígena*, 47 (1987), 630–45.

OMASUYO. See AYMARA.

OMURANO. The Omurano were a group of Zaparoan*-speaking Amerindians whose traditional homeland was along the Urituyacu River, a tributary of the Marañon River in the Peruvian Amazon. They have also been known historically as the Humurana, Umurano, Roamaina, and Numurana. They were first contacted by Spaniards in 1641 and used regionally as interpreters. Smallpox and measles epidemics reduced the Omurano population from 10,000 people in 1654 to only 1,500 in 1660. In the last half of the seventeenth century, the Jesuits tried unsuccessfully to missionize the Omurano, but only a handful of the Indians stayed in the settlements. Disease continued to hurt the Omurano, as did the rubber boom of the late nineteenth and early twentieth centuries, which brought mestizo collectors into their region. By 1930, the Omurano population was down to only several dozen people. Some neighboring Indians have claimed that severe epidemics completely destroyed the Omurano in the late 1950s and early 1960s, although there may still be a few surviving Indians in Peru who are aware of their Omurano heritage. Nevertheless, the tribe is extinct as a sociological unit.

REFERENCE: Darcy Ribeiro and Mary Ruth Wise, *Los grupos étnicos de la amazona peruana*, 1978.

ONA. See SELK'NAM.

ONGWA. See HOTÍ.

ONICOIN. See SHARANAHUA.

ONOTO. See PARAUJANO.

OPATORO. See LENCA.

OPINADKOM. See ARÁRA.

ORARI. See BORÓRO.

ORAW-IT. See WARRAU.

ORCOCOYANA. See URUKUYÁNA.

ORECHÓN. See OREJÓN.

OREGÓN. See OREJÓN.

OREJÓN. A Witoto* (Huitoto) people, the Orejón (Orejon-Koto, Koto, Coto, Oregón, Orechon, Payaguá, and Tutapi) are a small group of Amerindian people who today live along the Napo, Algodon, Yanayacu, Sucusari, and Putumayo rivers in the districts of Napo, Pebas, Putumayo, and Las Amazonas in the province of Maynas, Loreto, in Peru. Roman Catholic missionaries established missions along the Orejón in the 1680s, but the Indians abandoned them in the 1720s when they feared being made into slaves. Severe epidemics hurt them in the mid-eighteenth century, as did the rubber boom of the late nineteenth and early twentieth centuries. In 1925, the Orejón population exceeded 500 people. Like other tropical forest people, the Orejón support themselves in a subsistence hunting and horticultural economy and also perform migrant labor in order to raise cash for trade goods. Although indigenous traditions survive among older Orejón, most tribal members under the age of 40 have adopted Western values and dress; they speak Spanish. The current Orejón population consists of approximately 300 people, of whom an increasing number are bilingual in Quechua or Spanish. Intermarriage with neighboring Indians and mestizos is rapidly increasing.

REFERENCES: Darcy Ribeiro and Mary Ruth Wise, *Los grupos étnicos de la amazona peruana*, 1978; Gustavus Solís F., "Multilinguismo y extinciones de lenguas," *América Indígena*, 47 (1987), 630–45; Stefano Varese, *The Forest Indians in the Present Political Situation of Peru*, 1972.

OREJÓN-KOTO. See OREJÓN.

ORELHA DE PAU. See NUMBIAI.

ORIO. See CHAMACOCO.

ORKOKOYÁNA. See WAYÁNA.

ORO AT. The Oro At are a subtribe of the Pakaanóva* Indians of western Rondônia in Brazil. Traditionally, the Oro At lived between the Pacaas Novas and the Oura Preta rivers; they intermarried with the Oro Nao* and the Oro Eu.* The Oro At were pacified in 1961 when agents of the government Indian service came into permanent contact with them. In the subsequent epidemics that hit the Oro At, their population declined by more than half, down to fewer than 100 people. Today there are Oro At living on the Post Rio Negro Ocaia on the Pacaas Novas River. See PAKAANÓVA.

ORO EU. The Oro Eu are a subtribe of the Pakaanova* Indians of western Rondônia in Brazil. Traditionally, the Oro Eu lived at the headquarters of the Pacaas Nova River. They were linguistically and culturally very close to the Oro At* and the Oro Nao.* Missionaries from the New Tribes Mission reached the Oro Eu in 1956 in order to treat them for a severe outbreak of flu and measles. Within three years, the Oro Nao population had declined from approximately 400 people to fewer than 150. See PAKAANÓVA.

ORO MUN. The Oro Mun are a subtribe of the Pakaanóva* Indians of western Rondônia in Brazil. Traditionally, the Oro Mun were scattered from the Ribeirao to the headwaters of the Mutum Paraná River. They are very closely related to the Oro Waram* and the Oro Waramxijein.* Government Indian agents established permanent contact with the Oro Mun in 1960 and persuaded them to visit the post on the Madeira-Mamoré Railroad regularly, but when severe flue epidemics erupted within a few weeks, the Oro Mun fled back into the forests and avoided contact for several more years. See PAKAANÓVA.

ORO NAO. The Oro Nao are a subtribe of the Pakaanóva* Indians of western Rondônia in Brazil. Traditionally, the Oro Nao lived along the southern tributaries of the Pacaas Novas River, the Dois Irmaos River, and the Novo River where they pursued a tropical forest existence. Missionaries from the New Tribes Mission reached the Oro Nao in 1956 in order to treat them for a severe outbreak of flu and measles. Within three years the Oro Nao population had declined from approximately 400 people to fewer than 100. Today they live on the upper waters of the Oura Preta River. See PAKAANÓVA.

OROTINA. See MANGUE.

ORO WARAM. The Oro Waram are a subtribe of the Pakaanóva* Indians of western Rondônia in Brazil. Traditionally, they lived in an area reaching from the upper Lage River to the Bananeira River. In 1960, the Oro Waram slaughtered several neo-Brazilians; in the ensuing uproar, government agents realized that they either had to establish permanent contact with the Oro Waram or watch the Indians face a genocidal reaction by settlers. Government Indian agents established permanent contact with the Oro Waram that year. See PAKAANÓVA.

ORO WARMXIJEIN. The Oro Waramxijein are a subtribe of the Pakaanóva* Indians of western Rondônia in Brazil. They traditionally pursued a horticultural existence from the Ribeirao River to the headwaters of the Mutum Paraná River. In 1960, government Indian agents persuaded the Oro Waramxijein to regularly visit the post on the Madeira-Mamoré Railroad. When severe flu epidemics erupted within a few weeks, the Oro Waram fled back into the forests and avoided contact for several more years. See PAKAANÓVA.

OROWARI. See PAKAANÓVA.

OSA. See BRUNKA.

OTANABE. See MUNICHE.

OTANAVE. See MUNICHE.

OTAVALO. The Otavalos are a group of several thousand Amerindians living in Imbabura Province of the highlands of Ecuador. Their language is a Quechuan* dialect, which they adopted after Roman Catholic missionaries used it as their *lingua franca* in converting the Otavalo. They are descendants of the pre-conquest Cara tribe. During the period of Incan expansion, the Otavalos successfully resisted conquest and have since maintained a powerful sense of identity. They have also been able to maintain their independence in recent years because of their economic prosperity. The Otavalos are known widely throughout Ecuador and Peru for their woolen textiles. That industry provides them with a source of cash that has given the Otavalo a standard of living higher than that of most neo-Ecuadorians and mestizos in the highlands. Most Otavalo Indians are subsistence farmers who raise beans, barley, maize, quinoa, and wheat.

REFERENCES: John Collier, *The Awakening Valley*, 1971; Jed Arthur Cooper, *The School in Otavalo Indian Society*, 1965; Thomas E. Weil, ed., *Area Handbook for Ecuador*, 1971; Gladys R. Villavicencio, *Relaciones interétnicas en Otavalo-Ecuador*, 1973.

OTOGE. See APINAYÉ.

OTOMACO. See ACHAGUA.

OTÚKE. See OTÚKI.

OTÚKI. The Otúki (Otúqui, Otúke) are a group of Amerindians from an isolated linguistic group who once lived in the tropical forests of eastern Brazil. Their depopulation was accelerated by the rubber boom of the late nineteenth and early twentieth centuries, when neo-Bolivian and neo-Brazilian rubber collectors enslaved many of the Otúki and brought deadly diseases to others. Although the Otúki ceased to function as a differentiated social group in the mid-twentieth century, there are still detribalized, acculturated neo-Bolivians who are aware of their distant Otúki roots.

REFERENCE: S. Lyman Tyler, *Indians of South America*, 1976.

OTÚQUI. See OTÚKI.

OUAITIADEHO. See KADUVEO.

OUAPISHÁNA. See WAPISHÁNA.

OUAPISIÁNA. See WAPISHÁNA.

OUAVAOUS. See WARRAU.

OUAYEOUE. See WAIWÁI.

OUITOTO. See WITOTO.

OUPINAGEE. See APINAYÉ.

OUYÁNA. See URUKUYÁNA.

OYAMPÍ. See OYANPÍK.

OYÁNA. See URUKUYÁNA.

OYANPÍK. The Oyanpík (Oyampík, Oyampí, Oaimpík, Oyambí, Aipí, Aiapí, Uajapí, Oaiapí, Guyapí, Ayapí, Guaiapy, Waiapí, Wayampí, and Wayapí) are a small group of Tupi*-speaking Amerindians who once lived in Surinam and on the Brazilian coast north of the mouth of the Amazon River. In the eighteenth century, they migrated there from points south of the Amazon and joined with the Portuguese in slave-hunting expeditions against the Karib*-speaking people of Surinam. Around 1800, they migrated into what is today Surinam, but they were suffering a population decline from epidemic disease. By the 1940s, the Oyanpík had begun to live in close proximity with the Emerilon* people, and most of them have recently been absorbed by the Karib-speaking tribes of Surinam. The Oyanpík tribe no longer exists as the functional unit of the past, but there are nearly 300 individuals who are aware of their Oyanpík roots. They live along the Oyapok River and in a village near Camopi. Because of the isolation of their region and its general inaccessibility to tourists, the Oyanpík have been able to maintain a relatively traditional way of life.

REFERENCES: Edwin Brooks, et al., *Tribes of the Amazon Basin, Brazil, 1972,* 1973; Walter Dostal, *The Situation of the Indian in South America,* 1972; Robert Lee Spires, "As línguas falados do Brasil," *América Indígena,* 47 (1987), 455–79; Theodore L. Stoddard, ed., *Indians of Brazil in the Twentieth Century,* 1967.

P

PA'ANKOTSHONK. See TEHUELCHE.

PA'ANKUN'K. See TEHUELCHE.

PAATSIAGA. See ANDOKE.

PABANOTÓN. See YEKUANA.

PACAA-NÓVO. See PAKAANÓVA.

PACAGUARA. See PACANUARA.

PACAHANOVA. See PAKAANÓVA.

PACAHUARA. See PACANUARA.

PACAJUDEUS. See KADUVEO.

PACANHUA. See PAKANÁWA.

PACANUARA. The Pacanaura (Pacaguara, Pacahuara, Pakawara, Pacavara) are a tiny group of Panoan*-speaking Amerindians who until recently tried to keep their distance from all neo-Bolivians. At one time, their subtribes included the Sinabu (Shinabu, Ginabo, Gritones) and Capuibo. The Pacanuara lived between the Beni River and the lower Madre de Dios River in the province of F. Román in the department of Pando in Bolivia. Today there are only a handful of the Pacanuara still alive. Although they are still familiar with the aboriginal language, they no longer have sufficient numbers to sustain tribal ceremonial life. Population expansion by neo-Bolivians has steadily reduced their tribal economic base. In fact, the tribe does not function as a differentiated social unit. The most recent figures put the tribal population at only 10 people. They are all members of a single nuclear family that lives in Arroyo Ivón.

REFERENCES: Brian M. Boom, *Ethnobotany of the Chácobo Indians, Beni, Bolivia*, 1987; Harold Key and Mary Key, *Bolivian Indian Tribes: Classification, Bibliography, and Map of Present Language Distribution*, 1967; Jürgen Riester, *Indians of Eastern Bolivia: Aspects of Their Present Situation*, 1975; Graciela Zolezzi and J. Riester, "Lenguas indígenas del oriente boliviano clasificación preliminar," *América Indígena*, 47 (1987), 425–33.

PACASA. See AYMARA.

PACAVARA. See PACANUARA.

PADAHURI. See YANOAMA.

PÁECE. See PÁEZ.

PÁEZ. The Páez (Páece) Indians are a Páezan*-speaking group of farmers who live on the eastern slopes of the Central Cordillera mountain range of Colombia, east of the department of Cauca, in the municipalities of Páez and Inza. Smaller Páez settlements can be found on the western slopes of the mountains as well as on the Pacific Coast and in the eastern lowlands. In recent years, thousands of Páez Indians have migrated to the cities in search of work. Along the Moras River, the Páez raise maize, beans, and potatoes, and along the lower Moras, they produce some sugar cane. The Páez call themselves the "Nasa." There are a number of Páez subtribes, including the Tierradentro, Tacueyo, Pitayo, Jambalo, Totoro, Caldono, Toribio, Corinto, and Paniquita. All of the dialects except Paniquita are mutually intelligible. They raise such warm country crops as sugar cane, coca, manioc, plantains, and bananas along the Páez River, with some coffee that they treat as a cash crop. In recent years, they have also turned to dairy livestock as well. Politically they are organized into reservation communities—called *resguardos*—presided over by councils called *cabildos*. All property is owned communally, not individually.

At the time of the conquest, the Páez inhabited the banks of the Páez River, the lower Moras River, and the valley of La Plata to the southeast. The conquest gradually drove them west to the mountain slopes. Páez communities appeared at Pitayo, Jambalo, Toribio-Tacueyo, Quichaya, Caldono, Pueblo Nuevo, and Paniquitia. In the eighteenth century, the colonial *encomiendo* gave way to wage labor systems, especially when neo-Colombians became interested in producing chinchona bark. During the twentieth century, the Páez Indians have become more politically active in protecting their way of life from government intrusion. Along with the neighboring Gambiano* Indians, they established the *Commando Quintín Lame*, a guerrilla organization, in 1985. Government attempts to question Páez title to their land has inspired the guerrilla activity. There are approximately 70,000 members of the Páez Indian group. Of that total, approximately 458 were living on the government Indian reservation of Agua Negra, as well as 425 on the Tumbichucue reservation in 1988.

REFERENCES: Ministerio de Gobierno, *Aspetos de la cultura material de grupos étnicos de Colombia*, 1979; Sutti R. Ortiz, *Uncertainties in Peasant Farming: A Colombian Case*, 1973; Jorge P. Osterling, *Democracy in Colombia: Clientelist Politics and Guerrilla Warfare*, 1989; Joanna Rappaport, "Mythic Images, Historical Thought, and Printed Texts: The Páez and the Written Word," *Journal of Anthropological Research*, 43 (1987), 43–67; Joanna Rappaport, "Territory and Tradition: The Ethnohistory of the Páez of Colombia," Ph.D. dissertation, University of Illinois, 1982.

PÁEZAN. The term "Páezan" refers to a group of languages that are part of the larger Chibchan* affiliation of Amerindian languages. Included in the Paezan group during the historical era were the following languages: Allentiac, Andoke,* Atacama, Barbacoa, Betoi,* Chimu, Chocó,* Itonama,* Jirajira, Murá,* Páez,* Timucua, and Warrau.*

REFERENCE: Joseph H. Greenberg, *Language in the Americas*, 1987.

PAHAYA. See PAYA.

PAI. See SECOYA.

PAIAGUÁ. On the eve of the Portuguese arrival in Brazil in the sixteenth century, the Paiaguá numbered approximately 6,000 people. Closely related to the Guaycuru,* they were a river tribe who controlled the Paraguay River in the seventeenth century. They attacked the Spanish advance up the river, whether Jesuit missionaries, government soldiers, or adventurers. Paulista bandeirantes failed to enslave the Paiaguá in the seventeenth centuries, but not because they did not try. When the discovery of gold brought large numbers of Portuguese settlers to Cuiaba in the early eighteenth century, the Paiaguá put up a fierce resistance, fighting a skilled guerrilla war. They destroyed expedition after expedition sent up the Paraguay River to pacify, convert, or enslave them. But in 1734, a huge Portuguese military expedition went up the river and slaughtered more than 600 Paiaguá, a defeat from which the tribe never recovered. After that, the Paiaguá retreated into the swamps and suffered further ravages from disease and wars with neighboring tribes. By the end of the eighteenth century, the tribe had been reduced to only a few hundred people. By the 1860s, the Paiaguá were living on the beaches of Asunción selling firewood and fish to support themselves. There were two branches of the tribe, a northern group called Saringue and a southern group called the Maca (Magatch, Agaces, or

Siakua). Today only a few dozen Paiaguá exist. They live on an island reservation just outside Asunción, Paraguay.

REFERENCE: John Hemming, *Red Gold: The Conquest of the Brazilian Indians, 1500–1760*, 1978.

PAĪ-CAYUĀ. The Paī-Cayuā (Paī-Tavyterā, Paī-Tavyerā) are a large tribe of Guaraní*-speaking Indians who today inhabit the forests of eastern Paraguay. They came under the influence of Jesuit missionaries in the eighteenth century but returned to the forests, where they continue to practice a slash-and-burn agriculture for the production of maize, their staple. Because the settlement of eastern Paraguay occurred very slowly in the twentieth century, the Paī-Cayuā were spared massive dislocation until recently. In the 1970s, large-scale hydroelectric projects along the Paraná River brought construction workers and new settlers. High soybean prices and government land policies encouraging settlement have led to the deforestation of large areas of eastern Paraguay and new pressures on the Paī-Cayuā. Today there are 14,000 Paī-Cayuā Indians scattered over 40,000 square kilometers of land, primarily in the department of Amambay in northeastern Paraguay and across the border in the state of Mato Grosso, Brazil. About 10,000 of the Paī-Cayuā live on the Paraguayan side of the border and the rest in Brazil. The Paī-Cayuā raise manioc and hunt for game; they are known to raise small numbers of pigs, ducks, and chickens. They also work as laborers on local ranches and coffee plantations. Today the Paī-Cayuā use Western metal technology, shotguns, and Western dress, but they retain their ancient religious ceremonies and group identity. Because they have no titles to their land, development projects and increased settlement have reduced their opportunities for hunting and fishing. The Paī-Cayuā are a desperately poor people.

REFERENCES: Miguel Chase-Sardi, ''La situación actual de los indígenas en el Paraguay,'' in George Grunberg, *La situación del indígena in América del Sul*, 1972; David Maybury-Lewis and James Howe, *The Indian Peoples of Paraguay: Their Plight and Their Prospects*, 1980.

PAICONE. See PAUNACA.

PAICONECA. See PAUNACA.

PAIGNKENKEN. See TEHUELCHE.

PAII. See KAWAHÍB.

PAIKISE. See MUNDURUKÚ.

PAIKYCE. See MUNDURUKÚ.

PAIMERÚ. The Paimerú Indians are a subtribe of the Tiriyó* tribe. They live in the Tumucumaque Indian Park in Brazil, in the state of Pará just south of Surinam. See TIRIYÓ.

PAIQUIZE. See MUNDURUKÚ.

PAĨ-TAVIYERÃ. See PAĨ-CAYUÃ.

PAĨ-TAVYERÃ. See PAĨ-CAYUÃ.

PAITÉR. See SURUÍ.

PAJONALINO. The Pajonalino are a major division of the Campa* Indians of the Peruvian Amazon. They call themselves the Asheninca or Atsiri and they live in the region of the Gran Pajonal in upper jungle regions between 3,000 and 6,000 feet in altitude. In the 1940s, heavy settlement of the Gran Pajonal by neo-Peruvians began. Catholic and Protestant missionaries established mission settlements there, but despite those incursions, the Pajonalino have remained monolingual and have acculturated very little. They are also known for their hostility to neo-Peruvians as well as to many other Indian groups. The Pajonalino are subsistence farmers, raising maize and manioc, and periodically they head off on long hunting and fishing trips. For men, up to half of their time is spent hunting and fishing, although the bulk of the tribe's protein comes from agriculture. An increasing number of the Pajonalinos, however, are beginning to take up manual labor as a way of earning cash for trade goods. At the present time, there are approximately 4,000 members of the Pajonalino group.

REFERENCE: Darcy Ribeiro and Mary Ruth Wise, *Los grupos étnicos de la amazona peruana*, 1978.

PAKAA NOVA. See PAKAANÓVA.

PAKAANÓVA. The Pakaanóvas (Pacahanóva, Pacaa Nóvos, Pacaanóva), also known as the Orowari, Jarú, or Uomo, are a tribe of Amerindians who are part of the isolated Txapakúra* (Chapakuran) language group between the Guaporé and Jiparaná rivers in the states of Rondônia and Mato Grosso in Brazil. They call themselves the "Wari." In particular, the Pakaanóvas live between the Pacaas Novas and the Ouro Preto rivers, both of which are tributaries of the Mamoré River in Rondônia. There are six subgroups of the Pakaanóvas: the Oro Nao, Oro At, and Oro Eu all speak mutually intelligible dialects, while the Oro Waram, Oro Waramxijein, and Oro Mun are more different. Historically, there has been a great deal of interaction among these subgroups, including joint festivals and intermarriages. By the late 1600s, the Pakaanóvas were already experiencing European diseases, even though most of these came through indirect contact with other Indians. Jesuit missionaries began establishing missions in their area in the early 1700s. Once the Jesuits were expelled from the New World, the Pakaanóvas fled deep into the forests and avoided contact for the next 150 years.

Although missionaries, explorers, and rubber gatherers contacted and fought with the Pakaanóvas during the eighteenth, nineteenth, and twentieth centuries, drastically reducing the tribal population from its peak of around 2,000 people, the Pakaanóvas were not pacified by the Brazilian government until the late 1950s. By that time, rubber collectors had settled throughout the area of the Pacaas Novas River. Although the Pakaanóvas Indians have adopted metal tools and work for cash to buy these goods, they remain relatively isolated from neo-Brazilian society. Government resettlement policies brought tens of thousands of peasants into the region in the 1950s and 1960s, and the discovery of cassiterite, the ore from which tin is mined, brought miners and mining companies. Diseases severely affected the Indians. Their group population, which fell to around 300 people in the 1950s, has recovered to around 900 people today.

REFERENCES: David Maybury-Lewis, *In the Path of the Polonoreste: Endangered Peoples of Western Brazil*, 1981; Robert Lee Spires, "As línguas faladas do Brasil," *América Indígena*, 47 (1987), 455–79; Theodore L. Stoddard, ed., *Indians of Brazil in the Twentieth Century*, 1967.

PAKARÁRA. In the municipality of Floresta, in the state of Pernambuco, Brazil, there is a group of highly assimilated Amerindians who call themselves the Pakarára. They live in the sierras of Cacaria and Arapua. Although no trace of their aboriginal language or culture survives and they pursue an economic lifestyle indistinguishable from that of surrounding neo-Brazilians, the Pakarára still maintain a sense of ethnic identity that sets them apart. They view themselves as an indigenous people.

REFERENCE: Theodore L. Stoddard, ed., *Indians of Brazil in the Twentieth Century*, 1967.

PAKIDAI. The Pakidai (Surara) are an unacculturated group of the Yanoama* linguistic group of southern Venezuela and northern Brazil. In particular, they are closely related to the Shiriana or Xiriana branch of the Yanoama and live along the Demeni, Araca, and Padauiri rivers in approximately ten villages. See YANOAMA.

PALANOA. See BARASÁNA.

PALICUR. See PALIKUR.

PALIKUR. The Palikur (Palicur) are an Amerindian group of people who originally spoke an Arawak* dialect but who today are highly acculturated. These are approximately 700 Palikur, most of whom live in two villages on the Urucaua River in the territory of Amapá, Brazil. About 200 Palikur live across the border in French Guiana, where they have abandoned the marshy savannas of the Oyapok estuary, a traditional homeland, for St. Georges de l'Oyapok where their children attend school. Leaving their homeland, however, with its protein-rich fishing environment, has hurt them economically, turning them into manual laborers suffering from poverty and disorganization. Aboriginal Palikur culture has all but disappeared, and large numbers of the Indians supplement their subsistence horticulture with marginal labor to provide cash for consumer goods. All of the Palikur speak Portuguese in Brazil and French Creole in Surinam, and most of them use these as their primary languages.

REFERENCES: Walter Dostal, ed., *The Situation of the Indian in South America*, 1972; Robert Lee Spires, "As línguas faladas do Brasil," *América Indígena*, 47 (1987), 455–79; Theodore L. Stoddard, ed., *Indians of Brazil in the Twentieth Century*, 1967.

PALMELA. The Palmelas were a group of Karib*-speaking Amerindians who in the late 1800s lived a riverine lifestyle in what is today the state of Rondônia, Brazil. They lived along the Guaporé River near its confluence with the Branco River just north of the contemporary border with Bolivia. They are not native to the area, since most of the other tribes living in southern Rondônia are of Tupian extraction. Scholars suspect that the Palmela are descendents of Indian oarsmen whom Portuguese merchants brought into the areas centuries before. When the rubber boom of the late nineteenth century brought thousands of neo-Brazilian collectors into Rondônia, the Palmelas were devastated by violence and disease; they entered a population decline from which they have never recovered. By the 1920s, there were fewer than 100 members of the tribe still alive, and most of them were gone by the 1940s. The Brazilian government announced that the Palmela were extinct as a tribe in 1956. Today there are probably a few people living in Rondônia who are aware of at least part of their ancestry in Palmela culture, but the tribe no longer exists.

REFERENCE: Theodore L. Stoddard, ed., *Indians of Brazil in the Twentieth Century*, 1967.

PAMARÍ. See PAUMARÍ.

PAMAURÍ. See PAUMARÍ.

PAMBADEQUE. See COCAMILLA.

PAMIWA. See CUBEO.

PAMMARÍ. See PAUMARÍ.

PAMOA. See TATUYO.

PAMOA. See BARASÁNA.

PANA. See PANOBO.

PANAGOTÓ. See PIANOKOTÓ.

PANAMAKA. See SUMU.

PANARE. The Panare are a Karib*-speaking Amerindian people who occupy the northwestern corner of the Cedeño district of the state of Bolívar in Venezuela. They call themselves E'napa. They live in a 20,000-square-kilometer triangle bordered by the Suapare, Cuchivero, and Orinoco rivers. They are descendents of the Payuros and Oyé. Although the Panare have historically had to deal with a succession of Jesuit and Capuchin missionaries, settlers, anthropologists, and government officials, they have maintained a remarkable cultural identity, resisting all but the most rudimentary examples of European technology—metal tools. They usually live at the junction of the savanna and the forests and plant gardens along fertile river bottoms. Although the bulk of their nourishment comes from horticulture, the Panare still view hunting and fishing as more important activities. By the early 1980s, the Panare numbered approximately 2,500 people living in fifty villages. Their population was increasing in numbers and expanding in area.

REFERENCES: Jean-Paul Dumont, *The Headman and I: Ambiguity and Ambivalence in the Fieldworker Experience*, 1978; *Under the Rainbow: Nature and Supernature among the Panare Indians*, 1976; Paul Henley, *The Panare: Tradition and Change in the Amazonian Frontier*, 1982.

PANCARÁRU. See PANKARÁRU.

PANCÁRE. See PANKARÁRU.

PANCHO. The Pancho Indians are a Nahuat-speaking tribe who probably are full-blooded descendents of the Pipil* Indians. Today the Pancho number only a few hundred people and are concentrated in and around Panchimalco, El Salvador.

REFERENCE: Howard Blutstein, *Area Handbook for El Salvador*, 1971.

PANDABEQUEO. See COCAMILLA.

PANEROA. The Paneroa (Tsola, Tsoloa) are an Eastern Tukanoan* language tribe of Amerindians who lived in the Vaupés River drainage region of Colombia. The upper Vaupés River has been a very isolated place until recently, even though various anthropologists, Roman Catholic priests, and Protestant missionaries have moved into the area since 1900. The Colombian government today is trying to encourage settlement of the region, but development has been very slow. The Paneroa have contacts with many other Indian tribes but not much contact with Europeans. The tribe today includes several hundred people.

REFERENCE: Arthur P. Sorenson, Jr., "Multilingualism in the Northwest Amazon," *American Anthropologist*, 69 (1967), 670–84.

PANGOA. See CAMPA.

PANIQUITA. See PÁEZ.

PANKARÁRA. The Pankarára (Pankaráre) are a group of fewer than 300 people who today live about 40 miles northeast of Rodelas on the São Francisco River in the Caciara and Arapua highlands of the state of Pernambuco, Brazil. A highly mestizo people, they are descendants of the Pankarára Indians who once roamed widely throughout what is today Pernambuco. The Pankarára were known in the region as early as 1696 when they occupied a small Jesuit mission with a number of other tribes. Today the Pankarára, although aware of their Indian origins, are Portuguese-speaking people who worship as Roman Catholics and work in the local cash economy as small farmers and laborers. They retain nothing of their aboriginal culture except a sense of group identity. Like other groups in the region, the Pankarára are threatened by the Itaparica Hydroelectric Project on the Sao Francisco River that may well flood much of their land.

REFERENCES: Paul L.Aspelin and Silvio Coelho dos Santos, *Indian Areas Threatened by Hydroelectric Projects in Brazil*, 1981; Theodore L. Stoddard, ed., *Indians of Brazil in the Twentieth Century*, 1967.

PANKARÁRU. The Pankaráru (Pancaráru) are an assimilated group of approximately 3,000 people who are descendents of the Pankarára tribe of Amerindians. As early as the 1690s, the Pankaráru were inhabiting several islands in the São Francisco River in Brazil; they moved to their present location on the banks of the river in 1802. Most anthropologists think the Pankaráru represent a case of recent ethnogenesis, in which descendents and survivors of several other tribal groups who had been gathered in Jesuit missions in the sixteenth century assimilated together and formed a new group. Although they retain none of their tribal culture, language, or religion, the Pankaráru do have an elaborate volume of ceremonial lore that distinguishes their cultural life from that of surrounding mestizos. They live on a reservation of the Brazilian Indian Service, the Pancaru Indian Park, about twenty miles from Petrolandia in the state of Pernambuco, Brazil. They still divide themselves into two general groups—the Pankáru and the Pancáre—and retain an identity as a people separate from the larger neo-Brazilian society. The Pankaráru are integrated into the local regional economy primarily as laborers and small farmers. The greatest existing threat to the Pankararu Indians is the Itaparica Hydroelectric Project on the São Francisco River that may well flood much of their land.

REFERENCES: Paul L. Aspelin and Silvio Coelho dos Santos, *Indian Areas Threatened by Hydroelectric Projects in Brazil*, 1981; Theodore L. Stoddard, ed., *Indians of Brazil in the Twentieth Century*, 1967.

PANKARU. See PANKARÁRU.

PANO. See PANOBO.

PANO. See SETEBO.

PANOAN. Panoan refers to a group of South American Indian languages that form part of the larger Macro-Pano-Tacanan language group. Panoan speakers were widely distributed throughout Brazil, Peru, and Bolivia, and included the following tribal languages: Amahuaca* (Amawaca), Kaxináwa* (Kaxanáwa,

Cashinahua, Cashinawa), Capanahua (Capanáwa), Cashibo,* Conibo,* Shipibo,* Marinahua (Marináwa), Marobo, Nocaman, Panobo* (Pano), Kulina*
(Culino, Curino), Jaminahua, Jumá, Mayá,* Mayorúna* (Maruba, Marubo),
Nastanahua, Nixinahua, Parannahua, Poyanahua (Poyanawa*), Remo, Shami-
nahua, Tushinahua (Tushinawa), Waninahua (Catoquino, Katukína*), Yahu-
anahua (Yawanáwa), Yumanahua, Arasaeri* (Arasaire), Atsahuaca (Atsawaca
or Chaspa), Yamaica (Haauneiri), Karipúna,* Chácobo,* Pacanuara* (Paca-
wara), and Tamanahua (Tamanawa).
   REFERENCE: Cestmir Loukotka, *Classification of South American Indian Languages*,
1968.

PANOBO. The Panobo are a Panoan*-speaking group of Amerindians few of
whom survived the epidemics, slaving expeditions, rubber booms, and settlement
patterns of neo-Peruvian civilization. They have been known historically as the
Manoa, Pano, Pana, and Pelado, as well as Panobo, although their name for
themselves is Wariapana (Huariapana). By the mid–1920s, there were only 200
of the Panobo still alive, and they were widely dispersed along the Ucayali River.
They had also mixed heavily with the Setebo Indians. By the late 1950s, only
a handful of older Panobo still spoke the native language; the others had adopted
Quechua* or Spanish as their primary language. Although there is not a Panobo
community in existence anymore, there are probably individuals in Peruvian
society who are aware of their Panobo background.
   REFERENCE: Darcy Ribeiro and Mary Ruth Wise, *Los grupos étnicos de la amazona
peruana*, 1978.

PANOBO. See SETEBO.

PAPARO. See CHOCÓ.

PARACANA. See PARAKANA.

PARAFURI. See YANOAMA.

PARAGUAYAN TOBA. See TOBA.

PARAHURI. See PARIHURI.

PARAKÁNA. The Parakána are a Tupi*-speaking tribe of Amerindians who
live southwest of the city of Belém, on the middle Tocantins River and at the
headwaters of the Pacaja River, in the state of Pará, Brazil. They currently
occupy three different sites. These are the Pucuri and Parakanan reservations,
located about 60 and 90 kilometers respectively south of the town of Tucuri, in
the municipalities of Tucuri and Jatobal, Pará; a third site is located along the
headwaters of the Cajazeiras River in the municipality of Itupiranga. Historically,

the tribe has remained quite isolated from neo-Brazilian society. Ever since the early 1900s, the Parakána Indians have been the objects of a variety of pacification efforts, most of them unsuccessful. But construction of the Tocantins Railroad brought workers into Parakana land between 1905 and its completion in 1944; although the Indians resisted the construction workers, often violently, the project established permanent contact between the tribe and neo-Brazilian society. In 1953, the Brazilian Indian Protection Service established a government post and attracted 190 Parakána Indians to live there. By 1954, more than 50 of those Indians had died of influenza, and the others had fled the post for their lives in the jungle again. For sixteen years, there was little contact between neo-Brazilians and the Parakaná until construction of the Trans-Amazon Highway brought more settlers. The Brazilian government again established a post among the Parakána and attempted to pacify them; once again influenza destroyed large numbers of tribal members. The Parakána were attracted to the village post, which became known as Espiritu Santo, but they were plagued by poverty and disease, particularly influenza and venereal disease. By the late 1970s, the Parakaña population was fewer than 100 people, and virtually all of those were reduced to begging for a living. Another 150 Parakána were scattered out in groups of individual families. Tribal culture has been severely damaged by depopulation and contact with neo-Brazilians. Moreover, those surviving Parakána people have been threatened by the Tucuri Hydroelectric Project, which may well flood much of their land and relocate the Trans-Amazon Highway much closer to them. They are suffering from high disease rates, severe poverty, and cultural dislocation.

REFERENCES: Paul L. Aspelin and Silvio Coelho dos Santos, *Indian Areas Threatened by Hydroelectric Projects in Brazil*, 1981; Shelton H. Davis, *Victims of the Miracle: Development and the Indians of Brazil*, 1977; Robert Lee Spires, "As línguas faladas do Brasil," *América Indígena*, 47 (1987), 455–79.

PARAKATEYE. See GAVIÃO.

PARAMONA. See PATAMUNO.

PARAMUNI. See PATAMUNO.

PARANAPURA. The Paranapura (Chebero-Munichi, Xevero-Munichi) were originally Jebero* Indians who moved to the region of the Paranapura River in Peru to escape Portuguese slavers in the seventeenth century. On the Paranapura River, they intermarried with the Muniche and eventually adopted the Muniche* language. In 1654, many of them settled at the Mission of Nuesta Senora de Loreto de Paranapura, where they began a long population decline. The term "Paranapura" is still used occasionally to describe Indians, probably Jebero or Muniche, living in that area.

REFERENCE: Stefano Varese, *The Forest Indians in the Present Political Situation of Peru*, 1972.

PARANAWAT. The Paranawat people are a tiny surviving group of Kawahíb*
Indians. The Kawahib once ranged over a large area of the Tapajós-Madeira
River Basin in what is today the state of Amazonas, Brazil, but in the eighteenth
century, they disintegrated into a series of many separate tribes because of the
aggressive expansion of the Mundurukú* Indians. One of the small tribes emerging from the larger Kawahíb group was the Pavahawat. Rubber collectors and
gold prospectors in the early twentieth century put more pressure on the Paranawat, drastically reducing their population to the point that ceremonial life
was no longer possible. Today there are fewer than 50 Paranawat left. They are
living, intermixed with Wirafed* and Tukunafed* Indians, along the Riosinho,
Leitao, Muqui, and Cacoal rivers. Most of them work as laborers on ranches
and rubber plantations in the area and are in permanent contact with neo-Brazilian
society, which is slowly acculturating them.

REFERENCE: Theodore L. Stoddard, ed., *Indians of Brazil in the Twentieth Century*,
1967.

PARAOGWAN. See PARAUJANO.

PARAOKAN. See PARAUJANO.

PARAUANO. See PARAUJANO.

PARAUJANO. The Paraujano Indians, who call themselves the Anuu, live on
the northwestern side of Lake Maracaibo in northwestern Venezuela, between
Sinamaica Lagoon, Nazaret de El Moján, and Santa Rosa de Agua in the state
of Zulia. They are part of the Arawakan* linguistic family. The Paraujano were
contacted by Alonso de Ojeda and Amerigo Vespucci in 1499. They are descendents of the Quiriquire, Jirajira, and Caquetio Indians who at the time of
the conquest dominated northwestern Venezuela. Over the years, they have also
been identified as the Onotos, Alcojolados, Aliles, Sinamaicas, Toas, and Za-
paras, while the most prominent alternate spellings of their name have been
Parhowka, Paraqgwan, Parauano, Parawkan, Paraokan, and Paraogwan. Although the Paraujano are becoming increasingly acculturated to neo-Venezuelan
values and integrated into the regional cash economy, primarily in a transition
from subsistence to commercial fishing, they still maintain a strong awareness
of their Indian heritage. Beginning in the 1970s, there was an increasing rate of
intermarriage between Paraujanos and neo-Venezuelans. Still, by the mid–1980s,
the Paraujano population exceeded 2,600 people. The most highly assimilated
of the Paraujano live in the towns of El Barro, Cano Morita, La Boquita, and
Boca del Cano.

REFERENCES: Ministerio de Estado para la Cultura, *Arte indígena de Venezuela*,
1983; Estéban Emilio Mosonyi, ''La revitalización lingüística y la realidad venezolano,''
América Indígena, 47 (1987), 553–61.

PARAWGWAN. Se PARAUJANO.

PARAWKAN. See PARAUJANO.

PARECÍ. The Parecí Indians (Paresí, Paressí, Paretí, Halití) are a tribe of tropical forest people who live in northwestern Mato Grosso, Brazil, between the Parecí River and the upper Juruena River. They call themselves the Ariti and are a southern branch of the Arawakan* language group. Their homeland is the high, dry plateau that separates northern and southern South America. Historically, they supported themselves by hunting, fishing, and raising sweet manioc and maize. There were once four major divisions of the Parecí: the Parecí proper; the Kashinití* (Cashinití, Kaxinití) who lived along the Soumidoro, Sepotuba, and Sucuriu-na rivers; the Waimaré* (Uaimaré, Mambaré) who lived along the upper Verde and Sacre rivers; and the Kozárene* (Cozarini, Kozárini, Cabishi, Paressí-Cabishi, Cabishi-Parecí) who lived in the watershed of the Juba, Cabacai, Jaurú, Guaporé, Verde, Papagaio, Burity, and Juruena rivers. Today the Kashiniti live on the Sumidouro, Agua Verde, and Sepotuba rivers; the Kozárene are on the headwaters of those three rivers as well as the Juba, Cabacal, Jauru, Guaporé, and Juruena rivers; the Waimaré Indians live along the Verde, Sacre, and Papagaio rivers. In the eighteenth century, the Parecí, because of their highly religious, peaceful value system, were targeted as easy prey for the slave markets of the Cuiabá gold mines. The Parecí population, which stood at 10,000 to 20,000 people before the Portuguese conquest, began a precipitous decline due to slavery, relocation, and disease. By the middle of the nineteenth century, there were approximately 250 Kashinití, 400 Waimaré, and 500 Kozárene still alive. The number of all three groups combined dropped to about 150 in the 1920s. At that time, the tribe received help from the Brazilian Indian Protection Service, even though disease still haunted them. Today most of the Parecí live in small towns and villages along the Cuiabá-Porto Velho Road and on the Parecí Reservation north of the road. There are approximately 640 Pareci living today, most of whom still speak their native tongue. They customarily wear Western-style clothes and adopt a posture of quiet docility when near neo-Brazilians. They nevertheless are profoundly aware of their tribal identity. During the 1970s and 1980s, Daniel Cabixí, a Parecí, emerged as a leader in the national Indian movement and succeeded in having three reservations of more than 90,000 acres set aside for them.

REFERENCES: Robin Hanbury-Tenison, *A Question of Survival for the Indians of Brazil*, 1973; John Hemming, *Red Gold: The Conquest of the Brazilian Indians, 1500–1760*, 1978; David Maybury-Lewis, *In the Path of Polonoreste: Endangered Peoples of Western Brazil*, 1981; Robert Lee Spires, "As Línguas Faladas do Brasil," *América Indígena*, 47 (1987), 455–79.

PARENISATI. See CAMPA DEL ALTO PERENE.

PARENTINTIN. See PARINTINTIN.

PARESÍ. See PARECÍ.

PARESSÍ. See PARECÍ.

PARESSÍ-CABISHÍ. See PARECÍ.

PARETÍ. See PARECÍ.

PARHOWKA. See PARAUJANO.

PARIA. See AYMARA.

PARIANA. See OMÁGUA.

PARI-BI-TETE. See APIACÁ.

PARIHURI. The Parihuri are an unacculturated group of the Yanoama* linguistic family of southern Venezuela and northern Brazil. In particular, they are
closely related to the Shiriana or Xiriana branch of the Yanoama and live along
the Parima River in approximately ten villages. See YANOAMA.

PARIKOTO. See PARUKOTO.

PARINTINTÍN. Parintintín may be the original name for the Kawahib* people,
a large tribe of Amerindians from the Tapajós-Madeira River Basin in Brazil
who were broken up in the eighteenth century by the expansion of the more
aggressive Mundurukú* Indians. Today the Parintintín, or Parintintín-Kawahíb,
are a small tribe of perhaps 120 Indians who live in three villages on the Madeira
River, the Ipixuna River, and the Marmelos River in the state of Amazonas,
Brazil. Their language is of Tupi* extraction. See KAWAHÍB.
    REFERENCE: Waud H. Kracke, *Force and Persuasion: Leadership in an Amazonian
Society*, 1978.

PARIRI. The Pariri are a subtribe of the Yukpa* Indians of northwestern Venezuela. They traditionally pursued a subsistence, farming life along the Yasa
River. The Pariri today number approximately 120 people. See YUKPA.

PARITÍN. See KAWAHÍB.

PAROKOTO. See PARUKOTO.

PARQUENAHUA. The Parquenahua are a tiny group of Amerindians who live along the Panagua and Cashpajali rivers in the Peruvian Amazon. They speak a Panoan* language and may be a subtribe of the Yaminawa,* although they maintain a distinct identity. Little is known about the Parquenahua except that their numbers probably total about 200 people and they pursue a tropical forest existence. They are isolated from neo-Peruvian society.

REFERENCE: Darcy Ribeiro and Mary Ruth Wise, *Los grupos étnicos de la amazona peruana*, 1978.

PARTAMONA. See PATAMUNO.

PARUA. See KAIABÍ.

PARUKOTO. The Parukoto are a Karib*-speaking group of Amerindians inhabiting the northern Amazon basin of Venezuela, Brazil, and Guyana. They have also been known as the Arekuna,* Karamaracoto, Parikoto, Purukoto, Ipuricoto, Parakuto, Purucoto, Purucutu, Progoto, Porocoto, Porokoto, and Taurépane. Like other tropical forest people, the Parukoto plant gardens to raise their staple crops, particularly manioc, and spend a good deal of their time hunting and fishing. They were first reached by William Farabee's anthropological expedition in 1914. In recent years, the Parukoto have become increasingly dependent on European technology, particularly metal tools and clothing. There are two major Parukoto groups, each distantly related to the other. The Parukoto-Pemón live near the Uraricapara River in southeastern Venezuela, while the Parukoto-Xaruma (Parukoto-Charuma) are located on the upper Mapuera River. Anthropologists have also divided the Parukoto-Pemón into three subgroups: the Arekuna, Kamarakoto (Camarakoto), and Taurépan. Both groups have recently undergone sustained population growth, primarily because of high fertility rates and basic medical care provided by local Protestant missionaries. Between 1937 and 1987, the Parukoto-Pemón increased from 1,600 people to more than 11,000. The Parukoto-Xaruma today total approximately 3,500 people. The greatest threat to the Parukoto now comes from the development of alluvial diamond mining in their region, which is attracting unprecedented numbers of outsiders to their homeland. Along with the fact that the Parukoto have always been willing to marry outside the tribe to other Indians, especially the Makushi,* Akawaio,* Patamuno,* and Yekuana,* this influx has contributed to a broadening sense of ethnicity.

REFERENCES: Estéban Emilio Mosonyi, "La revitalización lingüística y la realidad venezolano," *América Indígena*, 47 (1987), 553–61; David John Thomas, "Pemón Demography, Kinship, and Trade," Ph.D. dissertation, University of Michigan, 1973; David

John Thomas, *Order Without Government: The Society of Pemón Indians of Venezuela*, 1982.

PARUKOTO-CHARUMA. See PARUKOTO.

PARUKOTO-XARUMA. See PARUKOTO.

PARUKUTU. See PARUKOTO.

PASCO. See QUECHUA.

PASTO. The Pasto were a large tribe of the Cauca Valley in southwestern Colombia at the time of the Spanish conquest, but they did not survive as a tribal entity. The last speakers of the aboriginal Pasto language died in the mid–1800s, and the language died with them. But although the Pasto language and the overt elements of Pasto culture disappeared, there are still approximately 16,000 people scattered throughout southwestern Colombia and northwestern Ecuador who are descendants of the Pasto. They are integrated into the local economy as subsistence farmers, migrant laborers, quinine extractors, and miners, but they maintain a distinct identity as Indian people and have generally tried to avoid intermarriage with surrounding mestizos and blacks.

REFERENCE: Eduardo Nalo Martínez, *Etnohistória de los Pastos*, 1977; Joanne Rappaport, "History and Everyday Life in the Colombian Andes," *Man*, 23 (1988), 718–39.

PATAGONE. See TEHUELCHE.

PATAMONA. See PATAMUNO.

PATAMUNO. The Patamuno—or Partamona, Patamona, Paramona, and Paramuni—are a subtribe of the Akawáios.* They speak a Karib* language. Today they live in the northern Pakaraima Mountains from the Ireng River in the west to the Kaieteur escarpment in the east in Guyana and in far southeastern Venezuela. Their main villages are in the North Pakaraimas in such villages as Paramakatoi, Kurukubaru, Chenapau, Kamana, and Kató. A smaller concentration of Patamuno Indians can be found at Monkey Mountain in the South Pakaraimas and at Mahdia and Tumatumari in the Essequibo area. The Patamuno are highly acculturated Amerindians increasingly integrated into neo-Guyanese technology, values, and cash economy. Today they total approximately 2,500 people.

REFERENCES: Audrey Butt-Colson, "Birth Customs of the Akawáios," in J. M. Beattie and R. G. Leinhardt, eds., *Studies in Social Anthropology in Memory of E.E. Evans-Pritchard*, 1975; Estéban Emilio Mosonyi, "La revitalización lingüística y la realidad venezolano," *América Indígena*, 47 (1987), 553–61; Andrew Sanders, *The Powerless People*, 1987; David John Thomas, *Order Without Government: The Society of Pemón Indians of Venezuela*, 1982.

PATASHÓ. See PATAXÓ.

PATAXÓ. The Pataxó (Patashó, Pataxó-Hãhãhãi) once lived in the dense wood-lands between the Mucuri and Arassuai rivers in the state of Bahia, Brazil. At the time of the Portuguese conquest, there were more than 6,000 Pataxó Indians, but they declined rapidly after contact with the Portuguese. Several independent bands of the Pataxo were still functioning as social units in 1900, scattered around the Rio das Contas in southern Bahia. Large numbers of neo-Brazilians had by then invaded their territory, and local governments did nothing to protect Pataxó land. Extermination of the Pataxó in order to clear land for cacao plan-tations became commonplace. By the 1960s, there were only a handful of full-blooded Pataxó Indians, but hundreds of other mixed-blood Pataxó possessed strong tribal identities. In 1982, the Pataxó Indians on the Paraguacu-Caramuru Reservation, who had been living in the state of Minas Gerais, decided to return to their tribal homelands, but their migration precipitated violence from local ranchers. Their numbers have continued to decline in the 1970s and 1980s. Today fewer than 50 people of Pataxo descent survive, most of them near Itaquira at the Caramuru Indian Park, in the state of Bahia. Demographers estimate that there are approximately 1,700 people in Bahia who are of Pataxó extraction and 1,200 of Pataxó-Hãhãhãhi descent.

REFERENCES: Ordep T. Serra, "The Pataxó of Bahia: Persecution and Discrimi-nation Continue," *Cultural Survival Quarterly*, 13 (1989), 16–17; Robert Lee Spires, "As línguas faladas do Brasil," *América Indígena*, 47 (1987), 455–79.

PATAXÓ-HÃHÃHÃI. See PATAXÓ.

PAU CERNA. See PAUSERNA.

PAUMARÍ. Also known historically as the Paumary, Pammarí, Pamaurí, Ku-rukúru, Purupúru, and Wayai, the Paumarí are an Arawá*-speaking people who today occupy several sites in the state of Amazonas in northwestern Brazil. They live primarily in small villages of several nuclear families. One group lives near Lake Marraha, while the others can be found on such tributaries of the Purus River as the Sepatini, Ituxi, Big Mamoria, and Tapoa rivers. Like other tropical forest tribes, the Paumarí plant manioc as their staple, but they are also widely known for their prowess as fishermen, especially turtle fishermen. They are a surviving subtribe of the now-extinct Purupúru people, who once numbered 5,000 people and who in the seventeenth century occupied the Purus River to its mouth. The last time the Purupúru were heard from was in the mid–1800s. By that time, the Paumarí population was falling, and men were working as rubber gatherers and lumberjacks for other Brazilians. Today there are approximately 280 mem-bers of the Paumarí tribe in Brazil.

REFERENCES: Mary Ann Odmark and Rachel Landin, "On Paumarí Social Orga-nization," in William R. Merrifield, ed., *South American Kinship: Eight Kinship Systems*

From Brazil and Colombia, 1985; Robert Lee Spires, "As línguas faladas do Brasil," *América Indígena*, 47 (1987), 455–79.

PAUMARY. See PAUMARÍ.

PAUMUCA. See CHIQUITANO.

PAUNA. See PAUNACA.

PAUNACA. The Paunaca (Paiconeca, Paicone, Pauna, Paunaka, Pawnaka) are a small, Arawakan*-speaking group of Amerindians who today live near Concepcion in the province of Ñuflo de Chávez in the department of Santa Cruz, Bolivia. In 1707, the Paunaca joined the Roman Catholic mission settlement of Concepción with the Uñape and Carababa Indians. They stayed there for more than a century, although about a third of the tribe retreated back into the forests. In the twentieth century, the Paunaca moved up toward the headwaters of the Río Blanco to increase their distance from neo-Bolivianos. Today there are only about 180 Paunaca Indians. They are increasingly acculturated to the local economy and society. They are in a state of rapid detribalization and no longer use the aboriginal language. Many live among the Chiriguano* Indians.

REFERENCES: Jürgen Riester, *Indians of Eastern Bolivia: Aspects of Their Present Situation*, 1975; Graciela Zolezzi and J. Riester, "Lenguas indígenas del oriente boliviano clasificacion preliminar," *América Indígena*, 47 (1987), 425–33.

PAUNAKA. See PAUNACA.

PAUSERNA. The Pauserna (Pau Cerna, Itatin, Carabere, Araibayba, Moterequoa) are a tiny, functionally extinct group of Amerindians who live in the northwestern corner of the department of Santa Cruz in Bolivia. They call themselves the Guarasug'we. They are descendents of the Guaraní.* Most likely they migrated to Bolivia from Paraguay centuries before when the Guaraní attacked the frontiers of the Incan empire. They were one tribe with the Guarayu (Guarayo) until Spanish missionaries settled the Guarayu on missions. Those Guarayu who did not go into the missions became known as Pausernas. They lived on the left side of the Guaporé River. The Pauserna were essentially a hunting and foraging tribe although they adapted to communal horticulture. They had little contact with neo-Bolivian society until after 1880 when the rubber boom brought large numbers of rubber collectors into their territory. At the time, they numbered approximately 300 people. Since 1930, they have lived between the Paragua River and the Guaporé River in the province of Velasco. They recently gave up the production of manioc and switched to rice and caripo. Their population went into a period of sustained decline in the twentieth century. From approximately 130 people in 1930, the Pauserna declined to 60 people in 1965 to fewer than 30 in the 1970s, with the majority of them elderly people. Those few Pauserna who still survive make their living by collecting rubber and ipecacuanha, which neo-Bolivian merchants sell to pharmaceutical laboratories.

REFERENCES: Brian M. Boom, *Ethnobotany of the Chácobo Indians, Beni, Bolivia*, 1987; Harold Key and Mary Key, *Bolivian Indian Tribes: Classification, Bibliography, and Map of Present Language Distribution*, 1967; Jürgen Riester, *Los Guarasug'we: Crónica de sus ultimos dias*, 1977.

PAWANA. See YEKUANA.

PAWATE. See PARANAWAT.

PAWNAKA. See PAUNACA.

PAWYER. See PAYA.

PAYA. The Paya (Pesch, Pech) Indians are a tribe living in and around the towns of Dulce Nombre de Culmi and Santa Maria del Carbón in the department of Olancho in Honduras. There are also scattered settlements in the neighboring departments of Colón and Gracias a Dios. The Paya are closely related to the Jicaque.* Christopher Columbus first encountered the Paya on his third voyage to the New World in 1498, and he called them Taia. At the time, there were thousands of Paya ranging from the Aguan River Valley and the Wanks River south to the Olancho and Jamastrau valleys. They were a semi-nomadic, agricultural people who raised tubers. European diseases decimated the Paya, as did raids from the neighboring Miskito* Indians, particularly after the British had armed them. The Miskito drove the Paya up the river valleys into the interior of Honduras. By the 1920s, the Paya numbered only 600 people. By the early 1980s, Paya numbers had dropped even more, down to only a few hundred people who still spoke the language, but another 1,000 people consider themselves Paya Indians. Despite the population decline, the tribe still survives as a self-conscious entity. An even smaller group, the Seco, are a Payan people living on the Tinto River. Over the years, the Paya Indians have also been known as the Poya, Poyer, Poyai, Popya, Pawyer, and Pahaya. In 1978, the Paya joined with several other tribes to form the National Federation of Tribes for the Liberation of the Honduran Indian. Today approximately 1,800 people claim Paya ancestry, but fewer than 20 of them are full bloods.

REFERENCES: R. S. Chamberlain, *The Conquest and Colonization of Honduras, 1502–1550*, 1967; Leon Kolankiewicz, "The Pesch of Honduras Face Uncertain Prospects," *Cultural Survival Quarterly*, 13 (1989), 34–37; L. Fernando Cruz Sandoval, "Los indios de Honduras y la situación de sus recursos naturales," *América Indígena*, 44 (1984), 423–46; Demetrio Sodi and Espinosa de Derbez, "Honduras," *Indian Yearbook*, 22 (1962), 63–65.

PAYAGUÁ. See OREJÓN.

PAYNI-KEN. See TEHUELCHE.

PEBA. See YAGUA.

PEBO. See COGUI.

PECH. See PAYA.

PEGUENCHE. See PEHUENCHE.

PEHUENCHE. The Pehuenche (Peguenche) were a foraging people whose economy revolved around the pinon, a pine tree fruit that they collected and used to make bread and beverages. In the sixteenth and seventeenth centuries, the Pehuenches fell under the influence of the Mapuche* Indians, an Araucanian* people, and eventually merged with them, losing their own tribal identity. See ARAUCANIAN.

PELADO. See PANOBO.

PEMÓN. See PARUKOTO.

PEMÓNG. See AREKUNA.

PEÑOKI. See PEÑOQUI.

PEÑOQUI. The Peñoqui (Peñoki) were a tribe of Amerindians who spoke a Chiquitoan language and lived in eastern Bolivia. The Jesuits settled the small tribe at the Mission of San José in the early eighteenth century. At the mission, the Peñoqui soon lost their aboriginal language and adopted the Piñoco dialect. Their tribal population began a long decline from which it never recovered, although until just recently, and perhaps even still, there are detribalized, acculturated neo-Bolivians vaguely aware of their Peñoqui background.
    REFERENCE: S. Lyman Tyler, *Indians of South America*, 1976.

PESCH. See PAYA.

PIALPIE. See COAIQUER.

PIANOI. The Pianoi are a sub-group of the Aramagotó,* who are themselves a subtribe of the Tiriyó.* They have been known among other Tiriyó for their suspiciousness about outsiders, neo-Brazilians as well as other Indians. See TIRIYÓ.

PIANOKOTÓ. The Pianokotó (Maracho, Marahtxo, Pianakotó, Pianocotó, Pianoghotto, Pianogotó, Piannacotou, and Piannocotou) are most likely a subtribe of the Tiriyó* who have so mixed with other Tiriyó subtribes in recent years that they have ceased to exist as a self-conscious social unit. Today the Pianokotó and the Tiriyó have become essentially the same tribe and live on the upper and eastern tributaries of the Trombetas River in the state of Pará, Brazil, and across the border in Surinam. See TIRIYÓ.

PIAPOCO. The Piapoco (Yapaco, Cuipoco, Deja, Enagua, and Dzase) Indians are a small, tropical forest group of people who once inhabited the territory drained by the María and Cuinacia rivers near the border of Colombia and Venezuela. They are members of the Arawak* linguistic family; their self-designation is Tsese. Today they live in the vicinity of the Guaviare, Vichada, Meta, and Orinoco rivers in the territory of Vichada in Colombia and in adjacent areas of Venezuela. When Jesuit missionaries moved into the area in the sixteenth century, the Piapoco moved to stay away from them; they relocated repeatedly over the years to avoid rubber collectors, European and mestizo settlers, and cattle ranchers. In the 1920s, the Piapoco adopted Western-style clothing, and most gradually lost use of the aboriginal language, adopting Spanish instead. They are subsistence farmers whose diet revolves around the cultivation of manioc. The Piapoco also raise maize, rice, bananas, chickens, and pigs. Since 1966, the Summer Institute of Linguistics has worked among them. Today the Piapoco number approximately 10,000 people and live primarily as subsistence farmers or day laborers. There are approximately 275 Piapoco living on the government Indian reservation of Corozal-Tapapojo, as well as 30 on the Yuri Brazo Amanaven reservation, 110 on the Giro Brazo Amanaven reservation, 329 on the Morocoto Buenavista reservation, 180 on the Ministas Miralindo reservation, 434 on the Pueblo Nuevo Laguna Colorada reservation, and 130 on the Murcielago-Altamira reservation.

REFERENCES: Lubio Cardozo, *Cuentas indígenas venezolanos*, 1968; Ministerio de Gobierno, *Aspetos de la cultura material de los grupos étnicos de Colombia*, 1979; Estéban Emilio Mosonyi, "La revitalización lingüística y la realidad venezolano," *América Indígena*, 47 (1987), 553–61.

PIAROA. The Piaroa (Fiaroa, Fiaroankomo) are a tropical forest, Sálivan*-speaking people living along the tributaries of the Orinoco River in the Guiana Highlands of Venezuela and just across the border in Colombia. In the 1750s, they were called the Sipapo. Most of the nearly 7,000 Piaroa live in the federal territory of Amazonas. The largest concentrations of Piaroa live near the Atures Rapids of the Orinoco, along the Sipapo River, an Orinoco tributary, and along such Sipapo tributaries as the Autana, Cuao, and Guayapo rivers. They have historically been called the Atures people, because of their location near rapids of the same name, and as the Macos. The Piaroa called themselves the "Wotuha" (Tuha). Although the Piaroa were victimized by Karib* slave traders in the seventeenth centuries and by Jesuit missionaries in the eighteenth, their relative isolation helped protect them from annihilation. They have been widely known by other Indians because of their ability to supply curare, a poisonous drug used in war and hunting. Since the tribe values peace and tranquility, not aggressiveness, as the greatest of virtues, it was their geographic position, not their resistance, that preserved them from the ravages of European civilization. The Piaroa knew that deadly sicknesses always accompanied contact with whites, so they avoided whites whenever possible. The Piaroa still live as they have for centuries. They hunt and fish but only to supplement their horticulture. The Piaroa maintain individually owned gardens of two to four acres in which they raise their staple—bitter yuca—along with potatoes, squash, bananas, maize, pineapple, sugar cane, peppers, and cotton. In 1988, there were approximately 112 Piaroa living on a Colombian government reservation at Cano Zama, as well as 175 at the Mataven Fruta reservation and 111 at the Cumaral Brazo Amanaven reservation.

REFERENCES: Joanna Overing Kaplan, *The Piaroa: A People of the Orinoco Basin*, 1975; Estéban Emilio Mosonyi, "La revitalización lingüística y la realidad venezolano," *América Indígena*, 47 (1987), 553–61.

PIBA-YAGUA. See YAGUA.

PICONE. See PICUNCHE.

PICUNCHE. The Picunche (Picanos) were the northernmost of the Araucanian* Indian people of Chile. Pedro de Valdivia and the Spaniards arrived in Chile in 1540 and, despite great resistance, conquered the Picunche and put them to work on cattle ranches, horse ranches, and gold mines. They sustained a rapid population loss in the sixteenth century and by the early seventeenth century had for the most part disappeared into the surrounding mestizo society. See ARAUCANIANS.

PIDA-DIAPÁ. See KATUKÍNA.

PIJAO. The Pijao Indians of southwestern Colombia are part of the Páezan* language group and historically were closely related to their neighbors, the Páez tribe. They were first contacted by the Spanish in 1538 when Sebastián de Benalcazar reached them; they put up a vicious resistance to his invasion. They then inhabited the eastern slopes of the Andes mountains from La Plata to Ibague; the Páez River was their southwestern limit. Because of the ruggedness of their tribal territory, they were able to hold out against the Spanish invasion. The Spanish fought a bloody struggle with the Pijao for more than twenty years, bringing the tribe to the edge of extinction. They were a horticultural people who raised potatoes and tubers. Today there are 163 Indians living on the Colombian government reservation of Tinajas who claim to be Pijao Indians.

REFERENCE: Blaz Telban, *Grupos étnicos de Colombia: Etnografía y Bibliografía*, 1988.

PILAGÁ. The Pilagá—also known historically as the Toba-Pilagá, Western Toba, Pilacá, Pitilagá, Yapitalgá, Zapitalagá, Pitelahá, Pitaleaes, and Ai—are a Guaycuruan-speaking people of the Gran Chaco in lower South America. Until recently, they had retained many of their aboriginal habits. There are approximately 800 Pilaga living along the middle Pilcomayo River in Paraguay; in Argentina there are large settlements of Pilagá in Las Lomitas, El Descanso, Campo del Cielo, and Pozo de los Chancos. Their territory was once much wider than that, particularly after they acquired use of the horse in the seventeenth century. In the eighteenth and nineteenth centuries, Spanish mission policies and the increasing presence of European immigrants gradually reduced Pilagá territory. Their tribal population exceeded 2,000 people in the 1930s, but a devastating smallpox epidemic in 1940 killed half of the tribe. The tribal population has since declined because of assimilation into the neighboring mestizo culture. The Pilagá have been greatly influenced by evangelical Protestant missionaries in the 1950s, 1960s, and 1970s. During the last two decades, the Pilagá have turned to cotton cultivation, along with their subsistence crops, to provide the cash they need to function in the regional economy.

REFERENCES: Jules Henry, *Doll Play of Pilaga Indian Children*, 1974; Isabel Hernández, "Los pueblos y las lenguas aborígenes en la actualidad," *América Indígena*, 47 (1987), 409–23; Sara Josefina Newberry, "Los Pilagá: Su religión a sus mitos de origen," *América Indígena*, 33 (1973), 757–69; Johannes Wilbert and Karin Simoneau, *Folk Literature of the Toba Indians*, 1982.

PILCOSUMI. See CAMPA.

PINAGÉ. See APINAYÉ.

PINARÉ. See APINAYÉ.

PINCHE. See TAUSHIRO.

PINCHI. See TAUSHIRO.

PIOCHE. See SECOYA.

PIOJÉ. See SECOYA.

PIPIL. The Pipil are a Nahuat-speaking people who today live in western El Salvador, primarily in and around Cuisnahuat and Santo Domingo de Guzmán, with smaller groups in Honduras and Nicaragua. Once a large, advanced urban civilization, the tribe moved to El Salvador during a series of migrations beginning in the eighth century and continuing into the fourteenth. There they founded the kingdom of Cuzcatlán and largely displaced the Pocomám who were living there. By 1350, the Pipil had absorbed most of the other tribes living in El Salvador. Although the tribe was not completely centralized, the ruling group in Cuzcatlán dominated all the Pipil. The Pipil probably came from central and southern Mexico because of the expansion of the Toltec empire there. They put up a fierce resistance to the Spaniards, defeating Pedro de Alvarado's expedition at the Battle of Acajutla on June 8, 1524. Alvarado came back in 1525 and crushed the Pipil, bringing on a drastic population decline, although they were not completely subdued until 1539. They survived the missionization process of the Catholic friars, as well as government land policies in the nineteenth and twentieth centuries. Today there are approximately 2,000 Pipil living an indigenous lifestyle in El Salvador, Honduras, and Nicaragua.

REFERENCES: William R. Fowler, "Ethnohistoric Sources on the Pipil-Nicarao of Central America: Critical Analysis," *Ethnohistory*, 32 (1982), 37–62; Robert C. West and John P. Augelli, *Middle America: Its Lands and Peoples*, 1966.

PÍRA. See PÍRO.

PIRAHÃ. The Pirahã (Pirianaus, Piaarhaus, Piraheus, Piriahai, Piriahã, and Pinyaha) are a subtribe of the Múra* Indians. Known for their suspicion of outsiders, they are scattered along the Marmelos, Maici, Manicoré, and Capana rivers in the state of Amazonas, Brazil. A tropical forest people, the Piraha support themselves by hunting, a little fishing, and the production of manioc in communal gardens. The tribe remained extremely isolated from European civilization until the early 1900s when rubber collectors disrupted their habitat, precipitating a severe population decline. Today the Pirahã total approximately 200 people.

REFERENCE: Robert Lee Spires, "As Línguas Faladas do Brasil," *América Indígena*, 47 (1987), 455–79.

PIRATAPUIO. See PIRA-TAPUYA.

PIRA-TAPUYA. An Eastern Tukanoan* language tribe of Amerindians, the Pira-Tapuya (Piriatapuya, Paratapuio, Uaicama) today are concentrated on the lower Papuri River and in the villages of Teresita, Africa, and Piramiri in the Vaupés River drainage region of Colombia and in the state of Amazonas, Brazil. Some of them have moved recently to such cities as Meta and Bogotá looking for wage-laboring jobs. They call themselves the Waikena (Wakada, Waikana, Uaikena) and are probably a subtribe of the Uanana.* There were sporadic European contacts with the Pira-Tapuya in the eighteenth and nineteenth centuries. Portuguese missions were established temporarily along the upper Vaupés in the 1780s, but systematic evangelization of the tribe did not begin until 1914 when Roman Catholic priests established missions on the Papuri River. Theodor Koch-Grünberg began ethnological studies of the Pira-Tapuya at the same time. Protestant missionaries made their way into the region after World

War II, eventually making nominal converts of a minority of Pira-Tapuya. The tribal economy focuses on the production of bitter manioc and fishing; hunting is quite secondary, although in recent years the tribe has become increasingly dependent on such European technology as fishhooks, shotguns, and machetes, as well as on increased manioc production for sale. Contact with whites has also led to the development of small-scale animal husbandry, primarily hogs and poultry. There are several subtribes of the Pira-Tapuya. The Busada live in the region of the lower Papuri River near Leticia, Amazonas; the Kedada are on the lower Papuri, the Wehetara near the town of Teresita, the Bua across the Brazilian border, and the Soariapode and the Ditiapode outside the town of Teresitas.

In the 1960s and 1970s, the Colombian government began to encourage colonization of the Vaupés River basin, but settlement there has been very slow. The Pira-Tapuya interact with other Indian tribes in the area but rarely with whites, except for missionaries and rubber collectors, because of the extreme geographical isolation of the area. There are approximately 1,300 Pira-Tapuya today who acknowledge tribal membership. Of those, approximately 400 still speak the tribal language. The Pira-Tapuya are increasingly becoming acculturated. Use of the aboriginal language is now confined to older adults, while young people, although they still understand Pira-Tapuyan, use Spanish. To outsiders, the Pira-Tapuya appear to be little different from surrounding campesino farmers. They raise sugar cane, maize, coffee, and various fruit products. The majority of the tribe resides in Colombia.

REFERENCES: Ministerio de Gobierno, *Aspetos de la cultura material de los grupos étnicos de Colombia*, 1979; Jean A. Jackson, *The Fish People: Linguistic Exogamy and Tukanoan Identity in Northwest Amazonia*, 1983; Gerardo Reichel-Dolmatoff, *Amazonian Cosmos: The Sexual and Religious Symbolism of the Tukano Indians*, 1985; Robert Lee Spires, "As línguas faladas do Brasil," *América Indígena*, 47 (1987), 455–79.

PÍRIO. See PÍRO.

PÍRIU. See APURUI.

PÍRO. The Píro (Pírio, Pírro, Píra, Simirinche, Simiranch, Chontader, Chontaquiro) are an Arawakan*-speaking group of Amerindians who live in small scattered groups in the forests on the Urubamba, Cushabatay, and Madre de Dios rivers in the Peruvian Amazon and between the upper Iaco and Acre rivers in the state of Acre, Brazil. They call themselves the Yine. Their particular homeland is near the junction of the Brazilian-Bolivian-Peruvian borders. They are divided into two subgroups: the Manitenéri* (Manetenéri, Manetinéri, Manienéri, Maniteneiri, Manitinéri, and Manichenéri) and the Maxinéri.* The Manitenéri today number approximately 560 people and the Maxinéri approximately 345 people. An interfluvial people, the Manitenéri generally avoid river life, preferring to gather food and hunt in the open forests between the rivers. In Brazil, the Píro are referred to as one of the subtribes, while in Peru the generic Píro is used. In Peru, the Píro live primarily on the banks of the Urubamba and the Paucartambo rivers, with some on the Ucayali and Madre de Dios rivers. The Píro bitterly resisted the first contacts with Spanish missionaries in the seventeenth and eighteenth centuries, and the first missions were not established among them until 1795 and 1809. They were devastated by rubber collectors in the late nineteenth and early twentieth centuries. In the process of dislocation, they intermarried with individuals of many other dislocated tribes, giving their culture a new identity. They thereby lost their clan system social structure. Since 1920, the Píro population has increased from 500 to 2,000 people, but today they are rapidly acculturating. Most of them understand Spanish or Portuguese.

REFERENCES: Ricardo Alvarez, *Los Piros: Hijos dioses*, 1970; Peter Gow, "The Perverse Child: Desire in a Native Amazonian Subsistence Economy," *Man*, 24 (1989), 567–82; Robert Lee Spires, "As línguas faladas do Brasil," *América Indígena*, 47 (1987), 455–79; Theodore L. Stoddard, ed., *Indians of Brazil in the Twentieth Century*, 1967.

PÍRRO. See PÍRO.

PISABO. The Pisabo (Pisagua, Pisahua) are a tiny group of Amerindians who today live in the Peruvian and Brazilian Amazon. They are part of the Panoan* language group. A tropical forest people who have been extremely isolated and intent on avoiding contact with neo-Peruvians and neo-Brazilians, the Pisabo number approximately 100 people. In 1973, they attacked a petroleum exploration group between the Tapiche and Blanco rivers in Peru. During the late 1970s, the Mayorúna* Indians said they knew that some Pisabo had migrated into Brazil.

REFERENCE: Darcy Ribeiro and Mary Ruth Wise, *Los grupos étnicos de la amazona peruana*, 1978.

PISAGUA. See PISABO.

PISAHUA. See PISABO.

PISHQUIBO. The Pishquibo (Pisquibo) are a group of Amerindians descended from Panoan*-speaking people and living in the region of the Pisqui River in eastern Peru. They are very closely related to the Shipibo* and may represent a very conservative, transitional group of them. Once a horticultural people who lived by the production of manioc, the Pishquibo today remain a subsistence agricultural people. They are now also in permanent contact with the neo-Peruvian economy and work part-time and seasonally as laborers to raise the cash they need for trade goods. The Pishquibo number more than 1,000 people, and the vast majority still speak their tribal language.

REFERENCES: Peter G. Roe, "Art and Residence Among the Shipibo Indians of Peru: A Study in Microacculturation," *American Anthropology*, 82 (1980), 42–71; Stefano Varese, *The Forest Indians in the Present Political Situation of Peru*, 1972.

PISIATARI. See CAMPA.

PISINÁHUA. See SHARANÁHUA.

PISISUMI. See CAMPA.

PISQUIBO. See PISHQUIBO.

PITALEAE. See PILAGÁ.

PITAYO. See PÁEZ.

PITELAHA. See PILAGÁ.

PITILAGÁ. See PILAGÁ.

PITUIARÓ. The Pituiaró are an extremely small, highly isolated group of
Amerindians who are part of the Northern Kayapó* group. Like the other Kayapó
people, they are a Gê*-speaking tribal group and have a reputation for social
fracturing into smaller and smaller groups. The Pituiaró population today is
approximately 60 people. They separated from the Kuben-Kran-Kêgn* Indians
around 1941 and then moved southeast to the headwaters of the Rio Fresco.
They are a tropical forest people who are extremely suspicious of neo-Brazilians
and were still resisting contact in the 1980s.
   REFERENCE: Paul L. Aspelin and Silvio Coelho dos Santos, *Indian Groups Threatened by Hydroelectric Projects in Brazil*, 1981.

PLAYERO. The Playero are a small tribe of Amerindians who live on the
Arauca River in the intendency of Arauca in Colombia; some also live on the
Venezuelan side of the Arauca River. They are closely related historically to
the Guahibo,* and some people consider them a subtribe of the Guahibo. Their
language is part of the Guahibo group of languages. They practice a subsistence
agriculture, raising plantains, maize, manioc, and sugar cane, as well as chickens.
They supplement their protein needs by hunting. In the mid–1980s, the Playero
population stood at nearly 200 people.
   REFERENCE: Leah B. Ellis and Linda Criswell, eds., *Estudiemos las culturas indígenas de Colombia*, 1984.

POCANAHUA. See MORUNAHAU.

POCOMÁN. The Pocomán (Pokomám) are a Kekchian Maya* people located
in the departments of Guatemala, Jalapa, Esquintla, and Chiquimula, Guatemala.
Smaller numbers have also migrated to El Salvador. In the fifteenth century,
they fell under the domination of the Quiché* Maya, and although they overthrew

Quiché oppression early in the 1500s, they fell under Spanish control in the 1530s. Disease, relocation, and warfare dramatically reduced the Pocomán population in the sixteenth century, but it stabilized in the seventeenth. Like other Mayans, the Pocomán were a settled, agricultural people who lived off the cultivation of maize and beans. In the late 1800s, the government of Guatemala, pressured by powerful agricultural interests, began forcibly transferring tribal land to private ownership, reducing most of the Pocomán to peasant or migrant laborer status. Their poverty produced political unrest after World War II, which in turn brought bloody reprisals against Mayan activists. In the 1980s, perhaps 25 percent of the Pocomán emigrated to the United States, leaving approximately 50,000 members of the tribe behind in Guatemala and El Salvador.

REFERENCES: Jim Handy, *Gift of the Devil: A History of Guatemala*, 1984; W. George Lovell, *Conquest and Survival in Colonial Guatemala: A Historical Geography of the Cuchumatan Highlands, 1500–1821*, 1984; W. George Lovell, "Surviving Conquest: The Maya of Guatemala in Historical Perspective," *Latin American Research Review*, 23 (1988), 25–58; Gloria Tujab, "Lenguas indígenas que se encuentran en vias de extinción," *América Indígena*, 47 (1987), 529–33.

POKANGA. See BARÁ.

POKANGA-TAPUYA. See BARÁ.

POKOMCHÍ. The Pokomchí are a Kekchian Mayan* people living in the departments of Alta Verapaz and Baja Verapaz, Guatemala. In the century before the Spanish conquest, the Pokomchí came under the domination of the Quiché,* but no sooner had they thrown off Quiché control than Spanish domination began in the 1520s and 1530s. During the next several centuries, the Pokomchí population declined rapidly from disease but then stabilized. During the nineteenth century, the Pokomchí had to fight against the land hunger of mestizo peasants and the policies of the Guatemalan government, which wanted to convert their communal lands to private ownership. The Pokomchí protested but the alienation of their land occurred anyway, gradually reducing their holdings and transforming them into peasants and migrant laborers. After World War II, the Pokomchí became dissatisfied politically and were attracted to left-wing political movements promising a return of their land. The Guatemalan government reacted to their political insurgency with savage repression, sending large numbers of Pokomchí fleeing to Mexico and the United States. In the 1980s, there were more than 60,000 Pokomchí still in Guatemala.

REFERENCES: Robert M. Carmack, *The Quiché Mayas of Utatlán: The Evolution of a Highland Guatemalan Kingdom*, 1981; Melanie A. Counce and William V. Davidson, "Indians of Central America 1980s," *Cultural Survival Quarterly*, 13 (1989), 38–41; John W. Fox, *Quiché Conquest: Centralism and Regionalism in Highland Guatemalan State Development*, 1978; Jim Handy, *Gift of the Devil: A History of Guatemala*, 1984.

POKOSÍ. See BRIBRI.

POPYA. See PAYA.

POROCOTO. See PARUKOTO.

POROKOTO. See PARUKOTO.

POTIGUAR. See POTIGUARA.

POTIGUARA. The Potiguara (Potivara, Cannibals, Cannibaliers, Potiguar) are a Tupi*-speaking group of Amerindians who today are fully integrated into neo-Brazilian society. At the time of the Portuguese conquest, the Potiguara totaled more than 90,000 people living along the Atlantic coast of Brazil north of Pernambuco. Fierce warriors, they put up a violent resistance to Portuguese expansion and allied themselves with the French in the late sixteenth century. They battled the Portuguese throughout the sixteenth century; between 1603 and 1654 the Potiguara also allied themselves with the Dutch empire in hopes of expelling them. By the middle of the seventeenth century, however, the Potiguara had entered Jesuit missions and they had allied with the Portuguese against the French, Dutch, and other Indian tribes by the end of the century. As a reward, the Portuguese began giving the surviving Potiguara substantial land grants. By the eighteenth century, the Potiguara were well into the acculturation process, accommodating themselves to the Portuguese language, Roman Catholicism, and the regional cash economy. Today there are more than 1,500 Potiguara living in villages scattered along the coast in the state of Paraíba, especially at Traição Bay. In essence they are a mestizo people who speak Portuguese and function in the local culture. Still, the Potiguara are aware of their Indian origins.

REFERENCE: Theodore L. Stoddard, ed., *Indians of Brazil in the Twentieth Century*, 1967.

POTORERA. See POTURERO.

POTURERO. The Poturero (Potorera) were a tribe of Amerindians who once spoke a Zamucoan* language and lived in eastern Bolivia. They were a large tribe inhabiting the forests of the northern Chaco, close to the San Rafael and Aguas Calientes rivers and the missions of Santo Corazón and San Juan Bautista. By the early twentieth century, they had moved out of the missions and into the forests along the Tucabaca River between Santiago and Corumba. The rubber boom of the early twentieth century sent the Poturero down the road to extinction, even though there are probably some neo-Bolivians who are vaguely aware of their Poturero background.

REFERENCE: S. Lyman Tyler, *Indians of South America*, 1976.

POYA. See PAYA.

POYAI. See PAYA.

POYANÁWA. The Poyanáwa are today a small Amerindian tribe pursuing a tropical forest, subsistence existence on the Upper Moa River, a tributary of the Juma, in the state of Acre, Brazil. Their language is part of the Panoan* linguistic family. Because of the geographic isolation of the region, the Poyanáwa avoided sustained contact with neo-Brazilians until the late nineteenth and early twentieth centuries when the rubber boom devastated tribal life. Disease, murder, and ecological change decimated the tribe; at that time, the tribal population exceeded 500 people. In 1913, they were pacified by the government Indian service, which established a post among them, but the Poyanáwa population was in a state of rapid decline. Today there are about 100 Poyanáwa left alive, some of whom still speak the old language but are also fluent in Portuguese. Most live on rubber plantations at the upper Rio Moa.

REFERENCES: Robert Lee Spires, "As línguas faladas do Brasil," *América Indígena*, 47 (1987), 455–79; Theodore L. Stoddard, ed., *Indians of Brazil in the Twentieth Century*, 1967.

POYENISATI. See CAQUINTE.

POYER. See PAYA.

POZA. See MAKUNA.

PRINSU. See SUMU.

PROGOTO. See PARUKOTO.

PROUYÁNA. The Prouyána (Ragú) are a subtribe of the Tiriyó* Indians of Brazil and Surinam. A tropical forest people conditioned to slash-and-burn agriculture, the Prouyána in the 1960s were attracted to a Roman Catholic mission and began the acculturation process. See TIRIYÓ.

PUCAPACURI. See MACHIGUENGA.

PUCAPACURI. See TUYUNEIRI.

PUCA-UMA. See IQUITO.

PUELCHE. The Puelche (Puelchu) were an Amerindian tribe occupying territory east of the Picunche, the northernmost Araucanian* tribe in what are today Chile and Argentina. In the eighteenth century, the Puelche were absorbed by the Mapuche* Indians. See ARAUCANIANS.

PUELCHU. See PUELCHE.

PUINAHUA. See POYANÁWA.

PUINABE. See PUINAVE.

PUINABI. See PUINAVE.

PUINABO. See PUINAVE.

PUINAHUA. See PUINAVE.

PUINAVE. The Puinave (Puinabe, Puinabi, Puinabo, Guaipujinave, Caberre, Winavi) Indians are a small tropical forest group of people who once inhabited the territory drained by the Nooquene and Inírida rivers in the territory of Guainía, Colombia, near the border of Colombia and Venezuela. Some have also moved across the border into Venezuela and Brazil. Many descendents of the Puinave live on the Orinoco River near the mouths of the Guiviare and Atabapo rivers. When Jesuit missionaries moved into the area in the sixteenth century, the Puinave moved to stay away from them; they have relocated repeatedly over the years to avoid rubber collectors, European and mestizo settlers, and cattle ranchers. Today the Puinave number approximately 1,800 people and are primarily concentrated in the territory of Guainía in Colombia and near San Fernando de Atabapo in the Federal Amazonas Territory of Venezuela. Because of the pressures of acculturation, they are rapidly reaching the point of extinction as a functional social group. They still tend to live in extended families of five or six small groups, however. In 1988, there were approximately 184 Puinave living on the Colombian government reservation at Coayare-El Coco, as well as 490 at the Remanzo-Chorro Bocón reservation, 326 at the Caranacoa-Yuri-Laguna Morocoto reservation, 138 at the Almikdon-La Gelba reservation, 186 at the Bachaco Buena Vista reservation, 265 at the Guaco Bajo y Guaco Alto reservation, and 103 at the Cano Bocón Brazo Amanaven reservation.

REFERENCES: Lubio Cardozo, *Cuentas indígenas venezolanos*, 1968; Marc de Civrieux, *Watunna: An Orinoco Creation Cycle*, 1980; Estéban Emilio Mosonyi, "La revitalización lingüística y la realidad venezolano," *América Indígena*, 47 (1987), 553–61.

PUKINA. See PUQUINA.

PUKIRIERI. See ARASAERI.

PUKIRIERI. See TOYERI.

PUKOBYÉ. See GAVIÃO.

PUKOPYÉ. See GAVIÃO.

PUKU-DIAPÁ. See KATUKÍNA.

PUME. See YARURO.

PUNCURI. See TOYERI.

PUNTALE. See COAIQUER.

PUQUINA. The Puquina (Pukina) people are part of an isolated linguistic group around the Lake Titicaca area of Bolivia. Most of them did not survive the first Incan and then the Spanish conquest, except for the Uru* and the Shipaya.* See URU and SHIPAYA.

PUQUIRI. See MASCO.

PURÓ. The Puró Indians are a tiny group of Amerindians who are part of the larger Northern Kayapó* group. They speak a Gê* language and are known for their extreme suspicion of other Indians as well as neo-Brazilians. The Puró are a tropical forest people whose economy has revolved around foraging, hunting, and fishing, as well as limited horticulture. They separated from the Mekranotí* Indians near the upper Iriri River in 1940 and headed downstream. As late as the mid–1980s, the Puró were studiously avoiding contact with the larger neo-Brazilian society.

REFERENCE: Paul L. Aspelin and Silvio Coelho dos Santos, *Indian Areas Threatened by Hydroelectric Projects in Brazil*, 1981.

PURUBORÁ. A part of the Tupi* language group, the Puruborá (Buruborá) once numbered several thousand people and lived at the headwaters of the São Miguel River in what is today the state of Rondônia, Brazil. They experienced a serious population decline in the 1730s when thousands of neo-Brazilian rubber collectors invaded their tribal homeland. A tropical forest people, they were subsequently devastated by the rubber collectors of the nineteenth and early twentieth centuries and suffered rapid population decline. At present, the Puruborá number fewer than 100 people but they are in fairly constant contact with a post of the Brazilian government Indian service. Tribal identity and functional social life are still intact, although declining numbers are threatening that. Most of the Puruborá still speak the native language, although increasing numbers are becoming familiar with Portuguese.

REFERENCES: Robert Lee Spires, ''As línguas faladas do Brasil,'' *América Indígena*, 47 (1987), 455–79; Theodore L. Stoddard, ed., *Indians of Brazil in the Twentieth Century*, 1967.

PURUCOTO. See PARUKOTO.

PURUKOTO. See PARUKOTO.

PURUPURU. See PAUMARÍ.

Q

QAWASQAR. The Qawasqar Indians of Tierra del Fuego were essentially a Stone Age people with a sea-based lifestyle. They roamed the coastal seashores widely, looking for shellfish and beached sea mammals. The Qawasqar population stood at 4,000 people in 1850, but a series of tuberculosis and syphilis epidemics decimated them. In 1884, their population had dropped to 950 people, and the decline continued unabated, dropping to 490 in 1885, 150 in 1925, 100 in 1946, 60 in 1953, and 47 in 1971. The Chilean government passed legislation in the 1920s to protect the Qawasqar, and in the 1960s they were settled on a reserve at Puerto Eden. Medical treatment at a substantial level reached the Qawasqar in 1986 and probably averted their total extinction. Most of the surviving Qawasqar work as day laborers on local fishing boats.

REFERENCE: "The Qawasqar Indians of Tierra del Fuego," *Cultural Survival Quarterly*, 11 (1987), 83–84.

QHECHWA. See QUECHUA.

QOLLA. The term "Qolla" (Colla, Coya) has been used for years to describe the Aymara* Indians of Peru and Bolivia, but also to identify a surviving Aymara subtribe that today numbers in the thousands and inhabits the Lake Titicaca basin in Peru and Bolivia. They pursue an Andean lifestyle that revolves around the production of maize, beans, potatoes, and llamas. It is not uncommon for the Qolla to speak several languages, including Aymara, Quechua,* and Spanish. Despite the fact that more and more of them have adopted Quechua as a *lingua franca*, the Qolla maintain a strong sense of ethnic identity and enjoy a cultural life still centered on tribal values.

REFERENCE: Ralph Bolton, "Aggression and Hypoglycemia Among the Qollas: A Study in Psychological Anthropology," *Ethnology*, 12 (1973), 227–58.

QOLLAHUAYA. The Qollahuaya (Collohuaya, Callawalla, Callahuaya, Kallawaya, Kollasuyo) are an Andean subculture of Aymara* affiliation found in the area around Lake Titicaca in Peru and Bolivia. They are particularly concentrated in the province of Bautista Saavedra in Bolivia. Historically they have been a subtribe of the Aymara but have managed to maintain a strong sense of ethnic identity. Before the arrival of the Spanish, they were known as court physicians to the Incas, and their renown for herbal remedies is still widespread throughout Latin America. When the Spaniards arrived, the Qollahuaya adopted the horse and increased their range as healers and practitioners of folk medicine. It is not uncommon today for the Qollahuaya to speak four languages—Quechua,* Qollahuaya, Spanish, and Aymara. Among other Indians in the Andean region, the Qollahuaya retain a prestigious reputation. Today there are more than 16,000 members of the Qollahuaya tribe.

REFERENCES: Joseph W. Bastien, "Qollahuaya Andean Body Concepts: A Topographical-Hydraulic Model of Physiology," *American Anthropologist*, 87 (1985), 595–611; Ralph Bolton, "Aggression and Hypoglycemia Among the Qollas: A Study in Psychological Anthropology," *Ethnology*, 12 (1973), 227–58; Louis Girault, *Kallawaya: Guérisseurs Itinérants des Andes*, 1984.

QUAINACONA. See TERÉNO.

QUAQUA. See MAPOYO.

QUECHUA. Quechua (Kechua, Quichua, Kichwa, Keshwa, Quichua) is the language spoken today by the descendents of the Incas (Inka), as well as by the tribes they conquered, in Peru, Ecuador, Colombia, and Bolivia. The Inca Empire was one of the great civilizations of Mesoamerica, and of the world, at the time of European expansion in the sixteenth century. The origins of the Inca are shrouded in myth and pre-history. Virtually all Amerindian tribes have mythologized their tribal origins. Most tribes maintained a theology that claimed that when god or the "Great Spirit" created the earth, he or she first created that tribe's particular homeland and then finished the rest of the world. The first people created were that particular tribe, after which the rest of the people of the world were created. The Incas were no exception. In their particular legend, the sun created a son and a daughter—Manco Capac and his sister Mama Ocllo—and placed them on an island in Lake Titicaca. He gave them a special golden rod and told them to search throughout the region and settle where they could plunge the staff into the earth. Manco Capac and Mama Ocllo did as they were instructed, built the city of Cuzco, and founded the Inca Empire.

Archaeologists and ethnologists have of course developed a different theory for early Incan history. The primary theory today is that a tribe known as the Incas migrated into the Peruvian Andes from the region of Lake Titicaca to the

Cuzco Valley around A.D. 1000. They were an extremely expansion-minded people who eventually managed to subdue an empire of nearly 400,000 square miles which stretched from the area of present-day Quito in Ecuador to Tucumán in Argentina. Their imperial success was due to economic as well as political strength. According to the major chroniclers of the time, the Incas were able to eliminate hunger and destitution within the empire. Unsurpassed in their agricultural prowess, the Incas changed Andean deserts and mountain slopes into arable land with systems of terraces, aqueducts, irrigation canals, and dams. They also stored commodity surpluses in royal granaries and warehouses, which enabled them to avoid starvation during times of famine.

But in addition to their economic abilities, the Incas were usually even-handed in their imposition of colonial status on conquered areas. The Incas always tried to secure new territory by persuasion rather than violence. After deciding on a new region to be subjugated, the Incas sent diplomats to convince the people of the advantages of being a part of the empire. When several attempts at persuasion failed, the Incas would then send in troops, but even the act of conquest was restrained. Inca warriors were forbidden to take captives, rape women, impose taxes, or loot homes and businesses. Once the conquest was over, the Incas sent public officials, road builders, and artisans to build fortresses, government offices, highways, aqueducts, dams, irrigation systems, canals, and terraces. While building temples to their own sun god, the Incas also showed respect for local deities. The Incas allowed local dialects to exist privately but insisted on Quechua as the language of government and commerce. Finally, the Incas brought the conquered chiefs to Cuzco for political training and then returned them to their homelands to preside over the Inca empire. Not surprisingly, the Incas were the most successful empire builders of all the pre-Columbian Indians. Their political control and Quechua language spread widely.

In the 1530s and early 1540s, however, the Spanish *conquistadores*, led by Francisco Pizarro, swiftly brought the Inca empire under control. Spanish firearms and horses gave them tremendous advantages in mobility and firepower, and European diseases, to which the Indians had no immunities, devastated tribal populations. The absolutism of the Inca empire itself proved to be a great Spanish advantage. When Pizarro executed Atahuallpa, the Inca ruler, he found that the masses of Indians in the Inca empire had no intention of resisting. They simply viewed Spanish despotism as something similar to Inca despotism.

When the Spaniards arrived in the sixteenth century, they employed Quechua as a *lingua franca* for the *ecomiendas* as well as the missions. As a result, Quechua became a dominant linguistic and ethnic force in the highlands of west central South America. Today, the northern-most Quechuan-speaking tribe in South America are the Inga* of Colombia. The Almaguero are another Quechuan dialect in Colombia. There are also another 20,000 Quechuan-speaking Indians in Argentina, particularly in the barrios of Buenos Aires. They are classified as the Catamarca-La Rioja and Santiago del Estero groups. With more than ten million native speakers, Quechua is by far the largest Indian language spoken in either North America or South America. The center of Quechua is in the highlands of Peru, Bolivia, and Ecuador, but it has also spread to the highland areas of southern Colombia, northern Chile and Argentina, the west coast of Peru, and the lowlands of Peru and Bolivia on the east slope of the Andes Mountains. The Quechuan-speaking people in Ecuador include such groups as the Quijos,* Tenas, Otavalos,* Salasacas,* and the Saraguros.* Dynamic and expansionist, Quechua has displaced many other native languages in its region of dominance. In the Peruvian and Bolivian highlands, more than 90 percent of the people understood Quechua, 80 percent speak it, and 50 percent know only it. Quechua is not, however, a monolithic tribal entity. Because it was super-imposed by Incas and Spaniards on other tribes and dialects, there are powerful centrifugal ethnic forces among the various Quechua subtribes, who are identified either by their original tribal name—such as the Chachapoya or Chocorbo (Cho-corvo)—or by the village and region in Peru or Bolivia in which they live, such as the Arequipa or the Huamachuco. Other prominent Quechua-speaking groups in Peru are the Alama,* Ancash, Ayacucho, Cajamarca, Chasutino, Huanuco, Junin, Lama,* Lima, Mayna, Pasco, and Ucayali.

There is a tremendous diversity among the Quechua-speaking people, enough to divide them into many different ethnic groups. Linguists identify two separate Quechuan language groups and seven distinct Quechuan languages: Ayacucho-Cuzco, Ancash-Huanuco, Yaru-Huanuco, Jauja-Huanca, Yauyos, Cañaris-Cajamarca, and Chachapoyas-Lamas. Several million Quechua-speaking Indians have crowded into Lima, Peru, and La Paz, Bolivia, looking for work in recent years. There they haved learned to speak Spanish as well as to integrate them-selves into the urban cash economy. In Bolivia, the Valley of Cochabamba is the center of Quechua culture, and fidelity to the language is very powerful. In Chuquisaca, the dialect is somewhat different but most people are monolingual. South of Potosi, on the other hand, most of the Quechuan Indians are bilingual and are increasingly acculturated to neo-Bolivian values and culture. North of La Paz, in the provinces of Muñecas, Bautista Saavedra, and Franz Tamayo, the Indians are monolingual in a pre-Columbian Quechua dialect.

REFERENCES: Paul T. Baker, *Man in the Andes: Multidisciplinary Study of High-Altitude Quechua*, 1976; Lyle Campbell, *Quichoan Linguistic Prehistory*, 1977; Isabel Hernández, "Los pueblos y las lenguas aborígenes in la actualidad," *América Indígena*, 47 (1987), 409–23; Billie Jean Isbell, *To Defend Ourselves: Ecology and Ritual in an Andean Village*, 1978; Harold Osborne, *Indians of the Andes: Aymaras and Quechuas*, 1940; Arthur P. Sorenson, Jr., "South American Indian Linguistics at the Turn of the Seventies," in Daniel R. Gross, ed., *Peoples and Cultures of Native South America*, 1973; Alfredo Torero, *El Quechua y la historia social Andina*, 1974.

QUENTUSE. See MACÁ.

QUEQUEXQUE. See TÉRRABA.

QUICHÉ. The Quiché are the largest tribe of Mayan* Indians in contemporary Guatemala. Militarily aggressive, politically centralized, and culturally well-developed, the Quiché came to dominate much of the Guatemalan highlands in the fifteenth century, conquering the resident tribes but making a number of enemies in the process. They lived in large agricultural settlements and used a hieroglyphic writing system that was preserved in their holy book of scriptures, the *Popul Vuh*. By the late fifteenth century, the Quiché were fighting several guerrilla wars against their vassal tribes, particularly the Cakchiquel,* Tzutujil,* Ixil,* and Uspantecs.* Early in the 1500s, on the eve of the Spanish conquest, the Quiché lost control of much of their empire. When the Spanish invaders reached Guatemala in the 1520s and attacked the Quiché nation, they formed alliances with such tribes as the Cakchiquel and Tzutujil to defeat the Quiché. Under the leadership of Tecum Uman, the Quiché put up a heroic resistance to Pedro de Alvarado's expedition of conquest, but the Spaniards soon defeated them. Quiché resistance erupted periodically during the colonial period, with the last major uprising against the Spanish occurring in 1815.

During the nineteenth century, the Quiché had to fight against the land hunger of mestizo peasants and the policies of the Guatemalan government, which wanted to convert Quiché communal lands to private ownership. The Quiché protested but the alienation of their land occurred anyway, gradually reducing their holdings and transforming the Quiché into peasants and migrant laborers. After World War II, the Quiché became more and more dissatisfied politically and were attracted to left-wing political movements that promised the return of their land. The Guatemalan government reacted to their political insurgency with savage repression, sending large numbers of Quiché fleeing to Mexico and the United States. In the 1980s, there were more than 1,000,000 Quiché still in Guatemala, most of them in the departments of Huehuetenango, Chimaltenango, Quezaltenango, Totonicapan, Quiché, Baja Verapaz, Retalhuleu, Suchitepequez, Solola, and Escuintla.

REFERENCES: Lyle Campbell, *Quichean Linguistic Prehistory*, 1977; Robert M. Carmack, *The Quiché Mayas of Utatlan: The Evolution of a Highland Guatemalan Kingdom*, 1981; John W. Fox, *Quiché Conquest: Centralism and Regionalism in Highland Guatemalan State Development*, 1978; Jim Handy, *Gift of the Devil: A History of Guatemala*, 1984; Carroll Edward Mace, *Two Spanish-Quiché Dance-Dramas of Rabinal*, 1970.

QUICHEAN. The term "Quichean" refers to a group of Mayan* languages prominent in highland Central America. Included in the Quichean group are the Quiché,* Cakchiquel,* Tzutujil,* Uspantec,* and Rabinal languages.

REFERENCE: Richard E. Moore, *Historical Dictionary of Guatemala*, 1973.

QUICHUA. The term "Quichua" is most commonly used in Ecuador to refer to Quechua* Indians.

REFERENCE: Albert William Bork and Georg Maier, *Historical Dictionary of Ecuador*, 1973.

QUIJO. The Quijo, also known historically as the Kicho, Quixo, Napo, and Santa Rosino, are a Chibchan*-language Amerindian people who occupy land between the Coca and Napo rivers in the Ecuadorian Montana. Their culture was traditionally a cross between that of the Andean uplands—potato cultivation, gold metallurgy, and mummification—and that of the Amazonian forests—slash-and-burn agriculture to raise manioc and sweet potatoes and hunting with a blowgun. In 1536, Gonzalo Dias de Piñeda became the first European to contact them. Their tribal population dropped from 30,000 to 2,000 people in the next 30 years. The Quijo enjoyed wide trading relationships with other Indians by the late seventeenth century, when they exchanged their own woven cloth and tobacco for trade goods. Roman Catholic priests established missions among the Quijo. Over the centuries, the tribe lost most of its aboriginal culture. They converted to Christianity and became quite critical of the animistic religions of the Amazonian tribes. Today the Quijo are primarily Roman Catholic in religion and have abandoned the Chibchan-Quijo language for either Quechua or Spanish. Although they still retain a sense of tribal identity, they are in an advanced stage of acculturation.

REFERENCES: Udo Oberem, "Trade and Trade Goods in the Ecuadorian Montana," *Folk*, 8–9 (1967), 243–58; Norman E. Whitten, Jr., "Jungle Quechua Ethnicity: An Ecuadorian Case Study," in Leo Despres, ed., *Ethnicity and Resource Competition in Plural Societies*, 1975, 51–71.

QUILACO. See AYMARA.

QUILLACA. See AYMARA.

QUILLACINGA. The Quillacinga (Quillasinga, Killacinga) were a large Amerindian tribe living in southwestern Colombia and northeastern Ecuador at the time of the Spanish conquest. Although neither the tribal language nor group social identity survived the conquest, the Indians did, adopting Quechua* as their primary language and Roman Catholicism as their religion. Today there are more than 70,000 detribalized Indians living in what used to be Quillacinga territory. Occasionally the term "Quillacinga" is still used to refer to them. They are remnants of the now-extinct Quillacinga and Pasto* Indians. The vast majority of the Quillacinga today work as farmers and laborers and are indistinguishable from the surrounding mestizo culture.

REFERENCE: Myriam Jiméno and Adolfo Triana Antorveza, *Estado y minorias étnicas de Colombia*, 1985.

QUINAQUI. See ESSEJJA.

QUINTIMIRI. See CAMPA.

QUIRRUBU. See ACHAGUA.

QUITIRRISÍ. The Quitirrisí are a thoroughly detribalized group of Amerindians living today in north central Costa Rica. At the time of the Spanish conquest, the Quitirrisí were spread over a much larger area, but disease and the dislocations of conquest drastically reduced their population. Today the Quitirrisí number approximately 500 people, but they speak Spanish and have a lifestyle nearly identical to that of the surrounding mestizo population.

REFERENCE: Melanie A. Counce and William V. Douglas, "Indians of Central America 1980s," *Cultural Survival Quarterly*, 13 (1989), 38–41.

QUITO. See IQUITO.

QUITURRAN. See IQUITO.

QUIVA. See CUIVA.

QUIXO. See QUIJO.

R

RABINAL ACHÍ. See ACHÍ.

RAGU. See PROUYANA.

RAMA. Today there are approximately 700 Rama Indians in the departments of Zelaya Norte, Zelaya Sur, and Río San Juan on the Atlantic side of Nicaragua, most of them living around the Bluefield Lagoons. At the time of the Spanish conquest, the Rama were one of the subtribes of the Voto Indians. They put up a fierce resistance to the Spaniards, and, because of the isolation of the Atlantic coast of Nicaragua, they were able to maintain their tribal identity. During that conquest period, a process of ethnogenesis occurred, from which the contemporary Rama people emerged out of the mix of the Voto, Suerre, and Guetar Indians. The Voto, Suerre, and Guetar eventually became extinct. The Rama suffered from Miskito* domination during the seventeenth and eighteenth centuries. The English arrived on the Nicaraguan coast in 1589 and by 1640 had formed an alliance with the Miskito. The Rama population declined as a result of European diseases and their violent resistance against the Spanish, British, and Miskito. During the 1980s, the Rama suffered from the revolutionary wars in Nicaragua but also succeeded in getting themselves included in the 1987 decision of the government to create an autonomous political zone in eastern Nicaragua.

REFERENCES: CIDCA, *Ethnic Groups and the Nation State: The Case of the Atlantic Coast in Nicaragua*, 1987; David Close, *Nicaragua: Politics, Economics and Society*, 1988; Anne Manuel, "No Place to be Neutral: The Plight of the Sumu Indians," *Commonweal*, 115 (1988), 107; Linda Newsom, *Indian Survival in Colonial Nicaragua*, 1987; Bernard Nietschmann, *The Distribution of Miskito, Sumu and Rama Indians in East Nicaragua*, 1969; Albert Wiggins, "Colonialism and Revolution: Nicaraguan Sandinism and the Liberation of the Miskito, Sumu and Rama Peoples.'' *Akwesane Notes*, 13 (1982), 44–58.

RAMARÁMA. The term ''Ramaráma'' refers to a small linguistic family of Amerindian groups that were native to what is today the state of Rondônia in Brazil. Originally, the Ramaráma family included the Ramaráma* tribe proper, the Arára* (Urúku, Karo), and the Itogapúk* (Ntogapíd), but the Ramaráma have disappeared as a viable sociological unit.

REFERENCE: Robert Lee Spires, ''As línguas faladas do Brasil,'' *América Indígena*, 47 (1987), 455–79.

RAMARÁMA. The Ramaráma were a group of Tupi*-speaking Amerindians who were part of the larger Kawahíb* group. They were a sizable tribe of riverine people who fished and hunted along the Anari and Machadinho rivers, which are both tributaries of the Jiparaná River, in what is today the state of Rondônia. They also raised manioc in communal gardens to supplement their diet. When rubber collectors poured into Rondônia in the 1880s, they devastated the Ramaráma with violence and disease. The tribe never recovered from the onslaught. Their tribal population declined rapidly and by the 1930s they were having trouble maintaining ceremonial life. Subsequent population declines destroyed the tribe as a functioning social unit, although there are still isolated individuals in Rondônia who are aware of their Ramarâma heritage.

REFERENCE: Theodore L. Stoddard, ed., *Indians of Brazil in the Twentieth Century*, 1967.

RAMCÓCAMECRA. See CANELA.

RAMKÓKAMEKRA. See CANELA.

RANGU-PIKI. See TIRIYÓ.

RANKÓKAMEKRA. See CANELA.

RECUYENNE. See URUKUYÁNA.

REMO. The Remo (Rheno), also known as the Sakuya, were a group of Amerindians who spoke a Panoan* language and lived in the northwestern reaches of the state of Acre, Brazil, and along the Juruamirin River, a branch of the Juruá River, in Peru. In 1690, the Remo population exceeded 3,000 people. Their traditional enemies were the Shipibo* and Conibo.* Some of the Remo joined a Franciscan mission, along with the Píro,* in the eighteenth century, but others avoided the missions for fear of being attacked by the Conibo. In 1870, they finally joined the Roman Catholic mission in Shunaumana, but they were attacked and nearly destroyed that year by the Conibo. Many of the survivors became Shipibo and Conibo slaves. In the 1960s, some Kapanáwa* Indians claimed to have spent nearly a year with a small group of surviving Remo Indians near Tapiche, Peru; they also claimed that the Remo then went over into Brazil where they were controlled by a neo-Brazilian labor boss. Several Brazilian anthropologists think there are a few surviving Remo with the Pisabo.* Today there is no remnant of the Remo language or culture, although there are isolated individuals in Brazil who are aware of their Remo ancestry.

REFERENCES: Darcy Ribeiro and Mary Ruth Wise, *Los grupos étnicos de la amazona peruana*, 1978; Theodore L. Stoddard, ed., *Indians of Brazil in the Twentieth Century*, 1967; Stefano Varese, *The Forest Indians in the Present Political Situation of Peru*, 1972.

RESIGARO. The Resigaro (Resigero, Ressigaro, Resiguaro) are a group of Amerindians who in recent years have become almost completely detribalized. Today there are hundreds of Resigaro Indians living along the Ampiyacu, Yaguasyacu, and Putumayo rivers in the districts of Pebas and Putumayo in the province of Maynas, Loreto, in Peru. Others live along the Guacaya, Miriti, and Apaporis rivers in the territory of Amazonas in Colombia, where they are closely associated with the Tanimuko* Indians. Only 10 Resigaro still speak the aboriginal language. The others speak Quechua* and function as mestizos in the regional cash economy while some have associated themselves with the Bora* and Ocaina* Indians. There were sporadic European contacts with the Resigaro in the eighteenth and nineteenth centuries. Portuguese missions were established temporarily along the Upper Vaupés River in the 1780s, but systematic evangelization of the tribe did not begin until 1914 when Roman Catholic priests established missions in the area. Anthropologists reached the Resigaro early in the 1900s, and Protestant missionaries made their way into the region after World War II. By that time, the Resigaro had been devastated by the diseases and dislocation brought by the rubber collectors. The tribal economy focuses on the production of bitter manioc and fishing; hunting is quite secondary, although in recent years the tribe has become increasingly dependent on such European technology as fishhooks, shotguns, and machetes, as well as on increased manioc production for sale. Contact with whites has also led to the development of small-scale animal husbandry, primarily hogs and poultry. The Resigaro no longer function as a well-differentiated social or tribal unit.

REFERENCES: Kaj Arhem, *Makuna Social Organization: A Study in Descent, Alliance and the Formation of Corporate Groups in the North-Western Amazon*, 1981; Myriam Jiméno and Adolfo Triana Antorveza, *Estado y minorias étnicas en Colombia*, 1985; Gerardo Reichel-Dolmatoff, *Amazonian Cosmos: The Sexual and Religious Symbolism of the Tukano Indians*, 1985; Arthur P. Sorenson, Jr., "Multilingualism in the Northwest Amazon," *American Anthropologist*, 69 (1967), 670–84.

RESIGERO. See RESIGARO.

RESIGGARO. See RESIGARO.

RESIGUARO. See RESIGARO.

REYESANO. The Reyesano Indians today live in the small community of Reyes in the department of El Beni on the right bank of the Alto Beni River in Bolivia. Spaniards first contacted the Reyesano in the 1530s when the expedition of Pedro Anzules de Campo-Redondo reached the Beni River. Franciscan missionaries established missions among the Reyesano at the end of the seventeenth century, converting them to Roman Catholicism. Many Reyesano also adopted the Quechua* language at the time because of its use by the missionaries. Today there are approximately 1,200 Reyesano living in organized villages along the Beni River where they are increasingly acculturated and integrated into the local cash economy. They have been thoroughly detribalized in recent years and no longer speak the aboriginal language. They are laborers, subsistence farmers, and cattle raisers.

REFERENCES: Brian M. Boom, *Ethnobotany of the Chácobo Indians, Beni, Bolivia*, 1987; Harold Key and Mary Key, *Bolivian Indian Tribes: Classification, Bibliography, and Map of Present Language Distribution*, 1967; Pedro Plaza Martínez and Juan Carvajal Carvajal, *Etnías y lenguas de Bolivia*, 1985; Graciela Zolezzi and J. Riester, "Lenguas indígenas del oriente boliviano clasificación preliminar," *América Indígena*, 47 (1987), 425–33.

RHENO. See REMO.

RIKBAKCA. See ARIKPAKTSÁ.

RIKBAKTSA. See ARIKPAKTSÁ.

RIMACHU. See MAYNA.

RIONEGRINO. The Rionegrino are a subtribe of the Yukpa* Indians of northwestern Venezuela. Their traditional homeland was along the Negro River near the Colombian border, where they followed a subsistence agricultural way of life in the tropical forests. Today the Rionegrinos total approximately 140 people. See YUKPA.

RIVER CAMPA. See CAMPA.

ROAMAINA. See OMURANO.

RODELA. The Rodela (Tuxá, Tushá) are a thoroughly assimilated group of Amerindians who today number approximately 200 people and live on a government Indian post on the São Francisco River near the city of Rodelas in the state of Bahia, Brazil. They no longer speak the Indian language or formally use any elements of tribal culture. The Rodela participate in the local cash economy and are essentially a mestizo people functioning in neo-Brazilian society. Nevertheless, they keep alive an identity as a people with a conscious Indian heritage.

REFERENCE: Theodore L. Stoddard, ed., *Indians of Brazil in the Twentieth Century*, 1967.

ROEAMASA. See MAKUNA.

ROKORONA. See PAKAANÓVA.

ROUCOUYENNE. See URUKUYÁNA.

RUCANA. See URUKUYÁNA.

RUCUYEN. See URUKUYÁNA.

RUCUYENNE. See URUKUYÁNA.

RUMA. See SECOYA.

RUMO. See SECOYA.

S

SABANÊ. The Sabanês (Sabonê) are a subtribe of the Nambiquára* Indians, even though their language is totally unintelligible to other Nambiquára Indians. Today there are only a dozen or so Sabanês still alive who are conscious of their specific tribal heritage; they live in heavily jungled territory at the headwaters of the Roosevelt River near the town of Vilhena in the state of Rondônia, Brazil. They call themselves the "Kolimisi." They once occupied a broad area and were divided into several bands. When neo-Brazilians constructed telephone lines through their territory, they suffered from successive epidemics of measles and influenza. A horrible measles attack all but destroyed them in 1963. When they were attacked shortly thereafter by the Cinta Larga,* the Sabanê fled close to neo-Brazilian settlements for protection. Ethnologists estimate that their extinction is only a decade away.

REFERENCES: David Maybury-Lewis et al., *In the Path of Polonoreste: Endangered Peoples of Western Brazil*, 1981; David Price and Cecil E. Cook, Jr., "The Present Situation of the Nambiquara," *American Anthropologist*, 71 (1969), 688–91; Robert Lee Spires, "As línguas faladas do Brasil," *América Indígena*, 47 (1987), 455–79.

SABATINI. See ARAONA.

SABONÊ. See SABANÊ.

SABRILE. See JAPRERÍA.

SACAPULTECO. The Sacapulteco are a Mayan* Indian group living in and around the municipality of Sacapulas in the department of Quiché in the highlands of west central Guatemala. The Sacapultecos still live a settled agricultural lifestyle, raising maize, beans, and avocados for their own food and sugar cane for a cash crop. Although they still have a number of communal agricultural plots, the transition to individual ownership, which government policies began promoting at the end of the nineteenth century and accelerated after World War II, has been a continuing process. Most of the 22,000 Sacapulteco Indians still speak a Mayan dialect as their primary language, although most of them also speak Spanish. In recent years, there has been increasing political insurgency among the Sacapultecos because of the loss of their communal lands and their reduction to peasant and migrant laboring status in Guatemala. During the 1980s, repressive government policies against them and other Mayan groups triggered a wave of emigration from the Guatemalan highlands to Mexico and the United States.

REFERENCES: W. George Lovell, *Conquest and Survival in Colonial Guatemala: A Historical Geography of the Cuchumutan Highlands, 1500–1821*, 1985; "Surviving Conquest: The Maya of Guatemala in Historical Perspective," *Latin American Research Review*, 23 (1988), 25–58.

SADEDNDESU. See NAMBIQUÁRA.

SAKUYA. See REMO.

SALAMÃI. See MONDÉ.

SALASACA. The Salasacas are an Amerindian people of the intermontane basins of the sierra of Ecuador. They are concentrated in the province of Tungurahua, southeast of the city of Ambato, in the Andean highlands of central Ecuador. In the late fifteenth century, the Salasacas came under the domination of the Peruvian Incas, but that oppression only lasted for 50 years until the Spaniards crushed the Incan empire. Archeologists suspect that the Incas relocated the Salasacas from Bolivia to Ecuador. Spanish missionaries and settlers soon reached the Salasacas, and because the missionaries used Quechua* as a *lingua franca*, the Salasacas lost their own language and began speaking Quechua in the sixteenth century. Over the centuries, the Salasacas maintained a great degree of independence from hacienda labor and tenant farmer status. Because they have not been dependent for sustenance on whites for several generations, the Salasacas are still a highly independent ethnic group. They generally try to avoid working as laborers for neo-Ecuadorians, preferring their own subsistence lifestyle. They are surrounded by a large mestizo population but there are relatively few intermarriages. There are more than 5,000 Salasaca Indians living today in Tungurahua province, and most of them are landholding peasant farmers.

REFERENCES: Joseph B. Casagrande, "Strategies for Survival: The Indians of Highland Ecuador," in Dwight B. Heath, ed., *Contemporary Cultures and Societies of Latin America*, 1974, 93–107; Thomas E. Weil et al., *Area Handbook for Ecuador*, 1973.

SÁLIBA. See SÁLIVA.

SÁLIUA. See SÁLIVA.

SÁLIVA. The Sáliva (Sáliba, Sáliua) are a tropical forest group of Amerindians who at the time of the conquest lived on the Orinoco River from the Atuares Rapids northward to the mouth of the Arauca River, as well as along the Cinaruco River. Like other tropical forest people, the Sáliva were primarily farmers who raised sweet manioc, maize, and chili peppers. After the arrival of the Spaniards, they adopted banana cultivation as a major horticultural endeavor as well. The Sáliva came under attack from Karib* Indians in the early nineteenth century and fled south toward the Vichada River. Many of them joined Jesuit missions there until the expulsion of the Jesuits in 1767. Today the Sáliva live along the Guaviare River near the junction of the department of Meta and the territories of Vaupés, Guainía, and Vichada in Colombia. Some Sáliva also live across the border in Venezuela. Those opposite Orocue on the right bank of the Meta River are highly acculturated. Still, most Sáliva maintain a strong sense of Indian identity even though they are increasingly acculturating to the neo-Colombian economy. In 1988, there were approximately 69 Sáliva Indians living on the Colombian government Indian reservation at Consejo; 313 on the El Duya, San Juanito, and Paravare reservations; 70 on the Macucuana reservation; 88 on the Santa Rosalía reservation; 34 on the El Suspiro o Rincón del Socorro reservation; and 28 on the El Saladillo reservation. They are closely related to the Piaroa.* Today, the Sáliva population totals approximately 2,000 people.

REFERENCES: Leah B. Ellis and Linda Criswell, eds., *Estudiemos las culturas indígenas de Colombia*, 1984; Myriam Jiméno and Adolfo Triana Antorveza, *Estado y minorias étnicas en Colombia*, 1985; Nancy Morey, "Ethnohistory of the Colombian and Venezuelan Llanos," Ph.D. dissertation, University of Utah, 1975; R. V. Morey, "Notes on the Sáliva of Eastern Colombia," *Current Anthropology*, 13 (1972), 144–47.

SALUMÁ. The Salumá (Enawene-nawe) are a tropical forest tribe of Amerindians who today live on the upper Anamu River in the northwestern region of the state of Pará, Brazil, and across the border in Surinam. Only about 150 members of the tribe are still alive and functioning as a group, and they are in intermittent contact with neo-Brazilian and neo-Surinamese society. Most of them still use their tribal language in private conversation and nurture their primary ethnic identity as Salumá Indians.

REFERENCES: Robert Lee Spires, "As línguas faladas do Brasil," *América Indígena*, 47 (1987), 455–79; Theodore L. Stoddard, ed., *Indians of Brazil in the Twentieth Century*, 1967.

SAMUKU. See ZAMUCO.

SANAMAIKA. See MONDÉ.

SANAPANÁ. The Sanapaná, or Kyisapang, are a Lengua*-Maskoy-speaking tribe of Amerindians living in the Gran Chaco of Paraguay. They are particularly concentrated on the Galvan and Salado rivers, stretching from Laguna Castilla to just outside Puerto Casado in the department of Boquerón. There are two distinct subgroups of the Sanapaná—the Sanapaná and the Sapuquis. The Sanapaná traditionally cultivated small gardens ranging from four to eight acres and supplemented their diet through hunting and fishing. In recent years, however, they have been drawn inexorably into the regional cash economy, particularly because of their desire for cotton cloth, hunting rifles and shotguns, ammunition, and high quality tools. Increasingly the Sanapaná can be found as wage laborers on large Mennonite farms and ranches in the Paraguayan Chaco. Because of the influence of the Mennonites, many of the Sanapaná have converted to Christianity, and large numbers of the Sanapaná understand Guaraní and Spanish. The process of economic integration is making more and more Sanapaná familiar with the Spanish language and the cultural processes of mestizo society. In the mid–1980s, the Paraguayan government claimed that there were 2,000 members of the Sanapaná tribe. The South American Missionary Society, the Mennonite Central Committee, the New Tribes Mission, and the Salesians all conduct missionary work among the Sanapaná.

REFERENCES: Harriet Klein and Louisa Stark, "Indian Tribes of the Paraguayan Chaco," *Anthropological Linguistics*, 19 (1977), 378–402; David Maybury-Lewis and James Howe, *The Indian Peoples of Paraguay: Their Plight and Their Prospects*, 1980.

SAN BLAS CUNA. See CUNA.

SANEMÁ. See SANUMÁ.

SAN GERANO. The San Gerano people are a subtribe of the Yuko* Indians of northeastern Colombia. Their traditional homeland was along the Roncón River where they lived a horticultural existence, raising manioc, maize, and beans, among other crops. By the 1970s, however, the San Gerano population had dropped to fewer than 10 people, effectively eliminating them as a self-conscious sociological unit. See YUKO.

SANGIRENI. See CAMPA.

SANHA. See MALAYO.

SANJA. See MALAYO.

SANKA. See MALAYO.

SANOMÁ. See SANUMÁ.

SANTA MARÍA. See SECOYA.

SANTA ROSINO. See QUIJO.

SANTIAGO DEL ESPERO. See QUECHUA.

SANUMÁ. The Sanumá (Sanemá), whose language is a subgroup of the Yanoama* family, live in the mountain range that separates the Orinoco River from the Amazon basin. They have also been known historically as the Ciriana people.

They live in the upper Auaris River Valley in the northwest corner of Roraima in northern Brazil. At the present time the tribal population is approximately 2,300 people. They live in villages of between 30 and 50 people and are a hunting and foraging people with some horticultural abilities. They depend very heavily on hunting game birds and gathering wild forest products. Their main crops are bitter manioc, plantains, and bananas, while their most sought-after game animals are tapirs, peccaries, monkeys, and armadillos. Their extreme geographic isolation has protected them from the worst depredations of European civilization. The main Sanumá contacts outside their own people are with Makiritáre Indians.

REFERENCES: M.E.M. Colchester, "The Economy, Ecology, and Ethnobiology of the Sanumá of South Venezuela," Ph.D. dissertation, Oxford University, 1982; Alcida R. Ramos, "How the Sanumá Acquire Their Names," *Ethnology*, 13 (1974), 171–86; Kenneth I. Taylor, "Body and Spirit Among the Sanumá (Yanoama) of North Brazil," in David L. Browman and Ronald A. Schwartz, eds., *Spirits, Shamans, and Stars: Perspectives from South America*, 1979.

SAPE. See KALIANA.

SAPITERI. See SIRINEIRI.

SAPRIRÍA. See JAPRERÍA.

SAPUQUIS. See SANAPANÁ.

SAPUYA. See KARIRÍ.

SARA. See ARAONA.

SARAGURO. The Saraguro are an Amerindian people of the intermontane basins of the sierra of Ecuador. They are concentrated in the province of Loja in the Andean highlands of southern Ecuador. In the late fifteenth century, the Saraguros came under the domination of the Peruvian Incas, who probably relocated them from Bolivia to Ecuador, but that oppression only lasted for 50 years until the Spaniards crushed the Incan empire. Spanish missionaries and settlers soon reached the Saraguros, and because the missionaries used Quechua* as a *lingua franca*, the Saraguros lost their own language and began speaking Quechua in the sixteenth century. Over the centuries the Saraguros maintained a great degree of independence from hacienda labor and tenant farmer status. Because they have not depended on whites for sustenance for several generations, the Saraguros are still a highly independent ethnic group. There are more than 10,000 Saraguros Indians living today in Loja Province, and most of them are landholding peasant farmers. In recent years, the Saraguros have also colonized the Ecuadorean Oriente, moving into the Yacuambi River Valley where they have expropriated Jívaro* land and established large farms where they raise manioc, sugar cane, and bananas. More and more are also turning to cattle raising.

REFERENCES: Joseph B. Casagrande, "Strategies for Survival: The Indians of Highland Ecuador," in Dwight B. Heath, ed., *Contemporary Cultures and Societies of Latin America*, 1974, 93–107; Roberto Santana, *Campesinado indígena y el desafío de la modernidad*, 1983; Thomas E. Weil et al., *Area Handbook for Ecuador*, 1973.

SARAMO. See ITONAMA.

SARARÉ. The Sararé Indians, occasionally referred to as Kabixí* (though not the Karib*-speaking Kabixí), are a subtribe of the Nambiquára* Indians. There are fewer than 100 of them living on the Sararé River in the southern reaches of the state of Mato Grosso, Brazil. See NAMBIQUÁRA.

SARAVECA. See SARAVEKA.

SARAVEKA. The Saraveka (Saraveca) are an Arawakan* group of Amerindians who have remained independent and hostile to neo-Bolivian and neo-Brazilian society. They are a tropical forest people who have lived in the northeast reaches of the province of Velasco in the department of Santa Cruz in Bolivia and across the border in Brazil. For more than a century, most of the Saraveka lived on the Verde River, a tributary of the Guaporé River. They probably migrated to that region from an original homeland in the area of the Xingú River and the Amazon Basin. Although the rubber boom of the late nineteenth and early twentieth centuries adversely affected the Saraveka, as it did so many other tropical forest tribes in northern South America, they have maintained a powerful sense of isolation and tribal identity.

REFERENCE: Pedro Plaza Martínez and Juan Carvajal Carvajal, *Etnías y lenguas de Bolivia*, 1985.

SATARÉ. See MAWÉ.

SATERÉ. See MAWÉ.

SATIPO. See CAMPA.

SAWEDNDESU. See NAMBIQUÁRA.

SAYACO. See AMAHUACA.

SCHETIBO. See SETEBO.

SEBONDOY. See KAMSÁ.

SECO. See PAYÁ.

SECOYA. The Secoya (Sekoya) are a western Tukanoan* tribe of Amerindians who are remnants of the Encabellado (Pioche, Piojé) people, who occupied a large territory between the Napo River and the Putumayo River in northeastern

Ecuador in the seventeenth century. They call themselves the Pai. Other subgroups and names for the Secoya have been Icaguate, Ycahuate, Cieguaje, Santa María, Tarapotot, Angutera, Angotero, Angutero, Ancutere, Anckutere, Ancutena, Ruma, Rumo, and Macaguaje. Jesuit and Franciscan missionaries tried unsuccessfully to pacify the Encabellado in the seventeenth and eighteenth centuries. In the process of resisting, the tribe declined drastically in numbers, from warfare with other Indian tribes and from European-imported diseases. Along with the Siona, the Secoya are the survivors of the Encabellado. The destruction of the Encabellado by Spaniards was especially severe after the Indians murdered Father Francisco Real in 1744. The survivors became a semi-nomadic people who avoided contact with Europeans and mestizos. The modern population of the Secoya is around 500 people who are scattered around the Aguarico River in Ecuador, the Angusilla and Yubineto rivers in Peru, and the Putumayo River in Colombia. In 1988, there were 124 Secoya-Siona Indians living on the Colombian government reservation at Buenavista, as well as 145 on the El Tablero reservation and 97 on the El Hacha reservation. Today they practice a mixed subsistence economy involving shifting cultivation, fishing, hunting, and collecting. Horticulture provides the bulk of their diet by far. They also work occasionally as oarsmen and porters carrying freight between the Putumayo, Aguarico, and Napo rivers. The Secoya sell chickens and rice in order to obtain pork, sugar, salt, bread, kerosene, and metal tools. There are two functioning linguistic divisions of the Secoya—the Angotero* and the Piojé. Capuchin missionaries as well as those from the Summer Institute of Linguistics have worked periodically among the Secoya. Most of the Secoya speak their native tongue, and relatively few are fluent in Spanish. Recent oil discoveries in their area, however, have increased their contact with neo-Ecuadoreans and neo-Peruvians.

REFERENCES: Stefano Varese, *The Forest Indians in the Present Political Situation of Peru*, 1972; William T. Vickers, "The Territorial Dimensions of Siona-Secoya and Encabellado Adaptation," in Raymond B. Hames and William T. Vickers, eds., *Adaptive Responses of Native Amazonians*, 1983, 46–68; William T. Vickers, "Tropical Forest Mimicry in Swidden: A Reassessment of Geertz's Model, with Amazonian Data," *Human Ecology*, 11 (1983), 35–46.

SECULUSEPA. See AGUANO.

SEKOYA. See SECOYA.

SELK'NAM. The Selk'nam, also known historically as the Shelk'nam and the Ona, were once a hunting and fishing tribe which occupied the Great Island of Tierra del Fuego at the southernmost tip of South America. When Ferdinand Magellan's expedition passed through the straits in 1520, the Selk'nam warned neighboring tribes of the strange ships by lighting huge signal fires, and the Spaniards dubbed the island "Tierra del Fuego" or "Land of Fire." Spanish explorer Pedro Sarmiento de Gamboa first contacted the Selk'nam in 1579. The

Selk'nam's close neighbors, the Haush, were contacted by Spanish explorers in 1619. During the next 250 years, a series of Spanish, English, and Dutch exploring, commercial, and fishing expeditions established contact with the Selk'nam, and the encounters were often violent. Nevertheless, the Selk'nam survived largely intact until the late 1800s. In the 1880s and 1890s, increasingly large numbers of European settlers were attracted to Selk'nam land by alluvial gold discoveries and by the broad grasslands that were perfect for raising sheep. Farmers, sheep ranchers, and gold seekers hired professional killers to hunt down the Selk'nam; a genocidal attack ensued. Salesian missionaries gathered the Selk'nam into missions in the 1890s, but the transition from nomadic hunting to the confining mission life was too much emotionally for the tribe. A rapid population decline set in. What the hired killers did not do, diseases such as influenza, tuberculosis, pneumonia, and measles accomplished. The Selk'nam population dropped from 4,000 people in 1880 to 500 in 1905. Today there are only 5 or 6 people on the Great Island who still claim Selk'nam origins. The Haush are completely extinct.

REFERENCES: Anne Chapman, *Drama and Power in a Hunting Society: The Selk'nam of Tierra del Fuego*, 1982; Isabel Hernández, "Los pueblos y las lenguas aborígenes en la actualidad," *América Indígena*, 47 (1987), 409–23.

SEMIGAE. See SHIMIGAE.

SEPUANABO. See CAMPA.

SERÉNTE. See XERÉNTE.

SERRANO. See PUELCHE.

SETEBO. The Setebo (Settebo, Shetebo, Ssetebo, Schetibo, Sitibo, Xitipo, Jitipo, Gitibo, Pano, Manoita, Puinahua, Sensi, and Panobo) were once a large, Panoan*-speaking tribe of the Ucayali River in east central Peru. Although Spanish missionaries established several unsuccessful missions among the Setebo in 1657, many of the Indians rebelled shortly thereafter and the missionaries left. Smallpox epidemics in 1670 and 1680 decimated the Setebo population. In the eighteenth century, the Setebo sought the protection of Spanish missionaries because of bloody raids from the Shipibo,* but in the 1770s and 1780s the Setebo participated in a number of rebellions against the missions along the Ucayali River. Early in the 1800s, many Setebo joined Franciscan missions in the region; after a severe smallpox epidemic in 1860, many Indians and missionaries left the area. By the 1930s, there were several hundred Setebo still alive in the area, working as subsistence farmers. By then, population decline due to acculturation had replaced smallpox as the greatest enemy to tribal identity. Today the Setebo tribe no longer functions as a social unit but there are still isolated individuals who are aware of their Setebo heritage. Virtually all of them, however, have intermarried with the Shipibo and are living with them in the Ucayali valley of Peru.

REFERENCE: Lucille Eakin, Erwin Lauriault, and Harry Boonstra, *People of the Ucayali: The Shipibo and Conibo of Peru*, 1986.

SETTEBO. See SETEBO.

SEUENI. See WITOTO.

SHAHINDAHUA. See SHAHINDAWA.

SHAHINDAWA. The Shahindawa (Shahindahua, Chandinahua) are a group of Amerindians who are descended from Panoan*-speaking people and live in the region of the Embira and Riozinho rivers in eastern Peru. Once a horticultural people who lived by the production of manioc, the Shahindawa today remain a subsistence agricultural group, but they are now in permanent contact with the neo-Peruvian economy and work part-time and seasonally as laborers to earn the cash they need for trade goods. The Shahindawa number more than 1,000 people, although the vast majority of them speak Spanish. They are a subgroup of the Yamináwa.* See YAMINÁWA.

SHAKRIABÁ. See XABRIABÁ.

SHAMATIRI. See YANOAMA.

SHAMBOIÁ. See XAMBOIÁ.

SHAODAWA. See YAMINÁWA.

SHAONAHUA. See YAMINÁWA.

SHAPARRU. The Shaparru are a subtribe of the Yukpa* Indians of northwestern Venezuela. Their traditional tribal land neighbored that of the Irapa people near the Tukuku River. They have pursued a subsistence agricultural lifestyle typical of tropical forest Indians. Today their total population is around 50 people. See YUKPA.

SHAPARU. See SHAPARRU.

SHAPRA. The Shapra Indians are called the Murato by outsiders. That is an incorrect designation. The Murato Indians once lived near Lake Rimachi but have long been extinct. The heart of Shapra land is on the Sicuanga and Pushaga rivers, both tributaries of the Morona River. Along with the Candoshi,* to whom they are closely related, the Shapra are probably descendents of the now extinct

Maina tribe, which was devastated by Spanish *encomenderos* and diseases in the late sixteenth and early seventeenth centuries. The Maina were living on the lower Marona River in the late nineteenth century, but have since become extinct. The colonization of their lands along the Pastaza River was never effectively undertaken by neo-Peruvians. After the Jesuit expulsion in 1767, the entire area remained little traveled until well into the twentieth century. Early in the 1900s, when the wild rubber boom began, the Shapra retreated to more isolated areas, especially to the headwaters of the Nucuray River, a tributary of the Marañon River. Today the Shapra sell relatively little agricultural produce in the regional market; their agricultural practices are relatively unaffected by outside influences. They raise plantains, maize, manioc, beans, peanuts, and sweet potatoes. Few of them speak Spanish, and their sense of tribal identity is strong.

REFERENCES: Anthony Stocks, "Candoshi and Cocamilla Swidden in Eastern Peru," *Human Ecology*, 11 (1983), 69–84; Sheila C. Tuggy, "Candoshi Behavior Change," in William R. Merrifield, ed., *Five Amazonian Studies on World View and Cultural Change*, 1985, 5–40.

SHARANÁHUA. The Sharanáhua, also identified historically as Pisináhua or Marináwa* (Marináhua, Aguti), live near the upper Purús River in eastern Peru and western Brazil. They are part of the Panoan*-language family. They call themselves the Onicoin; the major subgroups of the Sharanáhua include the Marináwa, Mastanáhua, and Sharanáhua. Around 1900, the Sharanáhua left their tribal homeland near the headwaters of the Taruaca River because they were being crowded by other Indian tribes fleeing the rubber gatherers in Brazil. The Sharanáhua reached the Upper Purús region in the 1940s. Those were difficult years for the tribe. Between 1925 and 1950, the Sharanáhua lost half of their population because of epidemics of whooping cough and measles. Although the Sharanáhua plant maize, manioc, peanuts, bananas, and plantains in small plots, they are primarily an interfluvial people who settle along small streams and depend on fishing and hunting for their protein. In the 1960s, the Sharanáhua adopted canoes and fish nets to improve their fishing production and began to dress like other Peruvians. The Sharanáhua population today exceeds 1,500 people and is slowly expanding. Although some Sharanáhua work as migrant laborers in the neo-Peruvian economy, the tribe maintains a strong sense of identity. They keep their distance from other Peruvians.

REFERENCES: Darcy Ribeiro and Mary Ruth Wise, *Los grupos etnicos de la Amazona Peruana*, 1978; Janet Siskind, *To Hunt in the Morning*, 1973; Janet Siskind, "Tropical Forest Hunters and the Economy of Sex," in Daniel R. Gross, ed., *Peoples and Cultures of Native South America*, 1973, 122–40; Stefano Varese, *The Forest Indians in the Present Political Situation in Peru*, 1972.

SHAVÁNTE. See AKWĒ-XAVÁNTE.

SHAYABIT. See CHAYAVITA.

SHELK'NAM. See SELK'NAM.

SHEMIGAE. See SHIMIGAE.

SHERÉNTE. See XERÉNTE.

SHETEBO. See SETEBO.

SHICHA'AM. See ASHLUSLAY.

SHIKANA. See HOTÍ.

SHIKRÍ. See XIKRĨN.

SHILIVERI. The Shiliveri were a group of Amerindians who were part of the Harakmbet* linguistic group. Their traditional homeland was between the Sirineiri* and Toyeri* on the Shiliva and Wandakhwe rivers in southeastern Peru. A tropical forest people, the Shiliveri were devastated by the rubber boom of 1894–1920 when rubber collectors brought disease and slavery to them. Subsequent epidemics of smallpox and influenza in the 1950s and 1960s eventually destroyed the tribe. Today there are only one or two Shiliveri survivors who remember their tribal identity.
 REFERENCE: Andrew Gray, "Perspectives on Amarakaeri History," in Harald O. Sklar and Frank Salomon, eds., *Natives and Neighbors in South America: Anthropological Essays*, 1987, 299–329.

SHIMACU. See URARINA.

SHIMAKU. See URARINA.

SHIMIGAE. The Shimigae (Shemigae, Semigae, Gae, Chimigae, Ando, Andoa) are an Amerindian group whose language is part of the Zaparo* linguistic family. They are concentrated on the Pastaza River, in the province of Alto Amazonas, Loreto, in Peru. In the distant historical past, the Shimigae and the Andoa were probably different dialectic groups, but they merged under the pressure of the Spanish conquest. Before the arrival of the Spanish, they lived between the Pastaza and Morona rivers, but in 1582 many of the Shimigae went to work on the encomiendas, others were moved to the Borja region of Peru. They lived at Roman Catholic missions in the seventeenth and early eighteenth centuries. There they were constantly subject to attack by the Jívaro* and Murato Indians, which, along with contact with Europeans, rapidly reduced their population. By 1850 the Shimigae population had declined to only 450 people; by 1925, there were only 12 families still surviving. Today there are fewer than 10 Shimigae Indians who still speak the aboriginal language, but they also speak

Spanish and Quechua,* although Quechua is their primary language. Culturally they are integrated with the Quechua. Use of the native language is rapidly approaching extinction.

REFERENCE: Darcy Ribeiro and Mary Ruth Wise, *Los grupos étnicos de la amazonia peruana*, 1978.

SHIMIZYA. See CHIMILA

SHINABU. See PACANAURA.

SHIPANAHUA. See XIPINÁWA.

SHIPANÁWA. See XIPINÁWA.

SHIPAYA. The Shipaya (Xipaia, Chipaya) are a group of Amerindians who speak the only surviving Puquina* language in South America. For centuries they have lived in the dry, agriculturally poor section of the Charangas in western Bolivia, between Potosí and Oruro in the Altiplano. They are despised by the neighboring Aymara* Indians and by neo-Bolivians who look upon them as an especially primitive people. The Shipaya are closely related to the Qolla* of southern Bolivia. Because of the dry weather and poor soil of their region, the Shipaya have been known for making a living by trading llamas, sheep milk, and cheese to the neighboring Aymara in exchange for quinoa and potatoes. They also travel widely in search of work to generate cash. For many years, the Shipaya population has been declining, primarily because they have been gradually absorbed by the Aymara. Today there are approximately 800 Shipaya, and most of them are bilingual in Shipaya and Aymara, with some also knowing Spanish and/or Quechua.* Among themselves, however, they use their own language.

REFERENCES: Brian M. Boom, *Ethnobotany of the Chácobo Indians, Beni, Bolivia*, 1987; Alain Chednevière, *Vanishing Tribes: Primitive Man on Earth*, 1987; Harold Key and Mary Key, *Bolivian Indian Tribes: Classification, Bibliography, and Map of Present Language Distribution*, 1967; Pedro Plaza Martínez and Juan Carvajal Carvajal, *Etnías y lenguas de Bolivia*, 1985; F. T. Murillo et al., "The Chipaya of Bolivia: Dermatoglyphics and Ethnic Relationships," *American Journal of Physical Anthropology*, 46 (1977), 45–50.

SHIPIBO. The Shipibo are a Panoan*-speaking tribe of Amerindians on both sides of the Ucalayi River and its branches—the Cushabatay, Maqui, Yapacti, Cashiboya, Cushucayo, Aguaytia, Utaquines, Abujao Tamaya, Pachitea, Tahuania, and Cohenhua rivers—in the selva of eastern Peru. Originally they lived on the upper Aguaytia River until neighboring Cashibo* Indians drove them out of the area. Historically, the Shipibo have also been known as Chipeo, Chipio, Chepeo, Shipipo, Ssipipo, Calliseca, Chama, Manamabobo, Manava, and Pisquibo. They are a slash-and-burn horticultural people who supplement their staple diet of sweet manioc with animal protein from the fish, aquatic mammals, and reptiles near the river. The Shipibo generally live on old ox-bow lakes and natural levees, and they travel by canoe. They tend to avoid venturing into the jungle. Between 1657 and 1680, Spanish soldiers and missionaries carried out a bloody campaign to bring the Shipibo into missions. Once they had succeeded, a smallpox epidemic in 1680 destroyed most tribal members. They remained under Jesuit influence between 1686 and 1698 before rebelling and killing the missionaries. Jesuit and Franciscan missionaries succeeded in bringing large numbers of Shipibo back to the missions in the 1760s, by which time the tribal population had stabilized. Today there are more than 16,000 Shipibo living in perhaps 100 villages in a floodplain environment that provides fertile soil for their staple product, the banana, as well as the ability to raise maize, beans, and manioc and to hunt and fish.

Until the 1960s, the Shipibo maintained a largely indigenous lifestyle, but in the 1970s they were drawn inexorably into the regional cash economy because of their use of outboard motors and fuel, shotguns and ammunition, and manufactured clothing. Virtually all of the Shipibo men have abandoned the traditional *cushma* for Westernized shirts and trousers; large numbers of them work as laborers for Spanish-speaking employers. But the Shipibo have managed to maintain a powerful sense of ethnic identity in spite of the surrounding pressures to acculturate. The school system for the Shipibo maintains a system of bilingual instruction, and the tribe has an indigenous newspaper. Commercial radio also broadcasts locally in Shipibo. Most people understand Spanish as well, although they do not employ it in private conversations. In terms of economics, most Shipibo function on a subsistence level, with their protein needs being supplied by hunting and fishing. Although the Shipibo population continues to increase, use of the tribal language has recently started to decline as increasing numbers of people use Spanish. The Shipibo-Conibo range from fairly well-acculturated people, like those who live near the city of Pucallpa, to less acculturated people who live farther up river.

REFERENCES: Clifford A. Behrens, "The Cultural Ecology of Dietary Change Accompanying Changing Activity Patterns among the Shipibo," *Human Ecology*, 14 (1986), 367–96; Clifford A. Behrens, "Time Allocation and Meat Procurement Among the Shipibo Indians of Eastern Peru," *Human Ecology*, 9 (1981), 189–220; Roland W. Bergman, *Amazon Economics: The Simplicity of Shipibo Indian Wealth*, 1980; Lucille Eakin, Erwin Lauriault, and Harry Boonstra, *People of the Ucayali: The Shipibo and Conibo of Peru*, 1986; Peter G. Roe, "Art and Residence Among the Shipibo Indians of Peru: A Study in Microacculturation," *American Anthropologist*, 82 (1980), 42–71.

SHIPIPO. See SHIPIBO.

SHIRIANA. See YANOAMA.

SHIRIANNA. See YANOAMA.

SHIRINERI. See SIRINEIRI.

SHIRISHANA. See YANOAMA.

SHIRIXANA. See YANOAMA.

SHIVAKUADENI. See DANÍ.

SHIWILA. See JEBERO.

SHOCÓ. The Shocó (Shocú, Shokó, Xokó) are a highly acculturated group of Amerindians whose origins are virtually unknown because they have so thoroughly mixed with neo-Brazilian society. They all speak Portuguese as their primary language and retain no vestiges of the aboriginal tongue. They no longer function as an organized tribe or participate in any tribal ceremonies. There are approximately 200 people who still consider themselves Shocó, and they live in several tiny groups in the cities of Porto Real do Colegio and Olho d'Agua do Meio in the state of Alagoas and in São Pedro in the state of Sergipe. Some of them receive assistance from the government Indian service. Most of them work as laborers.

REFERENCES: Clarice Novaes Da Mota, "Kariri-Shokó and Shokó Mode of Utilization of Medicinal Plants in the Context of Modern Northeastern Brazil," Ph.D. dissertation, University of Texas, 1987; Beatriz Gois Dantas, *Terrados indios Xocó: Estudos e documentos*, 1980; Theodore L. Stoddard, ed., *Indians of Brazil in the Twentieth Century*, 1967.

SHOCÚ. See SHOCÓ.

SHOKLÉNG. See AWEIKOMA.

SHOKÓ. See SHOCÓ.

SHUAR. The Shuar (Shuara) are part of the isolated Jívaroan* language group. They are a tribe of Amerindians living in the Amazon basin of southeastern Ecuador, particularly along the Upano and Bobonaza rivers in the provinces of Morona-Santiago and Zamora-Chinchipe and across the border in contiguous areas of Peru. They are more properly known as the Jívaro.* The Shuar have traditionally functioned in a political system based on a balance of power among autonomous groups engaged in constant warfare, feuding, shifting alliances, and trade. They have pursued an economic lifestyle consistent with that of other tropical forest people. But the Shuar have recently succeeded in making a political adaptation that has strengthened their ability to resist assimilation in neo-Peruvian society. Contact with the national society and with missionaries led in 1968 to the establishment of the Federation of Shuar Centers, a hierarchical, representative political organization that dramatically reduced Shuar feuding and civil warfare. The Shuar have been successful in accepting some features of the dominant culture without becoming politically subservient. The federation has become the key in preventing them from becoming a colonized people. Although its hierarchical political values are alien to Shuar culture, the tribe has accepted it in order to secure land titles and political recognition from neo-Ecuadorians and neo-Peruvians. Today there are three groups of the Shuar Indians. About 1,800 Shuar are very isolated in the Ecuadorian interior east of the Sierra de Cutucu. A much larger group of Shuar lives in the Upano Valley and is in constant contact with Salesian missionaries and neo-Ecuadorian farmers. Most of them work for the missionaries or the farmers. The third Shuar group lives along the Zamora River in close contact with Franciscan missionaries and neo-Ecuadorian farmers. The Shuar probably total about 24,000 people.

REFERENCE: Janet Wall Hendricks, "Power and Knowledge: Discourse and Ideological Transformation among the Shuar," *American Ethnologist*, 15 (1988), 216–38.

SHUARA. See SHUAR.

SHUKAHAMÃE. See MENTUKTÍRE.

SIBUNDOY. See KAMSÁ.

SICASICA. See AYMARA.

SICUANI. See ACHAGUA.

SICUANI. See SIKUANI.

SIKIANA. The Sikiana are a Karib*-speaking tribe of Amerindians who live along the Surinam border in the northwestern region of the state of Pará, Brazil. In particular, they live between the Cafuini River and the headwaters of the Turuna and Itapi rivers. Although they have adopted neo-Brazilian clothing and technology and have adjusted to a typical slash-and-burn subsistence agriculture, the Sikiana maintain a strong sense of tribal identity, and large numbers of the tribe still speak the native language. Their numbers today are probably fewer than 200 people. In the sixteenth and seventeenth centuries, the Sikiana ranged widely throughout their region, earning a reputation for exchange and trade among the Indians of the llanos, jungle, Andes, and Orinoco basin. Not until the end of the eighteenth century did their mobility decline. They then settled into a subsistence agricultural existence, raising manioc as their staple.

REFERENCE: Theodore L. Stoddard, ed., *Indians of Brazil in the Twentieth Century*, 1967.

SIKUANI. See ACHAGUA.

SIKUANI. The Sikuani Indians are a subtribe of the Guahibo* people of Venezuela and Colombia. Like the other Guahibo tribes, they call themselves Hiwi. Actually, the term Sikuani is ambiguous, inconsistent, and not a tribal division recognized by the Guahibo people. It is instead a designation imposed on one large group of Guahibo Indians. In Venezuela and Colombia, the Sikuani total several thousand people. A foraging people who generally disdain agriculture, they range widely across the Capanaparo, Ariporo, Agua Clara, and Meta River drainage systems in the savannas of western Venezuela and eastern Colombia. They live right in the middle of the Orinoco plains, an area of immense, grassy savannas dotted with palms and small shrubs. Unlike riverine tribes who lived along the major tributaries penetrating the South American interior and were devastated by contact with Europeans, the Sikuani were able to maintain an isolation because they were an interfluvial people who lived as nomadic hunters. In the 1970s and 1980s, economic development and settlement of eastern Colombia and western Venezuela, however, have placed new pressures on the Sikuani.
    REFERENCE: Walter Coppens, *Los aborígenes de Venezuela*, 1983.

SILAN. See SUMU.

SILVENO. See GAMBIANO.

SIMIRANCH. See PÍRO.

SIMIRANCHE. See PÍRO.

SIMIZA. See CHIMILA.

SIMZA. See CHIMILA.

SINABO. See PACANUARA.

SINAMAICA. See PARAUJANO.

SINDAGUA. See COAIQUER.

SIONA. The Siona (Sioni, Ceona, Cioni, and Ceno) are a Western Tukanoan* group of Amerindians who inhabited the upper Putumayo River in southern Colombia, from the region of Santiago and Sibundoy to the equator. They call themselves the Gatuya Paín. Jesuit missionaries first reached them in 1600, as did Franciscans in 1635, but the Indians rebelled against the missions and the priests abandoned them. The Jesuits and Franciscans returned in the early 1700s, but the Siona rebelled against them again in the 1740s, forcing the abandonment of the missions. By the nineteenth century, however, the Siona had adopted metal technology to improve their hunts and their manioc gardens. Slowly they became integrated into the regional cash economy. Today there are approximately 350 Siona Indians, most of whom live in the communities of Buena Vista, Granada, and Pinuna on the Upper Putumayo River and the tributaries of the Caquetá River in the intendency of Putumayo. The villages of Eno and Shu-shufindi on the Aguarico River are primarily Siona. Siona also live on the right bank of the Putumayo River, from the Cuhembi River to the Colombian frontier and on both sides of the lower San Miguel River. In recent years, there has been considerable intermarriage between Siona Indians and the Secoya* in Cuyabeno and with the Kofán.* The most isolated Sionas are those on the Aguarico River. The others are scattered downriver where they have mixed with the white and black population. The Summer Institute of Linguistics has been among the Siona since 1960. Most Siona have adopted Western dress and food, plant cash crops, and speak Spanish as a first language. There are a small number of Siona at the Carmelite Mission in the Putumayo region of Ecuador, as well as others in the provinces of Napo and Pastaza in Ecuador.

REFERENCES: E. Jean Langdon, "The Siona Medical System: Beliefs and Behavior," Ph.D. dissertation, Tulane University, 1974; "Yagé Among the Siona: Cultural Patterns in Visions," in David L. Browman and Ronald A. Schwartz, eds., *Spirits, Shamans, and Stars: Perspectives from South America*, 1979; William T. Vickers, "Tropical Forest Mimicry in Swidden: A Reassessment of Geertz's Model, with Amazonian Data," *Human Ecology*, 11 (1983), 35–46.

SIPACAPENSE. The Sipacapense are a small Mayan* Indian group living in and around the municipality of Sipacapa in the department of San Marcos in the highlands of southwestern Guatemala. The region is generally inaccessible by road. The Sipacapense still live a settled agricultural lifestyle, raising maize, beans, and avocados for their own food and oranges and lemons as cash crops, although delivery of these products to market is a difficult process. Although they still have a number of communal agricultural plots, the transition to individual ownership, which government policies began at the end of the nineteenth century and accelerated after World War II, has been a continuing process. Most of the 4,000 Sipacapense Indians still speak their Mayan dialect as their primary language, although most of them also speak Spanish.

REFERENCES: W. George Lovell, *Conquest and Survival in Colonial Guatemala: A Historical Geography of the Cuchumutan Highlands, 1500–1821*, 1985; "Surviving Conquest: The Maya of Guatemala in Historical Perspective," *Latin American Research Review*, 23 (1988), 25–58.

SIPAPO. See PIAROA.

SIRANA. See XIRIANA.

SIRIANO. The Siriano (Suriano, Surira) are a small tropical forest tribe of Amerindians who live along the Papuri and Vina rivers in the territory of Vaupés in Colombia. They are part of the Eastern Tukano* linguistic group. Another group of Sirianos dwells on the Ti River, a tributary of the Paca River. There were sporadic European contacts with the Siriano in the eighteenth and nineteenth centuries. Portuguese missions were established temporarily along the upper Vaupés in the 1780s, but systematic evangelization of the tribe did not begin until 1914 when Roman Catholic priests established missions in the area. Protestant missionaries made their way into the region after World War II. The tribal economy focuses on the production of bitter manioc and fishing; hunting is quite secondary, although in recent years the tribe has become increasingly dependent on such European technology as fishhooks, shotguns, and machetes, as well as increased manioc production for sale. Contact with whites has also led to the development of small-scale animal husbandry, primarily hogs and poultry. In the 1960s and 1970s, the Colombian government began to encourage colonization of the Vaupés River basin, but settlement there has been very slow. The Siriano interact with other Indian tribes in the area but less often with whites, except for missionaries and rubber collectors, because of the extreme geographical isolation of the area. There are 1,900 Siriano today, of whom several hundred speak the native language.

REFERENCES: Myriam Jiméno and Adolfo Triana Antorveza, *Estado y minorias étnicas en Colombia*, 1985; Gerardo Reichel-Dolmatoff, *Amazonian Cosmos: The Sexual and Religious Symbolism of the Tukano Indians*, 1985.

SIRINEIRI. The Sirineiri (Sapiteri, Shirineri, Sirineri, Sirineyri, Sireneire) are a small Amerindian group living on the Upper Madre de Dios, Marcapata, upper Pucapuca, and upper Chilive rivers in the tropical forests of eastern Peru. Some scholars have traditionally classified them as an Arawakan* group, but they are actually part of the Harakmbet* language family. They remained generally free of European contact until the late nineteenth century when the rubber boom brought them a host of diseases and violence. Since then, several smallpox and influenza epidemics have devastated them. A tropical forest people, the Sirineiri are subsistence farmers who raise manioc, bananas, and a variety of other products on communal farms. There are probably 400 people who are aware of their tribal heritage, but there are relatively few of them who are full-bloods and speak the language. Most of those live with some Kisambaeri* on the Pukiri River or with the Amarakaeri.*

REFERENCES: Andrew Gray, "Perspectives on Amarakaeri History," in Harald O. Sklar and Frank Salomon, eds., *Natives and Neighbors in South America: Anthropological Essays*, 1987, 299–329; Darcy Ribeiro and Mary Ruth Wise, *Los grupos étnicos de la amazona peruana*, 1978; Stefano Varese, *The Forest Indians in the Present Political Situation of Peru*, 1972.

SIRINERI. See SIRINEIRI.

SIRIONÓ. The Sirionó (Chorí), known among themselves and some of their Indian neighbors as the Mbia, were once a nomadic, foraging people who spoke a Tupi*-Guaraní* language. Today they live within a 200-square-mile area in northeastern Bolivia, especially in the departments of El Beni and Santa Cruz. They are between the San Martín and Negro rivers and near the upper Machado River northeast of Trinidad. The Sirionó were originally a Guaraní people of the Gran Chaco who migrated north into the dense forests of northeastern Bolivia. Their culture, based on a foraging economy, was quite different from the more technologically advanced surrounding tribes. Although the Sirionó cultivated gardens where they raised some maize and manioc, they were essentially small game hunters who prized meat as the staple of their diet. The Sirionó were contacted by Europeans in the 1690s. In the 1700s, the Jesuits tried but failed to gather them into their mission system. By the late nineteenth and early twentieth centuries, however, the Sirionó were becoming increasingly acculturated, with large numbers of them abandoning the aboriginal life in favor of migrant and unskilled labor on cattle ranches, missions, and farms, where their lifestyle came to resemble those of forced laborers and landless peasants. Most Sirionó live a subsistence lifestyle, raising maize, manioc, and rice on small plots and hunting, fishing, and foraging to supplement their diet. Today the Sirionó number approximately 1,000 people, with only a handful still wandering nomadically in the Cerro Blanco mountains. Most still employ the aboriginal language.

REFERENCES: Brian M. Boom, *Ethnobotany of the Chácobo Indians, Beni, Bolivia*, 1987; Allan R. Holmberg, *Nomads of the Long Bow: The Sirionó of Eastern Bolivia*, 1960; Barry L. Isaac, "The Sirionó of Eastern Bolivia: A Reassessment," *Human Ecology*, 5 (1977), 137–54; Pedro Plaza Martínez and Juan Carvajal Carvajal, *Etnías y lenguas de Bolivia*, 1985; Harold W. Scheffler and Floyd G. Lounsbury, *A Study in Structural Semantics: The Siriono Kinship System*, 1971.

SITIBO. See SETEBO.

SIUSY-TAPUYA. See BANÍWA.

SIWAIHSU. See NAMBIQUÁRA.

SIWARO. See JÍVARO.

SOARIAPODE. See PIRA-TAPUYA.

SOKOMBA. The Sokomba are a subtribe of the Yuko* Indians of northeastern Colombia. They total only 30 people today and live in a village along the Roncón River where they still pursue a largely subsistence way of life. See YUKO.

SOLOTÍ. See CHOROTÉ.

SONENES. See ESSEJJA.

SOTEGARAIK. See ASHLUSLAY.

SOTIAGAI. See ASHLUSLAY.

SOUTHERN BARASÁNA. See BARASÁNA.

SOUTHERN CAYAPÓ. See KAYAPÓ.

SOUTHERN CHOCÓ. See CHOCÓ.

SOUTHERN CHOROTÉ. See CHOROTÉ.

SOUTHERN GUAYMÍ. See GUAYMÍ.

SOUTHERN KAIAPÓ. See KAYAPÓ.

SOUTHERN KAYAPÓ. See KAYAPÓ.

SOUTHERN MOTILONES. See BARÍ.

SOUTHERN NAMBIQUÁRA. See NAMBIQUÁRA.

SOUTHERN TEHUELCHE. See TEHUELCHE.

SOWA. See ASHLUSLAY.

SOWUASH. See ASHLUSLAY.

SSETEBO. See SETEBO.

SSIMAKU. See URARINA.

SSIPIPO. See SHIPIBO.

SUCURIYU-TAPUYA. See BANÍWA.

SUERRE. See RAMA.

SUHIN. See SUYÁ.

SUIÁ. See SUYÁ.

SUMO. See SUMU.

SUMU. Today there are approximately 7,000 Sumu (Sumo) Indians in the departments of Zelaya and Río San Juan on the Atlantic side of Nicaragua and another 350 in Honduras. At the time of the Spanish conquest, the Sumu were of the most extensive Indians groups in Central America. The major Sumu subgroups were the Matagalpans, located in the present-day departments of Chontales and Matagalpa; the Ulwa (Ulua, Wulwa, Olua, Ohlwa), located from the tributaries of the Escondido River north to the Coco River and as far west as Somoto; and the Twahka (Twaxha, Twa'ka, Taguaca), located from the Prinzapolka River north into eastern Honduras. There were other subgroups as well, including the Paanamaka, Kukra, Bawihka, Yusku, Prinsu, Boa, Silan, and Ku. Most of those original groups no longer function as individual social entities, although many Sumu are still aware of their subtribal identities. The Sumu put up a fierce resistance to the Spaniards. Because of the isolation of the Atlantic coast of Nicaragua, they were able to maintain their tribal identity. The Sumu suffered from Miskito* domination during the seventeenth and eighteenth centuries. The English arrived on the Nicaraguan coast in 1589 and by 1640 had formed an alliance with the Miskito. The Sumu population declined as a result of European diseases and violent resistance against the Spanish, British, and Miskito. In the western portion of their homeland, there has also been considerable assimilation into the surrounding Spanish-speaking mestizo population. During the 1980s, the Sumu suffered from the revolutionary wars in Nicaragua but also succeeded in getting themselves included in the 1987 decision of the government to create an autonomous political zone for the Sumu in eastern Nicaragua. Most anthropologists argue today that there are three Sumu groups still functioning. The Paanamaka Sumu are the largest, and most of them live near the mining town of Bonanza. The Twakha Sumu live in the province of Waspan in the western part of the department of Jinotega. The Ulva Sumu are scattered along the Grande and Prinzapolka rivers.

    REFERENCES: CIDCA, *Ethnic Groups and the Nation State: The Case of the Atlantic Coast in Nicaragua*, 1987; David Close, *Nicaragua: Politics, Economics and Society*, 1988; Anne Manuel, "No Place to be Neutral: The Plight of the Sumu Indians," *Commonweal*, 115 (1988), 107; Linda Newsom, *Indian Survival in Colonial Nicaragua*, 1987; L. Fernando Cruz Sandoval, "Los Indios de Honduras y la situación de sus recurcos naturales," *América Indígena*, 44 (1984), 423–46.

SURARA. See PAKIDAI.

SURIANA. See SIRIANO.

SURINÍ. See ASURINÍ.

SURIRA. See SIRIANO.

SUROMASA. See MAKUNA.

SURUÍ. The Suruí (Paitér) are a Tupi*-speaking group of Amerindians who today live in southeastern Rondônia, Brazil. Scholars estimate that at the time of the Portuguese conquest, the Suruí population exceeded 8,000 people. Like other Tupi peoples in Brazil, they lived much closer to the Atlantic coast then. Portuguese settlement forced them into the interior, and diseases dramatically reduced their population. The Suruí practiced a slash-and-burn agriculture to raise manioc and maize, and hunted and fished to supplement their diet. There was no really peaceful contact between the Suruí and Brazilian society until 1969 when some Suruí settled at the new Aripuanã Indian Park in the area. Within a few years, however, large mining companies were sending prospectors and settlers into the park with the tacit approval of the Brazilian government. The Suruí immediately fell victim to high rates of tuberculosis, influenza, and hepatitis, which produced a serious population decline. Today Brazilian demographers estimate that the Suruí population is only 300 people. Those numbers have declined from 700 Suruí in 1969. They are under considerable pressure from Brazilian nut gatherers and land developers. During the early 1980s, the Suruí violently resisted the presence of neo-Brazilian settlers on their land. Still, they have also grown heavily dependent on money, clothing, guns, ammunition, fishing lines, fish hooks, soap, flashlights, and batteries—needs that are increasingly integrating them into the cash economy.

REFERENCES: Betty Mindlin Lafer, "The Surui," in David Maybury-Lewis, *In the Path of the Polonoreste: Endangered Peoples of Western Brazil*, 1981, 53–54; Carolyn Bontkes and William R. Merrifield, "On Suruí (Tupian) Social Organization," in William R. Merrifield, ed., *South American Kinship: Eight Kinship Systems from Brazil and Colombia*, 1985, 5–34; "Suruí Appeal for International Support," *Cultural Survival Quarterly*, 13 (1989), 27–29.

SURUÍ. The Suruí (Mudjetíre, Mujetíre) are an Amerindian people who live on the Tocantins River and on the Sororo, a tributary of the Itacaiunas River, in the state of Pará, Brazil. They are a tropical forest people who support themselves by hunting and fishing and by raising sweet manioc in communal gardens. Contacts with neo-Brazilians in the twentieth century have dramatically reduced the Suruí population. The Suruí were first contacted by neo-Brazilian settlers in 1920 near a local ranch, but the first peaceful contact was in 1953 when a Roman Catholic missionary settled temporarily among them. At the time, the Suruí population numbered approximately 100 people. In 1960, a local "businessman" invited 25 hunters into Suruí territory to collect animal skins; they broke up the village and put many of the Suruí women into prostitution. By 1961 the Suruí population had dropped to only 40 people. That population decline then stabilized and was back up to about 80 people in the early 1980s.

REFERENCES: Paul L. Aspelin and Silvio Coelho dos Santos, *Indian Areas Threatened by Hydroelectric Projects in Brazil*, 1981; Edwin Brooks et al., *Tribes of the Amazon Basin in Brazil 1972*, 1973; Robert Lee Spires, "As línguas faladas do Brasil," *América Indígena*, 47 (1987), 455–79.

SUSA. The Susa are a subtribe of the Yuko* Indians of northeastern Colombia. Today they live a tropical forest existence of manioc horticulture, hunting, and fishing and total approximately 110 people. Their tribal land is on the Espiritu Santo River. See YUKO.

SUWERI. The Suweri were a group of Amerindians who formed part of the Harakmbet* linguistic group. Their traditional homeland was between the Amarakaeri* and Wachapaeri* Indians on the Wandakhwe River in southeastern Peru. A tropical forest people, the Suweri were devastated by the rubber boom of 1894–1920 when rubber collectors brought disease and slavery to them. Subsequent epidemics of smallpox and influenza in the 1950s and 1960s eventually destroyed the tribe. Today there are only one or two Suweri survivors who remember their tribal identity.

REFERENCE: Andrew Gray, "Perspectives on Amarakaeri History," in Harald O. Sklar and Frank Salomon, eds., *Natives and Neighbors in South America: Anthropological Essays*, 1987, 299–329.

SUYÁ. The Suyá (Suiá), also known as the Tsuva, are a Gê*-speaking people of the northern Mato Grosso in Brazil. In the early 1800s, they entered the Xingú River area by coming down the Ronuro River. The Suyá were actually two separate groups until 1970. The Eastern Suyá lived on the Upper Xingú River while the Western Suyá, also known as the Tapayúna (Tapanyúna, Tapanhúna) or Beico do Pau,* were three hundred miles to the west, between the Arinos River and the Sangue River in Mato Grosso. The first European known to have contacted the Eastern Suyá was the German anthropologist and explorer Karl Von den Steinen, who reached them in 1884. In 1915, the Eastern Suyá were devastated by attacks from the Juruna* and Northern Kayapó.* Their population was so reduced that they could no longer sustain a traditional ceremonial life. Brazilian anthropologists reached them in 1959. A few years later they convinced the Eastern Suyá to move to the protection of the Xingú Indian Reserve. In 1968, Brazilian anthropologists and journalists reached the Western Suyá, but they also brought along a flu virus that reduced the tribal population from over 400 people to just 40. They too then moved to the Xingú Indian Reserve. By the mid–1980s, there were approximately 100 Eastern Suyá alive and about 50 Western Suyá.

REFERENCES: Robin Hanbury-Tenison, *A Question of Survival for the Indians of Brazil*, 1973; Anthony Seeger, "Nature and Culture and Their Transformation in the Cosmology and Social Organization of the Suyá, a Gê-Speaking Tribe of Central Brazil," Ph.D. dissertation, University of Chicago, 1974; Anthony Seeger, *Nature and Society in Central Brazil: The Suyá Indians of Mato Grosso*, 1981; Robert Lee Spires, "As línguas faladas do Brasil," *América Indígena*, 47 (1987), 455–79.

T

TABAINO. The Tabaino (Taibano, Taiwano, Eduria) are an Eastern Tukanoan* tribe of Amerindians who lived in the Vaupés River drainage region of Colombia, primarily at the confluence of the Cananri and Apaporis rivers in the territory of Vaupés. The upper Vaupés River has been a very isolated place until recently, even though various anthropologists, Roman Catholic priests, and Protestant missionaries have moved into the area since 1900. The tribe was decimated by the arrival of large numbers of Brazilian and Colombian rubber collectors in the early 1900s and again during World War II. The Colombian government today is trying to encourage settlement of the region, but development has been very slow. The Tabaino have contacts with many other Indian tribes but not much contact with Europeans. A riverine people, the Tabaino are skilled canoemen and fisherman who live on the fish and river animals of the area. They also practice a slash-and-burn agriculture to raise manioc. Although they are gradually being integrated into the regional cash economy, the approximately 100 members of the Tabaino tribe today retain a sense of tribal identity. They are closely related to the Southern Barasána, and some anthropologists consider them a subtribe. The Summer Institute of Linguistics has been working among the Tabaino since 1960. In recent years, the influences of a market economy and evangelical religion have accelerated the acculturation process.

REFERENCES: Myriam Jimeno and Adolfo Triana Antorveza, *Estado y minorias étnicas en Colombia*, 1985; Jean A. Jackson, *The Fish People: Linguistic Exogamy and Tukanoan Identity in Northwest Amazonia*, 1983; Arthur P. Sorenson, Jr., "Multilingualism in the Northwest Amazon," *American Anthropologist*, 69 (1967), 670–684.

TABOTIROJEJEAMASA. See MAKUNA.

TACANA. The Tacana (Takana) Indians today live in the province of Iturralde in the department of La Paz in Bolivia. They can also be found in and around the communities of Ixiamas, Tumupasa, and San Buenaventura in northwestern Bolivia, at the foot of the Andes mountains, and along the Beni, Tuichi, upper Madidi, and Madre de Dios rivers. Spaniards first contacted the Tacana in the 1530s when the expedition of Pedro Anzules de Campo-Redondo reached the Beni River. Franciscan missionaries established missions among the Tacana at the end of the seventeenth century, converting them to Roman Catholicism. Many Tacana also adopted the Quechua* language at the time because of its use by the missionaries. Today there are approximately 5,000 Tacana living in organized villages along the Beni River where they are increasingly acculturated and integrated into the local cash economy. They are laborers, subsistence farmers, and cattle raisers. The Tacana sense of tribal identity is declining and most of them are bilingual.

REFERENCES: Brian M. Boom, *Ethnobotany of the Chácobo Indians, Beni, Bolivia,* 1987; Harold Key and Mary Key, *Bolivian Indian Tribes: Classification, Bibliography, and Map of Present Language Distribution,* 1967; John Ottaviano, *Notas sobre la cultura Tacana,* 1980; Graciela Zolezzi and J. Riester, "Lenguas indígenas del oriente boliviano clasificación preliminar," *América Indígena,* 47 (1987), 425–33.

TACANAN. The term "Tacanan" is used to refer to a small group of Amerindian languages closely related to the Panoan* linguistic family. The Tacanan languages were concentrated in Bolivia at the time of the conquest and included the Arasaeri,* Cavineña,* Essejja,* Guarizo, Guarayo,* Mabenaro, Reyesano,* Sapiboca, and Tacana* (Araona or Toromona).

REFERENCES: Joseph H. Greenberg, *Language in the Americas,* 1987; Mary Ritchie Key, *Comparative Tacanan Phonology: With Cavinena Phonology and Notes on Pano-Tacanan Relationships,* 1968.

TACANECO. The Tacaneco are a Mayan*-language group living in the highlands of Guatemala. Today they total more than 42,000 people. They still make a living from the production of corn and beans on communal lands, although in recent years their severe poverty, as well as government policies that increasingly convert large amounts of their land to individual ownership, have forced many Tacaneco men to seek employment as migrant laborers. Until the 1970s, the Tacaneco settlements could be reached only by footpath, a circumstance that had protected them from the worst depredations of European and mestizo civilization. Road construction in the 1970s ended that isolation. In the 1980s, political repression by a right-wing government in Guatemala precipitated a large-scale emigration of Tacanecans to the United States.

REFERENCES: George Black, *Guatemala: The Making of a Revolution,* 1984; W. George Lovell, "Surviving Conquest: The Maya of Guatemala in Historical Perspective," *Latin American Research Review,* 23 (1988), 25–58.

TACUEYO. See PÁEZ

TADE. See ARAONA.

TADO. The Tado people are a group of Amerindians who today live in the department of Chocó at the mouth of the San Juan River in western Colombia. Their language is part of the Chocó subfamily of the larger Chibchan* linguistic group. They are an agricultural people who primarily raise sugar cane and plantains, along with maize and rice as secondary products. Although they raise some domestic livestock, most of their meat protein comes from hunting. In recent years, the settlement of the Pacific coast by mestizos and Afro-Americans has increased the pressures of acculturation on the Tado. At present, there are approximately 1,000 members of the Tado group.
  REFERENCE: Leah B. Ellis and Linda Criswell, eds., *Estudiemos las culturas indígenas de Colombia*, 1984.

TAGNANI. See NAMBIQUÁRA.

TAGUACA. See JICAQUE.

TAGUACA. See SUMU.

TAIA. See PAYÁ.

TAIATE. See NAMBIQUÁRA.

TAIBANO. See TABAINO.

TAÍNO. The Taíno were a huge group of perhaps millions of Amerindians occupying Cuba, Hispaniola, and Puerto Rico at the time of the Spanish conquest of the West Indies in the 1490s and early 1500s. They spoke an Arawakan* language. Conventional wisdom among scholars accepts as fact the complete destruction of the Taíno people by 1550, mostly because of disease. Over the years, however, meetings with small numbers of Indian people in Cuba and Puerto Rico have been reported. Miguel Rodríguez Ferrar, a Spanish scientist, encountered Indian communities on the eastern tip of Cuba in 1847, and José Martí, the great leader of Cuban independence, claimed to have lived briefly with some Indian groups in Cuba in 1895. Although the Taíno Indians were indeed destroyed as a functional social group, there survived in Puerto Rico and Cuba a few people whose ancestry retained a strong indigenous profile. Today there are a few hundred people in the Baracoa region of eastern Cuba as well as in the mountainous regions of western Puerto Rico who have strong Indian roots. Although they speak Spanish, are Roman Catholic, are integrated into the local economy, and have no sense of a peculiarly Taíno background, they are evertheless aware of their Indian ancestry.

REFERENCES: José Barreiro, "Indians in Cuba," *Cultural Survival Quarterly*, 13 (1989), 56–60; Jesse Walter Fewkes, *The Aborigines of Puerto Rico and Neighboring Islands*, 1907.

TAIWANO. See TABAINO.

TAKANA. See TACANA.

TAKSHIK. See TOBA.

TAKUATEP. The Takuatep were a group of Amerindians who once spoke a Tupi* language and lived on the right bank of the Jiparaná River in what is today the state of Rondônia, Brazil. They probably reached Rondônia in the early eighteenth century after fleeing the Portuguese in eastern Brazil. The rubber boom of the late 1800s and early 1900s doomed them. Large numbers of rubber collectors swarmed into Rondônia, bringing with them violence, economic exploitation, and disease. The Takuatep tribe did not survive after its population went into a rapid decline. They were also victimized by the Mundurukú* Indians. By the 1930s the Takuatep no longer functioned as a tribal culture, and by the 1950s there were no longer any full-blooded members of the tribe. Nevertheless, there are still individuals in Rondonia who are aware of their Takuatep ancestry.
   REFERENCE: Theodore L. Stoddard, ed., *Indians of Brazil in the Twentieth Century*, 1967.

TALAMANCA. The term "Talamanca" refers to a subtribe of the Bribri* in Costa Rica as well as a large group of Chibchan*-language tribes, including the Dorasque, Changuena, Terraba,* Brunka, Bribri, and Cabécare.*
   REFERENCE: Elías Zamora Acosta, *Etnografía histórica de Costa Rica (1561–1615)*, 1980.

TALIASERI. See TARIANA.

TAMA. The Tama are a Western Tukanoan* group of Amerindians who have for the most part merged with the Coreguaje* and Karijona* Indians. They live along the Cagua, the Caquetá, and the Upper Putumayo rivers in the department of Caquetá, Colombia. See COREGUAJE.

TAMAKURIDENI. See DANÍ.

TAMANÁWA. The Tamanáwa (Tamináua) are a small group of Amerindians who today live outside of Feijo on the border of the states of Amazonas and Acre in western Brazil. Sometimes called Kanamarí (Canamarí), the Tamanáwa are descended from Panoan*-speaking tribal ancestors now extinct as a differentiated social group. Because of their geographical location, the Tamanáwa were generally isloated from any sustained contact with neo-Brazilians until the late nineteenth and early twentieth centuries when rubber collectors savaged them. Many Tamanáwa were slaughtered or enslaved while others died of diseases. By the 1940s, there were fewer than 100 members of the tribe, and they were increasingly integrated into the local economy as laborers. Ceremonial life could not be sustained because of declining tribal numbers. Today there are only a few isolated individuals still living who have a conscious sense of their Tamanáwa origins.

REFERENCE: Theodore L. Stoddard, ed., *Indians of Brazil in the Twentieth Century*, 1967.

TAMBEOPE. See KAIWÁ.

TAMBOPATA. See ESSEJJA.

TAMBOPATA-GUARAYÓ. See ESSEJJA.

TAME. See TUNEBO.

TAMINAUA. See TAMANÁWA.

TAMPA. See CAMPA.

TANIMBOKA. See TANIMUKO.

TANIMUCA. See TANIMUKO.

TANIMUCO. See TANIMUKO.

TANIMUKA. See TANIMUKO.

TANIMUKO. The Tanimuko (Tanimuco, Tanimuka, Tanimboka) are a small group of Amerindians who live in the Vaupés River drainage region of the territory of Amazonas in Colombia. In particular, they live along the Guacaya, Miriti, and Apaporis rivers. They live and speak a language nearly identical to that of the Resigaro* Indians and call themselves the Ufaina. They are part of the Eastern Tukanoan* linguistic family. There were sporadic European contacts with the Tanimuko in the eighteenth and nineteenth centuries. Portuguese missions were established temporarily along the upper Vaupés in the 1780s, but systematic envangelization of the tribe did not begin until 1914 when Roman Catholic priests established missions in the area. Anthropologists reached the Tanimuko early in the 1900s, and Protestant missionaries made their way into the region after World War II. The tribal economy focuses on the production of bitter manioc and fishing; hunting is quite secondary, although in recent years the tribe has become increasingly dependent on such European technology as fishhooks, shotguns, and machetes, as well as on increased manioc production for sale. They are also known for their foraging abilities. Contact with whites has also led to the development of small-scale animal husbandry, primarily hogs and poultry. In the 1960s and 1970s, the Colombian government began to encourage colonization of the Vaupés River basin, but settlement there has been very slow. The Tanimuko interact with other Indian tribes in the area but less often with whites because of the extreme geographical isolation of the area. There are approximately 450 Tanimuko and Resigaro today who acknowledge tribal membership and speak the native language. Nearly 380 of them live on the Colombian government Indian reservation of Yaigoje-Rio Apaporis.

REFERENCES: Kaj Arhem, *Makuna Social Organization: A Study in Descent, Alliance and the Formation of Corporate Groups in the North-Western Amazon*, 1981; Myriam Jiméno and Adolfo Triana Antorveza, *Estado y minorias éthicas en Colombia*, 1985; Gerardo Reichel-Dolmatoff, *Amazonian Cosmos: The Sexual and Religious Symbolism of the Tukano Indians*, 1985; Arthur P. Sorenson, Jr., "Multilingualism in the Northwest Amazon," *American Anthropologist*, 69 (1967), 670–84.

TANYGUA. See AVÁ-CHIRIPÁ.

TAPAKARA. See KAWAHÍB.

TAPANHÚNA. See BEICO DO PAU.

TAPANYÚNA. See BEICO DO PAU.

TAPARITA. See ACHAGUA.

TAPAYÚNA. See BEICO DO PAU.

TAPIETÉ. The Tapieté (Guasurango, Tapii) are a Tupi-Guaraní*-speaking tribe of Amerindians most of whom live in the Gran Chaco of Paraguay, with a handful in southeastern Bolivia, between the upper Pilcomayo River and the Paraguayan border. Originally they inhabited the desert areas stretching from the upper Pilcomayo River to the lower Parapiti River. Although the Tapieté have a tribal culture very similar to that of the Mataco* and Chorote*, their language is the Guaraní dialect of the Chiriguano.* Since the time of the Spanish conquest, the Tapieté have also been identified by the terms Tapii, Yanaygua (Yanaigua), Yana, and Nanaigua. Today the Tapieté number approximately 1,100 people in Paraguay, and they are increasingly integrated into the regional economy of the Gran Chaco as wage laborers on larger ranches and plantations. There are only about 50 of them living in Bolivia, where they are concentrated in the western, northwestern, and central Chaco. Nevertheless, their sense of cultural identity remains strong, although most of them have abandoned their aboriginal language in favor of Guaraní. Many Tapieté are farmers who raise a variety of products, but an increasing number are wage laborers. Roman Catholic missionaries from the Oblates of Mary Immaculate maintain several missions among the Tapieté.

REFERENCES: Harriet Klein and Louisa Stark, "Indian Tribes of the Paraguayan Chaco," *Anthropological Linguistics*, 19 (1977), 378–402; John Renshaw, "Property, Resources and Equality among the Indians of the Paraguayan Chaco," *Man*, 23 (1988), 334–52; Pedro Plaza Martínez and Juan Carvajal Carvajal, *Ethnías y lenguas de Bolivia*, 1985; Graciela Zolezzi and J. Riester, "Lenguas indígenas del oriente boliviano clasificacion preliminar," *América Indígena*, 47 (1987), 425–33.

TAPIOCA. See WAIWAI.

TAPIRAPÉ. The Tapirapé Indians live today in only one village, which is located at the mouth of the Tapirapé River in the northern reaches of the state of Mato Grosso, Brazil. Their language is part of the Tupi*-Guaraní* family. Since they are surrounded by Gê*-speaking people, the Tapirapé are probably recent arrivals to the area. At the time of the European conquest, there were approximately 3,000 Tapirapé Indians, but that number fell to 1,500 people living in five villages by 1900. Most of the population decline came from attacks by neighborhing Kayapó* tribes on the north and Karajá* people on the east. The Tapirapé lived in the tropical forest, practicing a slash-and-burn garden agriculture to raise manioc, hunting game on the neighboring savannas, and fishing on the Tapirapé River. Tapirapé isolation ended in 1910 when Brazilian settlers began putting pressure on the Kayapó and Karajá who pushed into Tapirapé territory. A malaria epidemic destroyed half the Tapirapé population. Dominican missionaries brought tools to the tribe in the early 1900s but did not disturb the culture, at least not intentionally. Disease and Kayapó attacks continued to decimate the Tapirapé population in the twentieth century, reducing the tribe to one village and 200 people by the 1980s.

REFERENCES: Judith Shapiro, *Ceremonial Redistribution in Tapirapé Society*, 1968; Robert Lee Spires, "As línguas faladas do Brasil," *América Indígena*, 47 (1987), 455–79; Charles Wagley, *Welcome of Tears: The Tapirapé Indians of Central Brazil*, 1977.

TARANU. See ARAONA.

TARAPOTO. See SECOYA.

TARENA. See TERÉNO.

TAKIAKA. See BRIBRI.

TARIANA. The Tariana (Tariano, Taliaseri) Indians are a nearly extinct group of Arawakan* people who live in the general region of the Papuri and Vaupés rivers in the territory of Vaupés in Colombia and across the border in Brazil. Their nucleus today is in Brazil. They are considered a subtribe of the Tukano.* At the present time, there are fewer than 100 people who claim a Tariana heritage, and only 30 of them speak Tariana. Another 1,000 people maintain a social affiliation with the group. Those who do not speak Tariana speak Tukano. There are several hundred other people, however, who do not maintain a sense of Tariano identity but who are aware of their ancestry. Altogether there are approximately 1,600 people connected with the Tariana tribe. Missionaries relocated the Tariana to the Papuri and Vaupés area from their original homeland on the Içana and Aiari rivers. They are primarily a nomadic people who are able to raise manioc but prefer a hunting and fishing existence.

REFERENCES: Gerardo Reichel-Dolmatoff, *Amazonian Cosmos: The Sexual and Religious Symbolism of the Tukano Indians*, 1979; Robert Lee Spires, "As línguas faladas do Brasil," *America Indígena*, 47 (1987), 455–79.

TARUMA. The Taruma, also known historically as the Aroaqui, were once an Arawak*-language tribe inhabiting the headwaters of the Essequibo, Kuyuwini, and Cassiquity rivers in what is today Guyana. Once located in the Amazon basin of Brazil, they migrated north in the eighteenth century. By the middle of the nineteenth century, their numbers exceeded 500 people. Their lifestyle was typical of a tropical forest people—cultivating manioc as their staple and hunting and fishing to supplement the protein in their diet. In the mid–1920s, an influenza epidemic devastated the Tarumas, killing most members and rendering the tribe extinct as a self-conscious social unit. As late as the early 1980s, a handful of Taruma descendents was still aware of tribal origins.

REFERENCE: W. Edwards and K. Gibson, "An Ethnohistory of Amerindians in Guyana," *Ethnohistory*, 26 (Spring 1979), 161–65.

TASIO. See CAMPA.

TATU-TAPUYO. See TATUYO.

TATUYO. The Tatuyo, also known as the Pamoa, Suna, or the Tatu-tapuyo, are an Eastern Tukanoan*-language tribe of Amerindians who lived near the Karapanas River of the Vaupés drainage region of the territory of Vaupés, Colombia. The upper Vaupés River has been a very isolated place until recently, even though various anthropologists, Roman Catholic priests, and Protestant missionaries have moved into the area since 1900. The Colombian government today is trying to encourage settlement of the region, but development has been very slow. Although the Tatuyo have adopted Western clothing and metal technology and have contacts with many other Indian tribes, they do not have much contact with neo-Colombians. Since 1969, a group from the Summer Institute of Linguistics has worked among them. Today they still pursue a typical tropical forest culture, raising manioc as their staple and supplementing their diet with hunting and fishing. The Tatuyo total approximately 500 people.

REFERENCES: Darna L. Dufour, "Nutrition in the Northwest Amazon: Household Dietary Intake and Time-Energy Expenditure," in Raymond B. Hames and William T. Vickers, eds., *Adaptive Responses of Native Amazonians*, 1983, 329–355; Darna L.

Dufour, "Time and Energy Expenditure of Indigenous Women Horticulturalists in the Northwest Amazon," *American Journal of Physical Anthropology*, 65 (1984), 37–46; Myriam Jimeno and Adolfo Triana Andorveza, *Estado y minorias étnicas en Colombia*, 1985; Arthur P. Sorenson, Jr., "Multilingualism in the Northwest Amazon," *American Anthropologist*, 69 (1967), 670–84.

TAUARDE. See NAMBIQUÁRA.

TAULIPÁNG. The Taulipáng (Taurepã, Tarepáng, Jaricuna) are an Amerindian tribe of Karib* extraction who live today in villages on the mountainsides near Roraima and Pacaraima close to the border junction of Guyana, Brazil, and Venezuela. They are called Arekuna* (Aricuni) in Brazil. Large numbers of the Taulipáng were slaughtered during the mass immigration of neo-Brazilians in the mid-nineteenth century, forcing the Taulipáng into close association with the Matushí. Their subsistence economy broke down in the early 1900s when they became increasingly integrated into the local market economy. Today there are approximately 1,500 Taulipáng Indians, most of whom live in Guyana and Venezuela. Although the Taulipáng are conscious of their tribal heritage and group identity, their primary languages are increasingly becoming Portuguese and Spanish.

REFERENCE: Erich Molritz von Hornbostel, *The Music of the Makushi, Taulipang, and Yekuana Indians*, 1969.

TAUNDE. See NAMBIQUÁRA.

TAUPANE. See JICAQUE.

TAUREPAN. See PARUKOTO.

TAUREPÁN. See TAULIPÁNG.

TAUREPÁNG. See TAULIPÁNG.

TAUSHIRO. The Taushiro (Pinche, Pinchi) are an Amerindian group whose language is most likely part of the Zaparo* linguistic family, although scholars remain divided over the issue. They call themselves the Ite'chi. There are two major subdivisions of the Taushiro: the Einontu'tua and the Antontu'tua. They are concentrated along the Aucayacu and Tigre rivers in the district of Tigre in the province of Loreto, Loreto District, Peru. Father Tomás Santos visited them in 1684, and in 1698 Spanish missionaries established two missions among them. At that time, the Taushiro population exceeded 2,500 people. Diseases and enslavement rapidly reduced their population; by 1850 the Taushiro population had dropped to 100 people. A severe epidemic in 1960 reduced them further to only 70 people. Today there are approximately 125 Taushiro Indians, but only a dozen or so use the native language which is declining rapidly. The Taushiro are adopting Quechua,* Spanish, or even one of the local Jívaroan* languages. Although the Taushiro are becoming detribalized, they still define themselves as Indians and maintain a cultural separation from neo-Peruvian society.

REFERENCES: Darcy Ribeiro and Mary Ruth Wise, *Los grupos étnicos de la amazona peruana*, 1978; Gustavus Solís F., "Multilinguismo y extinciones de lenguas," *América Indígena*, 47 (1987), 630–45.

TA'UUSHN. See TEHUELCHE.

TAVASHAY. See ASHLUSLAY.

TAWAI. See KATUKÍNA.

TAWANDE. See NAMBIQUÁRA.

TAWENDE. See NAMBIQUÁRA.

TCHEOUELCHE. See TEHUELCHE.

TCHIGUEBO. See KADUVEO.

TCHIKAO. See TXIJKÃO.

TCHONEK. See TEHUELCHE.

TCHUKARRAMEI. See TXUKAHAMEI.

TECHBI. See TÉRRABA.

TECHI. See TÉRRABA.

TECO. See TECTITECO.

TECTITECO. The Tectiteco (Teco) are a small Mayan* Indian group living in and around the municipality of Tectitán in the department of Huehuetenango in the highlands of western Guatemala. The region is generally inaccessible by road. The Tectiteco still live a settled agricultural lifestyle, raising maize, beans, and bananas for their own food and sugar cane as a cash crop, although delivery of the product to market is a difficult process. Although the Tectiteco still have a number of communal agricultural plots, the transition to individual ownership, which government policies initiated at the end of the nineteenth century and accelerated after World War II, has been a continuing process. Most of the 7,000 Tectiteco Indians still speak their Mayan dialect as their primary language, although most of them also speak Spanish. At any given moment, large numbers of them are on the road looking for work, usually in Mexico.

REFERENCES: W. George Lovell, *Conquest and Survival in Colonial Guatemala: A Historical Geography of the Cochumutan Highlands, 1500–1821*, 1985; "Surviving Conquest: The Maya of Guatemala in Historical Perspective," *Latin American Research Review*, 23 (1988), 25–58; Gloria Tujab, "Lenguas indígenas que se encuentran en vias de extinción," *América Indígena*, 47 (1987), 529–33.

TEGUELCHE. See TEHUELCHE.

TEHUELCHE. At the time of the Spanish discovery of the New World, the Tehuelches were an Indian tribe occupying the region known today as Patagonia, the vast area of southern Argentina between the Colorado River in the north and the Strait of Magellan in the south. The Tehuelche also penetrated somewhat farther north into the adjacent Pampa. When Ferdinand Magellan sailed through the strait that now bears his name, he encountered and traded with the Tehuelche. During the next 150 years, another 8 European exploration parties had contact with the tribe. The Southern Tehuelche or Aonikenk (Ahonicanka, Ahoniken, Ahonnekenke, Ahonekenke, Aoniken, Aonik, Aonukun'k, Aoniko-tshonk, Aonikenke, Kenk, Harwaneki, Hawaneki, Haveniken, Huanaiker-Tsonik, and Inaken) occupied the region between the Chubut River and the Strait of Magellan, while the Northern Tehuelche or Gununa-kene (Payni-ken, Paignkenken, Pa'ankun'k, and Pa'ankotshonk) lived between the Colorado and Chabut rivers. A small third group of Tehuelche spoke a dialect known as Teuesh (Ta'uushn, Tehuesh, Tehueshen, Teuesson, Tehueshenk, The-ushene, and De-ushene).

Before 1670, the Tehuelche were a nomadic, foraging people. After 1670, from either the Spaniards or the Mapuche,* they adopted the use of the horse, especially the Northern Tehuelche, and became a wide-ranging hunting people. Late in the eighteenth century, Mapuche expansion began to pose serious problems for the Tehuelche, who were no match for the warlike Mapuche. A smallpox epidemic devastated the tribe between 1809 and 1812. The rapid population decline set in motion by Mapuche attacks and smallpox was completed in the late nineteenth and early twentieth centuries by increasing European settlement of Patagonia and government military campaigns against the tribe. These resulted in acute culture loss and the mestization of the tribal population. The 10,000 Tehuelche people had been reduced to only 500 people by 1900. The tribe has since almost ceased to exist as a self-conscious social entity, although there are elderly Tehuelche who are still aware of their tribal heritage. At present, approximately 50 Tehuelche live on a small reserve at Camushu Aike in Argentina. Historically, the Tehuelche have also been known as Patagonians, Chonik, Choneca, Choanik, Chouqui, Choonke, Tchonek, Tsonik, and various spellings of Tehuelche (Tuelche, Toelchi, Toelche, Tewelche, Thehuelche, Theguel-che, Teguelche, Tehuelci, Toelchu, Tuelchu, Thuelchu, Tehuelhet, Tehueleto, Chehuelchu, Cheuelchu, and Tcheouelche, and Tsoneca.

REFERENCES: Isabel Hernández, "Los pueblos y las lenguas aborígenes en la actualidad," *América Indígena*, 47 (1987), 409–23; "The Qawasqar Indians of Tierra del

Fuego,'' *Cultural Survival Quarterly*, 11 (1987), 83–84; Johannes Wilbert and Karin Somoneau, *Folk Literature of the Tehuelche Indians*, 1985.

TEHUELCI. See TEHUELCHE.

TEHUELETO. See TEHUELCHE.

TEHUELHET. See TEHUELCHE.

TEHUESH. See TEHUELCHE.

TEHUESHEN. See TEHUELCHE.

TEHUESHENK. See TEHUELCHE.

TEJUCA. See TUYUKA.

TELEMBIE. See COAIQUER.

TEMBE. See TENETEHÁRA.

TEMBKUA. See KAIWÁ.

TEMOMOYAMI. See WINAO.

TENA. See QUECHUA.

TENETEHÁRA. The Tenetehára are a Tupi*-Guaraní*-language people who live in northeastern Brazil. They have also been known historically as the Tembé and the Guajajará.* Today they function in two separate groups. The Guajajará-Tenetehára live in the region of the state of Maranhão that is drained by the Mearim, Grajau, and Pindaré rivers. The Tembé-Tenetehára of the state of Pará live along the Gurupi, Guama, and Capim rivers. They live in dense tropical forests and work as farmers, raising maize and manioc. Europeans first reached the Tenetehára early in the 1600s, and in the seventeenth century the Jesuits managed to place several thousand tribal members temporarily in missions; the Tenetehára then numbered approximately 12,000 people. Contact with European diseases brought the inevitable population decline, but the Tenetehára proved to be one of the most adaptable of the Brazilian tribes, no doubt because their homeland was not along the main routes in the Portuguese penetration of the continent. Not until the late nineteenth and early twentieth centuries did some Tenetehára begin to become integrated into the European economy as wage laborers. Although the Tenetehára are now in constant contact with other Brazilians, they have managed to maintain a number of their aboriginal cultural practices. Approximately 7,000 Tenetehára live today in the states of Maranhão and Pará. Of that total, the Tembé account for approximately 400 people. Most of them are highly integrated into neo-Brazilian culture.

REFERENCES: Michael Gomes, "The Ethnic Survival of the Tenetehára Indians of Maranhão, Brazil," Ph.D. dissertation, University of Florida, 1977; Robert Lee Spires, "As línguas faladas do Brasil," *América Indígena*, 47 (1987), 455–79; Charles Wagley and Eduardo Galvão, *The Tenetehára Indians of Brazil: A Culture in Transition*, 1949.

TENHAREM. See BOCA PRETA.

TENHARÍM. See BOCA PRETA.

TEQUIRACA. See AWISHIRI.

TERÉNA. See TERÉNO.

TERÉNO. The Teréno (Taréna, Terenoa, Teréna, Etelena, Ethlena) Indians are descendents of the old Guaná tribe, which was closely associated with the Guaycurú* (Mbaya) throughout much of the colonial period in Brazil and Paraguay. The Guaná people are the southernmost representatives of the Arawakan* language family in South America. They called themselves the Chana, which the Spaniards often transcribed as Chané. For generations, the Guaná had worked as servants and slaves to the Guaycuru, even though they vastly outnumbered them. The major subtribes of the Chané were the Layana,* Niguecactemic (Neguecaga temigii or Neguecatemigi, Niguicactemia, Neguicactemi), Kinikinão* (Equiniquinao, Equiliquinao, Quainaconas), Echoaladi (Hechoaladi, Charabana, Choarana, Echenoana, Chualas), and the Chana-Bohave, Chana-Mbegua, and Chana-Timbu. Before the Portuguese conquest, there were between 15,000 and 25,000 members of the Guaná tribe, divided into a western group living on the Andes slopes and an eastern group in the Paraguayan Chaco. By the mid-nineteenth century, the western group had merged and disappeared into the Chiriguano* tribe while the eastern groups had moved out of the Chaco, broken the dominance of the Guaycurú, and resettled into the region around Miranda, Brazil, where the Teréno were the largest representative of the tribe, and in northern Argentina. Today the Teréno, with remnants of the Chané and the Kinikinão, total approximately 10,000 people. Although they have adjusted to the Brazilian economy, they still suffer from terribly poor economic circumstances. They live between the Miranda and Aquidauana rivers in the state of Mato Grosso, Brazil. The Teréno maintain their tribal language and identity. Another 2,500 Teréno live in the province of Salta in Argentina, especially in Tuyunti, Aguaray, and Campo Durán. Although very similar to the Chiriguano, the Teréno maintain a strong sense of ethnic distinctiveness. Most of those in Argentina work in sugar mills. Franciscan priests work among several Teréno groups. A handful of Teréno live in the southeastern region of the department of Santa Cruz in Bolivia.

REFERENCES: Robin Hanbury-Tenison, *A Question of Survival for the Indians of Brazil*, 1973; John Hemming, *Red Gold: The Conquest of the Brazilian Indians, 1500–1760*, 1978; Isabel Hernández, "Los pueblos y las lenguas aborígenes en la actualidad," *América Indígena*, 47 (1987), 409–23; Andrés Serbin, "Las organizaciones indígenas en la Argentina," *América Indígena*, 41 (1981), 407–34; Robert Lee Spires, "As línguas faladas do Brasil," *América Indígena*, 47 (1987), 455–79.

TERENOA. See TERÉNO.

TERIAKA. See BRIBRI.

TERIBE. The Teribe are a small Amerindian group living today in Panama, particularly in Bocas del Toro Province along the Teribe, San Juan, and Changuinola rivers. They are closely related to the Chibchan*-language people known as Terrabas in Costa Rica. There are just over 1,000 people who identify closely with the Teribe Indians, and most of them work as laborers and subsistence farmers in Panama. Large numbers of them still speak the Teribe language.

REFERENCES: Carol Koontz and Joanne Anderson, "Connectives in Teribe Discourse," in Robert E. Longacre, ed., *Discourse Grammar: Studies in Indigenous Languages in Colombia, Panama, and Ecuador*, 2 (1977), 95–132; Arysteides Turpana, "Lenguas indígenas," *América Indígena*, 47 (1987), 614–25.

TÉRRABA. The Térrabas—also known as the Tírub, Tírribi, and Térrebe— live in the lowlands between the Sixaola River and the Changuinola River in what is today Costa Rica and across the border on the Atlantic side of Panama. Approximately 500 Térraba are in Costa Rica, although the vast majority of them are detribalized. Other Térrabas, known as the Tojar, live on the islands at the mouths of the rivers. The Térrabas have also included such subtribes as the Teshbi (Techi, Techbi, Tichbi), Depso, Lari, Uren, Norteño, Quequexque, and Brururau. A Talamancan-speaking people of the Chibchan* language group, the Térrabas were moved by the Spaniards to missions in southeastern Costa Rica in the eighteenth century, and in the nineteenth century they were conquered by the Bribri.* By the twentieth century, the Térrabas lived in close proximity to the Borucas and had mixed with them. Like the Borucas, the Térrabas are primarily a mestizo people with little of their Indian culture still visible. They are Roman Catholic in religion, speak Spanish as their primary language, and own land privately as individuals. The Térraba also frequently work as day laborers to earn the cash they need for the regional economy. In the 1980s, there were only a few dozen people in Costa Rica still identifying themselves as Térrabas, and not all of them spoke the Indian dialect.

REFERENCES: Howard I. Blutstein, *Area Handbook for Costa Rica*, 1971; Melanie A. Counce and William V. Douglas, "Indians of Central America 1980s," *Cultural Survival Quarterly*, 13 (1989), 38–41; Rudolf Schuller, *Las lenguas indígenas de Centro America: Con especial referencia a los idiomas aborígenes de Costa Rica*, 1928.

TÉRREBE. See TÉRRABA.

TETETE. The Tetete are a nearly extinct group of Tukanoan*-speaking, jungle-dwelling Amerindians native to the provinces of Napo and Pastaza in Ecuador. They are scattered between the Pacayacu, Cuyabeno, Aguarico, and San Miguel rivers. Some ethnologists believe that the Tetete were a remnant of a group of Secoya* Indians who left the main group of their tribe in the late nineteenth century. The Tetete were isolated until the rubber boom of the early twentieth century, when disease and exploitation dramatically reduced their population. When the Capuchin order created the mission of Apostolic Prefecture of Aguarico in 1954, a number of Tetete Indians settled there and lived among Siona,* Kofán,* Cushma,* Yumbo,* and Auca* Indians. They were a tropical forest people whose traditional lifestyle valued hunting and fishing over agriculture, although in recent years they have become more adept at raising manioc and bananas. Capuchin schools have acculturated the descendents of the Tetete, while the presence of so many other Indians has brought about their detribalization. There are still several dozen Tetete isolated in the jungles, but at the missions there are only a handful of people, most of them very elderly, who understand the aboriginal language and maintain a consciousness of their tribal membership.

REFERENCES: Walter Dostal, ed., *The Situation of the Indian in South America*, 1972; S. Lyman Tyler, *Indians of South America*, 1976.

TEUESH. See TEHUELCHE.

TEUESSON. See TEHUELCHE.

TEUI. See KAIOVÁ.

TEWELCHE. See TEHUELCHE.

THAMPA. See CAMPA.

THEGUEL-CHE. See TEHUELCHE.

THEUELCHE. See TEHUELCHE.

THE-USHENE. See TEHUELCHE.

THUELCHU. See TEHUELCHE.

TIATINAGUA. See ESSEJJA.

TIBILO. See AGUANO.

TIBITIBI. See WARRAU.

TICHBI. See TÉRRABA.

TICUNA. See TUKUNA.

TIERRADENTRO. See PÁEZ.

TIKUNA. See TUKUNA.

TIMBIRA. The Timbira are a group of Gê*-speaking tribes who occupy the high steppes and dry forests in the Maranhão area of central Brazil. Today they are divided into the Western Timbira and Eastern Timbira groups. The Western Timbira group is confined to the Apinayé* tribe, while the contemporary Eastern Timbira group includes the Canela,* Krikatí,* Krahô,* and Gavião* tribes. All of the Timbira are a horticultural people raising maize, manioc, and beans, and hunting and fishing to supplement their diets.

REFERENCES: Robert Da Matta, "Myth and Anti-myth among the Timbira," in Pierre Maranda and Elli Kongas Maranda, eds., *Structural Analysis of Oral Tradition*, 1971, 88–109; Curt Nimuendajú, *The Eastern Timbira*, 1946.

TIMINABA. See CHAMACOCO.

TIMINAVA. See CHAMACOCO.

TIRIYÓ. The Tiriyó (called Trió by the Surinamese and Yawí by other Indians in the region) are a group of Amerindians who live in the equatorial rain forest along the border between Brazil and Surinam. They lived on the Tapanahony and Paloemeu rivers in Surinam and along the East and West Parú and Marapi rivers in Brazil. Most of those in Brazil live in the Tumucumaque Indian Park. The Dutch explorer Roger Schomburgk first reached them in 1843, and in the early 1900s a number of other Dutch exploration groups contacted the Tiriyó. Candido Rondon, the founder of the Brazilian Indian Protection Service, contacted the Tiriyó in 1928. More consistent contact with this tropical, horticultural people, however, did not come until 1959 and 1960. The Protestant America Door-to-Life Gospel Mission was built near the Tiriyó in 1959, as was a Roman Catholic mission run by Franciscans. Both Brazil and Surinam also constructed airstrips near the Tiriyó in 1960. By the early 1960s, most members of the tribe had moved to or near the missions. Today there are approximately 1,000 members of the Tiriyó tribe, and they are divided into thirteen subtribes. Most of them live on the Surinam side of the border. Approximately 270 are in Brazil. The Pianokotó* (Marahtxo, Maracho, Maraso), Okomoyána (Maipuridjana or Waripi), Prouyána* (Rangu-Piki, Proyána), Arimihotó, Paimerú,* Kirikirigotó,* Armagotó, and Aramichó are friendly with neo-Brazilians and neo-Surinamese,

while the Akuriyó,* Wayarikure, Wama, Kukuyána,* Pianoi, and Tiriyometesem* are suspicious of contact.

REFERENCES: Robin Hanbury-Tenison, *A Question of Survival for the Indians of Brazil*, 1973; Peter Rivière, *Marriage Among the Trió: A Principle of Social Organization*, 1979; Robert Lee Spires, "As línguas faladas do Brasil," *América Indígena*, 47 (1987), 455–79.

TIRIYOMETESEM. The Tiriyometesem are a subtribe of the Tiriyó* of the Brazilian-Surinam border. Among other Tiriyó, the Tiriyometesem are almost legendary for their suspicion of outsiders, and there is no contact with them at the present. Some anthropologists even doubt the existence of the Tiriyometesem. See TIRIYÓ.

TÍRRIBI. See TÉRRABA.

TÍRUB. See TÉRRABA.

TIVILO. See AGUANO.

TIVITIVA. See WARRAU.

TIVITIVI. See WARRAU.

TOA. See PARAUJANO.

TOBA. The Toba (Emok) are a Guaycuruan*-speaking people living in the Gran Chaco of lower South America. Their current population exceeds 39,000 people, although they are in a state of rapid assimilation with the surrounding mestizo population. The Toba are geographically and culturally subdivided into four major groups: the Argentine Toba (Eastern Toba or Takshik), who live between the lower Pilcomayo and Bermejo rivers; the Paraguayan Toba (Eastern Toba or Toba-miri), who live along the lower Pilcomayo River; the Bolivian Toba (Western Toba), who dwell in the region of the upper Pilcomayo and Bermejo rivers; and the Toba-Pilagá (Pilagá*), who live along the middle Pilcomayo River. They should not be confused with the Toba-Maskoy* of Paraguay. Europeans first encountered the Toba in the mid-sixteenth century, and Roman Catholic missionaries reached the Toba in 1590. In the seventeenth century, the Toba domesticated the horse and began to range widely throughout the Gran Chaco as nomadic hunters and warriors. Jesuits and Franciscans gathered some Toba into missions in the late seventeenth and eighteenth centuries, but the Toba resisted acculturation. As late as 1924, the Toba rose up in rebellion against settlers encroaching on their land; Argentinian troops were called in to crush the rebellion. By that time, they had made the transition from hunting and gathering to cotton cultivation and gardening. Protestant evangelical religions have recently made rapid progress in converting the Toba, most of whom now profess loyalty to one of those faiths. Historically the Toba have also been known as Tocoytus, Natekebit, Nata'kebit, Nactocovit, Ntocouit, Ntokowit, Yncanabacte, Toco'it, and Frentones.

REFERENCES: Isabel Hernández, "Los pueblos y las lenguas aborígenes en la actualidad," *América Indígena*, 47 (1987), 109–23; Rafael Karsten, *The Toba Indians of the Bolivan Gran Chaco*, 1967; Elmer S. Miller, "The Argentine Toba," *Ethnology*, 10 (1971), 149–49; Johannes Wilbert and Karin Simoneau, *Folk Literature of the Toba Indians*, 1982; S. Shapiro, "The Toba Indians of Bolivia," *América Indígena*, 22 (1962), 241–45; B. J. Susnik, "Estudios Emok-Toba," *Boletín de la Sociedad del Paraguay*, 7 (1962), 12–29.

TOBA-MASKOY. The Toba-Maskoy (Mascoy, Maskoy, Mascoi, Machicuy, Cabanatith, and Tujetge) are a Lengua*-Maskoy-speaking Indian tribe of the Paraguayan Gran Chaco who historically have represented a fusion of Guaycuruan-speaking Toba* bands and Maskoy bands. When the Europeans first arrived on their land in the eighteenth century, the Toba-Maskoy were a nomadic, foraging people with a simple material culture. Many of them adapted to the horse in the eighteenth century and increased the range of their hunting activities. Today the Toba-Maskoy have become somewhat more acculturated to European lifestyles, especially in thier economic adjustment, where they have made the transition to farming and ranching labor. Most of them work as wage laborers on the large Mennonite farms in the area or work small tribal plots of land and run a few head of cattle or sheep. In the mid–1980s, there were approximately 1,400 Toba-Maskoy Indians in Paraguay.

REFERENCES: Harriet Klein and Louisa Stark, "Indian Tribes of the Paraguayan Chaco," *Anthropological Linguistics*, 19 (1977), 378–402; David Maybury-Lewis and James Howe, *The Indian Peoples of Paraguay: Their Plight and Their Prospects*, 1980; John Renshaw, "Property, Resources and Equality among the Indians of the Paraguayan Chaco," *Man*, 23 (1988), 334–52.

TOBA-MIRI. See TOBA.

TOBA-PILAGA. See PILAGÁ.

TOCO-IT. See TOBA.

TOCOKIRU. See NAMBIQUAŔA.

TOEBEHE. See KAWAHÍB.

TOELCHE. See TEHUELCHE.

TOELCHI. See TEHUELCHE.

TOELCHU. See TEHUELCHE.

TOEPEHE. See KAWAHÍB.

TOJAR. See TÉRRABA.

TOL. See JICAQUE.

TOLPAN. See JICAQUE.

TOMARXA. See CHAMACOCO.

TOMRAXO. See CHAMACOCO.

TONIC. See TEHUELCHE.

TONORE. See TUNULI.

TOOTHLE. See MACÁ.

TOPEHE. See KAWAHÍB.

TORÁ. The Torá Indians are a small, Txapakuran*-speaking group of people who today live in the state of Amazonas in Brazil. Their contemporary population is approximately 250 people, and they maintain a strong sense of ethnic identity, even though their tropical forest way of life is being limited by the expanding regional cash economy and their own desire for trade goods. The Torá numbered in the thousands of people as late as the end of the nineteenth century, but the rubber boom in the state of Amazonas in the early 1900s and again during the 1940s devastated them. In recent years their population has stabilized.

REFERENCE: Robert Lee Spires, "As línguas faladas do Brasil," *América Indígena*, 47 (1987), 455–79.

TORIBIO. See PÁEZ.

TOROMONA. The Toromona are a small group of Tacanan*-speaking Amerindians who today live in the department of La Paz between the Alto Madidi, Tuichi, and Beni rivers in Bolivia. When they were first contacted by the Spanish in the sixteenth century, they were a foraging tribe living largely on the Brazil nut and other roots, insects, and small animals. Franciscan missionaries began working with the Toromona Indians in the seventeenth century and are still among them. In 1764 the Franciscans moved more than 100 Toromona to Ixiamas. Their numbers today are so small that the tribe verges on extinction.

REFERENCES: Pedro Plaza Martínez and Juan Carvajal Carvajal, *Etnías y lenguas de Bolivia*, 1985; Graciela Zolezzi and J. Riester, "Lenguas indígenas del oriente boliviano clasificación preliminar," *América Indígena*, 47 (1987), 425–33.

TORRUPAN. See JICAQUE.

TOTORO. See PÁEZ.

TOVOK. See ASHLUSLAY.

TOWOTHLE. See MACÁ.

TOYERI. The Toyeri (Tuyuneiri, Pucapacuri) are a small group of Amerindians whose language is part of the Harakmbet* (Hate) linguistic family. A tropical forest people, their traditional homeland was along the Madre de Dios River from its upper reaches down to below the Inambari River in southeastern Peru. They are very closely related linguistically to the Sirineiri.* There are three subgroups of the Toyeri, known as Toyeri, Manuquiari, and Pukirieri (Puncuri). There are approximately 35 Toyeri, 50 Manuquiari, and 50 Pukirieri. Some claim the Pukirieri are a subtribe of the Amarakaeri.* Today the Toyeri live on the Tono, Pinipini, and Pilcopata rivers in Peru, with some scattered as well on the lower Inambari River and on the Chaupimayo River. During the rubber boom from 1894 to 1920, the Toyeri were almost completely destroyed by disease, slavery, and exploitation. In the past 25 years, the Toyeri have become the most acculturated of all the Harakmbet peoples.

REFERENCES: Andrew Gray, "Perspectives on Amarakaeri History," in Harald O. Sklar and Frank Salomon, eds., *Natives and Neighbors in South America: Anthropological Essays*, 1987, 299–329; Darcy Ribeiro and Mary Ruth Wise, *Los grupos étnicos de la amazona peruana*, 1978.

TOYPEHE. See KAWAHÍB.

TRINITARIO. See MOXO.

TRIÓ. See TIRIYÓ.

TRUKA. The Truka are a small group of Amerindians numbering approximately 450 people. They live on Assunção Island in the São Francisco River in the state of Pernambuco, Brazil. The Truka are an agricultural people, descendents of typical tropical forest Indians of Brazil, but in the 1980s they faced ecological, economic, and cultural disaster. Large agribusiness concerns have been steadily driving the Truka off Assunção Island in order to gain access to their land and convert it from subsistence to commercial agriculture, while the Itaparica Hydroelectric Project on the São Francisco River has threatened to flood much of the land they had left. The Truka Indians face relocation from their traditional homeland in the 1990s.

REFERENCE: Paul L. Aspelin and Silvio Coelho dos Santos, *Indian Areas Threatened by Hydroelectric Projects in Brazil*, 1981.

TRUMÁI. The Trumái are a linguistically independent group of Amerindians who today live at the headwaters of the Xingú River in upper Mato Grosso, Brazil. They first encountered Europeans in 1884 when the anthropological expedition of Karl Von den Steinen reached them. At the time, the Trumái numbered several thousand people. They had only recently arrived at the upper Xingú, migrating there from the southeast where the pressure of white colonization had driven them out. They were a typical tropical forest people, raising manioc as their staple and supplementing their diet by hunting and fishing. But the Trumái fell victim to European diseases and Indian violence, particularly at the hands of the Suyá.* Their population entered a state of rapid decline in the twentieth century, dropping to 45 people in 1940 and only 35 in 1955. At that point, tribal ceremonial life could no longer be sustained. By the early 1980s, there were only about 20 Trumái still alive who remembered their tribal heritage and understood the native language. They were elderly people who lived among other Indians at Posto Leonardo in Mato Grosso, Brazil.

REFERENCES: Anne Sutherland Louis, "Alliance or Descent: The Trumái Indians of Central Brazil," *Man*, 6 (1971), 18–29; Robert F. Murphy and Buell Quain, *The Trumái Indians of Central Brazil*, 1967; Robert Lee Spires, "As línguas faladas no Brasil," *América Indígena*, 47 (1987), 455–79.

TSATCHELA. See COLORADO.

TSESE. See PIAPOCO.

TSHAAHUI. See CHAYAVITA.

TSOLA. See PANEROA.

TSOLOTÍ. See CHOROTÉ.

TSONECA. See TEHUELCHE.

TSONIK. See TEHUELCHE.

TTE. See ASHLUSLAY.

TUAMA. See ARAONA.

TUBARAO. See AIKANÁ.

TUCANO. See TUKANO.

TUCUNA. See TUKANO.

TUCUNDIAPA. See KATUKÍNA.

TUELCHE. See TEHUELCHE.

TUELCHU. See TEHUELCHE.

TUJETGE. See TOBA-MASKOY.

TUKANA. The term Tukana, in addition to its direct reference to the Dachsea Indians, also refers to a large group of Amerindian languages that extended from the Vaupés River basin in Brazil to the adjoining areas of Colombia, Ecuador, Brazil, and Peru. The Western Tukanoan* languages included such groups as the Piojé, Datuana,* Macaguaje, Makuna,* Sara, Siona,* Tama,* Tanimuko,* Uantia, Yahuna,* Yupua, Coretu, and Secoya,* while the Eastern Tukanoan languages consisted of such groups as the Barasána,* Bará,* Erulia, Karapána,* Siana, Tatapuyo, Wayána,* Yaruti, Desana,* Tuyuka,* Uanana,* Cubeo,* Suriana, Yeba-masa,* and Tukano.*

REFERENCE: Cestmir Loukotka, *Classification of South American Indian Languages*, 1968.

TUKANO. The Tukano (Tukana, Tucano), also known by the self-designation Dachsea (Datxea, Dahseye), are a tropical forest tribe of Amerindians who live along the Paca River at the headwaters of the Papuri River, primarily in the region of Uacaricuara in southeastern Colombia and northern Brazil. They are part of the Eastern Tukano language group. Today the Tukano number nearly 10,000 people. There were sporadic European contacts with the Tukano in the eighteeneth and nineteenth centuries. Portuguese missions were established temporarily along the upper Vaupés River in the 1780s, but systematic evangelization of the tribe did not begin until 1914 when Roman Catholic priests established missions on the Papuri River. Theodor Koch-Grünberg began ethnological studies of the Tukano at the same time. Protestant missionaries made their way into the region after World War II, eventually making nominal converts of a minority of Tukano. The tribal economy focuses on producing bitter manioc and fishing; hunting is quite secondary, although in recent years the tribe has become increasingly dependent on such European technology as fishhooks, shotguns, and machetes, as well as on increased manioc production for sale. Contact with whites has also led to the development of small-scale animal husbandry, primarily hogs and poultry. The contemporary population of the Tukano proper exceeds 6,000 people, most of whom live in Brazil. The Tukano include such subtribes as the Pokanga, who number approximately 500 people; the Arapaso* (Arapaco,

Konea), approximately 270 people; the Miriti-Tapuaya* (Miriti, Neenoa), about 50 people; and the Tariana,* nearly 1,600 people.

REFERENCES: Janet Chernela, "Endangered Ideologies: Tukano Fishing Taboos," *Cultural Survival Quarterly*, 11 (1987), 50–52; Jean A. Jackson, *The Fish People: Linguistic Exogamy and Tukanoan Identity*, 1983; Robert Lee Spires, "As línguas faladas do Brasil," *América Indígena*, 47 (1987), 455–79.

TUKANO-MAKÚ. See MAKÚ.

TUKUKU. See IRAPA.

TUKUMAFED. See TUKUNAFED.

TUKUM-DIAPÁ. See KATUKÍNA.

TUKUNA. The Tukuna (Ticuna, Tikuna) are a very large tribe of Amerindians located between the lower Amazon and Putumayo rivers in Peru, Colombia, and Brazil. They call themselves the Duuxuga. They are particularly concentrated near Leticia in the territory of Amazonas in Colombia; on the Amazon River between Cajocuma Island in Peru and the Tocantins River in Brazil; and around Lakes Caballococha and Cushillococha in the department of Loreto in Peru. Those members of the tribe who live in Peru are in a state of advanced acculturation, and there is considerable intertribal migration across the international frontiers. The Tukuna in Colombia and Brazil are in permanent contact with neo-Colombians and neo-Brazilians, but their sense of tribal identity is stronger. The traditional enemies of the Tukuna were the Omagua* Indians, but when the Spanish and Portuguese wiped out the Omágua, the Tukuna began to expand. Rubber collectors came into contact with the Tukuna in the twentieth century, but when the rubber boom ended, the Tukuna returned to their semi-nomadic way of life, in which they supported themselves by foraging, hunting, and fishing. The Association of Baptists for World Evangelization has worked among them for years. There are more than 18,000 Tukuna today who acknowledge tribal membership and speak the native language. About 1,500 of them are in Colombia, 3,000 in Peru, and nearly 14,000 in Brazil. In 1988, approximately 720 Tukuna were living on Colombian government reservations at Mocagua, Macedonia, El Vergel, and Zaragoza, as well as 282 at the Arara reservation, 270 at the San Antonio de Los Lagos and San Sebastian reservations, 210 at the Santa Sofía and El Progreso reservation, and 192 at the Nazareth reservation.

REFERENCES: Linda Leigh Glenboski, *The Enthnobotany of the Tukuna Indians, Amazonas, Colombia*, 1983; Myriam Jiméno and Adolfo Triana Antorveza, *Estado y minorias étnicas en Colombia*, 1985; Darcy Ribeiro and Mary Ruth Wise, *Los grupos étnicos de la amazona peruana*, 1978; Gustavo Solís F., "Multilinguismo y extinciones de lenguas," *América Indígena*, 47 (1987), 630–45; Robert Lee Spires, "As línguas faladas do Brasil," *América Indígena*, 47 (1987), 455–79.

TUKUNAFED. The Tukunafed (Tukumafed) people are a tiny surviving group of Kawahíb* Indians. The Kawahíb once ranged over a large area of the Tapajós-Madeira River Basin in what is today the state of Amazonas, Brazil, but in the eighteenth century, they dispersed into a series of many separate tribes because of the aggressive expansion of the Mundurukú* Indians. One of the small tribes emerging from the larger Kawahíb group was the Tukunafed. Rubber collectors and gold prospectors in the early twentieth century put more pressure on the Tukunafed, drastically reducing their population to the point that ceremonial life was no longer possible. Today there are fewer than 50 Tukunafed left, and they, intermixed with Paranawat and Wirafed Indians, are living along the Riosinho, Leitao, Muqui, and Cacoal rivers. Most of them work as laborers on ranches and rubber plantations in the area and are in permanent contact with neo-Brazilian society, to which they are slowly acculturating.

REFERENCE: Theodore L. Stoddard, ed., *Indians of Brazil in the Twentieth Century*, 1967.

TULE. See CUNA.

TUMRAH. See CHAMACOCO.

TUNEBO. The Tunebo (Luna, Tunevo, Tame) are a Chibchan*-speaking group of Amerindians native to the intendency of Arauco and the departments of Boyacá and Norte de Santander in Colombia. They can also be found in the forests of San Camilo, west of the state of Apure in Venezuela. Their general homeland is in the eastern Andes in an area called Sararé. The Tunebo are a semi-nomadic hunting and foraging people who live on the fringes of the llanos and the mountains, primarily confining themselves to the headwaters of the llanos rivers. They avoided extinction during the conquest period by constantly moving to elude the Spaniards. They remain today suspicious of neo-Colombians, preferring their own cultural and ethnic independence. Since 1964, the Summer Institute of Linguistics has maintained a presence among the Tunebo. Today there are more than 3,500 Tunebo Indians who still speak the native language. Of that total, approximately 1,200 live at the Colombian government Indian reservation of Cobraria, along with 207 at the Tauretes-Agua Blanca reservation, 58 at the Tunebo de Angostura reservation, and 150 at the Chaparral-Barronegro reservation. They are an overwhelmingly agricultural people. There are two identifiable subtribes of the Tunebo. The Agua Blanco Tunebo live in the departments of Santander and Norte de Santander. They total approximately 700 people. The Barro Negro Tunebo, who number 400 people, live in the intendency of Casanare. The acculturation process is accelerating among the Tunebo because of the expanding market economy, the influence of evangelical Protestants in the area, and the impact of formal education on children.

REFERENCES: Howard I. Blutstein, *Area Handbook for Colombia*, 1977; Leah B. Ellis and Linda Criswell, eds., *Estudiemos las culturas indigenas de Colombia*, 1984;

Maria Marquéz V., *Los Tunebo*, 1979; Nancy Morey, "Ethnohistory of the Colombian and Venezuelan Llanos," Ph.D. dissertation, University of Utah, 1975.

TUNEVO. See TUNEBO.

TUNO. See ARAONA.

TUNULI. See TXIKÃO.

TÙPARÍ. The term "Tùparí" refers to a small linguistic group within the larger Tupi* family. The Tùparí proper, the Wayoró* (Ajurú), and the Makuráp* speak Tùparí dialects.
   REFERENCE: Robert Lee Spires, "As línguas faladas do Brasil," *América Indígena* 47 (1987), 455–79.

TÙPARÍ. The Tùparí were a tribe of Tupi*-speaking Indians who once numbered several thousand people; they lived in the heavily forested jungles near the headwaters of the Branco River in what is today the state of Rondônia, Brazil. Beginning in the eighteenth century, the region witnessed a steady traffic of explorers, missionaries, and anthropologists, and in the nineteenth century rubber collectors arrived. In the process, the Tùparí underwent rapid depopulation. By the early 1960s, only 50 members of the tribe were still alive, and the tribe had ceased to exist as a functional social unit. Since then the Tùparí have remained in permanent contact with neo-Brazilian society. From death and assimilation into the mestizo culture, their numbers have dropped even more. Today only a handful of people are left alive who still remember their Tùparí tribal origins. They live on the right bank of the Branco River.
   REFERENCES: Franz Caspar, *Tupari*, 1956; Robert Lee Spires, "As línguas faladas do Brasil," *América Indígena*, 47 (1987), 455–79; Theodore L. Stoddard, ed., *Indians of Brazil in the Twentieth Century*, 1967.

TUPI. The term "Tupi" (Tupy) refers to a huge linguistic group of Amerindian tribes who occupied eastern Brazil at the time of the Portuguese conquest in the sixteenth century. Just when the Portuguese were arriving in Brazil, the Tupi tribes were expanding out of their base in Paraguay and driving the existing foraging tribes into the Brazilian interior. A vicious battle raged between Tupi-speaking and Gê*-speaking Indians for dominance in eastern and southern Brazil; the Tupi prevailed. The Tupi groups then fractured into many tribes. Many of these tribes practiced a ritualistic exocannibalism that gave the Portuguese a moral excuse for exterminating them. Warfare was also a ceremonial ritual among the Tupi, against other Indian groups as well as against one another, so they were unable to develop the unity necessary to resist Portuguese conquest.
   Their own penchant for migration, as well as the inexorable expansion of Portuguese civilization in Brazil, eventually scattered the various Tupi tribes all over Brazil and other regions of South America. The Tupi tribes included the

Sirionó,* Chiriguano,* Guarayo,* and Pauserna* in Bolivia; the Guaraní* in Argentina, Brazil, and Paraguay; the Cocama* in Peru; the Kaiwa* in Paraguay and Brazil; the Omágua* in Brazil and Peru; the Oyanpík*-Emerion* in French Guiana and Brazil; and the Tapieté,* Chané, and Aché* in Paraguay. In addition to these Tupi-speaking tribes, there were dozens of Tupi peoples located throughout Brazil, including the Apiacá* (Apiaká), Auetí,* Canoeiro,* Kamaiurá* (Camayurá), Kawahíb* (Cawahíb), Pawate (Parinintín,* Wirafed*), Kayabí* (Cayabí), Sheta, Takunape (Tacunyape), Tapirapé,* Tenetehára* (Anambe, Guayayara, Guajajára,* Manajé, Tembé, Turiwára,* Urúbu), Tupi-Guaraní (Tupinamba), Neengatú (Nheengatú*), Arara,* Ramaráma,* Urukú, Urumí, Ariken,* Kabixiana,* Karitiana,* Arúa, Digut, Mondé,* Guarategaya (Amniape, Kanoê, Mekén), Kepikiriwat,* Makuráp,* Tùparí,* Wayoro* (Apichum), Kuruáya* (Curuáya), Mundurukú,* Manitsawa, Shipaya,* Juruna,* and Purubora.*

REFERENCES: Joseph H. Greenberg, *Language in the Americas*, 1987; John Hemming, *Red Gold: The Conquest of the Brazilian Indians, 1500–1760*, 1978.

TUPI-KAWAHÍB. The Tupi*-Kawahíb* are a Tupi-speaking people who were part of the Kawahíb tribe before Mundurukú* attacks in the eighteenth century split the tribe into several groups. The Tupi-Kawahíb then migrated from the upper Tapajós River area west to the upper Machado River. Today they number perhaps 200 people. See KAWAHÍB.

TUPI-MODERNO. See NHEENGATÚ.

TUPINAKI. The Tupinaki are a thoroughly detribalized group of Indians who live near Jequié on the Rio das Cantas in the state of Bahia, Brazil. There is no trace of their original Tupi* language or any ceremonial survival of the aboriginal culture. These people function in the local regional cash economy and live in a manner indistinguishable from the surrounding neo-Brazilian mestizos. Their ancestors were pacified in the early eighteenth century by Jesuit missionaries. All that remains of tribal culture is a generic sense of identity as an Indian people.

REFERENCE: Theodore L. Stoddard, ed., *Indians of Brazil in the Twentieth Century*, 1967.

TUPINAMBA. "Tupinamba" is a generic term generally applied to all the Tupi*-Guaraní* tribes of Amerindians living in eastern Brazil at the time of the Portuguese conquest.

REFERENCES: Donald W. Forsyth, "The Beginning of Brazilian Anthropology: Jesuits and Tupinamba Cannibalism," *Journal of Anthropological Research*, 39 (1983), 147–78; John Hemming, *Red Gold: The Conquest of the Brazilian Indians, 1500–1760*, 1978.

TUPY. See TUPI.

TURIMNAINAI. See WAKUENAI.

TURIWA. See AMANAYÉ.

TURIWARA. The Turiwara, sometimes called the Anambé, were a Tupian language group of Amerindians closely related to the Urúbu* tribe. They occupied villages along the lower Tocantins River in Brazil. By the 1860s, the Turiwara had migrated to the Capim River below the Acarajucana Rapids. They moved again in the 1880s, this time to villages along the Acara Grande River. At the time of the conquest, the Turiwara numbered in the thousands, but disease and warfare rendered the tribe extinct as a sociological unit by the 1940s. In 1942, anthropologists could locate only 14 members of the tribe still alive, all closely associated with the Tembé or Urúbu. There were, however, several dozen Turiwara whom they had not located. By the 1980s, there were approximately 60 Turiwara left alive, most of whom lived on the Caiari River, a tributary of the Moju River in the state of Pará, Brazil.

REFERENCES: Francis Huxley, *Affable Savages*, 1966; Robert Lee Spires, "As línguas faladas do Brasil," *América Indígena*, 47 (1987), 455–79.

TUSHA. See RODELA.

TUSHINAWA. See TUXINÁWA.

TUTAPI. See OREJÓN.

TUXÁ. At a Brazilian government Indian post—Rodelas Indian Park—near the city of Belém do São Francisco in the state of Bahia, there is a group of highly acculturated people who call themselves the Tuxá or Rodela and who consider themselves Indians. Scholars estimate that the Tuxá have been in the area since the late 1600s. Although they all speak Portuguese as their only language, work as farmers in the local economy, and have no traces of aboriginal ceremonial life, they nevertheless consider themselves Indians and nurture an ethnic identity that separates them from the surrounding society. Their population is approximately 500 people, and they live in single, large villages. Since there is no farmland for them on the banks of the river, the Tuxá are known to work land on islands in the São Francisco River. Most of their protein comes from fishing, and they are excellent canoeists. The greatest threat to the Tuxá Indians is the Itaparica Dam Hydroelectric Project, which will completely flood their land.

REFERENCES: Paul L. Aspelin and Silvio Coelho dos Santos, *Indian Areas Threatened by Hydroelectric Projects in Brazil*, 1981; Theodore L. Stoddard, ed., *Indians of Brazil in the Twentieth Century*, 1967.

TUXINÁWA. There are several hundred people living in the state of Acre, Brazil, along the Envira River, who are descendents of the Tuxináwa Indians, a Panoan*-speaking people who once lived in much larger numbers in the region. Today they are thoroughly integrated in the local economy and have lost all vestiges of their aboriginal language and culture. Nevertheless, in spite of speaking Portuguese and working as subsistence farmers and laborers, they are aware of their Indian ancestry and retain an identification of themselves as Tuxináwa people.

REFERENCE: Theodore L. Stoddard, ed., *Indians of Brazil in the Twentieth Century*, 1967.

TUYONERI. See TOYERI.

TUYUCA. See TUYUKA.

TUYUCO. See TUYUKA.

TUYUKA. The Tuyuka (Tuyuca, Tejuca, Dochkafuara, Dohkapoara) are an Eastern Tukanoan* tribe of Amerindians who live on the Inambu River, a tributary of the Papuri River, on the Abiyu River, and in Uacaricuara, Colombia. Another group lives along the Tiquié River. There were sporadic European contacts with the Tuyuka in the eighteenth and nineteenth centuries. Portuguese missions were established temporarily along the upper Vaupés in the 1780s, but systematic evangelization of the tribe did not begin until 1914 when Roman Catholic priests established missions in the area. Protestant missionaries made their way into the region after World War II. The tribal economy focuses on the production of bitter manioc and fishing; hunting is quite secondary, although in recent years the tribe has become increasingly dependent on such European technology as fishhooks, shotguns, and machetes, as well as on increased manioc production for sale. Contact with whites has also led to the development of small-scale animal husbandry, primarily hogs and poultry. In the 1960s and 1970s, the Colombian government began to encourage colonization of the Vaupés River basin, but settlement there has been very slow. The Tuyuka interact with other Indian tribes in the area but not as often with whites because of the extreme geographical isolation of the area. The Summer Institute of Linguistics established a unit among the Tuyuka in 1970. There are approximately 650 Tuyuka today who acknowledge tribal membership and speak the native language, but because of the impact of the market economy, evangelical missionary work, and government schools, the processes of acculturation and detribalization are accelerating.

REFERENCES: Gerardo Reichel-Dolmatoff, *Amazonian Cosmos: The Sexual and Religious Symbolism of the Tukano Indians*, 1985; Blaz Telban, *Grupos étnicos de Colombia: Etnografía y bibliografía*, 1987.

TUYUNEIRI. See TOYERI.

TWAHKA. See SUMU.

TWÁKA. See SUMU.

TWAXHA. See SUMU.

TXAKAMEKRA. The Txakamekra, also known as the Mateiros, were a group of Gê*-speaking people who once belonged to the Timbira* group of Brazilian Amerindians. They pursued a hunting and foraging lifestyle, with occasional gardening, and roamed widely around what is today the state of Maranhão. They lived on the savannas near the Rio das Flores, a tributary of the Mearim. By the early twentieth century, their numbers were so few that they joined forces with the Ramkókamekra Canela* and ceased to exist as a differentiated social unit. Nevertheless, there are still individuals in the area who are aware that their heritage is both Canela and Txakamekra.
REFERENCE: Theodore L. Stoddard, ed., *Indians of Brazil in the Twentieth Century*, 1967.

TXAPAKÚRA. The term "Txapakúra" (Chapacúra, Chapakúra) refers to a small, isolated linguistic family of Amerindian groups scattered from the right bank of the Guaporé River to the tributaries of the right bank of the Madeira River in the state of Rondônia, Brazil, and in Bolivia. The Txapakúra people once included the Huayan, Tora,* Urupa, Pakaanóva,* Moré*, Huachi, Txapakúra, Itoreauhip, Napé, Quitemo, Cumana, and Wanyam tribes.
REFERENCES: Harriet E. Manelis Klein and Louis R. Stark, *South American Indian Languages: Retrospect and Prospect*, 1985; Robert Lee Spires, "As línguas faladas do Brasil," *América Indígena*, 47 (1987), 455–79; Theodore L. Stoddard, ed., *Indians of Brazil in the Twentieth Century*, 1967.

TXIKÃO. The Txikão (Tunuli) today are a pacified tribe of approximately 100 people living in the Xingú Indian Park of northern Mato Grosso, Brazil. They occupy the region around the Jatoba River. Historically, the Txikão were known for their raids down the Batovi and Kurizevo rivers, where they would assault the Waurá,* Mehinácu,* and Nafuquá* Indians. They are part of the Karib* language family. The Txikão were first discovered in the 1880s when the German anthropologist Karl Von den Steinen reached the headwaters of the Xingú River above the Von Martius Rapids, but there was little or no contact after that with neo-Brazilians until the early 1960s. In the 1950s, the Txikão had a small village on the Batovi River, and they conducted a number of deadly raids into the Xingú Park area, but in 1961, an intertribal group of Xingú Indians led by the Waurá attacked the Txikão and killed most of them. The survivors fled to the Jatoba River area, where Orlando and Cláudio Villas Boas contacted them in 1964. They moved the Txikão to the government Indian post at Posto Leonardo in

1967 to protect them from incoming gold prospectors. Although the Txikão plant corn, manioc, cotton, urucu, and calabash, they do not rely on agriculture for most of their sustenance. Hunting, fishing, and fruit-picking play a larger role in the Txikão economy than in the economies of the other Xingú tribes. Although pacified, the Txikão are known for their extraordinary suspicion of outsiders.

REFERENCES: Orlando Villas Boas and Cláudio Villas Boas, *Xingú: The Indians, Their Myths*, 1973; Robert Lee Spires, "As línguas faladas do Brasil," *América Indígena*, 47 (1987), 455–79.

TXIRIPÁ. See AVÁ-CHIRIPÁ.

TXUKAHAMÃI. The term "Txukahamãi" (Txukahemei, Txukarramãe, Txukarramãi) is a name employed inside the Xingú Indian Park in the state of Mato Grosso, Brazil. It is actually a word from the Juruna* language that means "men without a bow." More specifically, it refers to the Mentuktíre* Indians, a Northern Kayapó* group of Gê*-speaking Amerindians who today dwell inside the park. See MENTUKTÍRE.

TXUKAHAMEI. See TXUKAHAMÃI.

TXUKARRAMÃE. See TXUKAHAMÃI.

TXUKARRAMÃI. See TXUKAHAMÃI.

TXUNHUA-DJAPÁ. The Txunhua-Djapa are a tiny tropical forest group of Amerindians now verging on extinction. They speak a language from the Katukína* linguistic family and live in the state of Amazonas, Brazil, along the Rio Pedras. Today they number only 37 people. See KATUKÍNA.

TYNYRO. See AYOREO.

TZUTUHILE. See TZUTUJIL.

TZUTUJIL. The Tzutujil, also known as the "Tzutuhile" or "Zutuhil," are a Quiché* Mayan* group who originally migrated to the Guatemalan highlands from Tulan, the ancient Toltec capital. They settled near Lake Atitlán, occupying a large region on the southwestern reaches of the lake and producing a wide variety of agricultural products for food and also cacao for trade. When the Spanish conqueror Pedro de Alvarado and his troops reached Guatemala in the mid–1520s, the Tzutujil put up a fierce resistance, but they could not stand up to the superior technology or the Europeans or the devastation wrought by smallpox, mumps, and measles. The Tzutujil underwent a catastrophic population decline in the sixteenth century, dropping from perhaps 100,000 people to only a few thousand. Late in the 1500s, Franciscan missionaries relocated many

Tzutujil to their present-day capital Santiago Atitlán. The Spanish *congregaciones* had a powerful impact on the Tzutujil, particularly in precipitating the loss of their ancestral lands. Virtually all of the lowland piedmont lands were lost to Spanish coffee plantations, while the Tzutujil held on to some of the highland property. During the seventeenth and eighteenth centuries, the entire Tzutujil population was gradually depressed into a class of peasant cultivators who were largely absorbed by the Spanish political system. Although Guatemalan politicians in the nineteenth and twentieth centuries transformed Tzutujil landholdings from communal to individual forms of proprietorship, the Tzutujil have been very conservative in recent years, keeping their individual holdings despite intense demands from other Guatemalan farmers and corporations. By the 1980s, the Tzutujil population numbered nearly 90,000 people.

REFERENCES: W. George Lovell, "Surviving Conquest: The Maya of Guatemala in Historical Perspective," *Latin American Research Review* 23 (Number 2, 1988), 25–58; Sandra L. Orellano, "Ethnohistorical and Archaeological Boundaries of the Tzutujil Maya," *Ethnohistory*, 20 (1973), 125–42; Sandra L. Orellano, *The Tzutujil Maya: Continuity and Change, 1250–1630*, 1989.

U

UAIANA. See YURITI-TAPUYA.

UAICA. See YANOAMA.

UAICAMA. See PIRA-TAPUYA.

UAIKENA. See PIRA-TAPUYA.

UAIMARE. See WAIMARE.

UAIQUIRE. See WOKIARE.

UAJÁNA. See URUKUYÁNA.

UAJAPI. See OYANPÍK.

UAMIRI. See YAWAPERI.

UAMUE. See ATICUM.

UANANA. The Uanana (Uamana, Uanano, Guanano, Wanana, Wanano), also described historically as the Ananas, are an Eastern Tukanoan* language group of Amerindians who occupy the banks of the Vaupés River from Uaracapuri Falls in Colombia to Yavarete, Brazil. Their principal settlements are Villa Santa Cruz, Villa Fatima, and Yapima. They practice hunting, fishing, and gardening in a tropical rain forest and wide river habitat. They call themselves Kotiria, or the "people of the river." There were sporadic European contacts with the Uanana in the eighteenth and nineteenth centuries. Portuguese missions were established temporarily along the upper Vaupés in the 1780s, but systematic evangelization of the tribe did not begin until 1914 when Roman Catholic priests established missions in the area. Theodor Koch-Grünberg began ethnological studies of the Uanana at the same time. Protestant missionaries made their way into the region after World War II, eventually making nominal converts of a minority of Uanana. The tribal economy focuses on the production of bitter manioc and fishing; hunting is quite secondary, although in recent years the tribe has become increasingly dependent on such European technology as fishhooks, shotguns, and machetes, as well as on increased manioc production for sale. Contact with whites has also led to the development of small-scale animal husbandry, primarily hogs and poultry, as well as the wearing of Western clothing. There are nearly 1,700 Uanana today who acknowledge tribal membership and speak the native language.

REFERENCES: Janet M. Chernela, "Gender, Language, and Placement in Uanano Songs," *Journal of Latin American Lore*, 14 (1988), 193–206; Janet M. Chernela, "Some Considerations of Gender and Myth in a Northwest Amazonian Society," in Richard R. Randolph, William M. Schneider, and May N. Diaz, eds., *Dialectics and Gender: Anthropological Approaches*, 1988, 67–79; Janet M. Chernela, "Hierarchy and Economy of the Uanano (Kotiria) Speaking Peoples of the Middle Uaupés Basin," Ph.D. dissertation, Columbia University, 1983; Janet M. Chernela, "Indigenous Fishing in the Neodotropics: The Tukanoan Uanano of the Blackwater Uaupés River in Brazil and Colombia," *Interciéncia*, 10 (1985), 78–86; Jean A. Jackson, *The Fish People: Linguistic Exogamy and Tukanoan Identity in Northwest Amazonia*, 1983; Gerardo Reichel-Dolmatoff, *Amazonian Cosmos: The Sexual and Religious Symbolism of the Tukano Indians*, 1985.

UANANO. See UANANA.

UARAKENA. See WARIKYÁNA.

UARAO. See WARRAU.

UARAU. See WARRAU.

UARAUNO. See WARRAU.

UARAW. See WARRAU.

UARIQUENA. See WARIKYÁNA.

UAROW. See WARRAU.

UATADEO. See KADUVEO.

UA-TEO-TE-UO. See KADUVEO.

UAUI. See ARAONA.

UBDE. See MAKÚ.

UBINA. See AYMARA.

UCATAQUERRI. See ACHAGUA.

UCAYALI. See COCAMA.

UCAYALI. See QUECHUA.

UCAYALINO. The Ucayalino are a major division of the Campa* Indians of the Peruvian Amazon. They live primarily along the Sheshea, Ucayali, and Pachitea rivers, as well as such tributaries as the Apurucayali, Bajo Pichi, Palcazu, and Yurua rivers. Some of them also live across the border in Brazil. The Ucayalino were in sporadic contact with neo-Peruvian society by the late nineteenth century, and many of them lived on a Franciscan mission at Cahuapanas. When priests cruelly punished a Ucayalino student in 1925, the Ucayalino burned down the mission. A Peruvian military expedition set out to punish them so the Ucayalino fled into the jungles. There they mixed heavily with the Amuesha along the Bajo Palcazu River. Although the Ucayalino have traditionally been a subsistence agricultural people, many of them have turned to commercial agriculture in recent years, especially the production of rice for sale in cash markets. Large numbers of Ucayalino men are also engaged in rubber extraction. At present the Ucayalino population exceeds 5,000 people.

REFERENCE: Darcy Ribeiro and Mary Ruth Wise, *Los grupos étnicos de la amazona peruana*, 1978.

UCHUMI. See URU.

UFAINA. See TANIMUKA.

UGUANO. See AGUANO.

UHITISCHE. See APINAYÉ.

UIAPII. The Uiapii are a Tupi*-language group of Amerindians who are concentrated in two regions in the state of Pará, Brazil: near the Mapuera River and west of the Trombetas River, both just south of the Brazilian border with Guyana. Demographers estimate that the total population of Uiapii is approximately 140 people. They live a subsistence lifestyle of hunting small game and raising manioc as their major protein source. Although the tribe has accepted a number of items of Western technology, they still nurture a separate ethnic identity and try to maintain their social isolation.

REFERENCE: Edwin Brooks, et al., *Tribes of the Amazon Basin, Brazil, 1972*, 1973.

UIQUIARE. See WOKIARE.

UIQUIRE. See WOKIARE.

UIRAUASU-TAPUYO. See WITOTO.

UITOTO. See WITOTO.

ULUA. See SUMU.

ULVA. See SUMU.

ULWA. See SUMU.

UMAUA. See OMÁGUA.

UMOTINA. The Umotina (Umutina, Umotima, Barbados) are a group of Boróro* Amerindians who once spoke a Gê* language. They pursued a nomadic hunting and foraging lifestyle in the forested areas between the upper Paraguay river and the Sepotuba River in what is today the state of Mato Grosso, Brazil. Agents from the Brazilian government Indian service first pacified them in 1918, bringing them into permanent contact with neo-Brazilians during the next 15 years. By the 1940s, they were in a state of rapid acculturation and population decline, with some tribal members moving to a government Indian post in the municipality of Barra dos Bugres in Mato Grosso. Today there are approximately 160 individuals who claim Umotina descent living in Mato Grosso, but they are highly integrated into neo-Brazilian society. Only two or three of them still speak the language. Despite the acculturation process, they retain a strong sense of ethnic identity.

REFERENCES: Harald Schultz, *Vinte e tres indios resistem a civilizacao*, 1953; Robert Lee Spires, ''As Línguas Faladas do Brasil,'' *América Indígena*, 47 (1987), 455–79; Theodore L. Stoddard, ed., *Indians of Brazil in the Twentieth Century*, 1967.

UMUAMASA. See MAKUNA.

UMURANO. See OMURANO.

UMUTINA. See UMOTINA.

UNCONINO. See CAMPA.

UNIVERRENAY. See ACHAGUA.

UOMO. See PAKAANÓVA.

UPANAVADENÍ. See DANÍ.

UPURI. See URUKUYÁNA.

URANICO. See ARAONA.

URARINA. The Urarina (Itakule, Itucale, Ytucali, Singacuchusca, Cingacu-chusca, Arucui, Arucuye, Ssimaku, Shimacu, Chimacu, Chambira, Chambirino, and Cimarron) are a group of Amerindians living north of the Marañon River on the tributaries of the Chambira and Urituyacu rivers in Peru. There is still much debate and indecision among ethnolgists about the classification of the Urarina language. They were traditionally divided into two groups, the Urarina proper and the Itakule. Spanish missionaries working among the Cocama first contacted the Itakule in 1653, when many of them were settled on missions in the area. In 1738, the Urarina joined a mission of their own on the Chambira River. The Itakule eventually joined them and assimilated. By 1800, disease had reduced the Urarina population to approximately 600 people. Although it stabilized and began to increase, severe epidemics in the early 1950s devastated the tribe, and the survivors scattered into the jungles. Today they live in small, scattered groups, practicing a subsistence agriculture; many of them are under the control of labor bosses. At present, there are approximately 5,000 people in Peru who are aware of their Urarina ancestry.

REFERENCES: Darcy Ribeiro and Mary Ruth Wise, *Los grupos étnicos de la amazona peruana*, 1978; Stefano Varese, *The Forest People in the Present Political Situation of Peru*, 1972.

URINAMA. See BRIBRI.

URINI. See ASURINÍ.

URO. See URU.

UROCOLLA. See URU.

UROQUILLA. See URU.

URU. The Uru—also known historically as the Uro, Huno, Ochomazo, Ochozuma, Uchumi, Kjotsuni, Bukina, Pukina, Puquina,* Urocolla, Uroquilla, and
Yuracare (not the Yuracare* of eastern Bolivia)—were a Puquina-speaking tribe
of Amerindians who lived on floating rafts on Lake Titicaca in Boliva. They
were a fishing and foraging people who ate raw fish, roots, and insects; they
avoided agriculture. The Uru suffered much from the Incan and Spanish conquests in the fifteenth and sixteenth centuries, and since then they faced pressure
from expanding Aymara*- and Quechua*-speaking people. The Uru population
dwindled to about 100 people in 1930, and anthropologists estimate that the last
full-blooded Uru Indians died out in the early 1960s. Today there are Indian
descendents of the Uru living on the floating reed platforms of Lake Titicaca,
but they now speak primarily Aymara and have adopted an Aymara lifestyle.
They have also adopted an agricultural lifestyle, raising potatoes and quinoa.
There are perhaps 20 people there among the Aymara who are direct descendents
of the Uru.
    REFERENCES: Victor Englebart, "Reed People of Titicaca," *Natural History*, 91
(1982), 34–36; Pedro Plaza Martínez and Juan Carvajal Carvajal, *Etnías y lenguas de
Bolivia*, 1985.

URUAK. See AUAKÉ.

URUBÚ. The Urubú (Urubú-Kaapór, Ka'apór) are a Tupi*-Guaraníí*-language
people who live in the jungles between the Gurupí and Turiacu rivers in the
northern reaches of the state of Maranhão in Brazil. They arrived in that region
only in the early 1900s after migrating from further south in Maranhão. The
Urubú began to flee to the northwest in the 1870s. Their former habitat—an
interfluvial region drained by the Capim, Guama, and Piria rivers in the state
of Pará—was being invaded by settlers and soldiers. Since the Urubu were known
for their ferocity, the Brazilian government did not establish regular contact with
them until 1928. Before then, the Urubu frequently raided small towns and
hamlets looking for metal tools. They also remained at war with such neighboring
tribes as the Krem-yé*, Guajá,* and Guajajára.* Like many other tropical forest
tribes, the Urubú are an interfluvial people who practice a shifting, subsistence
horticulture to raise manioc, but prefer to avoid the rivers, building their villages

and planting their gardens in the jungles. Most of their protein comes from hunting and foraging. In the early 1980s, the Brazilian government estimated that there were still approximately 500 Urubú indians living in fourteen villages who, except for the use of metal tools and some Western clothing, still maintained a strong tribal identity. Although their lands have been invaded by gold prospectors, rubber collectors, resin gatherers, and farmers, they have managed to maintain their cultural integrity and ethnic identity.

REFERENCES: William Balée, "Ka'apór Ritual Hunting," *Human Ecology*, 13 (1985), 485–510; William Balée, "Nomenclature Patterns in Ka'apór Ethnohistory," *Journal of Ethnobiology*, 9 (1989), 1–24; Francis Huxley, *Affable Savages*, 1966; Robert Lee Spires, "As línguas faladas do Brasil," *América Indígena*, 47 (1987), 455–79; Theodore L. Stoddard, ed., *Indians of Brazil in the Twentieth Century*, 1967.

URUBU-DIAPA. See KATUKÍNA.

URUBÚ-KAAPÓR. See URUBÚ.

URUBÚ-TAPUYA. See KARUTANA.

URUEU-WAU-WÁU. The Urueu-Wau-Wáu are a tropical forest tribe living on a 7,000-square-mile reserve of primeval forest in western Rondônia, Brazil. Because of their location, the tribe escaped the worst effects of the sixteenth- and seventeenth-century epidemics and the slave trading that decimated so many Brazilian Indians. Today their tribal land is recognized by the Brazilian government and is off-limits to settlers. The Urueu-Wau-Wáu have been known to kill intruders periodically; in 1979 and 1980, for excample, they murdered several neo-Brazilian colonists. European contact with the tribe has been minimal. Construction of a permanent fort on the Guaporé River restricted tribal movement to the south, and the completion of a railroad in 1872 established a new boundary on the northwest. In 1960, the government completed Highway 364, which established the northeastern boundary. Although the official census in the late 1970s placed the tribal membership at 350, there are probably only about 200 Urueu-Wau-Wáu alive today. They still practice an indigenous lifestyle of hunting and subsistence horticulture in the rain forest.

REFERENCES: Loren McIntyre, "Last Days of Eden: Rondônia Urueu-Wau-Wáu Indians," *National Geographic*, 174 (December 1988), 800–17; Robert Lee Spires, "As línguas faladas do Brasil," *América Indígena*, 47 (1987), 455–79.

URUKU. See ARAONA.

URUKUENA. See URUKUYÁNA.

URUKUIÁNA. See URUKUYÁNA.

URUKUYÁNA. The Urukuyána (Wayána, Uarakena, Urukuena, Urukuiána) are a small Karib*-speaking group of Amerindians who today live on the headwaters of the Jari, Paru de Leste, Itani, and Paruma rivers along the border between French Guiana and Brazil, with the majority of the 100 or so members of the tribe in the territory of Amapá in Brazil. A few scattered Urukuyána live in southern Surinam. There they are in permanent contact with neo-Brazilian society and are closely associated with the Wayána* tribe. They practice a subsistence horticulture typical of tropical forest tribes, with seasonal migrant labor to provide cash for trade goods. Historically, the Urukuyána and its sub-tribes have also been known as the Guyána, Oyána, Ojána, Ajána, Ouyána, Uajána, Upuri, Opeoeroei, Rucána, Rucuyen, Rucuyenne, Orcocoyána, Orko-koyána, Urucuiána, Alucuyána, and Alukuyána.

REFERENCES: John LaPointe, ''Residence Patterns and Wayána Social Organization,'' Ph.D. dissertation, Columbia University, 1970; Robert Lee Spires, ''As línguas faladas do Brasil,'' *América Indígena*, 47 (1987), 455–79; Theodore L. Stoddard, ed., *Indians of Brazil in the Twentieth Century*, 1967.

URUMI. The Urumi are an almost extinct group of Tupi*-speaking Amerindians who once lived along the Jiparaná River, between the Taruma and Madeirinha rivers, in what is today the state of Rondônia, Brazil. They migrated there from points east in the eighteenth century to escape the Portuguese conquest, but in the late 1800s, the Urumi fell victim to the rubber collectors who invaded Rondônia and exploited and killed the Indians. The Urumi entered a population decline from which they have never recovered. By the 1920s, their numbers were under 100 people; soon after they lost the population base to sustain tribal ceremonial life. Although the tribe is extinct today as a social unit, there are still individuals in Brazil who are aware of their Urumi roots.

REFERENCE: Theodore L. Stoddard, ed., *Indians of Brazil in the Twentieth Century*, 1967.

URUPÁ. The Urupá are a small tribe of Amerindians who today live in the Madeira basin, on the Urupá and Jamari rivers, in the state of Rondônia, Brazil, at the headwaters of the Urupá River. Closely related to the Pakaanóvas,* they are part of the Txapakúra* language family. The Urupá were uncontacted by neo-Brazilians until the 1730s when gold prospectors reached their territory. The subsequent epidemics started the Urupá on the long road to extinction. Early in the twentieth century, rubber collectors precipitated another decline that has brought the Urupá nearly to extinction. Today there are two groups of people with Urupá roots, together totaling approximately 150 Indians. One group is scattered along the Urupá River and the other lives at a government Indian post on the upper Jamari River. The Urupá are in permanent contact with neo-Brazilian society.

REFERENCES: Robert Lee Spires, ''As línguas faladas do Brasil,'' *América Indígena*, 47 (1987), 455–79; Theodore L. Stoddard, ed., *Indians of Brazil in the Twentieth Century*, 1967.

USPANTEC. The Uspantecs are a small Quichean Maya* group of Indians who live in the highlands of the department of Quiché in Guatemala. In the fifteenth century, they fell under the domination of the Quiché Maya, and although they overthrew Quiché oppression early in the 1500s, they fell under Spanish control in the 1530s. Disease, relocation, and warfare dramatically reduced the Uspantec population in the sixteenth century, but it stabilized in the 1600s. Like other Mayans, the Uspantecs were a settled agricultural people who lived off the cultivation of maize and beans. In the late 1800s, the government of Guatemala, pressured by powerful agricultural interests, began forcibly transferring tribal land to private ownership, reducing most Uspantecs to peasant or migrant laborer status. Their poverty produced political unrest after World War II, which in turn led to bloody reprisals against Mayan activists. In the 1980s, perhaps 25 percent of Uspantecs emigrated to the United States, leaving approximately 2,000 members of the tribe behind in Guatemala.

REFERENCES: Jim Handy, *Gift of the Devil: A History of Guatemala*, 1984; W. George Lovell, *Conquest and Survival in Colonial Guatemala: A Historical Geography of the Cuchumatan Highlands, 1500–1821*, 1984; W. George Lovell, "Surviving Conquest: The Maya of Guatemala in Historical Perspective," *Latin American Research Review*, 23 (1988), 25–58.

UTINSCHE. See APINAYÉ.

V

VACACOCHA. See AWISHIRI.

VACACOCHA. See ARABELA.

VALIENTE. See BRIBRI.

VAPIDIÁNA. See WAPISHÁNA.

VARRA. See WARRAU.

VARASHADENÍ. See DANÍ.

VAYENA. See WAYÁNA.

VEADO. See ASURINÍ.

VEJO. See MATACO.

VEJOZ. See MATACO.

VELICHE. See HUILLICHE.

VENTEGUEBO. See KADUVEO.

VEYANA. See WAYÁNA.

VIAKSHI. See VIAKSI.

VIAKSI. The Viaksi are a subtribe of the Yukpa* Indians of northwestern Venezuela. They traditionally lived along the Santa Rosa de Aguas Negras River right at the Colombian border, where they have followed a tropical forest lifestyle revolving around the production of manioc, maize, and beans. The tribal identity, however, has ceased to exist in the last twenty years. By the mid–1970s, there were fewer than 10 Viaksi people still alive, and they were living among other Yukpa subtribes in the Uykpa Indian Reserve. See YUKPA.

VICIETA. See BRIBRI.

VINTUKUA. See IKA.

VOQUEARE. See WOKIARE.

VOTO. See RAMA.

W

WACAWAÍ. See AKAWÁIO.

WACHIPAERI. The Wachipaeri (Huachipaire, Huachipaeri, Huachipary) is the last remnant, and probably a fusion, of several very closely related bands of Amerindians who once occupied the Q'eros, Cosnipata, Pilcopata, Tono, and Pini-pini river valleys of the department of Cuzco in the province of Paucartambo in the district of Cosnipata in eastern Peru. The Wachipaeri are part of the Harakmbet* (Hate) language family, a relatively small and isolated group. Soon after the Spanish arrived in Peru in the 1530s, they contacted the Wachipaeri, and ever since then, the Wachipaeri have been in continuous contact with neo-Peruvians, as well as with their Machiguenga* and Quechua*-speaking neighbors. They have adopted the use of steel tools, chickens, and Western clothing. Still, the Wachipaeri have maintained a strong tribal identity. In 1900, the tribe numbered perhaps 700 people, but they have decline since then from disease. A smallpox epidemic in 1948 reduced the Wachipaeri from 200 to only 70 people. Both Protestants and Catholics established missions among the Wachipaeri in the 1950s. Today many of them live at the missions and speak Spanish. The total number of full-blood Wachipaeri is approximately 150. Although they are in contact with the Machiguenga Indians, Quechua-speaking Indians, mestizos, and whites, the Wachipaeri retain a strong sense of tribal identity.

REFERENCES: Andrew Gray, "Perspectives on Amarakaeri History," in Harald O. Sklar and Frank Salomon, eds., *Natives and Neighbors in South America: Anthropological Essays*, 1987, 299–329; Patricia J. Lyon, "Change in Wachipaeri Marriage Patterns," in Kenneth M. Kensinger, ed., *Marriage Practices in Lowland South America*, 1984, 252–64; Patricia J. Lyon, "Singing as a Social Interaction among the Wachipaeri of Eastern Peru," Ph.D. dissertation, University of California, Berkeley, 1967; Patricia Lyon, "Dislocación tribal y clasificaciones lingüísticas en la zona del Río Madre de

Dios,'' *Actas y Memorias*, 5 (1975), 185–207; Darcy Ribeiro and Mary Ruth Wise, *Los grupos étnicos de la amazona peruana*, 1978; Stefano Varese, *The Forest Indians in the Present Political Situation of Peru*, 1972.

WADIUPARANIN. See KATUKÍNA.

WAHAI. See KAWAHÍB.

WAHARIBO. See GUAHIBO.

WAHYARA. See YURITI-TAPUYA.

WAIANA. See YURITI-TAPUYA.

WAIAPÍ. See OYANPÍK.

WAICÁ. See AKAWÁIO.

WAICÁ. See YANOAMA.

WAIKÁ. See AKAWÁIO.

WAIKA. See YANOAMA.

WAIKANA. See PIRA-TAPUYA.

WAIKATDESU. See NAMBIQUÁRA.

WAIKINO. See PIRA-TAPUYA.

WAIMAHA. See BARÁ.

WAIMAJA. See BARÁ.

WAIMARÉ. The Waimaré are a subgroup of Arawak*-speaking Amerindians whose larger tribal affiliation is with the Parecí* Indians. Their homeland is along the Verde, Sacre, and Papagaio rivers in Brazil. Although the Waimaré intermarry with such other Parecí subgroups as the Kashiniti* and Kozarene*, they still maintain a strong ethnic identity as Waimaré. See PARECÍ.

WAIMIRI. See YAWAPERI.

WAIOMGOMO. See MAYONGÓNG.

WAIOMIRI. See YAWAPERI.

WAIWÁI. The Waiwái, also known historically as the Woyamana, Waiwe, Tapioca, and Ouayeone, are a Karib*-language people living in the rain forests of Brazil and Guyana. When they were first contacted by Europeans in 1837, they were living in one village near the Essequibo River in Guyana and two villages on the Mapuera River in Brazil. In the 1890s, large numbers of Waiwái were slaughtered by other Indians. Gradually more and more Waiwá migrated to Guyana where they have remained close to Protestant missionaries near Mauika village on the upper Essequibo River. Early in the 1970s, when those missionaries relocated to Brazil, many Waiwái followed them. Today there are approximately 1,000 Waiwái, most of them near the Brazilian-Guyana border where they continue to pursue a slash-and-burn agriculture and a largely indigenous lifestyle. Compared to most Amerindian groups, the Waiwái have maintained larger segments of their traditional life because of the geographical isolation of their homeland in the southern Rupununi area.

REFERENCES: Ronald R. Dagon, *Current Agricultural Practices Among the Waiwai*, 1967; W. Edwards and K. Gibson, "An Ethnohistory of Amerindians in Guyana," *Ethnohistory*, 26 (Spring 1979), 161–75; Kenneth Sugrim, *Some Historical and Demographic Information on the Amerindians of Guyana*, 1977; Niels Fock, Waiwái: Religion and Society of an Amazonian Tribe, 1963; George P. Mentore, "Waiwái Women: The Basis of Wealth and Power," *Man*, 22 (1987), 511–22; Jens Yde, *Material Culture of the Waiwái*, 1965.

WAIWE. See WAIWÁI.

WAIYAN. See WAYÁNA.

WAKADA. See PIRA-TAPUYA.

WAKALITDESU. See NAMBIQUÁRA.

WAKATANERI. See AMARAKAERI.

WAKONA. The Wakona are an Amerindian group of people of unknown language extraction who today live in the municipality of Palmeira dos Indios in the state of Alagoas, Brazil. They are virtually indistinguishable from their neo-Brazilian neighbors in terms of economic lifestyle, in which they are laborers or subsistence farmers. They retain no remnants of their aboriginal language or culture, but they still define themselves as Wakona Indians and maintain a strong

sense of ethnic identity. The Brazilian government Indian service provides assistance to more than 1,000 people who consider themselves part of this group.
   REFERENCE: Theodore L. Stoddard, ed., *Indians of Brazil in the Twentieth Century*, 1967.

WAKUÉNAI. The Wakuénai Indians live along the Guainía River in the Venezuelan Amazonian basin and along the Içana River across the Brazilian border. In Venezuela, there are five Wakuénai dialects—Curripaco,* Curricarro, Oh-hon, Eh-hen, and Namé. Of those, Curripaco is the most widely spoken. Neo-Venezuelans and neo-Colombians often call the Wakuénai the "Curripaco." Across the border in Brazil, the Wakuénai are often called the Baníwa* (Baníva, Maníbas, Karutána, Carutána, Korekaru, and Baníba), the principal tribe on the Içana River. Actually, the term Baníwa should not be confused with the Baníwa people of Venezuela, an Arawakan* people whose language is not intelligible to Wakuénai people. The Karú subtribe is located on the lower Içana, while the Karupaka are on the upper Içana. There are other subgroups, such as the Hohodene, Wariperidakena, Kumadamnainai, Adzaneni, Dzawinai, Turimnainai, and Guarequena. There are also some Wakuénai in contiguous areas of Colombia, whose subtribes include the Hohodene, Kadaupuritana, Sucuriuy-Tapuya, Siusy-Tapuya, Ira-Tapuya, Acuti-Tapuya, and Kawa-Tapuya. The Venezuelan and Brazilian Wakuénai dialects are quite distinct. Today they number more than 4,500 people and live on government posts along the middle Içana and Ayeri rivers in the state of Amazonas. They still emphasize hunting and fishing over farming, although subsistence agriculture and day labor are becoming more and more significant economically.
   Ever since the sixteenth century, the processes of acculturation have affected the Wakuénai. In the early 1700s, Jesuit missionaries arrived in the area and introduced Nheengatú* as the language they wanted all Indians to speak. Portuguese slave traders entered the region in the 1740s and 1750s, but the Wakuénai managed to survive them. In the 1780s, however, smallpox, measles, and flu began to take their toll on the tribe. They are a tropical forest people whose economic life revolves around slash-and-burn cultivation of manioc. In the nineteenth century, the Wakuénai underwent another severe population decline from European diseases, even though most of them came from contact with other Indians. They also suffered from exploitive government labor policies in Brazil and Venezuela in the 1850s. A rubber boom in the 1940s introduced more social dislocation when neo-Brazilians and neo-Venezuelans flooded into their tribal territory. Protestant missionaries from the New Tribes Mission built an installation in Wakuénai territory and began eradicating traditional social customs governing marriage and other family ceremonial rituals. Government programs in Venezuela, Brazil, and Colombia in the 1970s have brought more European and mestizo settlers into the area, forcing a migration of the Wakuénai from the upper Guainía and Içana rivers to the lower Guainía River in Venezuela. Large numbers of Wakuénai have also moved from the rural countryside to towns and

cities in search of work. Today the Brazilian Wakuénai number more than 1,600 people, while the Wakuénai in Venezuela include more than 3,000 people.

REFERENCES: Lubio Cardozo, *Cuentas indígenas venezolanos*, 1968; Ministerio de Estado para la Cultura, *Arte Indigéna de Venezuela*, 1983; Jonathan Hill, "Music, Myth, and Communication in Wakuenai Society," Ph.D. dissertation, Indiana University, 1979; Jonathan D. Hill, "Ritual Production of Environmental History Among the Arawakan Wakuenai of Venezuala," *Human Ecology*, 17 (1989), 237–57; Jonathan Hill and Emilio F. Moran, "Adaptive Strategies of Wakuenai People to the Oligotrophic Rain Forest of the Río Negro Basin," in Raymond B. Hames and William T. Vickers, eds., *Adaptive Responses of Native Amazonians*, 1983, 113–33.

WAMA. The Wama are a subtribe of the Tiriyó* Indians of the equatorial rain forest along the border between Brazil and Surinam. They are considered an inaccessible group because of their suspiciousness toward neo-Brazilians and neo-Surinamese. See TIRIYÓ.

WAMBISA. See HUAMBISA.

WAMONAE. See CUIVA.

WAMUTANARA. See BARASÁNA.

WANACO. See BARASÁNA.

WANAI. See MAPOYO.

WANÁM. The Wanám (Huanyam) were a group of Amerindians once native to the region of southern Rondônia in Brazil. They lived on the Cautarinho and Manoel rivers near their confluence with the Guaporé. The rubber booms of the twentieth century destroyed the tribe because of the violence and diseases brought in by neo-Brazilians. The surviving Wanám went to live with neighboring groups. Although the Wanám people did not survive, their language did, at least among the Kabixí Indians living on the São Miguel River.

REFERENCE: David Maybury-Lewis, ed., *In the Path of the Polonoreste: Endangered Peoples of Western Brazil*, 1981.

WANANA. See UANANA.

WANANA. The term "Wanana," in addition to its reference to the Uanano group, is also used generically in southern Colombia and northwestern Brazil to describe any Indian whose language is part of the Tukano* group.

REFERENCE: Theodore L. Stoddard ed., *Indians of Brazil in the Twentieth Century*, 1967.

WANANO. See UANANA.

WANINAWA. See KATUKINA.

WAO. See WAORANI.

WAORANI. The Waorani (Huaorani, Wao) are a linguistically isolated group of Amerindians who live in the moist tropical forest of an area bounded by the Napo, Curaray, and Villano rivers in eastern Ecuador. They call themselves the Auca. Traditionally the Waorani have been an interfluvial people lacking canoes who avoided large rivers whenever possible. They constructed their villages on the tops of hills or ridges and planted their gardens, where they raise manioc and plantains, on the slopes of hills. The first permanent contact with Europeans did not occur until 1958 when there were approximately 500 Waorani living in an area of 7,000 square miles. Recent road construction has brought many neo-Ecuadorean settlers into the area, reducing Waorani territory, especially in Yasuni National Park, where several groups of Waorani live. Ecuadorean government policies in the 1980s, which have encouraged business and economic development of the Amazon region, are also dislocating the Waorani people. Oil exports that fuel the national economy have hastened the development of the oil-rich Amazon. Despite the support of such groups as the Confederation of Indian Nations of the Ecuadorian Amazon, the alienation of Waorani land continues unimpeded. By the early 1980s, there were nearly 600 members of the tribe occupying about 700 square miles.

REFERENCES: Nina Orville, "Road Construction Threatens Huaorani in Ecuador," *Cultural Survival Quarterly*, 12 (1988), 43–46; James Yost, "Twenty Years of Contact: The Mechanisms of Change in Wao ("Auca") Culture," in Norman E. Whitten, Jr., *Cultural Transformation and Ethnicity in Modern Ecuador*, 1981, 78–96.

WAPICHAŃA. See WAPISHÁNA.

WAPICHIYÁNA. See WAPISHÁNA.

WAPIDIAN. See WAPISHÁNA.

WAPISHÁNA. The Wapishana are an Arawak*-speaking people who migrated north from the Río Negro area, up the Branco River, and across what is today the political boundary with Brazil and onto the southern savannas of Guyana by the early 1800s. Large numbers of them are concentrated on the southern Rupununi River. The Wapishána are also located in the far southeastern corner of Venezuela. This migration brought them to their present territory by 1810. In the process of the migration, the Amariba (Amaripa), a subtribe of the Wapishána, lost their separate identity and merged with the larger group. By the late nineteenth century, the Wapishána had absorbed the Atorai, also known historically as the Atorya, Attaraya, Attorraidi, Atorad, Daurai, Dauri, and Tauri. A subtribe of the Atorai, known as the Maopityan (Mapidian, Maopidian, Mapidian, Pidian, and Moonpidenne), were simultaneously absorbed by the Wapishána. By 1920, the Paraviyana (Parauiana, Paravilhana, Parauillana, Palauiyang, and Parauana), a Karib*-speaking tribe, were likewise assimilated by the Wapishána. The Wapishána, like the other tribes of Guyana, practice slash-and-burn agriculture to raise their staple crop, manioc. Many of the Wapishána have recently begun cattle-raising operations, and they are among the most economically prosperous Indian groups in Guyana. Today the Wapishána number approximately 6,000 people and are increasingly acculturated and integrated into the regional cash economy. Their main settlements in Guyana are located at Aishalton, Achiwib, Awaruwaunawa, Dadanawa, Maruranawa, Sauiwau, and Shea. In Brazil they are located on the lower Uraricuera River, west of the upper Branco River. Historically they have also been known as the Wapichána, Wapichiyána, Wapidian, Wapitxana, Warpeshana, Ouapisiana, Guapishana, Ouapishane, Mapeshana, and Vapidiana.

REFERENCES: W. Edwards and K. Gibson, "An Ethnohistory of Amerindians in Guayana," *Ethnohistory*, 26 (Spring 1979), 161–75; Andrew Sanders, *The Powerless People*, 1987: Robert Lee Spires, "As línguas faladas do Brasil," *América Indígena*, 47 (1987), 455–79; Kenneth Sugrim, *Some Historical and Demographic Information on the Amerindians of Guyana*, 1977.

WAPISIÁNA. See WAPISHÁNA.

WAPITXÁNA. See WAPISHÁNA.

WARAO. The Warao (Guarao, Guarauno) are a closely related subtribe of the Warrau* who occupy a small area in northeastern Venezuela along the border with Guyana, especially in the Orinoco delta of the Delta Amacura Territory, east of Monacas and south of Sucre. A riverine people, the Warao call themselves the Canoe People because of the canoe's significance to their way of life. They spend a great deal of time hunting and fishing, but they also raise manioc and rice as staples. The Warao survived contact with European civilization primarily because of their equatorial delta habitat, which European settlers tended to avoid. Those Warao living on the fringes of the delta are more acculturated, while those residing inland are more traditional in their values. Since the 1960s, the Warao have been oppressed and exploited by local sawmill owners and rice planters, whose labor demands have caused severe health problems. At present, the Warao number only about 150 people and are verging on extinction as a well-differentiated social group.

REFERENCES: Estéban Emilio Mosonyi, "La revitalización lingüística y la realidad venezolano," *América Indígena*, 47 (1987), 553–61; Ministerio de Estado para la Cultura, *Arte indígena de Venezuela*, 1983; María Matilde Suárez, *Los Warao: Indígenas del delta del Orinoco*, 1968.

WARAU. See WARRAU.

WARAUETI. See WARRAU.

WARAWEETE. See WARRAU.

WAREKENA. See WARIKYÁNA.

WAREQUENA. See WARIKYÁNA.

WARI. See DESANA.

WARI. See PAKAANÓVA.

WARIAPANO. See PANOBO.

WARIKYÁNA. The Warikyána today are a collection of about ten subgroups of Amerindians who once spoke Arawakan* dialects and lived close to the central Trombetas River in the state of Pará, Brazil. They are part of a smaller Arhuac linguistic family. After the Treaty of Madrid consolidated Portugal's claim to the region, Portuguese military and colonizing expeditions brought permanent contact to the Warikyána, whose population began a rapid decline from its total of 3,000 to 4,000 at the time of the European arrival in the New World. Historically, the Warikyána have been known as Arikiena, Arekena, Arequena, Guariquena, Guarequena,* Uarekena, Uariquena, Warequena, Werekena, and Warekena. Today their numbers are down to fewer than 300 people, and they no longer function as a differentiated tribal group.
REFERENCES: Estéban Emilio Mosonyi, "La revitalización lingüística y la realidad venezolano," *América Indígena*, 47 (1987), 553–61; Robert Lee Spires, "As línguas faladas do Brasil," *América Indígena*, 47 (1987), 455–79; Theodore L. Stoddard, ed., *Indians of Brazil in the Twentieth Century*, 1967.

WARIPERIDAKENA. See WAKUENAI.

WARIPI. See OKOMOYÁNA.

WARIWA-TAPUYA. See MAKÚ.

WAROUWEN. See WARRAU.

WAROW. See WARRAU.

WARPESHANA. See WAPISHÁNA.

WARRAN. See WARRAU.

WARRAU. The Warrau are a tropical forest people occupying the lowland swamps of the Orinoco Delta in Guyana, Surinam, and Venezuela, especially the swampy lands of the Delta Amacura Territory. The English explorer Sir

Walter Raleigh first contacted the Warrau in the late 1500s, but it was not until the 1680s that missions were established among them. The Warrau resisted, some fleeing to Dutch Guiana and becoming the source of the present Warrau population along the Corentyne River. Most of the Warrau live in the swamps between the Orinoco River and the Pomeroon River. Archeologists postulate that the Warrau arrived in those swamps because they were fleeing Arawakan* and Karib* expansion into the coastal regions. The Warrau population has been relatively stable over the years, primarily because the inaccessibility of the swamps protected them from Europeans as well as from other Indians. At the end of the eighteenth century, the Warrau population was estimated at approximately 6,000 people. By 1950, the Warrau population was still near 6,000 people, and today it exceeds 15,000. Most of them are concentrated in a 7,000-square-kilometer area between Mariusa and the Amicuro region south of the Wirinoko River.

The Warrau are skilled boat builders, and they fish from boats using harpoons. Their staple, however, is the starchy pith of the ite palm, which they mix with a variety of other food products. The leaves of the ite palm are also used for roofing houses, making shoes, and constructing ropes and fibers. By the 1960s, some Warrau had adopted a primitive agriculture, but most still practice a fishing and foraging life.

The Warrau language constitutes its own language group. There are some subtribes of the Warrau still in existence, including the Mariusa and the Chaguan (also Chaugane or Ciawani). Extinct subtribes and historical synonyms of the Warrau include the Araote, Farute, Guarau, Guaraon, Guaraunan, Guarauana, Guarauno, Guaraune, Guaraounoe, Guaranu, Guarano, Guararini, Guaraoun, Guaraouno, Guaranne, Houaroux, Oraw-it, Ouavaous, Tibitibi, Tivitivi, Tivitiva, Uarau, Uarao, Uarauno, Uaraw, Uarow, Varaa, Warau, Warow, Warraw, Warrow, Warran, Warao, Warouwen, Warray, Waraweete, and Waraueti.

REFERENCES: W. Edwards and K. Gibson, "An Ethnohistory of Amerindians in Guyana," *Ethnohistory*, 26 (1979), 161–75; H. Dieter Heinen, "Adaptive Changes in a Tribal Economy: A Case Study of the Winikina-Warao, "Ph.D. dissertation, University of California at Los Angeles, 1972; Colin Henfrey, *The Gentle People: A Journey Among the Indian Tribes of Guiana*, 1964; Johannes Wilbert, *Demographic and Biological Studies of the Warao Indians*, 1980.

WARRAW. See WARRAU.

WARRAY. See WARRAU.

WARROW. See WARRAU.

WARUWARU. See HOTI.

WASAMA. The Wasama are a subtribe of the Yukpa* Indians of northwestern Venezuala. Their traditional land was along the Yasa River, near the Pariri Indians,* another Yukpa subtribe. The Wasama today total approximately 70 people. See YUKPA.

WASUHSU. See NAMBIQUÁRA.

WAUNANA. The Waunana (Nonama, Noanama) are an Amerindian group of nearly 3,000 people who are part of the Chocó* linguistic family. The Waunana originally lived in the lower San Juan River basin in the department of Chocó in Colombia, but in recent years up to one-third of them have migrated across the border to the province of Darién in Panama. Approximately 2,000 of the Waunana now live in Colombia and 1,000 in Panama. There are 129 Waunana Indians living on the Papayo reservation in Colombia, as well as 168 on the Togoroma reservation, 165 on the Docordo-Balsalito reservation, 104 on the Chachajo reservation, 326 on the Cabeceras o Puerto Pizario reservation, 90 on the Tiosilidio reservation, 172 on the Burujon o La Union San Bernardo reservation, 229 on the Chagpien-Tordo reservation, 42 on the Río Dagua reservation, 256 on the Union Choco-San Cristobal reservation, 647 on the Bellavista y Union Pitalito o Río Siguirisua-Docampado reservation, 312 on the Río Taparal reservation, 372 on the Río Pichima reservation, 307 on the Santa María de Pangala reservation, 146 on the Río Curiche reservation, 215 on the Río Orpua reservation, and 500 on the Puado, Matare, La Lerma and Terdo reservation.

The Waunana Indians are a tropical forest tribe. Vasco Núñez de Balboa first contacted the Chocó in 1511 and encountered fierce resistance. After those first encounters, there was little contact until 1654 when Spanish missionaries worked to concentrate and convert the Chocó. During those encounters, they also made contact with the Waunana. The Waunana resisted the concentration efforts by moving farther upriver from the Panamanian and Colombian coasts. Franciscan and Jesuit missionaries reached them nonetheless, as did slavers who wanted to work them in the gold mines. The Waunana population entered a long period of decline. Today the tribe practices a slash-and-burn agriculture and lives primarily on plantains, bananas, sweet manioc, sugar cane, and maize. They usually live in round houses without walls. Many of the Waunana speak Spanish. Since World War II, they have increasingly intermarried with black Colombians migrating to the Pacific coast of Colombia.

REFERENCES: Ronald Binder, "Thematic Linkage in Waunana Discourse," in Robert Longacre, ed., *Discourse Grammar: Studies in indigenous languages of Colombia, Panama, and Ecuador*, 2 (1977), 159–90; Blaz Telban, *Grupos étnicos de Colombia: Etnografía y Bibliografía*, 1988.

WAURÁ. The Waurá (Wauru, Uaura, Aura) are a small tropical forest tribe living on a small tributary near the headwaters of the Xingú River in upper Mato Grosso, Brazil. The tribe speaks an Arawakan* language. The Waura were not contacted by Europeans until surveying and anthropological expeditions made it up the Xingú River in the late nineteenth century. All of the Waurá today live in a few small villages and total fewer than 130 people. They fish and practice a slash-and-burn agriculture to produce their staple, manioc. Although the Waurá are linguistically distinct from their other tribal neighbors on the Xingú River, they interact with them both socially and culturally. Today the Waurá are protected by their residence in the Xingú Indian Park, where they are in intermittent contact with neo-Brazilians. They are also widely known as the diplomats of the Xingú Indian Park for their ability to communicate with different tribes and to resolve disputes among them.

REFERENCES: Edwin Brooks, et al., *Tribes of the Amazon Basin, Brazil*, 1972, 1973; Robin Hanbury-Tenison, *A Question of Survival for the Indians of Brazil*, 1973; Orlando Villas Boas and Cláudio Villas Boas, *Xingú: The Indians, Their Myths*, 1973; Robert Lee Spires, "As línguas faladas do Brasil," *América Indígena*, 47 (1987), 455–79.

WAYACULE. See TIRIYÓ.

WAYAI. See PAUMARÍ.

WAYAMPÍ. See OYANPÍK.

WAYÁNA. The Wayana (Waiyána, Guayána, Vayéna, Ouyána, Urukuyána, Orkokoyána, Ojána, Oyána, Oepoeroei), along with the Urukuyana, belong to a small group of Karib* -speaking Amerindians. The French called them Roucouyennes (Rucana, Rucuyen, Rucuyenne) because of the red urucum dye that they used to paint themselves. Until the 1940s, they were relatively unmolested and were able to pursue a tropical forest existence along what is today the Brazilian-Surinamese border. In Surinam and French Guiana, they live near the Tapanahony and Paloemeu rivers and on the Maroni and Litani rivers. By the 1950s, they were in permanent contact with neo-Brazilian society and increasingly dependent on trade goods. During the 1960s, the Wayána in French Guiana were increasingly drawn away from their villages above the Litani Falls toward Maripasoula, a trading post and tourist center. They fell victim to tuberculosis, syphilis, and malaria, although medical missionaries from the West Indies Mission helped them stabilize their population in the 1970s. Today there are fewer than 50 people who still live as Wayana Indians, the others having moved into neo-Brazilian society. See URUKUYÁNA.

WAYANAZE. See KAINGÁNG.

WAYAPÍ. See OYANPÍK.

WAYARIKULE. See WAYARIKURE.

WAYARIKURE. The Wayarikure (Wayacule, Wayarikule) are a subtribe of the Tiriyó* Indians of Brazil and Surinam. Although there may be a few Wayarikure still alive and aware of their heritage, the group no longer exists as a self-conscious entity. See TIRIYÓ.

WAYKA. See AKAWÁIO.

WAYORÓ. The Wayoró (Ajurú) were a group of Amerindians who lived in what is today the state of Rondônia, Brazil. Their language is part of the Tupi* linguistic family and to the Makuráp* subfamily. Their traditional homeland has been at the headwaters of the Colorado River. A tropical forest people who lived by hunting and horticulture, the Wayoró first encountered neo-Brazilians in the 1730s when gold prospectors flooded into their territory, bringing slavery and disease with them. The Wayoró were decimated by the rubber boom in Rondônia in the early 1900s and again during World War II. The rubber collectors brought violence, disease, and forced labor to the Wayoró people, and their population declined so drastically that they could no longer maintain traditional ceremonial life. In the late 1950s, a small group of Wayoró lived at Ribeirão on the Madeira-Mamoré railroad. Today there are approximately 40 people living in Rondônia, primarily near the Branco River, who are aware of their Wayoró heritage and understand the language, but the tribe is no longer a viable social unit.

REFERENCES: David Maybury-Lewis, ed., *In the Path of the Polonoreste: Endangered Peoples of Western Brazil*, 1981; Robert Lee Spires, "As línguas faladas do Brasil," *América Indígena*, 47 (1987), 455–79.

WAYUU. See GUAJIRO.

WAZAIZARA. See GUARATEGAJA.

WECIARE. See WOKIARE.

WEHETARA. See PIRA-TAPUYA.

WEIDYENYE. See MUNDURUKÚ.

WEJWO. See MATACO.

WEREKENA. See WARIKYÁNA.

WESTERN BAKIRI. See BAKIRÍ.

WESTERN BORORO. See BORÓRO.

WESTERN SUYA. See BEICO DO PAU.

WESTERN TIMBIRA. See APINAYÉ.

WESTERN TOBA. See TOBA.

WIAUNYEN. See MUNDURUKÚ.

WINAO. The Winao (Guinau) were an Arawakan*-speaking group of Amerindians who were recently absorbed by the Makiritáre. They called themselves the Temomoyami. See YEKUANA.

WINAVI. See PUINAVE.

WINTAPERI. See AMARAKAERI.

WIRAFED. The Wirafed people are a tiny surviving group of Kawahíb* Indians. The Kawahíb once ranged over a large area of the Tapajós-Madeira River Basin in what is today the state of Amazonas, Brazil, but in the eighteenth century they dispersed into a series of many separate tribes because of the aggressive expansion of the Munduruкú* Indians. One of the small tribes emerging from the larger Kawahíb group was the Wirafed. Rubber collectors and gold prospectors in the early twentieth century put more pressure on the Wirafed, drastically reducing their population to the point that ceremonial life was no longer possible. Today there are fewer than 50 Wirafed left, and they are living, intermixed with Paranawat* and Tukunafed* Indians, along the Riosinho, Leitao, Muqui, and Cacoal rivers. Most of them work as laborers on ranches and rubber plantations in the area and are in permanent contact with neo-Brazilian society, to which they are slowly acculturating.

REFERENCE: Theodore L. Stoddard, ed., *Indians of Brazil in the Twentieth Century*, 1967.

WITOTO. The Witoto (Uitoto, Fitita, Huito, Huitoto, Hitote, Ouitoto, Huitata, Guitoto, Murui, Kaime, Xura, Seueni, Jayruya, Mekka, Meneca, Menekka, Bue) are a tribe of perhaps 12,000 Amerindians who live upstream of Araracuara on the Caquetá River in the Colombian and Peruvian Amazon. The two great ceremonial divisions of the Witoto are the Murui,* who live in the western reaches of their territory, and the Muinane,* who live in the east. These Muinane should not be confused with the Bora*-speaking Muinane. Today the Muinane have largely been absorbed by the Murui. Another division—the Meneca— consists of approximately 1,600 people along the Putumayo and Ampiyacu rivers in Colombia and Peru. There are also other Witoto settlements in the departments of Caqueta, Vaupés, Amazonas, and Meta in Colombia. In 1988, approximately 300 Witoto were living on the Kilometro 6 y 11-Carretera Leticia-Tarapaca reservation in Colombia; there were also 262 Witoto on the Puerto Sabalo y Los Monos reservation, 256 on the Monochoa reservation, 56 on the El Quince reservation, 140 on the Witora reservation, 158 on the Samaritana reservation, 196 on the Jirijiri reservation, and 10,400 on the Predio Putumayo reservation. Other Witoto dialects include Nonuya (Noanawa, Noaname, Achote, Achiote), and Ocaina* (Okaina, Dukaiya). Their language is Tupian in its origins, and approximately 1,700 Witoto still speak it. The Witoto were first contacted by Europeans in the early seventeenth century, but sustained contact did not come until the late nineteenth century. Although hunting and fishing consume a great deal of their time and hold great symbolic importance in Witoto culture, most of the tribe's nutrients come from the manioc, maize, sweet potatoes, plaintains, and bananas that they raise in tribal gardens. Until the end of the nineteenth century, the Witoto numbered more than 40,000 people, but the wild rubber boom of the 1890s and early 1900s devastated them, bringing thousands of neo-Colombians and their diseases into Witoto territory and drastically reducing their population. Until the twentieth century, they lived on the Caraparana and Igar-aparana rivers, but in the 1930s they began an outmigration and headed for more isolated sites in the Amazon jungles. Large numbers of the Witoto and their subtribes were dislocated and moved, the vast majority dying from disease or being assimilated into neo-Colombian society.

REFERENCES: Michael J. Eden and Angela Andrade, "Ecological Aspects of Swid-den Cultivation among the Andoke and Witoto Indians of the Colombian Amazon," *Human Ecology*, 15 (1987), 339–59; Ministerio de Gobierno, *Aspetos de la cultura material de grupos étnicos de Colombia*, 1979.

WITOTOAN. The term "Witotoan" is used by linguists to refer to a small group of Amerindian languages. At one time, the Witotoan languages included those of the Andoquero and Witoto* Indians of Colombia; the Coeruna Indians of Brazil; and the Ocaina,* Orejón,* Nonuya,* and Achiote Indians of Peru.

REFERENCES: Harriet E. Manelis Klein and Louisa R. Stark, *South American Indian Languages: Retrospect and Prospect*, 1985; Geoffrey K. Pullum, ed., *Handbook of Amazonian Languages*, 1986.

WIWI. See MALAYO.

WOKIARE. The Wokiare (Wociare, Uiquiare, Uiquire, Uaiquire, Weciare, and Guaikiare) are descendents of the Karib*-speaking Voqueares who lived at the headwaters of the Paru River in the Orinoco River drainage area of Guyana and Venezuela. They are extremely close relatives of the Yabarana* and in recent years have largely been absorbed by them. See YABARANA.

WORROW. See WARRAU.

WOTUHA. See PIAROA.

WOYAMANA. See WAIWÁI.

WUHANA. See MAKUNA.

WULWA. See SUMU.

X

XAGUETEO. See KADUVEO.

XAKLÉNG. See AWEIKOMA.

XAKRIABÁ. The Xakriabá (Shacriabá, Chikriabá, Xikriabá) were an Akwẽ*-speaking Gê* people who lived in the Tocantins River drainage area of central Brazil. In the eighteenth century, the Xakriabá accepted settlement on the great reservations, or aldeias, and gradually disapppeared as a tribal unit. Most anthropologists believe that the Xakriabá are extinct as a functioning social unit, although periodically in recent years the Brazilian government has received reports that isolated individuals claiming to be Xakriabá are living in the state of Minas Gerais. At present, there are approximately 3,500 people of known Xakriabá descent who live in the State of Mato Grosso, Brazil, but they speak Portuguese and are assimilated into the larger society.

REFERENCES: David Maybury-Lewis, *Dialectical Societies: The Gê and Boróro of Central Brazil*, 1979; Robert Lee Spires, "As línguas faladas do Brasil," *América Indígena*, 47 (1987), 455–79.

XAMATARI. The Xamatari (Shamatari) are a branch of the Yanoama* linguistic group of southeastern Venezuela and northern Brazil. They live in the Serra Parima Mountains and pursue a highly isolated lifestyle. See YANOAMA.

XAMBIOÁ. The Xambioá (Shambioá) are a subgroup of the Karajá* tribe of Brazil. Today there are fewer than 100 Xambioá living near the rapids of the Araguaia River. See KARAJÁ.

XARÚMA. The Xarúma are a highly isolated tribe of Amerindians who speak a Karib* language and live an isolated existence on the savannas of the northwestern region of the state of Pará, Brazil, just south of the Guyanese border. As a savanna people. they devote much of their time to a subsistence economy that revolves around hunting and gathering. They have adopted metal technology from neo-Brazilians, but have resisted most other forms of acculturation. Anthropologists place the Xarúma population at approximately 300 people.

REFERENCE: Edwin Brooks, et al., *Tribes of the Amazon Basin, Brazil, 1972*, 1973.

XAVÁNTE. Approximately 4,400 Xavánte (A'we, Akuen, Chavante, Shavante) Indians now live in the eastern part of northern Mato Grosso State in central Brazil, between the Rio das Mortes and the upper tributaries of the Xingú River. They can also be found at the headwaters of the Batovi and Teles Peres rivers. The Xavánte occupy nine villages, each of which either has a Brazilian government Indian post or is attached to a Salesian mission. The Xavánte belong to the Gê* branch of the Gê language family. When first contacted by Europeans in the eighteenth century, the tribe was living east of the Araguaia River in what is today Goiás State. At the time, they were one people with the Xerénte* (Sherénte). The Xavánte briefly accepted resettlement to a reservation in Goiás in the 1780s but soon left, crossing the Tocantins River and splitting from the Xerénte. By staying west of the frontier line, the Xavánte maintained their cultural integrity until the 1950s by violently resisting contact with neo-Brazilians and striking terror into them. Until the early 1970s, the Xavánte depended for the most part on wild foods, spending much of their time on long, nomadic trips to hunt and gather food. They spent only one month in the year working on their manioc, maize, and bean gardens. Their lifestyle changed dramatically in the 1960s, when huge neo-Brazilian cattle ranches and rice plantations surrounded their homeland. Today the Xavánte have only one long hunt a year, and it is confined to the reservation. They have successfully made the transition to agriculture, with rice as their main product.

REFERENCES: Nancy M. Flowers, "Seasonal Factors in Subsistence, Nutrition, and Child Growth in a Central Brazilian Indian Community," in Raymond B. Hames and William T. Vickers, eds., *Adaptive Responses of Native Amazonians*, 1983, 357–90; David Maybury-Lewis, *Akwe-Shavante Society*, 1974; Robert Lee Spires, "As línguas faladas do Brasil," *América Indígena*, 47 (1987), 455–79; Dennis Warner et al., "Subsistence Productivity and Hunting Effort in Native South America," *Human Ecology*, 7 (1979), 303–15.

XEBERO. See JEBERO.

XERENO-MUNICHI. See PARANAPURA.

XERÉNTE. The Xerénte (Serente, Sherente, Cherente) are a Gê*-speaking people who occupied the east bank of the Tocantins River in Brazil. In the eighteenth century, when Portuguese gold seekers contacted the Xerénte in what is now central and northern Goiás, the Xerénte were united with the Akwẽ*-Xavánte* people. Between 1800 and 1820, however, the Akwẽ-Xavánte decided to leave the area in order to get out of touch with the Portuguese. They crossed the Tocantins River and headed west, while the Xerénte remained behind on the Tocantins. Because the Tocantins was an artery for advancing colonization, the Xerénte were soon surrounded by neo-Brazilian settlers, while the Xavánte were free to pursue an aboriginal lifestyle further west. Roman Catholic and Protestant missionaries have been in close contact with the Xerénte for more than a century, and the Brazilian Indian Service maintains two posts for them. All Xerénte men and women speak Portuguese as a second language, although their private language remains the native tongue. Using simple tools, they practice a slash-and-burn agriculture that differs little from that of poor neo-Brazilian backwoodsmen. The Xerénte do not maintain livestock, and they are frequently accused of killing other people's cattle. At present, there are approximately 1,000 members of the Xerénte tribe, who live near the Tocantinia Indian Park in the state of Goiás, Brazil.

REFERENCES: Nancy M. Flowers, "Seasonal Factors in Subsistence, Nutrition, and Child Growth in a Central Brazilian Indian Community," in Raymond B. Hames and William T. Vickers, eds., *Adaptive Responses of Native Amazonians*, 1983, 179–202; David Maybury-Lewis, *Dialectical Societies: The Gê and Bororo of Central Brazil*, 1979; Robert Lee Spires, "As línguas faladas do Brasil," *América Indígena*, 47 (1987), 455–79.

XETÁ. See ARÉ.

XEVERO. See JEBERO.

XIBITAONO. The Xibitaono were a small colony of the Cocama* Indians who lived on the Santiago River near Santiago de las Montanas in Peru. See COCAMA.

XICAQUE. See JICAQUE.

XICRÍN. See XIKRÍN.

XIKRÍ. See XIKRÍN.

XIKRIABÁ. See XAKRIABÁ.

XIKRÍN. The Xikrín (Xikrí, Xicrín, Shikrí, Diore, Djore) are part of the Gê* linguistic family and are a Northern Kayapó* tribe of Amerindians. They inhabit the lands around the Caetete River, a left tributary of the Itacaiunas River, itself a tributary of the Tocantins, as well as the Bacajá reservation on the middle Bacajá River in the state of Pará, Brazil. Originially part of the Gorotíre* tribe, they split off and gradually migrated up the Fresco River toward the Tocantins.

Anthropologists reached the tribe in the 1890s, but early in the 1900s the Xikrín came into bloody conflict with neo-Brazilian rubber gatherers; those hostilities continued until the 1950s. Similar conflicts with nut gatherers led to extermination expeditions against the Xikrín. The Xikrín tribe today numbers approximately 450 people still residing in their same habitat. There are two subgroups of the Xikrín—the Itacayunas and the Bacajá, or Bemontíre. French Dominican priests and the Brazilian Indian Foundation are in regular contact with the tribe. The major threat facing the Xikrín is the recent discovery of huge iron ore deposits near them in Serra dos Carajas. Industrial development and population influx to work the mines will have a dramatic impact on the tribe.

REFERENCES: Raymond Caron, *Curé d'Indiens*, 1971; Protasio Frikel, "Notes on the Present Situation of the Xikrín Indians of the Rio Caetete," *Revista do Museo Paulista*, 14 (1963), 145–58; Robert Lee Spires, "As línguas faladas do Brasil," *América Indígena*, 47 (1987), 455–79.

XINCA. The Xinca are a tiny, nearly extinct group of Amerindians who today live in Taxisco, Chiquimulilla, and Guazacapan in the department of Sante Rosa, Guatemala. Closely associated historically with the Lenca* of Guatemala, the Xinca are from an isolated linguistic group. They could not survive the conquest pressures of Spanish settlers in the sixteenth and seventeenth centuries nor more recent acculturation pressures. The Xinca tribe does not really function anymore. As late as the 1970s, there were 55 aged people who still spoke Xinca, but their numbers had declined to only 6 people by 1987. All of them are old and bilingual, employing Spanish most of the time. There are, however, approximately 3,500 other people in Guatemala who identify themselves as Xinca Indians, even though they use Spanish as their primary language.

REFERENCES: Melanie A. Counce and William V. Davidson, "Indians of Central America 1980s," *Cultural Survival Quarterly*, 13 (1989), 39–41; Gloria Tujab, "Lenguas indígenas que se encuentran en vias de extinción," *América Indígena*, 47 (1987), 529–33.

XIPAIA. See SHIPAYA.

XIPINAW. See XIPIANÁWA.

XIPINÁWA. There are several hundred people of Amerindian descent who call themselves Xipináwa (Shipináwa, Shipináhua) and are descendents of a Panoan*-speaking people who lived in what is today the southern region of the states of Amazonas and Acre. They have lost the use of their aboriginal language and appear to be no different from surrounding mestizos who make a living as laborers and subsistence farmers. Nevertheless, the Xipináwa, even without a tribal organization or surviving tribal ceremonies, still view themselves as Indians with Xipináwa ancestry.

REFERENCE: Theodore L. Stoddard, ed., *Indians of Brazil in the Twentieth Century*, 1967.

XIRIANA. The Xiriana (Siriana) are an extremely isolated Amerindian group of people who live on the Mucajai, Uraricara, Erico, Branco, and Paragua rivers in northwestern Brazil and across the border in Venezuela. They are a semi-nomadic people who rely on horticulture only sparingly and prefer hunting and fishing along the rivers and streams of the area. They still speak the native language, part of the Xiriana group, although more and more tribal members are becoming familiar with Portuguese and Spanish.

REFERENCE: Theodore L. Stoddard, ed., *Indians of Brazil in the Twentieth Century*, 1967.

XIRIANA. Not to be confused with the Xiriana of the northwestern Rio Branco region of Brazil along the Venezuelan border, the Xiriana are a tiny, isolated group of Arawakan*-speaking Amerindians who live along several tributaries of the Rio Negro in the state of Amazonas, Brazil, near the Venezuelan border. They pursue a riverine lifestyle and plant manioc in tribal gardens. Although they have developed a taste for modern trade goods, they nurture a strong sense of tribal identity and separateness. Increasing numbers of the Xiriana are coming to understand Portuguese and Spanish.

REFERENCE: Theodore L. Stoddard, ed., *Indians of Brazil in the Twentieth Century*, 1967.

XITIBO. See SETEBO.

XÍVARI. See JÍVARO.

XOGLÉNG. See AWEIKOMA.

XOKLÉNG. See AWEIKOMA.

XOKÓ. See SHOCÓ.

XOKRE. See AWEIKOMA.

XOKRENG. See AWEIKOMA.

XORSHIO. See CHAMACOCO.

XUIKINA-WO. See CHOROTÉ.

XUKURÚ. The Xukurú are descendents of a tribe of Amerindians who once lived in what is today the state of Pernambuco, Brazil. As late as the 1930s, they still had a separate tribal identity. Although they speak Portuguese and no longer function socially or culturally as an Indian tribe, their vocabulary is still replete with surviving Xukurú words. There are approximately 1,500 people of

Xukurú descent living today as mestizos near the city of Cimbres in the state of Pernambuco.

REFERENCE: Theodore L. Stoddard, ed., *Indians of Brazil in the Twentieth Century*, 1967.

XUKURÚ-KARIRÍ. Until the 1930s, the Natu, Xoko, and Xukurú were separate tribal entities of Amerindians living in the states of Pernambuco and Alagoas, Brazil. During the last thirty years, those three groups ceased to function as differentiated social units because of population decline and acculturation; intermarriage occurred among them. Emerging from that assimilation was a new group of people who, under the influence of messianic religious cult leaders, began to call themselves Xukurú-Karirí. Today there are approximately 700 people who identify themselves as Xukurú-Karirí. Thoroughly acculturated to neo-Brazilian society, they live in the state of Alagoas. They do have, however, an Indian identity, and many of them live in such national Indian parks as the Alfredo Damasco Indian Park and the Ireneu Indian Park.

REFRENCE: Theodore L. Stoddard, ed., *Indians of Brazil in the Twentieth Century*, 1967.

XURA. See WITOTO.

Y

YABAÁNA. See YABARÁNA.

YABARÁNA. The Yabaránaa (Yabaana, Guaiquairo) are a Karib*-speaking tribe of Amerindians who live on the headwaters of the Marauia and Cauaboris rivers, both tributaries of the Rio Negro, in the state of Amazonas, Brazil. They can also be found in the vicinity of San Juan de Manapiare in the federal territory of Amazonas in Venezuela. The Yabarána live a riverine existence near the Venezuelan border and, although they have a growing affinity for neo-Brazilian trade goods, they are in only intermittent contact with the larger society. Yabarána society was totally disrupted by the twentieth-century rubber boom, and today fewer than 50 people still speak the aboriginal language. Nearly 20,000 other people live along the middle Ventauri River in Venezuela who do not speak the language or associate as a tribal entity but who still are aware of their Yabarána ancestry. The aboriginal culture is all but extinct, but a sense of ethnicity survives.

REFERENCES: Estéban Emilio Mosonyi, "La revitalización lingüística y la realidad venezolaña," *América Indígena*, 47 (1987), 653–62; Theodore L. Stoddard, ed., *Indians of Brazil in the Twentieth Century*, 1967; Johannes Wilbert, *Zur Kenntnis der Yabarana*, 1959.

YABUTI. See JABUTÍ.

YAGANO. See YAHGAN.

YAGUA. The Yagua (Peba, Piba-Yagua, Yahua, Llagua, Nixamvo, Mishara, Yava) are a tropical forest people who speak a language from the Peban family. They call themselves the Nihamwo. They traditionally lived on the headwaters of the Yaguas River and the Upper Guerari River in Peru, where they practiced a slash-and-burn horticulture with sweet manioc as their staple. In the mid-eighteenth century, several hundred Yagua Indians joined the Mission of San Ignacio, which the Jesuits administered. The Yagua were always closely associated with the Peba tribe, and the two groups had virtually fused together by the twentieth century. The rubber boom of the late nineteenth and early twentieth centuries devastated the Yagua, and they were hurt again by a smallpox epidemic in the 1930s. They are not becoming extinct at all, although their relatively recent adoption of Western dress has rendered them less visible. The Yagua live in communities of one to twenty families, although most of the communities consist of three to four houses of the typical Amazon style of frame buildings on stilts. Today the tribe numbers approximately 5,000 people, most of whom function as subsistence farmers in permanent contact with neo-Peruvian society. They are concentrated along the Napo, Orosa, Arambaza, Cajocuma, Atacuari, and Yavari rivers. Approximately 50 Yagua live across the border in the commissary of Amazonas in Colombia. There are also a few Yagua families in Brazil. They raise plantains, bananas, sweet manioc, sugar cane, pineapples, papaya, sweet potatoes, and potatoes.

REFERENCES: Jean-Pierre Chaumeil, *Between Zoo and Slavery: The Yagua of Eastern Peru in Their Present Situation*, 1984; Paul Stewart Powlison, *Yagua Mythology: Epic Tendencies in a New World Mythology*, 1985; Stefano Varese, *The Forest Indians in the Present Political Situation of Peru*, 1972.

YAGUMA. The Yaguma were a Karib*-speaking people who lived east of the Culuene River beyond the Tanguro tributary in the Upper Xingú Basin of Central Brazil. Sometime before establishment of the Xingú Indian Park in 1961, the Yaguma ceased to exist as a tribe, although a few elderly members of the tribe are still alive, residing with other groups.

REFERENCE: Ellen B. Basso, *The Kalapalo Indians of Central Brazil*, 1973.

YAHGAN. The Yahgan (Yagano, Yamana) are a foraging tribe of Amerindians who once lived in the Beagle Channel of Tierra del Fuego in Argentina. Although the Yahgan came into contact with Spanish maritime explorers in the early 1500s, there was no really sustained contact until the nineteenth century. The Yahgan were a nomadic people who traveled along the coast in long canoes that were able to hold several families. They lived off shellfish, seals, fish, and birds and lived in small, temporary, grass huts. Until the late nineteenth century, the Yahgan population totaled approximately 3,000 people, but a rapid decline set in once the tribe came into frequent contact with neo-Argentinian settlers. Typhoid, whooping cough, and smallpox epidemics decimated the tribe. By the mid–1880s, there were only 400 Yahgan still alive, and they declined in numbers to 200 in 1900 and 100 in 1913. Today there are only a handful of people in Chile and Argentina who are still aware of their Yahgan heritage. They live in the tiny village of Ukika near Puerto Williams on the Isle of Navariño in Chile.

REFERENCES: Martin Gusinde, *Los Indios de Tierra del Fuego*, 1982; Johannes Wilbert and Karin Simoneau, *Folk Tales of the Yamana*, 1977.

YAHUA. See YAGUA.

YAHUNA. The Yahuna are a nearly extinct tribe of Amerindians whose traditional homeland was along the Yapiya, Popeyaca, and Icapuya rivers, all of which are tributaries of the Apaporis River in Colombia. The Yahuna were contacted by Jesuit missionaries in the seventeenth century, and subsequently by Franciscans and Augustinians, but it was the rubber collectors and slavers of the late nineteenth and early twentieth centuries who destroyed the tribe. Today there are only about 40 Yahuna still alive, and they have adopted the language and culture of the Tanimuko* and Makuna* Indians, since they now live among them and have intermarried with them.

REFERENCES: Patricio von Hildebrand, "Observaciones preliminares sobre utilización de tierras y fauna por los indígenas del río Miriti-Paraná," *Revista Colombiana de Antropología*, 18 (1975), 183–292.

YAHUP. See MAKÚ.

YALUDNDE. See NAMBIQUÁRA.

YAMAMADÍ. The Yamamadí (Iamamadí, Jamamadí, Jamamandí, Kapinamarí, Kapana, Amamatí, Jamamirí, and Anamarí) are an Arawakan*-speaking group of Amerindians who occupy approximately a dozen sites on the west side of the Purús River, stretching from the southern tributaries of the Tapaua River to the mouth of the Iaco River in the state of Amazonas in Brazil. At the time of the Portuguese conquest at the beginning of the sixteenth century, there were more than 4,000 Yamamadí Indians, but disease and dislocation rapidly reduced those numbers. The rubber boom of the late 1800s and early 1900s further devastated them, particularly when neo-Brazilian rubber gatherers enslaved many Yamamadí to help them with their work. Today there are approximately 500 Yamamadí Indians, all in permanent contact with neo-Brazilian society. Many speak Portuguese as well as the tribal language, and all are acculturated to neo-Brazilian trade goods and clothing.

REFERENCES: Robert Lee Spires, "As línguas faladas do Brasil," *América Indígena*, 47 (1987), 455–79; Theodore L. Stoddard, ed., *Indians of Brazil in the Twentieth Century*, 1967.

YAMANA. See YAHGAN.

YAMEO. The Yameo were a group of Amerindians who spoke a Peban language and lived along the Marañon and Amazon rivers, from the mouth of the Tigre River to the Nanay River. Early in the seventeenth century, neo-Peruvian slavers reached the Yameo, who violently resisted the contact. Spanish missionaries established settlements among them in the 1680s and 1690s, but the contact brought diseases that reduced the Yameo population from 8,000 in 1690 to only 1,000 in 1767, when the Jesuit missionaries left. The demographic decline continued, with the Yameo population falling to 240 in 1851, 150 in 1860, and 50 in 1925. By that time, all but three of them spoke Spanish, Cocama*, or Quechua* as their primary language. Although there are no more Yameo Indians alive, there may still be isolated individuals in Peru who are aware of their Yameo heritage.

REFERENCE: Darcy Ribeiro and Mary Ruth Wise, *Los grupos étnicos de la amazona peruana*, 1978.

YAMINÁWA. The Yamináwa (Jamináwa, Jaminaua, Iamináwa, Yamináhua, Yumináwa) are an Amerindian tribe of Panoan*-speaking people scattered widely in several small villages in the state of Acre, Brazil, along the lower Chandless River, the lower Iaco River, the Acre River above the town of Brasilia; on the Juruá River, as well as in the Curiuja Basin of the Piedras River in Peru; on the Acre River 200 kilometers west of Cobija; and on the Tahuamanu River 70 kilometers west of Porveir in Bolivia. The primary Yamináwa subgroups are the Masronhua (Masrodawa), Chandináhua (Chanináwa), Nishináhua (Nishidáwa), Chitonáhua (Chitodáwa), and Shaonáhua (Shaodáwa). The rubber boom of 1894–1920 devastated the Yamináwa, drastically reducing their population because of slavery, violence, and disease. The Yamináwa total approximately 1,000 people and are in a state of permanent contact with neo-Brazilian and neo-Peruvian society, speaking Portuguese and Spanish, wearing Western clothing, and working as laborers to generate cash for trade goods. That permanent contact did not begin until 20 to 30 years ago. They still maintain a sense of tribal identity, however. Traditionally a hunting, fishing, and foraging people, the Yamináwa have recently turned to agriculture, although their proclivity for changing residence in their tribal territory makes farming a marginal pursuit.

REFERENCE: Kim Hill, "Macronutrient Modifications of Optimal Foraging Theory: An Approach Using Indifferent Curves Applied to Some Modern Foragers," *Human Ecology*, 16 (1988), 157–98; Pedro Plaza Martínez and Juan Carvajal Carvajal, *Etnías y lenguas de Bolivia*, 1985; Gustavo Solís F., "Multilinguismo y extinciones de lenguas," *América Indígena*, 47 (1987), 630–45; Graham Townsley, "The Outside Overwhelms: Yaminahua Dual Organization and Its Decline," in Harald O. Sklar and Frank Salomon, eds., *Natives and Neighbors in South America: Anthropological Essays*, 1987, 355–72.

YAMINIHUA. See YAMINÁWA.

YANA. See TAPIETÉ.

YANACONA. The term "Yanacona" is widely used in Ecuador to describe Indians, usually Quechua*-speaking, who work as servants in the homes of well-to-do neo-Ecuadoreans.

REFERENCE: Albert William Bork and Georg Maier, *Historical Dictionary of Ecuador*, 1973.

YANAIGUA. See TAPIETÉ.

YANAM. See YANOAMA.

YANAPERO. The term "Yanapero" is used in Ecuador to describe Amerindians who are detached from a tribal setting and permanently attached to a hacienda or latifundia estate as permanent peasants. They have no land of their own and are usually caught in extraordinarily difficult economic situations.
REFERENCE: S. Lyman Tyler, *Indians of South America*, 1976.

YANAYGUA. See TAPIETÉ.

YANESHA. See AMUESHA.

YANOAMA. The term Yanoama (Yainomá, Yanohami, Yanomami, Yanomani, Yanomám, Yanám, Yanomamo, Yanomami, Ninám) is a linguistic term referring to one of the largest groups of suriving Amerindians in Amazonian South America. There are four main subgroups of the Yanoama people. The northern group is the Sanumá (Sanimá, Sanomá); the central lowland group consists of the Orinoco Waiká (Uaica, Oico) and the Ocama Waiká; the central mountain group, which is composed of the Cobari of the upper Ocama and Matacuni rivers, the Barafiri (Barajiri) on the upper Buuta-u and Majecodo rivers, and the Yanamaya of the Orinoco headwaters; and the southern group, termed the Yainomá (Yanomán, Yanomám) or Shamatiri (Xamatari), which extends into northern Brazil. Historically, the following terms have also been used by explorers and other Indians when referring to the Yanoama: Aiwateri, Shirishana, Shirixana, Shiriana, Shirianna, Xiriana, Xirishana, Crishana, Kirishana, Guaharibo, Guajaribo, Guaharivo, Guariba, Waika, Guaica, Guaika, Uaica, Shamatari, Xamatari, Padahuri, Pakidai, Parafuri, and Parahuri.

Over the centuries, the Yanoama have been extremely isolated in the Parima highlands of southern Venezuela and northern Brazil, with little to no contact with other Indians or with Europeans and mestizos. While all the other tropical forest people surrounding the Yanoama cultivate manioc, the Yanoama raise plantains as their staple. They did not develop a river culture, preferring land travel. Their 30,000-square-mile habitat is centered at the Sierra Parima and extends east along the axis of the Sierra Pacaraima to include on the north the headwaters of such important tributaries of the lower Orinoco as the Erebato-Caura and Paragua-Caroni, and on the south the small headwater streams that enter the Uraricoera-Branco system. The Yanoama also occupy the headwaters of several Rio Negro tributaries, the headwaters of the Mavaca River, and the headwaters of the Yatua and Siapa rivers. Systematic neo-Venezuelan contact with the Yanoama did not really begin until the 1970s. Today the Yanoama total more than 20,000 people and still live an aboriginal lifestyle. During the 1980s, however, penetration of Yanoama territory by neo-Brazilian settlers and gold prospectors increased dramatically. In 1988, to satisfy the demands of economic developers, the Brazilian government reduced Yanoama land from 8 million to only 2.5 million hectares, and the land was divided into 19 noncontiguous areas. The decision will no doubt accelerate the decline of the Yanoama.

REFERENCES: "Brazilian Government Reduces Yanomami Territory by 70 Percent," *Cultural Survival Quarterly*, 13 (1989), 47; Napoleon A. Chagnon, *Yanomamo: The Fierce People*, 1968; Raymond B. Hames, "Monoculture, Polyculture, and Polyvariety in Tropical Forest Swidden Cultivation," *Human Ecology*, 11 (1983), 13–34; "Roraima, Brazil: A Death Warning," *Cultural Survival Quarterly*, 13 (1989), 59–62; William J. Smole, *The Yanoama Indians: A Cultural Geography*, 1976; Robert Lee Spires, "As línguas faladas do Brasil," *América Indígena*, 47 (1987), 455–79.

YANOHAMI. See YANOAMA.

YANOMAM. See YANOAMA.

YANOMAMI. See YANOAMA.

YANOMANI. See YANOAMA.

YANOMANO. See YANOAMA.

YANOMAYA. See YANOAMA.

YAPITALAGA. See PILAGÁ.

YAPOCO. See PIAPOCO.

YARI. The Yari Indians are a small group of Amerindians living in the department of Caquetá, near the Yari River, in Colombia. They have maintained a powerful sense of isolation from neo-Colombian society over the centuries, but disease has nevertheless devastated them. The Yari pursue a subsistence lifestyle of hunting and gathering, as well as planting manioc to provide a steady protein source. Their population has dropped below 100 people and extinction as a tribe is likely in the next several decades.

REFERENCE: Leah B. Ellis and Linda Criswell, eds., *Estudiemos las culturas indígenas de Colombia*, 1984.

YARUMA. The Yaruma were a group of Amerindians who existed as a Gê*-speaking tribe. They pursued a tropical forest, horticultural existence on the Tanguro River in the Xingú River drainage area of Brazil, but they were constantly at war with their mortal enemies, the Kuikúru.* Eventually, in the early decades of the twentieth century, the Kuikúru almost wiped out the Yaruma people. Those Yaruma who did survive went to live with the Suyá* Indians, who spoke a similar Gê language. Over the years, the Yaruma have merged with the Suyá, although there may still be individuals among the Suyá who are aware of their Yaruma roots.

REFERENCE: Adrian Crowell, *The Tribe That Hides From Man*, 1979.

YARURA. See YARURO.

YARURO. The Yaruro (Yarura) are a tribe of Amerindians who have been living for centuries in the llanos, or dry plains, of southern Venezuela, particularly in the southern part of the state of Apure. They call themselves the Pume. They are distantly related to the Chibchan* language group. Jesuits established the first missions among the Yaruro in 1739, but the Indians were loath to remain in one place. Tribal population dropped because of diseases imported by Europeans, but it stabilized in the late eighteenth century. The flood-covered llanos have forced the Yaruro to live on west-to-east flowing rivers. In the rainy season, the Yaruro practice a slash-and-burn horticulture to raise manioc, corn, plantains, and several other crops, but during the dry season they primarily fish along the rivers and hunt such river animals as turtles and crocodiles. Although the Yaruro have adopted much European metal technology—fishhooks, knives, and machetes—their tribal value system has maintained its resiliency. At the beginning of the twentieth century, anthropologists were convinced that the Yaruro were headed for extinction, but the tribe recovered as a social group, even though its political organization no longer functions. Their tribal population today totals nearly 4,000 people.

REFERENCES: Anthony Leeds, "The Ideology of the Yaruro Indians in Relation to Socio-economic Organization," *Anthropológica*, 9 (1960), 1–10; Philippe Mitrani, "Santé et maladie chez un groupe d'indiens du bassin de l'Orenque; les Yaruro de l'Apure," Ph.D. dissertation, University of Paris, 1976; Estéban Emilio Mosonyi, "La revitalización lingüística y la realidad Venezolana,"*América Indígena*, 47 (1987), 653–61.

YATE. See FULNIÓ.

YAUAPITÍ. See IAUALAPITÍ.

YAUARANA. See YEKUANA.

YAULAPITÍ. See IAUALAPITÍ.

YAUNA. See MAKUNA.

YAVA. See YAGUA.

YAWALAPITÍ. See IAUALAPITÍ.

YAWAPERI. Also known historically as the Waimiri-Atroarí, Atroarí, Atruahí, Krixána, Krishána, and Waiomirí, the Yawaperi are an Amerindian tribe of more than 2,000 people who live today in a large jungle refuge between the Alalau,

Uatuma, and Jauaperi rivers north of Manaus in Brazil. Their traditional homeland occupied a vast area east of the Rio Branco and the Rio Negro rivers, south
to the junction of the Rio Negro with the Amazon and east through the Urubu,
Uatuma, and Jatapu River basins. Of Karib* extraction, the Yawaperi have been
widely known for the past century for their aggressiveness. In the 1860s, when
neo-Brazilians began settling on Yawaperi territory, the tribe launched an all-
out war, inviting military assaults against themselves by government officials.
War prevailed throughout the 1860s and 1870s against the Yawaperi. Peaceful
co-existence emerged in the 1890s, but only because settlement in Yawaperi
territory declined. The Indians lived in the forests between Manaus and the
savannas of the upper Branco River, a generally isolated region. From the 1920s
to the 1970s, the Yawaperi killed almost all intruders—settlers, priests, and
scientists. In the mid–1970s, when the government-built Manaus-Boa Vista highway cut through Yawaperi territory, the Indians again fought back, killing dozens
of Indian agents and construction workers. Although peaceful contacts with the
Yawaperi increased in the 1980s, their accommodation to neo-Brazilian society
has been tenuous at best. Many of the existing Yawaperi villages are threatened
by flooding from the Balbina Regional Hydroelectric Project.

REFERENCES: Paul L. Aspelin and Silvio Coelho dos Santos, *Indian Areas Threatened by Hydroelectric Projects in Brazil*, 1981; Shelton H. Davis, *Victims of the Miracle:
Development and the Indians of Brazil*, 1977; Robert Lee Spires, "As línguas faladas
do Brasil," *América Indígena*, 47 (1987), 455–79.

YAWARANA. See YEKUANA.

YAWARETA-TAPIIYA. See KAWAHÍB.

YAWI. See TIRIYÓ.

YCAHUATE. See SECOYA.

YEBÁ-MASÃ. A small Eastern Tukanoan* lanugage tribe of Amerindians, the
Yebá-Masã (Yepá-Mahsã, Yepa-Matso) live in the Vaupés River drainage region
of southeastern Colombia and in the state of Amazonas, Brazil. There were
sporadic European contacts with the Yebá-Masã in the eighteenth and nineteenth
centuries. Portuguese missions were established temporarily along the upper
Vaupés in the 1780s, but systematic evangelization of the tribe did not begin
until 1914 when Roman Catholic priests established missions there. Protestant
missionaries made some inroads after World War I. The tribal economy revolves
around manioc production. The Yebá-Masã interact with other Indian tribes in
the area but rarely with whites, except for missionaries and rubber collectors,
because of the extreme geographical isolation of the area. There are several
hundred Yebá-Masã today who acknowledge tribal membership and speak the
native language. The majority of the tribe resides in Colombia.

REFERENCES: Jean A. Jackson, *The Fish People: Linguistic Exogamy and Tukanoan Identity in Northwest Amazonia*, 1983; Gerardo Reichel-Dolmatoff, *Amazonian Cosmos: The Sexual and Religious Symbolism of the Tukano Indians*, 1985; Robert Lee Spires, "As línguas faladas do Brasil," *Américá Indígena*, 47 (1987), 455–79.

YEBÁ-MATSÁ. See YEBÁ-MASÁ.

YECUANA. See YEKUANA.

YE'CUANA. See YEKUANA.

YEKUANA. The Yekuana are a Karib*-language group of tropical forest Amerindians who live along the Merevari, Paraba, Mazaruni, Erebato, and Cunaracuni rivers in the eastern part of the federal territory of Amazonas and the southern reaches of the state of Bolívar, Venezuela. They also dwell in a small section of northern Brazil. Historically, they have also been known as Yekuana (Dekuhana, Decuana, Iekuana, Yekuhana, Ye'cuana, Yecuana), Maingcóng (Maiongking, Maiongcóng, Maiongkóng, Mayongóng, Mayonggóng, Maschongcóng, Maschongkóng), Munangone, Waiomgomo, Makiritáre (Maquiritáre, Maquitáre, Markitáre), and Yawarana (Yahaurana). Anthropologists have recognized four Yejuana subtribes: The Kunuhana (Kunuana), Ihuruhana, Dekuana, and Yekuana. The homeland of the Yekuana has been one of the most isolated in South America, which explains why they remain one of the least acculturated of American Indian tribes. Manuel Román, the Jesuit missionary, first contacted them in 1744, and intermittent contacts by other Europeans occurred over the next two centuries. The Yekuana population numbers approximately 3,000 people in Venezuela and several hundred in Brazil. They still pursue a largely indigenous lifestyle, except for the use of metal gardening, hunting, and fishing tools. Their way of life is typical of other interfluvial people in Amazonia. Their average village size is approximately 45 people. Tribal members speak their Karib dialect, although some members understand Spanish or Portuguese. By the 1970s and 1980s, however, the Yekuana were increasingly being influenced by the local market economy. Those forces are inevitably helping to acculturate them.

REFERENCES: David M. Guss, *To Weave and Sing: Art, Symbol, and Narrative in the South American Rain Forest*, 1989; Nelly Arvelo-Jimenez, "Political Relations in a Tribal Society: A Study of the Ye'cuana Indians of Venezuela," Ph.D. dissertation, Cornell University, 1971; Marc de Civrieux, *Watunna: An Orinoco Creation Cycle*, 1980; Blanche Reine Delas Pourrut, "Les indiens Maquiritaires du bassin de l-Orenoque au Venezuela: modes de vie, traditions. Exportation d'une mentalité," Ph.D. dissertation, University of Paris, 1979.

YEKUHANA. See YEKUANA.

YE'KWANA. See YEKUANA.

YEKWANA. See YEKUANA.

YEPÁ-MAHSÃ. See YEBÁ-MASÃ.

YETE. See OMÁGUA.

YHUATA. See OMÁGUA.

YINE. See PÍRO.

YITAA. See ASHLUSLAY.

YNCANABACTE. See TOBA.

YODUNSU. See NAMBIQUÁRA.

YOHOP. See MAKÚ.

YOKPA. See JAPRERÍA.

YOWA. The Yowa are a subtribe of the Yuko* Indians of northeastern Colombia. Traditionally they occupied land along a tributary of the Maracas River, where they were a subsistence agricultural people. In recent years, however, the Yowa have ceased to exist as a self-conscious social unit, particularly since their tribal population dipped below 20 people in the late 1960s. See YUKO.

YOWANA. See HOTI.

YOWUXUA. See CHOROTÉ.

YOXWAHA. See CHOROTÉ.

YTUCALI. See URARINA.

YUANA. See HOTÍ.

YUCATECO. The Yucatecos are a Yucatec Mayan* people living today in northern Belize. They fled to British Honduras from Mexico during the bloody Caste War of 1847–1853 and continued to live the Mayan lifestyle of settled, communal agriculture raising maize and beans. In the twentieth century, the

Yucatecos have become increasingly assimilated in Belize, but primarily to Hispanic rather than to Anglo values. Much of their communal land has been converted to individual ownership by government land policies. Protestants have made religious inroads among them, but the Yucatecos are still largely Roman Catholic and speak Yucateco as their primary language. Today there are approximately 6,200 Yucatecos in Belize.

REFERENCES: O. Nigel Bolland and Assael Shoman, *Land in Belize, 1765–1871*, 1977; William V. Davidson, "The Amerindians of Belize," *América Indígena*, 47 (1987), 9–22; J. Eric Thompson, *The Maya of Belize*, 1977.

YUCO. See YUKO.

YUCPA. See YUKPA.

YUCUNA. See YUKUNA.

YUGURA. See LECO.

YUHUANA. See MAPOYO.

YUHUP. See MAKÚ.

YUKI. See YUQUI.

YUKO. The Yuko (Yuco) Indians are of Karib* extraction and today inhabit the river valleys of northeastern Colombia along the border with Venezuela. They are divided into eight fiercely independent subtribes: the Iroka,* Las Candelas*, Manaure*, Maraca*, San Genaro*, Sokomba*, Susa*, and Yowa.* In 1988, approximately 264 Yuko were living on the Colombian government reservation at Iroka, and another 274 were on the reservation at Sokorpa. A tropical forest people who relied heavily on manioc horticulture, the Yuko have been traditionally known for their intertribal as well as intratribal warfare, their aggressiveness, and their strong sense of tribal and subtribal identity. Spanish explorers hunting for the legendary gold of El Dorado slaughtered large numbers of the Yuko in the 1530s, and most of the surviving Indians retreated deep into the highlands. For a brief period, Spaniards enticed some Yuko to descend and live on *encomiendas* in the 1550s, but the Indians soon retreated into the mountains. Capuchin missionaries attracted some Yuko down again in the mid–1600s, but by that time neo-Colombian settlers were living on Yuko ancestral lands. Periodic violence erupted between the Yuko and the settlers, which did not really subside until the early 1960s. A Capuchin mission was established among the Yuko in 1960, but unlike the Venezuelan government and the Yukpa,* Colombia did not establish a protected reservation for the Yuko. Neo-Colombian settlers are still alienating more and more Yuko tribal land. Today there are nearly 900

Yuko Indians in Colombia. Through acculturation to European clothing and technology, as well as to the regional cash economy, the Indians are slowly being incorporated into the larger society.

REFERENCES: Bruce Olson, *For This Cross I'll Kill You*, 1973; Kenneth Ruddle, *The Yukpa Cultivation System: A Study of Shifting Cultivation in Colombia and Venezuela*, 1974.

YUKPA. The Yukpa (Yucpa, Yupa, Chaques, Chakes) Indians are of Karib* extraction and today inhabit the river valleys of northwestern Venezuela, in the state of Zulia, along the border with Colombia. At the time of the conquest, they ranged over the general area from the Catatumbo River to the Río Negro in the Maracaibo Lake Basin. They are divided into eight fiercely independent subtribes: the Irapa* (Tukukus), Japreria* (Sabril, Sapriria), Macoita* (Macoas), Paririi,* Shaparru* (Shaparu, Chaparro), Viaksi* (Viakshi), Wasama,* and Rionegrinos.* Over the years, they have also been known to neo-Venezuelans as the tame Motilones* or the Motilones of the North. A tropical forest people who relied heavily on manioc horticulture, the Yupka have been traditionally known for their intertribal as well as intratribal warfare, their aggressiveness, and their strong sense of tribal and subtribal identity. Spanish explorers hunting for the legendary gold of El Dorado slaughtered large numbers of the Yukpa in the 1530s, and most of the surviving Indians retreated deep into the Sierra de Perija mountains. For a brief period, Spaniards enticed some Yukpa to descend and live on *encomiendas* in the 1550s, but the Indians soon retreated to the mountains. Capuchin missionaries attracted some Yukpa down again in the mid–1600s, but by that time neo-Venezuelan settlers were living on Yukpa ancestral lands. Periodic violence erupted between the Yukpa and the settlers, which did not really subside until the early 1960s. The Venezuelan government established an official Indian reserve for the Yukpa in 1960 in the eastern foothills of the Sierra de Perija mountains. Gradually the Yukpa descended from the mountains. The protection of the Indian reserve guaranteed Yukpa land and dramatically reduced the hostility between the Indians and neo-Venezuelans. A missionary group known as the Plymouth Brethren began working with the Yukpa in the late 1960s. Today there are more than 3,000 Yukpa Indians in Venezuela. Through acculturation to European clothing and technology, as well as to the regional cash economy, the Indians are slowly being incorporated into the larger society.

REFERENCES: Estéban Emilio Mosonyi, "La revitalización lingüística y la realidad venezolana," *América Indígena*, 47 (1987), 653–61; Kenneth Ruddle, *The Yukpa Cultivation System: A Study of Shifting Cultivation in Colombia and Venezuela*, 1974; Johannes Wilbert, *Yupa Folktales*, 1974.

YUKUNA. The Yukuna (Yucuna, Matapi) are a tribe of Amerindians who live along the Miriti-Paraná River in the Vaupés River drainage area of the territory of Amazonas, Colombia. They speak a language that is part of the larger Arawakan* linguistic family and call themselves the Camejeya. The Yukuna are a riverine people known for their excellence as canoemen and river navigators.

The Yukuna make a living by fishing and hunting river animals, as well as by cultivating bitter manioc and a variety of other crops in tribal gardens. They remained almost completely isolated until neo-Colombian rubber gatherers penetrated thier territory in the late nineteenth century, as did missionaries, who brought Christianity and European diseases. Since then, the Yukuna population dropped precipitously but is now stabilized. They are divided into three surviving subgroups: Jeruiwa, Jurumi, and Imikie. Most of them retain a strong sense of their tribal origins, even though they are being integrated into the regional cash economy because of their adoption of trade goods. Since 1963, the Yukuna have had to deal with the presence of the Summer Institute of Linguistics among them. In 1988, there were 1,200 Yukuna Indians living on the Colombian government reservation at Miriti-Paraná, as well as 355 on the Comeyafu reservation and 143 on the Puerto Cordoba reservation. The Yukunas live in very close association with the Matapi, Tanimuka, and Mirana Indians.

REFERENCES: Christine Hugh-Jones, *From the Milk River: Spatial and Temporal Processes in Northwest Amazonia*, 1979; Myriam Jiméno and Adolfo Triana Antorveza, *Estado y minorias étnicas en Colombia*, 1985; Pierre Yves-Jacopin, "On the Syntactic Structure of Myth, or the Yukuna Invention of Speech," *Cultural Anthropology*, 3 (1988), 131–59.

YULE. See CUNA.

YUMA. See ARÁRA.

YUMA. See ARAONA.

YUMBO. The Yumbo (Huumbo) were an Amerindian group of Panzaleo-language extraction who at the time of the conquest occupied the western slopes of the Andes in contemporary Ecuador. Although the term has been used to describe Amerindians living between the southern boundary of Colombia and the Río Coca in the Ecuadorian montana, it is of little use ethnically, since it has also become a generic term for describing lowland Indian people on both the eastern and western slopes of the Andes in Ecuador. In particular, it refers to approximately 50,000 Quechua-speaking Indians who are descendents of a post-conquest mix between such groups as the Quijos,* Canelas,* Baezas, and others.

REFERENCES: Udo Oberem, "Trade and Trade Goods in the Ecuadorian Montana," *Folk*, 8–9 (1967), 243–58; Frank Salomon, "Killing the Yumbo," in Norman E. Whitten, Jr., ed., *Cultural Transformations and Ethnicity in Modern Ecuador*, 1981, 162–208.

YUMINÁWA. See YAMINÁWA.

YUNGAS. The term "Yungas" is a generic word used to describe the cool, wet valleys of the eastern side of the Andes Mountains in Bolivia. The Yungas are known for their rich agricultural potential in the valleys at 7,000 to 9,000 feet in altitude. Among many neo-Bolivians, the term "Yunga" has also been applied to any individual of Amerindian ancestry living as an Indian in that region.

REFERENCE: *Encyclopedia of Indians of the Americas*, 2 (1974), 178.

YUPA. See YUKPA.

YUQUÍ. The Yuquí (Yukí) Indians are a tiny Amerindian group in eastern Bolivia show speak a Tupi*-Guaraní* language. Today they can be found south of the upper Ichilo River in the province of Carrasco in the department of Cochabamba. When they were first contacted by the Spanish in 1548, the Yuquí were part of the Sirionó* tribe. Jesuit priests missionized the Sirionó in the seventeenth century, but the nomadic Indians had a difficult time there because they hated the sedentary, agricultural lifestyle. Some of the Sirionó escaped from the missions and headed back into the forests. Among those nomadic Sirionó were some who evolved into the Yuquí. In the late 1950s, the government of Bolivia initiated a series of colonization projects near Yuquí territory, and conflict developed immediately. Fundamentalist Protestant missionaries also began working with them. By 1969, the Yuquí population had dropped to only 43 people. At that time, they gave up their nomadic existence and settled on a mission on the banks of the Chimore River, which is a tributary of the Ichilo. By the mid–1980s, the Yuquí population had increased to 73 people. Today there are fewer still who speak the Yuquí dialect. The Yuquí are willing to consume such agricultural products as corn, plantains, manioc, and rice, but they still prefer to hunt and fish.

REFERENCES: Pedro Plaza Martínez and Juan Carvajal Carvajal, *Etnías y lenguas de Bolivia*, 1985; Allyn MacLean Stearman, "The Yuquí Connection: Another Look at Siriono Deculturation," *American Anthropologist*, 86 (1984), 630–50; Allyn M. Stearman, *Yuquí: Forest Nomads in a Changing World*, 1989.

YURÁ. The Yura are a Quechua*-speaking people who live within a 2,000-square-mile area of the department of Potosí in Bolivia. They are concentrated particularly in the canton of Yurá. When the Spaniards first arrived in the area in the 1530s, the Yurá were scrambling to maintain their ethnic identity against the recently imposed Incan empire; over the centuries, they have developed a number of techniques for resisting acculturation. By the mid–1980s, there were approximately 6,000 Yurá Indians living in about 100 villages and hamlets of the main river valleys. They continue to be an agricultural people, raising twelve varieties of maize, as well as beans, squash, and potatoes, on elaborately irrigated plots of land. In recent years, most Yurá families have added sheep or goat raising to their economy, herding the animals on communal pastures. Most children do not stay in school long because they yearn to go to the fields with their parents and begin farming. Yurá-Quechua remains the primary language of the vast majority of the Yurá. Although men have recently adopted the clothing of the surrounding mestizo society, Yurá women remain in their traditional dress.

REFERENCE: Roger Neil Rasnake, *Domination and Cultural Survival: Authority and Power among an Andean People*, 1988.

YURACARÉ. The Yuracaré (Conis, Cuchis, Enetes) are a tribe of Amerindians living in the departments of El Beni and Cochabamba between the Sucre, Ichilo, and Chapare rivers in Bolivia. Their language is from an isolated, independent family. At the time of the conquest, their territory stretched throughout the tropical forests from the eastern foothills of the Andes to Cochabamba. Roman Catholic missionaries established missions among them in the 1760s, but the Yuracaré resisted their eforts. The Yuracaré numbered 1,500 people in 1800 and fewer than 1,000 in 1900. Their current population exceeds 2,500 people. Today the Yuracaré have a strong sense of ethnic identity and are bilingual. They make a living selling handicrafts for cash and pursuing a subsistence agricultural way of life, supplemented by hunting and fishing.

REFERENCES: Brian M. Boom, *Ethnobotany of the Chácobo Indians, Beni, Bolivia*, 1987; Pedro Plaza Martínez and Juan Carvajal Carvajal, *Etnías y lenguas de Bolivia*, 1985; Graciela Zolezzi and J. Riester, "'Lenguas indígenas del oriente Boliviano clasificación preliminar," *América Indígena*, 47 (1987), 425–33.

YURACARÉ. See URU.

YURAPARI-TAPUYA. See KARUTÁNA.

YURITI-TAPUYA. See YURUTI.

YURO. See YURACARÉ.

YURUCARITIA. See YURUKARIKA.

YURUKARIKA. The Yurukarika (Yurucaritia) are an almost extinct group of Amerindians who once lived in the province of Velasco in the department of Santa Cruz in Bolivia. Spanish explorers ascending the Paraguay in the mid- and late sixteenth century probably encountered the Yurukarika, who were then a tropical forest people who hunted and fished for their livelihood. Always a small group, the Yurukarika avoided contact with neo-Bolivians until the rubber boom of the late nineteenth and early twentieth centuries devastated them. The Yurukarika population declined rapidly because of disease and exploitation. The tribe had ceased to function as a differentiated social unit by the late 1950s. Today there are only 2 members of the tribe still alive.

REFERENCE: Pedro Plaza Martínez and Juan Carvajal Carvajal, *Etnías y lenguas de Bolivia*, 1985.

YURPARI-TAPUYA. See KARUTÁNA.

YURUTI. The Yuruti are a small, Eastern Tukanoan*-speaking Amerindian people of the Vaupés River drainage area of Colombia. They are particularly concentrated in the communities of San Luis and Consuelo on the Paca River. Traditionally they have been a horticultural people, raising bitter manioc as their staple and fishing to supplement their diet. Hunting has been of only secondary importance. Their first contacts with Europeans probably came in 1784 when the Portuguese explorer Manuel da Gama da Lobo da Almada ascended the Vaupés River. Jesuit and Carmelite missionaries also had sporadic contacts with the Yuruti, but the isolated geography of the Vaupés jungles prevented much European exploitation. The Yuruti population was devastated by the rubber boom of the late nineteenth and early twentieth centuries but then stabilized after World War II. By that time, they had adopted the metal technology of Europeans and have been gradually integrating, though very slowly, into the regional cash economy of the area, selling manioc-based farinha flour as well as their own labor. The Yuruti population today is approximately 1,000 people who live in scattered multi-family settlements.

REFERENCES: Jean A. Jackson, *The Fish People: Linguistic Exogamy and Tukanoan Identity in Northwest Amazonia*, 1983; Myriam Jiméno and Adolfo Triana Antorveza, *Estado y minorias étnicas en Colombia*, 1985; Gerardo Reichel-Dolmatoff, *Amazonian Cosmos: The Sexual and Religious Symbolism of the Tukano Indians*, 1985; Robert Lee Spires, "As línguas faladas do Brasil," *América Indígena*, 47 (1987), 455–79.

YUSKU. See SUMU.

Z

ZAGORENI. See CAMPA.

ZAMUCO. The term "Zamuco" (Samuku) refers to a small linguistic family of Amerindian languages concentrated in the department of Santa Cruz, Bolivia, and across the border in western Paraguay. It includes the Chamacoco* and Ayoreo* (Zamuco proper) tribal groups in Bolivia and Paraguay.

REFERENCE: Cestmir Loukotka, *Classification of South American Indian Languages*, 1968.

ZAMUCO. See MOXO.

ZAPARA. See PARAUJANO.

ZAPARA. See ZAPARO.

ZAPARO. The Zaparo (Zapara, Kayapwe) were a group of Amerindians who spoke a Zaparoan language and lived between the Napo and Pastazo rivers in Peru and Ecuador. The first European contact with the Zaparo occurred at the confluence of the Curaray and Noximo rivers in 1848; some Zaparo were also living on the banks of the Bobonazo River. The Zaparo population then exceeded 1,000 people, but in the late nineteenth and into the twentieth centuries the Zaparo declined in numbers and became integrated with Quechua*-speaking Indians in Ecuador and Peru. They ceased to function as a sociological unit and ceased to exist as a linguistic group. It is possible, however, that there are a few isolated individuals among Quechua-speakers in Peru and Ecuador who are aware of their Zaparoan ancestry.

REFERENCE: Darcy Ribeiro and Mary Ruth Wise, *Los grupos étnicos de la amazona peruana*, 1978.

ZAPAROAN. The term Zaparoan refers to a small linguistic group of Amerindian languages located historically in the highlands of Ecuador. The tribal languages traditionally included in the Zaparoan group are Andoa (Ando, Shimigae*), Iquito* (Cahuarano*), Arabela,* and Zaparo* proper. The Iquito and Andoa dialects still function, although the Zaparo tribes, which once ranged widely throughout eastern Peru and Ecuador, declined rapidly in number in the seventeenth and eighteenth centuries because of disease and enslavement. During the rubber booms of the early twentieth century, many surviving Zaparo migrated into Peru. Those who survived adopted a riverine lifestyle—hunting, fishing, and practicing swidden horticulture on territory shared with the Achuara* people. There are still several thousand Zaparoan speakers in Ecuador and Peru, but there is also a stigma about being of Zaparoan descent, so many Zaparoan people are bilingual in Spanish and/or Quechua.*

REFERENCES: David G. Swett, "The Population of the Upper Amazon Valley, 17th and 18th Centuries," M.A. thesis, University of Wisconsin, Madison, 1969; Gustavo Solís F., "Multilinguismo y extinctiones de lenguas," *América Indígena*, 47 (1987), 631–45; Norman E. Whitten, Jr., *Sacha Runa: Ethnicity and Adaptation of Ecuadorian Jungle Quechua*, 1976.

ZAPITALAGA. See PILAGÁ.

ZATCHILA. See COLORADO.

ZIVARO. See JÍVARO.

ZORÓ. The Zoró are a tribe of approximately 175 Amerindians who once lived in the northwestern edge of the state of Mato Grosso, Brazil, near the border with Bolivia. Their language is part of the Mondé* linguistic family, and related tribes include the Gavião,* Cinta Larga,* Suruí,* and Arára.* A tropical forest people who lived by hunting and horticulture, the Zoró were decimated by the rubber boom in Rondônia in the early 1900s and again during World War II. The rubber collectors brought violence, disease, and forced labor to the Zoró people, and their population declined so drastically that they had difficulty maintaining traditional ceremonial life. Official contact with the Zoró tribe by the Brazilian government did not take place until 1977. Mortal enemies of the Suruí, the Zoró were still at war with them off and on in the early 1980s. In 1986, the Zoró were integrated into the Aripuanã Park, but in recent years their land has been invaded by thousands of neo-Brazilian settlers, precipitating several acts of violence on both sides. Today the tribe has been reduced to near complete dependency on government or philanthropic handouts. The New Tribes Mission has converted most of the Zoró to Christianity, and the Indians are abandoning most of their traditional rituals. Today the Zoró are all Baptists. The Brazilian government has located all 200 of the Zoró in a single village and rigidly controls their economic and political life. A few of the Zoró, however, still violently resist the intrusions of outsiders.

REFERENCES: Denny Moore, "The Gavião, Zoró, and Arara Indians," in David Maybury-Lewis, *In the Path of the Polonoreste: Endangered Peoples of Western Brazil*, 1981, 46–62; Mario Silva, "Zoró Indians Prepare for War," *Cultural Survival Quarterly*, 11 (1987), 32–33; Robert Lee Spires, "As línguas faladas do Brasil," *América Indígena*, 47 (1987), 455–79.

ZUTUHIL. See TZUTUJIL.

Appendix A

TRIBES BY COUNTRY

ARGENTINA

Araucanian
Ashluslay
Auca
Aymara
Chiriguano
Choroté
Diaguita
Guaycurú
Macá
Mataco
Mocoví
Pilagá
Tehuelche
Teréna
Toba

BELIZE

Garífuna
Kekchí
Maya-Mopan
Miskito

BOLIVIA

Araona
Aymara
Ayoreo
Baure
Canichana
Cavineña
Cayuvava
Chácobo
Chamacoco
Chimane
Chiquitano
Chiriguano
Churupa
Essejja
Guarayu
Itonama
Izoceño
Jora
Jukumani
Kilemoka
Kusikia
Laymi
Leco
Mataco
Moncoca
Moré
Movima
Moxo
Pacahuara
Paunaca

Pauserna
Poturero
Qollahuaya
Quechua
Reyesano
Saraveka
Shipaya
Sirionó
Tacana
Tapieté
Toba
Toromona
Txapakúra
Uru

BRAZIL

Agavotoküeng
Aikaná
Aipatse
Aiwateri
Akuriyo
Akwẽ
Amahuaca
Amanayé
Amniape
Anambé
Apalaí
Apâniekra
Apiacá
Apinayé
Apurinã
Aramagotó
Aramichó
Arára
Arawine
Aré
Arekuna
Arikapú
Arikên
Arimihotó
Aripaktsá
Aruá
Aruashí
Asuriní
Atikum
Atruahí
Auaicu

Auakê
Auetí
Avá
Avá-Chiripá
Aweikoma
Baenan
Bakirí
Banavá-Jafi
Baníwa
Bará
Barawána
Boca Negra
Boca Preta
Boróro
Botocudo
Campé
Cayuishána
Cinta Larga
Daní
Desana
Diarrói
Emerion
Ewarhoyana
Fulniô
Galera
Galibí
Gavião
Gorotíre
Guajá
Guajajára
Guató
Gueren
Hixkaryána
Huarí
Iaualapití
Iawano
Iñapari
Ingarikó
Ipotewát
Ipurinã
Irántxe
Itogapúk
Jabutí
Jaruára
Javaé
Júma
Juruna
Kabixí

Kabixiańa
Kaduveo
Kaimbé
Kaingáng
Kaiová
Kaiwá
Kakwa
Kalapalo
Kamaiurá
Kamakán
Kambiwa
Kámpa
Kanamarí
Kanoê
Kapanáwa
Karajá
Karapanã
Kararaô
Karipúna
Karitiána
Karutána
Kashiniti
Katawian
Katawixí
Katukína
Kawahíb
Kaxararí
Kaxináwa
Kaxuiána
Kayabí
Kayapó
Kepkiriwat
Kinikinão
Kirikirigotó
Kiriri
Koaiá
Kokraimôro
Kozarene
Krahô
Kreen-Akarôre
Krem-Yé
Krenkatẽyé
Krikatí
Kuben-Kragnotíre
Kuben-Kran-Kêgn
Kuikúru
Kukuyána
Kulína

Kunuhána
Kuruáya
Kutenabu
Layana
Makú
Makuráp
Makushí
Mamaindè
Manairisu
Manitenéri
Mapidian
Marináwa
Marubo
Matipú
Matse
Mawé
Maxakalí
Maxinéri
Mayá
Mayorúna
Mehinácu
Mekém
Mekranotí
Mentuktíre
Miarra
Mondé
Morerebi
Mundurukú
Murá
Murui
Nafuquá
Nambiquára
Naruvót
Natú
Nukuíni
Numbaia
Ofayé
Okomoyána
Omágua
Oyanpík
Pãi-Cayuã
Paimerú
Pakaanóva
Pakanáwa
Pakarára
Pakidai
Palikur
Palmela

Pankarára
Pankaráru
Parakána
Paranawat
Parecí
Parihuri
Parintintín
Parukoto
Pataxó
Paumarí
Pianoi
Pianokotó
Pirahã
Pira-Tapuya
Píro
Pisabo
Pituiaró
Potiguara
Poyanáwa
Prouyána
Puró
Puruborá
Ramaráma
Remo
Rodela
Sabanê
Salumá
Sanumá
Sararé
Saraveka
Sharanáhua
Shocó
Sikiana
Suriana
Suruí
Suyá
Takuatep
Tamanáwa
Tapayúna
Tapirapé
Tariana
Taulipáng
Tenetehára
Teréno
Timbira
Tiriyó
Torá
Truka

Trumái
Tukano
Tukuna
Tukunafed
Tùparí
Tupinaki
Turiwara
Tuxá
Tuxináwa
Txakamekra
Txapakúra
Txikão
Txukarramãe
Txunhua-Djapá
Uiapii
Umotina
Unanana
Urubú
Urueu-Wau-Wáu
Urukuyána
Urumi
Urupá
Yekuana
Zoró

CHILE

Alacaluf
Araucanian
Auca
Aymara
Huilliche
Mapuche
Qawasqar
Selknam

COLOMBIA

Achagua
Amorua
Andoke
Angotero
Arapaso
Arhuaco
Bará
Barasána
Baré

Barí
Betoi
Bora
Buhayana
Caramanta
Chami
Chibcha
Chimila
Chocó
Coaquier
Cogui
Coreguaje
Coyaima
Cubeo
Cuiva
Cuna
Curripaco
Datuana
Desana
Eduria
Embera
Epena
Fa'ai
Gambiano
Guahibo
Guajiro
Guaviare
Guayabero
Guayquerí
Ika
Imihata
Inga
Iroka
Kabiyeri
Kamsá
Karabayo
Karapana
Karijona
Katío
Kofán
Letuana
Makaguane
Makú
Makuna
Malayo
Manaure
Mirana
Miriti-Tapuya

Murui
Nonuya
Nukak
Ocaina
Páez
Paneroa
Pasto
Piapoco
Piaroa
Pira-Tapuya
Puinave
Quechua
Quillacinga
Sáliva
San Gerano
Sanha
Siona
Siriano
Sokomba
Susa
Tabaino
Tado
Tama
Tanimuko
Tariana
Tatuyo
Tukano
Tukuna
Tunebo
Tuyuka
Uanana
Waunana
Yagua
Yahuna
Yari

COSTA RICA

Bribri
Brunka
Cabecare
Chaniguena
Guatuso
Nicarao
Talamanca
Teribe
Terraba

ECUADOR

Achuara
Alama
Auca
Canelo
Colorado
Cushma
Huambisa
Jívaro
Kofán
Mayna
Otavalo
Quechua
Quillacinga
Salasaca
Saraguro
Secoya
Shuar
Tetete
Zaparo

EL SALVADOR

Cacaopera
Chortí
Lenca
Nicarao
Pancho
Pocomán

FRENCH GUIANA

Emerion
Galibí
Locono
Palikur
Urukuyána

GUATAMALA

Acateco
Achí
Aguacateca
Cakchiquel
Chortí
Guatemala

Itza
Ixil
Jacaltec
Kanjobal
Kekchí
Mam
Maya-Mopan
Miskito
Pocomán
Pokómchi
Quiché
Sacapulteco
Sipacapense
Tacaneco
Tectiteco
Tzutujil
Uspantec

GUYANA

Akawáio
Arekuna
Ingarikó
Locono
Makushí
Parukoto
Patamuno
Taruma
Taulipáng
Warao

HONDURAS

Cacaopera
Chortí
Garífuna
Jicaque
Lenca
Miskito
Paya
Pipil

NICARAGUA

Cacaopera
Garífuna
Miskito

Nicarao
Pipil
Rama
Sumu

PANAMA

Chocó
Cuiva
Guaymí

PARAGUAY

Aché
Angaité
Ashluslay
Avá-Chiripá
Ayoreo
Chamacoco
Chiriguano
Choroté
Kaduveo
Kaskiha
Lengua
Macá
Mataco
Paiagua
Pãi-Cayuã
Pilagá
Sanapana
Tapieté
Toba
Toba-Maskoy

PERU

Achuara
Aguano
Aguaruna
Alama
Amahuaca
Amarakaeri
Amniape
Amuesha
Angotero
Arabela
Arasaeri

Ashinanca
Awishiri
Aymara
Bora
Cahuarano
Campa
Candoshi
Canela
Canelo
Caquinte
Cashibo
Chamicuro
Chayavita
Cholón
Cocama
Cocamilla
Conibo
Cujareno
Guarayo
Harakmbet
Huachipaire
Huambisa
Iawano
Iñapari
Iquito
Isconahua
Jaqarú
Jebero
Jívaro
Kapanawa
Kawki
Kaxinawa
Kaxuiana
Kayabí
Kayapó
Kisamberi
Kulina
Lama
Machiguenga
Marinawa
Masco
Mastanahua
Matse
Mayna
Mayoruna
Morunahua
Muniche
Murui

Nomatsiguenga
Ocaina
Omagua
Omurano
Orejón
Pajonalino
Panobo
Paranapura
Parquenahua
Piro
Pisabo
Pishquibo
Quechua
Resigaro
Secoya
Setebo
Shahindawa
Sharanahua
Shiliveri
Shimigae
Shipibo
Shuar
Sirineiri
Suweri
Taushiro
Toyeri
Tukuna
Tuyuneiri
Ucayalino
Urarina
Zaparo

SURINAM

Akuriyó
Aramagotó
Aramichó
Arimihotó
Katawian
Kukuyána
Locono
Mapidian
Okomoyána
Oyanpík
Pianokotó
Saluma
Sikiana
Tiriyó

VENEZUELA

Achagua
Aiwateri
Akawáio
Amorua
Arahuac
Arekuna
Auake
Baníwa
Baré
Barí
Cuiva
Curripaco
Guahibo
Guajiro
Guayqueri
Hoti
Irapa
Japrería
Kaliana
Kariña
Locono
Macoita
Makiritaire
Makushí
Mandawaka
Mapoyo
Pakidai
Panare
Paraujano
Parihuri
Pariri
Parukoto
Patamuno
Piapoco
Piaroa
Puinave
Shaparru
Taulipáng
Warao

Appendix B

CHRONOLOGY OF THE CONQUEST OF CENTRAL AND SOUTH AMERICA

1492—Christopher Columbus discovers America, encountering Arawak Indians in the Bahamas, Cuba, and Hispaniola.

1493—Columbus begins the exploration of the Greater Antilles and encounters the Karib Indians. The conquest of the Arawak and Karib Indians in the Caribbean islands begins.

1494—Treaty of Tordesillas divides the New World between Spain and Portugal.

1498—Columbus encounters the Paya Indians of Honduras.

1499—Alonso de Ojeda of Spain begins his exploratory voyage to the northern coast of South America and makes contact with the Guajiro Indians. Amerigo Vespucci contacts the Paraujano Indians in northwestern Venezuela.

1500—Pedro Cabral claims Brazil for the Portuguese. Vicente Pinzón discovers the mouth of the Amazon River.

1501—Rodrigo de Bastidas of Spain discovers the west coast of Colombia. Ojeda discovers the Gulf of Uraba.

1502—King Manoel of Portugal licenses Lisbon merchants to import brazilwood from the New World. Trade relations with the Tupi-speaking tribes of the Brazilian coast are established.

1508—Spaniards begin the conquest of Puerto Rico.

1509—Spaniards begin the conquest of Jamaica.

1510—Ojeda begins the conquest of the northern Colombia lowlands.

1511—Diego Velásquez of Spain begins the conquest of Cuba. Vasco Núñez de Balboa of Spain establishes first contact with the Chocó Indians of Panama and Colombia.

1513—Balboa crosses Panama and discovers the Pacific Ocean.

1514—Velásquez completes the conquest of Cuba.

1515—Robert Dudley and Walter Raleigh of England explore the Orinoco River.

1516—Pedro de Gómez of Spain begins the conquest of the Guaymí Indians of Panama and Costa Rica.

1519—Ferdinand Magellan, a Portuguese mariner sailing for Spain, begins his circumnavigation of the globe. Spaniard Hernán Cortés begins the conquest of Mexico.

1520—Magellan makes contact with the Tehuelche Indians of Argentina.

1522—Many Chorotega Indians of Costa Rica convert to Roman Catholicism.

1524—Spaniard Pedro de Alvarado's expedition of conquest reaches the various lowland tribes of El Salvador, Guatamala, and Honduras.

1525—Spaniard Rodrigo de Bastidas begins the conquest of the Chibchan Indians of Colombia. Gonzalo de Alvarado of Spain conquers the Mam Indians of Guatemala.

1526—The Cakchiquel Indians rebel. Sebastián Cabot, an Italian sailing under the Spanish flag, makes contact with the Querandi Indians of Argentina.

1527—Alvar Núñez Cabeza de Vaca begins his expedition to the Río de la Plata region of South America, traveling 1,000 miles across southern Brazil to Asunción, Paraguay. Spaniard Juan de Ampues begins the conquest of the Indian tribes of the Lake Maracaibo basin in Venezuela.

1529—Pedro de Alvarado begins the conquest of the highland tribes of Guatemala.

1532—Portugal establishes its first permanent settlements in Brazil; the process of driving the Tupi-speaking people of the coastal regions into the interior begins. Spaniard Francisco Pizarro defeats the Inca emperor at the Battle of Cajamarca.

1533—Pizarro executes the Inca emperor Atahuallpa. Spaniards conquer Cuzco, Peru, and subdue the Inca empire. The city of Cartagena, Colombia, is established. Diego de Aguero and Pedro Martínez de Moguer reach the Aymara Indians of Peru and Bolivia.

1534—Pedro Anzules de Campo-Redondo of Spain establishes first contact with the Cavineña and Reyesano Indians of Bolivia.

1535—Sebastián de Benalcazar of Spain founds the city of Quito, Ecuador. Spaniard Diego de Almagro begins the conquest of the Aymara.

1536—Gonzalo Dias de Piñeda of Spain first encounters the Quijo Indians of Ecuador. The Querandi Indians of Argentina (now extinct) fight pitched battles with the expedition of Pedro de Mendoza, and the Manco Inca rebellion begins in Cuzco, Peru. Spaniard Alonso de Heredía explores the Cauca Valley of Colombia.

1537—The city of Asunción, Paraguay, is established in Guaraní territory.

1538—Benalcazar reaches the Pijao Indians of Colombia. Hernán Pérez de Quesada of Spain completes an expedition into the Vaupés River area.

1539—Payagua Indians in the Gran Chaco massacre the expedition of Spaniard Juan de Ayolas. Spanish settlement of the Cauca Valley of Colombia begins. The expedition of Pedro Anzules de Campo-Redondo establishes first contact with Tacanan-speaking Indians in eastern Bolivia.

1540—Pedro de Valdivia of Spain launches his expedition and wars against the Araucanian Indians of Chile. Francisco de Orellana of Spain begins an expedition to trace the Amazon River from its headwaters in the Andes to its outlet in the Atlantic Ocean.

1542—Domingo Martínez de Irala of Spain ascends the Paraguay River and makes first contact with a variety of Chiquitoan-speaking Indian tribes of eastern Bolivia. Spanish explorers make first contact with the Omágua Indians of the Amazon River. Cabeza de Vaca's expedition attacks the Mbaya Guaycuru in the Gran Chaco. New laws go into effect, and neo-Peruvian settlers begin moving into the Huallaga and Marañon river valleys of Peru.

1545—The Ñuflo de Chávez of Spain expedition attacks the Mbaya Indians of the Gran Chaco.

1548—Spanish missionaries and explorers establish contact with the Sirionó Indians of Bolivia.

1549—Spaniards establish first contact with the Aguaruna Indians in northern Peru.

1553—Araucanians destroy the city of Concepción, Chile, but Spanish explorers establish first contact with the Chonó Indians of Chile. Martínez de Irala establishes contact with the Naperu, Mbaya, Chané, and Tamacosi Indians of the Gran Chaco, the last being long since extinct.

1554—Pedro de Ursua of Spain establishes first contact with the Lama Indians of Peru.

1557—Ñuflo de Chávez begins the conquest of the Chiquitano and Churupa Indians of Bolivia. Juan Salinas Loyola establishes first contact with the Cocama, Cocamilla, and Huambisa Indians of Peru. Spanish soldiers begin the conquest of the Patangoro and Amani Indians on the eastern slope of the Cordillera Central in Colombia.

1562—Francisco Benalcazar of Spain conquers the Gambiano Indians of Colombia.

1564—Neo-Bolivian settlers first enter the territory of the Chiriguano Indians of Bolivia, precipitating a long history of violent interaction.

1565—Diego de Lozada of Spain establishes the city of Caracas and begins the conquest of the tribes of north central Venezuela.

1572—Spanish explorers first contact the Machiguenga Indians of Peru.

1577—Pijao Indians rebel in many areas in Colombia.

1579—Pedro Sarmiento de Gamboa of Spain first contacts the Selk'nam Indians of Tierra del Fuego.

1580—Spanish explorers establish first contact with the Baure Indians of Bolivia. Sarmiento de Gamboa establishes contact with the Ona Indians of Tierra del Fuego.

1582—Miguel Cabello de Balboa of Spain contacts the Leco Indians of Bolivia.

1583—Spain establishes a colony in the Río de la Plata area; the Querandi uprising begins in Argentina.

1587—Luis de Tapia of Spain first contacts the Arhuaco and Malayo Indians of Colombia.

1588—Jesuit missionaries first arrive in Ascunción, Paraguay.

1589—The British government forges an alliance with the Miskito Indians in what is today Nicaragua. Father Reginaldo de Lizarraga establishes contact with the Huarpe Indians of Argentina and Chile (now extinct).

1590—Spanish missionaries first reach the Toba Indians of Argentina and Paraguay.

1593—Jesuit missionaries begin working among the Araucanian Indians of Chile.

1595—Sir Walter Raleigh first contacts the Makushí Indians of Venezuela.

1598—A large-scale Araucanian rebellion begins.

1599—Jesuit missionaries establish missions among the Kofán Indians in Ecuador and Colombia.

1600—Jesuit missionaries establish missions among the Siona Indians of Colombia.

1603—The Potiguara Indians establish an alliance with the Dutch to resist Portuguese expansion in Brazil. Spanish officials launch a war of extermination against the Páez Indians of Colombia.

1609—Europeans first contact the Tiriyó people of the Brazilian-Surinam border area. Jesuit missionaries establish missions among the Chonó Indians of Chile.

1610—Portuguese settlers first contact the Guajajára Indians.

1613—A French expedition establishes contact with the Pacajá Indians of Brazil.

1615—A Portuguese expedition first encounters the Tenetehára Indians of Brazil.

1617—The Baure Indians of Bolivia successfully resist Spanish expeditions of conquest.

1619—Spanish explorers first reach the Huash Indians of Tierra del Fuego (now extinct).

1620—Roman Catholic missionaries establish contact with the Awishira Indians of eastern Peru.

1621—Franciscan missionaries first reach the Chimane Indians of Bolivia.

1623—British and French missionaries settle St. Kitts but disease destroys the Karib Indians there.

1624—Jacques L'Hermite of France establishes contact with the Yaghan Indians of Tierra del Fuego.

1628—Spaniards establish contact with the Mataco Indians of northern Argentina, Paraguay, and Bolivia.

1630—Most Achagua Indians of Venezuela and Colombia settle on Jesuit missions. The Avé-Chiripá Indians of Paraguay and Brazil begin entering Jesuit missions. Portuguese troops conquer the Guaitaca Indians of Brazil (now extinct).

1631—Franciscan and Jesuit missions are established among the Indian tribes of the Upper Huallaga River Valley in Peru.

1635—Franciscan missionaries contact the Amuesha and Campa Indians of Peru.

1639—Jesuit missionaries begin to establish themselves on the Xingú River in Brazil.

1640—Jesuits establish the Concepción de Xeveros Mission among the Jebero Indians of Peru.

1641—Spanish explorers first reach the Omurano Indians of Peru while slavers begin to decimate the Omágua Indians of the Amazon Valley.

1644—Franciscan missionaries begin their work among the Payanso Indians of Peru. The Xebero Revolt begins in Peru.

1649—Jesuits establish the mission of Santa María de Huallaga among the Cocama and Cocamilla.

1650—Jesuit missionaries establish missions among the Guahibo, Cuiva, and Sáliva Indians of Venezuela and Colombia.

1654—Smallpox and measles epidemics devastate the Omurana Indians of Peru. The Potiguara Indians of Brazil abrogate their alliance with the Dutch. The Portuguese in Belém launch a war of extermination against the Arúa Indians. The Aguano

Indians of Peru enter a mission on the Huallaga River, while Jesuit missionaries convert large numbers of Lama and other tribes in Peru.

1655—A series of epidemic diseases all but destroys the Mayorúna Indians of Peru.

1656—The Pacajá Indians of Brazil begin entering Jesuit missions.

1657—Spanish soldiers and missionaries launch a war against the Shipibo Indians of Peru that lasts until 1670. Father Alonso Cabellero establishes first contact with the Setebo Indians of Peru.

1658—Jesuit missionaries begin to gather the Pauxi Indians of Brazil (now extinct) into mission settlements.

1661—The Mbaya uprising, which lasts on and off for more than a century, begins in the Gran Chaco.

1664—Jesuit missionaries convert most of the Lama Indians of Peru and place them in mission settlements.

1665—Some Awishira Indians begin moving to the Roman Catholic mission at San Miguel, Peru. Some Baure Indians of Bolivia begin relocating to the Jesuit missions at San Nicolas, San Joaquin, and Concepción.

1669—The Jesuits establish a mission among the Tupinamba Indians of Brazil.

1670—Smallpox epidemics decimate the Setebo Indians of Peru as well as many other tribes of the Peruvian and Ecuadorian montana. The Tehuelche Indians of Argentina begin to domesticate the horse.

1673—Angel de Peredo launches a campaign against the Indians of the Gran Chaco.

1675—Franciscan missionaries establish contact with the Campa Indians of Peru.

1676—Franciscan missionaries convert large numbers of Hibito (extinct) and Cholón Indians in Peru.

1678—Franciscan missionaries begin their work among the Tacanan-speaking Indians of eastern Bolivia.

1680—A severe smallpox epidemic breaks out among the Shipibo Indians of Peru.

1682—The Amuesha Indians rebel against Franciscan missionaries in Brazil. Bartolomé Bueno founds the city of Santa Anna, Brazil, and establishes contact with the Karajá Indians.

1684—Smallpox epidemics begin to sweep through the Cocama and Cocamilla Indians of Peru. Jesuit missionaries establish missions among the Moxo Indians of Bolivia.

1685—The Yuruna-Tacunyape Indians revolt in Brazil. Franciscan and Jesuit missionaries begin their work among the Conibo Indians of Peru.

1686—Dominican missionaries contact the Amahuaca Indians of Peru and Brazil, and the Conibo Indians of Peru begin settling in Jesuit missions. Roman Catholic missionaries also establish missions among the Orejón Indians of Peru. Large numbers of Shipibo Indians of Peru join Jesuit missions. Jesuit missionaries begin their work among the Omágua Indians of Peru and Brazil. The Simiranche and Píro Indians rebel in Peru.

1687—Great Britain establishes a protectorate over the Miskito Indians in Nicaragua.

1688—Jesuit missionaries settle the Aizuare Indians of the Amazon Valley of Brazil (now extinct) on missions to protect them from slavers.

1690—Spanish soldiers place the Churapa Indians of eastern Bolivia under Jesuit control, and Jesuit missionaries begin their work among the Chiriguano Indians of Bolivia.

1693—Capuchin missionaries establish a mission among the Arhuaco and Malayo Indians of Colombia. Agustín Zapata reaches the Canichana and Cayuvava Indians of Bolivia.

1694—Jesuit missionaries make contact with the Mawé Indians of Brazil.

1695—Gold is discovered in Minas Gerais, Brazil, bringing tens of thousands of prospectors and devastatiing tribal life. Zapata begins to missionize the Canichana and Cayuvava Indians of Bolivia. Jesuit priest Cipriano Barrace establishes a mission among the Guarayu Indians of eastern Bolivia and makes contact with the Sirionó Indians.

1698—Conibo and Shipibo revolts against Jesuit missionaries begin.

1699—Jesuit missionaries begin to build missions and to settle the Achagua, Guaiqueri, Palenque, Piritu, Caberre, Puinave, Saliva, and Piapoco Indians of Colombia and Venezuela.

1701—The Aruá Indians rebel in Brazil.

1707—The Paunaca, Unape, and Carababa Indians join the Roman Catholic mission at Concepción, Bolivia. The Shimigae Rebellion begins in Peru.

1708—Jesuits peacefully settle many Yurimagua Indians on missions in the Amazon Valley.

1710—Estéban Urizar y Arespacochaga conquers the Lule-Vilela Indians of the Gran Chaco (now extinct) and begins the conquest of the Malbala Indians.

1711—Father Juan Bautista de Zea discovers the Morotoco Indians of the Gran Chaco.

1718—A smallpox epidemic all but destroys the Calchaquí Indians of the Gran Chaco. Portuguese slavers begin to disrupt the Indian tribes of Mato Grosso, Brazil, and of eastern Bolivia.

1719—A Portuguese expedition under João da Barros da Guerra slaughters large numbers of Torá Indians in western Brazil and eastern Bolivia.

1720—Brazilian explorers reach Boróro territory in north central Mato Grosso and displace the Indians, dividing them into the Eastern and the Western Boróro. Neo-Bolivian settlers enslave thousands of Itonama Indians.

1723—The Araucanian Rebellion begins.

1724—Worried about being sold as slaves, the Orejón begin abandoning the mission settlements in Peru.

1726—Jesuit missionaries begin to missionize the Zamuco and Cucurare Indians of the Gran Chaco.

1727—A large-scale Chiriguano revolt takes place in Bolivia against Jesuit missions.

1732—Neo-Brazilian gold prospectors establish contact with the various tribes in what is today the state of Rondônia.

1734—A large Portuguese military expedition heads up the Paraguay River and slaughters large numbers of Paiagua Indians.

1735—The Jesuits begin a successful missionization process among the Vilela Indians of the Gran Chaco.

1736—A gold rush begins in Mato Grosso, Brazil.

1737—Spanish missionaries contact the Iquito Indians of Peru and settle them on missions.

1738—The Urarina join the Roman Catholic mission on the Chambira River in Peru.

1739—Jesuits establish missions among the Yaruro Indians of Brazil.

1740—The Southern Payagua Indians settle in Asunción, Paraguay. Another Araucanian rebellion begins in Chile.

1742—The Tarma Rebellion begins in Peru. Tarma are now extinct.

1743—A Siona rebellion begins in Colombia. Jesuit missionaries begin the successful missionization of the Mocoví Indians of the Gran Chaco.

1744—Jesuit priest Manuel Román establishes contact with the Yekuana Indians of Venezuela.

1748—Roman Catholic missionaries reach the Cahuarano Indians of Peru, and Jesuit missionaries begin to missionize the Abipón Indians of the Gran Chaco (now extinct).

1749—The expedition of João Gonçalves da Fonseca establishes contact with the Murá Indians of Brazil.

1750—The Treaty of Madrid establishes the boundary between the Portuguese and Spanish empires in South America. Portuguese missionaries first reach the Letuana Indians of Colombia. Jesuit missionaries establish contact with the Yuruna and Shipaya Indians of the Xingú River in Brazil. Portugal officially abolishes Indian slavery.

1751—Kayapó Indians attack the city of Goiás, Brazil.

1753—The Atahuallpa Revolt takes place in Peru.

1754—Governor Francisco Xavier da Mendonça Furtado begins his first journey up the Amazon River in Brazil. Measles epidemics devastate the Campé Indians in Rondônia, Brazil.

1755—Sebastião José da Pombal of Portugal establishes the Law of Liberty for Indians under Portuguese control. Portugal also passes legislation removing all temporal control over Indians from missionaries. Pinto da Silveira slaughters the Karajá Indians on Bananal Island in Brazil.

1756—A combined Spanish-Portuguese army attacks and destroys the Guaraní of the Sete Povos missions at Caibate in Rio Grande do Sul, Brazil. The Seven Years' War begins. Portugal declares war on Spain. The Baré Indians of Colombia and Venezuela begin settling in Roman Catholic missions in Solano, Santa Rosa de Amanadona, and San Carlos de Río Negro, while Jesuits begin to missionize the Toba and Mataco Indians of the Gran Chaco.

1757—Governor Mendonça Furtado establishes the "Directorate" for the Amazon Indians in Brazil. The conquest of the Akroa Indians (now extinct) of northern Goiás in Brazil begins. Many Indians at Lamalonga on the Middle Negro River in Brazil rebel. Spanish missionaries first reach the Cashibo Indians of Peru. Franciscan missionaries begin their work among the Chiriguano Indians of Bolivia.

1758—Governor Mendonça Furtado begins his journey on the Negro River in Brazil.

1759—The Jesuits are expelled from the Portuguese empire, including Brazil.

1762—The Portuguese establish forts at São Gabriel on the Vaupés River and Marabitanas on the Negro River in Brazil.

1763—The capital of Brazil is moved from Salvador (Bahia) to Rio de Janeiro. The Seven Years' War ends.

1764—Portuguese expeditions defeat the Guenguen and Akroá Indians in Piaui, Brazil.

1766—A smallpox epidemic devastates the Chamicuro Indians of Peru. Roman Catholic missionaries establish a mission for the Laytana Indians of Paraguay. Another Araucanian rebellion begins in Chile.

1767—The Jesuits are expelled from the Spanish empire. Portuguese expeditions begin to explore the Guarapuava plains in Paraná, Brazil, and Portuguese authorities establish control over the Coroado Indians of Brazil.

1768—José Monteiro da Noronha begins the exploration of the Rio Negro River in Brazil. Franciscan and Dominican missionaries begin resettling Conibo Indians on the former Jesuit missions. A smallpox epidemic sweeps through the Chamicura Indians of Peru.

1769—Captain James Cook of Great Britain visits several tribes in Tierra del Fuego.

1770—Jaõa Leme do Prado establishes contact with the Nambiquára Indians of Brazil.

1772—The first peaceful contact between neo-Colombian settlers and the Barí Indians is established.

1774—The Portuguese capture Spanish troops on the upper Branco River. Neo-Brazilian settlers first contact the Apinayé Indians in the northern reaches of Goiás, Brazil. The Brazilian gold rush of the 1750s and 1760s begins to decline. The Portuguese launch a war of extermination against the Murá Indians of Brazil.

1775—The Portuguese build Fort São Joaquim on the Branco River and Fort Coimbra on the Paraguay River. Pinto da Fonseca's expedition makes peace with the Karajá Indians on the Araguaia River.

1776—Spanish priest Francisco Marcos establishes a mission among the Yuracare Indians of Bolivia.

1777—The Treaty of San Ildefonso redefines the boundaries between Brazil and Paraguay, returning a number of mission areas to Spain.

1778—The Guaycuru Indians attack Fort Coimbra on the Paraguay River. The Portuguese build Fort Albuquerque on the Paraguay River.

1779—Capuchin missionaries begin to collect the Chake, Mape, Motilones, Sabril, Coyamo, and Aratomo Indians of Colombia into missions. The Chayanta Rebellion begins in Peru.

1780—Francisco Gabino Arias founds missions for the Mocoví and Toba Indians in the Gran Chaco. The Tupac Amaru Rebellion begins in Peru, as does the Mundurukú Rebellion in Brazil. Severe epidemics afflict the Wakuénai Indians in Colombia and Brazil.

1781—The Guaycuru sign a peace treaty with the Portuguese. The Southern Kayapó move to *aldeias* settlements near Goiás, Brazil. Portuguese boundary commissioners explore the upper Negro River, the Branco River, and the Vaupés River. A large-scale rebellion of Aymara Indians occurs in Bolivia.

1782—Francisco Requeña y Herrera and Teodosio Chermont explore the Japura River.

1783—Ricardo Franco de Almeida Serra begins the exploration of the upper Guaporé and Paraguay rivers.

1784—Alexander Rodrigues Ferreira begins his scientific expeditions to the Amazon, Negro, and Branco rivers. Bishop Caetano Brandão begins his expeditions up the Amazon River. Portuguese explorer Manual de Gama Lobo do Almada ascends the Vaupés River and begins to establish missions there.

1785—The Murá tribe on the Solimões, Madeira, and Negro rivers surrenders to the Portuguese.

1787—The Xavánte settle at the *aldeia* at Carretao north of Goias.

1790—The Makushí on the upper Branco River rebel against the increase in neo-Brazilian settlement and are driven off their tribal lands. Northern Payagua Indians settle in Asunción, Paraguay. A smallpox epidemic destroys the Guanaca Indians of Colombia.

1791—Neo-Brazilian settlers first contact the Apiacá Indians in northern Mato Grosso, Brazil.

1792—Tomás de Souza Villa Real begins his expeditions on the Araguaia and Tocantins rivers.

1794—The Baure and Guarayo Indians of eastern Bolivia begin to enter Roman Catholic missions.

1795—The Mundurukú living on the Tapajós River surrender and are relocated to the lower Tapajós and Amazon rivers. Spanish missionaries establish a mission among the Píro Indians of Brazil.

1796—British troops defeat the Garífuna on St. Vincent Island and relocate them to the Bay Islands in the Gulf of Honduras.

1797—The Portuguese build Fort São João das Duas Barras at the confluence of the Araguaia and Tocantins rivers.

1798—Portuguese soldiers slaughter large numbers of Wapishána and Parviana Indians in raids along the upper Branco River.

1799—The Puri in Paraiba, Brazil (now extinct), agree to settle in the Queluz mission, and the Mundurukú of Brazil settle in missions as well.

1802—European settlers first learn of the Chamacoco Indians of the Gran Chaco.

1806—Canela Indians begin their raids on cattle ranches in Maranhão, Brazil.

1808—The neo-Brazilians launch war against the Botocudo and the Kaingáng.

1809—Pinto de Magalhães defeats the Krahó Indians and establishes the Carolina settlement on the Tocantins River. The Kaingáng Indians in Guarapuava, Brazil, begin to surrender in increasing numbers, while peaceful contact is established with the Krahó Indians of the state of Goiás, Brazil. A smallpox epidemic sweeps through the Tehuelche Indians of Argentina. The first successful mission among the Píro Indians of Peru is established.

1810—Father Chagas Lima establishes a mission among the Kaingáng in Paraná, Brazil.

1812—Smallpox epidemics bring devastation to the Canela Indians of Brazil.

1813—Karajá, Xavánte, and Apinayé Indians attack and destroy the Santa Maria settlement on the Araguaia River. Guido Marliere begins his work among the Coroado, Coropo, and Puri Indians in Minas Gerais, Brazil.

1814—A large-scale rebellion of Aymara Indians of Bolivia breaks out. Neo-Brazilians launch a war of extermination against the Krenkatëyé Indians of the Tocantins-Araguaia River drainage system of Brazil.

1815—A Portuguese military expedition slaughters Timbira Indians near the Carolina settlement on the Tocantins River. The Quiché Rebellion begins in Guatamala.

1816—The beginning of war between Brazil and Paraguay leads to the slaughter of thousands of Guaraní Indians.

1817—A Portuguese military expedition is launched against the Western Boróro near Cuiaba, Brazil. J. B. von Spix and C.P.F. von Martius begin their exploration from São Pãolo to the upper Amazon and Negro rivers. Portuguese officials settle the Kamacán Indians on government *aldeias*. Epidemic diseases devastate the Kapanáwa Indians of Peru.

1818—The Barí Indians retreat into the jungles of the Maracaibo basin in northeastern Colombia and northwestern Venezuela to end their contact with white society.

1819—Marliere begins the pacification of the Botocudo on the upper Doce River.

1820—The expedition of Francisco Lopes da Sa reaches the Tapayúna and Apiacá Indians of Brazil.

1822—Emperor Dom Pedro II declares the independence of Brazil.

1823—Charles Macintosh invents waterproof rubber material, greatly stimulating the demand for raw rubber.

1826—Baron Georg von Langsdorff begins his expedition to Cuiaba and down the Arinos-Tapajós River system.

1828—Mawé Indians of Brazil begin to settle on the Tapajós River mission in Brazil.

1830—Capuchin missionaries establish a mission for the Kaiwá Indians of Mato Grosso, Brazil.

1832—Ipecac boom brings tens of thousands of neo-Brazilian collectors into Mato Grosso and southern Rondônia, Brazil.

1833—European settlers first contact the Ashluslay Indians of Paraguay.

1835—The Cabano Rebellion begins in Brazil.

1836—The Cabano capture Manaus, Brazil.

1837—Europeans establish contact with the Waiwai Indians of Brazil and Guyana.

1838—Murá Indians slaughter a group of Brazilian government forces under Ambrosio Pedro Ayres.

1839—An amnesty ends the Cabano rebellion. Robert and Richard Schomburgk begin their explorations in northern Brazil.

1840—Italian Capuchin missionaries arrive in Brazil.

1842—Brazilian settlers establish contact with the Anambé Indians. Father Silva Fraga converts large numbers of Boróro Indians near Cabacal, Brazil. Prince Adalbert and Count von Bismarck visit the Xingú River region.

1843—A large-scale civil war breaks out among the Kaingáng Indians of Santa Catarina and Rio Grande do Sul, Brazil. Dutch explorer Robert Schomburgk first reaches the Tiriyó Indians of Surinam.

1844—Baron Silva Machado Antonina begins his attempt to settle and pacify the Kaiwá Indians in Paraná, Brazil.

1845—Brazil passes the Imperial Laws on Indians.

1846—The Count of Castelnau explores the Araguaia and Tocantins rivers.

1847—Miguel Rodriguez Ferrar, a Spanish anthropologist, reports the existence of surviving Indian people on the eastern tip of Cuba.

1848—The Henry Bates and Alfred Wallace scientific expeditions begin on the Amazon River. Neo-Peruvian settlers make contact with the Zaparo Indians. Capuchin missionaries begin work among the Araucanian Indians of Chile. Dictator Carlos Antonio López of Paraguay forces all Guaraní out of the mission settlements and into the general population.

1849—Father Rafael de Taggia relocates the Krahó Indians to the Tocantins River.

1850—Coffee plantations begin to spread west in São Pãolo, Brazil.

1852—Father de Taggia again relocates the Krahó in Brazil. The Karajá Indians destroy the Santa Maria presidio on the Araguaia River in Brazil. Teofilo Otoni begins his colony of Filadelfia among the Botocudo of Mucuri, Brazil. Capuchin missionaries establish a mission among the Kinikinao Indians of southern Mato Grosso.

1856—The Avá Indians begin their reign of terror throughout northern Goiás, Brazil.

1857—A Brazilian military expedition of extermination all but destroys the Gavião Indians of Pará and Maranhão, Brazil.

1859—Brazilian settlers slaughter large numbers of Kaingáng in Guarapuava.

1860—The Tenetehára Indians rebel in Maranhão, Brazil. A smallpox epidemic breaks out among the tribes of the Peruvian and Ecuadorian montana.

1863—Brazilian settlers commence warfare against the Waimiri and Atroarí Indians in Jauaperi on the lower Negro River.

1864—The Paraguay-Brazil War begins, bringing catastrophe to large numbers of Guaraní, Guato, Guaycuru, and Teréna Indians. William Chandless begins his exploration of the Purús, Acre, and Juruá River systems in Brazil.

1866—Brazil opens the Amazon River system to foreign shipping. The Chiriguano Revolt begins in Bolivia. The government of Chile establishes a reservation policy for the Mapuche Indians.

1869—The Mapuche Rebellion begins.

1871—In Brazil, Couto de Magalhães establishes his steamship line on the Araguaia River, while João Barbosa Rodrigues begins his exploration of the Trombetas River there. Arára Indians gather at the São Francisco Mission on the Machado River, and Turiwara and Tembé Indians begin to settle at the Pracateua Mission on the Capim River, all in Brazil. The government of Guatemala passes legislation to convert Indian tribal lands to individual ownership, precipitating widespread opposition among Mayan Indians.

1872—Railroad construction from Campinas, Brazil, deep into São Pãolo Province invades Kaingáng territory. Kabixí Indians begin a series of attacks on neo-Brazilian settlements and mining camps in Mato Grosso and southern Rondônia, Brazil. Roman Catholic missionaries begin to gather the Amanayé, Tembé, and Turiwara Indians of the Capim River area of Brazil into missions.

1873—Brazil launches a military expedition against the Eastern Boróro in Coroado. Capuchin missionaries establish the Itambacuri mission among the Botocodu.

1874—The Chiriguano Revolt begins in Bolivia.

1877—Jules Crevaux explores the Jari and Paru River systems in Brazil, while a measles epidemic devastates the Kulína Indians there.

1879—F. X. Lopes de Araujo explores the region of the Brazil-Venezuela border. Salesian missionaries begin working among the Araucanian Indians of Chile.

1880—The last major Araucanian rebellion begins.

1881—Brazil closes its presidios on the Araguaia River. The Franciscans establish successful missions among the Cubeo, Tukano, and Uanana Indians of the Vaupés region of Colombia and Brazil.

1884—Barbosa Rodrigues contacts the Waimiri-Atroarí on the Jauaperi River in Brazil. Karl Von den Steinen begins his first descent of the Xingú River.

1885—Antonio José Duarte pacifies some Eastern Boróro in Brazil, and Henri Coudreau travels from the Branco River to the upper Trombetas River there.

1886—Rubber collectors establish permanent contact with the Witoto Indians of Colombia and Brazil.

1887—Karl Von den Steinen begins his second expedition to the upper Xingú River, and Antonio Labre explores the Acre River to the Madre de Dios River region in Brazil. F. A. Pimenta Buenos explores the border region between Brazil and British Guiana. The South American Evangelical Society begins its work among the Gran Chaco tribes, while British missionaries begin work among the Lengua.

1888—Salesian missionaries establish a mission for the Alacaluf Indians of Chile.

1889—The establishment of the Peruvian Corporation opens millions of acres of land in eastern Peru to developers and settlers.

1890—Cândido Rondon begins to construct the Cuiaba-Goiás telegraph in Brazil.

1891—A large-scale massacre of Chiriguano Indians begins in Bolivia.

1894—The great South American rubber boom begins and wreaks havoc among the jungle tribes of Brazil, Bolivia, Peru, Venezuela, and Colombia. The Asuriní Rebellion begins in the middle Xingú River region of central Brazil.

1895—Salesian missionaries take over the Boróro *aldeias*. Henri Coudreau begins his exploration of several river systems in Pará, Brazil.

1896—Father Gil Vilanova of the Dominican order contacts the Kayapó and founds Conceiçao do Araguaia in Brazil. Hermann Meyer begins his first expedition up the Xingú River. Control of the Miskito Indians shifts from Great Britain to Nicaragua.

1899—Hermann Meyer begins his second expedition up the Xingú River.

1900—Rondon begins to construct the telegraph from Cuiaba to Corumba in Brazil. The

Tenetehára Indians rebel in Maranhão, Brazil, after suffering a severe measles epidemic; Brazil begins a war of extermination against them.

1901—Tenetehára Indians rebel near Barra do Corda, Maranhão, Brazil.

1903—Theodore Koch-Grünberg contacts tribes in the regions of the Vaupés, Içana, and Negro rivers in Brazil and Colombia.

1904—Baníwa Indians flee the military forces of Tomás Fuñes in Venezuela and cross the border to live in Brazil.

1906—Rondon begins construction of telegraph lines north and west out of Cuiaba, Brazil.

1907—Construction of the Madeira-Mamoré Railway begins in Brazil. Protestant and Catholic missions are established among the Cuna Indians of Panama. Rondon makes contact with the Nambiquára Indians of Brazil.

1908—Atrocities against Indians by rubber collectors in the Putomayo River area of Brazil and Peru lead to an international investigation headed by Roger Casement of Great Britain.

1910—Rondon agrees to head the newly established Indian Protection Service in Brazil. The Brazilian Indian Protection Service pacifies the last band of the Botocudo Indians. Petroleum prospectors enter the Vaupés River drainage area of Colombia and Venezuela.

1911—The last Kaingáng group is peacefully settled in the state of São Pãolo, Brazil.

1912—Rondon pacifies the Kepkiriwat Indians of Rondônia, Brazil, and the Brazilian Indian Protection Service establishes contact with the Tapirapé Indians of Brazil.

1913—Rondon discovers the Arikén Indians in Brazil, and the Brazilian Indian Protection Service pacifies the Poyanáwa Indians.

1914—The Brazilian government establishes peaceful contact with the Aweikoma Indians, and some relocate to a reservation outside the town of Ibirama. Roman Catholic missionaries establish a series of missions among the Eastern Tukano Indians of the Vaupés River drainage area of Colombia and Brazil. Dominican missionaries begin work among the Tapirapé Indians of Brazil.

1915—The expedition of Pyrineus de Souza establishes contact with the Kayabí Indians of Brazil.

1916—The Juruna Indians avoid extinction at the hands of rubber collectors by migrating up the Xingú River, above the Von Martius Rapids in Brazil. The Toba Rebellion begins in Argentina and Paraguay.

1920—The rubber boom collapses.

1922—The Brazilian Indian Protection Service establishes peaceful contact with the Parintintín Indians.

1923—German anthropologist Curt Nimuendajú establishes peaceful contact with the Kawahíb Indians of Brazil. William Farrabee's anthropological expedition contacts the Parukoto Indians of the northern Amazon basin. The government of Chile passes legislation to protect the Qawasqar Indians.

1924—The Brazilian Indian Protection Service pacifies large numbers of Kayabí Indians in the state of Mato Grosso. Another Toba Rebellion begins in Argentina and Paraguay. British Honduras establishes special reservations for the Maya tribes.

1925—An Ucayali Rebellion begins in Peru, and a Cuna Rebellion begins in Panama.

1927—Asuriní Indians in the Tocantins River area of Brazil attack railroad construction workers.

1928—Rondon establishes contact with the Tiriyó Indians of Surinam. The Brazilian Indian Protection Service establishes regular contact with the Urubú Indians.

1929—The Christian and Missionary Alliance places Protestant missionaries among the Gambiano Indians of Colombia.

1930—The discovery of gold in Ecuador brings an invasion of neo-Ecuadorians into Jívaro land. Panama creates a large reserve of original land for the San Blas Cuna Indians.

1932—The Chaco War between Paraguay and Bolivia begins.

1935—The Chaco War between Paraguay and Bolivia, which results in the deaths of tens of thousands of Indians, ends. The outbreak of war between Peru and Colombia devastates the Matapi Indians of Colombia. Heinrich Snethlage establishes peaceful contact with the Moré Indians of eastern Bolivia.

1936—The Brazilian Indian Protection Service pacifies the Gorotíre Indians in Para. The Pilagá Indians of the Gran Chaco place themselves under the control of the South American Missionary Society, a Protestant group.

1940—The outbreak of World War II creates a new rubber boom that inflicts more damage on the jungle Indians of Brazil, Bolivia, Peru, Ecuador, Colombia, and Venezuela. Neo-Brazilian cattle ranchers attack the Krahó Indians in the state of Goiás. A smallpox epidemic kills large numbers of Pilagá Indians in Argentina and Paraguay.

1945—Father Ismael Barrio establishes contact with the Arabela Indians of Peru.

1946—Neo-Paraguayan and neo-Bolivian settlers establish peaceful contact with the Ayoreo Indians.

1947—The New Tribes Mission begins its work among the Wakuénai Indians of Colombia and Brazil.

1948—Mass settlement of the Colombian and Venezuelan llanos begins and threatens the tribes living there. A smallpox epidemic devastates the Wachipaeri Indians of Peru.

1949—Orlando and Cláudio Villas Boas contact the Juruna Indians of Brazil.

1950—A smallpox epidemic devastates the Kulína Indians of Brazil.

1952—Orlando and Cláudio Villas Boas convince the Kayabí Indians to relocate inside the Xingú Indian Park in Brazil. Construction of the Tocantins Railroad in Brazil invades Parakana land.

1953—The Cuiva Indians of Venezuela and Colombia begin a series of attacks on cattle ranches. Roman Catholic missionaries establish peaceful contact with the Surui Indians of Brazil, and Brazilian government anthropologists pacify several groups of Tupi-speaking Asuriní Indians.

1954—Capuchin missionaries settle large numbers of Cushma Indians of Ecuador on the mission at Apostolic Prefecture de Aguarico. Large numbers of Tetete, Auca, Yumbo, Kofán, and Siona Indians join them there. The first contact with the Heta

Indians of Parana, Brazil, is made. The Mentuktíre Indians relocate to the Xingú Indian Park in Brazil.

1955—The Summer Institute of Linguistics begins work among the Kozarene Indians of Brazil.

1956—Auca Indians of Ecuador slaughter five missionaries, and Awishiri Indians of eastern Peru kill six missionaries. The New Tribes Mission begins work among the Pakaanova Indians of Brazil.

1957—The Brazilian government uses Gavião Indians to contact the Arára Indians in eastern Rondônia and establishes peaceful contact with the Kokraimôro.

1959—The Protestant-America Door-to-Life Gospel Mission establishes itself among the Tiriyó Indians of Brazil and Surinam.

1960—The Summer Institute of Linguistics begins work among the Siona and Tabaino Indians of Colombia. The government of Venezuela establishes a reservation for the Yukpa Indians. Orlando and Cláudio Villas Boas make contact with the Suyá Indians of Brazil.

1961—Protestant missionaries contact the Aripaktsa Indians in northwestern Mato Grosso, Brazil. The government of Brazil formally establishes the Xingú Indian Park. Anthropologists from the Royal Geographical Society of London discover the Kreen-Akarôre Indians in Mato Grosso, Brazil.

1962—The Eastern Suyá Indians relocate to the Xingú Indian Park in Brazil.

1963—The Arruda and Junquiera Company, a Brazilian rubber concern, launches a military strike against the Cinta Larga Indians of Rondônia, Brazil. The World Evangelization Crusade and Summer Institute of Linguistics begin work among the Guahibo of Colombia and Venezuela. Measles all but destroys the Sabané Indians of Brazil. The Mekranotí Indians of Brazil enter the Xingú Indian Park.

1964—The New Tribes Mission establishes peaceful contact with the Araona Indians of Bolivia. The Summer Institute of Linguistics begins work among the Guajiro and Tunebo Indians of Colombia and Venezuela. Orlando and Cláudio Villas Boas establish contact with the Txikão Indians of Brazil.

1965—The Summer Institute of Linguistics establishes permanent contact with the Barasána Indians of Colombia. The Beico do Pau Indians, suffering from a flu epidemic, are relocated to the Xingú Indian Park.

1966—Measles epidemics devastate the Kararão Indians of Pará, Brazil. The Summer Institute of Linguistics begins work among the Piapoco Indians of Colombia and Venezuela.

1967—The Brazilian government establishes the Aripuanã Indian Park in the state of Rondônia, Brazil.

1969—A severe polio epidemic devastates the Awishiri Indians of eastern Peru. The Summer Institute of Linguistics begins work among the Chimila and Tatuyo Indians of Colombia.

1971—Paraguayans begin a near-genocidal war against the Aché Indians. Petroleum exploration brings destruction to the tribes of the Peruvian Amazon.

1972—Brazilian government social workers establish peaceful contact with the Asuriní Indians. Ayoreo Indians agree to settle at the New Tribes Mission at Faro Moro,

Paraguay, and at the Salesian mission at Maria Auxiliadora. Systematic contact with the Yanoama Indians of Brazil and Venezuela begins.

1973—The government of Peru establishes a reservation for the Mayorúna Indians. Pisabo Indians attack oil exploration groups between the Tapiche and Blanco rivers in Peru.

1974—Orlando and Cláudio Villas Boas convince the Kreen-Akarôre Indians to relocate to the Xingú Indian Park in Brazil.

1975—Influenza and tuberculosis epidemics devastate the Cinta Larga and Suruí Indians of Brazil. Brazilian government agents establish peaceful contact with the Guajá Indians in Maranhão, Brazil. The Guerrilla Army of the Poor begins recruiting Mayan Indians in Guatemala.

1977—Brazilian government anthropologists establish contact with the Zoró Indians.

1978—Guatemalan government troops slaughter more than 100 Kekchí Indians. Pesch and Jicaque Indians, along with representatives of other tribes, form the National Federation of Tribes for the Liberation of the Honduran Indian.

1979—The Urueu-Wau-Wáu uprising begins in Brazil. The Sandinista Revolution in Nicaragua brings new pressures to assimilate the Miskito, Sumo, and Rama Indians.

1980—A severe measles epidemic sweeps through the Negro and Guainía River areas of Venezuela.

1984—Frustrated Brazilian ranchers begin a violent campaign of eviction against the Pataxó Indians.

1985—The Gambiano and Páez Indians of Colombia establish the Commando Quintin Lamé, a guerrilla organization to resist seizures of their land. The Zoró Rebellion erupts in Brazil. Shining Path guerrilla movement gains ground in central Peru.

1986—The Zoró Indians are relocated to the Aripuanã Indian Park in Brazil. Several Ayoreo Indians are killed when the New Tribes Mission attempts to relocate them in Brazil.

1987—Kayapó Indian leaders join with the leaders of 28 other Brazilian Indian tribes to oppose hydroelectric development of the Amazon Basin, and the Union of Indigenous Nations in Brazil demands constitutional protection for indigenous people.

1988—The Brazilian government announces its intention to demarcate Yanoama land. The Confederation of Indian Nations of the Ecuadorian Amazon demands protection of Indian land rights.

SELECTED
BIBLIOGRAPHY

GENERAL

Alvarsson, Jan-Ake. *Bolivia: Indianland*. 1980.

Aspelin, Paul Leslie, and Silvio Coelho dos Santos. *Indian Areas Threatened by Hydroelectric Projects in Brazil*. 1981.

Aveni, Anthony, and Gordon Brotherston, eds. *Ethnoastronomy and Archaeoastronomy in the American Tropics*. 1982.

Baker, Paul T. *Man in the Andes: Multidisciplinary Study of High-Altitude Quechua*. 1976.

Balée, William. "Cultural Forests of the Amazon." *Garden*, 11 (1987), 12–14, 32.

Balée, William. "Indigenous Adaptation to Amazonian Palm Forests." *Principes*, 32 (1988), 47–54.

Bamberger, Joan. "The Myth of Matriarchy: Why Men Rule in Primitive Society." In M. Zimbalist Rosaldo and Lawrence Lamphere, eds., *Women, Culture and Society*. 1974. Pp. 263–80.

Barreiro, José. "Indians in Cuba." *Cultural Survival Quarterly*, 13 (1989), 56–60.

Bastien, Joseph William. *Mountain of the Condor: Metaphor and Ritual in an Andean Ayllu*. 1978.

Beattie, J. M., and R. G. Leinhardt, eds. *Studies in Social Anthropology in Memory of E. E. Evans-Pritchard*. 1975.

Beckerman, Stephen. "The Abundance of Protein in Amazonia: A Reply to Gross." *American Anthropologist*, 81 (1979), 533–60.

Bennett Ross, John. "Ecology and the Problem of Tribe: A Critique of the Hobbesian Model of Preindustrial Warfare." In Eric Ross, ed., *Beyond the Myths of Culture: Essays in Cultural Materialism*. 1980. Pp. 33–60.

Berglund, Steffan. *The New Indianism: A Threat Against Imperialism and Underdevelopment*. 1979.

Berglund, Steffan. *Resisting Poverty: Perspectives on Participation and Social Development: The Case of CRIC and the Eastern Rural Region of Cauca in Colombia*. 1982.

Bharati, Agehananda, ed. *The Realm of the Extra-Human Senses: Ideas and Actions*. 1976.

Bisilliat, Maureen. *Xingu: Tribal Territory*. 1979.

Black, George. *Guatemala: The Making of a Revolution*. 1984.

Bodard, Lucien. *Green Hell: Massacre of the Brazilian Indians*. 1971.

Bodard, Lucien. *Massacre on the Amazon*. 1971.

Bolton, Ralph. *Andean Kinship and Marriage*. 1977.

Borque, Susan Carolyn. *Denial and Reaffirmation of Ethnic Identities: A Comparative Examination of Guatemalan and Peruvian Communities*. 1978.

Borque, Susan C., and Kay Barbara Warren. *Women of the Andes: Patriarchy and Social Change in Two Peruvian Towns*. 1981.

Bossen, Laurel. "Plantations and Labor Force Discrimination in Guatemala." *Current Anthropology*, 23 (1982), 263–68.

Bray, Warwick, and Colin Dollery. "Coca Chewing and High Altitude Stress: A Spurious Correlation." *Current Anthropology*, 24 (1983), 269–82.

Broadbent, Sylvia M. "The Formation of Peasant Society in Central Colombia." *Ethnohistory*, 28 (1981), 259–77.

Brooks, Edwin, Rene Fuerst, John Hemming, and Francis Huxley. *Tribes of the Amazon Basin, Brazil 1972*. 1973.

Browman, David L. *Peasants, Primitives and Proletariat: The Struggle for Identity in South America*. 1979.

Browman, David L., and Ronald A. Schwartz, eds. *Spirits, Shamans, and Stars: Perspectives from South America*. 1979.

Brush, Stephen B. "The Environment and Native Andean Agriculture." *America Indigena*, 40 (1980), 161–72.

Brush, Stephen B. *Mountain, Field, and Family: The Economy and Human Ecology of an Andean Valley*. 1977.

Caraman, Philip. *The Lost Paradise: The Jesuit Republic in South America*. 1976.

Carneiro, Robert Leonard. *Anthropological Investigations in Amazonia: Selected Papers*. 1985.

Carneiro, Robert Leonard. "The Transition from Hunting to Horticulture in the Amazon Basin." *Eighth Congress of Anthropological and Ethnological Sciences* (1970), 244–48.

Carter, William E. *Coca in Bolivia*. 1980.

Chapin, Mac. "The 500,000 Invisible Indians of El Salvador." *Cultural Survival Quarterly*, 13 (1989), 11–20.

Chesser, Barbara. "The Anthropomorphic Personal Guardian Spirit in Aboriginal South America." *Journal of Latin American Lore*, 1 (1975), 107–26.

Chevalier, Jacques M. *Civilization and the Stolen Gift: Capital, Kin, and Cult in Eastern Peru*. 1982.

Chiappino, Jean. *The Brazilian Indigenous Problem and Policy: The Aripuanã Park*. 1975.

Chibnik, Michael, and Wil de Jong. "Agricultural Labor Organization in Ribereiro Communities of the Peruvian Amazon." *Ethnology*, 28 (1989), 75–95.

CIDCA. *Ethnic Groups and the Nation State: The Case of the Atlantic Coast in Nicaragua.* 1987.

Civrieux, Marc de. *Watunna: An Orinoco Creation Cycle.* 1980.

Clark, K., and C. Uhl. "Farming, Fishing, and Fire in the History of the Upper Rio Negro Region of Venezuela." *Human Ecology*, 15 (1987), 1–26.

Coimbra, Carlos E. A., Jr. "Human Settlements, Demographic Patterns, and Epidemiology in Lowland Amazonia: The Case of Chagas's Disease." *American Anthropologist*, 90 (1988), 82–97.

Cook, N. David. *The People of the Colca Valley: A Population Study.* 1981.

Cordoba-Rios, Manuel. *The Stolen Chief: Adventures of a Captive in the Amazonas Jungle.* 1972.

Cordoba-Rios, Manuel. *Wizard of the Upper Amazon: The Story of Manuel Cordoba-Rios.* 1975.

Counce, Melanie A., and William V. Douglas. "Indians of Central America 1980s." *Cultural Survival Quarterly*, 13 (1989), 38–41.

Crain, Mary. "The Social Construction of a National Identity in Highland Ecuador." *Anthropological Quarterly*, 63 (1990), 43–59.

Cultural Survival. *Brazilian Indians and the Law.* 1981.

Cultural Survival. *El Salvador's Indians.* 1982.

Custred, Glynn. "Hunting Technologies in Andean Culture." *Journal de la Société des Américanistes*, 66 (1979), 7–19.

Davies, Thomas M. *Indian Integration in Peru: A Half Century of Experience, 1900–1948.* 1974.

Davis, Shelton H. *The Geological Imperative: Anthropology and Development in the Amazon Basin of South America.* 1976.

De Boer, William. "Buffer Zones in the Cultural Ecology of Aboriginal Amazonia: An Ethnohistorical Approach." *American Antiquity*, 48 (1981), 364–77.

Demarast, Arthur Andrew. *Viracocha: The Nature and Antiquity of the Andean High God.* 1981.

Deneven, William. "The Aboriginal Cultural Geography of the Llanos de Mojos of Bolivia." *Ibero-Americana*, 48 (1966), 1–185.

Deneven, William. "The Aboriginal Population of Western Amazonia in Relation to Habitat and Subsistence." *Revista Geográfica*, 72 (1970), 61–86.

Deneven, William, and Christian Padock, eds. *Swidden-Fallow Agroforestry in the Peruvian Amazon.* 1988.

Derbyshire, Desmond C., and Geoffrey K. Pullum. *Handbook of Amazonian Languages.* 1985.

Despres, Leo, ed. *Ethnicity and Resource Competition in Plural Societies.* 1975.

Dobkin de Rios, Marlene. *Visionary Vine: Psychedelic Healing in the Peruvian Amazon.* 1972.

Dostal, Walter, ed. *The Situation of the Indian in South America: Contributions to the Study of Inter-Ethnic Conflict in the Non-Andean Regions of South America.* 1972.

Dufour, Darna L. "Insects as Food: A Case Study from the Northwest Amazon." *American Anthropologist*, 89 (1987), 383–91.

Dufour, Darna L. "Nutrition in the Northwest Amazon: Household Dietary Intake and

Time-Energy Expenditure.'' In Raymond B. Hames and William T. Vickers, eds., *Adaptive Responses of Native Amazonians*. 1983. Pp. 329–55.

Edwards, Walter F. *Focus on Amerindians*. 1980.

Elder, Norman. *This Thing of Darkness: Elder's Amazon Notebooks*. 1979.

Ethnobotany in the Neotropics Symposium. *Ethnobotany in the Neotropics*. 1984.

Fagundes-Neto, U. R. ''Observations of the Alto Xingu Indians (Central Brazil) with Special Reference to the Nutritional Evaluation in Children.'' *American Journal of Clinical Nutrition*, 34 (1981), 2220–35.

Ferguson, R. Brian. ''Blood of the Leviathan: Western Contact and Warfare in Amazonia.'' *American Ethnologist*, 17 (1990), 237–57.

Ferguson, R. Brian. ''Ecological Consequences of Amazonian Warfare.'' *Ethnology*, 28 (1989), 249–64.

Ferguson, R. Brian. ''Game Wars? Ecology and Conflict in Amazonia.'' *Journal of Anthropological Research*, 45 (1989), 179–206.

Ferguson, R. Brian. ''War and the Sexes in Amazonia.'' In Richard E. Randolph, William M. Schneider, and May N. Diaz, eds., *Dialectics and Gender: Anthropological Approaches*. 1988. Pp. 136–54.

Ferguson, R. Brian, ed. *Warfare, Culture, and Environment*. 1984.

Fernside, Philip M. *Human Carrying Capacity of the Brazilian Rain Forest*. 1986.

Fine, Kathleen. ''Ideology, History, and Action in Cotocollao: A Barrio of Quito, Ecuador.'' Ph.D. diss., University of Illinois at Urbana-Champaign, 1986.

Fishman, O. M. ''Black Piedra among Brazilian Indians.'' *Revista do Instituto Medicina Tropical de São Pãolo*. 11 (1973), 527–34.

Flowers, Nancy. ''Seasonal Factors in Subsistence, Nutrition, and Child Growth in a Central Brazilian Indian Community.'' In Raymond B. Hames and William T. Vickers, eds., *Adaptive Responses of Native Amazonians*. 1983. Pp. 357–90.

Flowers, Nancy et al. ''Variations in Swidden Practices in Four Central Brazilian Indian Societies.'' *Human Ecology*, 10 (1982), 203–38.

Furst, Peter T., ed. *Flesh of the Gods: The Ritual Use of Hallucinogens*. 1972.

Gagliano, Joseph A. ''Coca and Popular Medicine in Peru: An Historical Analysis of Attitudes.'' In David L. Browman and Ronald A. Schwartz, eds., *Spirits, Shamans, and Stars: Perspectives from South America*. 1979. Pp. 39–54.

Galvão, Eduardo. ''Indians and Whites in the Brazilian Amazon.'' *Zeitschrift für Ethnologie*, 95 (1970), 220–30.

Global Report. *The Case for Political Asylum: Guatemala's Uprooted Indians*. 1978.

Golob, Andrew. ''The Upper Amazon in Historical Perspective.'' Ph.D. diss., City University of New York, 1982.

Gordon, Burton Le Roy. *Human Geography and Ecology in the Sinu Country of Colombia*. 1977.

Greenberg, Joseph H. *Language in the Americas*. Palo Alto, Calif.: Stanford University Press, 1987.

Gross, Daniel R. ''The Indians and the Brazilian Frontier.'' *Journal of International Affairs*, 36 (1982), 1–14.

Gross, Daniel R. ''A New Approach to Central Brazilian Social Organization.'' In Michael Martin, ed., *Contemporary Brazil*. 1979. Pp. 321–42.

Gross, Daniel R. ''Protein Capture and Cultural Development in the Amazon Basin.'' *American Anthropologist*, 77 (1975), 526–49.

Gross, Daniel R., et al. "Ecology and Acculturation Among Native Peoples of Central Brazil." *Science*, 206 (1979), 1043–50.

Gross, Daniel, and Barbara Underwood. "Technological Change and Caloric Costs: Sisal Agriculture in Northeast Brazil." *American Anthropologist*, 73 (1971), 725–40.

Gudeman, Stephen, and Alberto Rivera. "Colombian Conversations: The Strength of the Earth." *Current Anthropology*, 30 (1989), 267–82.

Guillet, David. "Terracing and Irrigation in the Peruvian Highlands." *Current Anthropology*, 28 (1987), 409–30.

Hames, Raymond B. *Adaptive Responses of Native Amazonians*. 1983.

Hames, Raymond B. "A Comparison of the Efficiencies of the Shotgun and the Bow in Neotropical Forest Hunting." *Human Ecology*, 7 (1979), 219–52.

Hames, Raymond B. *Studies in Hunting and Fishing in the Neotropics*. 1980.

Hames, Raymond B., and William Vickers. "Optimal Diet Breadth Theory as a Model to Explain Variability in Amazonian Hunting." *American Ethnologist*, 9 (1982), 358–78.

Hanbury-Tenison, Marika. *For Better, For Worse: To the Brazilian Jungles and Back Again*. 1972.

Hanbury-Tenison, Marika. *World's Apart: An Explorer's Life*. 1984.

Hanbury-Tenison, Robin. *A Question of Survival for the Indians of Brazil*. 1973.

Hanna, Joel M. "Coca Leaf Use in Southern Peru: Some Biological Aspects." *American Anthropologist*, 76 (1974), 281–96.

Harner, Michael J. *Hallucinogens and Shamanism*. 1973.

Harris, Marvin. "The Highland Heritage." In Daniel R. Gross, ed., *Peoples and Cultures in Native South America: An Anthropological Reader*. 1973. Pp. 411–32.

Hawkins, John. *Inverse Images: The Meaning of Culture, Ethnicity, and Family in Postcolonial Guatemala*. 1984.

Heath, Dwight, ed. *Contemporary Cultures and Societies of Latin America: A Reader in the Social Anthropology of Middle and South America*. 1974.

Heath, Ernest Gerald. *Brazilian Indian Archery: A Preliminary Ethno-Toxological Study of the Archery of the Brazilian Indians*. 1977.

Hefley, James C. *Unstilled Voices*. 1981.

Helguera, J. Leon. *Indigenismo in Colombia: A Facet of the National Identity Search, 1821–1973*. 1974.

Hemming, John. *Amazon Frontier: The Destruction of the Brazilian Indians*. 1987.

Hemming, John. *Red Gold: The Conquest of the Brazilian Indians*. 1978.

Hill, Jonathan D. *Rethinking History and Myth: Indigenous South American Perspectives on the Past*. 1988.

Hopper, Janice H. *Indians of Brazil in the Twentieth Century*. 1967.

Hugh-Jones, Christine. *From the Milk River: Spatial and Temporal Processes in Northwest Amazonia*. 1979.

Hugh-Jones, Stephen. *The Palm and the Pleiades: Initiation and Cosmology in Northwest Amazonia*. 1979.

Indigena and American Friends of Brazil. *Supysana: A Documentary Report on the Conditions of Indian Peoples in Brazil*. 1974.

Isbell, Billie Jean. "From Culture to Nature and Back Again." In Gary Urton, ed., *Animal Myths and Metaphors in South America*. 1985. Pp. 285–314.

Isbell, Billie Jean. *To Defend Ourselves: Ecology and Ritual in an Andean Village*. 1978.

Jackson, Jean E. *The Fish People: Linguistic Exogamy and Tukanoan Identity in Northwest Amazonia.* 1979.

Jackson, Jean E. "Recent Ethnography of Indigenous Northern Lowland South America." *Annual Review of Anthropology*, 4 (1975), 307–40.

Jackson, Jean E. "Vaupés Marriage Practices." In Kenneth M. Kensinger, ed., *Marriage Practices in Lowland South America.* 1984. Pp. 156–79.

Johnson, Allen. "Reductionism in Cultural Ecology: The Amazon Case." *Current Anthropology*, 23 (1982), 413–28.

Jones, Grant D. "Recent Ethnohistorical Works on Southeastern Mesoamerica." *Latin American Research Review*, 22 (1987), 214–42.

Junquiera, Carmen. *The Brazilian Indigenous Problem and Policy: The Example of the Xingú National Park.* 1973.

Kaplan, Abraham. "Cosmology as Ecological Analysis: A View from the Rain Forest." *Man*, 11 (1976), 307–18.

Kaplan, Joanne. "Amazonian Anthropology." *Journal of Latin American Lore*, 13 (1981), 151–64.

Kensinger, Kenneth M. *Food Taboos in Lowland South America.* 1981.

Kensinger, Kenneth M. *Sexual Ideologies in Lowland South America.* 1984.

Kensinger, Kenneth M., ed. *Marriage Practices in Lowland South America.* 1984.

Key, Mary Ritchie. *The Grouping of South American Indian Languages.* 1979.

Kiemen, Mathias Charles. *The Indian Policy of Portugal in the Amazon Region, 1614–1693.* 1973.

Kiltie, Richard. "More on Amazon Culture Ecology." *Current Anthropology*, 21 (1980), 541–44.

Kingsland, Rosemary. *A Saint Among Savages.* 1980.

Klein, Harriet, and Louisa Stark. "Indian Tribes of the Paraguayan Chaco." *Anthropological Linguistics*, 19 (1977), 378–402.

Klein, Harriet E. Manelis, and Louisa R. Stark, eds. *South American Indian Languages: Retrospect and Prospect.* 1985.

Kracke, Waud H. *Force and Persuasion: Leadership in an Amazonian Society.* 1978.

Kroeger, A. V. "Housing and Health in the Process of Cultural Adaptation: A Case Study Among Jungle and Highland Natives of Ecuador." *Journal of Tropical Medicine and Hygiene*, 83 (1980), 53–69.

Kroeger, A. V. "South American Indians Between Traditional and Modern Health Services in Rural Ecuador." *Bulletin of the Pan American Health Organization*, 16 (1982), 242–54.

Larson, Mildred L. *Bilingual Education: An Experience in Peruvian Amazonia.* 1981.

Lathrap, Donald W. "The Hunting Economies of the Tropical Forest Zone of South America: An Attempt at Historical Perspective." In Daniel R. Gross, ed. *Peoples and Cultures of Native South America: An Anthropological Reader.* 1973. Pp. 83–97.

Lathrap, Donald W. *The Upper Amazon.* 1970.

Lehmann, David, ed. *Ecology and Exchange in the Andes.* 1982.

Levi-Strauss, Claude. *The Elementary Structures of Kinship.* 1969.

Levi-Strauss, Claude. *From Honey to Ashes.* 1983.

Levi-Strauss, Claude. "Social Structures of Central and Eastern Brazil." In Daniel R. Gross, ed. *Peoples and Cultures of Native South America: An Anthropological Reader.* 1973. Pp. 263–76.

Lewellen, Ted C. "Aggression and Hypoglycemia in the Andes: Another Look at the Evidence." *Current Anthropology*, 22 (1981), 347–61.

Lewis, Norman. *Eastern Bolivia: The White Promised Land*. 1978.

Linares, Olga. "Garden Hunting in the American Tropics." *Human Ecology*, 4 (1976), 331–49.

Long, Jerry. *Amazonia Reborn*. 1970.

Longacre, Robert E., ed. *Discourse Grammar: Studies in Indigenous Languages of Colombia, Panama, and Ecuador*. 1976.

Loveland, Christine A., and Franklin V. Loveland. *Sex Roles and Social Change in Native Lower Central American Societies*. 1982.

Lovell, W. George. *Conquest and Survival in Colonial Guatemala: A Historical Geography of the Cuchumatan Highlands, 1500–1821*. 1984.

Lovell, W. George. "Surviving Conquest: The Maya of Guatemala in Historical Perspective." *Latin American Research Review*, 23 (1988), 25–58.

Lovin, Robin, and Frank Reynolds, ed. *Cosmogony and Ethical Order: New Studies in Comparative Ethics*. 1985.

Lowen, Jacob Abram. *Culture and Human Values: Christian Intervention in Anthropological Perspectives*. 1975.

Lozano, Eduardo. "Recent Books in Indian Literatures." *Latin American Indian Literatures*, 1 (1977), 41–60.

Lozano, Eduardo. "Recent Books on South American Indian Languages." *Latin American Indian Literatures*, 1 (1977), 97–122.

Lyon, Patricia J., ed. *Native South Americans: Ethnology of the Least Known Continent*. 1974.

Macdonald, Theodore. *Native Peoples and Economic Development: Six Case Studies from Latin America*. 1985.

Magana, Edmundo. "Note on Ethnoanthropological Notions of the Guiana Indians." *Anthropológica*, 24 (1982), 215–33.

Manz, Beatriz. *Refugees of a Hidden War: The Aftermath of Counterinsurgency in Guatemala*. 1988.

Maranda, Pierre, and Elli Kongas Maranda, eds. *Structural Analysis of Oral Tradition*. 1971.

Margolis, Maxine L., and William E. Carter, eds. *Brazil: Anthropological Perspectives: Essays in Honor of Charles Wagley*. 1979.

Masuda, Shozo, Izumi Shimada, and Craig Morin. *Andean Ecology and Civilization: An Interdisciplinary Perspective on Andean Ecological Complementarity*. 1985.

Matteson, Esther. *Comparative Studies in Amerindian Languages*. 1972.

Maybury-Lewis, David, Ed. *Dialectical Societies: The Gê and Bororo of Central Brazil*. 1979.

Maybury-Lewis, David, ed. *In the Path of the Polonoreste: Endangered Peoples of Western Brazil*. 1981.

Maybury-Lewis, David, and James Howe. *The Indian Peoples of Paraguay: Their Plight and Their Prospects*. 1980.

Mayer, Enrique. *A Tribute to the Household: Domestic Economy and the Encomienda in Colonial Peru*. 1982.

McClintock, Martin. *Guatemala: The American Connection, State Terror and Popular Resistance*. 1984.

Meggers, Betty. *Amazonia: Man and Culture in a Counterfeit Paradise*. 1971.

Meggers, Betty. "Application of the Biological Model of Diversification to Cultural Distributions in Tropical Lowland South America." *Biotropica*, 7 (1975), 141–61.

Meggers, Betty. "Resource Optimization and Environmental Limitation in Lowland South America." *Reviews in Anthropology*, 11 (1984), 288–93.

Melatti, Julio Cezar. "Myth and Shaman." In Patricia J. Lyon, ed., *Native South Americans: Ethnology of the Least Known Continent*. 1974. Pp. 267–75.

Merrifield, William L. *Five Amazonian Studies: On World View and Cultural Change*. 1985.

Migliazza, Ernesto. *The Integration of the Indigenous Peoples of the Territory of Roraima*. 1978.

Milton, Katharine. "Morphometric Features as Tribal Predictors in Northwestern Amazonia." *Annals of Human Ecology*, 10 (1983), 435–40.

Mitchell, William P. "Irrigation and Community in the Central Peruvian Highlands." *American Anthropologist*, 78 (1976), 25–44.

Moran, Emilio. *Developing the Amazon*. 1981.

Moran, Emilio F., and Rafael Herrera, eds. *Human Ecology in the Amazon*. 1984.

Morey, Nancy. "Ethnohistory of the Colombian and Venezuelan Llanos." Ph.D. diss., University of Utah, 1975.

Morey, Robert V., and John Marwitt. "Ecology, Economy and Warfare in Lowland South America." In Mark Nettleship et al., eds., *War: Its Causes and Correlates*. 1975. Pp. 439–50.

Murdock, George Peter. "South American Culture Areas." In Patricia J. Lyon, ed., *Native South Americans: Ethnology of the Least Known Continent*. 1974. Pp. 22–39.

Murphy, Robert F. "Lineage and Lineality in Lowland South America." In Maxine L. Margolis and William T. Carter, eds., *Brazil: Anthropological Perspectives: Essays in Honor of Charles Wagley*. 1979. Pp. 217–24.

Murphy, Robert F. "Social Structure and Sex Antagonism." In Daniel R. Gross, ed., *Peoples and Cultures of Native South America: An Anthropological Reader*. 1973. Pp. 213–25.

Myers, Sarah K. *Language Shift Among Migrants to Peru*. 1973.

Myers, Thomas P. "Spanish Contacts and Social Change on the Ucayali River, Peru." *Ethnohistory*, 21 (1974), 135–57.

Neel, James V. "Lessons from a 'Primitive' People." In Daniel R. Gross, ed., *Peoples and Cultures of Native South America: An Anthropological Reader*. 1973. Pp. 159–86.

Nelson, Charles, and Kevin Taylor. *Witness to Genocide—The Present Situation of Indians in Guatemala*. 1983.

Newsom, Linda. *The Cost of Conquest: Indian Decline in Honduras Under Spanish Rule*. 1986.

Newsom, Linda. *Indian Survival in Nicaragua*. 1987.

Niles, Susan A. *South American Indian Narrative, Theoretical and Analytical Approaches*. 1981.

Oberem, Udo. "Trade and Trade Goods in the Ecuadorian Montana." In Patricia J. Lyon, ed., *Native South Americans: Ethnology of the Least Known Continent*. 1974. Pp. 346–57.

Oberg, K. S. "Types of Social Structure among the Lowland Tribes of South and Central

America." In Daniel R. Gross, ed., *Peoples and Cultures of Native South America: An Anthropological Reader*. 1973. Pp. 189–212.

Orlove, Benjamin S. "Barter and Cash Sale on Lake Titicaca: A Test of Competing Approaches." *Current Anthropology*, 23 (1986), 85–106.

Ortiz, Roxanne D. *Indians of the Americas: Self-Determination and Human Rights*. 1974.

Ortiz, Sutti. *Uncertainties in Peasant Farming: A Colombia Case*. 1973.

Osterling, Jorge P. *Democracy in Colombia: Clientelist Politics and Guerrilla Warfare*. 1989.

Otter, Elizabeth. *Music and Dance of Indians and Mestizos in an Andean Valley of Peru*. 1985.

Overing, Joanna. "Images of Cannibalism, Death and Domination in a 'Non-Violent' Society." *Journal de la Société des Américanistes*, 72 (1986), 133–56.

Parry, John Horace. *The Discovery of South America*. 1979.

Penny, N. D., and J. R. Arias. *Insects of an Amazon Forest*. 1982.

Prance, G. T. "Ethnobotanical Comparison of Four Tribes of Amazonian Indians." *Acta Amazonica*, 2 (1972), 7–27.

Prance, G. T. "Quantitative Ethnobotany and the Case for Conservation in Amazonia." *Conservation Biology*, 1 (1987), 296–310.

Quitler, Jeffrey, and Terry Stocker. "Subsistence Economies and the Origins of Andean Complex Societies." *American Anthropologist*, 85 (1983), 545–62.

Rappaport, Joanne. "History and Everyday Life in the Colombian Andes." *Man*, 23 (1988), 718–39.

Rappaport, Joanne. "History, Myth, and the Dynamics of Territorial Maintenance in Tierradentro, Colombia." *American Ethnologist*, 12 (1985), 27–45.

Rasnake, Roger. "Images of Resistance to Colonial Domination." In Jonathan D. Hill, ed., *Rethinking History and Myth: Indigenous South American Perspectives on the Past*. 1988. Pp. 136–56.

Rausch, Jane M. *A Tropical Plains Frontier: The Llanos of Colombia, 1531–1831*. 1984.

Redekop, Calvin Hall. *Strangers Become Neighbors: Mennonite and Indigenous Relations in the Paraguayan Chaco*. 1980.

Reed, Robert. *Amazon Dream: Escape to the Unknown*. 1977.

Reichel-Dolmatoff, Gerardo. *Amazonian Cosmos: The Sexual and Religious Symbolism of the Tukano Indians*. 1971.

Reichel-Dolmatoff, Gerardo. "Biological and Social Aspects of the Yurupari Complex of the Colombian Vaupes Territory." *Journal of Latin American Lore*, 15 (1989), 95–135.

Reichel-Dolmatoff, Gerardo. "Cosmology as Ecological Analysis: A View from the Rain Forest." *Man*, 11 (1976), 307–18.

Reichel-Dolmatoff, Gerardo. "Tapir Avoidance in the Colombian Northwest Amazon." In Gary Urton, ed., *Animal Myths and Metaphors in South America*. 1985. Pp. 107–44.

Renshaw, John. "Property, Resources and Equality among the Indians of the Paraguayan Chaco." *Man*, 23 (1988), 334–352.

Ridgwell, W. M. *The Forgotten Tribes of Guyana*. 1972.

Riester, Jürgen. *Indians of Eastern Bolivia: Aspects of Their Present Situation*. 1972.

Rivière, Peter. *Individual and Society in Guiana: A Comparative Study of Amerindian Social Organization*. 1984.

Rodrigues, Aryon Dall'Inga. "Linguistic Groups of Amazonia." In Patricia J. Lyon, ed., *Native South Americans: Ethnology of the Least Known Continent.* 1974. Pp. 51–59.

Roe, Peter G. *The Cosmic Zygote: Cosmology in the Amazon Basin.* 1982.

Ross, Eric Barry. "Food Taboos, Diet, and Hunting Strategy: The Adaptation to Animals in Amazon Cultural Ecology." *Cultural Anthropology,* 19 (1978), 1–36.

Ross, Eric, and J. Bennett Ross. "Amazon Warfare." *Science,* 207 (1980), 590–91.

Roth, Walter Edmund. "Trade and Barter among the Guainía Indians." In Patricia J. Lyon, ed., *Native South Americans: Ethnology of the Least Known Continent.* 1974. Pp. 159–66.

Rowe, John Howland. "Linguistic Classification Problems in South America." In Patricia J. Lyon, ed., *Native South Americans: Ethnology of the Least Known Continent.* 1974. Pp. 43–50.

Rowe, John Howland. "A Review of the Outline of South American Cultures." In Patricia J. Lyon, ed., *Native South Americans: Ethnology of the Least Known Continent.* 1974. Pp. 40–42.

Salazar, Ernesto. *An Indian Federation in Lowland Ecuador.* 1977.

Salzano, Francisco M., and Sidia M. Callegari-Jacques. *South America Indians: A Case Study.* 1988.

Schmidt, Max. "Comments on Cultivated Plants and Agricultural Methods of South American Indians." In Patricia J. Lyon, ed., *Native South Americans: Ethnology of the Least Known Continent.* 1974. Pp. 60–71.

Schmink, Marianne, and Charles H. Wood, eds. *Frontier Expansion in Amazonia.* 1984.

Seigler, D. S., and J. T. Pereira. "Modernized Preparation of Cassava in the Llanos Orientales of Venezuela." *Economic Botany,* 35 (1981), 356–62.

Shapiro, Judith R. "Marriage Rules, Marriage Exchange, and the Definition of Marriage in Lowland South American Societies." In Kenneth M. Kensinger, ed., *Marriage Practices in Lowland South America.* 1984. Pp. 1–32.

Sinclair, Maurice. *Green Finger of God.* 1980.

Sklar, Harald O., and Frank Salomon, eds. *Natives and Neighbors in South America: Anthropological Essays.* 1987.

Smith, Nathan. "Utilization of Game along Brazil's Transamazon Highway." *Acta Amazonica,* 6 (1976), 455–66.

Smith, Richard Chase. *The Dialectics of Domination in Peru: The Native Communities and the Myth of the Vast Amazonian Emptiness.* 1982.

Sorenson, Arthur P. "Linguistic Exogamy and Personal Choice in Northwest Amazonia." In Kenneth M. Kensinger, ed., *Marriage Practices in Lowland South America.* 1984. Pp. 180–93.

Spalding, Karen. *Huarochiri: An Andean Society Under Inca and Spanish Rule.* 1984.

Spath, Charles. "Getting to the Meat of the Problem: Some Comments on Protein as a Limiting Factor in Amazonia." *American Anthropologist,* 83 (1981), 377–79.

Stephen, David, and Phillip Wearne. *Central America's Indians.* 1982.

Stern, Steve J. "The Struggle for Solidarity: Class, Culture, and Community in Highland Indian America." *Radical History Review,* 27 (1983), 21–45.

Sternberg, Herbert. *The Amazon River of Brazil.* 1975.

Steven, Hugh. *To the Ends of the Earth.* 1978.

Stutzman, Ronald. "Black Highlanders: Racism and Ethnic Stratification in Ecuadorian Sierra." Ph.D. diss., Washington University, St. Louis, 1974.

Sugrim, Kenneth. *Some Historical and Demographic Information on the Amerindians of Guyana*. 1977.

Sullivan, Lawrence E. *Icanchu's Drum: An Orientation to Meaning in South American Religions*. 1988.

Sweet, D. G. "A Rich Realm of Nature Destroyed: The Middle Amazon Valley, 1640–1750." Ph.D. diss., University of Wisconsin, Madison, 1975.

Tatunca, Nara. *The Chronicle of Akakor*. 1977.

Taussig, Michael T. *The Devil and Commodity Fetishism in South America*. 1980.

Taussig, Michael T. "Folk Healing and the Structure of Conquest in the Southwest Colombian Andes." *Journal of Latin American Lore*, 6 (1980), 217–78.

Taussig, Michael T. *Shamanism, Colonialism, and the Wild Man: A Study in Terror and Healing*. 1987.

Taylor, Kenneth, and Ramos Alcida. "Alliance or Descent: Some Amazonian Contrasts." *Man*, 10 (1975), 28–30.

Tschopik, Harry. *Highland Communities of Central Peru: A Regional Survey*. 1973.

Turner, Terence. "Animal Symbolism, Totemism and the Structure of Myth." In Gary Urton, ed. *Animal Myths and Metaphors in South America*. 1985. Pp. 49–106.

Tyler, S. Lyman. *The Indian Cause in Contemporary Brazilian Law*. 1981.

Tyler, S. Lyman. *Indians of Brazil, with Reference to Paraguay and Uruguay*. 1976.

Tyler, S. Lyman. *Indians of South America*, 1976.

Tyler, S. Lyman. *Two Worlds: The Indian Encounter with the European, 1492–1509*. 1988.

Uhl, Charles. "Studies of Forest Agricultural and Successional Environments in the Upper Rio Negro Region of the Amazon Basin." Ph.D. diss., Michigan State University, 1980.

Urban, Greg. "Ceremonial Dialogues in South America." *American Anthropologist*, 88 (1986), 371–86.

Urban, Greg. "Ritual Wailing in Amerindian Brazil." *American Anthropologist*, 90 (1988), 385–400.

Urton, Gary. *At the Crossroads of the Earth and Sky: An Andean Cosmology*. 1981.

Urton, Gary, ed. *Animal Myths and Metaphors in South America*. 1985.

Van den Berghe, Pierre L. *Class and Ethnicity in Peru*. 1974.

Varese, Stefano. *The Forest Indians in the Present Political Situation of Peru*. 1972.

Villas Boas, Orlando, and Claudio Villas Boas. *Xingu: The Indians, Their Myths*. 1973.

Walter, Lynn. *Ethnicity, Economy and the State in Ecuador*. 1981.

Wasserman, Tamara E. *Bolivian Indian Textiles: Traditional Designs and Costumes*. 1981.

Wauchope, Robert, ed. *Handbook of Middle American Indians*. 17 volumes. 1969.

Webster, Steven. "Interpretation of an Andean Social and Economic Formation." *Man*, 16 (1981), 616–33.

Weismantel, Mary J. *Food, Gender and Poverty in the Ecuadorian Andes*. 1988.

Werner, Dennis, et al. "Subsistence Productivity and Hunting Effort in Native South America." *Human Ecology*, 7 (1979), 303–15.

West, Robert C., and John Augelli. *Middle America: Its Land and People*. 1989.

Whitten, Dorothea, and Norman E. Whitten, Jr. *From Myth to Creation: Art from Amazonian Ecuador*. 1988.

Whyte, William Foote, and Giorgio Alberti. *Power, Politics, and Progressive Social Change in Rural Peru*. 1976.

Wiedemann, Inga. "Brazilian Hammocks." *Zeitschrift für Ethnologie*, 104 (1979), 105–33.

Wiedemann, Inga. "The Folklore of Coca in the South American Andes: Coca Pouches, Lime Calabashes, and Rituals." *Zeitschrift für Ethnologie*, 104 (1979), 278–343.

Wilbert, Johannes. "Geography and Telluric Lore of the Orinoco Delta." *Journal of Latin American Lore*, 5 (1979), 129–50.

Wilbert, Johannes. "Magico-Religious Use of Tobacco Among South American Indians." In David L. Browman and Ronald A. Schwartz, eds. *Spirits, Shamans, and Stars: South American Perspectives*. 1979. Pp. 13–38.

Wilbert, Johannes. *Navigators of the Orinoco: River Indians of Venezuela*. 1980.

Wilbert, Johannes. *Survivors of Eldorado: Four Indian Cultures of South America*. 1972.

Wilbert, Johannes. *Tobacco and Shamanism in South America*. 1987.

Wilk, Richard R. "The Search for Tradition in Southern Belize." *América Indígena*, 47 (1987), 77–96.

Wilk, Richard R., and Mac Chapin. "Belize: Land Tenure and Ethnicity." *Cultural Survival Quarterly*, 13 (1989), 41–44.

Wolf, Carolyn E. *Indians of North and South America*. 1977.

Wright, Robin, and Jonathan Hill. "History, Ritual, and Myth: Nineteenth Century Millenarian Movements in the Northwest Amazon." *Ethnohistory*, 33 (1986), 31–54.

Wright, Robin, and Sally Swensen, eds. *The New Tribes Mission in Amazonia*. 1982.

Yost, James, and Paul Kelley, "Shotguns, Blowguns, and Spears: The Analysis of Technological Efficiency." In Raymond B. Hames and William T. Vickers, eds. *Adaptive Responses of Native Amazonians*. 1983. Pp. 189–224.

ACHÉ

Clastres, Pierre. "The Guayakí." In Michael Bicchieri, ed., *Hunters and Gatherers Today: A Socioeconomic Study of Eleven Such Cultures in the Twentieth Century*. 1972. Pp. 138–74.

Hawkes, Kristen. "Aché at the Settlement: Contrasts Between Farming and Foraging." *Human Ecology*, 15 (1987), 133–62.

Hawkes, Kristen, et al. "Why Hunters Gather: Optimal Foraging and the Aché of Eastern Paraguay." *American Ethnologist*, 9 (1982), 379–91.

Hill, Kim, and Kristen Hawkes. "Neotropical Hunting among the Aché of Eastern Paraguay." In Raymond B. Hames and William T. Vickers, eds., *Adaptive Responses of Native Amazonians*. 1983. Pp. 139–88.

Hurtado, Ana Magdalena, et al. "Female Subsistence Strategies among Aché Hunter-Gatherers of Eastern Paraguay." *Human Ecology*, 13 (1985), 1–28.

Kaplan, Hillard, and Kim Hill. "Food Sharing among Aché Foragers: Tests of Explanatory Hypotheses." *Current Anthropology*, 26 (1985), 223–46.

Kaplan, Hillard, and Kim Hill. "Hunting Ability and Reproductive Success among Male Aché Foragers: Preliminary Results." *Current Anthropology*, 26 (1985), 131–33.

Kaplan, Hillard, et al. "Food Sharing among Aché Hunter Gatherers of Eastern Paraguay." *Current Anthropology*, 25 (1984), 113–16.

Munzel, Mark. *The Aché: Genocide Continues in Paraguay*. 1974.

ACHUARA

Bennett-Ross, Jane. "Effects of Contact on Revenge Hostilities among the Achuara Jívaro." In R. Brian Ferguson, ed., *Warfare, Culture and Environment*. 1984. Pp. 83–109.

Bennett-Ross, Jane. "Revenge Feuding among the Achuara Jívaro of the Northwest Peruvian Amazon." Ph.D. diss., Columbia University, 1986.

Descola, Paul. "From Scattered to Nucleated Settlement: A Process of Socio-Economic Change among the Achuar." In Norman E. Whitten, Jr., ed., *Cultural Transformation and Ethnicity in Modern Ecuador*. 1981. Pp. 614–46.

Kroger, Axel. "Housing and Health in the Process of Cultural Adaptation: A Case Study among Jungle and Highland Indians from Ecuador." *Zeitschrift für Ethnologie*, 104 (1979), 79–103.

Ross, Eric. "The Achuara Jívaro: Cultural Adaptation in the Upper Amazon." Ph.D. diss., Columbia University, 1976.

Ross, Eric. "Food Taboos, Diet, and Hunting Strategy: The Adaptation to Animals in Amazon Cultural Ecology." *Current Anthropology*, 19 (1978), 1–36.

Taylor, A. C. "God-Wealth: The Achuar and the Missions." In Norman E. Whitten, Jr., ed., *Cultural Transformation and Ethnicity in Modern Ecuador*. 1981. Pp. 647–76.

AGUARUNA

Bennett-Ross, Jane. "An Assessment of the Nutritional and Health Status of an Aguaruna Jívaro Community, Amazonas, Peru." *Ecology of Food and Nutrition*, 6 (1977), 69–81.

Bennett-Ross, Jane. "Ecology and the Problem of Tribe: A Critique of the Hobbesian Model of Preindustrial Warfare." In Eric Ross, ed., *Beyond the Myths of Culture: Essays in Cultural Materialism*. 1980. Pp. 33–60.

Berlin, Brent. "The Concept of Rank in Ethnobiological Classification: Some Evidence from Aguaruna Folk Botany." *American Ethnologist*, 3 (1976), 381–99.

Berlin, Brent, and Elois Ann Berlin. "Adaptation and Ethnozoological Classification: Theoretical Implications of Animal Resources and Diet of the Aguaruna and Huambisa." In Raymond B. Hames and William T. Vickers, eds., *Adaptive Responses of Native Amazonians*. 1983. Pp. 293–325.

Berlin, Brent, and Elois A. Berlin. "Aguaruna Color Categories." *American Ethnologist*, 2 (1975), 61–87.

Berlin, Brent, D. Breedlove, and P. Raven. "General Principles of Classification and Nomenclature in Folk Biology." *American Anthropologist*, 75 (1973), 214–42.

Berlin, Elois, and E. K. Markell. "An Assessment of the Nutritional and Health Status of an Aguaruna Jívaro Community, Amazonas, Peru." *Ecology of Food and Nutrition*, 6 (1977), 69–81.

Boster, James, Brent Berlin, and John O'Neill. "The Perceptual Bases of Ethnobiological Classification: Evidence from Aguaruna Jívaro Ornithology." *Journal of Ethnobiology*, 1 (1981), 95–108.

Brown, Michael F. *Tsewa's Gift: Magic and Meaning in an Amazonian Society*. 1986.

Siverts, Henning. *Tribal Survival in the Alto Marañón: The Aguaruna Case*. 1972.

AKAWÁIO

Amerindian Languages Project. *An Introduction to the Akawáio and Arekuna Peoples.*
   1977.

AKWĒ

Lopes da Silva, Aracy. "Social Practices and Ontology in Akwē-Xavánte Naming and
   Myth." *Ethnology*, 28 (1989), 331–41.

AMAHUACA

Carneiro, Robert. "On the Use of the Stone Axe by the Amahuaca Indians of Eastern
   Peru." *Ethnologische Zeitschrift Zurich*, 1 (1974), 107–22.
Dole, Gertrude. "Types of Amahuaca Pottery and Techniques of Its Construction."
   Ethnologische Zeitschrift Zurich, 1 (1974), 145–59.
Lamb, Frank Bruce. *Río Tigre and Beyond: The Amazon Jungle Medicine of Manual
   Cordova.* 1985.

ANDOKE

Witte, Paul. "Functions of the Andoke Copulative in Discourse and Sentence Structure."
   In Robert E. Longacre, ed., *Discourse Grammar: Studies in Indigenous Languages
   of Colombia, Panama, and Ecuador.* Volume III. 1977. Pp. 253–87.

APINAYÉ

Matta, Roberto da. "Apinayé Social Structure." Ph.D. diss., Harvard University, 1971.
Matta, Roberto da. "A Reconsideration of Apinayé Social Morphology." In David Gross,
   ed., *Peoples and Cultures of Native South America: An Anthropological Reader.*
   1973. Pp. 263–76.

ARAPACO

Chernela, Janet M. "Righting History in the Northwest Amazon: Myth, Structure, and
   History in an Arapaco Narrative." In Jonathan D. Hill, ed., *Rethinking History
   and Myth: Indigenous South American Perspectives on the Past.* 1988. Pp. 35–
   49.

ARÁRA

Moore, Denny. "The Gavião, Zoró, and Arára Indians." In David Maybury-Lewis, et
   al. *In the Path of the Polonoreste: Endangered Peoples of Western Brazil.* 1981.
   Pp. 46–52.

ARAUCANIAN

Hilger, M. Inez, and Margaret Mondloch. "Surnames and Time and Distance Measurements Among the Chilean Araucanians." In Patricia J. Lyon, ed., *Native South Americans: Ethnology of the Least Known Continent*. 1974.
Padden, Robert Charles. "Cultural Change and Military Resistance in Araucanian Chile, 1550–1730." In Patricia J. Lyon, ed., *Native South Americans: Ethnology of the Least Known Continent*. 1974. Pp. 327–42.

ARAWAK

Charlesworth, Ross. "Caribs and Arawaks." *Caribbean Quarterly*, 16 (1970), 52–59.
Drummond, Lee. "The Serpent's Children: Semiotics of Cultural Genesis in Arawak and Trobiand Myth." *American Ethnologist*, 8 (1981), 633–60.
Drummond, Lee. "Structure and Process in the Interpretation of South American Myth: The Arawak Dog Spirit People." *American Anthropologist*, 79 (1977), 842–68.
Hill, Jonathan. "Agnatic Sibling Relations and Rank in Northern Arawakan Myth and Social Life." In Jane Shapiro, ed., *Working Papers on South American Indians*. Number 7. 1984. Pp. 25–33.
Schwerin, Karl H. "Arawak, Carib, Gê, Tupi: Cultural Adaptation and Culture History in the Tropical Forest, South America." *39 Congreso Internacional de Americanistas*, 4 (1972), 136–78.

AREKUNA

Amerindian Languages Project. *An Introduction to the Akawáio and Arekuna Peoples*. 1977.

AUCA

Peeke, M. Catherine. *Preliminary Grammar of Auca*. 1973.
Yost, John. "Shotguns, Blowguns, and Spears: The Analysis of Technological Efficiency." In Raymond B. Hames and William T. Vickers, eds., *Adaptive Responses of Native Amazonians*. 1983. Pp. 189–224.
Yost, John. "Twenty Years of Contact: The Mechanisms of Change in Wao ("Auca") Culture." In Norman E. Whitten, Jr., ed., *Cultural Transformation and Ethnicity in Modern Ecuador*. 1981. Pp. 677–704.

AWEIKOMA

Urban, Greg. "Ceremonial Dialogues in South America." *American Anthropologist*, 88 (1986), 371–86.
Urban, Greg. "Interpretations of Inter-Cultural Contact: The Shokléng and Brazilian National Society, 1914–1916." *Ethnohistory*, 32 (1985), 224–45.

AYMARA

Abercrombie, Thomas. "The Politics of Sacrifice: An Aymara Cosmology." Ph.D. diss., Cornell University, 1987.

Apaza, Julio Turniri, ed. *The Indian Liberation and Social Rights Movement in Kollasuyu.* 1978.

Bastien, Joseph W. "A Shamanistic Curing Ritual of the Bolivia Aymara." *Journal of Latin American Lore,* 15 (1989), 73–94.

Beuchler, Hans C. *The Bolivian Aymara.* 1971.

Briggs, Lucy Therina and Domingo Llanque Chana. "Humor in Aymara Oral Narrative." *Latin American Indian Literatures,* 3 (1979), 1–10.

Cusicanqui, Silvia Rivera. *Oppressed but not Defeated: Peasant Struggles among the Aymara and Qhechwa in Bolivia, 1900–1980.* 1987.

Diaz, B. E. "The Multinational Andean Genetic and Health Program: II. Disease and Disability Among the Aymara." *Bulletin of the Pan American Health Organization,* 12 (1978), 219–35.

Dillon, Mary, and Thomas Abercrombie. "The Destroying Christ: An Aymara Myth of Conquest." In Jonathan D. Hill, ed., *Rethinking History and Myth: Indigenous South American Perspectives on the Past.* 1988. Pp. 50–77.

Gow, David. "The Gods and Social Change in the High Andes." Ph.D. diss., University of Wisconsin, 1976.

Gow, David. "The Roles of Christ and Inkarri in Andean Religion." *Journal of Latin American Lore,* 6 (1980), 279–98.

Hardman-de-Bautista, Martha James. *The Aymara Language in Its Social and Cultural Context.* 1981.

Harman, Inge Marie. "Collective Labor and Rituals of Reciprocity in the Southern Bolivian Andes." Ph.D. diss., Cornell University. 1987.

Johnson, Tim. "Coping with Austerity in Highland Bolivia." *Cultural Survival Quarterly,* 10 (1986), 12–15.

Johnsson, Mick. *Food and Culture Among Bolivian Aymara: Symbolic Expressions of Social Relations.* 1986.

Lewellen, T. C., Paul Brown, and Winifred Mitchell. "Aymara Indians—Adaptation and Survival in Southern Peru." *Cultural Survival Quarterly,* 10 (1986), 16–18.

Rasnake, Roger. "Carnaval in Yura: Ritual Reflections on Ayllu and State Relations." *American Ethnologist,* 13 (1982), 662–80.

Rasnake, Roger. "The Kurakhuna of Yura: Indigenous Authorities of Colonial Charcas and Contemporary Bolivia." Ph.D. diss., Cornell University, 1982.

Stinson, Sara. "Child Growth and the Economic Value of Children in Rural Bolivia." *Human Ecology,* 8 (1980), 89–104.

Stinson, Sara. "The Physical Growth of High Altitude Aymara Children." *American Journal of Physical Anthropology,* 52 (1980), 377–85.

AYOREO

Bormida, Marcelo. "Ayoreo Myths." *Latin American Indian Literatures,* 2 (1978), 1–13.

Nunez, Carmen Estela. "Asai, A Mythic Personage of the Ayoreo." *Latin American Indian Literatures*, 5 (1980), 64–67.

BANIWA

Wright, Robin. "History and Religion of the Baníwa Peoples of the Upper Río Negro Valley." Ph.D. diss., Stanford University, 1981.

BARA

Jackson, Jean. *Bará Cousin Terminology and Prescribed Language Aggregate Exogamy.* 1971.
Jackson, Jean. *Language, Marriage, and the Tribe: The Bará of Vaupés.* 1970.
Jackson, Jean. "Marriage and Linguistic Identity Among the Bará Indians of the Vaupés, Colombia." Ph.D. diss., Stanford University, 1972.
Jackson, Jean. "Vaupés Marriage: A Network System in the Northwest Amazon." *Regional Analysis*, 2 (1976), 65–93.

BARASANA

Hugh-Jones, Christine. *Food for Thought: Patterns of Production and Consumption in Pira-Paraná Society: Sex and Age as Principles of Social Differentiation.* 1979.
Hugh-Jones, Stephen. *A Social Anthropological Study of the Barasana Indians of the Vaupés Area of Colombia.* 1973.
Hugh-Jones, Stephen. "Like the Leaves on the Forest Floor: Space and Time in Barasana Ritual." *International Congress of Americanists*, 42 (1977), 205–15.
Hugh-Jones, Stephen. "The Pleiades and Scorpius in Barasana Cosmology." Ethnoastronomy and Archaeoastronomy in the American Tropics." *Academy of Science*, 385 (1982), 183–201.
Jackson, Jean. "A Description of Northern Barasana Phonology." *Linguistics*, 75 (1971), 86–92.
Jones, Wendel, and Paula Jones. *A Grammar Sketch of Barasano and Taiwano.* 1985.
Langdon, Thomas Allen. *Food Restrictions in the Medical System of the Barasana and Taiwano Indians of the Colombian Northwest Amazon.* 1983.
Smith, Richard. *Southern Barasano Grammar.* 1973.
Smith, Richard. "Southern Barasano Sentence Structure." In Robert E. Longacre, ed., *Discourse Grammar: Studies in Indigenous Languages of Colombia, Panama, and Ecuador.* 1977. Volume III. Pp. 175–206.
Smith, Richard, and Connie Smith. "Southern Barasano Phonemics." *Linguistics*, 75 (1971), 80–85.

BARÍ

Beckerman, Stephen. "The Cultural Energetics of the Barí (Motilones Bravos) of Northern Colombia." Ph.D. diss., University of New Mexico, 1975.
Beckerman, Stephen. "Fishing and Hunting by the Barí of Colombia." *Working Papers on South American Indians*, 2 (1980), 67–111.

Beckerman, Stephen. "Optimal Foraging Group Size for Human Population: The Case of Barí Fishing." *American Zoologist*, 23 (1983), 283–90.
Beckerman, Stephen. "The Use of Palms by the Barí Indians of the Maracaibo Basin." *Principes*, 22 (1977), 143–54.

BORORO

Crocker, J. Christopher. "The Mirrored Self: Identity and Ritual Invasion Among the Eastern Bororo." *Ethnology*, 16 (1977), 129–46.
Crocker, J. Christopher. *Vital Souls: Bororo Cosmology, Natural Symbolism, and Shamanism*. 1985.
Crocker, J. Christopher. "Why are the Bororo Matrilineal?" *Actes*, 2 (1977), 245–58.
Marsh, Charles R., Jr. "The Indians and The Whites: Two Bororo Texts." *Latin American Indian Literatures*, 1 (1977), 34–36.
Maybury-Lewis, David, ed. *Dialectical Societies: The Ge and Bororo of Central Brazil*. 1979.
Turner, Terence. "The Gê and Bororo Societies as Dialectical Systems: A General Model." In David Maybury-Lewis, ed., *Dialectical Societies: The Ge and Bororo of Central Brazil*. 1979. Pp. 147–78.
Werner, Denis, et al. "Subsistence Productivity and Hunting Effort in Native South America." *Human Ecology*, 7 (1979), 303–15.
Wilbert, Johannes. *Folk Literature of the Bororo Indians*. 1983.

CAMPA

Baker, Will. *Backward: An Essay on Indians, Time, and Photography*. 1983.
Stein, William W. *Civilization and the Stolen Gift: Capital, Kin, and Cult in Eastern Peru*. 1982.
Weiss, Gerald. *Campa Cosmology: The World of a Forest Tribe in South America*. 1975.

CANELA

Crocker, William H. "Canela Kinship and the Question of Matrilineality." In Maxine Margolis and W. Carter, eds., *Anthropological Perspectives*. 1979. Pp. 225–47.
Crocker, William H. "Canela 'Group' Recruitment and Perpetuity: Incipient 'Unilineality'?" *Actes*, 2 (1977), 259–75.
Crocker, William H. "The Non-Adaptation of a Savanna Indian Tribe (Canela, Brazil) to Forced, Forest Relocation: An Analysis of Factors." *Anais*, 1 (1972).
Crocker, William H. "Ultimate Reality and Meaning for the Ramkôkamekra-Canela, Eastern Timbira, Brazil: A Triadic Dualistic Cognitive Pattern." *Journal of Ultimate Reality and Meaning*, 6 (1983), 84–111.
Margolis, Maxine L., and William E. Carter, eds. *Brazil: Anthropological Perspectives: Essays in Honor of Charles Wagley*. 1979.

CANELO

Whitten, Dorothy S., and Norman E. Whitten, Jr. "Ceramics of the Canelos Quichua." *Natural History*, 87 (1978), 91–99, 152.

Whitten, Norman E., Jr. *Amazonian Ecuador: An Ethnic Interface in Ecological, Social, and Ideological Perspective*. 1978.
Whitten, Norman E., Jr. *Cultural Transformation and Ethnicity in Modern Ecuador*. 1981.
Whitten, Norman E., Jr. *Sicuanga Runa: The Other Side of Development in Amazonian Ecuador*. 1985.

CAVINEÑA

Key, Mary Ritchie. *Comparative Tacanan Phonology: With Cavineña Phonology and Notes on Pano-Tacanan Relationships*. 1968.

CHOCÓ

Bennett, Charles W. "Notes on Chocó Ecology in Darién Province, Panama." *Antropológica*, 24 (1968), 26–55.
Isaacson, Sven Erik. "Observations on Chocó Slash-Mulch Agriculture." *Arstyck*, (1975), 20–48.
Whitten, Norman E., Jr. "Strategies of Adaptive Mobility in the Colombian-Ecuadorean Littoral." *American Anthropologist*, 71 (1969), 228–37.

COAIQUER

Ehrenreich, Jeffrey. *Contact and Conflict: An Ethnographic Inquiry into the Impact of Racism, Ethnocide, and Social Change on the Egalitarian Coaiquer Indians of Ecuador*. 1984.
Hendriksen, Lee A., and Stephen H. Levinsohn. "Progression and Prominence in Cuaquier Discourse." In Robert E. Longacre, ed., *Discourse Grammar: Studies in Indigenous Languages of Colombia, Panama, and Ecuador*. Volume II. 1977. Pp. 43–68.
Kempf, Judith. "The Dynamics of Culture and Health: Disease and Curing among the Ecuadorian Coaiquer Indians under the Impact of Acculturation." Ph.D. diss., State University of New York at Albany, 1982.
Kempf, Judith. "The Politics of Curing Among the Coaiquer Indians." In Jeffrey Ehrenreich, ed., *Political Anthropology of Ecuador: Perspectives from Indigenous Cultures*. 1984. Pp. 107–28.
Osborn, Ann. "Alliance of Ground Level: The Kwaiker of Southern Colombia." *Revista de Antropologia*, 20 (1972), 209–15.

COCAMA

Faust, Norma. "Cocama Clause Types." *Tupi Studies*, 1 (1971), 73–105.

COCAMILLA

Stocks, Anthony. "Candoshi and Cocamilla Swidden in Eastern Peru." *Human Ecology*, 11 (1983), 69–84.

Stocks, Anthony. "The Invisible Indians: A History and Analysis of the Relations of the Cocamilla Indians of Loreto, Peru." Ph.D. diss., University of Florida, 1978.

COGUI

Chenevière, Alain. *Vanishing Tribes: Primitive Man on Earth.* 1987.
Reichel-Dolmatoff, Gerardo. "Cultural Change and Environmental Awareness: A Case Study of the Sierra Nevada de Santa Marta, Colombia." *Mountain Research and Development*, 2 (1982), 289–98.
Reichel-Dolmatoff, Gerardo. "Funerary Customs and Religious Symbolism Among the Kogi." In Patricia J. Lyon, ed., *Native South Americans: Ethnology of the Least Known Continent.* 1974. Pp. 289–301.
Reichel-Dolmatoff, Gerardo. "The Loom of Life: A Kogi Principle of Integration." *Journal of Latin American Lore*, 4 (1978), 5–27.
Reichel-Dolmatoff, Gerardo. "Some Kogi Models of the Bendoy." *Journal of Latin American Lore*, 10 (1984), 63–85.
Reichel-Dolmatoff, Gerardo. "Training for the Priesthood among the Kogi of Colombia." In Johannes Wilbert, ed., *Enculturation in Latin America: An Anthology.* 1976. Pp. 265–88.

CONIBO

DeBoer, William. "The Machete and the Cross: Conibo Trade in the Late Seventeenth Century." In Peter D. Francis, F. J. Xense, and P. G. Duke, eds., *Networks of the Past: Regional Interaction in Archaeology.* 1981. Pp. 31–47.
DeBoer, William. "Pillage and Production in the Amazon: A View Through the Conibo of the Ucayali Basin, Eastern Peru." *World Archaeology*, 18 (1986), 231–46.
Gebhart-Sayer, Angelika. "The Geometric Designs of the Shipibo-Conibo in Ritual Context." *Journal of Latin American Lore*, 11 (1985), 143–75.
Hern, Warren M. "High Fertility in a Peruvian Amazon Indian Village." *Human Ecology*, 5 (1977), 155–68.

COREGUAJE

Gralow, Francis, and William R. Merrifield. "A Preliminary Note on Coreguaje Kinship Terminology." In William R. Merrifield, ed., *South American Kinship: Eight Kinship Systems From Brazil and Colombia.* 1985. Pp. 43–54.

CUBEO

Goldman, Irving. "Cubeo Dietary Rules." *Working Papers on South American Indians*, 3 (1981), 143–56.
Goldman, Irving. "Perceptions of Nature and the Structure of Society: The Question of Cubeo Descent." *Dialectical Anthropology*, 1 (1976), 287–92.
Goldman, Irving. "Time, Space and Descent: The Cubeo Example." *Proceedings of the International Congress of Americanists*, 2 (1976), 175–84.

Salser, J. K. "Cubeo Acculturation to Coca and Its Social Implications." *Economic Botany*, 24 (1970), 182–86.
Salser, J. K. "Cubeo Phonemics." *Linguistics*, 75 (1971), 74–79.
Salser, J. K., and Neva Salser. "Some Features of Cubeo Discourse and Sentence Structure." In Robert E. Longacre, ed., *Discourse Grammar: Studies in Indigenous Languages of Colombia, Panama, and Ecuador*. Volume II. 1977. Pp. 253–72.

CUIVA

Arcand, Bernard. "Contribution to Cuiva Ethnography." Ph.D. diss., Cambridge University, 1972.
Arcand, Bernard. "The Cuiva Band." In David H. Turner and Gavin A. Smith, eds., *Challenging Anthropology: A Critical Introduction to Social and Cultural Anthropology*. 1979. Pp. 214–28.
Arcand, Bernard. "Cuiva Food Production." *Canadian Review of Sociology and Anthropology*, 13 (1976), 387–96.
Arcand, Bernard. "The Logic of Kinship: An Example of the Cuiva." *Actas*, 2 (1977), 19–34.
Arcand, Bernard. "Making Love is Like Eating Honey or Sweet Fruit—It Causes Cavities: An Essay on Cuiva Symbolism." *Yearbook of Symbolic Anthropology*, 1 (1978), 1–10.
Berg, Marie. *The Cuiva Language*. 1973.
Kerr, Isabel. "The Centrality of Dialogue in Cuiva Discourse and Sentence Structure." In Robert E. Longacre, ed., *Discourse Grammar: Studies in Indigenous Languages of Colombia, Panama, and Ecuador*. Volume III. 1977. Pp. 133–74.
Ortiz, Francisco. *The Present Situation and Future Prospects of the Cuiba of Casanare*. 1980.

CUNA

Arauz, Reina Torres de. "The Anthropology of Eastern Panama." *Bulletin of the Biological Society of Washington*, 2 (1972), 229–46.
Costello, Richard W. "Some Preliminary Findings on the Economic Structure of the San Blas Community." *Actas II Simposium Nacional de Antropologia y Ethohistoria de Panama* I (1971), 417–35.
Forster, Keith. "The Narrative Folklore in Border Cuna." In Robert E. Longacre, ed. *Discourse Grammar: Studies in Indigenous Languages of Colombia, Panama, and Ecuador*. Volume II. 1977. Pp. 1–24.
Hatley, Nancy Brennan. "Cooperativism and Enculturation among the Cuna Indians of San Blas." In Johannes Wilbert, ed., *Enculturation in Latin America*. 1976. Pp. 67–94.
Hirschfeld, Lawrence A. "Art in Cunaland: Ideology and Cultural Adaptation." *Man*, 12 (1971), 104–23.
Hirschfeld, Lawrence A. "Cuna Aesthetics: A Quantitative Analysis." *Ethnology*, 16 (1977), 147–66.
Howe, James. "The Effects of Cuna Writing: Political Systems." *Ethnology*, 18 (1978), 1–16.

Howe, James. "How the Cuna Keep Their Chiefs in Line." *Man*, 13 (1978), 537–53.
Kramer, Fritz W. "Literature Among the Cuna Indians." *Etnologiska Studier*, 30 (1970), 1–183.
Mattil, Edward L. *The Cuna Mola*. 1973.
McCosker, Sandra. "The Lullabies of the San Blas Cuna Indians of Panama." *Etnologiska Studier*, 33 (1974), 1–190.
McCosker, Sandra. "San Blas Cuna Lullabies: A Means of Informal Learning." In Johannes Wilbert, ed., *Enculturation in Latin America: An Anthology*. 1976. Pp. 29–68.
Moore, Alexander. "From Council to Legislature: Democracy, Parliamentarianism, and the San Blas Cuna." *American Anthropologist*, 86 (1984), 28–42.
Sherzer, Joel. *Kuna Ways of Speaking: An Ethnographic Perspective*. 1983.
Sherzer, Joel, and Greg Urban. *Native South American Discourse*. 1986.
Urban, Greg. "Ceremonial Dialogues in South America." *American Anthropologist*, 88 (1986), 371–86.
Wali, Alaka. "In Eastern Panama, Land is the Key to Survival." *Cultural Survival Quarterly*, 13 (1989), 25–29.

DESANA

Kaye, Jonathan Derek. *The Desano Verb: Problems in Semantics, Syntax, and Phonology*. 1970.
Kaye, Jonathan Derek. "Nasal Harmony in Desano." *Linguistic Inquiry*, 2 (1971), 37–56.
Reichel-Dolmatoff, Gerardo. *Basketry as Metaphor: A Study of Some Arts and Crafts of the Desana Indians of the Northwest Amazon*. 1985.
Reichel-Dolmatoff, Gerardo. "Brain and Mind in Desana Shamanism." *Journal of Latin American Lore*, 7 (1981), 73–98.
Reichel-Dolmatoff, Gerardo. "Some Source Materials on Desana Shamanistic Initiation." *Antropologica*, 51 (1979), 27–61.

EMBERA

Issacson, Sven Erik. *Embera: Territorial and Agrarian Structure in a Tropical Forest*. 1974.
Myers, Charles W. *A Dangerously Toxic New Frog (Phyllobates) Used by Embera Indians of Western Colombia, With Discussion of Blowgun Fabrication and Dart Poisoning*. 1978.
Wali, Alaka. "In Eastern Panama, Land is the Key to Survival." *Cultural Survival Quarterly*, 13 (1989), 25–29.

GAMBINO

Mendez, Harold Lopez. *Guambia*. 1980.
Sanchez, Juan Bautista. *The Drama of Life: A Study of Life Cycle Customs Among the Guambino, Colombia, South America*. 1978.

GARÍFUNA

Hutchinson, Janis, and Pamela J. Byard. "Family Resemblance for Anthropometric and Blood Pressure Measurement in Black Carib and Creoles From St. Vincent Island." *American Journal of Physical Anthropology*, 73 (1987), 33–40.

Palacio, Joseph O. "Age as a Source of Differentiation within a Garífuna Village in Southern Belize." *América Indígena*, 47 (1987), 97–120.

GAVIÃO

Lovold, Lars. "First He Locked Them In: A Creation Myth of the Gavião and the Zoró Indians of Brazil." In Harald O. Sklar and Frank Salomon, eds., *Natives and Neighbors in South America: Anthropological Essays*. 1987. Pp. 417–42.

GÊ

Margolis, Maxine L., and William E. Carter, eds. *Brazil: Anthropological Perspectives: Essays in Honor of Charles Wagley*. 1979.

Maybury-Lewis, David, ed. *Dialectical Societies: The Gê and Bororo of Central Brazil*. 1979.

Schwerin, Karl H. "Arawak, Carib, Gê, Tupi: Cultural Adaptation and Culture History in the Tropical Forest, South America." *39 Congreso Internacional de Americanistas*, 4 (1970), 136–78.

Turner, Terence. "The Gê and Bororo Societies as Dialectical Systems: A General Model." In David Maybury-Lewis, ed., *Dialectical Societies: The Gê and Bororo of Central Brazil*. 1979. Pp. 147–78.

GUAHIBO

Arcand, Bernard. *The Urgent Situation of the Cuiva Indians of Colombia*. 1972.

Balick, Michael J. "Economic Botany of the Guahibo Indians." *Economic Botany*, 33 (1979), 361–76.

Kondo, Victor F. "Participant Reference in Guahibo Narrative Discourse." In Robert E. Longacre, ed., *Discourse Grammar: Studies in Indigenous Languages of Colombia, Panama, and Ecuador*. Volume III. 1977. Pp. 25–44.

Morey, Nancy. "Ethnohistorical Evidence for Cultural Complexity in the Western Llanos of Venezuela and Eastern Llanos of Colombia." *Antropologica*, 45 (1976), 41–69.

Morey, Nancy. "Ethnohistory of the Colombian and Venezuelan Llanos." Ph.D. diss., University of Utah, 1975.

Morey, Nancy. "Guahibo Band Organization." *Antropologica*, 36 (1973), 83–95.

Morey, Nancy. *The Llanos Frontier: A Case for Aborted Development*. 1977.

Morey, Robert V. "Ecology and Culture Change among the Colombia Guahibo." Ph.D. diss., University of Pittsburgh, 1970.

Morey, Robert V. *The Guahibo: People of the Savanna*. 1974.

Morey, Robert V. "Warfare Patterns of the Colombian Guahibo." *Actas y Memorias del Congreso Internacional de Americanistas*, 4 (1970), 59–68.

Morey, Robert V., and David Jay Metzger. "The Guahibo: People of the Savannah." *Acta Etnológica y Lingüística*, 31 (1974).

GUAJIRO

Aschmann, Homer. "The Persistent Guajiro." *Natural History*, 84 (1975), 28–37.

Hernández, Deborah Pacini. *Resource Development and Indigenous People: The El Cerrejón Coal Project in Guajira, Colombia*. 1984.

Mansen, Richard, and Karis Mansen. "The Structure of Sentence and Paragraph in Guajiro Narrative Discourse." In Robert E. Longacre, ed., *Discourse Grammar: Studies in Indigenous Languages of Colombia, Panama, and Ecuador*. Volume I. 1976. Pp. 147–258.

Watson, Lawrence C. "Defense Mechanisms in Guajiro Personality and Culture." *Journal of Anthropological Research*, 30 (1974), 19–34.

Watson, Lawrence C. "The Education of the Cacique in Guajiro Society and Its Functional Implications." In Johannes Wilbert, ed., *Enculturation in Latin America: An Anthology*. 1976. Pp. 289–302.

Watson, Lawrence C. "Formal Education in Calinata: Learning and the Role of the Western School in a Guajiro Community." *Anthropological Quarterly*, 50 (1977), 91–97.

Watson, Lawrence C. "Marriage and Sexual Adjustment in Guajiro Society." *Ethnohistory*, 12 (April 1973), 153–62.

Watson, Lawrence C. *Self and Ideal in a Guajiro Life History*. 1970.

Watson, Lawrence C. "Urbanization and Identity Dissonance." *American Anthropologist*, 84 (1972), 1189–1207.

Watson, Lawrence C. "Urbanization and the Guajiro Matrifocal Family: Consequences for Socialization and Personality Development." *Antropológica*, 27 (1970), 3–23.

Watson, Lawrence C. "Urbanization, Cognition, and Socialization of Educational Values: The Case of the Guajiro Indians of Venezuela." In Johannes Wilbert, ed., *Enculturation in Latin America: An Anthology*. 1976. Pp. 395–414.

Watson-Franke, Maria-Barbara. "Social Pawns or Social Powers? The Position of Guajiro Women." *Antropológica*, 45 (1976), 19–40.

Watson-Franke, Maria-Barbara. "To Learn for Tomorrow: Enculturation of Girls and Its Importance among the Guajiro of Venezuela." In Johannes Wilbert, ed., *Enculturation in Latin America: An Anthology*. 1976. Pp. 191–212.

Watson-Franke, Maria-Barbara. "A Women's Profession in Guajiro Culture: Weaving." *Antropológica*, 45 (1976), 24–40.

Wilbert, Johannes. "Guajiro Kinship and the Eiruku Cycle." In Johannes Wilbert, ed., *The Social Anthropology of Latin America*. 1970. Pp. 306–57.

Wilbert, Johannes. "Kinsmen of Flesh and Blood: A Comment on Possible Socioeconomic Africanisms in Goajiro Indian Culture." *Contribution of the Latin American Anthropology Group*, 1 (1976), 58–66.

Wilbert, Johannes. "The Pastoralists: The Goajiro of the La Guajira Peninsula." In Wilbert, *Survivors of El Dorado: Four Indian Cultures of South America*. 1972. Pp. 163–205.

GUARANÍ

McNaspy, Clement J. *Lost Cities of Paraguay: Art and Architecture of the Jesuit Reductions, 1607–1767.* 1982.

GUAYMÍ

Arauz, Reina Torres de. "The Anthropology of Eastern Panama." *Bulletin of the Biological Society of Washington*, 2 (1972), 229–46.

HIXKARYANA

Derbyshire, Desmond C. *Hixkaryana and Linguistic Typology.* 1985.
Sherzer, Joel, and Greg Urban. *Native South American Discourse.* 1986.

HUAMBISA

Berlin, Brent, and Elois Ann Berlin. "Adaptation and Ethnozoological Classification: Theoretical Implications of Animal Resources and Diet of the Aguaruna and Huambisa." In Raymond B. Hames and William T. Vickers, eds., *Adaptive Responses of Native Amazonians.* 1983.

IKA

Tracy, Hubert P., and Stephen H. Levinsohn. "Participant Reference in Ica Expository Discourse." In Robert E. Longacre, ed., *Discourse Grammar: Studies in Indigenous Languages of Colombia, Panama, and Ecuador.* Volume III. 1977. Pp. 3–24.

INGANO

Gajdusek, Daniel Carleton. *Colombian Expeditions to the Noanama Indians of the Rio Siguirisua and to the Cofan and Ingano Indians of the Putumayo, August 22, 1970 to September 14, 1970.* 1972.

IXIL

"Counterinsurgency and the Development of Pole Strategy in Guatemala." *Cultural Survival Quarterly*, 12 (1988), 11–20.
Elliott, Ray. "Nebaj Ixil Unitary Kin Terms." In Helen L. Neuenswander and Dean E. Arnold, eds., *Cognitive Studies in Southern Mesoamerica.* 1981. Pp. 240–76.

JACALTEC

Collins, Ann. "Colonial Jacaltenango, Guatemala: The Formation of a Corporate Community." Ph.D. diss., Tulane University, 1980.

476   SELECTED BIBLIOGRAPHY

Stratmeyer, Dennis, and Jean Stratmeyer. "The Jacaltec Nawal and the Soul Bearer in
    Concepcion Huista." In Helen I. Neuenswander and Dean E. Arnold, eds., *Cog-
    nitive Studies of Southern Mesoamerica*. 1981. Pp. 126–55.

JICAQUE

Olfrogge, David F. "The Ethnoentemology of Some Jicaque (Tol) Categories of the
    Order Hymenoptera." In Helen L. Neuenswander and Dean E. Arnold, eds.,
    Cognitive Studies of Southern Mesoamerica. 1981. Pp. 160–80.
Olfrogge, Judith J., and Helen L. Neuenswander. "Colineality in Jicaque Cosmological,
    Socio-Political, and Kin Structures." In Helen L. Neuenswander and Dean E.
    Arnold, eds., *Cognitive Studies of Southern Mesoamerica*. 1981. Pp. 201–35.

JÍVARO

Boster, James. "A Comparison of the Diversity of Jivaroan Gardens with That of the
    Tropical Forest." *Human Ecology*, 11 (1983), 47–68.
Boster, James, Brent Berlin, and John O'Neill. "The Correspondence of Jivaroan to
    Scientific Ornithology." *American Anthropologist*, 88 (1986), 569–83.
Descola, Philippe. "Head-Shrinkers versus Shrinks: Jivaroan Dream Analysis." *Man*,
    24 (1989), 439–50.
Ferguson, Wilburn Henry. *The Son of Fergus: Discovery, Research, and Development
    of Primitive Jivaro Plant Extracts for Modern Chronic Disease Problems*. 1973.
Harner, Michael J. "The Supernatural World of the Jivaro Shaman." In Daniel R. Gross,
    ed., *Peoples and Cultures of Native South America: An Anthropological Reader*.
    1973. Pp. 347–57.
Ross, Eric. "Food Taboos, Diet, and Hunting Strategy: The Adaptation to Animals in
    Amazon Cultural Ecology." *Current Anthropology*, 19 (1978), 1–36.
Salazar, Ernesto. *An Indian Federation in Lowland Ecuador*. 1977.
Sherzer, Joel, and Greg Urban. *Native South American Discourse*. 1986.
Up de Graff, Fritz W. "Jivaro Field Clearing with Stone Axes." In Patricia J. Lyon,
    ed., *Native South Americans: Ethnology of the Least Known Continent*. 1974.
    Pp. 120–21.
Urban, Gary. "Ceremonial Dialogues in South America." *American Anthropologist*, 88
    (1986), 371–86.

JUKUMANI

Godoy, Richard. "Ecological Degradation and Agricultural Intensification in the Andean
    Highlands." *Human Ecology*, 12 (1984), 359–84.

KABIXÍ

Price, David. "Parecí, Cabixí, Nambiquára: A Case Study in the Western Classification
    of Native Peoples." *Journal de la Société des Américanistes*, 69 (1983), 129–
    48.

KADUVEO

Ribero, Darcy. "Kadiweu Kinship." In Patricia J. Lyon, ed., *Native South Americans: Ethnology of the Least Known Continent*. 1974. Pp. 167–83.

KAINGÁNG

Hicks, David. *Structural Analysis in Anthropology: Case Studies from Indonesia and Brazil*. 1978.

Weisemann, Ursula. "Purification among the Kaingang Indians Today." *Zeitschrift für Ethnologie*, 95 (1970), 104–13.

Weisemann, Ursula. "Time Distinctions in Kaingang." *Zeitschrift für Ethnologie*, 99 (1974), 120–30.

KALAPALO

Basso, Ellen B. *In Favor of Deceit: A Study of Tricksters in an Amazonian Society*. 1987.

Basso, Ellen B. "Kalapalo Affinity: Its Cultural and Social Contexts." *American Ethnologist*, 2 (1975), 207–28.

Basso, Ellen B. *A Musical View of the Universe: Kalapalo Myth and Ritual Performance*. 1985.

Sherzer, Joel, and Greg Urban. *Native South American Discourse*. 1986.

KAMSÁ

Howard, Linda. "Camsá: Certain Features of Verb Inflection as Related to Paragraph Types." In Robert E. Longacre, ed., *Discourse Grammar: Studies in Indigenous Languages of Colombia, Panama, and Ecuador*. Volume II. 1977. Pp. 273–98.

Taussig, Michael. *Folk Healing in Southwest Colombia*. 1975.

KANJOBAL

Burns, Allan F. "Resettlement in the US: Kanjobal Maya in Indiantown, Florida." *Cultural Survival Quarterly*, 12 (1988), 41–45.

KARAJÁ

Tavener, Christopher J. "The Karaja and the Brazilian Frontier." In Daniel R. Gross, ed., *Peoples and Cultures of Native South America: An Anthropological Reader*. 1973. Pp. 433–62.

KARIB

Basso, Ellen B. "Xingú Carib Kinship Terminology and Marriage: Another View." *Southwestern Journal of Anthropology*, 26 (1970), 402–16.

Charlesworth, Ross. "Caribs and Arawaks." *Caribbean Quarterly*, 16 (1970), 52–59.

Layng, Anthony."The Caribs of Dominica: Prospects for Structural Assimilation of a Territorial Minority." *Ethnic Groups*, 6 (1985), 209–21.
Layng, Anthony. *The Carib Reserve: Identity and Security in the West Indies*. 1983.
Magana, Edmundo, and Fabiola Jara. "The Carib Sky." *Journal de la Société des Américanistes*, 68 (1982), 105–23.
Owen, Nancy. "Land, Politics, and Ethnicity in a Carib Indian Community." *Ethnohistory*, 14 (1975), 385–93.
Riviere, Peter G. "Some Problems in the Comparative Study of Carib Societies." *Proceedings of the XL International Congress of Americanists*, 2 (1974), 639–43.
Schwerin, Karl H. "Arawak, Carib, Gê, Tupi: Cultural Adaptation and Culture History in the Tropical Forest, South America." *39 Congreso Internacional de Americanistas*, 4 (1972), 136–78.
Whitehead, Neil L. "Carib Cannibalism: The Historical Evidence." *Journal de la Société des Américanistes*, 70 (1984), 69–88.

KARIJONA

Schindler, Helmut. "Carijona and Manakini: An Opposition in the Mythology of a Carib Tribe." In Ellen B. Basso, ed., *Carib-Speaking Culture, Society, and Language*. 1977. Pp. 22–44.

KAWAHÍB

Kracke, Waud H. "Kagwahiv Moieties: Form Without Function." In Kenneth M. Kensinger, ed., *Marriage Practices in Lowland South America*. 1984. Pp. 99–126.
Kracke, Waud H. "Uxorilocality in Patriliny: Kagwahiv Filial Separation." *Ethos*, 4 (1975), 297–310.

KAXINÁWA

Der Marderosian, A. H. "The Use and Hallucinatory Principles of a Psycho-active Beverage of the Cashinahua Tribe (Amazon Basin)." *Drug Dependence*, 5 (1970), 7–15.
Kensinger, Kenneth M. "Cashinahua Notions of Social Time and Social Space." *Proceedings of the International Congress of Americanists*, 42nd Congress, 2 (1976), 233–44.
Kensinger, Kenneth M. *The Cashinahua of Eastern Peru*. 1975.
Kensinger, Kenneth M. "The Invisible People: Ostracism in Cashinahua Society." In Richard R. Randolph, William M. Schneider, and May N. Diaz, eds., *Dialectics and Gender: Anthropological Approaches*. 1988. Pp. 170–78.

KAYABÍ

Baruzzi, R. G., et al. "Occurrence of Lobo's Blastomycosis among 'Caiabi' Brazilian Indians." *International Journal of Dermatology*, 12 (1973), 356–62.

KAYAPÓ

Ayres, Marie, and F. M. Salzano. "Health Status of Brazilian Cayapó Indians." *Tropical and Geographical Medicine*, 24 (1972), 178–85.

Bamburger, Joan. "Exit and Voice in Central Brazil: The Politics of Flight in Kayapó Society." In David Maybury-Lewis, ed., *Dialectical Societies: The Gê and Bororo of Central Brazil*. 1979. Pp. 130–46.

Bamburger, Joan. "Naming and the Transmission of Status in a Central Brazilian Society." *Ethnology*, 13 (1974), 533–60.

Black, F. L., et al. "Nutritional Status of Brazilian Kayapó Indians." *Human Biology*, 49 (1977), 139–54.

Turner, Terence S. "History, Myth, and Social Consciousness among the Kayapó of Central Brazil." In Jonathan D. Hill, ed., *Rethinking History and Myth: Indigenous South American Perspectives on the Past*. 1988. Pp. 195–213.

Turner, Terence S. "Kayapó Plan Meeting to Discuss Dams." *Cultural Survival Quarterly*, 13 (1989), 20–24.

KOFÁN

Borman, M. B. "Cofán Paragraph Structure and Function." In Robert E. Longacre, ed., *Discourse Grammar: Studies in Indigenous Languages of Colombia, Panama, and Ecuador*. Volume III. 1977. Pp. 289–338.

Gajdusek, Daniel Carleton. *Colombian Expeditions to the Noanama Indians of the Río Siguirisua and to the Cofán and Ingano Indians of the Putumayo, August 22, 1970 to September 14, 1970*. 1972.

Robinson, Scott Studebaker. "Toward an Understanding of Kofán Shamanism." Ph.D. diss., Cornell University, 1979.

KREEN-AKARÔRE

Baruzzi, R. G., et al. "The Kreen-Akorôre: A Recently Contacted Indigenous Tribe." In Kenneth Elliott and James Whelan, eds., *Health and Disease in Tribal Societies*. 1977. Pp. 179–211.

Cowell, Adrian. *The Tribe that Hides from Man*. 1973.

KRIKATÍ

Sheffler, Harold W. "On Krikatí and Sirionó: A Reply to Lave." *American Anthropologist*, 78 (1976), 338–43.

KUIKÚRU

Carneiro, Robert L. "The Cultivation of Manioc among the Kuikúru of the Upper Xingú." In Raymond B. Hames and William T. Vickers, eds., *Adaptive Responses of Native Amazonians*. 1983. Pp. 65–111.

Carneiro, Robert L. "The Knowledge and Use of Rain Forest Trees by the Kuikúru

Indians of Central Brazil.'' In Robert Ford, ed., *The Nature and Status of Eth-nobotany*. 1978. Pp. 210–16.

Carneiro, Robert L. ''Recent Observations on Shamanism and Witchcraft Among the Kuikúru Indians of Central Brazil.'' *Annals of the New York Academy of Sciences*, 293 (1977), 215–28.

Dole, Gertrude. ''Anarchy Without Chaos: Alternatives to Political Authority Among the Kuikúru.'' In Marc J. Swartz, Victor W. Turner, and Arthur Tuden, eds., *Political Anthropology*. 1966. Pp. 73–87.

Dole, Gertrude. ''Shamanism and Political Control Among the Kuikúru.'' In David Gross, ed., *Peoples and Cultures of Native South America: An Anthropological Reader*. 1974. Pp. 294–307.

Dole, Gertrude. ''The Use of Manioc Among the Kuikúru: Some Interpretations.'' In Robert Ford, ed., *The Nature and Status of Ethnobotany*. 1978. Pp. 217–47.

LAYMI

Harris, Olivia. ''The Dead and Devils among the Bolivian Laymi.'' In Maurice Bloch and Jonathan Parry, eds., *Death and the Regeneration of Life*. 1982. Pp. 45–73.

MACHIGUENGA

Baer, Gerhard. ''Religion and Symbols: A Case in Point from Eastern Peru: The Mat-sigenka View of the Religious Dimension of Light.'' *Scripta Etnológica*, 6 (1981), 49–52.

Baer, Gerhard, and W. W. Snell. ''An Ayahuasca Ceremony among the Matsigenka (Eastern Peru).'' *Zeitschrift für Ethnologie*, 99 (1974), 63–80.

Baksh, Michael. ''Cultural Ecology and Change of the Machiguenga Indians of the Peruvian Amazon.'' Ph.D. diss., University of California at Los Angeles, 1984.

Hurtado, A. Magdalena, and Kim Hill. ''Experimental Studies of Tool Efficiency among Machiguenga Women and Implications for Root-Digging Foragers.'' *Journal of Anthropological Research*, 45 (1989), 207–18.

Johnson, Allen. ''The Energy Costs of Technology and the Changing Environment: A Machiguenga Case.'' In Harold Letchmann and Robert Merrill, eds., *Material Culture*. 1977. Pp. 155–67.

Johnson, Allen. ''Reductionism in Cultural Ecology: The Amazon Case.'' *Current Anthropology*, 23 (1982), 413–28.

Johnson, Allen, and Michael Baksh. ''Ecological and Structural Influences on the Pro-portions of Wild Foods in the Diets of Two Machiguenga Communities.'' In Marvin Harris and Eric Ross, eds., *Food and Evolution: Toward a Theory of Human Food Habits*. 1987.

Johnson, Allen, and Clifford A. Behrens. ''Nutritional Criteria in Machiguenga Food Production Decisions: A Linear-Programming Analysis.'' *Human Ecology*, 10 (1984), 167–89.

Johnson, Allen, Orna Johnson, and Michael Baksh. ''The Color of Emotions in Machi-guenga.'' *American Anthropologist*, 88 (1986), 674–81.

Johnson, Orna. ''Domestic Organization and Interpersonal Relations Among the Ma-chiguenga Indians of the Peruvian Amazon.'' Ph.D. diss., Columbia University, 1978.

Johnson, Orna. "The Social Context of Intimacy and Avoidance: A Videotape Study of Machiguenga Meals." *Ethnology*, 19 (1980), 353–66.

Johnson, Orna, and Allen Johnson. "Male/Female Relations and the Organization of Work in a Machiguenga Community." *American Ethnologist*, 2 (1976), 634–48.

Johnson, Orna, and Allen Johnson. "Oedipus in the Political Economy: Theme and Variations in Amazonia." In Richard R. Randolph, William M. Schneider, and May N. Diaz, eds., *Dialectics and Gender: Anthropological Approaches*. 1988. Pp. 38–56.

Montgomery, Edward, and Allen Johnson. "Machiguenga Energy Expenditure." *Ecology of Food and Nutrition*, 6 (1976), 97–105.

Rosengren, Dan. "Matsigenka Social Organization as Expressed in their Settlement Patterns." In Harald O. Sklar and Frank Salomon, eds., *Natives and Neighbors in South America: Anthropological Essays*. 1987. Pp. 329–54.

MAKÚ

Arhem, Kaj. "Wives for Sisters: The Management of Marriage Exchange in Northwest Amazonia." In Harald O. Sklar and Frank Salomon, eds., *Natives and Neighbors in South America: Anthropological Essays*. 1987. Pp. 130–77.

Milton, Katharine. "Protein and Carbohydrate Resources of the Makú Indians in Northwestern Amazonia." *American Anthropologist*, 86 (1984), 7–27.

Moore, Barbara J. "Some Discourse Features of Hupda Macú." In Robert E. Longacre, ed., *Discourse Grammar: Studies in Indigenous Languages of Colombia, Panama, and Ecuador*. Volume II. 1977. Pp. 25–42.

Reid, Howard. *Comparative Discussion of Maku and Tukanoan Social Structure*. 1977.

Reid, Howard. "Some Aspects of Movement, Growth, and Change among the Hupdu Makú Indians of Brazil." Ph.D. diss., Trinity College, Cambridge University, 1979.

Silverwood-Cope, Peter. "A Contribution to the Ethnography of the Colombian Maku." Ph.D. diss., Cambridge University, 1972.

MAKUNA

Arhem, Kaj. "Fishing and Hunting among the Makuna: Economy, Ideology, and Ecological Adaptation in the Northwest Amazon." *Arstryck*, 17 (1976), 27–44.

Arhem, Kaj. "The Makú, the Makuna, and the Guainía System: Transformation of Social Structure in Northern Lowland South America." *Ethnos*, 54 (1989), 5–22.

MAKUSHÍ

Hornbostel, Erich Molritz von. *Music of the Makuschi, Taulipáng, and Yekuana*. 1969.

MAM

Watanabe, John M. "From Saints to Shibboleths: Image, Structure, and Identity in Maya Religious Syncretism." *American Ethnologist*, 17 (1990), 131–50.

MAMINDÈ

Aspelin, Paul L. "The Anthropological Analysis of Tourism: Indirect Tourism and Political Economy in the Case of the Mamaindè of Mato Grosso, Brazil." *Annals of Tourism Research*, 4 (1977), 135–60.

MAPUCHE

Bergland, Steffan. *The National Integration of Mapuche: Ethnic Minority in Chile*. 1977.

Hilger, M. Inez, and Margaret Mondloch. "Surnames and Time and Distance Measurements Among the Chilean Araucanians." In Patricia J. Lyon, ed., *Native South Americans: Ethnology of the Least Known Continent*. 1974.

International Work Group for Indigenous Affairs. *The Mapuche Tragedy*. 1979.

Padden, Robert Charles. "Cultural Change and Military Resistance in Araucanian Chile, 1550–1730." In Patricia J. Lyon, ed., *Native South Americans: Ethnology of the Least Known Continent*. 1974. Pp. 327–42.

Robertson, Carol E. " 'Pulling the Ancestors': Performance, Practice, and Praxis in Mapuche Ordering." *Ethnomusicology*, 23 (1979), 395–416.

Robertson-DeCarbo, Carol E. "Lukutun: Text and Context in Mapuche Rogations." *Latin American Indian Lore*, 1 (1977), 67–78.

Stuchlik, Milan. *Life on a Half-Share: Mechanisms of Social Recruitment among the Mapuche of Southern Chile*. 1976.

Titiev, Mischa. "Social Singing Among the Mapuche." In Patricia J. Lyon, ed., *Native South Americans: Ethnology of the Least Known Continent*. 1974. Pp. 208–20.

MATACO

Barabas, Alicia M., and Miguel A. Bartolomé. "The Mythic Testimony of the Mataco." *Latin American Indian Lore*, 3 (1979), 76–85.

Palavecino, Enrique. "The Magic World of the Mataco." *Latin American Indian Lore*, 3 (1979), 61–75.

Rodriguez, Nemesio J. *Oppression in Argentina: The Mataco Case*. 1975.

MAYA

Brintnell, Douglas E. "A Model of Changing Group Relations in the Maya Highlands of Guatemala." *Journal of Anthropological Research*, 36 (1980), 294–315.

Brintnell, Douglas E. *Revolt Against the Dead: The Modernization of a Maya Community in the Highlands of Guatemala*. 1979.

Davis, Shelton H. "Land of Our Ancestors: A Study of Land Tenure and Inheritance in the Highlands of Guatemala." Ph.D. diss., Harvard University, 1970.

Early, John D. "Some Ethnographic Implications of an Ethnohistorical Perspective of the Civil-Religious Hierarchy Among the Highland Guatemala." *Ethnohistory*, 30 (1983), 185–202.

Edmonson, Munro S. *Meaning in Mayan Language*. 1973.

Farriss, Nancy M. *Maya Society Under Colonial Rule: The Collective Enterprise of Survival*. 1984.

Haba, Louis de la, and Joseph J. Scherschel. "Guatemala, Maya and Modern." *National Geographic*, 146 (1974), 661–89.

Hawkins, John. *Inverse Images: The Meaning of Culture, Ethnicity, and Family in Post-Colonial Guatemala*. 1984.

Hill, Robert M., and John Monaghan. *Continuities in Highland Maya Social Organization: Ethnohistory in Sacapulas, Guatemala*. 1987.

Jantzen, Carl R. "From Maya to Mennonite: Intercommunity Relationships in West Central Belize." *América Indígena*, 47 (1987), 169–92.

Lovell, W. George. *Conquest and Survival in Colonial Guatemala: A Historical Geography of the Cuchumatan Highlands, 1500–1821*. 1985.

Morrissey, R. C. "Continuity and Change in Backstrap Loom Textiles of Highland Guatemala." Ph.D. diss., University of Wisconsin-Madison, 1983.

Swetman, John. "An Ethnographic Test of Class and Pluralist Models of Guatemalan Ethnicity." *Journal of Anthropological Research*, 35 (1979), 350–60.

Tedlock, Barbara. *Time and the Highland Maya*. 1982.

Thompson, J. Eric. *The Maya of Belize*. 1977.

Warren, Kay B. *The Symbolism of Subordination: Indian Identity in a Guatemalan Town*. 1978.

Watanabe, John M. "From Saints to Shibboleths: Image, Structure, and Identity in Maya Religious Syncretism." *American Ethnologist*, 17 (1990), 131–50.

Watanabe, John M. "In the World of the Sun: A Cognitive Model of Mayan Cosmology." *Man*, 18 (1983), 710–28.

Willey, Gordon R. "Changing Conceptions of Lowland Maya Culture History." *Journal of Anthropological Research*, 40 (1984), 41–59.

MEHINÁKU

Gregor, Thomas A. "A Content Analysis of Mehináku Dreams." *Ethos*, 9 (1981), 353–90.

Gregor, Thomas A. "Dark Dreams about the White Man." *Natural History*, 92 (1983), 8–14.

Gregor, Thomas A. " 'Far, Far Away my Shadow Wandered . . . ': Dream Symbolism and Dream Theories of the Mehináku Indians of Brazil." *American Ethnologist*, 8 (1981), 709–20.

Gregor, Thomas A. "Privacy and Extramarital Affairs in a Tropical Forest Community." In Daniel R. Gross, ed., *Peoples and Cultures of Native South America: An Anthropological Reader*. 1973. Pp. 242–62.

Gregor, Thomas A. " 'She Who is Covered with Feces': The Dialectics of Gender among the Mehináku of Brazil." In Richard R. Randolph, William M. Schneider, and May N. Diaz, eds., *Dialectics and Gender: Anthropological Approaches*. 1988. Pp. 38–56.

Margolis, Maxine L., and William E. Carter, eds. *Brazil: Anthropological Perspectives: Essays in Honor of Charles Wagley*. 1979.

MEKRANOTÍ

Werner, Dennis. *Amazon Journey: An Anthropologist's Year Among Brazil's Mekranotí Indians*. 1984.

Werner, Dennis. "Chiefs and Presidents: A Comparison of Leadership Traits in the United States and among the Mekranotí of Central Brazil." *Ethos*, 10 (1982), 225–401.
Werner, Dennis. "Child Care and Influence among the Mekranotí of Central Brazil." *Social Roles*, 10 (1984), 395–404.
Werner, Dennis. "Gerontocracy among the Mekranotí of Central Brazil." *Anthropological Quarterly*, 54 (1981), 15–27.
Werner, Dennis. "Leadership Inheritance and Acculturation among the Mekranotí of Central Brazil." *Human Organization*, 41 (1982), 34–51.
Werner, Dennis. "The Making of a Mekranotí Chief: The Psychological and Social Determinants of Leadership in a Native South American Society." Ph.D. diss., City University of New York, 1980.
Werner, Dennis. "Why Do the Mekranotí Trek?" In Raymond B. Hames and William T. Vickers, eds., *Adaptive Responses of Native Amazonians*. 1983. Pp. 225–38.

MISKITO

Bourgeios, Paulo. "Class, Ethnicity and the State among the Miskito Amerindians of Northeastern Nicaragua." *Latin American Perspectives*, 8 (1981), 26–41.
CIDCA. *Ethnic Groups and the Nation State: The Case of the Atlantic Coast in Nicaragua.* 1987.
Helms, Mary W. "Miskito Slaving and Culture Contact: Ethnicity and Opportunity in an Expanding Population." *Journal of Anthropological Research*, 39 (1983), 179–97.
Nietschmann, Bernard. *Between Land and Water: The Subsistence Ecology of the Miskito Indians.* 1973.
Nietschmann, Bernard. "Hunting and Fishing Focus Among the Miskito Indians of Eastern Nicaragua." *Human Ecology*, 1 (1972), 41–68.
Nietschmann, Bernard. "The Limits to Protein." In Raymond B. Hames, ed., *Studies in Hunting and Fishing in the Neotropics*. Volume 2. 1980. Pp. 131–37.
Ohland, Klaudine, and Robin Schneider, eds. *National Revolution and Indigenous Identity: The Conflict between Sandinists and Miskito Indians in Nicaragua's Atlantic Coast.* 1983.
Olien, Michael D. "The Miskito Kings and the Line of Succession." *Journal of Anthropological Research*, 39 (1983), 198–241.
Wiggins, Albert. "Colonialism and Revolution: Nicaraguan Sandinism and the Liberation of the Miskito, Sumu and Rama Peoples." *Akwesane Notes*, 13 (1982), 44–58.

MUINANE

Walton, James. "Muinane Diagnostic Use of Narcotics." *Economic Botany*, 24 (1970), 187–88.
Walton, James. "Participant Reference and Introducers in Muinane Clause and Paragraph." In Robert E. Longacre, ed., *Discourse Grammar: Studies in Indigenous Languages of Colombia, Panama, and Ecuador*. Volume III. 1977. Pp. 45–66.

MUNDURUKÚ

Burkhalter, S. Brian. *Amazon Gold Rush: Markets and the Mundurukú Indians.* 1983.
Burkhalter, S. Brian. "Sexual Antagonism and Play in Mundurucu Society: The Fun is in the Chase." In Richard R. Randolph, William M. Schneider, and May N. Diaz, eds., *Dialectics and Gender: Anthropological Approaches.* 1988. Pp. 38–56.
Johnson, Orna, and Allen Johnson. "Oedipus in the Political Economy: Theme and Variations in Amazonia." In Richard R. Randolph, William M. Schneider, and May N. Diaz, eds., *Dialectics and Gender: Anthropological Approaches.* 1988. Pp. 38–56.
Margolis, Maxine L., and William E. Carter, eds. *Brazil: Anthropological Perspectives: Essays in Honor of Charles Wagley.* 1979.
Murphy, Robert F., and Yolanda Murphy. "Women, Work, and Property in a South American Tribe." In Stanley Diamond, ed., *Theory and Practice: Essays Presented to Gene Weltfish.* 1980. Pp. 179–94.
Murphy, Yolanda, and Robert F. Murphy. *Women of the Forest.* 1974.
Ramos, Alcida. "Mundurucú: Social Change or False Problem?" *American Ethnologist,* 5 (1978), 675–89.

NAMBIQUÁRA

Aspelin, Paul L. "The Anthropological Analysis of Tourism: Indirect Tourism and Political Economy in the Case of the Mamaindè of Mato Grosso, Brazil." *Annals of Tourism Research,* 4 (1977), 135–60.
Aspelin, Paul L. *External Articulation and Domestic Production: The Artifact Trade of the Mamaindè of Northwestern Mato Grosso, Brazil.* 1975.
Aspelin, Paul L. "Nambicuára Economic Dualism: Levi-Strauss in the Garden Once Again." *Bij-dragen tot de Taal, Land-en Volkenkunde,* 132 (1976), 135–60.
Price, P. David. "The Nambiquára." In David Maybury-Lewis, et al. *In the Path of the Polonoreste: Endangered Peoples of Western Brazil.* 1981. Pp. 23–27.
Price, P. David "Nambiquára Leadership." *American Ethnologist,* 8 (1981), 686–708.
Price, P. David. "Parecí, Cabixí, Nambiquára: A Case Study in the Western Classification of Native Peoples." *Journal de la Société des Américanistes,* 69 (1983), 129–48.

NICARAO

Fowler, William R. *The Cultural Evolution of Ancient Nahua Civilizations: The Pipil-Nicarao of Central America.* 1989.

NOANAMA

Gajdusek, Daniel Carleton. *Colombian Expeditions to the Noanama Indians of the Rio Siguirisua and to the Cofán and Ingano Indians of the Putumayo, August 22, 1970 to September 14, 1970.* 1972.

NOMATSIGUENGA

Wise, Mary Ruth. *Identification of Participants in Discourse: A Study of Aspects of Form and Meaning in Nomatsiguenga.* 1971.

OYANPÍK

Black, F. L., et al. "Failure of Linguistic Relationships to Predict Genetic Distances Between the Waiapi and Other Tribes of Lower Amazonia." *American Journal of Physical Anthropology*, 60 (1983), 327–35.
Campbell, Alan Tormaid. *To Square With Genesis: Causal Statements and Shamanism in Wayapi.* 1989.

PÁEZ

Gerdel, Florence L., and Marianna C. Slocum. "Páez Discourse, Paragraph and Sentence." In Robert E. Longacre, ed., *Discourse Grammar: Studies in Indigenous Languages of Colombia, Panama, and Ecuador.* Volume I. 1976. Pp. 259–443.
Ortiz, Sutti R. "The Stimulation of Work: Labour and Value among Paez Farmers." In Sandra Wallman, ed., *Social Anthropology of Work.* 1979. Pp. 207–28.
Rappaport, Joanna. "History, Myth, and the Dynamics of Territorial Maintenance in Tierradentro, Colombia." *American Ethnologist*, 26 (1985), 27–45.

PAKAANÓVA

Price, P. David. "The Indians of Western Rondônia." In David Maybury-Lewis, et al. *In the Path of the Polonoreste: Endangered Peoples of Western Brazil.* 1981. Pp. 38–45.

PANARE

Henley, Paul. "The Internal Social Organization of the Panare of Venezuelan Guiana and Their Relations with the National Society." Ph.D. diss., Cambridge University, 1979.
Henley, Paul, and Marie-Claude Muller. "Panare Basketry: Means of Commercial Exchange and Artistic Expression." *Antropologica*, 49 (1978), 29–130.

PARECÍ

Price, P. David. "The Parecí." In David Maybury-Lewis, et al. *In the Path of the Polonoreste: Endangered Peoples of Western Brazil.* 1981. Pp. 28–33.
Price, P. David. "Parecí, Cabixí, Nambiquára: A Case Study in the Western Classification of Native Peoples." *Journal de la Société des Américanistes*, 69 (1983), 129–48.

PAUMARÍ

Chapman, Shirley. "Problems in Paumarí Acculturation." In William R. Merrifield, ed., *Five Amazonian Studies on World View and Cultural Change*. 1985. Pp. 71–79.
Odmark, Mary Ann, and Rachel Landin. "On Paumarí Social Organization." In William R. Merrifield, ed., *South American Kinship: Eight Kinship Systems From Brazil and Colombia*. 1985. Pp. 93–110.

PEMÓN

Krugh, Janice. "The Mythology of the Pemón Indians of Venezuela: A Survey of the Work of Fatherr Cesareo de Armellada." *Latin American Indian Literatures*, 4 (1980), 287–373.
Thomas, David John. *Order Without Government: The Society of the Pemon Indians of Venezuela*. 1982.

PIAROA

Boglar, Lajos. "Aspects of Story-Telling Among the Piaroa Indians." *Acta Ethnographica*, 19 (1970), 38–52.
Boglar, Lajos. "Creative Process in Ritual Art: Piaroa Indians, Venezuela." In David L. Browman and Ronald A. Schwartz, eds. *Spirits, Shamans, and Stars: South American Perspectives*. 1979. Pp. 233–40.
Eden, Michael. "Ecological Aspects among Piaroa and Guahibo Indians of the Upper Orinoco Basin." *Antropologica*, 39 (1974), 25–56.
Granero, Fernando Santos. "Power, Ideology, and the Ritual of Production in Lowland South America." *Man*, 21 (1986), 657–79.
Halmos, Ian. "Preliminary Report on Field Work among Piaroa Indians." *Revista Venezolana de Folklore*, 5 (1974), 58–73.
Kaplan, Joanna Overing. "Cognation, Endogamy, and Teknonymy: The Piaroa Example." *Southwestern Journal of Anthropology*, 28 (1972), 282–97.
Kaplan, Joanna Overing. "Dualism as an Expression of Difference and Danger: Marriage Exchange and Reciprocity among the Piaroa of Venezuela." In Kenneth M. Kensinger, ed., *Marriage Practices in Lowland South America*. 1984. Pp. 127–56.
Kaplan, Joanna Overing. "Endogamy and the Marriage Alliance: A Note on Continuity in Kindred-Based Groups." *Man*, 8 (1973), 555–70.

PIPIL

Fowler, William R. *The Cultural Evolution of Ancient Nahua Civilizations: The Pipil-Nicarao of Central America*. 1989.

PÍRO

Hugh-Jones, Christine. "Food for Thought—Patterns of Production and Consumption in Pira-Piraná Society." In J. L. Fontaine, ed., *Sex and Age as Principles of Social Differentiation*. 1978. Pp. 41–66.

Hugh-Jones, Christine. "Skin and Soul, the Round and the Straight: Social Time and Social Space in Pira-Paraná Society." *Proceedings of the International Congress of Americanists*, 42nd Congress, 2 (1977), 184–204.
Loffler, Lorenz, and Gerhard Baer. "The Kinship Terminology of the Piro, Eastern Peru." *Ethnologische Zietschrift*, 1 (1974), 257–82.
Matteson, Esther. *The Piro (Arawakan) Language*. 1965.

PUQUINA

Englebart, Victor. "Reed People of Titicaca." *Natural History*, 91 (1982), 34–38.

QOLLAHUAYA

Apaza, Julio Turniri, ed. *The Indian Liberation and Social Rights Movement in Kollasuyu*. 1978.
Bastien, Joseph William. "Exchange Between Andean and Western Medicine." *Social Science and Medicine*, 16 (1982), 795–803.
Bastien, Joseph William. *Healers of the Andes: Kallawaya Herbalists and Their Medicinal Plants*. 1987.
Bastien, Joseph William. "Herbal Curing by Qollahuaya Andeans." *Journal of Ethnopharmacology*, 6 (1987), 13–28.
Bastien, Joseph William. "Land Litigation in an Andean Ayllu from 1592 to 1972." *Ethnohistory*, 26 (1979), 101–31.
Bastien, Joseph William. *Mountain of the Condor: Metaphor and Ritual in an Andean Ayllu*. 1978.
Bastien, Joseph William. "Pharmacopeia of Qollahuaya Andeans." *Journal of Ethnopharmacology*, 8 (1983), 97–111.
Bastien, Joseph William. *Qollahuaya Rituals: An Ethnographic Account of the Symbolic Relations of Man and Land in an Andean Village*. 1973.
Bolivia Bulletin. "Traditional Medicine in Bolivia." *Cultural Survival Quarterly*, 12 (1988), 26–27.

QUECHUA

Albo, Xavier. *Social Constraints on Cochabamba Quechua*. 1970.
Allen, Catherine. "Body and Soul in Quechua Thought." *Journal of Latin American Lore*, 8 (1982), 179–96.
Apaza, Julio Turniri, ed. *The Indian Liberation and Social Rights Movement in Kollasuyu*. 1978.
Beals, Carleton. *The Incredible Incas: Yesterday and Today*. 1973.
Cusicanqui, Silvia Rivera. *Oppressed but not Defeated: Peasant Struggles among the Aymara and Qhechwa in Bolivia, 1900–1980*. 1987.
Gade, Daniel W. *Plants, Man and the Land in the Vilcanota Valley of Peru*. 1975.
Gifford, Douglas. *Carnival and Coca Leaf: Some Traditions of the Peruvian Quechua Ayllu*. 1976.
Gow, David. "The Gods and Social Change in the High Andes." Ph.D. diss., University of Wisconsin, 1976.

Gow, David. "The Roles of Christ and Inkarri in Andean Religion." *Journal of Latin American Lore*, 6 (1980), 279–98.

Grollig, Francis Xavier. *Incaic and Modern Peru*. 1979.

Harman, Inge-Maria. "Collective Labor and Rituals of Reciprocity in the Southern Bolivian Andes." Ph.D. diss., Cornell University, 1987.

Howard-Malverde, Rosaleen. "Quechua Tales from Canas Ecuador." Ph.D. diss., St. Andrew's University, 1984.

Howard-Malverde, Rosaleen. "Storytelling Strategies in Quechua Narrative Performance." *Journal of Latin American Lore*, 15 (1989), 3–71.

Johnson, Tim. "Coping with Austerity in Highland Bolivia." *Cultural Survival Quarterly*, 10 (1986), 12–15.

Kleymeyer, Charles B. *Social Interaction Between Quechua, Campesino, and Criollo*. 1973.

Mangurian, David. *Children of the Incas*. 1979.

Mayer, Enrique. *A Tribute to the Household: Domestic Economy and the Encomienda in Colonial Peru*. 1982.

Moles, Jerry A. "Decisions and Variability: The Usage of Address Terms, Pronouns, and Language by Quechua-Spanish Bilinguals in Peru." *Anthropological Linguistics*, 16 (1974), 442–63.

Moles, Jerry A. "What Does One Say to a Naked Lady? Validity, Variability, and Data Collection: A Peruvian Example." *Journal of Anthropological Research*, 34 (1978), 263–90.

Myers, Sarah K. *Language Shift Among Migrants to Lima, Peru*. 1973.

Newman, M. T. "Palm and Finger Prints of Quechua Indians from Vicos in the North Central Peruvian Sierra." *Human Biology*, 46 (1974), 519–30.

Nuñez del Prado B., Juan Victor. "The Supernatural World of the Quechua of Southern Peru as Seen from the Community of Qotobamba." In Patricia J. Lyon, ed., *Native South Americans: Ethnology of the Least Known Continent*. 1974. Pp. 238–50.

Nuñez del Prado C., Oscar. *Kuyo Chico: Applied Anthropology in an Indian Community*. 1973.

Rasnake, Roger. "Carnaval in Yura: Ritual Reflections on Ayllu and State Relations." *American Ethnologist*, 13 (1986), 662–80.

Rasnake, Roger. "The Kurahkuna of Yura: Indigenous Authorities of Colonial Charcas and Contemporary Bolivia." Ph.D. diss., Cornell University, 1982.

Reeve, Mary-Elizabeth. "Cauchu Uras: Lowland Quichua Histories of the Amazon Rubber Boom." In Jonathan D. Hill, ed., *Rethinking History and Myth: Indigenous South American Perspectives on the Past*. 1988. Pp. 19–34.

Reeve, Mary-Elizabeth. "Identity as Process: The Meaning of Runapura for Quichua Speakers of the Curaray River, Eastern Ecuador." Ph.D. diss., University of Illinois at Urbana-Champaign, 1985.

Silverman-Proust, Gail P. "Weaving Technique and Knowledge in the Cuzco Area of Peru." *Journal of Latin American Lore*, 14 (1988), 207–44.

Simmons, Roger A. *Palca and Pucara: A Study of the Effects of Revolution on Two Bolivian Haciendas*. 1974.

Sklar, Harold G. *The Warm Valley People: Duality and Land Reform Among the Quechua Indians of Highland Peru*. 1982.

Spalding, Karen. *Huarochiri: An Andean Society Under Inca and Spanish Rule*. 1984.

Stein, William W. *Changing Vicos Agriculture*. 1972.

Urton, Gary. *Animal Myths and Metaphors in South America*. 1985.

Urton, Gary. *At the Crossroads of the Earth and Sky: An Andean Cosmology*. 1981.

Wagner, Catherine Allen. *Coca, Chicha and Trago: Private and Communal Rituals in a Quechua Community*. 1978.

Whitten, Norman E., Jr. *Sacha Runa: Ethnicity and Adaptation of Ecuadorean Jungle Quichua*. 1976.

Zuidema, R. Tom. "The Lion in the City: Royal Symbols of Transition in Cuzco." In Gary Urton, ed., *Animal Myths and Metaphors in South America*. 1985. Pp. 183–250.

QUICHÉ

Carmack, Robert M. *Quichean Civilization*. 1973.

Henne, Marilyn G. "Quiché Food: Its Cognitive Structures." In Helen L. Neuenswander and Dean E. Arnold, eds., *Cognitive Studies in Southern Mesoamerica*. 1981. Pp. 66–91.

Horspool, G. A. "The Music of the Quiché Maya of Momostenango in its Cultural Setting." Ph.D. diss., University of California at Los Angeles, 1982.

Neuenswander, Helen L., and Shirley D. Souder. "The Hot-Cold Wet-Dry Syndrome Among the Quiché of Joyabaj." In Helen L. Neuenswander and Dean E. Arnold, eds., *Cognitive Studies of Southern Mesoamerica*. 1981. Pp. 94–124.

Tedlock, Barbara. "Sound Texture and Metaphor in Quiché Maya Ritual Language." *Current Anthropology*, 23 (1982), 269–72.

Tedlock, Barbara. *Time and the Highland Maya*. 1982.

Tedlock, Barbara, and Dennis Tedlock. "Text and Textile: Language and Technology in the Art of the Quiché Maya." *Journal of Anthropological Research*, 41 (1985), 121–46.

QUIJOS

Kroger, Axel. "Housing and Health in the Process of Cultural Adaptation: A Case Study among Jungle and Highland Indians from Ecuador." *Zeitschrift fur Ethnologie*, 104 (1979), 79–103.

Macdonald, Theodore. *Processes of Change in Amazonian Ecuador: Quijos Quichua Indians Become Cattlemen*. 1979.

Whitten, Norman E., Jr. *Sacha Runa: Ethnicity and Adaptation of Ecuadorian Jungle Quichua*. 1976.

RAMA

CIDCA. *Ethnic Groups and the Nation State: The Case of the Atlantic Coast in Nicaragua*. 1987.

Wiggins, Albert. "Colonialism and Revolution: Nicaraguan Sandinism and the Liberation of the Miskito, Sumu and Rama Peoples." *Akwesane Notes*, 13 (1982), 44–58.

SANUMÁ

Colchester, Marcus. "Myths and Legends of the Sanemá." *Antropológica*, 56 (1981), 25–126.

Fidalgo, O., and G. T. Prance. "The Ethnomycology of the Sanamá Indians." *Mycología*, 68 (1976), 201–210.

Ramos, Alcida. "How the Sanumá Acquire Their Names." *Ethnology*, 13 (1974), 171–86.

Ramos, Alcida. "The Social System of the Sanumá of Northern Brazil." Ph.D. diss., University of Wisconsin, Madison, 1972.

Taylor, Kenneth. "Raiding, Dueling, and Descent Group Membership among the Sanumá." *Actes du XLII Congrès International des Américanistes*, 2 (1976), 91–104.

Taylor, Kenneth. *Sanuma Fauna: Prohibitions and Classifications*. 1974.

Taylor, Kenneth. "Sanuma (Yanoama) Food Prohibitions: The Multiple Classification of Society and Fauna." Ph.D. diss., University of Wisconsin, Madison, 1972.

SARAGURO

Kroger, Axel. "Housing and Health in the Process of Cultural Adaptation: A Case Study among Jungle and Highland Indians from Ecuador." *Zeitschrift für Ethnologie*, 104 (1979), 79–103.

SECOYA

Steven, Hugh. *Never Touch a Tiger*. 1980.

Vickers, William. "An Analysis of Amazonian Hunting Yields as a Function of Settlement Age." In Raymond Hames, ed., *Studies in Hunting and Fishing in the Neo-Tropics*. 1978. Pp. 7–29.

Vickers, William. "Cultural Adaptation to Amazonian Habitats: The Siona-Secoya of Eastern Ecuador." Ph.D. diss., University of Florida, 1976.

Vickers, William. "Game Depletion Hypothesis of Amazonian Adaptation: Data from a Native Community." *Science*, 239 (1988), 1521–22.

Vickers, William. "Meat Is Meat: The Siona-Secoya and the Hunting Prowess—Sexual Reward Hypothesis." *Florida Latinamericanist*, 11 (1975), 1–5.

Vickers, William. "Native Amazonian Subsistence to Diverse Habitats: The Siona-Secoya of Ecuador." *Studies in Third World Societies*, 7 (1979), 6–36.

SELKNAM

Campos Menendez, Enrique. *Only the Wind: Legends of the Onas of Tierra del Fuego*. 1978.

Chapman, Anne MacKaye. "What's in a Name? Problems of Meaning and Denotation Apropos of a Corpus of Selk'nam Personal Names." *Journal de la Société des Américanistes*, 67 (1984), 327–57.

Wilbert, Johannes. *Folk Literature of the Selknam Indians*. 1975.

SHARANÁHUA

Siskind, Janet. "Kinship and Mode of Production." *American Anthropologist*, 80 (1978), 860–72.

SHIPAYA

Chenevière, Alain. *Vanishing Tribes: Primitive Man on Earth*. 1987.

SHIPIBO

Eakin, Lucille. *Nuevo Destino: The Life Story of a Shipibo Bilingual*. 1980.

Gebhart-Sayer, Angelika. "The Geometric Designs of the Shipibo-Conibo in Ritual Context." *Journal of Latin American Lore*, 11 (1985), 143–75.

Hanna, J. M., and P. T. Baker. "Comparative Heat Tolerance of Shipibo Indians and Peruvian Mestizos." *Human Biology*, 46 (1974), 69–80.

Hern, Warren M. "High Fertility in a Peruvian Amazon Indian Village." *Human Ecology*, 5 (1977), 155–68.

Lathrap, Donald W. "Shipibo Tourist Art." In Nelson H. Graburn, ed., *Ethnic and Tourist Arts: Cultural Expression from the Fourth World*. 1976. Pp. 197–207.

Lathrap, Donald W., Angelika Gebhart-Sayer, and Ann M. Mester. "The Roots of the Shipibo Art Style: Three Waves on Imariacocha or There Were 'Incas' before the Incas." *Journal of Latin American Lore*, 11 (1985), 31–119.

Levy, C. Daniel. "Histrionics in Culture." In Richard R. Randolph, William M. Schneider, and May N. Diaz, eds., *Dialectics and Gender: Anthropological Approaches*. 1988. Pp. 91–135.

Roe, Peter G. "The Josho Nahuanbo Are All Wet and Undercooked: Shipibo Views of the Whiteman and the Incas in Myth, Legend, and History." In Jonathan D. Hill, ed., *Rethinking History and Myth: Indigenous South American Perspectives on the Past*. 1988. Pp. 106–35.

Roe, Peter G., and Peter E. Siegel. "The Life History of a Shipibo Compound: Ethnoarchaeology in the Peruvian Montana." *Archaeology and Anthropology*, 5 (1982), 94–118.

Siegel, Peter E., and Peter G. Roe. "Shipibo Archaeo-ethnography: Site Formation Processes and Archaeological Interpretation." *World Archaeology*, 18 (1986), 96–115.

SHUAR

Kroger, Axel. "Housing and Health in the Process of Cultural Adaptation: A Case Study among Jungle and Highland Indians from Ecuador." *Zeitschrift für Ethnologie*, 104 (1979), 79–103.

Macdonald, Theodore Jr. "Shuar Children: Bilingual-Bicultural Education." *Cultural Survival Quarterly*, 10 (1986), 18–20.

SIONA

Langdon, E. Jean. "Power and Authority in Siona Political Process: The Rise and Demise of the Shaman." In Jeffrey Ehrenreich, ed., *Political Anthropology of Ecuador: Perspectives from Indigenous Cultures*. 1984. Pp. 129–56.

Langdon, E. Jean. "Siona Clothing and Adornment, or You Are What You Wear." In Justine Cordwell and Ronald Schwartz, eds., *The Fabrics of Culture: Anthropology of Clothing and Adornment*. 1979. Pp. 297–311.

Langdon, E. Jean. "The Siona Hallucinogenic Ritual: Its Meaning and Power." In John H. Morgan, ed., *Understanding Religion and Culture: Anthropological and Theological Perspectives*. 1975. Pp. 29–46.

Vickers, William. "An Analysis of Amazonian Hunting Yields as a Function of Settlement Age." In Raymond Hames, ed., *Studies in Hunting and Fishing in the Neo-Tropics*. 1978. Pp. 7–29.

Vickers, William. "Cultural Adaptation to Amazonian Habitats: The Siona-Secoya of Eastern Ecuador." Ph.D. diss., University of Florida, 1976.

Vickers, William. "Game Depletion Hypothesis of Amazonian Adaptation: Data from a Native Community." *Science*, 239 (1988), 1521–22.

Vickers, William. "Ideation and Adaptation: Traditional Belief and Modern Intervention in Siona-Secoya Religion." In Norman E. Whitten, Jr., ed., *Cultural Transformation and Ethnicity in Modern Ecuador*. 1981.

Vickers, William. "Meat Is Meat: The Siona-Secoya and the Hunting Prowess—Sexual Reward Hypothesis." *Florida Latinamericanist*, 11 (1975), 1–5.

Vickers, William. "Native Amazonian Subsistence to Diverse Habitats: The Siona-Secoya of Ecuador." *Studies in Third World Societies*, 7 (1979), 6–36.

Vickers, William. "The Territorial Dimension of Siona-Secoya and Encabellado Adaptation." In Raymond Hames and William Vickers, eds., *Adaptive Responses of Native Amazonians*. 1983. Pp. 451–78.

Wheeler, Alva. "Grammatical Structure in Siona Discourse." *International Review of General Linguistics*, 1 (1967), 60–77.

SIRIONÓ

Ingham, John M. "Are the Sirionó Raw or Cooked?" *American Anthropologist*, 73 (1971), 1092–99.

Sheffler, Harold W. "On Krikatí and Sirionó: A Reply to Lave." *American Anthropologist*, 78 (1976), 338–43.

Stearman, Allyn. *No Longer Nomads: The Sirionó Revisted*. 1987.

Stearman, Allyn. "Territory Folks." *Natural History*, 95 (1986), 6–9.

Stearman, Allyn. "The Yuqui Connection: Another Look at Sirionó Deculturation." *American Anthropologist*, 86 (1984), 630–50.

Wordick, F.J.E. "Review Article: Sirionó Kinship Terminology." *International Journal of American Linguistics*, 41 (1975), 242–85.

SUMU

CIDCA. *Ethnic Groups and the Nation State: The Case of the Atlantic Coast in Nicaragua*. 1987.

Dodds, David. "Miskito and Sumu Refugees: Caught in Conflict in Honduras." *Cultural Survival Quarterly*, 13 (1989), 3–5.

Wiggins, Albert. "Colonialism and Revolution: Nicaraguan Sandinism and the Liberation of the Miskito, Sumu and Rama Peoples." *Akwesane Notes*, 13 (1982), 44–58.

SURUÍ

Barrros Laraia, Roque de. "Polyandrous Adjustments in Suruí Society." In Patricia J. Lyon, ed., *Native South Americans: Ethnology of the Least Known Continent*. 1974. Pp. 370–72.

Bontkes, Carolyn, and William R. Merrifield. "On Suruí (Tupian) Social Organization." In William R. Merrifield, ed., *South American Kinship: Eight Kinship Systems from Brazil and Colombia*. 1985. Pp. 5–34.

SUYÁ

Seeger, Anthony. "The Meaning of Body Ornaments: A Suyá Example." *Ethnology*, 14 (1975), 211–24.

Seeger, Anthony. "What Can We Learn When They Sing? Vocal Genres of the Suyá Indians of Central Brazil." *Ethnomusicology*, 23 (1979), 373–94.

Sherzer, Joel, and Greg Urban. *Native South American Discourse*. 1986.

TABAINO

Langdon, Thomas. *Food Restrictions in the Medical System of the Barasana and Taiwano Indians of the Colombian Northwest Amazon*. 1983.

Langdon, Thomas. "Food Restrictions in the Medical System of the Barasana and Tawaino Indians of the Colombian Northwest Amazon." Ph.D. diss., Louisiana State University, 1975.

Langdon, Thomas. "Food Taboos and the Balance of Oppositions among the Barasana and Taiwano." *Working Papers on South American Indians*, 3 (1981), 55–75.

TATUYO

Whisler, Dave. "Some Aspects of Tatuyo Discourse." In Robert E. Longacre, ed., *Discourse Grammar: Studies in Indigenous Languages of Colombia, Panama, and Ecuador*. Volume III. 1977. Pp. 207–52.

TERÉNA

Salzano, Francisco M., and Roberto Cardoso de Oliveira. "Genetic Aspects of the Demography of Brazilian Teréna Indians." *Social Biology*, 17 (1970), 217–23.

TERIBE

Koontz, Carol. "Features of Dialogue Within Narrative Discourse in Teribe." In Robert E. Longacre, ed., *Discourse Grammar: Studies in Indigenous Languages of Colombia, Panama, and Ecuador*. Volume III. 1977. Pp. 111–32.

TIKUNA

Lovelace, J. K., et al. "Toxoplasmosis Among the Ticuna Indians in the State of Amazonas, Brazil." *Tropical and Geographical Medicine*, 30 (1978), 295–300.

TAMBIRA

Lave, Jean. "Eastern Timbira Moiety Systems in Time and Space: A Complex Structure."
Proceedings of the International Congress of Americanists, 42nd Congress, 2
(1976), 309–21.

TIRIYÓ

Gage, T. B., et al. "Estimating Mortality from Two Censuses: An Application to the
Trió of Surinam." *Human Biology*, 56 (1984), 489–501.
Gage, T. B., et al. "The Population Dynamics and Fertility of the Trió of Surinam."
Human Biology, 56 (1984), 691–701.
Riviere, Peter. "Factions and Exclusions in Two South American Village Systems." In
Milton Douglas, ed., *Witchcraft Confessions and Accusations*. 1970. Pp. 245–
55.
Riviere, Peter. "Of Women, Men and Manioc." In Harald O. Sklar and Frank Salomon,
eds., *Natives and Neighbors in South America: Anthropological Essays*. 1987.
Pp. 178–202.
Urban, Greg. "Ceremonial Dialogues in South America." *American Anthropologist*, 88
(1986), 371–86.
Van Mazijk, J. S., et al. "Measles and Measles Vaccine in Isolated Amerindian Tribes.
I. The 1971 Trió (Tiriyó) Epidemic." *Tropical and Geographical Medicine*, 34
(1982), 3–6.

TOBA

Barstow, Jean R. *Culture and Ideology: Anthropological Perspectives*. 1982.
Miller, Elmer S. "The Argentine Toba." *Ethnology*, 10 (1971), 149–59.
Miller, Elmer S. *Harmony and Dissonance in Argentine Toba Society*. 1980.
Sherzer, Joel, and Greg Urban. *Native South American Discourse*. 1986.
Wilbert, Johannes. *Folk Literature of the Toba Indians*. 1982.

TUKANO

Jackson, Jean Elizabeth. *The Fish People: Linguistic Exogamy and Tukanoan Identity in
Northwest Amazonia*. 1983.
Reichel-Dolmatoff, Gerardo. *Beyond the Milky Way: Hallucinatory Imagery of the Tukano
Indians*. 1978.
Welch, Betty. "Tucano Discourse, Paragraph, and Information Distribution Discourse."
In Robert E. Longacre, ed., *Discourse Grammar: Studies in Indigenous Languages
of Colombia, Panama, and Ecuador*. Volume II. 1977. Pp. 229–52.

West, Birdy. "Results of a Tucanoan Syntax Questionnaire Pilot Study." In Robert E. Longacre, ed., *Studies in Indigenous Languages of Colombia, Panama, and Ecuador*. Volume III. 1977. Pp. 339–75.

TUKUNA

Jobim, L. F., et al. "HLS Antigens of Tukuna Indians." *American Journal of Physical Anthropology*, 56 (1981), 285–90.
Seiler Baldinger, Anne Marie. *Yagua and Tukuna Hammocks: Female Dignity and Culture Identity*. 1985.

TUNEBO

Headland, Paul, and Stephen H. Levinsohn. "Prominence and Cohesion in Tunebo Discourse." In Robert E. Longacre, ed., *Discourse Grammar: Studies in Indigenous Languages of Colombia, Panama, and Ecuador*. Volume II. 1977. Pp. 133–58.

TUPI

Schwerin, Karl H. "Arawak, Carib, Ge, Tupi: Cultural Adaptation and Culture History in the Tropical Forest, South America." *39 Congreso Internacional de Americanistas*, 4 (1972), 136–78.

TUPINAMBA

Balee, William. "The Ecology of Ancient Tupi Warfare." In R. Brian Ferguson, ed., *Warfare, Culture, and Environment*. 1984. Pp. 241–65.
Forsyth, Donald W. "The Beginnings of Brazilian Anthropology: Jesuits and Tupinamba Cannibalism." *Journal of Anthropological Research*, 39 (1983), 147–78.

TZUTUJIL

Butler, James, and Dean E. Arnold. "Tzutujil Maize Classification in San Pedro La Laguna." In Helen L. Neuenswander and Dean E. Arnold, eds., *Cognitive Studies of Southern Mesoamerica*. 1981. Pp. 182–204.
Kieffer, Margaret Marlar. "Color and Emotions in Tzutujil Maya and Spanish." Ph.D. diss., University of California, Irvine, 1974.
O'Brien, Linda L. "Music Education and Innovation in a Traditional Tzutuhil-Maya Community." In Johannes Wilbert, ed., *Enculturation in Latin America: An Anthology*. 1976. Pp. 377–94.

UANANO

Chernela, Janet M. "Sexual Ideologies in Lowland South America." *Working Papers on South American Indians*, 5 (1984).

Chernela, Janet M. "The Sibling Relationship among the Uanano of the Northwest Amazon: The Case of Nicho." *Working Papers on South American Indians*, 7 (1985).

Chernela, Janet M. "Why One Culture Stays Put: A Case of Resistance to Change in Authority and Economic Structure in an Indigenous Community in Northwest Amazon." In John Hemming, ed., *The Frontier After a Decade of Colonization: Change in Amazonia*. Volume II. 1984. Pp. 228–36.

Waltz, Carolyn H. "Some Observations on Guanano Dialogue." In Robert E. Longacre, ed., *Discourse Grammar: Studies in Indigenous Languages of Colombia, Panama, and Ecuador*. Volume III. 1977. Pp. 67–110.

Waltz, Carolyn H. "Water, Rock, and Smoke: A Guanano View of the World." In William R. Merrifield, ed., *Five Amazonian Studies on World View and Cultural Change*. 1985. Pp. 41–52.

Waltz, Nathan E. "Discourse Functions of Guanano Sentences and Paragraphs." In Robert E. Longacre, ed., *Discourse Grammar: Studies in Indigenous Languages of Colombia, Panama, and Ecuador*. Volume I. 1976. Pp. 21–145.

URUBÚ

Balée, William. "The Ka'apór Indian Wars of Lower Amazonia, ca. 1825–1928." In Richard R. Randolph, William M. Schneider, and May N. Diaz, eds., *Dialectics and Gender: Anthropological Approaches*. 1988. Pp. 155–69.

Balée, William. "The Persistence of Ka'apór Culture." Ph.D. diss., Columbia University, 1984.

Kakumasu, Kiyoko. "Urubú-Kaapór Girls' Puberty Rites." In William R. Merrifield, ed., *Five Amazonian Studies on World View and Cultural View*. 1985. Pp. 74–89.

WAIWÁI

Urban, Greg. "Ceremonial Dialogues in South America." *American Anthropologist*, 88 (1986), 371–86.

WAKUENAI

Hill, Jonathan. "Agnatic Sibling Relations and Rank in Northern Arawakan Myth and Social Life." In Joan Shapiro, ed., *Working Papers on South American Indians*, 7 (1984), 25–33.

Hill, Jonathan. "Myth, Spirit-Naming, and the Art of Microtonal Rising: Childbirth Rituals of the Arawakan Wakuenai." *Latin American Music Review*, 6 (1985), 1–30.

Hill, Jonathan. "Social Equality and Ritual Hierarchy: The Arawakan Wakuenai of Venezuela." *American Ethnologist*, 11 (1984), 528–44.

Hill, Jonathan. "Wakuenai Society: A Processual-Structural Analysis of Indigenous Cultural Life in the Upper Río Negrro Basin." Ph.D. diss., Indiana University, 1983.

Hill, Jonathan, and Robin M. Wright. "Time, Narrative, and Ritual: Historical Interpretations from an Amazonian Society." In Jonathan D. Hill, ed., *Rethinking*

History and Myth: Indigenous South American Perspectives on the Past. 1988. Pp. 78–105.

WAORANI

Larrick, J. W., et al. "Patterns of Health and Disease Among the Waorani Indians of Eastern Ecuador." *Medical Anthropology*, 3 (1979), 147–89.

Orville, Nina. "Road Construction Threatens Huaorani in Ecuador." *Cultural Survival Quarterly*, 12 (1988), 43–47.

Yost, John. "People of the Forest: The Waorani." In George Ligabue, ed., *Ecuador in the Shadow of the Volcanoes*. 1977. Pp. 95–115.

WARAO

Fleischman, Mark L. "The Warao: A Study in Microevolution." Ph.D. diss., University of California at Los Angeles, 1975.

Heinen, Heinz Dieter. "Adaptative Changes in a Tribal Economy: A Case Study of the Winikina-Warao in Venezuela." Ph.D. diss., University of California at Los Angeles, 1972.

Heinen, Heinz Dieter. "Residence Rules and Household Cycles in a Warao Subtribe: The Case of Winikina." *Antropológica*, 31 (1972), 21–86.

Heinen, Heinz Dieter. "The Warao Indians of the Orinoco Delta: An Outline of Their Traditional Economic Organization and Inter-Relation with the National Economy." *Antropológica*, 34 (1975), 25–40.

Heinen, Heinz Dieter, and Kenneth Ruddle. "Ecology, Ritual, and Economic Organization in the Distribution of Palm Starch among the Warao of the Orinoco Delta." *Journal of Anthropological Research*, 30 (1974), 116–38.

Murphy, Robert L. "Deviance and Social Control I: What Makes Waru Run?" In Patricia J. Lyons, ed., *Native South Americans: Ethnology of the Least Known Continent*. 1974. Pp. 195–202.

Needham, Rodney. "The Evolution of Social Classification: A Commentary on the Warao Case." *Bijdragen tot de Taal, Land-en Volkenkunde*, 130 (1974), 16–43.

Olsen, Dale A. "Music-Induced Altered States of Consciousness Among Warao Shamans." *Journal of Latin American Lore*, 1 (1975), 19–34.

Suarez, Maria Matilde. "Terminology, Alliance, and Change in Warao Society." *Nieuwe West-Indische Gids*, 48 (1971), 56–122.

Wilbert, Johannes. *Demographic and Biological Studies of the Warao Indians.* 1980.

Wilbert, Johannes. "Eschatology in a Participatory Universe: Destinies of the Soul among the Warao Indians of Venezuela." In Elizabeth Benson, ed., *Death and the Afterlife in Pre-Columbian America*. 1975.

Wilbert, Johannes. "The Fishermen: The Warao of the Orinoco Delta." In J. Wilbert, ed., *Survivors of El Dorado: Four Indigenous Cultures of South America*. 1972. Pp. 65–115.

Wilbert, Johannes. "The House of the Swallow-Tailed Kite: Warao Myth and the Art of Thinking in Images." In Gary Urton, ed., *Animal Myths and Metaphors in South America*. 1985. Pp. 145–82.

Wilbert, Johannes. "To Become a Maker of Canoes: An Essay in Warao Enculturation."

In Johannes Wilbert, ed., *Enculturation in Latin America: An Anthology*. 1976. Pp. 303–58.

Wilbert, Johannes. "Tobacco and Shamanistic Ecstasy among the Warao Indians." In Peter T. Furst, ed., *Flesh of the Gods: The Ritual Use of Hallucinogens*. 1972.

Wilbert, Johannes. *Warao Basketry: Form and Function*. 1975.

WAURA

Coelho, Vera Pentoado. "Some Aspects of the Pottery of the Waura Indians." *Zeitschrift für Ethnologie*, 107 (1982), 335–54.

Ireland, Emilienne. "Cerebral Savage: The Whiteman as Symbol of Cleverness and Savagery in Waura Myth." In Jonathan D. Hill, ed., *Rethinking History and Myth: Indigenous South American Perspectives on the Past*. 1988. Pp. 157–73.

WAYANA

LaPointe, John. "Residence Patterns and Wayana Social Organization." Ph.D. diss., Columbia University, 1974.

WITOTO

Agnew, A. A. "Phonemes of Ocaina (Huitoto)." *International Journal of American Linguistics*, 23 (1975), 24–27.

Eden, Michael J., and Angela Andrade. "Ecological Aspects of Swidden Cultivation among the Andoke and Witoto Indians of the Colombia Amazon." *Human Ecology*, 15 (1987), 339–59.

XAVÁNTE

Da Mota, Clarice Novaes. "Karirí-Shokó and Shokó Mode of Utilization of Medicinal Plants in the Context of Modern Northeastern Brazil." Ph.D. diss., University of Texas, 1987.

Lopes da Silva, Aracy. "Social Practice and the Ontology in Akwē-Xavánte Naming and Myth." *Ethnology*, 28 (1989), 331–42.

Maybury-Lewis, David. *Akwē-Shavante Society*. 1974.

Neel, J. V. "Notes on the Effect of Measles and Measles Vaccine in a Virgin-Soil Population of South American Indians." *American Journal of Epidemiology*, 91 (1970), 418–29.

Sherzer, Joel, and Greg Urban. *Native South American Discourse*. 1986.

XERENTE

Maybury-Lewis, David. *The Savage and the Innocent*. 1965.

XIKRÍN

Frikel, Protasio. "Notes on the Present Situation of the Xikrín Indians of the Rio Caete."
    In Patricia J. Lyon, ed., *Native South Americans: Ethnology of the Least Known
    Continent.* 1974. Pp. 358–69.

YAGUA

Powlinson, Esther. "The Superhierarchical and Hierarchical Structure of Yagua Phon-
    ology." *Linguistics,* 75 (1971), 43–73.
Seiler Baldinger, Anne Marie. *Yagua and Tukuna Hammocks: Female Dignity and Culture
    Identity.* 1985.

YAHGAN

Gusinde, Martin. *Folk Literature of the Yamana Indians.* 1977.

YANOAMA

Albert, Bruce. "On Yanomami Violence: Inclusive Fitness or Ethnographer's Represen-
    tation." *Current Anthropology,* 30 (1989), 637–40.
Anthropology Resource Center. *The Yanoama Indian Park: A Call for Action.* 1981.
Booth, William. "Warfare over Yanomamo Indians." *Science,* 243 (1989), 1138–41.
"Brazilian Government Reduces Yanomami Territory by 70 Percent." *Cultural Survival
    Quarterly,* 13 (1989), 47.
Carneiro, Robert J. "Forest Clearance Among the Yanomamo, Observations and Impli-
    cations." *Antropologica,* 52 (1979), 39–76.
Carneiro, Robert J. "Tree Felling with the Stone Axe: An Experiment Carried out Among
    the Yanomamo Indians of Southern Venezuela." In Charles Kramer, ed., *Ethoar-
    chaeology: Implications of Ethnography for Archaeology.* 1979. Pp. 21–58.
Chagnon, Napoleon. "The Culture-Ecology of Shifting (Pioneering) Cultivation among
    the Yanomamo Indians." In David R. Gross, ed., *Peoples and Cultures of Native
    South America: An Anthropological Reader.* 1973. Pp. 126–42.
Chagnon, Napoleon. "Geneaology, Solidarity and Relatedness: Limits to Local Group
    Size and Patterns of Fissioning in an Expanding Population." *Yearbook of Physical
    Anthropology,* 19 (1975), 95–110.
Chagnon, Napoleon. "Highland New Guinea Models in the South American Lowlands."
    Working Papers on South American Indians, (1980) 111–30.
Chagnon, Napoleon. "Is Reproductive Success Equal in Egalitarian Societies?" In Na-
    poleon Chagnon and William Irons, eds., *Evolutionary Biology and Human Social
    Behavior.* 1979. Pp. 374–401.
Chagnon, Napoleon. "Kin Selection Theory, Kinship, Marriage, and Fitness among the
    Yanomamo Indians." In G. W. Barlow and J. N. Silverberg, *Sociobiology: Be-
    yond Nature/Nurture?* 1980. Pp. 545–71.
Chagnon, Napoleon. "Life Histories, Blood Revenge, and Warfare in a Tribal Popula-
    tion." *Science,* 239 (1988), 985–93.
Chagnon, Napoleon. "Mate Competition, Favoring Close Kin, and Village Fissioning

among the Yanomamo Indians." In Napoleon Chagnon and William Irons, eds., *Evolutionary Biology and Human Social Behavior.* 1979. Pp. 86–131.

Chagnon, Napoleon. "On Yanomamo Violence: Reply to Albert." *Current Anthropology,* 31 (1990), 49–53.

Chagnon, Napoleon. *Studying the Yanomamo.* 1974.

Chagnon, Napoleon. "Terminological Kinship: Genealogical Relatedness and Village Fissioning among the Yanomamo Indians." In Robert Alexander, ed., *Natural Selection and Social Behavior: Recent Research and New Theory.* 1981. Pp. 490–508.

Chagnon, Napoleon. "Tribal Social Organization and Genetic Microdifferentiation." In G. A. Harrison and A. J. Boyce, eds., *The Structure of Human Population.* 1972. Pp. 252–82.

Chagnon, Napoleon A., and Raymond B. Hames. "Protein Deficiency and Tribal Warfare in Amazonia: New Data." *Science,* 203 (1979), 910–13.

Chagnon, Napoleon, et al. "The Influence of Cultural Factors on the Demography and Pattern of Gene Flows from the Makiritare (Ye'kwana) to the Yanomamo Indians." *American Journal of Physical Anthropology,* 32 (1970), 339–49.

Chagnon, Napoleon A., et al. "Some Aspects of Drug Usage, Trade and Plant Domestication among the Yanomamo Indians of Brazil and Venezuela." *Acta Cientifica Venezolana,* 21 (1970), 186–293.

Chagnon, N. A., P. Le Quesne, and J. M. Cook. "Yanomamo Hallucinogens: Anthropological, Botanical, and Chemical Findings." *Current Anthropology,* 7 (1971), 3–32.

Cultural Survival. *The Impact of Contact: Two Case Studies.* 1983.

Early, John D., and John F. Peters. *The Population Dynamics of the Mucajai Yanomama.* 1990.

Ferguson, R. Brian. "Do Yanomamo Killers Have More Kids?" *American Ethnologist,* 16 (1989), 564–65.

Hames, Raymond B. "A Comparison of the Efficiencies of the Shotgun and the Bow in Neotropical Forest Hunting." *Human Ecology,* 7 (1979), 219–52.

Hames, Raymond B. "Game Depletion and Hunting Zone Rotation Among the Ye'kwana and Yanomamo of Amazonas, Venezuela." *Working Papers on South American Indians,* 2 (1980), 31–60.

Hames, Raymond B. "A Settlement Pattern of a Yanomamo Population Bloc: A Behavioral Ecological Interpretation." In Raymond B. Hames and William T. Vickers, eds., *Adaptive Responses of Native Amazonians.* 1983. Pp. 393–427.

Harris, Marvin. "Animal Capture and Yanomano Warfare: Retrospect and Prospect." *Journal of Anthropological Research,* 40 (1984), 183–201.

Harris, Marvin. "A Cultural Materialist Theory of Band and Village Warfare: The Yanomamo Test." In R. Brian Ferguson, ed., *Warfare, Culture, and Environment.* 1984. Pp. 111–40.

Harris, Marvin. "The Yanomamo and the Causes of War in Band and Village Societies." In Martin Margolis and William Carter, eds., *Brazil: Anthropological Perspectives.* 1979. Pp. 121–32.

Horgan, John. "The Violent Yanomamo." *Scientific American,* 258 (1988), 17–19.

Jank, Margaret. *Culture Shock.* 1977.

Lizot, Jacques. "Population, Resources, and Warfare Among the Yanomami." *Man,* 12 (1977), 497–517.

Lizot, Jacques. *Tales of the Yanomami: Daily Life in the Venezuelan Forest*. 1985.

Lizot, Jacques. *The Yanomami in the Face of Ethnocide*. 1976.

Margolis, Maxine L., and William E. Carter, eds., *Brazil: Anthropological Perspectives: Essays in Honor of Charles Wagley*. 1979.

Migliazza, Ernesto. "Yanomama Grammar and Intelligibility." Ph.D. diss., Indiana University, 1972.

Montgomery, Evelyn Ina. *With the Shiriana in Brazil*. 1970.

Peters, J. F. "Demography of the Shirishana." *Social Biology*, 21 (1974), 58–69.

Peters, J. F. "The Shirishana of the Yanomami: A Demographic Study." *Social Biology*, 27 (1980), 272–85.

Prance, G. T. "The Mycological Diet of the Yanoami Indians." *Mycologia*, 68 (1978), 248–50.

Ramos, Alcida R. "Reflecting on the Yanomami: Ethnographic Images and the Exotic." *Cultural Anthropology*, 2 (1987), 284–305.

Ramos, Alcida R. *The Yanoama in Brazil, 1979, and Yanoama Indian Park: Proposal and Justification*. 1979.

Ramos, Alcida R. "Yanomama Descent and Affinity: The Sanuma/Yanomama Contrast." *Actes du XLL Congrès International des Américanistes*, 2 (1977), 71–90.

"Roraima, Brazil: A Death Warning." *Cultural Survival Quarterly*, 13 (1989), 59–63.

Saffirio, Giovanni, and Raymond B. Hames. "The Forest and the Highway." In Kenneth Kensinger, ed., *The Impact of Contact: Two Yanomamo Cases*. 1983. Pp. 1–52.

Saffirio, Giovanni, and Richard Scaglion. "Hunting Efficiency in Acculturated and Un-acculturated Yanomama Villages." *Journal of Anthropological Research*, 38 (1982), 315–27.

Shapiro, Judith. "Alliance or Descent: Some Amazonian Contrasts." *Man*, 9 (1974), 305–06.

Shapiro, Judith. "Sex Roles and Social Structure Among the Yanomama of Northern Brazil." Ph.D. diss., Columbia University, 1972.

Smouse, P. E., et al. "The Impact of Random and Lineal Fission on the Genetic Divergence of Small Human Groups: A Case Study Among the Yanomama." *Genetics*, 98 (1981), 179–97.

Sponsel, Leslie. "Amazon Ecology and Adaptation." *Annual Review of Anthropology*, 15 (1986), 67–97.

Sponsel, Leslie. "Yanomama Warfare, Protein Capture, and Cultural Ecology: A Critical Analysis of the Arguments of the Opponents." *Interciencia*, 8 (1983), 204–10.

Tanis, R. J., et al. "The Genetic Structure of a Tribal Population, the Yanomama Indians. IX. Gene Frequencies for 18 Serum Protein and Erythrocyte Enzyme Systems in the Yanomama and Five Neighboring Tribes: Nine New Variants." *American Journal of Human Genetics*, 25 (1973), 655–76.

Urban, Greg. "Ceremonial Dialogues in South America." *American Anthropologist*, 88 (1986), 371–86.

Wilbert, Johannes. "The Hunters: The Yanomama of Territorio Amazonas." In J. Wilbert, ed., *Survivors of El Dorado: Four Indigenous Cultures of South America*. 1972. Pp. 13–65.

YEKUANA

Arvelo-Jiménez, Nelly. *The Dynamics of the Ye'cuana (Maquiritare) Political Systems: Stability and Crises*. 1973.

Arvelo-Jiminez, Nelly. "Political Relations in a Tribal Society: A Study of the Ye-cuana Indians of Venezuela." Ph.D. diss., Cornell University, 1971.

Chagnon, Napoleon et al. "The Influence of Cultural Factors on the Demography and Pattern of Gene Flows from the Makiritare (Ye'kwana) to the Yanomamo Indians." *American Journal of Physical Anthropology*, 32 (1970), 339–49.

Civrieux, Marc de. *Watunna: An Orinoco Creation Cycle*. 1980.

Coppens, Walter. *The Anatomy of a Land Invasion Scheme in Yekuana Territory, Venezuela*. 1972.

Frechione, John. "Economic Self-Development by Yekuana Amerinds in Southern Venezuela." Ph.D. diss., University of Pittsburgh, 1981.

Frechione, John. "Supervillage Formation in the Amazonian Terra Firme: The Case of Asenone." *Ethnology*, 29 (1990), 117–34.

Guss, David M. "Historical Incorporation Among the Makiritare: From Legend to Myth." *Journal of Latin American Lore*, 7 (1981), 23–35.

Guss, David. "Keeping It Oral: A Yekuana Ethnology." *American Ethnologist*, 13 (1986), 413–29.

Hames, Raymond B. "A Behavioral Account of the Division of Labor among the Ye'kwana of Southern Venezuela." Ph.D. diss., University of California, Santa Barbara, 1978.

Hames, Raymond B. "Game Depletion and Hunting Zone Rotation Among the Ye'kwana and Yanomamo of Amazonas, Venezuela." *Working Papers on South American Indians*, 2 (1980), 31–60.

Wilbert, Johannes. "The Cultivators: The Makiritare of Territorio Amazonas." In *Survivors of El Dorado: Four Indigenous Culture of South America*. 1972. Pp. 116–62.

Wilbert, Johannes. *Navigators of the Orinoco: River Indians of Venezuela*. 1980.

YUKPA

Diaz Ungria, Adelaide G. de, and Helia L. de Castillo. *Antropológica Física de los Indios Irapa*. 1971.

Ruddle, Kenneth. "The Human Use of Insects: Examples from the Yukpa." *Biotropica*, 5 (1973), 94–101.

Ruddle, Kenneth. "The Hunting Technology of the Maraca Indians." *Antropologica*, 30 (1971), 18–28.

YUMBO

Salomon, Frank. "Killing the Yumbo." In Norman E. Whitten, Jr., *Cultural Transformations and Ethnicity in Modern Ecuador*. 1981. Pp. 162–208.

YUQUÍ

Stearman, Allyn. "Yuqui Foragers in the Bolivian Amazon: Subsistence Strategies, Prestige, and Leadership in an Acculturating Society." *Journal of Anthropological Research*, 45 (1989), 219–44.

ZORÓ

Lovold, Lars. "First He Locked Them In: A Creation Myth of the Gavião and the Zoró
Indians of Brazil." In Harald O. Sklar and Frank Salomon, eds., *Natives and
Neighbors in South America: Anthropological Essays*. 1987. Pp. 417–42.

INDEX

Numbers in **bold** indicate main entries.

About the Author

JAMES S. OLSON is Professor of History, Sam Houston State University, Huntsville, Texas. His previously published books include *Historical Dictionary of European Imperialism, Historical Dictionary of the Vietnam War,* and *Historical Dictionary of the New Deal* (Greenwood Press, 1991, 1988 and 1985, respectively).